PENGUIN 🐧 CLASSICS WITHDRAWN

THE COMPLETE GILBERT & SULLIVAN

Playwright/lyricist WILLIAM S. GILBERT (1836–1911) and composer ARTHUR S. SULLIVAN (1842–1900) defined operetta or comic operas in Victorian England with a series of their internationally successful and timeless works known as the Savoy Operas.

ED GLINERT was born in Dalston, London, and read Classical Hebrew at Manchester University. In 1983 he set up *City Life*, Manchester's listings magazine, and he has since worked for *Radio Times*, *Private Eye* and *Mojo*. He is the co-author of Fodor's *Rock & Roll Traveler USA* and Fodor's *Rock & Roll Traveler Great Britain and Ireland*, and recently edited *The Diary of a Nobody* by George and Weedon Grossmith, and annotated two volumes of Sherlock Holmes stories, all for Penguin Classics.

MIKE LEIGH is a film-maker and dramatist. His 1999 film *Topsy-Turvy* examined Gilbert and Sullivan's world at the time of the original productions of *Princess Ida* and *The Mikado*. It won two Oscars. His other films include *Nuts in May*, *Life is Sweet*, *Naked*, *Secrets and Lies* and *Vera Drake*. Among his many plays are *Babies Grow Old*, *Abigail's Party*, *Ecstasy*, *Goose-Pimples* and *Two Thousand Years*. He is a Vice President of the Sir Arthur Sullivan Society.

The Complete
Gilbert & Sullivan

Edited by ED GLINERT
with an Introduction by MIKE LEIGH

PENGUIN BOOKS

PENGUIN CLASSICS

Published by the Penguin Group
Penguin Books Ltd, 80 Strand, London WC2R ORL, England
Penguin Group (USA) Inc., 375 Hudson Street, New York, New York 10014, USA
Penguin Group (Canada), 90 Eglinton Avenue East, Suite 700, Toronto, Ontario, Canada M4P 2Y3
(a division of Pearson Penguin Canada Inc.)
Penguin Ireland, 25 St Stephen's Green, Dublin 2, Ireland
(a division of Penguin Books Ltd)
Penguin Group (Australia), 250 Camberwell Road, Camberwell, Victoria 3124, Australia
(a division of Pearson Australia Group Pty Ltd)
Penguin Books India Pvt Ltd, 11, Community Centre, Panchsheel Park, New Delhi – 110 017, India
Penguin Group (NZ), 67 Apollo Drive, Rosedale, North Shore 0632, New Zealand
(a division of Pearson New Zealand Ltd)
Penguin Books (South Africa) (Pty) Ltd, 24 Sturdee Avenue, Rosebank, Johannesburg 2196, South Africa

Penguin Books Ltd, Registered Offices: 80 Strand, London WC2R ORL, England

www.penguin.com

First published 2006
Published in paperback in Penguin Classics 2008

1

Chronology, Notes and Further Reading copyright © Ed Glinert, 2006
Introduction copyright © Mike Leigh, 2006
All rights reserved

Typeset by Rowland Phototypesetting Ltd, Bury St Edmunds, Suffolk
Printed in England by Clays Ltd, St Ives plc

978-0-141-44129-0

www.greenpenguin.co.uk

Contents

Introduction

One night in 1999, Jim Broadbent and I were in the audience at the New York Film Festival. Our Gilbert and Sullivan film, *Topsy-Turvy*, in which Jim plays Gilbert, had been screened the previous evening. Tonight it was the turn of *Being John Malkovich*, Spike Jonze and Charlie Kaufman's delightful surreal comedy about people popping through a magic door and finding themselves inside John Malkovich's head, thus instantly becoming that film star.

Suddenly, Jim and I looked at each other. This was a quintessentially Gilbertian 'magic lozenge' plot. Having immersed ourselves for the previous couple of years in the life, work and preoccupations of W. S. Gilbert, we were well versed in his predilection for devices that turn you, with significant dramatic consequences, into somebody else, or into a different version of yourself.

The magic lozenge was the bugbear of Gilbert and Sullivan's working relationship. Every time Gilbert proposed the idea, Sullivan rejected it. He disliked fantastical devices that tampered with reality. He always wanted 'to set a story of human interest and probability' as he wrote to Gilbert in 1884.

Of course, they had done the lozenge in their first fully-fledged collaboration, *The Sorcerer*, with its love philtre. But what Sullivan failed to spot was that every one of the subsequent operas was a lozenge story without the lozenge, in that they all involve transformation of identity, and that, far from failing to deal with human emotions, Gilbert's metaphorical world enabled him to do precisely that, albeit in his own idiosyncratic way.

The inscription on Gilbert's memorial on the Thames Embankment in London reads, 'His Foe was Folly, and his Weapon Wit'. This is too coy. Gilbert saw the world as a chaotic place, in which our lives are brutal accidents of birth, fate and human blunder, a jungle of confusion and delusion, where we all aspire to be other than what we are, and where nobody is really who or what they seem to be.

Power. Status. Rank. Duty. Hypocrisy and affectation. Youth and old age. Gilbert's obsessions inform all these operas, his greatest being the arbitrary nature of society's absurd rules and regulations. He was a failed barrister in his youth and a lay magistrate in his old age. He loved the English legal world, not least for its theatricality, and he himself was compulsively litigious. But, for all his appearance as the very model of conservative respectability, his merciless lampooning of the heartless constraints of laws and etiquette reveal him, underneath it all, to have been a genuine free spirit and a true anarchist. Doubtless he would have denied these descriptions, but his subversive tendencies are beyond dispute, and he could hardly have been called a conformist.

The two principal elements of all the Savoy Operas are Law and Identity. Magic crops up in just three of them, but material change caused by supernatural intervention is only a variation on the manipulation of laws and rules. There are love stories galore, but for the most part these do not drive the plot, and taken out of context they are sentimental and dull. As such, they are seldom distinguishable from the common fodder of ordinary light musical theatre, or indeed of Victorian melodrama.

If a key to understanding the operas is to see Gilbert as an anarchist, it may also be useful to approach them as the work of a proto-surrealist. With great fluidity and freedom, he continually challenges our natural expectations, and he does this on two levels. First, within the framework of the story, he makes bizarre things happen, and turns the world on its head. Thus, the Learned Judge marries the Plaintiff, the soldiers metamorphose into aesthetes, and so on, and nearly every opera is resolved by a deft moving of the goalposts.

But concurrently, Gilbert plays with different levels of reality, using para-theatrical conventions, that is, making characters refer implicitly to the fact that they are on a stage in a play, outside the framework of the audience's willing suspension of disbelief.

> Am I alone,
>> And unobserved? I am!
> Then let me own
>> I'm an aesthetic sham!

Read the whole of this confession by Bunthorne in *Patience*. Gilbert's joke, of course, is that Bunthorne is not unobserved – the audience is watching him. And he can only be talking to the audience. He is not discovering something new about himself before our very eyes, unlike the soliloquies of Hamlet or Macbeth, or even Malvolio, which must be played as real people talking to themselves, with total psychological truth. When Shakespeare needs to talk to the audience as such, he invents a non-character, like the Chorus in *Henry V*.

The most extreme exercise in surrealism in this series is of course *The Mikado*, a puppet show cheerfully devoid of any sense of the real world as we know it. The far-fetched nature of its abstraction – it has nothing to do with Japan – and the craziness of its logic surely account for its being the most durable and popular of the operas. It abounds with para-theatrical devices:

KO-KO: Congratulate me, gentlemen, I've found a volunteer!
CHORUS: The Japanese equivalent for Hear, Hear, Hear!

And the Mikado himself observes, 'it's an unjust world, and virtue is triumphant only in theatrical performances'.

The Yeomen of the Guard, uniquely, is grounded in the real world and, as such, is the odd man out. It is probably a romantic rather than a comic opera, although it does contain some very funny moments, and the plot still involves disguise and mistaken identity.

'Comic operas' is what Gilbert and Sullivan called these shows. They are certainly not mere 'light' operas, which are soft-centred romantic offerings; nor are they 'operettas', which are frilly, frothy affairs, devoid of any shade of the dark side.

For it is their dark side, their hard edge, that so distinguishes the Savoy Operas. Perhaps they may more usefully be described as grotesque operas. Far from being pejorative, this epithet most accurately evokes their true nature and spirit.

Or are they not absurd operas? Gilbert undoubtedly anticipated the Theatre of the Absurd, as did Alfred Jarry, whose *Ubu Roi* outraged Paris audiences in 1896. Ionesco's *Rhinoceros* is surely a magic-lozenge play, albeit a mournfully unfunny one, and it is no surprise that Samuel Beckett was a confirmed G&S aficionado.

The operas have often been misunderstood. They are referred to as satires, which they are not. There may be satirical elements in *Iolanthe* or *Utopia Limited*, but Gilbert's true intention is never to draw specific parallels. He merely holds up his mirror to the world, and reflects on its madness. Similarly misunderstood is his much-criticized attitude to elderly women. He is not attacking them; he is doing no more than to lament the way life is. We all grow old, and the plain and the ugly have a harder time than the beautiful.

If these shows have fallen into disrepute over the years, it is because directors have failed to understand their raw edge. This results in boring, bland, sentimental, self-conscious, often gratuitously camp productions, which entirely miss the point.

What, then, is 'Gilbertian'? The word has been in the English language for over a century, and to understand it, we need to analyse the stylistic alchemy of Gilbert's art as a dramatist. As we have seen, he views the world through a distorting lens of irony and paradox. His genius is to fuse opposites with an imperceptible sleight of hand. The Gilbertian formula is to blend the surreal with the real, and the caricature with the natural. In other words, to tell a perfectly outrageous story in a completely deadpan way. Indeed, to disguise a subversive anarchist bomb as bourgeois respectability.

We have discussed Gilbert the surrealist. But he was also a master of theatrical naturalism. Between 1863 and 1911, he wrote over seventy plays. Apart from his comic operas, translations of Donizetti and Offenbach, pantomimes and burlesques, a substantial proportion of his popular work consisted of naturalistic fourth-wall plays, all of them Gilbertian in their irony. These ranged from *Engaged* (1877), a farce about greed, which still enjoys revivals in the twenty-first century, to *The Hooligan* (1911), in which a condemned simpleton suffers a fatal heart attack in his prison cell.

Gilbert belonged to a small group of dramatists who reacted against the undisciplined melodramatic mess of the earlier Victorian theatre, so accurately evoked by Dickens in his portrayal of Mr Crummles and his company in *Nicholas Nickleby*.

One of these was Tom Robertson, who was a major influence on Gilbert in two ways. As a dramatist, his so-called 'cup-and-saucer' plays like *Ours* (1866) and *Caste* (1867) depicted the world in a new, fresh, realistic way; and as a director (or stage-manager, as they called it in those days), he introduced Gilbert both to the revolutionary notion of disciplined rehearsals and to mise-en-scène or unity of style in the whole presentation – direction, design, music, acting.

Before this period, directing as we know it did not exist. On the continent, Wagner pioneered it at Bayreuth, as did the Duke of Saxe-Meiningen with his court theatre. In London, the actor-managers Macready, Kean, and, later, Irving, organized their productions around their own egocentric performances. But it was Robertson and Gilbert who were the first real directors, and Robertson's early death in 1871 left Gilbert as the main pioneer of this new craft.

That Gilbert was a good director is not in doubt. He was able to extract from his actors natural, clear performances, which served the Gilbertian requirements of outrageousness delivered straight. He knew what he wanted – and he got it, and he was certainly a perfectionist. But whether his famously confrontational personality made him something of a dogmatic autocrat, such as some of us modern practitioners in this field might question, is altogether another matter.

A further key to understanding Gilbert is to savour his talents as a visual artist. Had he never written a word, his work as an illustrator would have stood the test of time. All that survives in print now are his many drawings for the Bab Ballads, the comic verses he wrote for *Fun* magazine in the 1860s. These have been published over the years in various collections, including, most recently, James Ellis's definitive

Harvard University Press edition (1980). Gilbert added the *Songs of a Savoyard* – favourites from these operas – in editions from 1898, and in 2000 Jim Broadbent recorded a selection for Penguin Audiobooks, under my direction.

The Bab Ballads are masterpieces. They rank with Lewis Carroll and Edward Lear, and no appreciation of the Savoy Operas is complete without studying them. There are two reasons for this.

Firstly, they contain the sources for many of the ideas, themes and plots of the operas. Thus, for example, *HMS Pinafore* derives from 'Captain Reece':

> Of all the ships upon the blue
> No ship contained a better crew
> Than that of worthy CAPTAIN REECE,
> Commanding of *The Mantelpiece*.
>
> He was adored by all his men,
> For worthy CAPTAIN REECE, RN,
> Did all that lay within him to
> Promote the comfort of his crew.

Driven by duty, and committed to furnishing his crew's every last desire, the Captain agrees not only to supply all his female relations as their brides, but also to marry his boatswain's widowed mother himself:

> 'Well, well, the Chaplain I will seek,
> We'll all be married this day week –
> At yonder church upon the hill;
> It is my duty, and I will!'
>
> The sisters, cousins, aunts and niece,
> And widowed ma of CAPTAIN REECE,
> Attended there as they were bid;
> It was their duty, and they did.

Secondly, within the Bab verses, we find the two opposing strands of Gilbert's vision, the ridiculous and the real, the comic and the tragic. 'The Story of Prince Agib' begins:

Strike the concertina's melancholy string!
Blow the spirit-stirring harp like anything!
   Let the piano's martial blast
   Rouse the echoes of the past
For AGIB, the prince of Tartary, I sing!

Of AGIB, who, amid Tartaric scenes,
Wrote a lot of ballet-music in his teens:
   His gentle spirit rolls
   In the melody of souls –
Which is pretty, but I don't know what it means.

Of AGIB, who could readily, at sight,
Strum a march upon the loud Theodolite.
   He would diligently play
   On the Zoetrope all day,
And blow the gay Pantechnicon all night.

By contrast, in 'At a Pantomime', Gilbert describes the old men in the audience as they watch the actor on the stage:

The old ones, palsied, blear and hoar,
   Their breasts in anguish beat –
They've seen him seventy times before,
   How well they know the cheat!

They've seen that ghastly pantomime,
   They've felt its blighting breath,
They know that rollicking Christmas-time
   Meant cold and want and death –

Starvation – Poor law Union fare,
   And deadly cramps and chills,
And illness – illness everywhere –
And crime, and Christmas bills.

They know Old Christmas well, I ween,
　　Those men of ripened age;
They've often, often, often seen
　　That actor off the stage.

They see in his gay rotundity
　　A clumsy stuffed-out dress;
They see in the cup he waves on high
　　A tinselled emptiness.

Those aged men so lean and wan,
　　They've seen it all before;
They know they'll see the charlatan
　　But twice or three times more.

And so they bear with dance and song,
　　And crimson foil and green;
They wearily sit, and grimly long
　　For the Transformation Scene.

And here we come to the heart of the matter. Gilbert was, above all, a great poet. This volume is a cornucopia of delights. Open it randomly at any page, and you will not fail to find a gem. It is easy to understand how W. S. Gilbert so inspired Arthur Sullivan.

Each of these men was an extremely skilled craftsman in his own right. But the key to their success is that they knew how to write for each other. For all their legendary conflict, they had extraordinary rapport. Despite their contrasting personalities – Sullivan ebullient and jolly, Gilbert sardonic and dour – they shared a sense of humour. Nothing else Sullivan wrote holds a candle to the music provoked by Gilbert's inventive words. What he did to those words was to challenge and subvert them, and to enhance them by bringing out their flavour and their meaning by interlacing and surrounding them with unpredictable succulent riches.

Much of Sullivan's serious and other lighter work is interesting and enjoyable. Without the Savoy Operas, he would certainly deserve a place in the pantheon of minor composers, not only for

'The Lost Chord' and 'Onward, Christian Soldiers', but for such pieces as his 'Di Ballo' Overture, his Cello Concerto and his grand opera, *Ivanhoe*.

And the Bab Ballads alone would have earned Gilbert his place in posterity, although a dozen of his plays will stand up to revival when the world rediscovers them.

Nevertheless, it is obvious that without each other, both Gilbert and Sullivan would probably have sunk without trace. Together, they created a unique body of work that places them up there alongside Molière, Congreve, Sheridan, Rossini, Donizetti, Offenbach and Feydeau, even the Mozart of *Cosí fan tutte* and *The Marriage of Figaro*. They paved the way for Wilde, Pinero, Shaw and Noel Coward; and all the lyricists and composers of the great twentieth-century American musicals cited G&S as their major influence and inspiration.

Sullivan's frustration was that he never had time to write proper music: he was convinced that he frittered away his life and his talents on the trivia of the Savoy Operas. How wrong he was!

As I have said, these operas have been much discredited by stale productions. Of course, some people simply loathe them on principle, courtesy of pompous elderly relatives and schoolteachers with awful singing voices. Others associate them with suffering the ignominy of playing members of the opposite sex in school productions of dubious motivation.

But approached fresh, they are great shows – strong and youthful, and resonant with meaning. It was a joy to behold the whole cast falling in love with the material when we shot *Topsy-Turvy* – and the film crew, too!

When we were rehearsing the film, some of us went, somewhat apprehensively, to see King's College, London, Gilbert and Sullivan Society in *The Pirates of Penzance*. (King's was Gilbert's alma mater.) This turned out to be one of the great nights out at the theatre, as the young, amateur cast explored every moment with originality, wit and musical relish. It was hilarious, and it was hard to accept that it had not been somehow updated or rewritten. But not a word or a note had been touched.

The same was true of Martin Duncan's laser-sharp and deeply

refreshing 2003 production of *The Gondoliers* at Chichester, which at the time of writing is being explored afresh at the English National Opera. Staged in 1950s style, it is amazingly modern and real – and utterly Gilbertian. And again, not a word has been changed.

When the old D'Oyly Carte Company died its inevitable natural death a quarter of a century ago, one could have been forgiven for thinking these operas would share the same fate. Yet at that very time, Joseph Papp's brilliant New York version of *The Pirates* was enjoying world-wide success. Jonathan Miller followed, with his inspired *Mikado*, relocated to an English hotel in the 1920s.

The operas are now as popular as ever. Gilbert and Sullivan are probably amazed, if they are watching from up there. But I think it not the least bit remarkable.

Mike Leigh
March 2006

Chronology

W. S. GILBERT (1836–1911)

The early years of William Schwenck Gilbert are frustratingly shrouded in mystery and biographers have been unable to unearth any more information than Gilbert himself revealed. We know that he was descended from a family of Wiltshire yeomen and that his grandfather, a tea merchant, lived at the since demolished 17 Southampton Street, off London's Strand, where Gilbert was born. Of his mother, Anne Morris, we know little. His father, William Gilbert, was a naval surgeon and novelist. The middle name, Schwenck, was added in honour of his great aunt and godmother, Mary Schwenck.

ARTHUR SULLIVAN (1842–1900)

In contrast to W. S. Gilbert's vague early years, Arthur Sullivan enjoyed an uncomplicated childhood in Lambeth, south London. His father was a bandmaster at the Royal Military College, and the young Sullivan was composing at the age of eight, soon mastering a variety of wind instruments. In his late teens he won a scholarship to study in Leipzig, where Franz Liszt listened to his final thesis. His professional career was a never-to-be-resolved battle between his frustration at the populist glory he received for composing the Savoy Operas at the expense, he believed, of the greater artistic kudos he may have gained for being Britain's greatest nineteenth-century composer. Other than his collaborations with Gilbert, Sullivan composed the music to the hymn 'Onward Christian Soldiers', a grand opera, *Ivanhoe*, and several major choral works, including *The Light of the World*, *The Martyr of Antioch* and *The Golden Legend*.

1836 *18 November*, William Schwenck Gilbert born. He had three younger sisters, Jane, Maud and Florence. Spent early years touring Europe with his parents. His family nickname was 'Bab'.

1838 Kidnapped by bandits in Naples and ransomed for £25.

1842 *13 May*, Arthur Sullivan born.

1854 Longing to become a chorister, Sullivan pleads with his father to be allowed to join the Chapel Royal School with the entreaty, 'Father, Purcell was a Chapel Royal boy.' Duly gains a place.

1856 Sullivan wins joint first prize in a Mendelssohn competition and a place at the Royal Academy of Music.

1857 Gilbert graduates from King's College, London, with a BA and takes job at the Privy Council office in London. Begins writing farces and burlesques, all of which are rejected for publication.

1861 As 'Bab', Gilbert begins writing his Bab Ballads (published 1869) for *Fun*, a rival to *Punch*.

1862 *April 15*, Sullivan's orchestral suite to Shakespeare's *The Tempest* performed at the Crystal Palace in front of an audience that includes Charles Dickens, who tells him: 'I am not a music critic, but I do know that I have just listened to some very remarkable music.'

1863 Gilbert called to the Bar after studying law at the Inner Temple, London.

31 October, what may have been Gilbert's first play, *Uncle Baby*, performed at the Lyceum Theatre, Covent Garden, London, but doubt surrounds his authorship; it may be a collaboration with his father.

Sullivan composes his Symphony in E flat (the 'Irish Symphony'), first performed, successfully, at the Crystal Palace in March 1866.

1866 *29 December*, Gilbert's *Dulcamara, or The Little Duck and the Great Quack* performed at St James's Theatre, London. He later claimed it to be his first dramatic production.

1867 *6 August*, Gilbert marries Lucy Agnes Turner ('Kitty'), daughter of an Indian army officer, in Kensington; no children.

1869 *Autumn*, Gilbert and Sullivan meet at the Royal Gallery of Illustration, Lower Regent Street, London, during rehearsals for a Gilbert–Frederick Clay musical, *Ages Ago*.

1871 G&S collaborate for the first time on *Thespis; or, The Gods Grown Old*; *26 December*, opens at the Gaiety Theatre, London (its music now lost). Gilbert sees the openings of two non-musical plays: *On Guard* (Court Theatre, *28 October*) and *Pygmalion and Galatea* (Haymarket, *9 December*).

1875 *25 March*, *Trial By Jury* (published in the April 1868 edition of *Fun*) opens at the Royalty Theatre, London.

1877 *17 November*, *The Sorcerer*, their first deliberately planned collaboration, premiered at the Opéra Comique, London, by the Comedy Opera Company which was formed by Richard D'Oyly Carte to promote English light opera.

Sullivan's brother, Fred, who was playing the Judge in *Trial by Jury*, dies of pneumonia. The composer writes 'The Lost Chord' in his memory.

1878 *25 May*, *HMS Pinafore* premiered at the Opéra Comique. That year Gilbert's serious drama, *The Ne'er Do Weel*, flops.

1879 *Gretchen*, a blank verse tragedy, closes after three weeks. *30 December*, *The Pirates of Penzance* first performed at the Royal Bijou Theatre, Paignton, Devon.

1881 *23 April*, *Patience* opens at the Opéra Comique. Gilbert's other main work that year, *Foggerty's Fairy*, a supernatural farce, lasts only three weeks. *10 October*, the newly built Savoy Theatre (see *Patience* headnote), largely created with G&S productions in mind, opens in London with a performance of *Patience*.

1882 *25 November*, *Iolanthe* is premiered at the Savoy Theatre.

1883 *22 May*, Sullivan knighted.

1884 *5 January*, *Princess Ida* opens at the Savoy Theatre.

1885 *14 March*, *The Mikado* opens at the Savoy Theatre.

1886 *16 October*, Sullivan's oratorio, 'The Golden Legend', well received during the Leeds Festival.

1887 *22 January*, *Ruddigore* opens at the Savoy Theatre.

1888 *3 October*, *The Yeomen of the Guard* opens at the Savoy Theatre.

1889 *7 December*, *The Gondoliers* opens at the Savoy Theatre. G&S

partnership splits up acrimoniously soon after, following the so-called Great Carpet Quarrel (see headnote to *Utopia Limited*).

1891 *31 January*, Sullivan's only Grand Opera, *Ivanhoe*, opens at D'Oyly Carte's newly built English Opera House (now the Palace Theatre, Cambridge Circus), London.

1893 G&S reunited; 7 *October*, *Utopia Limited* opens at the Savoy Theatre.

1896 7 *March*, *The Grand Duke*, the last collaboration, opens at the Savoy Theatre. Gilbert goes into semi-retirement at Grim's Dyke, his Harrow mansion.

1897 27 *September*, Gilbert's *The Fortune Hunter*, a serious melo-drama, opens in Birmingham to poor reviews. He is so upset by its failure, writes nothing further until 1904, spending much time in his role as a magistrate in Harrow.

1900 22 *November*, Sullivan dies a lonely death in London after contracting bronchitis.

1906 *December*, D'Oyly Carte's widow, Helen Lenoir, begins series of Savoy Opera revivals under Gilbert's stage direction.

1907 22 *May*, Gilbert knighted.

1911 Premiere of his swan song, *The Hooligan*, a short piece inspired by Alexandre Dumas's *Derniers Jours d'un condamné à mort* (1829), about the last hours of a condemned convict.

1911 29 *May*, Gilbert dies of heart failure while attempting to rescue a young woman he is teaching to swim in his own lake. His last words were: 'Put your hands on my shoulders and don't struggle.'

THESPIS[1]

OR

THE GODS GROWN OLD

DRAMATIS PERSONAE

Gods

JUPITER ⎫
APOLLO ⎪ *(Aged Deities)*
MARS ⎬
DIANA ⎭
MERCURY

Thespians

THESPIS
SILLIMON
TIMIDON
TIPSEION
PREPOSTEROS
STUPIDAS
SPARKEION
NICEMIS
PRETTEIA
DAPHNE
CYMON

Chorus of Stars

ACT I – Ruined Temple on the Summit of Olympus
ACT II – The same Scene, with the Ruins Restored

ACT I

SCENE – *The ruins of the Temple of the Gods on the summit of Mount Olympus.*[2] *Picturesque shattered columns, overgrown with ivy, with entrances to temple (ruined). Fallen columns on the stage. Three broken pillars. At the back of the stage is the approach from the summit of the mountain. In the distance are the summits of adjacent mountains. At first all this is concealed by a thick fog, which clears presently.*

[*Enter through fog Chorus of Stars, coming off duty, as fatigued with their night's work.*]

CHORUS OF STARS: Throughout the night,
　　　　　　　　The constellations
　　　　　　　Have given light
　　　　　　　　From various stations.
　　　　　　　When midnight gloom
　　　　　　　　Falls on all nations,
　　　　　　　We will resume
　　　　　　　　Our occupations.

SOLO:　　　　　Our light, it's true,
　　　　　　　　Is not worth mention,
　　　　　　　What can we do
　　　　　　　　To gain attention,
　　　　　　　When, night and noon,
　　　　　　　　With vulgar glaring,
　　　　　　　A great big Moon
　　　　　　　　Is *always* flaring?

3

CHORUS: Throughout the night, etc.

[*During Chorus enter* DIANA,[3] *an elderly Goddess. She is carefully wrapped up in Cloaks, Shawls, etc. A hood is over her head, a respirator in her mouth, and galoshes on her feet. During the chorus she takes these things off, and discovers herself dressed in the usual costume of the Lunar Diana, the Goddess of the Moon.*]

DIANA [*shuddering*]: Ugh! How cold the nights are! I don't know how it is, but I seem to feel the night air a great deal more than I used to. But it is time for the sun to be rising. [*Calls*] Apollo.[4]

APOLLO [*within*]: Hollo!

DIANA: I've come off duty – it's time for you to be getting up.

[*Enter* APOLLO. *He is an elderly 'buck' with an air of assumed juvenility, and is dressed in dressing-gown and smoking cap.*]

APOLLO [*yawning*]: I shan't go out to-day. I was out yesterday and the day before and I want a little rest. I don't know how it is, but I seem to feel my work a great deal more than I used to.

DIANA: I'm sure these short days can't hurt you. Why, you don't rise till six and you're in bed again by five: you should have a turn at *my* work and see how you like that – out all night!

APOLLO: My dear sister, I don't envy you – though I remember when I did – But that was when I was a younger sun. I don't think I'm quite well. Perhaps a little change of air will do me good. I've a great mind to show myself in London this winter; they'll be very glad to see me. No! I shan't go out to-day. I shall send them this fine thick wholesome fog and they won't miss me. It's the best substitute for a blazing sun – and like most substitutes, nothing at all like the real thing. [*To fog*] Be off with you.

[*Fog clears away and discovers the scene described.*]

[*Hurried music.* MERCURY[5] *shoots up from behind precipice at back of stage. He carries several parcels afterwards described. He sits down, very much fatigued.*]

MERCURY: Home at last! A nice time I've had of it.

DIANA: You young scamp, you've been down all night again. This is the third time you've been out this week.

MERCURY: Well, *you're* a nice one to blow me up for that.

DIANA: *I* can't help being out all night.

MERCURY: And I can't help being down all night. The nature of

Mercury requires that he should go down when the sun sets, and rise again, when the sun rises.

DIANA: And what have you been doing?

MERCURY: Stealing on commission. There's a set of false teeth and a box of Life Pills – that's for Jupiter[6] – An invisible peruke[7] and a bottle of hair dye – that's for Apollo – A respirator and a pair of galoshes – that's for Cupid[8] – A full-bottomed chignon, some auricomous fluid, a box of pearl-powder, a pot of rouge, and a hare's foot[9] – that's for Venus.[10]

DIANA: Stealing! you ought to be ashamed of yourself!

MERCURY: Oh, as the god of thieves I must do something to justify my position.

DIANA *and* APOLLO [*contemptuously*]: Your position!

MERCURY: Oh I know it's nothing to boast of, even on earth. Up here, it's simply contemptible. Now that you gods are too old for your work, you've made me the miserable drudge of Olympus – groom, valet, postman, butler, commissionaire, maid of all work, parish beadle and original dustman.

APOLLO: Your Christmas boxes ought to be something considerable.

MERCURY: They ought to be, but they're not. I'm treated abominably. I make everybody and I'm nobody – I go everywhere and I'm nowhere – I do everything and I'm nothing. I've made thunder for Jupiter, odes for Apollo, battles for Mars[11] and love for Venus. I've married couples for Hymen,[12] and six weeks afterwards, I've divorced them for Cupid – and in return I get all the kicks while they pocket the halfpence. And in compensation for robbing me of the halfpence in question, what have they done for me?

APOLLO: Why they've – ha! ha! they've made you the god of thieves!

MERCURY: Very self-denying of them – there isn't one of them who hasn't a better claim to the distinction than I have.

SONG

MERCURY: Oh, I'm the celestial drudge,
                     From morning to night I must stop at it,
              On errands all day I must trudge,
                     And I stick to my work till I drop at it!

In summer I get up at one,
    (As a good-natured donkey I'm ranked for it),
Then I go and I light up the Sun,
    And Phoebus[13] Apollo gets thanked for it!
        Well, well, it's the way of the world,
          And will be through all its futurity;
          Though noodles are baroned and earled,
            There's nothing for clever obscurity!

I'm the slave of the gods, neck and heels,
    And I'm bound to obey, though I rate at 'em;
And I not only order their meals,
    But I cook 'em, and serve 'em, and wait at 'em.
Then I make all their nectar – I do –
    (Which a terrible liquor to rack us is)
And whenever I mix them a brew,
        Why all the thanksgivings are Bacchus's![14]
          Well, well, it's the way of the world, etc.

Then reading and writing I teach,
    And spelling books many I've edited!
And for bringing these arts within reach,
    That donkey Minerva[15] gets credited.
Then I scrape at the stars with a knife,
    And plate-powder[16] the moon (on the days for it),
And I hear all the world and his wife
        Awarding Diana the praise for it!
          Well, well, it's the way of the world, etc.

[*After song – very loud and majestic music is heard.*]

DIANA *and* MERCURY [*looking off*]: Why, who's this? Jupiter, by Jove!

    [*Enter* JUPITER, *an extremely old man, very decrepit with very thin straggling white beard. He wears a long braided dressing-gown, handsomely trimmed, and a silk night-cap on his head.* MERCURY *falls back respectfully as he enters.*]

JUPITER: Good day, Diana – ah, Apollo – Well, well, well, what's the matter? what's the matter?

DIANA: Why, that young scamp Mercury says that we do nothing, and leave all the duties of Olympus to him! Will you believe it, he actually says that our influence on earth is dropping down to *nil*.

JUPITER: Well, well – don't be hard on the lad – to tell you the truth, I'm not sure that he's very far wrong. Don't let it go any further, but, between ourselves, the sacrifices and votive offerings have fallen off terribly of late. Why, I can remember the time when people offered us human sacrifices – No mistake about it – human sacrifices! think of that!

DIANA: Ah! those good old days!

JUPITER: Then it fell off to oxen, pigs and sheep.

APOLLO: Well, there are worse things than oxen, pigs and sheep!

JUPITER: So I've found to my cost. My dear sir – between ourselves it's dropped off from one thing to another until it has positively dwindled down to preserved Australian beef! What do you think of that!

APOLLO: I don't like it at all.

JUPITER: You won't mention it – it might go further –

DIANA: It couldn't fare worse.

JUPITER: In short, matters have come to such a crisis that there's no mistake about it – something must be done to restore our influence, the only question is, *What?*

QUARTETTE

MERCURY [*coming forward in great alarm*]:
  [*Enter* MARS.]

           Oh incident unprecedented!
           I hardly can believe it's true!

MARS: Why bless the boy, he's quite demented!
           Why, what's the matter, sir, with you?

APOLLO: Speak quickly, or you'll get a warning!

MERCURY: Why mortals up the mount are swarming,
           Our temple on Olympus storming,
             In hundreds – aye in thousands, too!

ALL: Goodness gracious,
    How audacious!
    Earth is spacious,
        Why come here?
    Our impeding
    Their proceeding
    Were good breeding,
        That is clear!

DIANA: Jupiter, hear my plea,
      Upon the mount if *they* light,
    There'll be an end of me,
      I won't be seen by daylight!

APOLLO: Tartarus[17] is the place
      These scoundrels you should send to –
    Should they behold my face
      My influence there's an end to!

JUPITER [*looking over precipice*]:
      What fools to give themselves so much exertion!

DIANA: " " A government survey, I'll make assertion!

APOLLO: " " Perhaps the Alpine club at their diversion!

MERCURY: " " They seem to be more like a 'Cook's
      Excursion'.[18]

ALL: Goodness gracious, etc.

APOLLO: If, mighty Jove, you value your existence,
      Send them a thunderbolt with your regards!

JUPITER: My thunderbolts, though valid at a distance,
      Are not effective at a hundred yards.

MERCURY: Let the moon's rays, Diana, strike 'em flighty,
      Make 'em all lunatics in various styles!

DIANA: My Lunar rays unhappily are mighty
      Only at many hundred thousand miles.

ALL: Goodness gracious, etc.

[*Exeunt* JUPITER, APOLLO, DIANA *and* MERCURY
into ruined temple.]

[*Enter* SPARKEION *and* NICEMIS *climbing mountain at back.*]

SPARKEION: Here we are at last on the very summit and we've left the others ever so far behind! Why, what's this?

NICEMIS: A ruined Palace! A Palace on the top of a mountain. I wonder who lives here? Some mighty king I dare say, with wealth beyond all counting, who came to live up here –

SPARKEION: To avoid his creditors! It's a lovely situation for a country house, though it's very much out of repair.

NICEMIS: Very inconvenient situation.

SPARKEION: Inconvenient?

NICEMIS: Yes – how are you to get butter, milk and eggs up here? No pigs – no poultry – no postman. Why, I should go mad.

SPARKEION: What a dear little practical mind it is! What a wife you will make!

NICEMIS: Don't be too sure – we are only partly married – the marriage ceremony lasts all day.

SPARKEION: I've no doubt at all about it. We shall be as happy as a king and queen, though we are only a strolling actor and actress.

NICEMIS: It's very kind of Thespis to celebrate our marriage day by giving the company a picnic on this lovely mountain.

SPARKEION: And still more kind to allow us to get so much ahead of all the others. Discreet Thespis! [*Kissing her.*]

NICEMIS: There now, get away, do! Remember the marriage ceremony is not yet completed.

SPARKEION: But it would be ungrateful to Thespis's discretion not to take advantage of it by improving the opportunity.

NICEMIS: Certainly not; get away.

SPARKEION: On second thoughts, the opportunity's so good it don't admit of improvement. There! [*Kisses her.*]

NICEMIS: How dare you kiss me before we are quite married.

SPARKEION: Attribute it to the intoxicating influence of the mountain air.

NICEMIS: Then we had better go down again. It is not right to expose ourselves to influences over which we have no control.

DUET – SPARKEION *and* NICEMIS

SPARKEION: Here far away from all the world,
　　　　　　　Dissension and derision,
　　　　　With Nature's wonders all unfurled
　　　　　　　To our delighted vision,
　　　　　　　　With no one here
　　　　　　　　　(At least in sight)
　　　　　　　　To interfere
　　　　　　　　　With our delight,
　　　　　　　And two fond lovers sever,
　　　　　　　　Oh do not free,
　　　　　　　　　Thine hand from mine,
　　　　　　　　I swear to thee
　　　　　　　　　My love is thine,
　　　　　　　For ever and for ever!

NICEMIS: On mountain top the air is keen,
　　　　　　　And most exhilarating,
　　　　　And we say things we do not mean
　　　　　　　In moments less elating.
　　　　　　　　So please to wait;
　　　　　　　　　For thoughts that crop
　　　　　　　　En tête-à-tête,
　　　　　　　　On mountain top,
　　　　　　　May not exactly tally
　　　　　　　　With those that you
　　　　　　　　　May entertain,
　　　　　　　　Returning to
　　　　　　　　　The sober plain
　　　　　Of yon relaxing valley.

SPARKEION: Very well – if you won't have anything to say to me, I know who will.

NICEMIS: Who will?

SPARKEION: Daphne[19] will.

NICEMIS: Daphne would flirt with anybody.

SPARKEION: Anybody would flirt with Daphne. She is quite as pretty as you and has twice as much back-hair.

NICEMIS: She has twice as much money, which may account for it.

SPARKEION: At all events *she* has appreciation. *She* likes good looks.

NICEMIS: We all like what we haven't got.

SPARKEION: *She* keeps her eyes open.

NICEMIS: Yes – one of them.

SPARKEION: Which one?

NICEMIS: The one she doesn't wink with.

SPARKEION: Well, I was engaged to her for six months, and if she still makes eyes at me, you must attribute it to force of habit. Besides, remember – we are only half-married at present.

NICEMIS: I suppose you mean that you are going to treat me as shamefully as you treated her. Very well, break it off it you like. *I* shall not offer any objection. Thespis used to be very attentive to me, and I'd just as soon be a manager's wife as a fifth-rate actor's!

[*Chorus heard, at first below, then enter* DAPHNE, PRETTEIA, PREPOSTEROS, STUPIDAS, TIPSEION, CYMON *and other members of* THESPIS*'s company climbing over rocks at back. All carry small baskets.*]

CHORUS – *with dance*

> Climbing over rocky mountain,
> Skipping rivulet and fountain,
> Passing where the willows quiver,
> By the ever-rolling river,
>   Swollen with the summer rain,
> Threading long and leafy mazes,
> Dotted with unnumbered daisies,
> Scaling rough and rugged passes,
> Climb the hardy lads and lasses,
>   Till the mountain top they gain.

FIRST VOICE: Fill the cup and tread the measure,
                        Make the most of fleeting leisure,
                        Hail it as a true ally,
                        Though it perish bye and bye!

SECOND VOICE: Every moment brings a treasure
                        Of its own especial pleasure;
                        Though the moments quickly die,
                        Greet them gaily as they fly!

THIRD VOICE: Far away from grief and care,
                        High up in the mountain air,
                        Let us live and reign alone
                        In a world that's all our own.

FOURTH VOICE: Here enthroned in the sky,
                        Far away from mortal eye,
                        We'll be gods and make decrees,
                        Those may honour them who please.

CHORUS: Fill the cup and tread the measure, etc.

[*After* CHORUS *and* COUPLETS, *enter* THESPIS *climbing over rocks.*]

THESPIS: Bless you, my people, bless you. Let the revels commence. After all, for thorough, unconstrained, unconventional enjoyment give me a picnic.

PREPOSTEROS [*very gloomily*]: Give him a picnic, somebody!

THESPIS: Be quiet, Preposteros – don't interrupt.

PREPOSTEROS: Ha! ha! shut up again! But no matter.

[STUPIDAS *endeavours, in pantomime, to reconcile him. Throughout the scene* PREPOSTEROS *shows symptoms of breaking out into a furious passion and* STUPIDAS *does all he can to pacify and restrain him.*]

THESPIS: The best of a picnic is that everybody contributes what he pleases, and nobody knows what anybody else has brought till the last moment. Now, unpack everybody, and let's see what there is for everybody.

NICEMIS: I have brought you – a bottle of soda water – for the claret cup.

DAPHNE: I have brought you – a lettuce for the lobster salad.

SPARKEION: A piece of ice – for the claret cup.

PRETTEIA: A bottle of vinegar – for the lobster salad.

CYMON: A bunch of burrage[20] for the claret cup!

TIPSEION: A hard-boiled egg – for the lobster salad!

STUPIDAS: One lump of sugar for the claret cup!

PREPOSTEROS: He has brought one lump of sugar for the claret cup! Ha! ha! ha! [*Laughing melodramatically.*]

STUPIDAS: Well, Preposteros, and what have *you* brought?

PREPOSTEROS: *I* have brought *two* lumps of the very best salt for the lobster salad.

THESPIS: Oh – is that all?

PREPOSTEROS: All! Ha! Ha! He asks if it is all! [STUPIDAS *consoles him.*]

THESPIS: But I say – this is capital, as far as it goes – nothing could be better, but it don't go far enough. The claret, for instance! I don't insist on claret – or a lobster – I don't insist on lobster, but a lobster salad without a lobster, why it isn't lobster salad. Here, Tipseion!

TIPSEION [*a very drunken bloated fellow, dressed however with scrupulous accuracy and wearing a large medal round his neck*]: My master? [*Falls on his knees to* THESPIS *and kisses his robe.*]

THESPIS: Get up – don't be a fool – Where's the claret? We arranged last week that you were to see to that?

TIPSEION: True, dear master – But then I was a drunkard!

THESPIS: You were.

TIPSEION: You engaged me to play convivial parts on the strength of my personal appearance.

THESPIS: I did.

TIPSEION: You then found that my habits interfered with my duties as low comedian.

THESPIS: True –

TIPSEION: You said yesterday that unless I took the pledge you would dismiss me from your company.

THESPIS: Quite so.

TIPSEION: Good. I have taken it. It is all I have taken since yesterday. My preserver! [*Embraces him.*]

THESPIS: Yes, but where's the wine?

TIPSEION: I left it behind, that I might not be tempted to violate my pledge.

PREPOSTEROS: Minion! [*Attempts to get at him – is restrained by* STUPIDAS.]

THESPIS: Now, Preposteros, what *is* the matter with you?

PREPOSTEROS: It is enough that I am down-trodden in my profession. I will not submit to imposition out of it. It is enough that as your heavy villain I get the worst of it every night in a combat of six. I will *not* submit to insult in the day time. I have come out, ha! ha! to enjoy myself!

THESPIS: But look here, you know – virtue only triumphs at night from seven to ten – vice gets the best of it during the other twenty-one hours. Won't that satisfy you? [STUPIDAS *endeavours to pacify him.*]

PREPOSTEROS [*irritated, to* STUPIDAS]: Ye are odious to my sight! get out of it!

STUPIDAS [*in great terror*]: What have I done?

THESPIS: Now *what* is it, Preposteros, *what* is it?

PREPOSTEROS: I a – hate him and would have his life!

THESPIS [*to* STUPIDAS]: That's it – he hates you and would have your life – now go and be merry.

STUPIDAS: Yes, but why does he hate me?

THESPIS: Oh – exactly. [*To* PREPOSTEROS] Why do you hate him?

PREPOSTEROS: Because he is a minion!

THESPIS: He hates you because you are a minion. It explains itself. Now go and enjoy yourselves. Ha! ha! It is well for those who *can* laugh – let them do so – there is no extra charge. The light-hearted cup and the convivial jest for them – but for me – what is there for me?

SILLIMON: There is some claret cup and lobster salad [*handing some*].

THESPIS [*taking it*]: Thank you. [*Resuming*] What is there for me but anxiety – ceaseless gnawing anxiety that tears at my very vitals and rends my peace of mind asunder? There is nothing whatever for me but anxiety of the nature I have just described. The charge of these thoughtless revellers is my unhappy lot. It is not a small charge and it is rightly termed a lot, because they are many. Oh why did the gods make me a manager?

SILLIMON [*as guessing a riddle*]: *Why* did the gods make him a manager?

SPARKEION: Why did the *gods* make him a manager?

DAPHNE: Why did the gods make *him* a manager?

PRETTEIA: Why did the gods make him a *manager*?

THESPIS: No-no – what are you talking about? what do you mean?

DAPHNE: I've got it – don't tell us –

ALL: No-no – because-because –

THESPIS [*annoyed*]: It isn't a conundrum – it's a misanthropical question. Why cannot I join you? [*Retires up-stage centre.*]

DAPHNE [*who is sitting with* SPARKEION *to the annoyance of* NICEMIS, *who is crying alone*]: I'm sure I don't know. We do not want you. Don't distress yourself on our account – we are getting on very comfortably – aren't we, Sparkeion?

SPARKEION: We are so happy that we don't miss the lobster or the claret. What are lobster and claret compared with the society of those we love! [*Embracing* DAPHNE.]

DAPHNE: Why, Nicemis, love, you are eating nothing. Aren't you happy, dear?

NICEMIS [*spitefully*]: *You* are *quite* welcome to *my* share of *everything. I* intend to console *myself* with the society of my manager. [*Takes* THESPIS*'s arm affectionately.*]

THESPIS: Here, I say – this won't do, you know – I can't allow it – at least before my company – besides, you are half-married to Sparkeion. Sparkeion, here's your half-wife impairing my influence before my company. Don't you know the story of the gentleman who undermined his influence by associating with his inferiors?

ALL: Yes, yes, – we know it.

PREPOSTEROS [*furiously*]: *I* do not know it! It's ever thus! Doomed
 to disappointment from my earliest years – [STUPIDAS *endeavours
 to console him.*]
THESPIS: There – that's enough. Preposteros – you *shall* hear it.

SONG

THESPIS: I once knew a chap who discharged a function
            On the North South East West Diddlesex[21] junction,
            He was conspicu*ous* exceeding,
            For his affable ways and his easy breeding.
            Although a Chairman of Directors,
            He was hand in glove with the ticket inspectors,
            He tipped the guards with bran-new fivers,
            And sang little songs to the engine drivers.
                'Twas told to me with great compunction,
                By one who had discharged with unction,
                A Chairman of Directors' function,
                On the North South East West Diddlesex junction.
                    Fol diddle, lol diddle, lol lol lay.

            Each Christmas day he gave each stoker
            A silver shovel and a golden poker,
            He'd button-hole flowers for the ticket sorters,
            And rich Bath-buns[22] for the outside porters.
            He'd mount the clerks on his first-class hunters,
            And he built little villas for the road-side shunters,
            And if any were fond of pigeon shooting,
            He'd ask them down to his place at Tooting.[23]
                'Twas told to me, etc.

            In course of time there spread a rumour
            That he did all this from a sense of humour,
            So instead of signalling and stoking,
            They gave themselves up to a course of joking.
            Whenever they knew that he was riding,
            They shunted his train on a lonely siding,

Or stopped all night in the middle of a tunnel,
On the plea that the boiler was a-coming through the
    funnel.
    'Twas told to me, etc.

If he wished to go to Perth or Stirling,
His train through several counties whirling,
Would set him down in a fit of larking,
At four a.m. in the wilds of Barking.[24]
This pleased his whim and seemed to strike it,
But the general Public did not like it.
The receipts fell, after a few repeatings,
And he got it hot at the Annual meetings.
    'Twas told to me, etc.

He followed out his whim with vigour,
The shares went down to a nominal figure.
These are the consequences all proceeding
From his affable ways and his easy breeding!
The line, with its rails and guards and peelers,
Was sold for a song to marine-store dealers,
The shareholders are all in the work'us,
And he sells pipe-lights in the Regent Circus.[25]
    'Twas told to me with much compunction,
    By one who had discharged with unction,
    A Chairman of Directors' function,
    On the North South East West Diddlesex junction,
        Fol diddle, lol diddle, lol lol lay!

It's very hard. As a man I am naturally of an easy disposition. As a manager, I am compelled to hold myself aloof, that my influence may not be deteriorated. As a man, I am inclined to fraternize with the pauper – as a manager I am compelled to walk about like this: Don't know yah! Don't know yah! don't know yah! [*Strides haughtily about the stage.*]

[JUPITER, MARS *and* APOLLO, *in full Olympian costume, appear on the three broken columns. Thespians scream.*]

JUPITER, MARS *and* APOLLO [*in recitative*]: Presumptuous mortal!

THESPIS [*same business*]: Don't know yah! Don't know yah!

JUPITER, MARS *and* APOLLO [*seated on three broken pillars, still in recitative*]: Presumptuous mortal!

THESPIS: I do not know you, I do not know you.

JUPITER, MARS *and* APOLLO [*standing on ground, recitative*]: Presumptuous mortal!

THESPIS [*recitative*]: Remove this person! [STUPIDAS *and* PREPOSTEROS *seize* APOLLO *and* MARS.]

JUPITER [*speaking*]: Stop, you evidently *don't* know me. Allow me to offer you my card. [*Throws flash paper.*]

THESPIS: Ah, yes, it's very pretty, but we don't want any at present. When we do our Christmas piece I'll let you know. [*Changing his manner*] Look here, you know, this is a private party and we haven't the pleasure of your acquaintance. There are a good many other mountains about, if you must have a mountain all to yourself. Don't make me let myself down before my company. [*Resuming*] Don't know yah! Don't know yah!

JUPITER: I am Jupiter, the King of the Gods. This is Apollo. This is Mars. [*All kneel to them except* THESPIS.]

THESPIS: Oh, then as I'm a respectable man, and rather particular about the company I keep, I think I'll go.

JUPITER: No-no – Stop a bit. We want to consult you on a matter of great importance. There! Now we are alone. Who are you?

THESPIS: I am Thespis of the Thessalian[26] Theatres.

JUPITER: The very man we want. Now as a judge of what the public likes, are you impressed with my appearance as the father of the gods?

THESPIS: Well, to be candid with you, I am not. In fact I'm disappointed.

JUPITER: Disappointed?

THESPIS: Yes, you see you're so much out of repair. No, you don't come up to my idea of the part. Bless you, I've played you often.

JUPITER: You have!

THESPIS: To be sure I have.

JUPITER: And how have you dressed the part?

THESPIS: Fine commanding party in the prime of life. Thunderbolt –

full beard – dignified manner – A good deal of this sort of thing: 'Don't know yah! Don't know yah! Don't know yah!' [*Imitating.*]

JUPITER [*much affected*]: I-I'm very much obliged to you. It's very good of you. I-I-I used to be like that. I can't tell you how much I feel it. And do you find I'm an impressive character to play?

THESPIS: Well, no, I can't say you are. In fact we don't use you much out of burlesque.

JUPITER: Burlesque! [*Offended, walks up-stage.*]

THESPIS: Yes, it's a painful subject; drop it, drop it. The fact is, you are not the gods you were – you're behind your age.

JUPITER: Well, but what are we to do? We feel that we ought to do something, but we don't know what.

THESPIS: Why don't you all go down to Earth, incog, mingle with the world, hear and see what people think of you, and judge for yourselves, as to the best means to take to restore your influence.

JUPITER: Ah, but what's to become of Olympus in the meantime?

THESPIS: Lor' bless you, don't distress yourself about that. I've a very clever company, used to take long parts on the shortest notice. Invest us with your powers and we'll fill your places till you return.

JUPITER [*aside*]: The offer is tempting. But suppose you fail?

THESPIS: Fail! Oh, we never fail in our profession. We've nothing but great successes!

JUPITER: Then it's a bargain?

THESPIS: It's a bargain. [*They shake hands on it.*]

JUPITER: And that you may not be entirely without assistance, we will leave you Mercury, and whenever you find yourself in a difficulty you can consult him.

[*Enter* MERCURY *through trap.*]

QUARTETTE – JUPITER, MERCURY, APOLLO, DIANA

JUPITER: So that's arranged – you take my place, my boy,
      While we make trial of a new existence.
    At length I shall be able to enjoy
      The pleasures I have envied from a distance.

MERCURY: Compelled upon Olympus here to stop,
    While other gods go down to play the hero,
  Don't be surprised if on this mountain top,
    You find your Mercury is down at zero!

APOLLO: To earth away! to join in mortal acts,
    And gather fresh materials to write on,
  Investigate more closely several facts,
    That I for centuries have thrown some light on!

DIANA: I, as the modest moon with crescent bow,
    Have always shown a light to nightly scandal,
  I must say I should like to go below,
    And find out if the game is worth the candle!

[*Enter all the Thespians, summoned by* MERCURY.]

MERCURY: Here come your people!

THESPIS: People better now!

AIR

THESPIS: While mighty Jove goes down below
    With all the other deities,
  I fill his place and wear his 'clo',
    The very part for me it is.
  To mother earth to make a track,
    They all are spurred and booted, too,
  And you will fill, till they come back,
    The parts you best are suited to.

CHORUS: Here's a pretty tale for future Iliads and Odysseys:[27]
  Mortals are about to personate the gods and
    goddesses.
  Now to set the world in order, we will work in unity;
  Jupiter's perplexity is Thespis' opportunity.

SOLO

SPARKEION: Phoebus am I, with golden ray,
    The God of Day, the God of Day.
When shadowy night has held her sway,
    I make the goddess fly.
'Tis mine the task to wake the world,
    In slumber curled, in slumber curled;
By me her charms are all unfurled,
    The God of Day am I!

CHORUS: The God of Day, the God of Day,
That part shall our Sparkeion play.
    Ha! ha! etc.
The rarest fun and rarest fare,
That ever fell to mortal share!
    Ha! ha! etc.

SOLO

NICEMIS: I am the Moon, the lamp of night.
    I show a light – I show a light.
With radiant sheen I put to flight
    The shadows of the sky.
By my fair rays, as you're aware,
    Gay lovers swear – gay lovers swear,
While graybeards sleep away their care,
    The lamp of night am I!

CHORUS: The lamp of night – the lamp of night,
Nicemis plays, to her delight,
    Ha! ha! ha! ha!
The rarest fun and rarest fare
That ever fell to mortal share,
    Ha! ha! ha! ha!

SOLO

TIMIDON: Mighty old Mars, the God of War,
　　I'm destined for – I'm destined for –
A terribly famous conqueror,
　　With sword upon his thigh.
When armies meet with eager shout,
　　And warlike rout, and warlike rout,
You'll find me there without a doubt.
　　The God of War am I!

CHORUS: The God of War, the God of War,
Great Timidon is destined for!
　　Ha! ha! ha! ha!
The rarest fun and rarest fare,
That ever fell to mortal share.
　　Ha! ha! ha! ha! etc.

SOLO

DAPHNE: When, as the fruit of warlike deeds,
　　The soldier bleeds, the soldier bleeds,
Calliope[28] crowns heroic deeds,
　　With immortality.
From mere oblivion I reclaim
　　The soldier's name, the soldier's name,
And write it on the roll of fame,
　　The Muse of Fame, am I!

CHORUS: The Muse of Fame, the Muse of Fame,
Calliope is Daphne's name,
　　Ha! ha! ha! ha!
The rarest fun and rarest fare,
That ever fell to mortal share!
　　Ha! ha! ha! ha!

TUTTI: Here's a pretty tale!

[*Enter procession of old gods. They come down very much aston-ished at all they see, then, passing by, ascend the platform that leads to the descent at the back.*]

GODS [JUPITER, DIANA *and* APOLLO, *in corner together*]:

We will go,
Down below,
Revels rare,
We will share.
    Ha! ha! ha!
With a gay
Holiday,
All unknown,
And alone.
    Ha! ha! ha!

TUTTI: Here's a pretty tale!

[*The Gods, including those who have lately entered in procession, group themselves on rising ground at back. The Thespians (kneel-ing) bid them farewell.*]

CURTAIN

ACT II

SCENE – *The same scene as in Act I, with the exception that in place of the ruins that filled the foreground of the stage, the interior of a magnificent temple is seen, showing the background of the scene of Act I, through the columns of the portico at the back. High throne, low seats below it.*

[*All the substitute gods and goddesses (that is to say, Thespians) are discovered grouped in picturesque attitudes about the stage, eating, drinking and smoking, and singing the following verses:*]

CHORUS: Of all symposia,[29]
    The best by half,
      Upon Olympus, here, await us,
  We eat Ambrosia,[30]
    And nectar quaff –
      It cheers but don't inebriate us.
  We know the fallacies
    Of human food,
      So please to pass Olympian rosy,
  We built up palaces,
    Where ruins stood,
      And find them much more snug and cosy.

SOLO

SILLIMON: To work and think, my dear,
                    Up here, would be,
                        The height of conscientious folly,
                  So eat and drink, my dear –
                    I like to see,
                        Young people gay – young people jolly!
                  Olympian food my love,
                    I'll lay long odds,
                        Will please your lips – those rosy portals.
                  What is the good, my love,
                    Of being gods,
                        If we must work like common mortals?

CHORUS: Of all symposia, etc.

> [*Exeuent all but* NICEMIS, *who is dressed as* DIANA, *and*
> PRETTEIA *who is dressed as* VENUS. *They take*
> SILLIMON'*s arm and bring him down-stage.*]

SILLIMON: Bless their little hearts, I can refuse them nothing. As the Olympian stage-manager I ought to be strict with them and make them do their duty, but I can't. Bless their little hearts, when I see the pretty little craft come sailing up to me with a wheedling smile on their pretty little figure-heads, I can't turn my back on 'em. I'm all bow, though I'm sure I try to be stern!

PRETTEIA: You certainly are a dear old thing.

SILLIMON: She says I'm a dear old thing! Deputy Venus says I'm a dear old thing!

NICEMIS: It's her affectionate habit to describe everybody in those terms. *I* am more particular, but still even *I* am bound to admit that you are certainly a very dear old thing.

SILLIMON: Deputy Venus says I'm a dear old thing, and deputy Diana, who is much more particular, endorses it! Who could be severe with such deputy divinities!

PRETTEIA: Do you know, I'm going to ask you a favour.

SILLIMON: Venus is going to ask me a favour!

PRETTEIA: You see, I am Venus.

SILLIMON: No one who saw your face would doubt it.

NICEMIS [*aside*]: No one who knew her *character* would!

PRETTEIA: Well, Venus, you know, is married to Mars.

SILLIMON: To Vulcan,[31] my dear, to Vulcan. The exact connubial relation of the different gods and goddesses is a point on which we must be extremely particular.

PRETTEIA: I beg your pardon – Venus is married to Mars.

NICEMIS: If she isn't married to Mars, she ought to be.

SILLIMON: Then that decides it – call it married to Mars.

PRETTEIA: Married to Vulcan or married to Mars, what does it signify?

SILLIMON: My dear, it's a matter on which I have no personal feeling whatever.

PRETTEIA: So that she is married to some one!

SILLIMON: Exactly, so that she is married to some one. Call it married to Mars.

PRETTEIA: Now here's my difficulty. Presumptios takes the place of Mars, and Presumptios is my father!

SILLIMON: Then why object to Vulcan?

PRETTEIA: Because Vulcan is my grandfather!

SILLIMON: But my dear, what an objection. You are playing a part till the real gods return. That's all! Whether you are supposed to be married to your father – or your grandfather, what does it matter? This passion for realism is the curse of the stage!

PRETTEIA: That's all very well, but I can't throw myself into a part that has already lasted a twelvemonth, when I have to make love to my father. It interferes with my conception of the characters. It spoils the part.

SILLIMON: Well, well, I'll see what can be done. [*Exit* PRETTEIA.] That's always the way with beginners, they've no imaginative power. A true artist ought to be superior to such considerations. [NICEMIS *comes down-stage.*] Well, Nicemis – I should say Diana – what's wrong with you? Don't you like your part?

NICEMIS: Oh, immensely! It's great fun.

SILLIMON: Don't you find it lonely out by yourself all night?

NICEMIS: Oh, but I'm *not* alone all night!

SILLIMON: But – I don't want to ask any injudicious questions – but who accompanies you?

NICEMIS: Who? why Sparkeion, of course.

SILLIMON: Sparkeion? Well, but Sparkeion is Phoebus Apollo. He's the Sun, you know.

[*Enter* SPARKEION.]

NICEMIS: Of course he is. I should catch my death of cold, in the night air, if he didn't accompany me.

SPARKEION: My dear Sillimon, it would never do for a young lady to be out alone all night. It wouldn't be respectable.

SILLIMON: There's a good deal of truth in that. But still – the Sun – at night – I don't like the idea. The original Diana always went out alone.

NICEMIS: I hope the original Diana is no rule for *me*. After all, what *does* it matter?

SILLIMON: To be sure – what *does* it matter?

SPARKEION: The sun at night, or in the daytime!

SILLIMON: So that he shines. That's all that's necessary. But poor Daphne, what will she say to this?

[*Exit* NICEMIS.]

SPARKEION: Oh, Daphne can console herself, young ladies soon get over this sort of thing. Did you never hear of the young lady who was engaged to cousin Robin?

SILLIMON: Never.

SPARKEION: Then I'll sing it to you.

SONG

SPARKEION: Little maid of Arcadee[32]
Sat on Cousin Robin's knee,
Though in form and face and limb,
Nobody could rival him.
He was brave and she was fair.
Truth, they made a pretty pair,
Happy little maiden, she!
Happy maid of Arcadee.

Moments fled as moments will,
Happily enough, until,
After, say, a month or two,
Robin did as Robins do.
Weary of his lover's play,
Jilted her and went away.
Wretched little maiden, she –
Wretched maid of Arcadee!

To her little home she crept,
There she sat her down and wept.
Maiden wept as maidens will –
Grew so thin and pale – until
Cousin Richard came to woo!
Then again the roses grew!
Happy little maiden, she –
Happy maid of Arcadee!

[*Exit* SPARKEION.]

SILLIMON: Well, Mercury, my boy, you've had a year's experience of us up here. How do we do it? I think we're rather an improvement on the original gods – don't you?

MERCURY: Well, you see, there's a good deal to be said on both sides of the question. You are certainly younger than the original gods, and, therefore, more active. On the other hand, they are certainly older than you, and have, therefore, more experience. On the whole, I prefer you, because your mistakes amuse me.

SONG

MERCURY: Olympus is now in a terrible muddle,
    The deputy deities all are at fault;
  They splutter and splash like a pig in the puddle,
    And dickens a one of 'em's earning his salt.
  For Thespis as Jove is a terrible blunder,
    Too nervous and timid – too easy and weak –
  Whenever he's called on to lighten or thunder,
    The thought of it keeps him awake for a week!

Then mighty Mars hasn't the pluck of a parrot,
　　When left in the dark he will quiver and quail;
And Vulcan has arms that would snap like a carrot,
　　Before he could drive in a tenpenny nail!
Then Venus's freckles are very repelling.
　　And Venus should *not* have a squint in her eyes;
The learned Minerva is weak in her spelling,
　　And scatters her h's all over the skies.

Then Pluto,[33] in kindhearted tenderness erring,
　　Can't make up his mind to let anyone die –
The *Times* has a paragraph ever recurring,
　　'Remarkable instance of longevity.'
On some it has come as a serious onus,
　　To others it's quite an advantage – in short,
While ev'ry Life Office declares a big bonus,
　　The poor undertakers are all in the court!

Then Cupid the rascal, forgetting his trade is
　　To make men and women impartially smart;
Will only shoot at pretty young ladies,
　　And never takes aim at a bachelor's heart.
The results of this freak – or whatever you term it –
　　Should cover the wicked young scamp with
　　　　disgrace;
While ev'ry young man is as shy as a hermit,
　　Young ladies are popping all over the place!

This wouldn't much matter – for bashful and shy men,
　　When skilfully handled, are certain to fall,
But alas that determined young bachelor Hymen
　　Refuses to wed anybody at all!
He swears that Love's flame is the vilest of arsons,
　　And looks upon marriage as quite a mistake;
Now what in the world's to become of the parsons,
　　And what of the artist who sugars the cake?

In short, you will see from the facts that I'm showing,
    The state of the case is exceedingly sad.
If Thespis's people go on as they're going,
    Olympus will certainly go to the bad!
From Jupiter downwards there isn't a dab in it,
    All of 'em quibble and shuffle and shirk;
A premier in Downing Street forming a cabinet,
    Couldn't find people less fit for their work!

[*Enter* THESPIS.]

THESPIS: Sillimon, you can retire.

SILLIMON: Sir, I –

THESPIS: Don't pretend you can't when I say you can. I've seen you do it, go. Well, Mercury, I've been in power one year to-day.

[*Exit* SILLIMON *bowing extravagantly.* THESPIS *imitates him.*]

MERCURY: One year to-day. How do you like ruling the world?

THESPIS: Like it! Why it's as straightforward as possible. Why there hasn't been a hitch of any kind since we came up here. Lor'! The airs you gods and goddesses give yourselves, are perfectly sickening. Why it's mere child's play!

MERCURY: Very simple, isn't it?

THESPIS: Simple! Why I could do it on my head!

MERCURY: Ah – I daresay you will do it on your head very soon.

THESPIS: What do you mean by *that*, Mercury?

MERCURY: I mean that when you've turned the world *quite* topsy-turvy you won't know whether you're standing on your head or your heels.

THESPIS: Well, but Mercury, it's all right at present.

MERCURY: Oh yes – as far as we know.

THESPIS: Well, but you know, we know as much as anybody knows, you know. I believe that the world's still going on.

MERCURY: Yes – as far as we can judge – much as usual.

THESPIS: Well, then, give the father of the Drama his due, Mercury. Don't be envious of the father of the Drama.

MERCURY: Well, but you see you leave so much to accident.

THESPIS: Well, Mercury, if I do, it's my principle. I am an easy man, and I like to make things as pleasant as possible. What did I do the day we took office? Why, I called the company together and I said to them: 'Here we are, you know, gods and goddesses, no mistake about it, the real thing. Well, we have certain duties to discharge; let's discharge them intelligently. Don't let us be hampered by routine and red tape and precedent; let's set the original gods an example, and put a liberal interpretation on our duties. If it occurs to any one to try an experiment in his own department, let him try it; if he fails there's no harm done; if he succeeds it is a distinct gain to society. Take it easy,' I said, 'and at the same time, make experiments. Don't hurry your work, do it slowly and do it well.' And here we are after a twelvemonth, and not a single complaint or a single petition has reached me.

MERCURY: No – not yet.

THESPIS: What do you mean by 'no, not yet'?

MERCURY: Well, you see, you don't understand these things. All the petitions that are addressed by men to Jupiter pass through my hands, and it's my duty to collect them and present them once a year.

THESPIS: Oh, only once a year?

MERCURY: Only once a year.

THESPIS: And the year is up –?

MERCURY: To-day.

THESPIS: Oh, then I suppose there are *some* complaints.

MERCURY: Yes, there *are some.*

THESPIS [*disturbed*]: Oh. Perhaps there are a good many?

MERCURY: There are, a good many.

THESPIS: Oh. Perhaps there are a thundering lot?

MERCURY: There are a thundering lot.

THESPIS [*very much disturbed*]: Oh!

MERCURY: You see you've been taking it so very easy – and so have most of your company.

THESPIS: Oh, who has been taking it easy?

MERCURY: Well, all except those who have been trying experiments.

THESPIS: Well, but I suppose the experiments are ingenious?

MERCURY: Yes, they are ingenious, but on the whole ill-judged. But it's time to go and summon your court.

THESPIS: What for?

MERCURY: To hear the complaints. In five minutes they will be here.   [*Exit.*]

THESPIS [*very uneasy*]: I don't know how it is, but there is something in that young man's manner that suggests that the Father of the gods has been taking it *too* easy. Perhaps it would have been better if I hadn't given my company so much scope. I wonder what they've been doing. I think I will curtail their discretion; though none of them appear to have much of the article it seems a pity to deprive 'em of what little they have.

   [*Enter* DAPHNE, *weeping.*]

THESPIS: Now, then, Daphne, what's the matter with you?

DAPHNE: Well, you know how disgracefully Sparkeion –

THESPIS [*correcting her*]: Apollo –

DAPHNE: Apollo, then – has treated me. He promised to marry me years ago, and now he's married to Nicemis.

THESPIS: Now look here. I can't go into that. You're in Olympus now and must behave accordingly. Drop your Daphne – assume your Calliope.

DAPHNE: Quite so. That's it! [*Mysteriously.*]

THESPIS: Oh – that is it? [*Puzzled.*]

DAPHNE: That is it, Thespis. I am Calliope the Muse of Fame. Very good. This morning I was in the Olympian library, and I took down the only book there. Here it is.

THESPIS [*taking it*]: Lemprière's Classical Dictionary.[34] The Olympian Peerage.

DAPHNE: Open it at Apollo.

THESPIS [*opens it*]: It is done.

DAPHNE: Read.

THESPIS: 'Apollo was several times married, among others to Issa,[35] Bolina,[36] Coronis,[37] Chymene,[38] Cyrene,[39] Chione,[40] Acacallis[41] and Calliope.'

DAPHNE: *And* Calliope.

THESPIS [*musing*]: Ha! I didn't know he was *married* to them.

DAPHNE [*severely*]: Sir! This is the Family Edition.

THESPIS: Quite so.

DAPHNE: You couldn't expect a lady to read any other?

THESPIS: On no consideration. But in the original version –

DAPHNE: I go by the Family Edition.

THESPIS: Then by the Family Edition, Apollo is your husband.

[*Enter* NICEMIS *and* SPARKEION.]

NICEMIS: Apollo *your* husband? He is *my* husband.

DAPHNE: I beg your pardon. He is *my* husband.

NICEMIS: Apollo is Sparkeion and he's married to *me*.

DAPHNE: Sparkeion is Apollo and he's married to *me*.

NICEMIS: He's my husband.

DAPHNE: He's your brother.

THESPIS: Look here, Apollo, whose husband are you? Don't let's have any row about it; whose husband are you?

SPARKEION: Upon my honour I don't know. I'm in a very delicate position, but I'll fall in with any arrangement Thespis may propose.

DAPHNE: I've just found out that he's my husband and yet he goes out every evening with that 'thing'!

THESPIS: Perhaps he's trying an experiment.

DAPHNE: I don't like my husband to make such experiments. The question is, who are we all and what is our relation to each other?

QUARTETTE

SPARKEION:	You're Diana, I'm Apollo –
	And Calliope is she.
DAPHNE:	He's your brother,
NICEMIS:	You're another.
	He has fairly married me.
DAPHNE:	By the rules of this fair spot,
	I'm his wife and you are not –

SPARKEION *and* DAPHNE:

By the rules of this fair spot,

$\left. \begin{array}{l} \text{I'm} \\ \text{She's} \end{array} \right\}$ his wife and you are not.

NICEMIS: By this golden wedding ring,

I'm his wife and you're a 'thing'.

DAPHNE, NICEMIS *and* SPARKEION:

> By this golden wedding ring,
>
> $\left.\begin{array}{l}\text{I'm}\\\text{She's}\end{array}\right\}$ his wife and you're a 'thing'.

ALL: Please will some one kindly tell us,

> Who are our respective kin?
>
> All of $\left\{\begin{array}{l}\text{us}\\\text{them}\end{array}\right\}$ are very jealous,
>
> Neither of $\left\{\begin{array}{l}\text{us}\\\text{them}\end{array}\right\}$ will give in.

NICEMIS: He's my husband, I declare,

> I espoused him properlee.

SPARKEION: That is true for I was there,

> And I saw her marry me.

DAPHNE: He's your brother – I'm his wife,

> If we go by Lemprière.

SPARKEION: So she is, upon my life,

> Really that seems very fair.

NICEMIS: You're my husband and no other,

SPARKEION: That is true enough, I swear,

DAPHNE: I'm his wife and you're his brother,

SPARKEION: If we go by Lemprière.

NICEMIS: It will surely be unfair,

> To decide by Lemprière [*crying*].

DAPHNE: It will surely be quite fair,

> To decide by Lemprière,

SPARKEION *and* THESPIS:

> How you settle I don't care,
>
> Leave it all to Lemprière.
>
> [*Spoken*] The Verdict:
>
> > As Sparkeion is Apollo
> >
> > > Up in this Olympian clime,
> >
> > Why, Nicemis, it will follow,
> >
> > > He's *her* husband, for the time – [*indicating*
> > > DAPHNE].
> >
> > When Sparkeion turns to mortal,
> >
> > > Joins once more the sons of men,

He may take *you* to his portal [*indicating*
    NICEMIS].
He will be *your* husband then.
That, oh that is my decision,
  'Cording to my mental vision.
Put an end to all collision,
    That, oh that is my decision.
My decision – my decision,

ALL: That, oh that is his decision,
His decision – his decision! etc.
        [*Exeunt* SPARKEION *with* DAPHNE, NICEMIS
                        weeping with THESPIS.]
[*Mysterious music. Enter* JUPITER, APOLLO *and* MARS, *from
below, at the back of stage. All wear cloaks as disguise and all
are masked.*]

RECITATIVE

JUPITER, APOLLO *and* MARS:
        Oh rage and fury! Oh shame and sorrow!
        We'll be resuming our ranks to-morrow.
        Since from Olympus we have departed,
        We've been distracted and brokenhearted.
        Oh wicked Thespis! Oh villain scurvy;
        Through him Olympus is topsy-turvy!
        Compelled to silence, to grin and bear it!
        He's caused our sorrow, and he shall share it.
        Where is the monster! Avenge his blunders;
        He has awakened Olympian thunders.

[*Enter* MERCURY.]
JUPITER [*recitative*]: Oh Monster!
APOLLO [*recitative*]:   Oh Monster!
MARS [*recitative*]:   Oh Monster!
MERCURY [*in great terror*]: Please, sir, what have I done, sir?
JUPITER: What did we leave you behind for?

MERCURY: Please, sir, that's the question I asked when you went away.

JUPITER: Was it not that Thespis might consult you whenever he was in a difficulty?

MERCURY: Well, here I've been, ready to be consulted, chock-full of reliable information – running over with celestial maxims – advice gratis ten to four – after twelve ring the night bell in cases of emergency.

JUPITER: And hasn't he consulted you?

MERCURY: Not he – he disagrees with me about everything.

JUPITER: He must have misunderstood me. I told him to consult you whenever he was in a fix.

MERCURY: He must have thought you said *in*sult. Why, whenever I open my mouth he jumps down my throat. It isn't pleasant to have a fellow constantly jumping down your throat – especially when he always disagrees with you. It's just the sort of thing I can't digest.

JUPITER [*in a rage*]: Send him here. I'll talk to him!

[*Enter* THESPIS. *He is much terrified.*]

JUPITER [*recitative*]: Oh Monster!

APOLLO [*recitative*]:   Oh Monster!

MARS [*recitative*]:   Oh Monster!

[THESPIS *sings in great terror, which he endeavours to conceal.*]

JUPITER: Well, sir, the year is up to-day.

APOLLO: And a nice mess you've made of it.

MARS: You've deranged the whole scheme of society!

THESPIS [*aside*]: There's going to be a row! [*Aloud and very familiarly*] My dear boy – I do assure you –

JUPITER [*recitative*]: Be respectful!

APOLLO [*recitative*]: Be respectful!

MARS [*recitative*]: Be respectful!

THESPIS: I don't know what you allude to. With the exception of getting our scene painter to 'run up' this temple, because we found the ruins draughty, we haven't touched a thing.

JUPITER [*recitative*]: Oh, story-teller!

APOLLO [*recitative*]: Oh, story-teller!

MARS [*recitative*]: Oh, story-teller!

THESPIS: My dear fellows, you're distressing yourselves unnecessarily. The court of Olympus is about to assemble to listen to the complaints of the year, if any. But there are none, or next to none. Let the Olympians assemble!

[*Enter* THESPIANS. THESPIS *takes chair.* JUPITER, APOLLO *and* MARS *sit below him.*]

THESPIS: Ladies and gentlemen. It seems that it is usual for the gods to assemble once a year to listen to mortal petitions. It don't seem to me to be a good plan, as work is liable to accumulate, but as I'm particularly anxious not to interfere with Olympian precedent, but to allow everything to go on as it has always been accustomed to go, why we'll say no more about it. [*Aside*] But how shall I account for your presence?

JUPITER: Say we are gentlemen of the press.

THESPIS: That all our proceedings may be perfectly open and above-board I have communicated with the most influential members of the Athenian press, and I beg to introduce to your notice three of its most distinguished members. They bear marks emblematic of the anonymous character of modern journalism. [*Business of introduction.* THESPIS *very uneasy.*] Now, then, if you're all ready we will begin.

MERCURY [*brings tremendous bundles of petitions*]: Here is the agenda.

THESPIS: What's that? The petitions?

MERCURY: Some of them. [*Opens one and reads.*] Ah, I thought there'd be a row about it.

THESPIS: Why, what's wrong now?

MERCURY: Why, it's been a foggy Friday in November for the last six months and the Athenians are tired of it.

THESPIS: There's no pleasing some people. This craving for perpetual change is the curse of the country. Friday's a very nice day.

MERCURY: So it is, but a Friday six months long – it gets monotonous.

JUPITER, APOLLO *and* MARS [*recitative, rising*]: It's perfectly ridiculous.

THESPIS [*calling them*]: It shall be arranged. Cymon!

CYMON [*as Time, with the usual attributes*]: Sir!

THESPIS [*introducing him to three gods*]: Allow me – Father Time – rather young at present but even Time must have a beginning. In course of Time, Time will grow older. Now then, Father Time, what's this about a wet Friday in November for the last six months?

CYMON: Well, the fact is, I've been trying an experiment. Seven days in the week is an awkward number. It can't be halved. Two's into seven won't go.

THESPIS [*tries it on his fingers*]: Quite so – quite so.

CYMON: So I abolished Saturday.

JUPITER, APOLLO *and* MARS: Oh, but – [*rising*].

THESPIS: Do be quiet. He's a very intelligent young man and knows what he is about. So you abolished Saturday. And how did you find it answered?

CYMON: Admirably.

THESPIS: You hear? He found it answered admirably.

CYMON: Yes, only Sunday refused to take its place.

THESPIS: Sunday refused to take its place?

CYMON: Sunday comes after Saturday – Sunday won't go on duty after Friday, Sunday's principles are very strict. That's where my experiment sticks.

THESPIS: Well, but why November? Come! why November?

CYMON: December can't begin till November has finished. November can't finish because he's abolished Saturday. There again my experiment sticks.

THESPIS: Well, but why wet? Come, now, why wet?

CYMON: Ah, that's your fault. You turned on the rain six months ago and you've forgot to turn it off again.

JUPITER, MARS *and* APOLLO [*rising – recitative*]: Oh, this is monstrous!

ALL: Order, order!

THESPIS: Gentlemen, pray be seated. [*To the others*] The liberty of the press, one can't help it. [*To the three gods*] It is easily settled. Athens has had a wet Friday in November for the last six months. Let them have a blazing Tuesday in July for the next twelve.

JUPITER, MARS *and* APOLLO: But –

ALL: Order, order!

THESPIS: Now, then, the next article.

MERCURY: Here's a petition from the Peace Society. They complain that there are no more battles.

MARS [*springing up*]: What!

THESPIS: Quiet there! Good dog – soho; Timidon!

TIMIDON [*as* MARS]: Here.

THESPIS: What's this about there being no battles?

TIMIDON: I've abolished battles; it's an experiment.

MARS [*springing up*]: Oh, come, I say –

THESPIS: Quiet, then! [*To* TIMIDON] Abolished battles?

TIMIDON: Yes, you told us on taking office to remember two things, to try experiments and to take it easy. I found I couldn't take it easy while there are any battles to attend to, so I tried the experiment and abolished battles. And then I took it easy. The Peace Society ought to be very much obliged to me.

THESPIS: Obliged to you? Why, confound it! since battles have been abolished war is universal.

TIMIDON: War universal?

THESPIS: To be sure it is! Now that nations can't fight, no two of 'em are on speaking terms. The dread of fighting was the only thing that kept them civil to each other. Let battles be restored and peace reign supreme.

MERCURY [*reads*]: Here's a petition from the associated wine merchants of Mytilene.[42]

THESPIS: Well, what's wrong with the associated wine merchants of Mytilene? Are there no grapes this year?

MERCURY: Plenty of grapes, more than usual.

THESPIS [*to the gods*]: You observe, there's no deception, there are more than usual.

MERCURY: There are plenty of grapes, only they are full of ginger beer.

THREE GODS: Oh, come, I say [*rising, they are put down by* THESPIS].

THESPIS: Eh? what? [*Much alarmed.*] Bacchus?

TIPSEION [*as* BACCHUS]: Here!

THESPIS: There seems to be something unusual with the grapes of Mytilene, they only grow ginger beer.

TIPSEION: And a very good thing too.

THESPIS: It's very nice in its way, but it is not what one looks for from grapes.

TIPSEION: Beloved master, a week before we came up here, you insisted on my taking the pledge. By so doing you rescued me from my otherwise inevitable misery. I cannot utter my thanks. Embrace me! [*Attempts to embrace him.*]

THESPIS: Get out, don't be a fool. Look here, you know you're the God of Wine.

TIPSEION: I am.

THESPIS [*very angry*]: Well, do you consider it consistent with your duty as the God of Wine to make the grapes yield nothing but ginger beer?

TIPSEION: Do you consider it consistent with my duty as a total abstainer, to grow anything stronger than ginger beer?

THESPIS: But your duty as the God of Wine –

TIPSEION: In every respect in which my duty as the God of Wine can be discharged consistently with my duty as a total abstainer, I will discharge it. But when the functions clash, everything must give way to the pledge. My preserver! [*Attempts to embrace him.*]

THESPIS: Don't be a confounded fool! This can be arranged. We can't give over the wine this year, but at least we can improve the ginger beer. Let all the ginger beer be extracted from it immediately.

JUPITER, MARS *and* APOLLO [*aside*]:

> We can't stand this,
> We can't stand this,
> It's much too strong,
> We can't stand this.
> It would be wrong,
> Extremely wrong,
> If we stood this,
>> If we stand this,
>> If we stand this,
>> We can't stand this.

DAPHNE, SPARKEION *and* NICEMIS:
> Great Jove, this interference,
>> Is more than we can stand;
> Of them make a clearance,
>> With your majestic hand.

JUPITER: This cool audacity, it beats us hollow! [*Removing mask*]
  I'm Jupiter!
MARS: I'm Mars!
APOLLO: I'm Apollo!
  [*Enter* DIANA, *and all the other Gods and Goddesses.*]
ALL [*kneeling with their foreheads on the ground*]:
> Jupiter, Mars and Apollo,
>> Have quitted the dwellings of men;
> The other gods quickly will follow,
>> And what will become of us then?

> Oh pardon us, Jove and Apollo,
>> Pardon us, Jupiter, Mars;
> Oh, see us in misery wallow,
>> Cursing our terrible stars.

[*Enter other Gods.*]

CHORUS AND BALLET

ALL THE THESPIANS:
> Let us remain, we beg of you pleadingly!
THREE GODS:
> Let them remain, they beg of us pleadingly!
THESPIANS: Life on Olympus suits us exceedingly,
GODS: Life on Olympus suits them exceedingly.
THESPIANS: Let us remain, we pray in humility,
GODS: Let 'em remain, they pray in humility.
THESPIANS: If we have shown some little ability –
GODS: If they have shown some little ability –
ALL: Let us remain, etc.

JUPITER: Enough, your reign is ended;
       Upon this sacred hill
    Let him be apprehended,
       And learn our awful will.
    Away to earth, contemptible comedians,
       And hear our curse, before we set you free;
    You shall all be eminent tragedians,
       Whom no one ever, ever goes to see!

ALL: We go to earth, contemptible comedians,
       We hear his curse before he sets us free,
    We shall all be eminent tragedians,
       Whom no one ever ever goes to see!

SILLIMON: Whom no one –
SPARKEION: Whom no one –
THESPIS: Whom *no* one –
ALL: Ever, ever goes to see.

   [*The Thespians are driven away by the Gods, who group themselves in attitudes of triumph.*]

BALLET DIVERTISSEMENT[43]

THESPIS: Now here you see the arrant folly
    Of doing your best to make things jolly.
    I've ruled the world like a chap in his senses;
    Observe the terrible consequences.
    Great Jupiter, whom nothing pleases,
    Splutters and swears and kicks up breezes,
    And sends us home, in a mood avengin',
    In double quick time like a railroad engine.

     All this he does without compunction,
     Because I have discharged with unction
     A highly complicated function,
     Complying with his own injunction.
        Fol, lol, lay.

CHORUS: All this he does, etc.

[*The Gods drive the Thespians away. The Thespians prepare to descend the mountain.*]

CURTAIN

TRIAL BY JURY

DRAMATIS PERSONAE

THE LEARNED JUDGE
THE PLAINTIFF
THE DEFENDANT
COUNSEL FOR THE PLAINTIFF
USHER
FOREMAN OF THE JURY
ASSOCIATE
FIRST BRIDESMAID

Chorus of Jurymen, Bridesmaids and Members of the Public

SCENE – *A Court of Justice.*

[*Barristers, Attorneys and Jurymen discovered.*]

CHORUS: Hark, the hour of ten is sounding:
                    Hearts with anxious fears are bounding,
                    Hall of Justice crowds surrounding,
                        Breathing hope and fear –
                    For to-day in this arena,
                    Summoned by a stern subpoena,
                    Edwin, sued by Angelina,[1]
                        Shortly will appear.

[*Enter* USHER]

SOLO

USHER: Now, Jurymen, hear my advice –
                    All kinds of vulgar prejudice
                        I pray you set aside:
                    With stern judicial frame of mind
                    From bias free of every kind,
                        This trial must be tried.
CHORUS: From bias free of every kind,
                    This trial must be tried.

[*During Chorus,* USHER *sings fortissimo, 'Silence in Court!'*]

USHER: Oh, listen to the plaintiff's case:
                    Observe the features of her face –

                The broken-hearted bride.
                Condole with her distress of mind:
                From bias free of every kind,
                    This trial must be tried!

CHORUS: From bias free, etc.

USHER: And when amid the plaintiff's shrieks,
                The ruffianly defendant speaks –
                    Upon the other side;
                What *he* may say you needn't mind –
                From bias free of every kind,
                    This trial must be tried!

CHORUS: From bias free, etc.

    [*Enter* DEFENDANT.]

RECITATIVE

DEFENDANT: Is this the Court of the Exchequer?[2]

ALL: It is!

DEFENDANT [*aside*]:
                Be firm, be firm, my pecker,
                Your evil star's in the ascendant!

ALL: Who are you?

DEFENDANT: I'm the Defendant!

CHORUS OF JURYMEN [*shaking their fists*]:
                Monster, dread our damages.
                    We're the jury,
                    Dread our fury!

DEFENDANT: Hear me, hear me, if you please,
                  These are very strange proceedings –
                For permit me to remark
                  On the merits of my pleadings,
                You're at present in the dark.

    [DEFENDANT *beckons to* JURYMEN – *they leave the box and gather round him as they sing the following:*]
                That's a very true remark –
                  On the merits of his pleadings
                We're at present in the dark!
                Ha! ha! – ha! ha!

SONG

DEFENDANT: When first my old, old love I knew,
      My bosom welled with joy;
  My riches at her feet I threw –
      I was a love-sick boy!
  No terms seemed too extravagant
      Upon her to employ –
  I used to mope, and sigh, and pant,
      Just like a love-sick boy!
          Tink-a-Tank – Tink-a-Tank.

  But joy incessant palls the sense;
      And love, unchanged, will cloy,
  And she became a bore intense
      Unto her love-sick boy!
  With fitful glimmer burnt my flame,
      And I grew cold and coy,
  At last, one morning, I became
      Another's love-sick boy.
          Tink-a-Tank – Tink-a-Tank.

CHORUS OF JURYMEN [*advancing stealthily*]:
  Oh, I was like that when a lad!
      A shocking young scamp of a rover,
  I behaved like a regular cad;
      But that sort of thing is all over.
  I'm now a respectable chap
      And shine with a virtue resplendent
  And, therefore, I haven't a scrap
      Of sympathy with the defendant!
        He shall treat us with awe,
        If there isn't a flaw,
  Singing so merrily – Trial-la-law!
  Trial-la-law – Trial-la-law!
  Singing so merrily – Trial-la-law!
[*They enter the Jury-box.*]

RECITATIVE

USHER [on Bench]:

  Silence in Court, and all attention lend.
  Behold your Judge! In due submission bend!

 [Enter JUDGE on Bench.]

CHORUS: All hail great Judge!
   To your bright rays
  We never grudge
   Ecstatic praise.
     All hail!
  May each decree
   As statute rank
  And never be
   Reversed in banc.[3]
     All hail!

RECITATIVE

JUDGE: For these kind words accept my thanks, I pray.
  A Breach of Promise[4] we've to try to-day.
  But firstly, if the time you'll not begrudge,
  I'll tell you how I came to be a Judge.

ALL: He'll tell us how he came to be a Judge!

SONG

JUDGE: When I, good friends, was called to the bar,
   I'd an appetite fresh and hearty,
  But I was, as many young barristers are,
   An impecunious party.
  I'd a swallow-tail coat of a beautiful blue –
   A brief which I bought of a booby –
  A couple of shirts and a collar or two,
   And a ring that looked like a ruby!

CHORUS: A couple of shirts, etc.

JUDGE: In Westminster Hall[5] I danced a dance,
                 Like a semi-despondent fury;
             For I thought I should never hit on a chance
                 Of addressing a British Jury –
             But I soon got tired of third-class journeys,
                 And dinners of bread and water;
             So I fell in love with a rich attorney's
                 Elderly, ugly daughter.

CHORUS: So he fell in love, etc.

JUDGE: The rich attorney, he jumped with joy,
                 And replied to my fond professions:
             'You shall reap the reward of your pluck, my boy,
                 At the Bailey[6] and Middlesex Sessions.[7]
             You'll soon get used to her looks,' said he,
                 'And a very nice girl you'll find her!
             She may very well pass for forty-three
                 In the dusk, with a light behind her!'

CHORUS: She may very well, etc.

JUDGE: The rich attorney was good as his word;
                 The briefs came trooping gaily,
             And every day my voice was heard
                 At the Sessions or Ancient Bailey.
             All thieves who could my fees afford
                 Relied on my orations,
             And many a burglar I've restored
                 To his friends and his relations.

CHORUS: And many a burglar, etc.

JUDGE: At length I became as rich as the Gurneys[8] –
                 An incubus[9] then I thought her,
             So I threw over that rich attorney's
                 Elderly, ugly daughter.
             The rich attorney my character high
                 Tried vainly to disparage –
             And now, if you please, I'm ready to try
                 This Breach of Promise of Marriage!

CHORUS: And now if you please, etc.

JUDGE: For now I am a judge!
ALL: And a good Judge too.
JUDGE: Yes, now I am a Judge!
ALL: And a good Judge too!

JUDGE: Though all my law is fudge,
                  Yet I'll never, never budge,
                  But I'll live and die a Judge!
ALL: And a good Judge too!

JUDGE [*pianissimo*]:
                  It was managed by a job –
ALL: And a good job too!
JUDGE: It was managed by a job!
ALL: And a good job too!

JUDGE: It is patent to the mob,
                  That my being made a nob
                  Was effected by a job.
ALL: And a good job too!

[*Enter* COUNSEL *for* PLAINTIFF. *He takes his place in front row of Counsel's seats.*]

RECITATIVE

COUNSEL: Swear thou the Jury!
USHER: Kneel, Jurymen, oh, kneel!
    [*All the* JURY *kneel in the Jury-box, and so are hidden from audience.*]
USHER: Oh, will you swear by yonder skies,
                  Whatever question may arise,
                  'Twixt rich and poor, 'twixt low and high,
                  That you will well and truly try?
JURY [*raising their hands, which alone are visible*]:
                  To all of this we make reply,
                  By the dull slate of yonder sky:
                  That we will well and truly try.
    [*All rise with the last note.*]

RECITATIVE

COUNSEL: Where is the Plaintiff?
            Let her now be brought.
USHER: Oh, Angelina! Come thou into Court!
            Angelina! Angelina!!

[*Enter the* BRIDESMAIDS.]

CHORUS

CHORUS OF BRIDESMAIDS:

Comes the broken flower –
    Comes the cheated maid –
Though the tempest lower,
    Rain and cloud will fade!
Take, oh take these posies:
    Though thy beauty rare
Shame the blushing roses,
    They are passing fair!
        Wear the flowers till they fade;
        Happy be thy life, oh maid!

[*The* JUDGE, *having taken a great fancy to* FIRST BRIDESMAID, *sends her a note by* USHER, *which she reads, kisses rapturously, and places in her bosom.*]
[*Enter* PLAINTIFF.]

SOLO

PLAINTIFF: O'er the season vernal,
                Time may cast a shade;
              Sunshine, if eternal,
                Makes the roses fade!
              Time may do his duty;
                Let the thief alone –
              Winter hath a beauty,
                That is all his own.
                    Fairest days are sun and shade:
                    I am no unhappy maid!

[*The* JUDGE *having by this time transferred his admiration to* PLAINTIFF, *directs the* USHER *to take the note from* FIRST BRIDESMAID *and hand it to* PLAINTIFF, *who reads it, kisses it rapturously and places it in her bosom.*]

CHORUS OF BRIDESMAIDS:

Comes the broken flower, etc.

JUDGE: Oh, never, never, never, since I joined the human
race,

Saw I so exquisitely fair a face.

JURY [*shaking their forefingers at him*]:

Ah, sly dog! Ah, sly dog!

JUDGE [*to* JURY]:

How say you? Is she not designed for capture?

FOREMAN [*after consulting with the* JURY]:

We've but one word, my lord, and that is – Rapture.

PLAINTIFF [*curtseying*]:

Your kindness, gentlemen, quite overpowers!

JURY: We love you fondly and would make you ours!

BRIDESMAIDS [*shaking their forefingers at* JURY]:

Ah, sly dogs! Ah, sly dogs!

RECITATIVE

COUNSEL: May it please you, my lud!
Gentlemen of the jury!

ARIA

COUNSEL: With a sense of deep emotion,
I approach this painful case;
For I never had a notion
That a man could be so base,
Or deceive a girl confiding,
Vows, *etcetera*, deriding.

ALL: He deceived a girl confiding,
Vows, *etcetera*, deriding.

54

[PLAINTIFF *falls sobbing on* COUNSEL'*s breast and remains there.*]

COUNSEL: See my interesting client,
        Victim of a heartless wile!
       See the traitor all defiant
        Wear a supercilious smile!
       Sweetly smiled my client on him,
       Coyly woo'd and gently won him.
ALL: Sweetly smiled, etc.
COUNSEL: Swiftly fled each honeyed hour
        Spent with this unmanly male!
       Camberwell[10] became a bower,
        Peckham[11] an Arcadian Vale,[12]
       Breathing concentrated otto![13]
       An existence *à la* Watteau.[14]
ALL: Bless us, concentrated otto! etc.
COUNSEL: Picture, then, my client naming,
        And insisting on the day:
       Picture him excuses framing –
        Going from her far away;
       Doubly criminal to do so,
       For the maid had bought her *trousseau*!
ALL: Doubly criminal, etc.
COUNSEL [*to* PLAINTIFF, *who weeps*]:
       Cheer up, my pretty – oh, cheer up!
JURY: Cheer up, cheer up, we love you!
   [COUNSEL *leads* PLAINTIFF *fondly into* Witness-box; he takes
   a tender leave of her, and resumes his place in Court.*]
   [PLAINTIFF *reels as if about to faint.*]
JUDGE: That she is reeling
        Is plain to see!
FOREMAN: If faint you're feeling
        Recline on me!
   [*She falls sobbing on to the* FOREMAN'*s breast.*]
PLAINTIFF [*feebly*]:
       I shall recover
        If left alone.

ALL [*shaking their fists at* DEFENDANT]:

Oh, perjured lover,

Atone! atone!

FOREMAN: Just like a father

I wish to be. [*Kissing her.*]

JUDGE [*approaching her*]:

Or, if you'd rather,

Recline on me!

[*She jumps on to Bench, sits down by the* JUDGE, *and falls sobbing on his breast.*]

COUNSEL: Oh! fetch some water

From far Cologne![15]

ALL: For this sad slaughter

Atone! atone!

JURY [*shaking fists at* DEFENDANT]:

Monster, monster, dread our fury –

There's the Judge, and we're the Jury!

Come! Substantial damages,

Dam–

USHER: Silence in Court!

SONG

DEFENDANT: Oh, gentlemen, listen, I pray,

Though I own that my heart has been ranging,

Of nature the laws I obey,

For nature is constantly changing.

The moon in her phases is found,

The time and the wind and the weather,

The months in succession come round,

And you don't find two Mondays together.

Consider the moral, I pray,

Nor bring a young fellow to sorrow,

Who loves this young lady to-day,

And loves that young lady to-morrow.

BRIDESMAIDS [*rushing forward, and kneeling to* JURY]:

Consider the moral, etc.

DEFENDANT: You cannot eat breakfast all day,
  Nor is it the act of a sinner,
When breakfast is taken away,
  To turn your attention to dinner;
And it's not in the range of belief,
  That you could hold him as a glutton,
Who, when he is tired of beef,
  Determines to tackle the mutton.
    But this I am willing to say,
      If it will appease her sorrow,
    I'll marry this lady to-day,
      And I'll marry the other to-morrow!

BRIDESMAIDS [*rushing forward as before*]:
  But this he is willing to say, etc.

RECITATIVE

JUDGE: That seems a reasonable proposition,
  To which, I think, your client may agree.

COUNSEL: But, I submit, my lord, with all submission,
  To marry two at once is Burglaree!

 [*Referring to law book.*]

  In the reign of James the Second,[16]
  It was generally reckoned
  As a very serious crime
  To marry two wives at one time.

 [*Hands book up to* JUDGE, *who reads it.*]

ALL: Oh, man of learning!

QUARTETTE – JUDGE, COUNSEL,
DEFENDANT, PLAINTIFF

JUDGE: A nice dilemma we have here,
  That calls for all our wit:

COUNSEL: And at this stage, it don't appear
  That we can settle it.

DEFENDANT [*in Witness-box*]:

> If I to wed the girl am loth
> A breach 'twill surely be –

PLAINTIFF: And if he goes and marries both,

> It counts as Burglaree!

ALL: A nice dilemma, etc.

DUET – PLAINTIFF *and* DEFENDANT

PLAINTIFF [*embracing him rapturously*]:

> I love him – I love him – with fervour unceasing
> I worship and madly adore;
> My blind adoration is always increasing,
> My loss I shall ever deplore.
> Oh, see what a blessing, what love and caressing
> I've lost, and remember it, pray,
> When you I'm addressing, are busy assessing
> The damages Edwin must pay!

DEFENDANT [*repelling her furiously*]:

> I smoke like a furnace – I'm always in liquor,
> A ruffian – a bully – a sot;
> I'm sure I should thrash her, perhaps I should kick her,
> I am such a very bad lot!
> I'm not prepossessing, as you may be guessing,
> She couldn't endure me a day;
> Recall my professing, when you are assessing
> The damages Edwin must pay!

[*She clings to him passionately; after a struggle, he throws her off into arms of* COUNSEL.]

JURY: We would be fairly acting,

> But this is most distracting!

RECITATIVE

JUDGE: The question, gentlemen – is one of liquor;

> You ask for guidance – this is my reply:

He says, when tipsy, he would thrash and kick
   her,
  Let's make him tipsy, gentlemen, and try!

COUNSEL: With all respect
I do object!

PLAINTIFF: I do object!

DEFENDANT: I don't object!

ALL: With all respect
We do object!

JUDGE [*tossing his books and papers about*]:
  All the legal furies seize you!
  No proposal seems to please you,
  I can't stop up here all day,
  I must shortly go away.
  Barristers, and you, attorneys,
  Set out on your homeward journeys;
  Gentle, simple-minded Usher,
  Get you, if you like, to Russ*her*;
  Put your briefs upon the shelf,
  I will marry her myself!

[*He comes down from Bench to floor of Court. He embraces* ANGELINA.]

FINALE

PLAINTIFF: Oh, joy unbounded,
With wealth surrounded,
The knell is sounded
    Of grief and woe.

COUNSEL: With love devoted
On you he's doated.
To castle moated
    Away they go.

DEFENDANT: I wonder whether
They'll live together
In marriage tether
    In manner true?

USHER:	It seems to me, sir,
	Of such as she, sir,
	A judge is he, sir,
	And a good judge too.
JUDGE:	Yes, I am a Judge.
ALL:	And a good Judge too!
JUDGE:	Yes, I am a Judge.
ALL:	And a good Judge too!
JUDGE:	Though homeward as you trudge,
	You declare my law is fudge,
	Yet of beauty I'm a judge.
ALL:	And a good Judge too!
JUDGE:	Though defendant is a snob.
ALL:	And a great snob too!
JUDGE:	Though defendant is a snob,
	I'll reward him from my fob.
ALL:	So we've settled with the job,
	And a good job too!

CURTAIN

THE SORCERER

DRAMATIS PERSONAE

SIR MARMADUKE POINTDEXTRE (*an Elderly Baronet*)
ALEXIS (*of the Grenadier Guards – his Son*)
DR DALY (*Vicar of Ploverleigh*)
NOTARY
JOHN WELLINGTON WELLS (*of J. W. Wells & Co., Family Sorcerers*)
LADY SANGAZURE (*a Lady of Ancient Lineage*)
ALINE (*her Daughter – betrothed to Alexis*)
MRS PARTLET (*a Pew-opener*)
CONSTANCE (*her Daughter*)

Chorus of Villagers

ACT I – Exterior of Sir Marmaduke's Mansion, mid-day
(*Twelve hours are supposed to elapse between Acts I and II*)
ACT II – Exterior of Sir Marmaduke's Mansion, midnight

ACT I

SCENE – *Exterior of* SIR MARMADUKE's *Elizabethan Mansion.*

CHORUS OF VILLAGERS:
> Ring forth, ye bells,
>> With clarion sound –
> Forget your knells,
>> For joys abound.
> Forget your notes
>> Of mournful lay,
> And from your throats
>> Pour joy to-day.

> For to-day young Alexis – young Alexis Pointdextre[1]
> Is betrothed to Aline – to Aline Sangazure,[2]
> And that pride of his sex is – of his sex is to be next her,
> At the feast on the green – on the green, oh, be sure!
>> Ring forth, ye bells, etc.
>>> [*Exeunt the men into house.*]
> [*Enter* MRS PARTLET[3] *with* CONSTANCE, *her daughter.*]

RECITATIVE

MRS P.: Constance, my daughter, why this strange depression?
The village rings with seasonable joy,
Because the young and amiable Alexis,
Heir to the great Sir Marmaduke Pointdextre,
Is plighted to Aline, the only daughter
Of Annabella, Lady Sangazure.

You, you alone are sad and out of spirits;
What is the reason? Speak, my daughter, speak!

CON.: Oh, mother, do not ask! If my complexion
From red to white should change in quick succession,
And then from white to red, oh, take no notice!
If my poor limbs should tremble with emotion,
Pay no attention, mother – it is nothing!
If long and deep-drawn sighs I chance to utter,
Oh, heed them not, their cause must ne'er be known!

[MRS PARTLET *motions to* CHORUS *to leave her with* CON-STANCE.]

[*Exeunt Ladies of* CHORUS.]

ARIA

CON.: When he is here,
     I sigh with pleasure –
When he is gone,
     I sigh with grief.
My hopeless fear
     No soul can measure –
His love alone
     Can give my aching heart relief!

When he is cold,
     I weep for sorrow –
When he is kind,
     I weep for joy.
My grief untold
     Knows no to-morrow –
My woe can find
     No hope, no solace, no alloy!

When I rejoice,
     He shows no pleasure.
When I am sad,
     It grieves him not.

His solemn voice
  Has tones I treasure –
My heart they glad,
  They solace my unhappy lot!

When I despond,
  My woe they chasten –
When I take heart,
  My hope they cheer;
With folly fond
  To him I hasten –
From him apart,
  My life is very sad and drear!

MRS P.: Come, tell me all about it! Do not fear –
I, too, have loved; but that was long ago!
Who is the object of your young affections?

CON.: Hush, mother! He is here!

[*Enter* DR DALY.[4] *He is pensive and does not see them.*]

MRS P. [*amazed*]:   Our reverend vicar!

CON.: Oh, pity me, my heart is almost broken!

MRS P.: My child, be comforted. To such an union
I shall not offer any opposition.
Take him – he's yours! May you and he be happy!

CON.: But, mother dear, he is not yours to give!

MRS P.: That's true, indeed!

CON.:   He might object!

MRS P.:   He might.
But come – take heart – I'll probe him on the subject.
Be comforted – leave this affair to me.

RECITATIVE

DR D.: The air is charged with amatory numbers –
  Soft madrigals, and dreamy lovers' lays.
Peace, peace, old heart! Why waken from its slumbers
  The aching memory of the old, old days?

BALLAD

DR D.:   Time was when Love and I were well acquainted.
            Time was when we walked ever hand in hand.
        A saintly youth, with worldly thought untainted,
            None better-loved than I in all the land!
        Time was, when maidens of the noblest station,
            Forsaking even military men,
        Would gaze upon me, rapt in adoration –
            Ah me, I was a fair young curate then!

        Had I a headache? sighed the maids assembled;
            Had I a cold? welled forth the silent tear;
        Did I look pale? then half a parish trembled;
            And when I coughed all thought the end was near!
        I had no care – no jealous doubts hung o'er me –
            For I was loved beyond all other men.
        Fled gilded dukes and belted earls[5] before me –
            Ah me, I was a pale young curate then!

[*At the conclusion of the ballad,* MRS PARTLET *comes forward with* CONSTANCE.]

MRS P.: Good day, reverend sir.

DR D.: Ah, good Mrs Partlet, I am glad to see you. And your little daughter, Constance! Why, she is quite a little woman, I declare!

CON. [*aside*]: Oh, mother, I cannot speak to him!

MRS P.: Yes, reverend sir, she is nearly eighteen, and as good a girl as ever stepped. [*Aside to* DR D.]: Ah, sir, I'm afraid I shall soon lose her!

DR D. [*aside to* MRS P.]: Dear me, you pain me very much. Is she delicate?

MRS P.: Oh no, sir – I don't mean that – but young girls look to get married.

DR D.: Oh, I take you. To be sure. But there's plenty of time for that. Four or five years hence, Mrs Partlet, four or five years hence. But when the time *does* come, I shall have much pleasure in marrying her myself –

CON. [*aside*]: Oh, mother!

DR D.: To some strapping young fellow in her own rank of life.

CON. [*in tears*]: He does *not* love me!

MRS P.: I have often wondered, reverend sir (if you'll excuse the liberty), that *you* have never married.

DR D. [*aside*]: Be still, my fluttering heart!

MRS P.: A clergyman's wife does so much good in a village. Besides that, you are not as young as you were, and before very long you will want somebody to nurse you, and look after your little comforts.

DR D.: Mrs Partlet, there is much truth in what you say. I am indeed getting on in years, and a helpmate would cheer my declining days. Time was when it might have been; but I have left it too long – I am an old fogy, now, am I not, my dear? [*to* CONSTANCE] – a very old fogy, indeed. Ha! ha! No, Mrs Partlet, my mind is quite made up. I shall live and die a solitary old bachelor.

CON.: Oh, mother, mother! [*Sobs on* MRS PARTLET's *bosom.*]

MRS P.: Come, come, dear one, don't fret. At a more fitting time we will try again – we will try again.

[*Exeunt* MRS PARTLET *and* CONSTANCE.]

DR D. [*looking after them*]: Poor little girl! I'm afraid she has something on her mind. She is rather comely. Time was when this old heart would have throbbed in double-time at the sight of such a fairy form! But tush! I am puling! Here comes the young Alexis with his proud and happy father. Let me dry this tell-tale tear!

[*Enter* SIR MARMADUKE *and* ALEXIS.]

RECITATIVE

DR D.:   Sir Marmaduke – my dear young friend, Alexis –
On this most happy, most auspicious plighting –
Permit me, as a true old friend, to tender
My best, my very best congratulations!

SIR M.:   Sir, you are most obleeging!

ALEXIS: Dr Daly,
My dear old tutor, and my valued pastor,
I thank you from the bottom of my heart!
[*Spoken through music.*]

DR D.:   May fortune bless you! may the middle distance
Of your young life be pleasant as the foreground –
The joyous foreground! and, when you have reached it,
May that which now is the far-off horizon
(But which will then become the middle distance),
In fruitful promise be exceeded only
By that which will have opened, in the meantime,
Into a new and glorious horizon!

SIR M.:   Dear Sir, that is an excellent example
Of an old school of stately compliment
To which I have, through life, been much addicted.
Will you obleege me with a copy of it,
In clerkly manuscript, that I myself
May use it on appropriate occasions?

DR D.:   Sir, you shall have a fairly-written copy
Ere Sol has sunk into his western slumbers!

[*Exit* DR DALY.]

SIR M. [*to* ALEXIS, *who is in a reverie*]: Come, come, my son – your
fiancée will be here in five minutes. Rouse yourself to receive her.

ALEXIS: Oh rapture!

SIR M.: Yes, you are a fortunate young fellow, and I will not disguise
from you that this union with the House of Sangazure realizes my
fondest wishes. Aline is rich and she comes of a sufficiently old
family, for she is the seven thousand and thirty-seventh in direct
descent from Helen of Troy.[6] True, there was a blot on the
escutcheon of that lady – that affair with Paris – but where is the
family, other than my own, in which there is no flaw? You are a
lucky fellow, sir – a very lucky fellow!

ALEXIS: Father, I am welling over with limpid joy! No sickling taint
of sorrow overlies the lucid lake of liquid love,[7] upon which, hand
in hand, Aline and I are to float into eternity!

SIR M.: Alexis, I desire that of your love for this young lady you do
not speak so openly. You are always singing ballads in praise of her
beauty, and you expect the very menials who wait behind your
chair, to chorus your ecstasies. It is not delicate.

ALEXIS: Father, a man who loves as I love –

SIR M.: Pooh pooh, sir! fifty years ago I madly loved your future mother-in-law, the Lady Sangazure, and I have reason to believe that she returned my love. But were we guilty of the indelicacy of publicly rushing into each other's arms, exclaiming –

'Oh, my adored one!' 'Beloved boy!'
'Ecstatic rapture!' 'Unmingled joy!'

which seems to be the modern fashion of love-making? No! it was 'Madam, I trust you are in the enjoyment of good health' – 'Sir, you are vastly polite, I protest I am mighty well' – and so forth. Much more delicate – much more respectful. But see – Aline approaches – let us retire, that she may compose herself for the interesting ceremony in which she is to play so important a part.

[*Exeunt* SIR MARMADUKE *and* ALEXIS.]
[*Enter* ALINE, *on terrace, preceded by Chorus of Girls.*]

CHORUS OF GIRLS:
With heart and with voice
Let us welcome this mating:
To the youth of her choice,
With a heart palpitating,
Comes the lovely Aline!

May their love never cloy!
May their bliss be unbounded!
With a halo of joy
May their lives be surrounded!
Heaven bless our Aline!

RECITATIVE

ALINE: My kindly friends, I thank you for this greeting,
And as you wish me every earthly joy,
I trust your wishes may have quick fulfilment!

ARIA

ALINE:

Oh, happy young heart!
  Comes thy young lord a-wooing
With joy in his eyes,
  And pride in his breast –
Make much of thy prize,
  For he is the best
That ever came a-suing.
  Yet – yet we must part,
              Young heart!
  Yet – yet we must part!

Oh, merry young heart,
  Bright are the days of thy wooing!
But happier far
  The days untried –
No sorrow can mar,
  When Love has tied
The knot there's no undoing.
  Then, never to part,
              Young heart!
  Then, never to part!

[*Enter* LADY SANGAZURE.]

RECITATIVE

LADY S.:

My child, I join in these congratulations:
Heed not the tear that dims this aged eye!
Old memories crowd upon me. Though I sorrow,
'Tis for myself, Aline, and not for thee!

BALLAD

LADY S.:   In days gone by, these eyes were bright,
       This bosom fair, these cheeks were rosy,
    This faded brow was snowy white,
       These lips were fresh as new-plucked posy;
    My girlish love he never guessed,
       Until the day when we were parted;
    I treasured it within my heart,
       And lived alone and broken-hearted.

    These cheeks are wan with age and care,
       These weary eyes have done their duty,
    As white as falling snow my hair,
       And faded all my girlish beauty.
    I see my every charm depart;
       But Memory's chain I cannot sever,
    For ah, within my poor old heart
       The fire of love burns bright as ever!

[*Enter* ALEXIS, *preceded by Chorus of Men.*]

CHORUS OF MEN AND WOMEN:
       With heart and with voice
         Let us welcome this mating;
       To the maid of his choice,
         With a heart palpitating,
         Comes Alexis the brave!

[SIR MARMADUKE *enters.* LADY SANGAZURE *and he exhibit signs of strong emotion at the sight of each other, which they endeavour to repress.* ALEXIS *and* ALINE *rush into each other's arms.*]

RECITATIVE

ALEXIS: Oh, my adored one!
ALINE: Beloved boy!
ALEXIS: Ecstatic rapture!
ALINE: Unmingled joy!

[*They retire up-stage.*]

DUET – SIR MARMADUKE *and*
LADY SANGAZURE

SIR M. [*with stately courtesy*]:

>Welcome joy, adieu to sadness!
>   As Aurora[8] gilds the day,
>So those eyes, twin orbs of gladness,
>   Chase the clouds of care away.
>Irresistible incentive
>   Bids me humbly kiss your hand;
>I'm your servant most attentive –
>   Most attentive to command!

[*Aside with frantic vehemence*]

>Wild with adoration!
>Mad with fascination!
>To indulge my lamentation
>   No occasion do I miss!
>Goaded to distraction
>By maddening inaction,
>I find some satisfaction
>   In apostrophe like this:
>   'Sangazure immortal,
>   Sangazure divine,
>   Welcome to my portal,
>   Angel, oh be mine!'

[*Aloud with much ceremony*]

>Irresistible incentive
>   Bids me humbly kiss your hand;
>I'm your servant most attentive –
>   Most attentive to command!

LADY S.:

>Sir, I thank you most politely
>   For your graceful courtesee;
>Compliment more true and knightly
>   Never yet was paid to me!

Chivalry is an ingredient
　　Sadly lacking in our land –
Sir, I am your most obedient,
　　Most obedient to command!

[*Aside with great vehemence*]
　　　　Wild with adoration!
　　　　Mad with fascination!
　　　　To indulge my lamentation
　　　　　No occasion do I miss!
　　　　Goaded to distraction
　　　　By maddening inaction,
　　　　I find some satisfaction
　　　　　In apostrophe like this:
　　　　　'Marmaduke immortal,
　　　　　　Marmaduke divine,
　　　　　Take me to thy portal,
　　　　　　Loved one, oh be mine!'

[*Aloud with much ceremony*]
　　　　Chivalry is an ingredient
　　　　　Sadly lacking in our land;
　　　　Sir, I am your most obedient,
　　　　　Most obedient to command!
[*During this the* NOTARY[9] *has entered, with marriage contract.*]

RECITATIVE

NOTARY:　　All is prepared for sealing and for signing,
　　　　　　The contract has been drafted as agreed;
　　　　　Approach the table, oh, ye lovers pining,
　　　　　　With hand and seal come execute the deed!
[ALEXIS *and* ALINE *advance and sign,* ALEXIS *supported by* SIR
MARMADUKE, ALINE *by her Mother.*]

CHORUS: See they sign, without a quiver, it –
                       Then to seal proceed.
                       They deliver it – they deliver it
                       As their Act and Deed!

ALEXIS: I deliver it – I deliver it
                         As my Act and Deed!

ALINE: I deliver it – I deliver it
                         As my Act and Deed!

CHORUS: With heart and with voice
                       Let us welcome this mating;
                     Leave them here to rejoice,
                       With true love palpitating,
                        Alexis the brave,
                        And the lovely Aline!

                            [*Exeunt all but* ALEXIS *and* ALINE.]

ALEXIS: At last we are alone! My darling, you are now irrevocably betrothed to me. Are you not very, very happy?

ALINE: Oh, Alexis, can you doubt it? Do I not love you beyond all on earth, and am I not beloved in return? Is not true love, faithfully given and faithfully returned, the source of every earthly joy?

ALEXIS: Of that there can be no doubt. Oh, that the world could be persuaded of the truth of that maxim! Oh, that the world would break down the artificial barriers of rank, wealth, education, age, beauty, habits, taste and temper, and recognize the glorious principle, that in marriage alone is to be found the panacea for every ill!

ALINE: Continue to preach that sweet doctrine, and you will succeed, oh, evangel of true happiness!

ALEXIS: I hope so, but as yet the cause progresses but slowly. Still I have made some converts to the principle, that men and women should be coupled in matrimony without distinction of rank. I have lectured on the subject at Mechanics' Institutes,[10] and the mechanics were unanimous in favour of my views. I have preached in workhouses, beershops and Lunatic Asylums, and I have been received with enthusiasm. I have addressed navvies on the advantages that would accrue to them if they married wealthy ladies of rank and not a navvy dissented!

ALINE: Noble fellows![11] And yet there are those who hold that the uneducated classes are not open to argument! And what do the countesses say?

ALEXIS: Why, at present, it can't be denied, the aristocracy hold aloof.

ALINE: Ah, the working man is the true Intelligence after all!

ALEXIS: He is a noble creature when he is quite sober. Yes, Aline, true happiness comes of true love, and true love should be independent of external influences. It should live upon itself and by itself – in itself love should live for love alone!

BALLAD

ALEXIS: Love feeds on many kinds of food, I know,
  Some love for rank, and some for duty:
Some give their hearts away for empty show,
  And others love for youth and beauty.
To love for money all the world is prone:
  Some love themselves, and live all lonely:
Give me the love that loves for love alone –
  I love that love – I love it only!

  What man for any other joy can thirst,
    Whose loving wife adores him duly?
  Want, misery, and care may do their worst,
    If loving woman loves you truly.
  A lover's thoughts are ever with his own –
    None truly loved is ever lonely:
  Give me the love that loves for love alone –
    I love that love – I love it only!

ALINE: Oh, Alexis, those are noble principles!

ALEXIS: Yes, Aline, and I am going to take a desperate step in support of them. Have you ever heard of the firm of J. W. Wells & Co., the old-established Family Sorcerers in St Mary Axe?[12]

ALINE: I have seen their advertisement.

ALEXIS: They have invented a philtre,[13] which, if report may be believed, is simply infallible. I intend to distribute it through the village, and within half an hour of my doing so there will not be an adult in the place who will not have learnt the secret of pure and lasting happiness. What do you say to that?

ALINE: Well, dear, of course a filter is a very useful thing in a house; but still I don't quite see that it is the sort of thing that places its possessor on the very pinnacle of earthly joy.

ALEXIS: Aline, you misunderstand me. I didn't say filter – I said a philtre.

ALINE [alarmed]: You don't mean a love-potion?

ALEXIS: On the contrary – I *do* mean a love-potion.

ALINE: Oh, Alexis! I don't think it would be right. I don't indeed. And then – a real magician! Oh, it would be downright wicked.

ALEXIS: Aline, is it, or is it not, a laudable object to steep the whole village up to its lips in love, and to couple them in matrimony without distinction of age, rank or fortune?

ALINE: Unquestionably, but –

ALEXIS: Then unpleasant as it must be to have recourse to supernatural aid, I must nevertheless pocket my aversion, in deference to the great and good end I have in view. [*Calling*] Hercules.[14]

[*Enter a Page from tent.*]

PAGE: Yes, sir.

ALEXIS: Is Mr Wells there?

PAGE: He's in the tent, sir – refreshing.

ALEXIS: Ask him to be so good as to step this way.

PAGE: Yes, sir.   [*Exit.*]

ALINE: Oh, but, Alexis! A real Sorcerer! Oh, I shall be frightened to death!

ALEXIS: I trust my Aline will not yield to fear while the strong right arm of her Alexis is here to protect her.

ALINE: It's nonsense, dear, to talk of your protecting me with your strong right arm, in face of the fact that this Family Sorcerer could change me into a guinea-pig before you could turn round.

ALEXIS: He *could* change you into a guinea-pig, no doubt, but it is most unlikely that he would take such a liberty. It's a most respectable firm, and I am sure he would never be guilty of so untradesmanlike an act.

[*Enter* MR WELLS *from tent.*]

MR W.: Good day, sir [ALINE *much terrified.*]

ALEXIS: Good day – I believe you are a Sorcerer.

MR W.: Yes, sir, we practise Necromancy in all its branches. We've a choice assortment of wishing-caps, divining-rods, amulets, charms and counter-charms. We can cast you a nativity at a low figure, and we have a horoscope at three-and-six that we can guarantee. Our Abudah chests, each containing a patent Hag[15] who comes out and prophesies disasters, with spring complete, are strongly recommended. Our Aladdin lamps are very chaste, and our Prophetic Tablets, foretelling everything – from a change of Ministry down to a rise in Unified[16] – are much enquired for. Our penny Curse – one of the cheapest things in the trade – is considered infallible. We have some very superior Blessings, too, but they're very little asked for. We've only sold one since Christmas – to a gentleman who bought it to send to his mother-in-law – but it turned out that he was afflicted in the head, and it's been returned on our hands. But our sale of penny Curses, especially on Saturday nights, is tremendous. We can't turn 'em out fast enough.

SONG

MR W.:   Oh! my name is John Wellington Wells,[17]
    I'm a dealer in magic and spells,
     In blessings and curses
     And ever-filled purses,
    In prophecies, witches and knells.

    If you want a proud foe to 'make tracks' –
    If you'd melt a rich uncle in wax[18] –
     You've but to look in
     On our resident Djinn,[19]
    Number seventy, Simmery Axe![20]

We've a first-class assortment of magic;
    And for raising a posthumous shade
With effects that are comic or tragic,
    There's no cheaper house in the trade.
Love-philtre – we've quantities of it;
    And for knowledge if any one burns,
We keep an extremely small prophet, a prophet
    Who brings us unbounded returns:

        For he can prophesy
        With a wink *of* his eye,
        Peep with security
        Into futurity,
        Sum up your history,
        Clear up a mystery,
        Humour proclivity
        For a nativity – for a nativity;
        With mirrors so magical,[21]
        Tetrapods[22] tragical,
        Bogies spectacular,
        Answers oracular,
        Facts astronomical,
        Solemn or comical,
        And, if you want it, he
        Makes a reduction on taking a quantity!

                    Oh!
If any one anything lacks,
He'll find it all ready in stacks,
        If he'll only look in
        On the resident Djinn,
Number seventy, Simmery Axe!

    He can raise you hosts
                Of ghosts,
And that without reflectors;
    And creepy things

78

With wings,
And gaunt and grisly spectres.
He can fill you crowds
Of shrouds,
And horrify you vastly;
He can rack your brains
With chains,
And gibberings grim and ghastly!

Then, if you plan it, he
Changes organity,
With an urbanity,
Full of Satanity,
Vexes humanity
With an inanity
Fatal to vanity –
Driving your foes to the verge of insanity!

Barring tautology,
In demonology,
'Lectro-biology,[23]
Mystic nosology,[24]
Spirit philology,[25]
High-class astrology,
Such is his knowledge, he
Isn't the man to require an apology!

Oh!
My name is John Wellington Wells,
I'm a dealer in magic and spells,
In blessings and curses
And ever-filled purses,
In prophecies, witches and knells.

If any one anything lacks,
He'll find it all ready in stacks,
    If he'll only look in
    On the resident Djinn,
Number seventy, Simmery Axe!

ALEXIS: I have sent for you to consult you on a very important matter.
I believe you advertise a Patent Oxy-Hydrogen Love-at-first-sight
Philtre?

MR W.: Sir, it is our leading article. [*Producing a phial.*]

ALEXIS: Now I want to know if you can confidently guarantee it as
possessing all the qualities you claim for it in your advertisement?

MR W.: Sir, we are not in the habit of puffing our goods. Ours is an
old-established house with a large family connection and every
assurance held out in the advertisement is fully realized. [*Hurt.*]

ALINE [*aside*]: Oh, Alexis, don't offend him! He'll change us into
something dreadful – I know he will!

ALEXIS: I am anxious from purely philanthropical motives to distribute this philtre, secretly, among the inhabitants of this village. I
shall of course require a quantity. How do you sell it?

MR W.: In buying a quantity, sir, we should strongly advise your
taking it in the wood, and drawing it off as you happen to want it.
We have it in four-and-a-half and nine gallon casks – also in pipes
and hogsheads for laying down, and we deduct 10 per cent for
prompt cash.

ALEXIS: I should mention that I am a Member of the Army and Navy
Stores.[26]

MR W.: In that case we deduct 25 per cent.

ALEXIS: Aline, the villagers will assemble to carouse in a few minutes.
Go and fetch the tea-pot.

ALINE: But, Alexis –

ALEXIS: My dear, you must obey me, if you please. Go and fetch the
tea-pot.

ALINE [*going*]: I'm sure Dr Daly would disapprove of it!   [*Exit.*]

ALEXIS: And how soon does it take effect?

MR W.: In twelve hours. Whoever drinks of it loses consciousness for
that period, and on waking falls in love, as a matter of course, with

the first lady he meets who has also tasted it, and his affection is at once returned. One trial will prove the fact.

[*Enter* ALINE *with large tea-pot.*]

ALEXIS: Good: then, Mr Wells, I shall feel obliged if you will at once pour as much philtre into this tea-pot as will suffice to affect the whole village.

ALINE: But bless me, Alexis, many of the villagers are married people!

MR W.: Madam, this philtre is compounded on the strictest principles. On married people it has no effect whatever. But are you quite sure that you have nerve enough to carry you through the fearful ordeal?

ALEXIS: In the good cause I fear nothing.

MR W.: Very good, then, we will proceed at once to the Incantation.

[*The stage grows dark.*]

INCANTATION[27]

MR W.:
> Sprites of earth and air –
> Fiends of flame and fire[28] –
> Demon souls,
> Come here in shoals,
> This dreadful deed inspire!
> Appear, appear, appear.

MALE VOICES:
> Good master, we are here!

MR W.:
> Noisome hags of night –
> Imps of deadly shade –
> Pallid ghosts,
> Arise in hosts,
> And lend me all your aid.
> Appear, appear, appear!

FEMALE VOICES:
> Good master, we are here!

ALEXIS [*aside*]:
> Hark, they assemble,
> These fiends of the night!

ALINE [*aside*]:
> Oh, Alexis, I tremble,
> Seek safety in flight!

ARIA

ALINE: Let us fly to a far-off land,
   Where peace and plenty dwell –
  Where the sigh of the silver strand
   Is echoed in every shell.
  To the joy that land will give,
   On the wings of Love we'll fly;
  In innocence there to live –
   In innocence there to die!

CHORUS OF SPIRITS:
   Too late – too late
    It may not be!
   That happy fate
    Is not for thee!

ALEXIS, ALINE *and* MR W.:
   Too late – too late,
    That may not be!
   That happy fate
    Is not for $\begin{cases} \text{me!} \\ \text{thee!} \end{cases}$

MR W.: Now shrivelled hags, with poison bags,
   Discharge your loathsome loads!
  Spit flame and fire, unholy choir!
   Belch forth your venom, toads!
  Ye demons fell, with yelp and yell,
   Shed curses far afield –
  Ye fiends of night, your filthy blight
   In noisome plenty yield!

MR W. [*pouring phial into tea-pot – flash*]:
   Number One!

CHORUS: It is done!

MR W. [*same business*]:
   Number Two! [*flash*]

CHORUS: One too few!

MR W. [*same business*]:
   Number Three! [*flash*]

CHORUS: Set us free!

Set us free – our work is done.
　Ha! ha! ha!
Set us free – our course is run!
　Ha! ha! ha!

ALINE *and* ALEXIS [*aside*]:

Let us fly to a far-off land,
　Where peace and plenty dwell –
Where the sigh of the silver strand
　Is echoed in every shell.

CHORUS OF FIENDS:

Ha! ha! ha! ha! ha! ha! ha! ha! ha! ha!

[*Stage grows light.* MR WELLS *beckons villagers. Enter villagers and all the* dramatis personae, *dancing joyously.* MRS PARTLET *and* MR WELLS *then distribute tea-cups.*]

CHORUS:　　　　Now to the banquet we press;
　　　　　　　　Now for the eggs, the ham;
　　　　　　Now for the mustard and cress,
　　　　　　　　Now for the strawberry jam!
　　　　　　Now for the tea of our host,
　　　　　　　　Now for the rollicking bun,
　　　　　　Now for the muffin and toast,
　　　　　　　　Now for the gay Sally Lunn![29]

WOMEN:　　　The eggs and the ham, and the strawberry jam!
MEN:　　　　The rollicking bun, and the gay Sally Lunn!
　　　　　　　　The rollicking, rollicking bun!

RECITATIVE

SIR M.:　　　　Be happy all – the feast is spread before ye;
　　　　　　　　Fear nothing, but enjoy yourselves, I pray!
　　　　　　Eat, aye, and drink – be merry, I implore ye,
　　　　　　　　For once let thoughtless Folly rule the day.

TEA-CUP BRINDISI[30]

SIR M.:　　　　Eat, drink and be gay,
　　　　　　　　Banish all worry and sorrow,

> Laugh gaily to-day,
> > Weep, if you're sorry, to-morrow!
> Come, pass the cup round –
> > I will go bail for the liquor;
> It's strong, I'll be bound,
> > For it was brewed by the vicar!

CHORUS:
> None so knowing as he
> At brewing a jorum[31] of tea,
> > Ha! ha!
> A pretty stiff jorum of tea.

TRIO

MR W., ALINE *and* ALEXIS [*aside*]:
> See – see – they drink –
> > All thought unheeding,
> The tea-cups clink,
> > They are exceeding!

> Their hearts will melt
> > In half-an-hour –
> Then will be felt
> > The potion's power!

[*During this verse* CONSTANCE *has brought a small tea-pot, kettle, caddy and cosy to* DR DALY. *He makes tea scientifically.*]

BRINDISI, 2nd verse

DR D. [*with the tea-pot*]:
> Pain, trouble, and care,
> > Misery, heart-ache and worry,
> Quick, out of your lair!
> > Get you all gone in a hurry!
> Toil, sorrow and plot,
> > Fly away quicker and quicker –
> Three spoons to the pot –
> > That is the brew of your vicar!

CHORUS: None so cunning as he
               At brewing a jorum of tea,
                    Ha! ha!
               A pretty stiff jorum of tea!

ENSEMBLE

ALEXIS *and* ALINE [*aside*]:
               Oh love, true love – unworldly, abiding!
                 Source of all pleasure – true fountain of joy –
               Oh love, true love – divinely confiding,
                 Exquisite treasure that knows no alloy –
               Oh love, true love, rich harvest of gladness,
                 Peace-bearing tillage – great garner of bliss –
               Oh love, true love, look down on our sadness –
                 Dwell in this village – oh, hear us in this!
[*It becomes evident by the strange conduct of the characters that
the charm is working. All rub their eyes, and stagger about the
stage as if under the influence of a narcotic.*]

TUTTI [*aside*]   ALEXIS, MR W. *and* ALINE [*aside*]
Oh, marvellous illusion!   A marvellous illusion!
  Oh, terrible surprise!   A terrible surprise
What is this strange confusion   Excites a strange confusion
  That veils my aching eyes?   Within their aching eyes –
I must regain my senses,   They must regain their senses,
  Restoring Reason's law,   Restoring Reason's law,
Or fearful inferences   Or fearful inferences
  Society will draw!   Society will draw!

[*Those who have partaken of the philtre struggle in vain against its
effects, and, at the end of the chorus, fall insensible on the stage.*]

END OF ACT I

ACT II

SCENE – *Exterior of* SIR MARMADUKE's *mansion by moonlight. All the peasantry are discovered asleep on the ground, as at the end of Act I.*

[*Enter* MR WELLS, *on tiptoe, followed by* ALEXIS *and* ALINE. MR WELLS *carries a dark lantern.*[32]]

TRIO – ALEXIS, ALINE *and* MR WELLS

'Tis twelve, I think,
  And at this mystic hour
The magic drink
  Should manifest its power.
Oh, slumbering forms,
  How little have ye guessed
The fire that warms
  Each apathetic breast!

ALEXIS: But stay, my father is not here!
ALINE: And pray where is my mother dear?
MR W.: I did not think it meet to see
A dame of lengthy pedigree,
  A Baronet[33] and KCB,[34]
  A Doctor of Divinity,[35]
  And that respectable QC,[36]
  All fast asleep, al-fresco-ly,
  And so I had them taken home
  And put to bed respectably!
  I trust my conduct meets your approbation.

ALEXIS: Sir, you have acted with discrimination,
    And shown more delicate appreciation
    Than we expect in persons of your station.

MR W.: But soft – they waken, one by one –
    The spell has worked – the deed is done!
    I would suggest that we retire.
    While Love, the Housemaid, lights her kitchen fire!
    [*Exeunt* MR WELLS, ALEXIS *and* ALINE, *on tiptoe, as the
    villagers stretch their arms, yawn, rub their eyes, and sit up.*]

MEN: Why, where be oi,[37] and what be oi a doin',
    A sleepin' out, just when the dews du rise?

GIRLS: Why, that's the very way your health to ruin,
    And don't seem quite respectable likewise!

MEN [*staring at girls*]:
    Eh, that's you!
    Only think o' that now!

GIRLS [*coyly*]: What may you be at, now?
    Tell me, du!

MEN [*admiringly*]: Eh, what a nose,
    And eh, what eyes, miss!
    Lips like a rose,
    And cheeks likewise, miss!

GIRLS [*coyly*]: Oi tell you true,
    Which I've never done, sir,
    Oi loike you
    As I never loiked none, sir!

ALL: Eh, but oi du loike you!

MEN: If you'll marry me, I'll dig for
    you and rake for you!

GIRLS: If you'll marry me, I'll scrub
    for you and bake for you!

MEN: If you'll marry me, all others
    I'll forsake for you!

ALL: All this will I du, if you'll marry me!

GIRLS: If you'll marry me, I'll cook for
    you and brew for you!

MEN: If you'll marry me, I've guineas
    not a few for you!

GIRLS: If you'll marry me, I'll take you
in and du for you!

ALL: All this will I du, if you'll marry me!
Eh, but oi du loike you!

COUNTRY DANCE

[*At end of dance, enter* CONSTANCE *in tears, leading* NOTARY,
who carries an ear-trumpet.]

ARIA

CON.: Dear friends, take pity on my lot,
My cup is not of nectar!
I long have loved – as who would not? –
Our kind and reverend rector.
Long years ago my love began
So sweetly – yet so sadly –
But when I saw this plain old man,
Away my old affection ran –
I found I loved him madly.
Oh!

[*To* NOTARY] You very, very plain old man,
I love, I love you madly!

CHORUS: You very, very plain old man,
She loves, she loves you madly!

NOT.: I am a very deaf old man,
And hear you very badly!

CON.: I know not why I love him so;
It is enchantment, surely!
He's dry and snuffy, deaf and slow,
Ill-tempered, weak and poorly!
He's ugly, and absurdly dressed,
And sixty-seven nearly,
He's everything that I detest,
But if the truth must be confessed,

    I love him very dearly!
     Oh!
[*To* NOTARY] You're everything that I detest,
    But still I love you dearly!
CHORUS: You're everything that girls detest,
    But still she loves you dearly!
NOT.:   I caught that line, but for the rest,
    I did not hear it clearly!

 [*During this verse* ALINE *and* ALEXIS *have entered at back
 unobserved.*]

ALEXIS: Oh joy! oh joy!
    The charm works well,
     And all are now united.
ALINE: The blind young boy
    Obeys the spell,
     Their troth they all have plighted!

ENSEMBLE

ALINE *and* ALEXIS	CONSTANCE	NOTARY
Oh joy! oh joy!	Oh, bitter joy!	Oh joy! oh joy!
The charm works well,	No words can tell	No words can tell
And all are now united!	How my poor heart is	My state of mind
The blind young boy	blighted!	delighted.
Obeys the spell,	They'll soon employ	They'll soon employ
Their troth they all have	A marriage bell,	A marriage bell,
plighted.	To say that we're united.	To say that we're united.
True happiness	I do confess	True happiness
Reigns everywhere,	A sorrow rare	Reigns everywhere,
And dwells with both the	My humbled spirit	And dwells with both the
sexes,	vexes,	sexes,
And all will bless	And none will bless	And all will bless
The thoughtful care	Example rare	Example rare
Of their beloved Alexis!	Of their beloved Alexis!	Of their beloved Alexis!

[*All, except* ALEXIS *and* ALINE, *exeunt lovingly.*]

ALINE: How joyful they all seem in their new-found happiness! The whole village has paired off in the happiest manner. And yet not a match has been made that the hollow world would not consider ill-advised!

ALEXIS: But we are wiser – far wiser – than the world. Observe the good that will become of these ill-assorted unions. The miserly wife will check the reckless expenditure of her too frivolous consort, the wealthy husband will shower innumerable bonnets on his penniless bride, and the young and lively spouse will cheer the declining days of her aged partner with comic songs unceasing!

ALINE: What a delightful prospect for him!

ALEXIS: But one thing remains to be done, that my happiness may be complete. We must drink the philtre ourselves, that I may be assured of your love for ever and ever.

ALINE: Oh, Alexis, do you doubt me? Is it necessary that such love as ours should be secured by artificial means? Oh, no, no, no!

ALEXIS: My dear Aline, time works terrible changes, and I want to place our love beyond the chance of change.

ALINE: Alexis, it is already far beyond that chance. Have faith in me, for my love can never, never change!

ALEXIS: Then you absolutely refuse?

ALINE: I do. If you cannot trust me, you have no right to love me – no right to be loved *by* me.

ALEXIS: Enough, Aline, I shall know how to interpret this refusal.

BALLAD

ALEXIS: Thou hast the power thy vaunted love
            To sanctify, all doubt above,
                Despite the gathering shade:
            To make that love of thine so sure
            That, come what may, it must endure
                Till time itself shall fade.
                    Thy love is but a flower
                    That fades within the hour!
                    If such thy love, oh, shame!
                    Call it by other name –
                        It is not love!

Thine is the power and thine alone,
To place me on so proud a throne
That kings might envy me!
A priceless throne of love untold,
More rare than orient pearl and gold.
But no! Thou wouldst be free!
Such love is like the ray
That dies within the day:
If such thy love, oh, shame!
Call it by other name –
It is not love!

[*Enter* DR DALY.]

DR D. [*musing*]: It is singular – it is very singular. It has overthrown all my calculations. It is distinctly opposed to the doctrine of averages. I cannot understand it.

ALINE: Dear Dr Daly, what has puzzled you?

DR D.: My dear, this village has not hitherto been addicted to marrying and giving in marriage. Hitherto the youths of this village have not been enterprising, and the maidens have been distinctly coy. Judge then of my surprise when I tell you that the whole village came to me in a body just now, and implored me to join them in matrimony with as little delay as possible. Even your excellent father has hinted to me that before very long it is not unlikely that he also may change his condition.

ALINE: Oh, Alexis – do you hear that? Are you not delighted?

ALEXIS: Yes. I confess that a union between your mother and my father would be a happy circumstance indeed. [*Crossing to* DR DALY] My dear sir – the news that you bring us is very gratifying.

DR D.: Yes – still, in my eyes, it has its melancholy side. This universal marrying recalls the happy days – now, alas, gone for ever – when I myself might have – but tush! I am puling. I am too old to marry – and yet, within the last half-hour, I have greatly yearned for companionship. I never remarked it before, but the young maidens of this village are very comely. So likewise are the middle-aged. Also the elderly. All are comely – and [*with a deep sigh*] all are engaged!

ALINE: Here comes your father.

[*Enter* SIR MARMADUKE *with* MRS PARTLET, *arm-in-arm.*]

ALINE *and* ALEXIS [*aside*]: Mrs Partlet!

SIR M.: Dr Daly, give me joy. Alexis, my dear boy, you will, I am sure, be pleased to hear that my declining days are not unlikely to be solaced by the companionship of this good, virtuous and amiable woman.

ALEXIS [*rather taken aback*]: My dear father, this is not altogether what I expected. I am certainly taken somewhat by surprise. Still it can hardly be necessary to assure you that any wife of yours is a mother of mine. [*Aside to* ALINE] It is not quite what I could have wished.

MRS P. [*crossing to* ALEXIS]: Oh, sir, I entreat your forgiveness. I am aware that socially I am not heverythink that could be desired, nor am I blessed with an abundance of worldly goods, but I can at least confer on your estimable father the great and priceless dowry of a true, tender and lovin' 'art!

ALEXIS [*coldly*]: I do not question it. After all, a faithful love is the true source of every earthly joy.

SIR M.: I knew that my boy would not blame his poor father for acting on the impulse of a heart that has never yet misled him. Zorah is not perhaps what the world calls beautiful –

DR D.: Still she is comely – distinctly comely. [*Sighs.*]

ALINE: Zorah is very good, and very clean, and honest, and quite, quite sober in her habits: and that is worth far more than beauty, dear Sir Marmaduke.

DR D.: Yes; beauty will fade and perish, but personal cleanliness is practically undying, for it can be renewed whenever it discovers symptoms of decay. My dear Sir Marmaduke, I heartily congratulate you. [*Sighs.*]

QUINTETTE – ALEXIS, ALINE, SIR MARMADUKE,
MRS PARTLET, DR DALY

ALEXIS:
    I rejoice that it's decided,
      Happy now will be his life,
    For my father is provided
      With a true and tender wife.

ALL: She will tend him, nurse him, mend him,
      Air his linen, dry his tears;
    Bless the thoughtful fates that send him
      Such a wife to soothe his years!

ALINE: No young giddy thoughtless maiden,
      Full of graces, airs and jeers –
    But a sober widow, laden
      With the weight of fifty years!

SIR M.:   No high-born exacting beauty,
      Blazing like a jewelled sun –
    But a wife who'll do her duty,
      As that duty should be done!

MRS P.:   I'm no saucy minx and giddy –
      Hussies such as them abound –
    But a clean and tidy widdy
      Well be-known for miles around!

DR D.:   All the village now have mated,
      All are happy as can be –
    I to live alone am fated:
      No one's left to marry me!

ALL: She will tend him, etc.
    [*Exeunt* SIR MARMADUKE, MRS PARTLET *and* ALINE, *with*
    ALEXIS. DR DALY *looks after them sentimentally, then exits*
                                with a sigh.]

[*Enter* MR WELLS.]

RECITATIVE

MR W.:   Oh, I have wrought much evil with my spells!
      And ill I can't undo!
    This is too bad of you, J. W. Wells –
      What wrong have they done you?

And see – another love-lorn lady comes –
Alas, poor stricken dame!
A gentle pensiveness her life benumbs –
And mine, alone, the blame!

[LADY SANGAZURE *enters. She is very melancholy.*]

LADY S.:   Alas! ah me! and well-a-day!
I sigh for love, and well I may,
For I am very old and grey.
But stay!

[*Sees* MR WELLS, *and becomes fascinated by him.*]

RECITATIVE

LADY S.:   What is this fairy form I see before me?

MR W.:   Oh, horrible! – she's going to adore me!
This last catastrophe is overpowering!

LADY S.:   Why do you glare at one with visage lowering?
For pity's sake recoil not thus from me!

MR W.:   My lady, leave me – this may never be!

DUET – LADY SANGAZURE *and* MR WELLS

MR W.:   Hate me! I drop my H's – have through life!

LADY S.:   Love me! I'll drop them too!

MR W.:   Hate me! I always eat peas with a knife!

LADY S.:   Love me! I'll eat like you!

MR W.:   Hate me! I spend the day at Rosherville![38]

LADY S.:   Love me! that joy I'll share!

MR W.:   Hate me! I often roll down One Tree Hill![39]

LADY S.:   Love me! I'll join you there!

LADY S.:   Love me! my prejudices I will drop!

MR W.:   Hate me! that's not enough!

LADY S.:   Love me! I'll come and help you in the shop!

MR W.:   Hate me! the life is rough!

LADY S.:   Love me! my grammar I will all forswear!

MR W.:   Hate me! abjure my lot!

LADY S.:   Love me! I'll stick sunflowers in my hair!
MR W.:   Hate me! they'll suit you not!

RECITATIVE

MR W.:   At what I am going to say be not enraged –
             I may not love you – for I am engaged!
LADY S. [*horrified*]:
             Engaged!
MR W.:   Engaged!
             To a maiden fair,
             With bright brown hair,
                 And a sweet and simple smile,
             Who waits for me
             By the sounding sea,
                 On a South Pacific isle.
MR W. [*aside*]:
             A lie! No maiden waits me there!
LADY S. [*mournfully*]:
             She has bright brown hair;
MR W. [*aside*]:
             A lie! No maiden smiles on me!
LADY S. [*mournfully*]:
             By the sounding sea!

ENSEMBLE

LADY SANGAZURE

Oh, agony, rage, despair!
The maiden has bright brown hair,
    And mine is as white as snow!
False man, it will be your fault,
If I go to my family vault,
    And bury my life-long woe!

MR WELLS

Oh, agony, rage, despair!
Oh, where will this end – oh, where?
    I should like very much to know!
It will certainly be my fault,
If she goes to her family vault,
    To bury her life-long woe!

BOTH: The family vault – the family vault.

It will certainly be $\left\{\begin{array}{c}\text{your}\\\text{my}\end{array}\right\}$ fault,

If $\left\{\begin{array}{c}\text{I go}\\\text{she goes}\end{array}\right\}$ to $\left\{\begin{array}{c}\text{my}\\\text{her}\end{array}\right\}$ family vault,

To bury $\left\{\begin{array}{c}\text{my}\\\text{her}\end{array}\right\}$ life-long woe!

[*Exit* LADY SANGAZURE, *in great anguish.*]

RECITATIVE

MR W.:   Oh, hideous doom – to scatter desolation,
        And sow the seeds of sorrow far and wide!
    To foster mésalliances[40] through the nation,
        And drive high-born old dames to suicide!
    Shall I subject myself to reprobation
        By leaving her in solitude to pine?
    No! come what may, I'll make her reparation,
        So, aged lady, take me! – I am thine!   [*Exit.*]

[*Enter* ALINE.]

ALINE: This was to have been the happiest day of my life – but I am
very far from happy! Alexis insists that I shall taste the philtre –
and when I try to persuade him that to do so would be an insult to
my pure and lasting love, he tells me that I object because I do not
desire that my love for him shall be eternal. Well [*sighing, and
producing a phial*], I can at least prove to him that, in that, he is
unjust!

RECITATIVE

        Alexis! Doubt me not, my loved one! See,
        Thine uttered will is sovereign law to me!
        All fear – all thought of ill I cast away!
        It is my darling's will, and I obey!
[*She drinks the philtre.*]
                The fearful deed is done,
                My love is near!

I go to meet my own
   In trembling fear!
If o'er us aught of ill
   Should cast a shade,
It was my darling's will,
   And I obeyed!

[*As* ALINE *is going off, she meets* DR DALY, *entering pensively. He is playing on a flageolet. Under the influence of the spell she at once becomes strangely fascinated by him, and exhibits every symptom of being hopelessly in love with him.*]

SONG

DR D.:

Oh, my voice is sad and low
And with timid step I go –
For with load of love o'erladen
I enquire of every maiden,
'Will you wed me, little lady?
Will you share my cottage shady?'
   Little lady answers 'No!
   Thank you for your kindly proffer –
   Good your heart, and full your coffer;
   Yet I must decline your offer –
      I'm engaged to So-and-so!'
         So-and-so!
         So-and-so! [*flageolet solo*]
   She's engaged to So-and-so!
What a rogue young hearts to pillage;
What a worker on Love's tillage!
Every maiden in the village
      Is engaged to So-and-so!
         So-and-so!
         So-and-so! [*flageolet solo*]
      All engaged to So-and-so!

[*At the end of the song* DR DALY *sees* ALINE, *and, under the influence of the potion, falls in love with her.*]

ENSEMBLE

ALINE *and* DR DALY:

> Oh, joyous boon! oh, mad delight;
> Oh, sun and moon! oh, day and night!
> > Rejoice, rejoice with me!
> Proclaim our joy, ye birds above –
> Ye brooklets, murmur forth our love,
> > In choral ecstasy:

ALINE: Oh, joyous boon!

DR D.: Oh, mad delight!

ALINE: Oh, sun and moon!

DR D.: Oh, day and night!

BOTH: Ye birds, and brooks, and fruitful trees,
> With choral joy delight the breeze –
> > Rejoice, rejoice with me!

[*Enter* ALEXIS.]

ALEXIS [*with rapture*]:

> Aline, my only love, my happiness!
> The philtre – you have tasted it?

ALINE [*with confusion*]: Yes! Yes!

ALEXIS: Oh, joy, mine, mine for ever, and for aye!
> [*Embraces her.*]

ALINE: Alexis, don't do that – you must not!

[DR DALY *interposes between them.*]

ALEXIS [*amazed*]: Why?

DUET – ALINE *and* DR DALY

ALINE: Alas! that lovers thus should meet:
> Oh, pity, pity me!
> Oh, charge me not with cold deceit;
> Oh, pity, pity me!
> You bade me drink – with trembling awe
> I drank, and, by the potion's law,
> I loved the very first I saw!
> Oh, pity, pity me!

DR D.:   My dear young friend, consolèd be –
                    We pity, pity you.
                In this I'm not an agent free –
                    We pity, pity you.
                Some most extraordinary spell
                O'er us has cast its magic fell –
                The consequence I need not tell.
                    We pity, pity you.

ENSEMBLE – DR DALY, ALEXIS *and* ALINE

            Some most extraordinary spell
            O'er $\left\{ \begin{array}{l} \text{us} \\ \text{them} \end{array} \right\}$ has cast its magic fell –
            The consequence $\left\{ \begin{array}{l} \text{we} \\ \text{they} \end{array} \right\}$ need not tell.
            $\left. \begin{array}{l} \text{We} \\ \text{They} \end{array} \right\}$ pity, pity $\left\{ \begin{array}{l} \text{thee!} \\ \text{me.} \end{array} \right.$

ALEXIS [*furiously*]:
                False one, begone – I spurn thee,
                To thy new lover turn thee!
                Thy perfidy all men shall know.
ALINE [*wildly*]: I could not help it!
ALEXIS [*calling off*]:   Come one, come all!
DR D.:   We could not help it!
ALEXIS [*calling off*]:   Obey my call!
ALINE [*wildly*]: I could not help it!
ALEXIS [*calling off*]:   Come hither, run!
DR D.:   We could not help it!
ALEXIS [*calling off*]:   Come, every one!
    [*Enter all the characters except* LADY SANGAZURE *and* MR
    WELLS.]
CHORUS: Oh, what is the matter, and what is the clatter?
            He's glowering at her, and threatens a blow!
        Oh, why does he batter the girl he did flatter?
            And why does the latter recoil from him so?

RECITATIVE

ALEXIS: Prepare for sad surprises –
                      My love Aline despises!
                      No thought of sorrow shames her –
                      Another lover claims her!
                 Be his, false girl, for better or for worse –
                 But, ere you leave me, may a lover's curse –

DR D. [*coming forward*]: Hold! Be just. This poor child drank the philtre at your instance. She hurried off to meet you – but, most unhappily, she met me instead. As you had administered the potion to both of us, the result was inevitable. But fear nothing from me – I will be no man's rival. I shall quit the country at once – and bury my sorrow in the congenial gloom of a Colonial Bishopric.

ALEXIS: My excellent old friend! [*Taking his hand – then turning to* MR WELLS, *who has entered with* LADY SANGAZURE.] Oh, Mr Wells, what, what is to be done?

MR W.: I do not know – and yet – there is one means by which this spell may be removed.

ALEXIS: Name it – oh, name it!

MR W.: Or you or I must yield up his life to Ahrimanes.[41] I would rather it were you. I should have no hesitation in sacrificing my own life to spare yours, but we take stock next week, and it would not be fair on the Co.

ALEXIS: True. Well, I am ready!

ALINE: No, no – Alexis – it must not be! Mr Wells, if he must die that all may be restored to their old loves, what is to become of me? I should be left out in the cold, with no love to be restored to!

MR W.: True – I did not think of that. [*To the others*] My friends, I appeal to you, and I will leave the decision in your hands.

FINALE

MR W.:   Or I or he
                      Must die!
                      Which shall it be?
                      Reply!

SIR M.:   Die thou!
             Thou art the cause of all offending!
DR D.:   Die thou!
             Yield thou to this decree unbending!
ALL: Die thou!
MR W.:   So be it! I submit! My fate is sealed.
             To public execration thus I yield!

[*Falls on trap.*]

             Be happy all – leave me to my despair –
             I go – it matters not with whom – or where!

[*Gong.*]

[*All quit their present partners, and rejoin their old lovers.* SIR
MARMADUKE *leaves* MRS PARTLET, *and goes to* LADY SANG-
AZURE. ALINE *leaves* DR DALY, *and goes to* ALEXIS. DR DALY
leaves ALINE, *and goes to* CONSTANCE. NOTARY *leaves* CON-
STANCE, *and goes to* MRS PARTLET. *All the* CHORUS *make a
corresponding change.*]

GENTLEMEN: Oh, my adored one!
LADIES: Unmingled joy!
GENTLEMEN: Ecstatic rapture!
LADIES: Beloved boy!

[*They embrace.*]

SIR M.:   Come to my mansion, all of you! At least
          We'll crown our rapture with another feast!

ENSEMBLE

SIR M., LADY S., ALEXIS, ALINE:
             Now to the banquet we press –
                Now for the eggs and the ham –
             Now for the mustard and cress –
                Now for the strawberry jam!
CHORUS: Now to the banquet, etc.
DR D., CON., NOT., MRS P.:
             Now for the tea of our host –
             Now for the rollicking bun –

Now for the muffin and toast –
Now for the gay Sally Lunn!
CHORUS: Now for the tea, etc.

GENERAL DANCE

[*During the symphony* MR WELLS *sinks through trap, amid red fire.*]

CURTAIN

HMS PINAFORE

OR

THE LASS THAT LOVED A SAILOR

DRAMATIS PERSONAE

THE RT HON. SIR JOSEPH PORTER, KCB (*First Lord of the Admiralty*)

CAPTAIN CORCORAN (*Commanding HMS* Pinafore)

TOM TUCKER (*Midshipmite*)

RALPH RACKSTRAW (*Able Seaman*)

DICK DEADEYE (*Able Seaman*)

BILL BOBSTAY (*Boatswain's Mate*)

BOB BECKET (*Carpenter's Mate*)

JOSEPHINE (*the Captain's Daughter*)

HEBE (*Sir Joseph's First Cousin*)

MRS CRIPPS (LITTLE BUTTERCUP) (*a Portsmouth Bumboat Woman*)

Chorus of First Lord's Sisters, his Cousins, his Aunts, Sailors, Marines, etc.

SCENE – Quarter-deck of HMS *Pinafore*, off Portsmouth

ACT I – Noon

ACT II – Night

ACT I

[*Sailors, led by* BOATSWAIN, *discovered cleaning brasswork, splicing rope, etc.*]

CHORUS: We sail the ocean blue,
And our saucy ship's a beauty;
We're sober men and true,
And attentive to our duty.
When the balls whistle free
O'er the bright blue sea,
We stand to our guns all day;
When at anchor we ride
On the Portsmouth[2] tide,
We have plenty of time to play.
[*Enter* LITTLE BUTTERCUP, *with large basket on her arm.*]

RECITATIVE

Hail, men-o'-war's men – safeguards of your nation,
Here is an end, at last, of all privation;
You've got your pay – spare all you can afford
To welcome Little Buttercup on board.

ARIA

BUT.:   For I'm called Little Buttercup – dear Little Buttercup,
        Though I could never tell why,
     But still I'm called Buttercup – poor Little Buttercup,
        Sweet Little Buttercup I!

     I've snuff and tobaccy, and excellent jacky,[3]
        I've scissors, and watches, and knives;
     I've ribbons and laces to set off the faces
        Of pretty young sweethearts and wives.

     I've treacle and toffee, I've tea and I've coffee,
        Soft tommy[4] and succulent chops;
     I've chickens and conies, and pretty polonies,[5]
        And excellent peppermint drops.

     Then buy of your Buttercup – dear Little Buttercup;
        Sailors should never be shy;
     So, buy of your Buttercup – poor Little Buttercup;
        Come, of your Buttercup buy!

BOAT.: Aye, Little Buttercup – and well called – for you're the rosiest, the roundest and the reddest beauty in all Spithead.[6]

BUT.: Red, am I? and round – and rosy! May be, for I have dissembled well! But hark ye, my merry friend – hast ever thought that beneath a gay and frivolous exterior there may lurk a canker-worm which is slowly but surely eating its way into one's very heart?

BOAT.: No, my lass, I can't say I've ever thought that.

[*Enter* DICK DEADEYE.[7] *He pushes through sailors, and comes down.*]

DICK: *I* have thought it often. [*All recoil from him.*]

BUT.: Yes, you look like it! What's the matter with the man? Isn't he well?

BOAT.: Don't take no heed of *him*; that's only poor Dick Deadeye.

DICK: I say – it's a beast of a name, ain't it – Dick Deadeye?

BUT.: It's not a nice name.

DICK: I'm ugly too, ain't I?

BUT.: You are certainly plain.

DICK: And I'm three-cornered too, ain't I?

BUT.: You are rather triangular.

DICK: Ha! ha! That's it. I'm ugly, and they hate me for it; for you all hate me, don't you?

ALL: We do!

DICK: There!

BOAT.: Well, Dick, we wouldn't go for to hurt any fellow-creature's feelings, but you can't expect a chap with such a name as Dick Deadeye to be a popular character – now can you?

DICK: No.

BOAT.: It's asking too much, ain't it?

DICK: It is. From such a face and form as mine the noblest sentiments sound like the black utterances of a depraved imagination. It is human nature – I am resigned.

RECITATIVE

BUT. [*looking down hatchway*]:

> But, tell me – who's the youth whose faltering feet
> With difficulty bear him on his course?

BOAT.: That is the smartest lad in all the fleet –
> Ralph Rackstraw!

BUT.: Ha! That name! Remorse! remorse!

[*Enter* RALPH *from hatchway.*]

MADRIGAL

RALPH:
> The Nightingale
> Sighed for the moon's bright ray,
> And told his tale
> In his own melodious way!
> He sang 'Ah, well-a-day!'

ALL:
> He sang 'Ah, well-a-day!'

          The lowly vale
    For the mountain vainly sighed,
        To his humble wail
    The echoing hills replied.
      They sang 'Ah, well-a-day!'

ALL: They sang 'Ah, well-a-day!'

RECITATIVE

    I know the value of a kindly chorus,
      But choruses yield little consolation
    When we have pain and sorrow too before us!
      I love – and love, alas, above my station!

BUT. [*aside*]: He loves – and loves a lass above his station!
ALL [*aside*]:   Yes, yes, the lass is much above his station!

                 [*Exit* LITTLE BUTTERCUP.]

BALLAD

RALPH: A maiden fair to see,
            The pearl of minstrelsy,
              A bud of blushing beauty;
            For whom proud nobles sigh,
            And with each other vie
              To do her menial's duty.

ALL: To do her menial's duty.

            A suitor, lowly born,
            With hopeless passion torn,
              And poor beyond denying,
            Has dared for her to pine
            At whose exalted shrine
              A world of wealth is sighing.

ALL: A world of wealth is sighing!

Unlearned he in aught
Save that which love has taught
  (For love had been his tutor);
Oh, pity, pity me –
Our captain's daughter she,
  And I that lowly suitor!

ALL: And he that lowly suitor!

BOAT.: Ah, my poor lad, you've climbed too high: our worthy captain's child won't have nothin' to say to a poor chap like you. Will she, lads?

ALL: No, no!

DICK: No, no, captains' daughters don't marry foremast hands.

ALL [*recoiling from him*]: Shame! shame!

BOAT.: Dick Deadeye, them sentiments o' yourn are a disgrace to our common natur'.

RALPH: But it's a strange anomaly, that the daughter of a man who hails from the quarter-deck may not love another who lays out on the fore-yard arm. For a man is but a man, whether he hoists his flag at the main-truck or his slacks on the main-deck.

DICK: Ah, it's a queer world!

RALPH: Dick Deadeye, I have no desire to press hardly on you, but such a revolutionary sentiment is enough to make an honest sailor shudder.

BOAT.: My lads, our gallant captain has come on deck; let us greet him as so brave an officer and so gallant a seaman deserves.

[*Enter* CAPTAIN CORCORAN.]

RECITATIVE

CAPT.:   My gallant crew, good morning.

ALL [*saluting*]:   Sir, good morning!

CAPT.:   I hope you're all quite well.

ALL [*as before*]:   Quite well; and you, sir?

CAPT.:   I am in reasonable health, and happy
                   To meet you all once more.

ALL [*as before*]:   You do us proud, sir!

SONG

CAPT.:	I am the Captain of the *Pinafore*;
ALL:	And a right good captain, too!
CAPT.:	You're very, very good,
	And be it understood,
	I command a right good crew,
ALL:	We're very, very good,
	And be it understood,
	He commands a right good crew.
CAPT.:	Though related to a peer,
	I can hand, reef and steer,
	And ship a selvagee;
	I am never known to quail
	At the fury of a gale,
	And I'm never, never sick at sea!
ALL:	What, never?
CAPT.:	No, never!
ALL:	What, *never*?
CAPT.:	Hardly ever![8]
ALL:	He's hardly ever sick at sea!
	Then give three cheers, and one cheer more,
	For the hardy Captain of the *Pinafore*!
CAPT.:	I do my best to satisfy you all –
ALL:	And with you we're quite content.
CAPT.:	You're exceedingly polite,
	And I think it only right
	To return the compliment.
ALL:	We're exceedingly polite,
	And he thinks it's only right
	To return the compliment.
CAPT.:	Bad language or abuse,
	I never, never use,
	Whatever the emergency;
	Though 'Bother it' I may
	Occasionally say,

I never use a big, big D–

ALL: What, never?

CAPT.: No, never!

ALL: What, *never*?

CAPT.: Hardly ever!

ALL: Hardly ever swears a big, big D–
Then give three cheers, and one cheer more,
For the well-bred Captain of the *Pinafore*!

[*After song exeunt all but* CAPTAIN.]

[*Enter* LITTLE BUTTERCUP.]

RECITATIVE

BUT.: Sir, you are sad! The silent eloquence
Of yonder tear that trembles on your eyelash
Proclaims a sorrow far more deep than common;
Confide in me – fear not – I am a mother!

CAPT.: Yes, Little Buttercup, I'm sad and sorry –
My daughter, Josephine, the fairest flower
That ever blossomed on ancestral timber,
Is sought in marriage by Sir Joseph Porter,[9]
Our Admiralty's First Lord, but for some reason
She does not seem to tackle kindly to it.

BUT. [*with emotion*]:
Ah, poor Sir Joseph! Ah, I know too well
The anguish of a heart that loves but vainly!
But see, here comes your most attractive daughter.
I go – Farewell!

[*Exit.*]

CAPT. [*looking after her*]:
A plump and pleasing person!

[*Exit.*]

[*Enter* JOSEPHINE, *twining some flowers which she carries in a small basket.*]

BALLAD

JOS.:   Sorry her lot who loves too well,
    Heavy the heart that hopes but vainly,
Sad are the sighs that own the spell,
    Uttered by eyes that speak too plainly;
      Heavy the sorrow that bows the head
      When love is alive and hope is dead!

Sad is the hour when sets the sun –
    Dark is the night to earth's poor daughters,
When to the ark the wearied one
    Flies from the empty waste of waters!
      Heavy the sorrow that bows the head
      When love is alive and hope is dead!

[*Enter* CAPTAIN.]

CAPT.: My child, I grieve to see that you are a prey to melancholy. You should look your best to-day, for Sir Joseph Porter, KCB,[10] will be here this afternoon to claim your promised hand.

JOS.: Ah, father, your words cut me to the quick. I can esteem – reverence – venerate Sir Joseph, for he is a great and good man; but oh, I cannot love him! My heart is already given.

CAPT. [*aside*]: It is then as I feared. [*Aloud*] Given? And to whom? Not to some gilded lordling?

JOS.: No, father – the object of my love is no lordling. Oh, pity me, for he is but a humble sailor on board your own ship!

CAPT.: Impossible!

JOS.: Yes, it is true – too true.

CAPT.: A common sailor? Oh fie!

JOS.: I blush for the weakness that allows me to cherish such a passion. I hate myself when I think of the depth to which I have stooped in permitting myself to think tenderly of one so ignobly born, but I love him! I love him! I love him! [*Weeps.*]

CAPT.: Come, my child, let us talk this over. In a matter of the heart I would not coerce my daughter – I attach but little value to rank or wealth, but the line must be drawn somewhere. A man in that station may be brave and worthy, but at every step he would commit solecisms that society would never pardon.

JOS.: Oh, I have thought of this night and day. But fear not, father, I have a heart, and therefore I love; but I am your daughter, and therefore I am proud. Though I carry my love with me to the tomb, he shall never, never know it.

CAPT.: You *are* my daughter after all. But see, Sir Joseph's barge approaches, manned by twelve trusty oarsmen and accompanied by the admiring crowd of sisters, cousins and aunts that attend him wherever he goes. Retire, my daughter, to your cabin – take this, his photograph, with you – it may help to bring you to a more reasonable frame of mind.

JOS.: My own thoughtful father!

> [*Exit* JOSEPHINE. CAPTAIN *remains and ascends the poop-deck.*]

BARCAROLLE[11]

FEMALE CHORUS. [*invisible*]:

> Over the bright blue sea
> Comes Sir Joseph Porter, KCB
> Wherever he may go
> Bang-bang the loud nine-pounders[12] go!
> Shout o'er the bright blue sea
> For Sir Joseph Porter, KCB.

[*During this the Crew have entered on tiptoe, listening attentively to the song.*]

CHORUS OF SAILORS:

> Sir Joseph's barge is seen,
> And its crowd of blushing beauties,
> We hope he'll find us clean,
> And attentive to our duties.
> We sail, we sail the ocean blue,
> And our saucy ship's a beauty.
> We're sober, sober men and true
> And attentive to our duty.

> We're smart and sober men,
> > And quite devoid of fe-ar,
> In all the Royal N.
> > None are so smart as we are.

[*Enter* SIR JOSEPH's *Female Relatives. They dance round stage.*]

REL.: Gaily tripping,
> > Lightly skipping,
> Flock the maidens to the shipping.

SAILORS: Flags and guns and pennants dipping!
> All the ladies love the shipping.

REL.: Sailors sprightly
> > Always rightly
> Welcome ladies so politely.

SAILORS: Ladies who can smile so brightly,
> Sailors welcome most politely.

CAPT. [*from poop*]:
> Now give three cheers, I'll lead the way.

ALL: Hurrah! hurrah! hurrah! hurray!

> > > [*Enter* SIR JOSEPH *with* COUSIN HEBE.]

SONG

SIR J.: I am the monarch of the sea,
> The ruler of the Queen's Navee,
> Whose praise Great Britain loudly chants.

COUSIN H.: And we are his sisters, and his cousins, and his aunts!

REL.: And we are his sisters, and his cousins, and his
> > aunts!

SIR J.: When at anchor here I ride,
> My bosom swells with pride,
> And I snap my fingers at a foeman's taunts

COUSIN H.: And so do his sisters, and his cousins, and his aunts!

ALL: And so do his sisters, and his cousins, and his
> > aunts!

SIR J.: But when the breezes blow,
> I generally go below,
> And seek the seclusion that a cabin grants!

COUSIN H.:   And so do his sisters, and his cousins, and his
                     aunts!

ALL: And so do his sisters, and his cousins, and his
                     aunts!
              His sisters and his cousins,
              Whom he reckons up by dozens,
                  And his aunts!

SONG

SIR J.:   When I was a lad I served a term
              As office boy to an Attorney's firm.
              I cleaned the windows and I swept the floor,
              And I polished up the handle of the big front door.
                  I polished up that handle so carefullee
                  That now I am the Ruler of the Queen's Navee!

CHORUS: He polished, etc.

SIR J.:   As office boy I made such a mark
              That they gave me the post of a junior clerk.
              I served the writs with a smile so bland,
              And I copied all the letters in a big round hand –
                  I copied all the letters in a hand so free,
                  That now I am the Ruler of the Queen's Navee!

CHORUS: He copied, etc.

SIR J.:   In serving writs I made such a name
              That an articled clerk[13] I soon became;
              I wore clean collars and a brand-new suit
              For the pass examination at the Institute.
                  And that pass examination did so well for me,
                  That now I am the Ruler of the Queen's Navee!

CHORUS: And that pass examination, etc.

SIR J.:   Of legal knowledge I acquired such a grip
              That they took me into the partnership.
               And that junior partnership, I ween,
              Was the only ship that I ever had seen.

> But that kind of ship so suited me,
> That now I am the Ruler of the Queen's Navee!

CHORUS:　　　But that kind, etc.

SIR J.:　　I grew so rich that I was sent
By a pocket borough[14] into Parliament.
I always voted at my party's call,
And I never thought of thinking for myself at all.
　　I thought so little, they rewarded me
　　By making me the Ruler of the Queen's Navee!

CHORUS:　　　He thought so little, etc.

SIR J.:　　Now landsmen all, whoever you may be,
If you want to rise to the top of the tree,
If your soul isn't fettered to an office stool,
Be careful to be guided by this golden rule –
　　Stick close to your desks and never go to sea,
　　And you all may be Rulers of the Queen's Navee!

CHORUS:　　　Stick close, etc.

SIR J.: You've a remarkably fine crew, Captain Corcoran.

CAPT.: It *is* a fine crew, Sir Joseph.

SIR J. [*examining a very small midshipman*]: A British sailor is a splendid fellow, Captain Corcoran.

CAPT.: A splendid fellow indeed, Sir Joseph.

SIR J.: I hope you treat your crew kindly, Captain Corcoran.

CAPT.: Indeed I hope so, Sir Joseph.

SIR J.: Never forget that they are the bulwarks of England's greatness, Captain Corcoran.

CAPT.: So I have always considered them, Sir Joseph.

SIR J.: No bullying, I trust – no strong language of any kind, eh?

CAPT.: Oh, never, Sir Joseph.

SIR J.: What, *never*?

CAPT.: Hardly ever, Sir Joseph. They are an excellent crew, and do their work thoroughly without it.

SIR J.: Don't patronize them, sir – pray, don't patronize them.

CAPT.: Certainly not, Sir Joseph.

SIR J.: That you are their captain is an accident of birth. I cannot permit these noble fellows to be patronized because an accident of birth has placed you above them and them below you.

CAPT.: I am the last person to insult a British sailor, Sir Joseph.

SIR J.: You are the last person who did, Captain Corcoran. Desire that splendid seaman to step forward.

[DICK *comes forward.*]

SIR J.: No, no, the other splendid seaman.

CAPT.: Ralph Rackstraw, three paces to the front – march!

SIR J. [*sternly*]: If what?

CAPT.: I beg your pardon – I don't think I understand you.

SIR J.: If you *please*.

CAPT.: Oh, yes, of course. If you please. [RALPH *steps forward.*]

SIR J.: You're a remarkably fine fellow.

RALPH: Yes, your honour.

SIR J.: And a first-rate seaman, I'll be bound.

RALPH: There's not a smarter topman in the Navy, your honour, though I say it who shouldn't.

SIR J.: Not at all. Proper self-respect, nothing more. Can you dance a hornpipe?[15]

RALPH: No, your honour.

SIR J.: That's a pity: all sailors should dance hornpipes. I will teach you one this evening, after dinner. Now tell me – don't be afraid – how does your captain treat you, eh?

RALPH: A better captain don't walk the deck, your honour.

ALL: Aye! Aye!

SIR J.: Good. I like to hear you speak well of your commanding officer; I daresay he don't deserve it, but still it does you credit. Can you sing?

RALPH: I can hum a little, your honour.

SIR J.: Then hum this at your leisure. [*Giving him MS music.*] It is a song that I have composed for the use of the Royal Navy. It is designed to encourage independence of thought and action in the lower branches of the service, and to teach the principle that a British sailor is any man's equal, excepting mine. Now, Captain Corcoran, a word with you in your cabin, on a tender and sentimental subject.

CAPT.: Aye, aye, Sir Joseph. [*Crossing.*] Boatswain, in commemoration of this joyous occasion, see that extra grog[16] is served out to the ship's company at seven bells.[17]

BOAT.: Beg pardon. If what, your honour?

CAPT.: If what? I don't think I understand you.

BOAT.: If you *please*, your honour.

CAPT.: What!

SIR J.: The gentleman is quite right. If you *please*.

CAPT. [*stamping his foot impatiently*]: If you *please*!　　　　　[*Exit.*]

SIR J.:　　　For I hold that on the seas
　　　　　The expression, 'if you please',
　　　　　　　A particularly gentlemanly tone implants.

COUSIN H.: And so do his sisters, and his cousins, and his aunts!

ALL:　　　And so do his sisters, and his cousins, and his aunts!

　　　　　　　[*Exeunt* SIR JOSEPH *and* RELATIVES.]

BOAT.: Ah! Sir Joseph's a true gentleman; courteous and considerate to the very humblest.

RALPH: True, Boatswain, but we are not the very humblest. Sir Joseph has explained our true position to us. As he says, a British seaman is any man's equal excepting his, and if Sir Joseph says that, is it not our duty to believe him?

ALL: Well spoke! well spoke!

DICK: You're on a wrong tack, and so is he. He means well, but he don't know. When people have to obey other people's orders, equality's out of the question.

ALL [*recoiling*]: Horrible! horrible!

BOAT.: Dick Deadeye, if you go for to infuriate this here ship's company too far, I won't answer for being able to hold 'em in. I'm shocked! that's what I am – shocked!

RALPH: Messmates, my mind's made up. I'll speak to the captain's daughter, and tell her, like an honest man, of the honest love I have for her.

ALL: Aye, aye!

RALPH: Is not my love as good as another's? Is not my heart as true as another's? Have I not hands and eyes and ears and limbs like another?

ALL: Aye, aye!

RALPH: True, I lack birth –

BOAT.: You've a berth on board this very ship.

RALPH: Well said – I had forgotten that. Messmates – what do you say? Do you approve my determination?

ALL: We do.

DICK: *I* don't.

BOAT.: What is to be done with this here hopeless chap? Let us sing him the song that Sir Joseph has kindly composed for us. Perhaps it will bring this here miserable creetur to a proper state of mind.

GLEE [18] – RALPH, BOATSWAIN, BOATSWAIN'S MATE
and CHORUS

A British tar is a soaring soul,
    As free as a mountain bird,
His energetic fist should be ready to resist
    A dictatorial word.
His nose should pant and his lip should curl,
His cheeks should flame and his brow should furl,
His bosom should heave and his heart should glow,
And his fist be ever ready for a knock-down blow.

CHORUS: His nose should pant, etc.

His eyes should flash with an inborn fire,
    His brow with scorn be wrung;
He never should bow down to a domineering frown,
    Or the tang of a tyrant tongue.
His foot should stamp and his throat should growl,
His hair should twirl and his face should scowl;
His eyes should flash and his breast protrude,
And this should be his customary attitude – [*pose*].

CHORUS: His foot should stamp, etc.

[*All dance off excepting* RALPH, *who remains, leaning pensively against bulwark.*]

[*Enter* JOSEPHINE *from cabin.*]

JOS.: It is useless – Sir Joseph's attentions nauseate me. I know that he is a truly great and good man, for he told me so himself, but to me he seems tedious, fretful and dictatorial. Yet his must be a mind of no common order, or he would not dare to teach my dear father to dance a hornpipe on the cabin table. [*Sees* RALPH.] Ralph Rackstraw! [*Overcome by emotion.*]

RALPH: Aye, lady – no other than poor Ralph Rackstraw!

JOS. [*aside*]: How my heart beats! [*Aloud*] And why poor, Ralph?

RALPH: I am poor in the essence of happiness, lady – rich only in never-ending unrest. In me there meet a combination of antithetical elements which are at eternal war with one another. Driven hither by objective influences – thither by subjective emotions – wafted one moment into blazing day, by mocking hope – plunged the next into the Cimmerian darkness[19] of tangible despair, I am but a living ganglion[20] of irreconcilable antagonisms. I hope I make myself clear, lady?

JOS.: Perfectly. [*Aside*] His simple eloquence goes to my heart. Oh, if I dared – but no, the thought is madness! [*Aloud*] Dismiss these foolish fancies, they torture you but needlessly. Come, make one effort.

RALPH [*aside*]: I will – one. [*Aloud*] Josephine!

JOS. [*indignantly*]: Sir!

RALPH: Aye, even though Jove's armoury[21] were launched at the head of the audacious mortal whose lips, unhallowed by relationship, dared to breathe that precious word, yet would I breathe it once, and then perchance be silent evermore. Josephine, in one brief breath I will concentrate the hopes, the doubts, the anxious fears of six weary months. Josephine, I am a British sailor, and I love you!

JOS.: Sir, this audacity! [*Aside*] Oh, my heart, my beating heart! [*Aloud*] This unwarrantable presumption on the part of a common sailor! [*Aside*] Common! oh, the irony of the word! [*Crossing, aloud*] Oh, sir, you forget the disparity in our ranks.

RALPH: I forget nothing, haughty lady. I love you desperately, my life is in your hand – I lay it at your feet! Give me hope, and what I lack in education and polite accomplishments, that I will endeavour to acquire. Drive me to despair, and in death alone I shall look for consolation. I am proud and cannot stoop to implore. I have spoken and I wait your word.

JOS.: You shall not wait long. Your proffered love I haughtily reject. Go, sir, and learn to cast your eyes on some village maiden in your own poor rank – they should be lowered before your captain's daughter!

DUET – JOSEPHINE *and* RALPH

JOS.:	Refrain, audacious tar,
	Your suit from pressing,
	Remember what you are,
	And whom addressing!
[*Aside*]	I'd laugh my rank to scorn
	In union holy,
	Were he more highly born
	Or I more lowly!
RALPH:	Proud lady, have your way,
	Unfeeling beauty!
	You speak and I obey,
	It is my duty!
	I am the lowliest tar
	That sails the water,
	And you, proud maiden, are
	My captain's daughter!
[*Aside*]	My heart with anguish torn
	Bows down before her,
	She laughs my love to scorn,
	Yet I adore her!

[*Repeat refrain, ensemble, then exit* JOSEPHINE *into cabin.*]

RALPH [*recitative*]:

> Can I survive this overbearing
> Or live a life of mad despairing,
> My proffered love despised, rejected?
> No, no, it's not to be expected!

[*Calling off*]

>   Messmates, ahoy!
>   Come here! Come here!

[*Enter* SAILORS, COUSIN HEBE *and* RELATIVES.]

ALL: Aye, aye, my boy,
>   What cheer, what cheer?
>   Now tell us, pray,
>   Without delay,
>   What does she say –
>   What cheer, what cheer?

RALPH [*to* COUSIN HEBE]:
>   The maiden treats my suit with scorn,
>   Rejects my humble gift, my lady;
>   She says I am ignobly born,
>   And cuts my hopes adrift, my lady.

ALL: Oh, cruel one.

DICK: She spurns your suit? Oho! Oho!
>   I told you so, I told you so.

SAILORS *and* RELATIVES:
>   Shall { we / they } submit? Are { we / they } but slaves?
>   Love comes alike to high and low –
>   Britannia's sailors rule the waves,
>   And shall they stoop to insult? No!

DICK: You must submit, you are but slaves;
>   A lady she! Oho! Oho!
>   You lowly toilers of the waves,
>   She spurns you all – I told you so!

RALPH: My friends, my leave of life I'm taking,
>   For oh, my heart, my heart is breaking.
>   When I am gone, oh, prithee tell
>   The maid that, as I died, I loved her well!

ALL [*turning away, weeping*]:
>   Of life, alas! his leave he's taking,
>   For ah! his faithful heart is breaking;
>   When he is gone we'll surely tell
>   The maid that, as he died, he loved her well.

[*During Chorus* BOATSWAIN *has loaded pistol, which he hands to* RALPH.]

RALPH: Be warned, my messmates all
                Who love in rank above you –
            For Josephine I fall!

[*Puts pistol to his head. All the sailors stop their ears.*]

[*Enter* JOSEPHINE *on deck.*]

JOS.:   Ah! stay your hand! I love you!

ALL: Ah! stay your hand – she loves you!

RALPH [*incredulously*]:
             Loves me?

JOS.:   Loves you!

ALL: Yes, yes – ah, yes, – she loves you!

ENSEMBLE – SAILORS, RELATIVES *and* JOSEPHINE

        Oh joy, oh rapture unforeseen,
        For now the sky is all serene;
        The god of day – the orb of love –
        Has hung his ensign high above,
            The sky is all ablaze.

        With wooing words and loving song,
        We'll chase the lagging hours along,
        And if $\left\{ \begin{array}{l} \text{I find} \\ \text{we find} \end{array} \right\}$ the maiden coy,
        $\left. \begin{array}{l} \text{I'll} \\ \text{We'll} \end{array} \right\}$ murmur forth decorous joy
          In dreamy roundelays!

DICK: He thinks he's won his Josephine,
        But though the sky is now serene,
        A frowning thunderbolt above
        May end their ill-assorted love
          Which now is all ablaze.

Our captain, ere the day is gone,
Will be extremely down upon
The wicked men who art employ
To make his Josephine less coy
    In many various ways.   *[Exit.]*

JOS.:	This very night,
COUSIN H.:	With bated breath
RALPH:	And muffled oar –
JOS.:	Without a light,
COUSIN H.:	As still as death,
RALPH:	We'll steal ashore.
JOS.:	A clergyman
RALPH:	Shall make us one
BOAT.:	At half-past ten,
JOS.:	And then we can
RALPH:	Return, for none
BOAT.:	Can part them then!
ALL:	This very night, etc.

[DICK *appears at hatchway.*]

DICK: Forbear, nor carry out the scheme you've
                  planned;
        She is a lady – you a foremast hand!
        Remember, she's your gallant captain's daughter,
        And you the meanest slave that crawls the water!

ALL: Back, vermin, back,
           Nor mock us!
         Back, vermin, back,
           You shock us!

                              [Exit DICK.]

    Let's give three cheers for the sailor's bride
    Who casts all thought of rank aside –
    Who gives up home and fortune too
    For the honest love of a sailor true!
        For a British tar is a soaring soul
          As free as a mountain bird!

His energetic fist should be ready to resist
A dictatorial word!
His foot should stamp and his throat should growl,
His hair should twirl and his face should scowl,
His eyes should flash and his breast protrude,
And this should be his customary attitude – [*pose*].

GENERAL DANCE

END OF ACT I

ACT II

Same Scene. Night. Awning removed. Moonlight.

[CAPTAIN *discovered singing on poop-deck, and accompanying himself on a mandolin.* LITTLE BUTTERCUP *seated on quarter-deck, gazing sentimentally at him.*]

SONG

CAPT.:　　　　Fair moon, to thee I sing,
　　　　　　　Bright regent of the heavens,
　　　　　　Say, why is everything
　　　　　　　Either at sixes or at sevens?
　　　　　　I have lived hitherto
　　　　　　　Free from breath of slander,
　　　　　　Beloved by all my crew –
　　　　　　　A really popular commander.
　　　　　　But now my kindly crew rebel,
　　　　　　　My daughter to a tar is partial,
　　　　　　Sir Joseph storms, and, sad to tell,
　　　　　　　He threatens a court martial!
　　　　　　　　Fair moon, to thee I sing,
　　　　　　　　　Bright regent of the heavens,
　　　　　　　　Say, why is everything
　　　　　　　　　Either at sixes or at sevens?

BUT.: How sweetly he carols forth his melody to the unconscious moon! Of whom is he thinking? Of some high-born beauty? It may be! Who is poor Little Buttercup that she should expect his glance to fall on one so lowly! And yet if he knew – if he only knew!

CAPT. [*coming down*]: Ah! Little Buttercup, still on board? That is not quite right, little one. It would have been more respectable to have gone on shore at dusk.

BUT.: True, dear Captain – but the recollection of your sad pale face seemed to chain me to the ship. I would fain see you smile before I go.

CAPT.: Ah! Little Buttercup, I fear it will be long before I recover my accustomed cheerfulness, for misfortunes crowd upon me, and all my old friends seem to have turned against me!

BUT.: Oh no – do not say 'all', dear Captain. That were unjust to one, at least.

CAPT.: True, for you are staunch to me. [*Aside*] If ever I gave my heart again, methinks it would be to such a one as this! [*Aloud*] I am touched to the heart by your innocent regard for me, and were we differently situated, I think I could have returned it. But as it is, I fear I can never be more to you than a friend.

BUT.: I understand! You hold aloof from me because you are rich and lofty – and I poor and lowly. But take care! The poor bumboat[22] woman has gipsy blood in her veins, and she can read destinies.

CAPT.: Destinies?

BUT.: There is a change in store for you!

CAPT.: A change?

BUT.: Aye – be prepared!

DUET – LITTLE BUTTERCUP *and* CAPTAIN

BUT.:   Things are seldom what they seem,
                     Skim milk masquerades as cream;
                     Highlows[23] pass as patent leathers;
                     Jackdaws strut in peacock's feathers.[24]

CAPT. [*puzzled*]:   Very true,
                     So they do.

BUT.:   Black sheep dwell in every fold;
                     All that glitters is not gold;[25]

Storks turn out to be but logs;[26]
Bulls are but inflated frogs.[27]

CAPT. [*puzzled*]:   So they be,
        Frequentlee.

BUT.:   Drops the wind and stops the mill;
Turbot is ambitious brill;
Gild the farthing[28] if you will,
Yet it is a farthing still.

CAPT. [*puzzled*]:   Yes, I know,
        That is so.
Though to catch your drift I'm striving,
    It is shady – it is shady;
I don't see at what you're driving,
    Mystic lady – mystic lady,

[*aside*]   Stern conviction's o'er me stealing,
That the mystic lady's dealing
In oracular revealing.

BUT. [*aside*]:   Stern conviction's o'er him stealing,
That the mystic lady's dealing
In oracular revealing.

BOTH: Yes, I know –
        That is so!

CAPT.:   Though I'm anything but clever,
I could talk like that for ever:
Once a cat was killed by care;
Only brave deserve the fair.[29]

BUT.:   Very true,
        So they do.

CAPT.:   Wink is often good as nod;[30]
Spoils the child who spares the rod;[31]
Thirsty lambs run foxy dangers;[32]
Dogs are found in many mangers.[33]

BUT.:   Frequentlee,
        I agree.

CAPT.:   Paw of cat the chestnut snatches;[34]
Worn-out garments show new patches;[35]

Only count the chick that hatches;[36]
Men are grown-up catchy-catchies.

BUT.: Yes, I know,
That is so.

[*aside*] Though to catch my drift he's striving,
I'll dissemble – I'll dissemble;
When he sees at what I'm driving,
Let him tremble – let him tremble!

ENSEMBLE – BUTTERCUP *and* CAPTAIN

Though a mystic tone $\left\{ \begin{array}{c} I \\ you \end{array} \right\}$ borrow,

$\left. \begin{array}{l} You will \\ I shall \end{array} \right\}$ learn the truth with sorrow,

Here to-day and gone to-morrow;
Yes, I know –
That is so!

[*At the end exit* LITTLE BUTTERCUP *melodramatically.*]

CAPT.: Incomprehensible as her utterances are, I nevertheless feel that they are dictated by a sincere regard for me. But to what new misery is she referring? Time alone can tell!

[*Enter* SIR JOSEPH.]

SIR J.: Captain Corcoran, I am much disappointed with your daughter. In fact, I don't think she will do.

CAPT.: She won't do, Sir Joseph!

SIR J.: I'm afraid not. The fact is, that although I have urged my suit with as much eloquence as is consistent with an official utterance, I have done so hitherto without success. How do you account for this?

CAPT.: Really, Sir Joseph, I hardly know. Josephine is of course sensible of your condescension.

SIR J.: She naturally would be.

CAPT.: But perhaps your exalted rank dazzles her.

SIR J.: You think it does?

CAPT.: I can hardly say; but she is a modest girl, and her social
position is far below your own. It may be that she feels she is not
worthy of you.

SIR J.: That is really a very sensible suggestion, and displays more
knowledge of human nature than I had given you credit for.

CAPT.: See, she comes. If your lordship would kindly reason with her
and assure her officially that it is a standing rule at the Admiralty
that love levels all ranks, her respect for an official utterance might
induce her to look upon your offer in its proper light.

SIR J.: It is not unlikely. I will adopt your suggestion. But soft, she is
here. Let us withdraw, and watch our opportunity.

[*Enter* JOSEPHINE *from cabin.* FIRST LORD *and* CAPTAIN
retire.]

SCENA[37]

JOS.:

The hours creep on apace,
My guilty heart is quaking!
Oh, that I might retrace
The step that I am taking!
Its folly it were easy to be showing,
What I am giving up and whither going.
On the one hand, papa's luxurious home,
Hung with ancestral armour and old brasses,
Carved oak and tapestry from distant Rome,
Rare 'blue and white'[38] Venetian finger-glasses,
Rich oriental rugs, luxurious sofa pillows,
And everything that isn't old, from Gillow's.[39]
And on the other, a dark and dingy room,
In some back street with stuffy children crying,
Where organs yell, and clacking housewives fume,
And clothes are hanging out all day a-drying.
With one cracked looking-glass to see your face in,
And dinner served up in a pudding basin!

A simple sailor, lowly born,
    Unlettered and unknown,
Who toils for bread from early morn
    Till half the night has flown!
No golden rank can he impart –
    No wealth of house or land –
No fortune save his trusty heart
    And honest brown right hand!
And yet he is so wondrous fair
That love for one so passing rare,
So peerless in his manly beauty,
Were little else than solemn duty!
Oh, god of love, and god of reason, say,
Which of you 'twain shall my poor heart obey!

[SIR JOSEPH *and* CAPTAIN *enter.*]

SIR J.: Madam, it has been represented to me that you are appalled by my exalted rank. I desire to convey to you officially my assurance, that if your hesitation is attributable to that circumstance, it is uncalled for.

JOS.: Oh! then your lordship is of opinion that married happiness is *not* inconsistent with discrepancy in rank?

SIR J.: I am officially of that opinion.

JOS.: That the high and the lowly may be truly happy together, provided that they truly love one another?

SIR J.: Madam, I desire to convey to you officially my opinion that love is a platform upon which all ranks meet.

JOS.: I thank you, Sir Joseph. I *did* hesitate, but I will hesitate no longer. [*Aside*] He little thinks how eloquently he has pleaded his rival's cause!

TRIO – SIR JOSEPH, CAPTAIN *and* JOSEPHINE

CAPT.:   Never mind the why and wherefore,
               Love can level ranks, and therefore,
               Though his lordship's station's mighty,

> Though stupendous be his brain,
> Though your tastes are mean and flighty
> And your fortune poor and plain,

CAPT. *and* SIR J.:

> Ring the merry bells on board-ship,
> Rend the air with warbling wild,
>
> For the union of $\left\{\begin{array}{c} \text{his} \\ \text{my} \end{array}\right\}$ lordship
>
> With a humble captain's child!

CAPT.:   For a humble captain's daughter –

JOS.:   For a gallant captain's daughter –

SIR J.:   And a lord who rules the water –

JOS. [*aside*]:   And a *tar* who ploughs the water!

ALL: Let the air with joy be laden,

> Rend with songs the air above,
> For the union of a maiden
> With the man who owns her love!

SIR J.:   Never mind the why and wherefore,

> Love can level ranks, and therefore,
> Though your nautical relation [*alluding to*
>   CAPTAIN]
> In my set could scarcely pass –
> Though you occupy a station
> In the lower middle class –

CAPT. *and* SIR J.:

> Ring the merry bells on board-ship,
> Rend the air with warbling wild,
>
> For the union of $\left\{\begin{array}{c} \text{my} \\ \text{his} \end{array}\right\}$ lordship
>
> With a humble captain's child!

CAPT.:   For a humble captain's daughter –

JOS.:   For a gallant captain's daughter –

SIR J.:   And a lord who rules the water –

JOS. [*aside*]:   And a *tar* who ploughs the water!

ALL: Let the air with joy be laden,

> Rend with songs the air above,

For the union of a maiden
　With the man who owns her love!
JOS.: Never mind the why and wherefore,
Love can level ranks, and therefore
I admit the jurisdiction;
　Ably have you played your part;
You have carried firm conviction
　To my hesitating heart.
CAPT. *and* SIR J.:
　Ring the merry bells on board-ship,
　　Rend the air with warbling wild,

For the union of $\left\{ \begin{array}{c} \text{my} \\ \text{his} \end{array} \right\}$ lordship

　　With a humble captain's child!
CAPT.: For a humble captain's daughter –
JOS.: For a gallant captain's daughter –
SIR J.: And a lord who rules the water –
JOS. [*aside*]: And a *tar* who ploughs the water!
　[*Aloud*] Let the air with joy be laden.
CAPT. *and* SIR J.:
　Ring the merry bells on board-ship –
JOS.: For the union of a maiden –
CAPT. *and* SIR J.:
　For her union with his lordship.
ALL: Rend with songs the air above
For the man who owns her love!

[*Exit* JOS.]

CAPT.: Sir Joseph, I cannot express to you my delight at the happy result of your eloquence. Your argument was unanswerable.

SIR J.: Captain Corcoran, it is one of the happiest characteristics of this glorious country that official utterances are invariably regarded as unanswerable. [*Exit.*]

CAPT.: At last my fond hopes are to be crowned. My only daughter is to be the bride of a Cabinet Minister. The prospect is Elysian.[40]

[*During this speech* DICK DEADEYE *has entered.*]

DICK: Captain.

CAPT.: Deadeye! You here? Don't! [*Recoiling from him.*]

DICK: Ah, don't shrink from me, Captain. I'm unpleasant to look at, and my name's agin me, but I ain't as bad as I seem.

CAPT.: What would you with me?

DICK [*mysteriously*]: I'm come to give you warning.

CAPT.: Indeed! do you propose to leave the Navy then?

DICK: No, no, you misunderstand me; listen!

DUET – CAPTAIN *and* DICK DEADEYE

DICK: Kind Captain, I've important information,
         Sing hey, the kind commander that you are,
      About a certain intimate relation,
         Sing hey, the merry maiden and the tar.

BOTH: The merry maiden and the tar.

CAPT.:   Good fellow, in conundrums you are speaking,
         Sing hey, the mystic sailor that you are;
      The answer to them vainly I am seeking;
         Sing hey, the merry maiden and the tar.

BOTH: The merry maiden and the tar.

DICK: Kind Captain, your young lady is a-sighing,
         Sing hey, the simple captain that you are,
      This very night with Rackstraw to be flying;
         Sing hey, the merry maiden and the tar.

BOTH: The merry maiden and the tar.

CAPT.:   Good fellow, you have given timely warning,
         Sing hey, the thoughtful sailor that you are,
      I'll talk to Master Rackstraw in the morning:
         Sing hey, the cat-o'-nine-tails[41] and the tar.
   [*Producing a 'cat'.*]

BOTH: The merry cat-o'-nine-tails and the tar!

CAPT.: Dick Deadeye – I thank you for your warning – I will at once take means to arrest their flight. This boat cloak will afford me ample disguise – So! [*Envelops himself in a mysterious cloak, hold-ing it before his face.*]

DICK: Ha, ha! They are foiled – foiled – foiled!

[*Enter Crew on tiptoe, with* RALPH *and* BOATSWAIN *meeting* JOSEPHINE, *who enters from cabin on tiptoe, with bundle of necessaries, and accompanied by* LITTLE BUTTERCUP.]

ENSEMBLE

Carefully on tiptoe stealing,
　　Breathing gently as we may,
Every step with caution feeling,
　　We will softly steal away.

[CAPTAIN *stamps – chord.*]

ALL [*much alarmed*]:

Goodness me –
　　Why, what was that?

DICK: Silent be,
　　It was the cat!

ALL [*reassured*]: It was – it was the cat!

CAPT. [*producing cat-o'-nine-tails*]:
　　They're right, it was the cat!

ALL: Pull ashore, in fashion steady,
　　Hymen[42] will defray the fare,
For a clergyman is ready
　　To unite the happy pair!

[*Stamp as before, and chord.*]

ALL: Goodness me,
　　Why, what was that?

DICK: Silent be,
　　Again the cat!

ALL: It was again that cat!

CAPT. [*aside*]: They're right, it was the cat!

CAPT. [*throwing off cloak*]:
　　Hold! [*All start.*]

Pretty daughter of mine,
  I insist upon knowing
  Where you may be going
With these sons of the brine,
  For my excellent crew,
Though foes they could thump any,
Are scarcely fit company,
  My daughter, for you.

CREW: Now, hark at that, do!
Though foes we could thump any,
We are scarcely fit company
For a lady like you!

RALPH: Proud officer, that haughty lip uncurl!
  Vain man, suppress that supercilious sneer,
For I have dared to love your matchless girl,
  A fact well known to all my messmates here!

CAPT.: Oh, horror!

RALPH AND JOS.:

$\left.\begin{matrix} I, \\ He, \end{matrix}\right\}$ humble, poor and lowly born,

The meanest in the port division –
  The butt of epauletted scorn –
The mark of quarter-deck derision –

$\left.\begin{matrix} \text{Have} \\ \text{Has} \end{matrix}\right\}$ dared to raise $\left\{\begin{matrix} \text{my} \\ \text{his} \end{matrix}\right.$ wormy eyes

Above the dust to which you'd mould $\left\{\begin{matrix} \text{me} \\ \text{him} \end{matrix}\right.$

  In manhood's glorious pride to rise,
$\left.\begin{matrix} \text{I am} \\ \text{He is} \end{matrix}\right\}$ an Englishman – behold $\left\{\begin{matrix} \text{me!} \\ \text{him!} \end{matrix}\right.$

ALL: He is an Englishman!

BOAT.: He is an Englishman!
  For he himself has said it,
  And it's greatly to his credit,
That he is an Englishman!

ALL: That he is an Englishman!

BOAT.:	For he might have been a Roosian,
	A French, or Turk, or Proosian,
	Or perhaps Itali-an!
ALL:	Or perhaps Itali-an!
BOAT.:	But in spite of all temptations
	To belong to other nations,
	He remains an Englishman!
ALL:	For in spite of all temptations, etc.

CAPT. [*trying to repress his anger*]:

> In uttering a reprobation
>> To any British tar,
> I try to speak with moderation,
>> But you have gone too far.
> I'm very sorry to disparage
>> A humble foremast lad,
> But to seek your captain's child in marriage,
>> Why, damme, it's too bad!

[*During this,* COUSIN HEBE *and Female Relatives have entered.*]

ALL [*shocked*]:

> Oh!

CAPT.: Yes, damme, it's too bad!

ALL: Oh!

CAPT. *and* DICK:

> Yes, damme, it's too bad.

[*During this,* SIR JOSEPH *has appeared on the poop-deck. He is horrified at the bad language.*]

COUSIN H.: Did you hear him – did you hear him?

> Oh, the monster overbearing!
> Don't go near him – don't go near him –
>> He is swearing – he is swearing!

SIR J.: My pain and my distress,

> I find it is not easy to express;
> My amazement – my surprise –
> You may learn from the expression of my eyes!

CAPT.:   My lord – one word – the facts are not before you
            The word was injudicious, I allow –
            But hear my explanation, I implore you,
            And you will be indignant too, I vow!

SIR J.:   I will hear of no defence,
            Attempt none if you're sensible.
            That word of evil sense
            Is wholly indefensible.
            Go, ribald, get you hence
            To your cabin with celerity.
            This is the consequence
            Of ill-advised asperity!
            [*Exit* CAPTAIN, *disgraced, followed by* JOSEPHINE.]

ALL: This is the consequence,
            Of ill-advised asperity!

SIR J.:   For I'll teach you all, ere long,
            To refrain from language strong.
            For I haven't any sympathy for ill-bred taunts!

COUSIN H.: No more have his sisters, nor his cousins, nor his
            aunts.

ALL: For he is an Englishman, etc.

SIR J.: Now, tell me, my fine fellow – for you *are* a fine fellow –

RALPH: Yes, your honour.

SIR J.: How came your captain so far to forget himself? I am quite
sure you had given him no cause for annoyance.

RALPH: Please your honour, it was thus-wise. You see I'm only a
topman – a mere foremast hand –

SIR J.: Don't be ashamed of that. Your position as a topman is a very
exalted one.

RALPH: Well, your honour, love burns as brightly in the fo'c'sle as it
does on the quarter-deck, and Josephine is the fairest bud that ever
blossomed upon the tree of a poor fellow's wildest hopes.

    [*Enter* JOSEPHINE; *she rushes to* RALPH'*s arms.*]

JOS.: Darling! [SIR JOSEPH *horrified.*]

RALPH: She is the figurehead of my ship of life – the bright beacon
that guides me into my port of happiness – the rarest, the purest

gem that ever sparkled on a poor but worthy fellow's trusting brow!

ALL: Very pretty, very pretty!

SIR J.: Insolent sailor, you shall repent this outrage. Seize him! [*Two Marines seize him and handcuff him.*]

JOS.: Oh, Sir Joseph, spare him, for I love him tenderly.

SIR J.: Pray, don't. I will teach this presumptuous mariner to discipline his affections. Have you such a thing as a dungeon on board?

ALL: We have!

DICK: They have!

SIR J.: Then load him with chains and take him there at once!

OCTETTE

RALPH: Farewell, my own,
               Light of my life, farewell!
            For crime unknown
               I go to a dungeon cell.

JOS.:   I will atone.
               In the meantime farewell!
            And all alone
               Rejoice in your dungeon cell!

SIR J.:   A bone, a bone
               I'll pick with this sailor fell;
            Let him be shown
               At once to his dungeon cell.

BOAT., DICK *and* COUSIN H.:
               He'll hear no tone
                  Of the maiden he loves so well!
               No telephone[43]
                  Communicates with his cell!

BUT. [*mysteriously*]:
               But when is known
                  The secret I have to tell,

> Wide will be thrown
>> The door of his dungeon cell.

ALL: For crime unknown
>> He goes to a dungeon cell!

>>>>> [RALPH *is led off in custody.*]

SIR J.:   My pain and my distress
> Again it is not easy to express.
> My amazement, my surprise,
> Again you may discover from my eyes.

ALL: How terrible the aspect of his eyes!

BUT.:   Hold! Ere upon your loss
>> You lay much stress,
> A long-concealèd crime
>> I would confess.

SONG

BUT.:   A many years ago,
> When I was young and charming,
>> As some of you may know,
> I practised baby-farming.[44]

ALL: Now this is most alarming!
> When she was young and charming,
> She practised baby-farming,
>> A many years ago.

BUT.:   Two tender babes I nussed:
>> One was of low condition,
> The other, upper crust,
>> A regular patrician.

ALL [*explaining to each other*]:
>> Now, this is the position:
>> One was of low condition,
>> The other a patrician,
>> A many years ago.

BUT.:   Oh, bitter is my cup!
>> However could I do it?

I mixed those children up,
　And not a creature knew it!

ALL:　However could you do it?
Some day, no doubt, you'll rue it,
Although no creature knew it,
　So many years ago.

BUT.:　In time each little waif
　Forsook his foster-mother,
The well-born babe was Ralph –
　Your captain was the other!!!

ALL:　They left their foster-mother,
The one was Ralph, our brother,
Our captain was the other,
　A many years ago.

SIR J.: Then I am to understand that Captain Corcoran and Ralph were exchanged in childhood's happy hour – that Ralph is really the Captain, and the Captain is Ralph?

BUT.: That is the idea I intended to convey, officially!

SIR J.: And very well you have conveyed it.

BUT.: Aye! aye! yer 'onour.

SIR J.: Dear me! Let them appear before me, at once!

　　[RALPH enters as CAPTAIN; CAPTAIN as a common sailor. JOSEPHINE rushes to his arms.]

JOS.: My father – a common sailor!

CAPT.: It is hard, is it not, my dear?

SIR J.: This is a very singular occurrence; I congratulate you both. [To RALPH] Desire that remarkably fine seaman to step forward.

RALPH: Corcoran. Three paces to the front – march!

CAPT.: If what?

RALPH: If what? I don't think I understand you.

CAPT.: If you please.

SIR J.: The gentleman is quite right. If you *please*.

RALPH: Oh! If you *please*. [CAPTAIN *steps forward*.]

SIR J. [to CAPTAIN]: You are an extremely fine fellow.

CAPT.: Yes, your honour.

SIR J.: So it seems that you were Ralph, and Ralph was you.

CAPT.: So it seems, your honour.

SIR J.: Well, I need not tell you that after this change in your condition, a marriage with your daughter will be out of the question.

CAPT.: Don't say that, your honour – love levels all ranks.

SIR J.: It does to a considerable extent, but it does not level them as much as that. [*Handing* JOSEPHINE *to* RALPH.] Here – take her, sir, and mind you treat her kindly.

RALPH AND JOS.: Oh bliss, oh rapture!

CAPT. AND BUT.: Oh rapture, oh bliss!

SIR J.: Sad my lot and sorry,
What shall I do? I cannot live alone!

COUSIN H.: Fear nothing – while I live I'll not desert you.
I'll soothe and comfort your declining days.

SIR J.: No, don't do that.

COUSIN H.: Yes, but indeed I'd rather –

SIR J. [*resigned*]: To-morrow morn our vows shall all be plighted,
Three loving pairs on the same day united!

QUARTETTE – JOSEPHINE, COUSIN HEBE, RALPH, DICK DEADEYE

Oh joy, oh rapture unforeseen,
The clouded sky is now serene,
The god of day – the orb of love,
Has hung his ensign high above,
   The sky is all ablaze.

With wooing words and loving song,
We'll chase the lagging hours along,
And if $\left\{ \begin{array}{c} \text{he finds} \\ \text{I find} \end{array} \right\}$ the maiden coy,
We'll murmur forth decorous joy,
   In dreamy roundelay.

CAPT.: For he's the Captain of the *Pinafore*.

ALL: And a right good captain too!

CAPT.:   And though before my fall
    I was captain of you all,
    I'm a member of the crew.
ALL: Although before his fall, etc.
CAPT.:   I shall marry with a wife,
    In my humble rank of life! [*turning to* BUTTERCUP]
      And you, my own, are she –
    I must wander to and fro,
    But wherever I may go,
      I shall never be untrue to thee!
ALL: What, never?
CAPT.:   No, never!
ALL: What, *never*?
CAPT.:   Hardly ever!
ALL: Hardly ever be untrue to thee.
    Then give three cheers, and one cheer more
    For the former Captain of the *Pinafore*.

BUT.:   For he loves Little Buttercup, dear Little Buttercup,
      Though I could never tell why;
    But still he loves Buttercup, poor Little Buttercup,
      Sweet Little Buttercup, aye!
ALL: For he loves, etc.

SIR J.:   I'm the monarch of the sea,
    And when I've married thee [*to* HEBE],
    I'll be true to the devotion that my love implants,
COUSIN H.:   Then good-bye to his sisters, and his cousins, and his
      aunts,
    Especially his cousins,
    Whom he reckons up by dozens,
    His sisters, and his cousins, and his aunts!

ALL: For he is an Englishman,
      And he himself hath said it,

And it's greatly to his credit
That he is an Englishman!

CURTAIN

THE PIRATES OF PENZANCE

OR

THE SLAVE OF DUTY

DRAMATIS PERSONAE

MAJOR-GENERAL STANLEY
THE PIRATE KING
SAMUEL (*his Lieutenant*)
FREDERIC (*the Pirate Apprentice*)
SERGEANT OF POLICE
MABEL
EDITH
KATE   (*General Stanley's Daughters*)
ISABEL
RUTH (*a Pirate Maid of all Work*)

Chorus of Pirates, Police and General Stanley's Daughters

ACT I – A Rocky Sea-shore on the Coast of Cornwall
ACT II – A Ruined Chapel by Moonlight

ACT I

SCENE – *A rocky sea-shore on the coast of Cornwall.*[1] *In the distance is a calm sea, on which a schooner is lying at anchor.*

[*As the curtain rises, groups of pirates are discovered – some drinking, some playing cards.* SAMUEL, *the Pirate Lieutenant, is going from one group to another, filling the cups from a flask.* FREDERIC *is seated in a despondent attitude at the back of the scene.*]

OPENING CHORUS

ALL: Pour, oh, pour the pirate sherry;
     Fill, oh, fill the pirate glass;
    And, to make us more than merry.
     Let the pirate bumper pass.

SAM.:   For to-day our pirate 'prentice
     Rises from indenture freed;
    Strong his arm and keen his scent is,
     He's a pirate now indeed!

ALL: Here's good luck to Frederic's ventures!
    Frederic's out of his indentures.

SAM.:   Two-and-twenty now he's rising,
     And alone he's fit to fly,
    Which we're bent on signalizing
     With unusual revelry.

ALL: Here's good luck to Frederic's ventures!
                Frederic's out of his indentures.
                Pour, oh, pour the pirate sherry, etc.

[FREDERIC *rises and comes forward with* PIRATE KING *who enters.*]

KING: Yes, Frederic, from to-day you rank as a full-blown member of our band.

ALL: Hurrah!

FRED.: My friends, I thank you all, from my heart for your kindly wishes. Would that I could repay them as they deserve!

KING: What do you mean?

FRED.: To-day I am out of my indentures, and to-day, I leave you for ever.

KING: But this is quite unaccountable; a keener hand at scuttling a Cunarder[2] or cutting out a P&O[3] never shipped a handspike.

FRED.: Yes, I have done my best for you. And why? It was my duty under my indentures, and I am the slave of duty. As a child I was regularly apprenticed to your band.[4] It was through an error – no matter, the mistake was ours, not yours, and I was in honour bound by it.

SAM.: An error? What error?

[RUTH *enters.*]

FRED.: I may not tell you; it would reflect upon my well-loved Ruth.

RUTH: Nay, dear master, my mind has long been gnawed by the cankering tooth of mystery. Better have it out at once.

SONG

RUTH:

    When Frederic was a little lad he proved so brave and daring,
    His father thought he'd 'prentice him to some career sea-faring.
    I was, alas! his nurserymaid, and so it fell to *my* lot
    To take and bind the promising boy apprentice to a *pilot* –
    A life not bad for a hardy lad, though surely not a high lot,
    Though I'm a nurse, you might do worse than make your boy a
        pilot.

I was a stupid nurserymaid, on breakers always steering,
And I did not catch the word aright, through being hard of
hearing;
Mistaking my instructions, which within my brain did gyrate,
I took and bound this promising boy apprentice to a *pirate*.
A sad mistake it was to make and doom him to a vile lot.
I bound him to a pirate – you – instead of to a pilot.

I soon found out, beyond all doubt, the scope of this disaster.
But I hadn't the face to return to my place, and break it to my
master.
A nurserymaid is not afraid of what you people *call* work,
So I made up my mind to go as a kind of piratical maid-of-all-
work.
And that is how you find me now, a member of your shy lot,
Which you wouldn't have found, had he been bound apprentice
to a pilot.

RUTH: Oh, pardon! Frederic, pardon! [*Kneels.*]

FRED.: Rise, sweet one, I have long pardoned you.

RUTH [*rises*]: The two words were so much alike!

FRED.: They were. They still are, though years have rolled over their
heads. But this afternoon my obligation ceases. Individually, I love
you all with affection unspeakable, but, collectively, I look upon
you with a disgust that amounts to absolute detestation. Oh! pity
me, my beloved friends, for such is my sense of duty that, once out
of my indentures, I shall feel myself bound to devote myself heart
and soul to your extermination!

ALL: Poor lad – poor lad! [*All weep.*]

KING: Well, Frederic, if you conscientiously feel that it is your duty
to destroy us, we cannot blame you for acting on that conviction.
Always act in accordance with the dictates of your conscience, my
boy, and chance the consequences.

SAM.: Besides, we can offer you but little temptation to remain with
us. We don't seem to make piracy pay. I'm sure I don't know why,
but we don't.

FRED.: *I* know why, but, alas! I mustn't tell you; it wouldn't be right.

KING: Why not, my boy? It's only half-past eleven and you are one of us until the clock strikes twelve.

SAM.: True, and until then you are bound to protect our interests.

ALL: Hear, hear!

FRED.: Well, then, it is my duty, as a pirate, to tell you that you are too tender-hearted. For instance, you make a point of never attacking a weaker party than yourselves, and when you attack a stronger party you invariably get thrashed.

KING: There is some truth in that.

FRED.: Then, again, you make a point of never molesting an orphan!

SAM.: Of course: we are orphans ourselves, and know what it is.

FRED.: Yes, but it has got about, and what is the consequence? Every one we capture says he's an orphan. The last three ships we took proved to be manned entirely by orphans, and so we had to let them go. One would think that Great Britain's mercantile navy was recruited solely from her orphan asylums – which we know is not the case.

SAM.: But, hang it all! you wouldn't have us absolutely merciless?

FRED.: There's my difficulty; until twelve o'clock I would, after twelve I wouldn't. Was ever a man placed in so delicate a situation?

RUTH: And Ruth, your own Ruth, whom you love so well, and who has won her middle-aged way into your boyish heart, what is to become of *her*?

KING: Oh, he will take you with him.

FRED.: Well, Ruth, I feel some little difficulty about you. It is true that I admire you very much, but I have been constantly at sea since I was eight years old, and yours is the only woman's face I have seen during that time. I think it is a sweet face.

RUTH: It is – oh, it is!

FRED.: I say I *think* it is; that is my impression. But as I have never had an opportunity of comparing you with other women, it is just possible I may be mistaken.

KING: True.

FRED.: What a terrible thing it would be if I were to marry this innocent person, and then find out that she is, on the whole, plain!

KING: Oh, Ruth is very well, very well indeed.

SAM.: Yes, there are the remains of a fine woman about Ruth.

FRED.: Do you really think so?

SAM.: I do.

FRED.: Then I will not be so selfish as to take her from you. In justice to her, and in consideration for you, I will leave her behind. [*Hands* RUTH *to* KING.]

KING: No, Frederic, this must not be. We are rough men who lead a rough life, but we are not so utterly heartless as to deprive thee of thy love. I think I am right in saying that there is not one here who would rob thee of this inestimable treasure for all the world holds dear.

ALL [*loudly*]: Not one!

KING: No, I thought there wasn't. Keep thy love, Frederic, keep thy love. [*Hands her back to* FREDERIC.]

FRED.: You're very good, I'm sure.

[*Exit* RUTH.]

KING: Well, it's the top of the tide, and we must be off. Farewell, Frederic. When your process of extermination begins, let our deaths be as swift and painless as you can conveniently make them.

FRED.: I will! By the love I have for you, I swear it! Would that you could render this extermination unnecessary by accompanying me back to civilization!

KING: No, Frederic, it cannot be. I don't think much of our profession, but, contrasted with respectability it is comparatively honest. No, Frederic, I shall live and die a Pirate King.

SONG

KING: Oh, better far to live and die
                 Under the brave black flag[5] I fly,
                 Than play a sanctimonious part,
                 With a pirate head and a pirate heart.
                 Away to the cheating world go you,
                 Where pirates all are well-to-do;
                 But I'll be true to the song I sing,
                 And live and die a Pirate King.
                    For I am a Pirate King.

ALL: You are!

	Hurrah for our Pirate King!
KING:	And it is, it is a glorious thing
	To be a Pirate King.
ALL:	Hurrah!
	Hurrah for our Pirate King!

KING:	When I sally forth to seek my prey
	I help myself in a royal way:
	I sink a few more ships, it's true,
	Than a well-bred monarch ought to do;
	But many a king on a first-class throne,
	If he wants to call his crown his own,
	Must manage somehow to get through
	More dirty work than ever *I* do,
	Though I am a Pirate King.
ALL:	You are!
	Hurrah for our Pirate King!
KING:	And it is, it is a glorious thing
	To be a Pirate King!
ALL:	It is!
	Hurrah for our Pirate King!

[*Exeunt all except* FREDERIC.]

[*Enter* RUTH.]

RUTH: Oh, take me with you! I cannot live if I am left behind.

FRED.: Ruth, I will be quite candid with you. You are very dear to me, as you know, but I must be circumspect. You see, you are considerably older than I. A lad of twenty-one usually looks for a wife of seventeen.

RUTH: A wife of seventeen! You will find me a wife of a thousand!

FRED.: No, but I shall find you a wife of forty-seven, and that is quite enough. Ruth, tell me candidly, and without reserve: compared with other women – how are *you*?

RUTH: I will answer you truthfully, master – I have a slight cold, but otherwise I am quite well.

FRED.: I am sorry for your cold, but I was referring rather to your personal appearance. Compared with other women, are you beautiful?

RUTH [*bashfully*]: I have been told so, dear master.

FRED.: Ah, but lately?

RUTH: Oh, no, years and years ago.

FRED.: What do you think of yourself?

RUTH: It is a delicate question to answer, but I think I am a fine woman.

FRED.: That is your candid opinion?

RUTH: Yes, I should be deceiving you if I told you otherwise.

FRED.: Thank you, Ruth, I believe you, for I am sure you would not practise on my inexperience; I wish to do the right thing, and if – I say *if* – you are really a fine woman, your age shall be no obstacle to our union! [*Chorus of Girls heard in the distance.*] Hark! Surely I hear voices! Who has ventured to approach our all but inaccessible lair? Can it be Custom House?[6] No, it does not sound like Custom House.

RUTH [*aside*]: Confusion! it is the voices of young girls! If he should see them I am lost.

FRED. [*looking off*]: By all that's marvellous, a bevy of beautiful maidens!

RUTH [*aside*]: Lost! lost! lost!

FRED.: How lovely! how surpassingly lovely is the plainest of them! What grace – what delicacy – what refinement! And Ruth – Ruth told me she was beautiful.

RECITATIVE

FRED.:   Oh, false one, you have deceived me!

RUTH: I have deceived you?

FRED.:   Yes, deceived me!

   [*Denouncing her.*]

DUET – FREDERIC *and* RUTH

FRED.:   You told me you were fair as gold!

RUTH [*wildly*]:   And, master, am I not so?

FRED.:   And now I see you're plain and old.

RUTH: I am sure I am not a jot so.

FRED.:   Upon my innocence you play.
RUTH: I'm not the one to plot so.
FRED.:   Your face is lined, your hair is grey.
RUTH: It's gradually got so.
FRED.:   Faithless woman, to deceive me,
                    I who trusted so!
RUTH: Master, master, do not leave me!
                    Hear me, ere you go!
                 My love without reflecting,
                 Oh, do not be rejecting.
           Take a maiden tender – her affection raw and green,
                 At very highest rating,
                 Has been accumulating
           Summers seventeen – summers seventeen.
                 Don't, beloved master,
                 Crush me with disaster.
           What is such a dower to the dower I have here?
                 My love unabating
                 Has been accumulating
           Forty-seven year – forty-seven year!

ENSEMBLE

RUTH	FREDERIC
Don't, beloved master,	Yes, your former master
Crush me with disaster.	Saves you from disaster.
What is such a dower to the dower I have here?	Your love would be uncomfortably, fervid, it is clear,
My love unabating	If, as you are stating,
Has been accumulating	It's been accumulating
Forty-seven year – forty-seven year!	Forty-seven year – forty-seven year!

[*At the end he renounces her, and she goes off in despair.*]

RECITATIVE

FRED.:   What shall I do? Before these gentle maidens
    I dare not show in this alarming costume.
    No, no, I must remain in close concealment
    Until I can appear in decent clothing!

[Hides in cave as the Girls enter climbing over the rocks.]

GIRLS: Climbing over rocky mountain,[7]
    Skipping rivulet and fountain,
    Passing where the willows quiver
    By the ever-rolling river,
       Swollen with the summer rain;
    Threading long and leafy mazes
    Dotted with unnumbered daisies;
    Scaling rough and rugged passes,
    Climb the hardy little lasses,
       Till the bright sea-shore they gain!

EDITH: Let us gaily tread the measure,
    Make the most of fleeting leisure;
    Hail it as a true ally,
    Though it perish by and by.

ALL: Hail it as a true ally,
       Though it perish by and by.

EDITH: Every moment brings a treasure
    Of its own especial pleasure,
    Though the moments quickly die,
    Greet them gaily as they fly.

KATE: Far away from toil and care,
    Revelling in fresh sea air,
    Here we live and reign alone
    In a world that's all our own.
    Here in this our rocky den,
    Far away from mortal men,

> We'll be queens, and make decrees –
> They may honour them who please.

ALL: Let us gaily tread the measure, etc.

KATE: What a picturesque spot! I wonder where we are!

EDITH: And I wonder where papa is. We have left him ever so far behind.

ISABEL: Oh, he will be here presently! Remember poor papa is not as young as we are, and we have come over a rather difficult country.

KATE: But how thoroughly delightful it is to be so entirely alone! Why, in all probability we are the first human beings who ever set foot on this enchanting spot.

ISABEL: Except the mermaids – it's the very place for mermaids.

KATE: Who are only human beings down to the waist.

EDITH: And who can't be said strictly to set *foot* anywhere. Tails they may, but feet they *cannot*.

KATE: But what shall we do until papa and the servants arrive with the luncheon?

EDITH: We are quite alone, and the sea is as smooth as glass. Suppose we take off our shoes and stockings and paddle?

ALL: Yes, yes! The very thing! [*They prepare to carry out the suggestion. They have all taken off one shoe, when* FREDERIC *comes forward from cave.*]

FRED. [*recitative*]:

    Stop, ladies, pray!

ALL [*hopping on one foot*]:

    A man!

FRED.:   I had intended
    Not to intrude myself upon your notice
    In this effective but alarming costume,
    But under these peculiar circumstances
    It is my bounden duty to inform you
    That your proceedings will not be unwitnessed!

EDITH: But who are you, sir? Speak! [*All hopping.*]

FRED.:   I am a pirate!

ALL [*recoiling, hopping*]:
> A pirate! Horror!

FRED.:   Ladies, do not shun me!
> This evening I renounce my wild profession;
> And to that end, oh, pure and peerless maidens!
> Oh, blushing buds of ever-blooming beauty!
> I, sore at heart, implore your kind assistance.

EDITH: How pitiful his tale!

KATE: How rare his beauty!

ALL: How pitiful his tale! How rare his beauty!

SONG

FRED.:   Oh, is there not one maiden breast
>   Which does not feel the moral beauty
> Of making worldly interest
>   Subordinate to sense of duty?
> Who would not give up willingly
>   All matrimonial ambition,
> To rescue such a one as I
>   From his unfortunate position?

ALL: Alas! there's not one maiden breast
>   Which seems to feel the moral beauty
> Of making worldly interest
>   Subordinate to sense of duty!

FRED.:   Oh, is there not one maiden here
>   Whose homely face and bad complexion
> Have caused all hopes to disappear
>   Of ever winning man's affection?
> To such a one, if such there be,
>   I swear by Heaven's arch above you,
> If you will cast your eyes on me –
>   However plain you be – I'll love you!

ALL: Alas! there's not one maiden here
              Whose homely face and bad complexion
          Have caused all hope to disappear
              Of ever winning man's affection!

FRED. [*in despair*]:
          Not one?
ALL: No, no – not one!
FRED.:   Not one?
ALL: No, no!
   [MABEL *enters*.]
MABEL: Yes, one!
ALL: 'Tis Mabel!
MABEL: Yes, 'tis Mabel!

RECITATIVE

MABEL: Oh, sisters, deaf to pity's name,
                    For shame!
          It's true that he has gone astray,
                    But pray
          Is that a reason good and true
                    Why you
          Should all be deaf to pity's name?

ALL [*aside*]:

          The question is, had he not been
              A thing of beauty,
          Would she be swayed by quite as keen
              A sense of duty?

MABEL: For shame, for shame, for shame!

SONG

MABEL: Poor wandering one!
          Though thou hast surely strayed,

Take heart of grace,
Thy steps retrace,
Poor wandering one!
Poor wandering one!
If such poor love as mine
Can help thee find
True peace of mind –
Why, take it, it is thine!
Take heart, fair days will shine;
Take any heart – take mine!

ALL:　　　　　Take heart; no danger lowers;
Take any heart – but ours!

　　　　　　　　　　[*Exeunt* MABEL *and* FREDERIC.]
　　[EDITH *beckons her sisters, who form in a semicircle around*
her.]

EDITH:　　　　What ought we to do,
Gentle sisters, say?
Propriety, we know,
Says we ought to stay;
While sympathy exclaims,
'Free them from your tether –
Play at other games –
Leave them here together.'

KATE:　　　　Her case may, any day,
Be yours, my dear, or mine.
Let her make her hay
While the sun doth shine.
Let us compromise,
(Our hearts are not of leather.)
Let us shut our eyes,
And talk about the weather.

GIRLS:　　　Yes, yes, let's talk about the weather.

CHATTERING CHORUS

How beautifully blue the sky,
The glass is rising very high,
Continue fine I hope it may,
And yet it rained but yesterday.
To-morrow it may pour again
(I hear the country wants some rain),
Yet people say, I know not why,
That we shall have a warm July.

[*Enter* MABEL *and* FREDERIC.]
[*During* MABEL's *solo the Girls continue to chatter pianissimo,
but listening eagerly all the time.*]

SOLO

MABEL: Did ever maiden wake
        From dream of homely duty,
To find her daylight break
        With such exceeding beauty?
Did ever maiden close
        Her eyes on waking sadness,
To dream of such exceeding gladness?

FRED.:   Oh, yes! ah, yes! this is exceeding gladness.

GIRLS: How beautifully blue the sky, etc.

SOLO

[*During this, Girls continue their chatter pianissimo as before,
but listening intently all the time.*]

FRED.:   Did ever pirate roll
        His soul in guilty dreaming,
And wake to find that soul
        With peace and virtue beaming?

ENSEMBLE

MABEL	FREDERIC	GIRLS
Did ever maiden wake, etc.	Did ever pirate roll, etc.	How beautifully blue the sky, etc.

RECITATIVE

FRED.:
Stay, we must not lose our senses;
    Men who stick at no offences
      Will anon be here.
Piracy their dreadful trade is;
    Pray you, get you hence, young ladies,
      While the coast is clear.

          [FREDERIC *and* MABEL *retire.*]

GIRLS:
No, we must not lose our senses,
    If they stick at no offences.
      We should not be here.
Piracy their dreadful trade is –
    Nice companions for young ladies!
      Let us disappear.

[*During this chorus the Pirates have entered stealthily, and formed in a semicircle behind the Girls. As the Girls move to go off each Pirate seizes a girl.* KING *seizes* EDITH *and* ISABEL, SAMUEL *seizes* KATE.]

ALL: Too late!
PIRATES: Ha! Ha!
ALL: Too late!
PIRATES: Ha! Ha!
Ha! ha! ha! ha! Ha! ha! ha! ha!

ENSEMBLE

[*Pirates pass in front of Girls.*]	[*Girls pass in front of Pirates.*]
PIRATES	GIRLS
Here's a first-rate opportunity	We have missed our opportunity
To get married with impunity,	Of escaping with impunity;
And indulge in the felicity	So farewell to the felicity
Of unbounded domesticity.	Of our maiden domesticity!
You shall quickly be parsonified,	We shall quickly be parsonified,
Conjugally matrimonified,	Conjugally matrimonified,
By a doctor of divinity,[8]	By a doctor of divinity,
Who resides in this vicinity.	Who resides in this vicinity.

RECITATIVE

MABEL [*coming forward*]:

      Hold, monsters! Ere your pirate caravanserai[9]
      Proceed, against our will, to wed us all,
      Just bear in mind that we are Wards in Chancery,[10]
      And father is a Major-General![11]

SAM. [*cowed*]:

      We'd better pause, or danger may befall,
      Their father is a Major-General.

GIRLS: Yes, yes; he is a Major-General!

[*The* MAJOR-GENERAL *has entered unnoticed, on rock.*]

GEN.:   Yes, I am a Major-General!

SAM.:   For he is a Major-General!

ALL: He is! Hurrah for the Major-General!

GEN.:   And it is – it is a glorious thing
      To be a Major-General!

ALL: It is! Hurrah for the Major-General!

SONG

GEN.:   I am the very model of a modern Major-General,
I've information vegetable, animal and mineral,
I know the kings of England, and I quote the fights
historical,
From Marathon to Waterloo,[12] in order categorical;
I'm very well acquainted too with matters mathematical,
I understand equations, both the simple and quadratical,[13]
About binomial theorem[14] I'm teeming with a lot o' news –
With many cheerful facts about the square of the
hypotenuse.[15]

ALL: With many cheerful facts, etc.

GEN.:   I'm very good at integral and differential calculus,[16]
I know the scientific names of beings animalculous;[17]
In short, in matters vegetable, animal and mineral,
I am the very model of a modern Major-General.

ALL: In short, in matters vegetable, animal and mineral,
He is the very model of a modern Major-General.

GEN.:   I know our mythic history, King Arthur's and Sir
Caradoc's,[18]
I answer hard acrostics,[19] I've a pretty taste for paradox,
I quote in elegiacs[20] all the crimes of Heliogabalus,[21]
In conics I can floor peculiarities parabolous.[22]
I can tell undoubted Raphaels from Gerard Dows and
Zoffanies,[23]
I know the croaking chorus from the *Frogs* of
Aristophanes,[24]
Then I can hum a fugue[25] of which I've heard the music's
din afore,
And whistle all the airs from that infernal nonsense
Pinafore.

ALL: And whistle all the airs, etc.

GEN.:   Then I can write a washing bill in Babylonic cuneiform,[26]
        And tell you every detail of Caractacus's[27] uniform;
        In short, in matters vegetable, animal and mineral,
        I am the very model of a modern Major-General.

ALL: In short, in matters vegetable, animal, and mineral,
        He is the very model of a modern Major-General.

GEN.:   In fact, when I know what is meant by 'mamelon'[28] and
           'ravelin',[29]
        When I can tell at sight a chassepôt rifle[30] from a javelin,
        When such affairs as sorties and surprises I'm more wary
           at,
        And when I know precisely what is meant by
           'commissariat',[31]
        When I have learnt what progress has been made in
           modern gunnery,
        When I know more of tactics than a novice in a nunnery;
        In short, when I've a smattering of elemental strategy,
        You'll say a better Major-Gener*al* has never *sat* a gee[32] –

ALL: You'll say a better, etc.

GEN.:   For my military knowledge, though I'm plucky and
           adventury,
        Has only been brought down to the beginning of the
           century;
        But still in matters vegetable, animal and mineral,
        I am the very model of a modern Major-General.

ALL: But still in matters vegetable, animal and mineral,
        He is the very model of a modern Major-General.

GEN.: And now that I've introduced myself I should like to have some
    idea of what's going on.

KATE: Oh, papa – we –

SAM.: Permit me, I'll explain in two words: we propose to marry your daughters.

GEN.: Dear me!

GIRLS: Against our wills, papa – against our wills!

GEN.: Oh, but you mustn't do that! May I ask – this is a picturesque uniform, but I'm not familiar with it. What are you?

KING: We are all single gentlemen.

GEN.: Yes, I gathered that – anything else?

KING: No, nothing else.

EDITH: Papa, don't believe them; they are pirates – the famous Pirates of Penzance!

GEN.: The Pirates of Penzance! I have often heard of them.

MABEL: All except this gentleman – [*indicating* FREDERIC] – who was a pirate once, but who is out of his indentures to-day, and who means to lead a blameless life evermore.

GEN.: But wait a bit. I object to pirates as sons-in-law.

KING: We object to Major-Generals as fathers-in-law. But we waive that point. We do not press it. We look over it.

GEN. [*aside*]: Hah! an idea! [*Aloud*] And do you mean to say that you would deliberately rob me of these, the sole remaining props of my old age, and leave me to go through the remainder of my life unfriended, unprotected and alone?

KING: Well, yes, that's the idea.

GEN.: Tell me, have you ever known what it is to be an orphan?

PIRATES [*disgusted*]: Oh, dash it all!

KING: Here we are again!

GEN.: I ask you, have you ever known what it is to be an orphan?

KING: Often!

GEN.: Yes, orphan. Have you ever known what it is to be one?

KING: I say, often.

ALL [*disgusted*]: Often, often, often. [*Turning away.*]

GEN.: I don't think we quite understand one another. I ask you, have you ever known what it is to be an orphan, and you say 'orphan'. As I understand you, you are merely repeating the word 'orphan' to show that you understand me.

KING: I didn't repeat the word often.

GEN.: Pardon me, you did indeed.

KING: I only repeated it once.

GEN.: True, but you repeated it.

KING: But not often.

GEN.: Stop: I think I see where we are getting confused. When you said 'orphan', did you mean 'orphan' – a person who has lost his parents, or 'often' – frequently?

KING: Ah! I beg pardon – I see what you mean – frequently.

GEN.: Ah! you said often – frequently.

KING: No, only once.

GEN. [*irritated*]: Exactly – you said often, frequently, only once.

RECITATIVE

GEN.:	Oh, men of dark and dismal fate,
	Forgo your cruel employ,
	Have pity on my lonely state,
	I am an orphan boy!
KING *and* SAM.:	An orphan boy?
GEN.:	An orphan boy!
PIRATES:	How sad – an orphan boy.

SOLO

GEN.:	These children whom you see
	Are all that I can call my own!
PIRATES:	Poor fellow!
GEN.:	Take them away from me
	And I shall be indeed alone.
PIRATES:	Poor fellow!
GEN.:	If pity you can feel,
	Leave me my sole remaining joy –
	See, at your feet they kneel;
	Your hearts you cannot steel
	Against the sad, sad tale of the lonely orphan boy!

PIRATES [*sobbing*]:   Poor fellow!
             See at our feet they kneel;
             Our hearts we cannot steel
             Against the sad, sad tale of the lonely orphan boy!
KING: The orphan boy!
SAM.:   The orphan boy!
ALL: The lonely orphan boy! Poor fellow!

ENSEMBLE

MAJOR-GENERAL [*aside*]	GIRLS [*aside*]	PIRATES [*aside*]
I'm telling a terrible story,	He's telling a terrible story,	If he's telling a terrible story,
But it doesn't diminish my glory;	Which will tend to diminish his glory;	He shall die by a death that is gory,
For they would have taken my daughters	Though they would have taken his daughters	One of the cruellest slaughters
Over the billowy waters,	Over the billowy waters.	That ever were known in these waters;
If I hadn't, in elegant diction,	It's easy, in elegant diction,	And we'll finish his moral affliction
Indulged in an innocent fiction;	To call it an innocent fiction,	By a very complete malediction,
Which is not in the same category	But it comes in the same category	As a compliment valedictory,
As a regular terrible story.	As a regular terrible story.	If he's telling a terrible story.

KING: Although our dark career
           Sometimes involves the crime of stealing,
        We rather think that we're
           Not altogether void of feeling.
        Although we live by strife,
           We're always sorry to begin it,
        For what, we ask, is life
           Without a touch of Poetry in it?

ALL [*kneeling*]:

> Hail, Poetry, thou heaven-born maid!
> Thou gildest e'en the pirate's trade:
> Hail, flowing fount of sentiment!
> All hail, Divine Emollient! [*All rise.*]

KING: You may go, for you're at liberty, our pirate rules
>   protect you,
> And honorary members of our band we do elect you!

SAM.:   For he is an orphan boy.

CHORUS: He is! Hurrah for the orphan boy.

GEN.:   And it sometimes is a useful thing
>   To be an orphan boy.

CHORUS: It is! Hurrah for the orphan boy!

> Oh, happy day, with joyous glee
> They will away and married be;
> Should it befall auspiciously,
> Our sisters all will bridesmaids be!

[RUTH *enters and comes down to* FREDERIC.]

RUTH: Oh, master, hear one word, I do implore you!
>   Remember Ruth, your Ruth, who kneels before you!

CHORUS: Yes, yes, remember Ruth, who kneels before you!

FRED. [*Pirates threaten* RUTH]:

> Away, you did deceive me!

CHORUS: Away, you did deceive him!

RUTH: Oh, do not leave me!

CHORUS: Oh, do not leave her!

FRED.:   Away, you grieve me!

CHORUS: Away, you grieve him!

FRED.:   I wish you'd leave me!

[FREDERIC *casts* RUTH *from him.*]

CHORUS: We wish you'd leave him!

ENSEMBLE

Pray observe the magnanimity

$\left.\begin{array}{l}\text{We}\\\text{They}\end{array}\right\}$ display to lace and dimity!

Never was such opportunity

To get married with impunity,

But $\left\{\begin{array}{l}\text{we}\\\text{they}\end{array}\right\}$ give up the felicity

Of unbounded domesticity,

Though a doctor of divinity

Resides in this vicinity.

[*Girls and* GENERAL *go up rocks, while Pirates indulge in a wild dance of delight on stage. The* GENERAL *produces a British flag, and the* PIRATE KING *produces a black flag with skull and cross-bones. Enter* RUTH, *who makes a final appeal to* FREDERIC, *who casts her from him.*]

END OF ACT I

ACT II

SCENE – *A Ruined Chapel*[33] *by Moonlight. Ruined Gothic windows at back.*

[MAJOR-GENERAL STANLEY *discovered seated pensively, surrounded by his daughters.*]

CHORUS

Oh, dry the glistening tear
   That dews that martial cheek;
Thy loving children hear,
   In them thy comfort seek.
With sympathetic care
   Their arms around thee creep,
For oh, they cannot bear
   To see their father weep!

[*Enter* MABEL.]

SOLO

MABEL: Dear father, why leave your bed
                 At this untimely hour,
            When happy daylight is dead,
                 And darksome dangers lower?
            See, heaven has lit her lamp,
                 The midnight hour is past,
            The chilly night air is damp,
                 And the dews are falling fast!

Dear father, why leave your bed
When happy daylight is dead?

[FREDERIC *enters.*]

MABEL: Oh, Frederic, cannot you, in the calm excellence of your wisdom, reconcile it with your conscience to say something that will relieve my father's sorrow?

FRED.: I will try, dear Mabel. But why does he sit, night after night, in this draughty old ruin?

GEN.: Why do I sit here? To escape from the pirates' clutches, I described myself as an orphan, and, heaven help me, I am no orphan! I come here to humble myself before the tombs of my ancestors, and to implore their pardon for having brought dishonour on the family escutcheon.

FRED.: But you forget, sir, you only bought the property a year ago, and the stucco in your baronial hall is scarcely dry.

GEN.: Frederic, in this chapel are ancestors: you cannot deny that. With the estate, I bought the chapel and its contents. I don't know whose ancestors they *were*, but I know whose ancestors they *are*, and I shudder to think that their descendant by purchase (if I may so describe myself) should have brought disgrace upon what, I have no doubt, was an unstained escutcheon.

FRED.: Be comforted. Had you not acted as you did, these reckless men would assuredly have called in the nearest clergyman, and have married your large family on the spot.

GEN.: I thank you for your proffered solace, but it is unavailing. I assure you, Frederic, that such is the anguish and remorse I feel at the abominable falsehood by which I escaped these easily deluded pirates, that I would go to their simple-minded chief this very night and confess all, did I not fear that the consequences would be most disastrous to myself. At what time does your expedition march against these scoundrels?

FRED.: At eleven, and before midnight I hope to have atoned for my involuntary association with the pestilent scourges by sweeping them from the face of the earth – and then, dear Mabel, you will be mine!

GEN.: Are your devoted followers at hand?

FRED.: They are, they only wait my orders.

RECITATIVE

GEN.:   Then, Frederic, let your escort lion-hearted
          Be summoned to receive a General's blessing,
          Ere they depart upon their dread adventure.

FRED.: Dear sir, they come.
          [*Enter Police, marching in single file. They form in line, facing
          audience.*]

SONG

SERG.:   When the foeman bares his steel,
                          Tarantara! tarantara!
          We uncomfortable feel,
                          Tarantara!
          And we find the wisest thing,
                          Tarantara! tarantara!
          Is to slap our chests and sing
                          Tarantara!
          For when threatened with emeutes,[34]
                          Tarantara! tarantara!
          And your heart is in your boots,
                          Tarantara!
          There is nothing brings it round,
                          Tarantara! tarantara!
          Like the trumpet's martial sound,
                          Tarantara! tarantara!
          Tarantara-ra-ra-ra-ra!
ALL: Tarantara-ra-ra-ra-ra!

MABEL: Go, ye heroes, go to glory,
          Though you die in combat gory,
          Ye shall live in song and story.
                  Go to immortality!
          Go to death, and go to slaughter;
          Die, and every Cornish daughter

With her tears your grave shall water.
Go, ye heroes, go and die!

ALL: Go, ye heroes, go and die!

POLICE: Though to us it's evident,
Tarantara! tarantara!
These intentions are well meant,
Tarantara!
Such expressions don't appear,
Tarantara! tarantara!
Calculated men to cheer,
Tarantara!
Who are going to meet their fate
In a highly nervous state,
Tarantara!
Still to us it's evident,
These intentions are well meant.
Tarantara!

EDITH: Go and do your best endeavour,
And before all links we sever,
We will say farewell for ever.
Go to glory and the grave!

GIRLS: For your foes are fierce and ruthless,
False, unmerciful and truthless.
Young and tender, old and toothless,
All in vain their mercy crave.

SERG.:   We observe too great a stress,
On the risks that on us press,
And of reference a lack
To our chance of coming back.
Still, perhaps it would be wise
Not to carp or criticize,
For it's very evident
These attentions are well meant.

ALL: Yes, to them it's evident
       Our attentions are well meant.
          Tarantara-ra-ra-ra-ra!

       Go, ye heroes, go to glory, etc.

ENSEMBLE

Chorus of all but Police	*Chorus of Police*
Go and do your best endeavour,	Such expressions don't appear,
	Tarantara, tarantara!
And before all links we sever	Calculated men to cheer,
	Tarantara!
We will say farewell for ever.	Who are going to their fate,
	Tarantara, tarantara!
Go to glory and the grave!	In a highly nervous state –
	Tarantara!
For your foes are fierce and ruthless,	We observe too great a stress,
	Tarantara, tarantara!
False, unmerciful and truthless.	On the risks that on us press,
	Tarantara!
Young and tender, old and toothless,	And of reference a lack,
	Tarantara, tarantara!
All in vain their mercy crave.	To our chance of coming back,
	Tarantara!

GEN.:   Away, away!
POLICE [*without moving*]:

        Yes, yes, we go.
GEN.:   These pirates slay.
POLICE: Tarantara!
GEN.:   Then do not stay.
POLICE: Tarantara!
GEN.:   Then why this delay?
POLICE: All right – we go.
       Yes, forward on the foe!

GEN.:   Yes, but you *don't* go!

POLICE: We go, we go!

              Yes, forward on the foe!

GEN.:   Yes, but you *don't* go!

ALL: At last they really go.

     [MABEL *tears herself from* FREDERIC *and exits, followed by
     her sisters, consoling her. The* MAJOR-GENERAL *and others
                       follow.* FREDERIC *remains.*]

RECITATIVE

FRED.:   Now for the pirates' lair! Oh, joy unbounded!

                  Oh, sweet relief! Oh, rapture unexampled!

                  At last I may atone, in some slight measure,

                  For the repeated acts of theft and pillage

                  Which, at a sense of duty's stern dictation,

                  I, circumstance's victim, have been guilty.

        [KING *and* RUTH *appear at the window, armed.*]

KING: Young Frederic! [*Covering him with pistol.*]

FRED.:   Who calls?

KING: Your late commander!

RUTH: And I, your little Ruth! [*Covering him with pistol.*]

FRED.:   Oh, mad intruders,

                  How dare ye face me? Know ye not, oh rash ones,

                  That I have doomed you to extermination?

       [KING *and* RUTH *hold a pistol to each ear.*]

KING: Have mercy on us, hear us, ere you slaughter.

FRED.:   I do not think I ought to listen to you.

                  Yet, mercy should alloy our stern resentment,

                  And so I will be merciful – say on!

TRIO – RUTH, PIRATE KING *and* FREDERIC

RUTH: When you had left our pirate fold

               We tried to raise our spirits faint,

          According to our customs old,

               With quips and quibbles quaint.

But all in vain the quips we heard,
 We lay and sobbed upon the rocks,
Until to somebody occurred
 A startling paradox.

FRED.:   A paradox?
KING [*laughing*]:   A paradox!
RUTH: A most ingenious paradox!
   We've quips and quibbles heard in flocks,
   But none to beat this paradox!
    Ha! ha! ha! ha! Ho! ho! ho! ho!

KING: We knew your taste for curious quips,
    For cranks and contradictions queer,
   And with the laughter on our lips,
    We wished you there to hear.
   We said, 'If we could tell it him,
    How Frederic would the joke enjoy!'
   And so we've risked both life and limb
    To tell it to our boy.

FRED. [*interested*]:
   That paradox? That paradox?
KING *and* RUTH [*laughing*]:
   That most ingenious paradox!
   We've quips and quibbles heard in flocks,
   But none to beat that paradox!
    Ha! ha! ha! ha! Ho! ho! ho! ho!

CHANT

KING: For some ridiculous reason, to which, however, I've no
   desire to be disloyal,
  Some person in authority, I don't know who, very likely the
   Astronomer Royal,[35]
  Has decided that, although for such a beastly month as
   February, twenty-eight days as a rule are plenty,
  One year in every four his days shall be reckoned as
   nine-and-twenty.

> Through some singular coincidence – I shouldn't be
>> surprised if it were owing to the agency of an ill-natured
>> fairy –
> You are the victim of this clumsy arrangement, having been
>> born in leap-year,[36] on the twenty-ninth of February,
> And so, by a simple arithmetical process, you'll easily
>> discover,
> That though you've lived twenty-one years, yet, if we go by
>> birthdays, you're only five and a little bit over!

RUTH: Ha! ha! ha! ha!

KING: Ho! ho! ho! ho!

FRED.: Dear me!
>> Let's see! [counting on fingers]
>> Yes, yes; with yours my figures do agree!

ALL: Ha! ha! ha! ha! Ho! ho! ho! ho! [FREDERIC more amused
>> than any.]

FRED.: How quaint the ways of Paradox!
>> At common sense she gaily mocks!
>> Though counting in the usual way,
>>> Years twenty-one I've been alive,
>> Yet, reckoning by my natal day,
>>> I am a little boy of five!

ALL: He is a little boy of five! Ha! ha!
>> A paradox, a paradox,
>> A most ingenious paradox!
>> Ha! ha! ha! ha! Ho! ho! ho! ho!

[RUTH and PIRATE KING throw themselves back on seats,
exhausted with laughter.]

FRED.: Upon my word, this is most curious – most absurdly whimsi-
cal. Five-and-a-quarter! No one would think it to look at me!

RUTH: You are glad now, I'll be bound, that you spared us. You
would never have forgiven yourself when you discovered that you
had killed *two of your comrades*.

FRED.: My comrades?

KING [*rises*]: I'm afraid you don't appreciate the delicacy of your
position. You were apprenticed to us –

FRED.: Until I reached my twenty-first year.

KING: No, until you reached your twenty-first *birthday* [*producing document*], and, going by birthdays, you are as yet only five-and-a-quarter.

FRED.: You don't mean to say you are going to hold me to that?

KING: No, we merely remind you of the fact, and leave the rest to your sense of duty.

RUTH: Your sense of duty!

FRED. [*wildly*]: Don't put it on that footing! As I was merciful to you just now, be merciful to me! I implore you not to insist on the letter of your bond just as the cup of happiness is at my lips!

RUTH: We insist on nothing; we content ourselves with pointing out to you *your duty.*

KING: Your duty!

FRED. [*after a pause*]: Well, you have appealed to my sense of duty, and my duty is only too clear. I abhor your infamous calling; I shudder at the thought that I have ever been mixed up with it; but duty is before all – at any price I will do my duty.

KING: Bravely spoken! Come, you are one of us once more.

FRED.: Lead on, I follow. [*Suddenly*] Oh, horror!

KING *and* RUTH: What is the matter?

FRED.: Ought I to tell you? No, no, I cannot do it; and yet, as one of your band –

KING: Speak out, I charge you by that sense of conscientiousness to which we have never yet appealed in vain.

FRED.: General Stanley,[37] the father of my Mabel –

KING *and* RUTH: Yes, yes!

FRED.: He escaped from you on the plea that he was an orphan!

KING: He did!

FRED.: It breaks my heart to betray the honoured father of the girl I adore, but as your apprentice I have no alternative. It is my duty to tell you that General Stanley is no orphan!

KING *and* RUTH: What!

FRED.: More than that, he never was one!

KING: Am I to understand that, to save his contemptible life, he dared to practise on our credulous simplicity? [FREDERIC *nods as he weeps.*] Our revenge shall be swift and terrible. We will go and collect our band and attack Tremorden Castle this very night.

FRED.: But – stay –

KING: Not a word! He is doomed!

TRIO

KING *and* RUTH	FREDERIC
Away, away! my heart's on fire,	Away, away! ere I expire –
I burn this base deception to repay,	I find my duty hard to do to-day!
This very night my vengeance dire	My heart is filled with anguish dire,
Shall glut itself in gore. Away, away!	It strikes me to the core. Away, away!

KING: With falsehood foul
He tricked us of our brides.
Let vengeance howl;
The Pirate so decides.
Our nature stern
He softened with his lies,
And, in return,
To-night the traitor dies.

ALL: Yes, yes! to-night the traitor dies.

RUTH: To-night he dies!
KING: Yes, or early to-morrow.
FRED.: His girls likewise?
RUTH: They will welter in sorrow.
KING: The one soft spot
FRED.: In their natures they cherish –
RUTH: And all who plot
KING: To abuse it shall perish!
ALL: Yes, all who plot
To abuse it shall perish!
Away, away! etc.

[*Exeunt* PIRATE KING *and* RUTH.]

[*Enter* MABEL.]

RECITATIVE – MABEL *and* FREDERIC

MABEL: All is prepared, your gallant crew await you.
          My Frederic in tears? It cannot be
          That lion-heart quails at the coming conflict?
FRED.:   No, Mabel, no. A terrible disclosure
          Has just been made! Mabel, my dearly-loved one,
          I bound myself to serve the pirate captain
          Until I reached my one-and-twentieth birthday –
MABEL: But you *are* twenty-one?
FRED.:   I've just discovered
          That I was born in leap-year, and that birthday
          Will not be reached by me till 1940.
MABEL: Oh, horrible! catastrophe appalling!
FRED.:   And so, farewell!
MABEL: No, no! Ah, Frederic, hear me.

DUET – MABEL *and* FREDERIC

MABEL: Stay, Frederic, stay!
              They have no legal claim,
              No shadow of a shame
              Will fall upon thy name.
          Stay, Frederic, stay!

FRED.:   Nay, Mabel, nay!
              To-night I quit these walls,
              The thought my soul appals,
              But when stern Duty calls,
          I must obey.

MABEL: Stay, Frederic, stay!
FRED.:   Nay, Mabel, nay!
MABEL: They have no claim –
FRED.:   But Duty's name!
              The thought my soul appals,
              But when stern Duty calls,
          I must obey.

BALLAD

MABEL: Ah, leave me not to pine
           Alone and desolate;
     No fate seemed fair as mine,
           No happiness so great!
     And nature, day by day,
           Has sung, in accents clear,
     This joyous roundelay,
           'He loves thee – he is here.
                Fa-la, fa-la, fa-la.'

FRED.:   Ah, must I leave thee here
           In endless night to dream,
     Where joy is dark and drear,
           And sorrow all supreme!
     Where nature, day by day,
           Will sing, in altered tone,
     This weary roundelay,
           'He loves thee – he is gone.
                Fa-la, fa-la, fa-la.'

     In 1940 I of age shall be,
     I'll then return, and claim you – I declare it!
MABEL: It seems so long!
FRED.:   Swear that, till then, you will be true to me.
MABEL: Yes, I'll be strong!
     By all the Stanleys dead and gone, I swear it!

ENSEMBLE

    Oh, here is love, and here is truth,
      And here is food for joyous laughter.
    He $\Big\}$ will be faithful to $\Big\{$ his $\Big\}$ sooth
    She   her
      Till we are wed, and even after.

What joy to know that though $\left\{ \begin{array}{l} he \\ I \end{array} \right\}$ must

Embrace piratical adventures,

$\left. \begin{array}{l} He \\ She \end{array} \right\}$ will be faithful to $\left\{ \begin{array}{l} his \\ her \end{array} \right\}$ trust

Till $\left\{ \begin{array}{l} he\ is \\ I\ am \end{array} \right\}$ out of $\left\{ \begin{array}{l} his \\ my \end{array} \right\}$ indentures!

FRED.:   Farewell! Adieu!

MABEL: The same to you!

BOTH: Farewell! Adieu!

> [FREDERIC *rushes to window and leaps out.*]

RECITATIVE

MABEL: Distraction! Frederic! loved one! oh return!
        With love I burn!

[*Recollecting*]

    Stay! I'm a Stanley! Even to the grave I will be brave.
    His conscience bids him give up love and all
        At duty's call;
    Mine teaches me that though I love him so,
        He is my foe.

MABEL [*almost fainting*]:

    No, I am brave! Oh, family descent,
    How great thy charm, thy sway how excellent!
    Come, one and all, undaunted men in blue,
    A crisis, now, affairs are coming to!

[*Enter Police, marching in single file.*]

SERG.:   Though in body and in mind,
        Tarantara, tarantara!
    We are timidly inclined,
        Tarantara!
    And anything but blind,
        Tarantara, tarantara!
    To the danger that's behind,
        Tarantara!

> Yet, when the danger's near,
>> Tarantara, tarantara!
> We manage to appear,
>> Tarantara!
> As insensible to fear
> As anybody here.
>> Tarantara, tarantara-ra-ra-ra-ra!

MABEL: Sergeant, approach! Young Frederic was to have led you to death and glory.

ALL: That is not a pleasant way of putting it.

MABEL: No matter; he will not so lead you, for he has allied himself once more with his old associates.

ALL: He has acted shamefully!

MABEL: You speak falsely. You know nothing about it. He has acted nobly.

ALL: He has acted nobly!

MABEL: Dearly as I loved him before, his heroic sacrifice to his sense of duty has endeared him to me tenfold. He has done his duty. I will do mine. Go ye and do yours.   [*Exit.*]

ALL: Right oh!

SERG.: This is perplexing.

ALL: We cannot understand it at all.

SERG.: Still, as he is actuated by a sense of duty –

ALL: That makes a difference, of course. At the same time we repeat, we cannot understand it at all.

SERG.: No matter; our course is clear. We must do our best to capture these pirates alone. It is most distressing to us to be the agents whereby our erring fellow-creatures are deprived of that liberty which is so dear to all – but we should have thought of that before we joined the Force.

ALL: We should!

SERG.: It is too late now!

ALL: It is!

SONG

SERG.:	When a felon's not engaged in his employment –
ALL:	His employment,
SERG.:	Or maturing his felonious little plans –
ALL:	Little plans,
SERG.:	His capacity for innocent enjoyment –
ALL:	'Cent enjoyment
SERG.:	Is just as great as any honest man's –
ALL:	Honest man's.
SERG.:	Our feelings we with difficulty smother –
ALL:	'Culty smother
SERG.:	When constabulary duty's to be done –
ALL:	To be done.
SERG.:	Ah, take one consideration with another –
ALL:	With another,
SERG.:	A policeman's lot is not a happy one –
ALL:	Happy one!
	When constabulary duty's to be done –
	To be done –
	The policeman's lot is not a happy one –
	Happy one!
SERG.:	When the enterprising burglar's not a-burgling –
ALL:	Not a-burgling,
SERG.:	When the cut-throat isn't occupied in crime –
ALL:	'Pied in crime,
SERG.:	He loves to hear the little brook a-gurgling –
ALL:	Brook a-gurgling,
SERG.:	And listen to the merry village chime –
ALL:	Village chime.
SERG.:	When the coster's finished jumping on his mother –
ALL:	On his mother,
SERG.:	He loves to lie a-basking in the sun –
ALL:	In the sun.
SERG.:	Ah, take one consideration with another –
ALL:	With another,

SERG.: The policeman's lot is not a happy one.
ALL: Happy one!
    When constabulary duty's to be done –
        To be done,
    The policeman's lot is not a happy one –
        Happy one!

[*Chorus of Pirates without, in the distance.*]
    A rollicking band of pirates we,
    Who, tired of tossing on the sea,
    Are trying their hand at a burglaree,
        With weapons grim and gory.

SERG.: Hush, hush! I hear them on the manor poaching,
    With stealthy step the pirates are approaching.

[*Chorus of Pirates, resumed nearer.*]
    We are not coming for plate or gold –
    A story General Stanley's told –
    We seek a penalty fifty-fold,
        For General Stanley's story.

POLICE: They seek a penalty –
PIRATES [*without*]: Fifty-fold,
    We seek a penalty –
POLICE: Fifty-fold,
ALL: We ⎫
    they ⎭ seek a penalty fifty-fold,
    For General Stanley's story.
POLICE: They come in force,
    The bold, burglarious elves;
    Our obvious course
    Is to conceal ourselves.
[*Police conceal themselves. As they do so, the Pirates are seen appearing at a ruined window. They enter cautiously, and come down-stage.* SAMUEL *is laden with burglarious tools and pistols, etc.*]

CHORUS

PIRATES [*very loud*]:

>> With cat-like tread,
>>> Upon our prey we steal,
>> In silence dread
>>> Our cautious way we feel.
>> No sound at all,
>>> We never speak a word,
>> A fly's foot-fall
>>> Would be distinctly heard –

POLICE [*pianissimo*]:   Tarantara, tarantara!

PIRATES: So stealthily the pirate creeps,
>> While all the household soundly sleeps.
>> Come, friends, who plough the sea,
>>> Truce to navigation,
>>> Take another station;
>> Let's vary piracee
>> With a little burglaree!

POLICE [*pianissimo*]:   Tarantara, tarantara!

SAM. [*distributing implements to various members of the gang*]:

>> Here's your crowbar and your centrebit,[38]
>> Your life-preserver – you may want to hit;
>> Your silent matches,[39] your dark lantern seize,
>> Take your file and your skeletonic keys.

[*Enter* KING, FREDERIC, *and* RUTH.]

ALL [*fortissimo*]:

>> With cat-like tread, etc.

RECITATIVE

FRED.:   Hush, hush, not a word! I see a light inside!
>> The Major-General comes, so quickly hide!

PIRATES: Yes, yes, the Major-General comes!

[*Exeunt* PIRATE KING, FREDERIC, SAMUEL *and* RUTH.]

POLICE: Yes, yes, the Major-General comes!

GEN. [*entering in dressing-gown, carrying a light*]:
>> Yes, yes, the Major-General comes!

SOLO

GEN.:   Tormented with the anguish dread
                   Of falsehood unatoned,
             I lay upon my sleepless bed,
                   And tossed and turned and groaned.
             The man who finds his conscience ache
                   No peace at all enjoys,
             And as I lay in bed awake
                   I thought I heard a noise.

PIRATES *and* POLICE:
             He thought he heard a noise – ha! ha!
             He thought he heard a noise – ha! ha! [*very loud*]

GEN.:   No, all is still
                    In dale, on hill;
                 My mind is set at ease.
                  So still the scene –
                   It must have been
                 The sighing of the breeze.

BALLAD

GEN.:   Sighing softly to the river
                   Comes the loving breeze,
             Setting nature all a-quiver,
                   Rustling through the trees –
ALL: Through the trees.
GEN.:   And the brook, in rippling measure,
                   Laughs for very love,
             While the poplars, in their pleasure,
                   Wave their arms above.

POLICE *and* PIRATES:
             Yes, the trees, for very love,
             Wave their leafy arms above,
                   River, river, little river,
                   May thy loving prosper ever.

> Heaven speed thee, poplar tree,
> May thy wooing happy be.

GEN.:
> Yet, the breeze is but a rover;
>> When he wings away,
> Brook and poplar mourn a lover!
>> Sighing well-a-day!

ALL:
>> Well-a-day!

GEN.:
> Ah! the doing and undoing,
>> That the rogue could tell!
> When the breeze is out a-wooing,
>> Who can woo so well?

POLICE *and* PIRATES:
> Shocking tales the rogue could tell
> Nobody can woo so well.
>> Pretty brook, thy dream is over,
>> For thy love is but a rover!
>> Sad the lot of poplar trees,
>> Courted by the fickle breeze!

[*Enter the* GENERAL's *daughters, all in white peignoirs and night-caps, and carrying lighted candles.*]

GIRLS:
> Now what is this, and what is that, and why does
>> father leave his rest
> At such a time of night as this, so very incompletely
>> dressed?
> Dear father is, and always was, the most methodical
>> of men!
> It's his invariable rule to go to bed at half-past ten.
> What strange occurrence can it be that calls dear
>> father from his rest
> At such a time of night as this, so very incompletely
>> dressed?

[*Enter* KING, SAMUEL *and* FREDERIC.]

KING:
> Forward, my men, and seize that General there!

[*They seize the* GENERAL.]

GIRLS:
> The pirates! the pirates! Oh, despair!

PIRATES: Yes, we're the pirates, so despair!
GEN.:   Frederic here! Oh, joy! Oh, rapture!
           Summon your men and effect their capture!
MABEL: Frederic, save us!
FRED.:   Beautiful Mabel,
           I would if I could, but I am not able.
PIRATES: He's telling the truth, he is not able.
KING: With base deceit
                 You worked upon our feelings!
               Revenge is sweet,
                 And flavours all our dealings!
               With courage rare
                 And resolution manly,
               For death prepare,
                 Unhappy General Stanley.

MABEL [*wildly*]:
               Is he to die, unshriven – unannealed?
GIRLS: Oh, spare him!
MABEL: Will no one in his cause a weapon wield?
GIRLS: Oh, spare him!
POLICE [*springing up*]:
               Yes, we are here, though hitherto concealed!
GIRLS: Oh, rapture!
POLICE: So to Constabulary, pirates, yield!
GIRLS: Oh, rapture!
    [*A struggle ensues between Pirates and Police. Eventually the
    Police are overcome, and fall prostrate, the Pirates standing over
    them with drawn swords.*]
CHORUS OF POLICE AND PIRATES:
               You ⎫
                   ⎬ triumph now, for well we trow
               We ⎭
                 Our mortal career's cut short,
               No pirate band will take its stand
                 At the Central Criminal Court.[40]
SERG.:   To gain a brief advantage you've contrived,
           But your proud triumph will not be long-lived.

KING: Don't say you are orphans, for we know that game.

SERG.:   On your allegiance we've a stronger claim –
         We charge you yield, in Queen Victoria's name!

KING [*baffled*]: You do!

POLICE: We do!
         We charge you yield, in Queen Victoria's name!
         [*Pirates kneel, Police stand over them triumphantly.*]

KING: We yield at once, with humbled mien,
         Because, with all our faults, we love our Queen.

POLICE: Yes, yes, with all their faults, they love their Queen.

GIRLS: Yes, yes, with all, etc.
         [*Police, holding Pirates by the collar, take out handkerchiefs and weep.*]

GEN.:   Away with them, and place them at the bar!
         [*Enter* RUTH.]

RUTH: One moment! let me tell you who they are.
         They are no members of the common throng;
         They are all noblemen who have gone wrong!

GEN.:   No Englishman unmoved that statement hears,
         Because, with all our faults, we love our House of Peers.

RECITATIVE

GEN.:   I pray you, pardon me, ex-Pirate King,
             Peers will be peers, and youth will have its fling.
             Resume your ranks and legislative duties,
             And take my daughters, all of whom are beauties.

FINALE

             Poor wandering ones!
                Though ye have surely strayed,
                Take heart of grace,
                Your steps retrace,
             Poor wandering ones!

Poor wandering ones!
　　If such poor love as ours
　　Can help you find
　　True peace of mind,
Why, take it, it is yours!
　　Poor wandering ones! etc.

CURTAIN

PATIENCE

OR

BUNTHORNE'S BRIDE

DRAMATIS PERSONAE

COLONEL CALVERLEY ⎫ (*Officers of*
MAJOR MURGATROYD ⎬ *Dragoon*
LIEUT. THE DUKE OF DUNSTABLE ⎭ *Guards*)
REGINALD BUNTHORNE (*a Fleshly Poet*)
ARCHIBALD GROSVENOR (*an Idyllic Poet*)
MR BUNTHORNE'S SOLICITOR
THE LADY ANGELA ⎫
THE LADY SAPHIR ⎬ (*Rapturous Maidens*)
THE LADY ELLA ⎪
THE LADY JANE ⎭
PATIENCE (*a Dairy Maid*)

Chorus of Rapturous Maidens and Officers of Dragoon Guards

ACT I – Exterior of Castle Bunthorne
ACT II – A Glade

ACT I

SCENE – *Exterior of Castle Bunthorne. Entrance to Castle by drawbridge over moat.*

[*Young ladies dressed in aesthetic draperies are grouped about the stage. They play on lutes, mandolins, etc., as they sing, and all are in the last stage of despair.* ANGELA, ELLA *and* SAPHIR *lead them.*]

CHORUS: Twenty[1] love-sick maidens we,
        Love-sick all against our will.
    Twenty years hence we shall be
        Twenty love-sick maidens still.
    Twenty love-sick maidens we,
    And we die for love of thee.

SOLO

ANG.:   Love feeds on hope, they say, or love will die[2] –
ALL: Ah, miserie!
ANG.:   Yet my love lives, although no hope have I!
ALL: Ah, miserie!
ANG.:   Alas, poor heart, go hide thyself away –
        To weeping concords tune thy roundelay!
        Ah, miserie!

CHORUS

All our love is all for one,
    Yet that love he heedeth not,
He is coy and cares for none,
    Sad and sorry is our lot!
            Ah, miserie!

SOLO

ELLA:
    Go, breaking heart,
        Go, dream of love requited;
    Go, foolish heart,
        Go, dream of lovers plighted;
    Go, madcap heart,
        Go, dream of never waking;
    And in thy dream
        Forget that thou art breaking!

CHORUS: Ah, miserie!

ELLA: Forget that thou art breaking!

CHORUS: Twenty love-sick maidens, etc.

ANG.: There is a strange magic in this love of ours! Rivals as we all
   are in the affections of our Reginald,[3] the very hopelessness of our
   love is a bond that binds us to one another!

SAPH.: Jealousy is merged in misery. While he, the very cynosure of
   our eyes and hearts, remains icy insensible – what have we to strive
   for?[4]

ELLA: The love of maidens is, to him, as interesting as the taxes!

SAPH.: Would that it were! He pays his taxes.

ANG.: And cherishes the receipts!

   [*Enter* LADY JANE.]

SAPH.: Happy receipts!

JANE [*suddenly*]: Fools!

ANG.: I beg your pardon?

JANE: Fools and blind! The man loves – wildly loves!

ANG.: But whom? None of us!

JANE: No, none of us. His weird fancy has lighted, for the nonce, on Patience, the village milkmaid!

SAPH.: On Patience? Oh, it cannot be!

JANE: Bah! But yesterday I caught him in her dairy, eating fresh butter with a tablespoon. To-day he is not well!

SAPH.: But Patience boasts that she has never loved – that love is, to her, a sealed book! Oh, he cannot be serious!

JANE: 'Tis but a fleeting fancy – 'twill quickly pass away. [*Aside*] Oh, Reginald, if you but knew what a wealth of golden love is waiting for you, stored up in this rugged old bosom of mine, the milkmaid's triumph would be short indeed!

[PATIENCE *appears on an eminence. She looks down with pity on the despondent Ladies.*]

RECITATIVE

PA.:   Still brooding on their mad infatuation!
          I thank thee, Love, thou comest not to me!
          Far happier I, free from thy ministration,
          Than dukes or duchesses who love can be!

SAPH. [*looking up*]:
          'Tis Patience – happy girl! Loved by a Poet!

PA.:   Your pardon, ladies. I intrude upon you. [*Going.*]

ANG.:   Nay, pretty child, come hither. Is it true
          That you have never loved?

PA.:   Most true indeed.

SOPRANOS: Most marvellous!

CONTRALTOS: And most deplorable!

SONG

PA.:   I cannot tell what this love may be
          That cometh to all, but not to me.
          It cannot be kind as they'd imply,
          Or why do these ladies sigh?
          It cannot be joy and rapture deep,
          Or why do these gentle ladies weep?

It cannot be blissful as 'tis said,
Or why are their eyes so wondrous red?

Though everywhere true love I see
A-coming to all, but not to me,
I cannot tell what this love may be!
For I am blithe and I am gay,
While they sit sighing night and day
Think of the gulf 'twixt them and me,
'Fal la la la!' – and 'Miserie!'

CHORUS: Yes, she is blithe, etc.

PA.:   If love is a thorn, they show no wit
Who foolishly hug and foster it.
If love is a weed, how simple they
Who gather it, day by day!
If love is a nettle that makes you smart,
Then why do you wear it next your heart?
And if it be none of these, say I,
Ah, why do you sit and sob and sigh?
Though everywhere, etc.

CHORUS: For she is blithe, etc.

ANG.: Ah, Patience, if you have never loved, you have never known true happiness! [*All sigh.*]

PA.: But the truly happy always seem to have so much on their minds. The truly happy never seem quite well.

JANE: There is a transcendentality of delirium – an acute accentuation of supremest ecstasy – which the earthy might easily mistake for indigestion. But it is *not* indigestion – it is aesthetic transfiguration! [*To the others*] Enough of babble. Come!

PA.: But stay, I have some news for you. The 35th Dragoon Guards[5] have halted in the village, and are even now on their way to this very spot.

ANG.: The 35th Dragoon Guards!

SAPH.: They are fleshly men, of full habit!

ELLA: We care nothing for Dragoon Guards!

PA.: But, bless me, you were all engaged to them a year ago!

SAPH.: A year ago!

ANG.: My poor child, you don't understand these things. A year ago they were very well in our eyes, but since then our tastes have been etherealized, our perceptions exalted. [*To others*] Come, it is time to lift up our voices in morning carol to our Reginald. Let us to his door.

[*The Ladies go off, two and two, into the Castle, singing refrain of 'Twenty love-sick maidens we', and accompanying themselves on harps and mandolins.* PATIENCE *watches them in surprise, as she climbs the rock by which she entered.*]

[*March. Enter Officers of Dragoon Guards, led by* MAJOR MURGATROYD.]

CHORUS OF DRAGOONS:

> The soldiers of our Queen
>   Are linked in friendly tether;
> Upon the battle scene
>   They fight the foe together.
> There every mother's son
>   Prepared to fight and fall is;
> The enemy of one
>   The enemy of all is!

[*Enter* COLONEL CALVERLEY.]

SONG

COL.:   If you want a receipt for that popular mystery,
>   Known to the world as a Heavy Dragoon,
> Take all the remarkable people in history,
>   Rattle them off to a popular tune.
> The pluck of Lord Nelson on board of the *Victory*[6] –
> Genius of Bismarck[7] devising a plan –
> The humour of Fielding[8] (which sounds contradictory) –
>   Coolness of Paget[9] about to trepan –
> The science of Jullien,[10] the eminent musico –
>   Wit of Macaulay,[11] who wrote of Queen Anne –

The pathos of Paddy, as rendered by Boucicault[12] –
    Style of the Bishop of Sodor and Man[13] –
The dash of a D'Orsay,[14] divested of quackery –
Narrative powers of Dickens and Thackeray –
Victor Emmanuel[15] – peak-haunting Peveril[16] –
Thomas Aquinas[17] and Doctor Sacheverell[18] –
    Tupper[19] and Tennyson – Daniel Defoe –
    Anthony Trollope and Mr Guizot![20]
        Take of these elements all that is fusible,
        Melt them all down in a pipkin or crucible,
        Set them to simmer and take off the scum,
        And a Heavy Dragoon is the residuum!

CHORUS: Yes! yes! yes! yes!
        A Heavy Dragoon is the residuum!

COL.:   If you want a receipt for this soldier-like paragon,
    Get at the wealth of the Czar (if you can) –
The family pride of a Spaniard from Aragon –
    Force of Mephisto[21] pronouncing a ban –
A smack of Lord Waterford,[22] reckless and rollicky –
    Swagger of Roderick,[23] heading his clan –
The keen penetration of Paddington Pollaky[24] –
    Grace of an Odalisque[25] on a divan –
The genius strategic of Caesar or Hannibal –
Skill of Sir Garnet[26] in thrashing a cannibal –
Flavour of Hamlet – the Stranger,[27] a touch of him –
Little of Manfred[28] (but not very much of him) –
    Beadle of Burlington[29] – Richardson's show[30] –
    Mr Micawber[31] and Madame Tussaud![32]
        Take of these elements all that is fusible,
        Melt them all down in a pipkin or crucible,
        Set them to simmer and take off the scum,
        And a Heavy Dragoon is the residuum!

ALL: Yes! yes! yes! yes!
        A Heavy Dragoon is the residuum!

COL.: Well, here we are once more on the scene of our former triumphs. But where's the Duke?

[*Enter the* DUKE OF DUNSTABLE, *listlessly, and in low spirits.*]

DUKE: Here I am! [*Sighs.*]

COL.: Come, cheer up, don't give way!

DUKE: Oh, for that, I'm as cheerful as a poor devil can be expected to be who has the misfortune to be a duke, with a thousand a day!

MAJ.: Humph! Most men would envy you!

DUKE: Envy *me*? Tell me, Major, are you fond of toffee?

MAJ.: Very!

COL.: We are all fond of toffee.

ALL: We are!

DUKE: Yes, and toffee in moderation is a capital thing. But to *live* on toffee – toffee for breakfast, toffee for dinner, toffee for tea – to have it supposed that you care for nothing *but* toffee, and that you would consider yourself insulted if anything but toffee were offered to you – how would you like *that*?

COL.: I can quite believe that, under those circumstances, even toffee would become monotonous.

DUKE: For 'toffee' read flattery, adulation and abject deference, carried to such a pitch that I began, at last, to think that man was born bent at an angle of forty-five degrees! Great Heavens, what is there to adulate in me! Am I particularly intelligent, or remarkably studious, or excruciatingly witty, or unusually accomplished, or exceptionally virtuous?

COL.: You're about as commonplace a young man as ever I saw.

ALL: You are!

DUKE: Exactly! That's it exactly! That describes me to a T! Thank you all very much! Well, I couldn't stand it any longer, so I joined this second-class cavalry regiment. In the Army, thought I, I shall be occasionally snubbed, perhaps even bullied, who knows? The thought was rapture, and here I am.

COL. [*looking off*]: Yes, and here are the ladies!

DUKE: But who is the gentleman with the long hair?

COL.: I don't know.

DUKE: He seems popular!

COL.: He *does* seem popular!

[BUNTHORNE *enters, followed by Ladies, two and two, singing and playing on harps as before. He is composing a poem, and quite absorbed. He sees no one, but walks across the stage, followed by Ladies. They take no notice of Dragoons – to the surprise and indignation of those Officers.*]

CHORUS OF LADIES:

> In a doleful train
> > Two and two we walk all day –
> For we love in vain!
> > None so sorrowful as they
> > > Who can only sigh and say,
> > > Woe is me, alackaday!

CHORUS OF DRAGOONS:

> Now is not this ridiculous – and is not this
> > preposterous?
> A thorough-paced absurdity – explain it if you can.
> Instead of rushing eagerly to cherish us and foster us,
> > They all prefer this melancholy literary man.
> > > Instead of slyly peering at us,
> > > Casting looks endearing at us,
> > Blushing at us, flushing at us – flirting with a fan;
> > They're actually sneering at us, fleering at us, jeering at
> > > us!
> > > Pretty sort of treatment for a military man!
> > > Pretty sort of treatment for a military man!

ANG.:   Mystic poet, hear our prayer,
> > Twenty love-sick maidens we –
> Young and wealthy, dark and fair –
> > All of county family.
> > > And we die for love of thee –
> > > Twenty love-sick maidens we!

CHORUS OF LADIES:

> Yes, we die for love of thee –
> Twenty love-sick maidens we!

BUN. [*aside – slyly*]:

> Though my book I seem to scan
>> In a rapt ecstatic way,
> Like a literary man
>> Who despises female clay,
> I hear plainly all they say,
> Twenty love-sick maidens they!

OFFICERS [*to each other*]:

> He hears plainly, etc.

SAPH.:

> Though so excellently wise,
>> For a moment mortal be,
> Deign to raise thy purple eyes
>> From thy heart-drawn poesy.
> Twenty love-sick maidens see –
> Each is kneeling on her knee! [*All kneel.*]

CHORUS OF LADIES:

> Twenty love-sick, etc.

BUN. [*aside*]:

> Though, as I remarked before,
>> Any one convinced would be
> That some transcendental lore
>> Is monopolizing me,
> Round the corner I can see
> Each is kneeling on her knee!

OFFICERS [*to each other*]:

> Round the corner, etc.

ENSEMBLE

OFFICERS	LADIES
Now is not this ridiculous, etc.	Mystic poet, hear our prayer, etc.

COL.: Angela! what is the meaning of this?

ANG.: Oh, sir, leave us; our minds are but ill-tuned to light love-talk.

MAJ.: But what in the world has come over you all?

JANE: Bunthorne! *He* has come over us. He has come among us, and he has idealized us.

DUKE: Has he succeeded in idealizing *you*?

JANE: He has!

DUKE: Good old Bunthorne!

JANE: My eyes are open; I droop despairingly; I am soulfully intense; I am limp and I cling!

[*During this* BUNTHORNE *is seen in all the agonies of composition. The Ladies are watching him intently as he writhes. At last he hits on the word he wants and writes it down. A general sense of relief.*]

BUN.: Finished! At last! Finished!

[*He staggers, overcome with the mental strain, into arms of* COLONEL.]

COL.: Are you better now?

BUN.: Yes – oh, it's you – I am better now. The poem is finished, and my soul had gone out into it. That was all. It was nothing worth mentioning, it occurs three times a day. [*Sees* PATIENCE, *who has entered during this scene.*] Ah, Patience! Dear Patience! [*Holds her hand; she seems frightened.*]

ANG.: Will it please you read it to us, sir?

SAPH.: This we supplicate. [*All kneel.*]

BUN.: Shall I?

ALL THE DRAGOONS: No!

BUN. [*annoyed – to* PATIENCE]: I will read it if *you* bid me!

PA. [*much frightened*]: You can if you like!

BUN.: It is a wild, weird, fleshly thing;[33] yet very tender, very yearning, very precious. It is called, 'Oh, Hollow! Hollow! Hollow!'[34]

PA.: Is it a hunting song?

BUN.: A hunting song? No, it is *not* a hunting song. It is the wail of the poet's heart on discovering that everything is commonplace. To understand it, cling passionately to one another and think of faint lilies.[35] [*They do so as he recites:*]

'OH, HOLLOW! HOLLOW! HOLLOW!'

What time the poet hath hymned
The writhing maid, lithe-limbed,
   Quivering on amaranthine asphodel,[36]
How can he paint her woes,
Knowing, as well he knows,
   That all can be set right with calomel?[37]

When from the poet's plinth
The amorous colocynth[38]
   Yearns for the aloe, faint with rapturous thrills,
How can he hymn their throes
Knowing, as well he knows,
   That they are only uncompounded pills?

Is it, and can it be,
Nature hath this decree,
   Nothing poetic in the world shall dwell?
Or that in all her works
Something poetic lurks,
   Even in colocynth and calomel?
         I cannot tell.

               [*Exit* BUNTHORNE.]

ANG.: How purely fragrant!

SAPH.: How earnestly precious!

PA.: Well, it seems to me to be nonsense.

SAPH.: Nonsense, yes, perhaps – but oh, what precious nonsense!

COL.: This is all very well, but you seem to forget that you are engaged
to us.

SAPH.: It can never be. You are not Empyrean.[39] You are not Della
Cruscan.[40] You are not even Early English.[41] Oh, be Early English
ere it is too late! [*Officers look at each other in astonishment.*]

JANE [*looking at uniform*]: Red and Yellow! Primary colours![42] Oh,
South Kensington![43]

DUKE: We didn't design our uniforms, but we don't see how they
could be improved.

JANE: No, you wouldn't. Still, there *is* a cobwebby grey velvet, with a tender bloom like cold gravy, which, made Florentine fourteenth-century, trimmed with Venetian leather and Spanish altar lace, and surmounted with something Japanese[44] – it matters not what – would at least be Early English! Come, maidens.

> [*Exeunt Maidens, two and two, singing refrain of 'Twenty love-sick maidens we'. The Officers watch them off in astonishment.*]

DUKE: Gentlemen, this is an insult to the British uniform –

COL.: A uniform that has been as successful in the courts of Venus as on the field of Mars!

SONG

COL.:
> When I first put this uniform on,
> I said, as I looked in the glass,
> 'It's one to a million
> That any civilian
> My figure and form will surpass.
> Gold lace has a charm for the fair,
> And I've plenty of that, and to spare,
> While a lover's professions,
> When uttered in Hessians,[45]
> Are eloquent everywhere!'
> A fact that I counted upon,
> When I first put this uniform on!

CHORUS OF DRAGOONS:
> By a simple coincidence, few
> Could ever have counted upon,
> The same thing occurred to me, too,
> When I first put this uniform on!

COL.:
> I said, when I first put it on,
> 'It is plain to the veriest dunce
> That every beauty
> Will feel it her duty
> To yield to its glamour at once.

They will see that I'm freely gold-laced
In a uniform handsome and chaste' –
   But the peripatetics[46]
   Of long-haired aesthetics
Are very much more to their taste –
     Which I never counted upon,
     When I first put this uniform on!

CHORUS: By a simple coincidence, few
     Could ever have reckoned upon,
   I didn't anticipate that,
     When I first put this uniform on!

                  [The Dragoons go off angrily.]
[Enter BUNTHORNE, *who changes his manner and becomes intensely melodramatic.]*

RECITATIVE *and* SONG

BUN.:   Am I alone,
     And unobserved? I am!
   Then let me own
     I'm an aesthetic sham!
   This air severe
     Is but a mere
         Veneer!
   This cynic smile
     Is but a wile
         Of guile!
   This costume chaste
     Is but good taste
         Misplaced!

     Let me confess!
A languid love for lilies does *not* blight me!
Lank limbs and haggard cheeks do *not* delight me!
   I do *not* care for dirty greens
     By any means.

I do *not* long for all one sees
    That's Japanese.
I am *not* fond of uttering platitudes
    In stained-glass attitudes.
In short, my mediaevalism's affectation,
Born of a morbid love of admiration!

SONG

BUN.: If you're anxious for to shine in the high aesthetic line as a
      man of culture rare,
You must get up all the germs of the transcendental terms,
    and plant them everywhere.
You must lie upon the daisies and discourse in novel
    phrases of your complicated state of mind,
The meaning doesn't matter if it's only idle chatter of a
    transcendental kind.
            And every one will say,
            As you walk your mystic way,
'If this young man expresses himself in terms too deep for *me*,
Why, what a very singularly deep young man this deep
    young man must be!'

Be eloquent in praise of the very dull old days which have
    long since passed away,
And convince 'em, if you can, that the reign of good Queen
    Anne was Culture's palmiest day.
Of course you will pooh-pooh whatever's fresh and new,
    and declare it's crude and mean,
For Art stopped short in the cultivated court of the Empress
    Josephine.[47]
            And every one will say,
            As you walk your mystic way,
'If that's not good enough for him which is good enough
    for *me*,
Why, what a very cultivated kind of youth this kind of
    youth must be!'

Then a sentimental passion of a vegetable fashion must
  excite your languid spleen,
An attachment *à la* Plato for a bashful young potato, or a
  not-too-French French bean!
Though the Philistines may jostle, you will rank as an
  apostle in the high aesthetic band,
If you walk down Piccadilly[48] with a poppy[49] or a lily[50] in
  your mediaeval hand.[51]
              And every one will say,
              As you walk your flowery way,
'If he's content with a vegetable love which would certainly
  not suit *me*,
Why, what a most particularly pure young man this pure
  young man must be!'

[*At the end of* BUNTHORNE'*s song* PATIENCE *enters. He sees
her.*]

Ah! Patience, come hither. I am pleased with thee. The bitter-hearted
one, who finds all else hollow, is pleased with thee. For you are not
hollow. *Are* you?

PA.: No, thanks, I have dined; but – I beg your pardon – I interrupt you.

BUN.: Life is made up of interruptions. The tortured soul, yearning
  for solitude, writhes under them. Oh, but my heart is a-weary! Oh,
  I am a cursed thing! Don't go.

PA.: Really, I'm very sorry –

BUN.: Tell me, girl, do you ever yearn?

PA. [*misunderstanding him*]: I earn my living.

BUN. [*impatiently*]: No, no! Do you know what it is to be heart-
  hungry? Do you know what it is to yearn for the Indefinable, and
  yet to be brought face to face, daily, with the Multiplication Table?
  Do you know what it is to seek oceans and to find puddles? – to
  long for whirlwinds and yet to have to do the best you can with the
  bellows? That's my case. Oh, I am a cursed thing! Don't go.

PA.: If you please, I don't understand you – you frighten me!

BUN.: Don't be frightened – it's only poetry.

PA.: Well, if that's poetry, I don't like poetry.

BUN. [*eagerly*]: Don't you? [*Aside*] Can I trust her? [*Aloud*] Patience, you don't like poetry – well, between you and me, *I* don't like poetry. It's hollow, unsubstantial – unsatisfactory. What's the use of yearning for Elysian Fields[52] when you know you can't get 'em, and would only let 'em out on building leases if you had 'em?

PA.: Sir, I –

BUN.: Patience, I have long loved you. Let me tell you a secret. I am not as bilious as I look. If you like, I will cut my hair. There is more innocent fun within me than a casual spectator would imagine. You have never seen me frolicsome. Be a good girl – a very good girl – and one day you shall. If you are fond of touch-and-go jocularity – this is the shop for it.

PA.: Sir, I will speak plainly. In the matter of love I am untaught. I have never loved but my great-aunt. But I am quite certain that, under any circumstances, I couldn't possibly love *you*.

BUN.: Oh, you think not?

PA.: I'm quite sure of it. Quite sure. Quite.

BUN.: Very good. Life is henceforth a blank. I don't care what becomes of me. I have only to ask that you will not abuse my confidence; though *you* despise me, I am extremely popular with the other young ladies.

PA.: I only ask that you will leave me and never renew the subject.

BUN.: Certainly. Broken-hearted and desolate, I go. [*Recites*]

> 'Oh, to be wafted away
>   From this black Aceldama[53] of sorrow,
> Where the dust of an earthy to-day
>   Is the earth of a dusty to-morrow!'

It is a little thing of my own. I call it 'Heart Foam'. I shall not publish it. Farewell! Patience, Patience, farewell! [*Exit.*]

PA.: What on earth does it all mean? Why does he love me? Why does he expect me to love him? He's not a relation! It frightens me!

[*Enter* ANGELA.]

ANG.: Why, Patience, what is the matter?

PA.: Lady Angela, tell me two things. Firstly, what on earth is this love that upsets everybody; and, secondly, how is it to be distinguished from insanity?

ANG.: Poor blind child! Oh, forgive her, Eros! Why, love is of all passions the most essential! It is the embodiment of purity, the abstraction of refinement! It is the one unselfish emotion in this whirlpool of grasping greed!

PA.: Oh, dear, oh! [*Beginning to cry.*]

ANG.: Why are you crying?

PA.: To think that I have lived all these years without having experienced this ennobling and unselfish passion! Why, what a wicked girl I must be! For it *is* unselfish, isn't it?

ANG.: Absolutely! Love that is tainted with selfishness is no love. Oh, try, try, try to love! It really isn't difficult if you give your whole mind to it.

PA.: I'll set about it at once. I won't go to bed until I'm head over ears in love with somebody.

ANG.: Noble girl! But is it possible that you have never loved anybody?

PA.: Yes, one.

ANG.: Ah! Whom?

PA.: My great-aunt –

ANG.: Great-aunts don't count.

PA.: Then there's nobody. At least – no, nobody. Not since I was a baby. But *that* doesn't count, I suppose.

ANG.: I don't know. Tell me all about it.

DUET – PATIENCE *and* ANGELA

PA.: Long years ago – fourteen, maybe –
        When but a tiny babe of four,
      Another baby played with me,
        My elder by a year or more;
      A little child of beauty rare,
      With marvellous eyes and wondrous hair,
      Who, in my child-eyes, seemed to me
      All that a little child should be!
            Ah, how we loved, that child and I!
              How pure our baby joy!
            How true our love – and, by the by,
              He was a little boy!
ANG.:   Ah, old, old tale of Cupid's touch!

I thought as much – I thought as much!
He *was* a little boy!

PA. [*shocked*]:

Pray don't misconstrue what I say –
Remember, pray – remember, pray,
He was a *little* boy!

ANG.:

No doubt! Yet, spite of all your pains,
The interesting fact remains –
He was a little *boy*!

ENSEMBLE: $\left\{\begin{array}{l}\text{Ah, yes, in}\\ \text{No doubt! Yet,}\end{array}\right\}$ spite of all $\left\{\begin{array}{l}\text{my}\\ \text{your}\end{array}\right\}$ pains, etc.

PA.:

Time fled, and one unhappy day –
   The first I'd ever known –
They took my little friend away,
   And left me weeping all alone!
Ah, how I sobbed, and how I cried,
Then I fell ill and nearly died,
And even now I weep apace
When I recall that baby face!
   We had one hope – one heart – one will –
      One life, in one employ;
   And, though it's not material, still
      He was a little *boy!*

ANG.:   Ah, old, old tale of Cupid's touch, etc.
PA.:   Pray don't misconstrue what I say, etc.
ANG.:   No doubt, yet spite of all your pains, etc.
PA.:   Ah, yes, in spite of all my pains, etc.

[*Exit* ANGELA.]

PA.: It's perfectly dreadful to think of the appalling state I must be in!
I had no idea that love was a duty. No wonder they all look so

unhappy! Upon my word, I hardly like to associate with myself. I don't think I'm respectable. I'll go at once and fall in love with – [*Enter* ARCHIBALD GROSVENOR.[54]] A stranger!

DUET – PATIENCE *and* GROSVENOR

GROS.: Prithee, pretty maiden – prithee, tell me true,
            (Hey, but I'm doleful, willow willow waly!)
        Have you e'er a lover a-dangling after you?
                Hey willow waly O!
                    I would fain discover
                    If you have a lover?
                Hey willow waly O!

PA.:   Gentle sir, my heart is frolicsome and free –
            (Hey, but he's doleful, willow willow waly!)
        Nobody I care for comes a-courting me –
                Hey willow waly O!
                    Nobody I care for
                    Comes a-courting – therefore,
                Hey willow waly O!

GROS.: Prithee, pretty maiden, will you marry me?
            (Hey, but I'm hopeful, willow willow waly!)
        I may say, at once, I'm a man of propertee[55]
                Hey willow waly O!
                    Money, I despise it;
                    Many people prize it,
                Hey willow waly O!

PA.:   Gentle sir, although to marry I design –
            (Hey, but he's hopeful, willow willow waly!)
        As yet I do not know you, and so I must decline.
                Hey willow waly O!
                    To other maidens go you –
                    As yet I do not know you,
                Hey willow waly O!

GROS.: Patience! Can it be that you don't recognize me?

PA.: Recognize you? No, indeed I don't!

GROS.: Have fifteen years so greatly changed me?

PA.: Fifteen years? What do you mean?

GROS.: Have you forgotten the friend of your youth, your Archibald? – your little playfellow? Oh, Chronos,[56] Chronos, this is too bad of you!

PA.: Archibald! Is it possible? Why, let me look! It is! It is! It must be! Oh, how happy I am! I thought we should never meet again! And how you've grown!

GROS.: Yes, Patience, I am much taller and much stouter than I was.

PA.: And how you've improved!

GROS.: Yes, Patience, I am very beautiful! [*Sighs.*]

PA.: But surely *that* doesn't make you unhappy?

GROS.: Yes, Patience. Gifted as I am with a beauty which probably has not its rival on earth, I am, nevertheless, utterly and completely miserable.

PA.: Oh – but why?

GROS.: My child-love for you has never faded. Conceive, then, the horror of my situation when I tell you that it is my hideous destiny to be madly loved at first sight by every woman I come across!

PA.: But why do you make yourself so picturesque? Why not disguise yourself, disfigure yourself, anything to escape this persecution?

GROS.: No, Patience, that may not be. These gifts – irksome as they are – were given to me for the enjoyment and delectation of my fellow-creatures. I am a trustee for Beauty, and it is my duty to see that the conditions of my trust are faithfully discharged.

PA.: And you, too, are a Poet?

GROS.: Yes, I am the Apostle of Simplicity. I am called 'Archibald the All-Right' – for I am infallible!

PA.: And is it possible that you condescend to love such a girl as I?

GROS.: Yes, Patience, is it not strange? I have loved you with a Florentine fourteenth-century frenzy for full fifteen years!

PA.: Oh, marvellous! I have hitherto been deaf to the voice of love. I seem now to know what love is! It has been revealed to me – it is Archibald Grosvenor!

GROS.: Yes, Patience, it is!

PA. [*as in a trance*]: We will never, never part!

GROS.: We will live and die together!

PA.: I swear it!

GROS.: We both swear it!

PA. [*recoiling from him*]: But – oh, horror!

GROS.: What's the matter?

PA.: Why, you are perfection! A source of endless ecstasy to all who know you!

GROS.: I know I am. Well?

PA.: Then, bless my heart, there can be nothing unselfish in loving *you*!

GROS.: Merciful powers! I never thought of that!

PA.: To monopolize those features on which all women love to linger! It would be unpardonable!

GROS.: Why, so it would! Oh, fatal perfection, again you interpose between me and my happiness!

PA.: Oh, if you were but a thought less beautiful than you are!

GROS.: Would that I were; but candour compels me to admit that I'm not!

PA.: Our duty is clear; we must part, and for ever!

GROS.: Oh, misery! And yet I cannot question the propriety of your decision. Farewell, Patience!

PA.: Farewell, Archibald! But stay!

GROS.: Yes, Patience?

PA.: Although I may not love *you* – for you are perfection – there is nothing to prevent your loving *me*. I am plain, homely, unattractive!

GROS.: Why, that's true!

PA.: The love of such a man as you for such a girl as I must be unselfish!

GROS.: Unselfishness itself!

DUET – PATIENCE *and* GROSVENOR

PA.:   Though to marry you would very selfish be –

GROS.:   Hey, but I'm doleful – willow willow waly!

PA.:   You may, all the same, continue loving me –

GROS.:   Hey willow waly O!
BOTH: All the world ignoring,
              $\left.\begin{array}{c}\text{You'll}\\\text{I'll}\end{array}\right\}$ go on adoring –
              Hey willow waly O!
              [*At the end, exeunt despairingly, in opposite directions.*]

FINALE

[*Enter* BUNTHORNE, *crowned with roses and hung about with garlands, and looking very miserable. He is led by* ANGELA *and* SAPHIR (*each of whom holds an end of the rose-garland by which he is bound*), *and accompanied by procession of Maidens. They are dancing classically, and playing on cymbals, double pipes, and other archaic instruments.*]

CHORUS: Let the merry cymbals sound,
                 Gaily pipe Pandaean pleasure,[57]
              With a Daphnephoric[58] bound
                 Tread a gay but classic measure.
              Every heart with hope is beating,
              For at this exciting meeting
                 Fickle Fortune will decide
                 Who shall be our Bunthorne's bride!

[*Enter Dragoons, led by* COLONEL, MAJOR *and* DUKE. *They are surprised at proceedings.*]

CHORUS OF DRAGOONS:
                 Now tell us, we pray you,
                 Why thus they array you –
                 Oh, poet, how say you –
                    What is it you've done?

DUKE: Of rite sacrificial,
                 By sentence judicial,
                 This seems the initial,
                    Then why don't you run?

COL.:
    They cannot have led you
    To hang or behead you,
    Nor may they *all* wed you,
        Unfortunate one!

CHORUS OF DRAGOONS:
    Then tell us, we pray you,
    Why thus they array you –
    Oh, poet, how say you –
        What is it you've done?

RECITATIVE

BUN.:
    Heart-broken at my Patience's barbarity,
        By the advice of my solicitor [*introducing his*
            SOLICITOR],
    In aid – in aid of a deserving charity,
        I've put myself up to be raffled for!

MAIDENS: By the advice of his solicitor
        He's put himself up to be raffled for!

DRAGOONS: Oh, horror! urged by his solicitor,
        He's put himself up to be raffled for!

MAIDENS: Oh, heaven's blessing on his solicitor!

DRAGOONS: A hideous curse on his solicitor!

    [*The* SOLICITOR, *horrified at the Dragoons' curse, rushes off.*]

COL.:
    Stay, we implore you,
      Before our hopes are blighted;
    You see before you
      The men to whom you're plighted!

CHORUS OF DRAGOONS:
    Stay we implore you,
    For we adore you;
    To us you're plighted
    To be united –
        Stay, we implore you!

SOLO

DUKE: Your maiden hearts, ah, do not steel
     To pity's eloquent appeal,
     Such conduct British soldiers feel.
 [*Aside to Dragoons*]
     Sigh, sigh, all sigh! [*They all sigh.*]

     To foeman's steel we rarely see
     A British soldier bend the knee,
     Yet, one and all, they kneel to ye –
 [*Aside to Dragoons*]
     Kneel, kneel, all kneel! [*They all kneel.*]

     Our soldiers very seldom cry,
     And yet – I need not tell you why –
     A tear-drop dews each martial eye!
 [*Aside to Dragoons*]
     Weep, weep, all weep! [*They all weep.*]

ENSEMBLE

     Our soldiers very seldom cry,
     And yet – I need not tell you why –
     A tear-drop dews each manly eye!
     Weep, weep, all weep!

BUN. [*who has been impatient during this appeal*]:
    Come, walk up, and purchase with avidity,
    Overcome your diffidence and natural timidity,
    Tickets for the raffle should be purchased with avidity,
     Put in half a guinea and a husband you may gain –
    Such a judge of blue-and-white[59] and other kinds of
      pottery –
    From early Oriental down to modern terra-cotta-ry –
    Put in half a guinea – you may draw him in a lottery –
     Such an opportunity may not occur again.

CHORUS: Such a judge of blue-and-white, etc.
            [*Maidens crowd up to purchase tickets; during this Dragoons
            dance in single file round stage, to express their indifference.*]
DRAGOONS: We've been thrown over, we're aware,
            But we don't care – but we don't care!
            There's fish in the sea, no doubt of it,
            As good as ever came out of it,
            And some day we shall get our share,
            So we don't care – so we don't care!
            [*During this the Maidens have been buying tickets. At last* JANE
            presents herself. BUNTHORNE *looks at her with aversion.*]

RECITATIVE

BUN.:   And are *you* going a ticket for to buy?
JANE [*surprised*]:
               Most certainly I am; why shouldn't I?
BUN. [*aside*]:   Oh, Fortune, this is hard! [*Aloud*] Blindfold your
                  eyes;
               Two minutes will decide who wins the prize!
               [*Maidens blindfold themselves.*]

CHORUS OF MAIDENS:
               Oh, Fortune, to my aching heart be kind!
               Like us, thou art blindfolded, but not blind! [*Each
                  uncovers one eye.*]
               Just raise your bandage, thus, that you may see,
               And give the prize, and give the prize to me! [*They
                  cover their eyes again.*]

BUN.:   Come, Lady Jane, I pray you draw the first!
JANE [*joyfully*]:
               He loves me best!
BUN. [*aside*]:   I want to know the worst!
               [JANE *puts hand in bag to draw ticket.* PATIENCE *enters and
               prevents her doing so.*]

PA.:   Hold! Stay your hand!

ALL [*uncovering their eyes:*   What means this interference?
         Of this bold girl I pray you make a clearance!

JANE: Away with you, and to your milk-pails go!

BUN. [*suddenly*]:
         She wants a ticket! Take a dozen!

PA.:   No!

SOLO

PA. [*kneeling to* BUNTHORNE]:
         If there be pardon in your breast
            For this poor penitent,
         Who, with remorseful thought opprest,
            Sincerely doth repent;
         If you, with one so lowly, still
            Desire to be allied,
         Then you may take me, if you will,
            For I will be your bride!

ALL: Oh, shameless one!
            Oh, bold-faced thing!
       Away you run,
            Go, take you wing,
       You shameless one!
            You bold-faced thing!

BUN.:   How strong is love! For many and many a week
         She's loved me fondly and has feared to speak,
         But Nature, for restraint too mighty far,
         Has burst the bonds of Art – and here we are!

PA.:   No, Mr Bunthorne, no – you're wrong again;
         Permit me – I'll endeavour to explain!

SONG

PA.:	True love must single-hearted be –
BUN.:	Exactly so!
PA.:	From every selfish fancy free –
BUN.:	Exactly so!
PA.:	No idle thought of gain or joy
	A maiden's fancy should employ –
	True love must be without alloy.
ALL:	Exactly so!
PA.:	Imposture to contempt must lead –
COL.:	Exactly so!
PA.:	Blind vanity's dissension's seed –
MAJ.:	Exactly so!
PA.:	It follows, then, a maiden who
	Devotes herself to loving *you* [*indicating* BUNTHORNE]
	Is prompted by no selfish view –
ALL:	Exactly so!

SAPH.: Are you resolved to wed this shameless one?

ANG.: Is there no chance for any other?

BUN. [*decisively*]: None! [*Embraces* PATIENCE.]

[*Exeunt* PATIENCE *and* BUNTHORNE.]

[ANGELA, SAPHIR *and* ELLA *take* COLONEL, DUKE *and* MAJOR *down-stage, while Girls gaze fondly at other Officers.*]

SESTETTE

I hear the soft note of the echoing voice
    Of an old, old love, long dead –
It whispers my sorrowing heart 'rejoice' –
    For the last sad tear is shed –

        The pain that is all but a pleasure will change
          For the pleasure that's all but pain,
        And never, oh never, this heart will range
          From that old, old love again!

[*Girls embrace Officers.*]

CHORUS: Yes, the pain that is all, etc. [*Embrace.*]

[*Enter* PATIENCE *and* BUNTHORNE.]
[*As the Dragoons and Girls are embracing, enter* GROSVENOR, *reading. He takes no notice of them, but comes slowly downstage, still reading. The Girls are all strangely fascinated by him, and gradually withdraw from Dragoons.*]

ANG.:   But who is this, whose god-like grace
                Proclaims he comes of noble race?
                And who is this, whose manly face
                Bears sorrow's interesting trace?

ENSEMBLE

TUTTI: Yes, who is this, etc.

GROS.:   I am a broken-hearted troubadour,
               Whose mind's aesthetic and whose tastes are pure!
ANG.:   Aesthetic! He is aesthetic!
GROS.:   Yes, yes – I am aesthetic
               And poetic!

ALL THE LADIES:
               Then, we love you!

[*The Girls leave Dragoons and group, kneeling, around* GROSVENOR. *Fury of* BUNTHORNE, *who recognizes a rival.*]

DRAGOONS: They love him! Horror!
BUN. *and* PA.: They love him! Horror!
GROS.:   They love me! Horror! Horror! Horror!

ENSEMBLE – TUTTI

GIRLS	PATIENCE
Oh, list while we a love confess	List, Reginald, while I confess
That words imperfectly express,	A love that's all unselfishness;
Those shell-like ears, ah, do not close	That it's unselfish, goodness knows,
To blighted love's distracting woes!	You won't dispute it, I suppose.
Nor be distressed, nor scandalized	For you are hideous – undersized,
If what we do is ill-advised,	And everything that I've despised,
Or we shall seek within the tomb	And I shall love you, I presume,
Relief from our appalling doom!	Until I sink into the tomb!

GROSVENOR	BUNTHORNE
Again my cursed comeliness	My jealousy I can't express,
Spreads hopeless anguish and distress;	Their love they openly confess,
Thine ears, oh, Fortune, do not close	His shell-like ear he does not close
To my intolerable woes.	To their recital of their woes –
Let me be hideous, undersized,	I'm more than angry and surprised,
Contemned, degraded, loathed,	I'm pained, and shocked, and
despised,	scandalized,
Or bid me seek within the tomb	But he shall meet a hideous doom
Relief from my detested doom!	Prepared for him by – I know whom!

DRAGOONS: Now is not this ridiculous, etc.

END OF ACT I

ACT II

SCENE – *A glade.*

[JANE *is discovered leaning on a violoncello, upon which she presently accompanies herself. Chorus of Maidens are heard singing in the distance.*]

JANE: The fickle crew have deserted Reginald and sworn allegiance to his rival, and all, forsooth, because he has glanced with passing favour on a puling milkmaid! Fools! of that fancy he will soon weary – and then I, who alone am faithful to him, shall reap my reward. But do not dally too long, Reginald, for my charms are ripe, Reginald, and already they are decaying. Better secure me ere I have gone too far!

RECITATIVE

JANE: Sad is that woman's lot who, year by year,
   Sees, one by one, her beauties disappear,
   When Time, grown weary of her heart-drawn sighs,
   Impatiently begins to 'dim her eyes'!
   Compelled, at last, in life's uncertain gloamings,
   To wreathe her wrinkled brow with well-saved 'combings',
   Reduced, with rouge, lip-salve and pearly grey,
   To 'make up' for lost time as best she may!

SONG

JANE:
    Silvered is the raven hair,
      Spreading is the parting straight,
    Mottled the complexion fair,
      Halting is the youthful gait,
    Hollow is the laughter free,
      Spectacled the limpid eye –
    Little will be left of me
      In the coming by and by!

    Fading is the taper waist,
      Shapeless grows the shapely limb,
    And although severely laced,
      Spreading is the figure trim!
    Stouter than I used to be,
      Still more corpulent grow I –
    There will be too much of me
      In the coming by and by!   [*Exit.*]

[*Enter* GROSVENOR, *followed by Maidens, two and two, each playing on an archaic instrument, as in Act I. He is reading abstractedly, as* BUNTHORNE *did in Act I, and pays no attention to them.*]

CHORUS OF MAIDENS:
    Turn, oh, turn in this direction,
      Shed, oh, shed a gentle smile,
    With a glance of sad perfection
      Our poor fainting hearts beguile!
    On such eyes as maidens cherish
      Let thy fond adorers gaze,
    Or incontinently perish
      In their all-consuming rays!
[*He sits – they group around him.*]

GROS. [*aside*]: The old, old tale. How rapturously these maidens love me, and how hopelessly! Oh, Patience, Patience, with the love of thee in my heart, what have I for these poor mad maidens but an unvalued pity? Alas, they will die of hopeless love for me, as I shall die of hopeless love for thee!

ANG.: Sir, will it please you read to us?

GROS. [*sighing*]: Yes, child, if you will. What shall I read?

ANG.: One of your own poems.

GROS.: One of my own poems? Better not, my child. *They* will not cure thee of thy love.

ELLA: Mr Bunthorne used to read us a poem of his own every day.

SAPH.: And, to do him justice, he read them extremely well.

GROS.: Oh, did he so? Well, who am I that I should take upon myself to withhold my gifts from you? What am I but a trustee? Here is a decalet[60] – a pure and simple thing, a very daisy – a babe might understand it. To appreciate it, it is not necessary to think of anything at all.

ANG.: Let us think of nothing at all!

GROS. [*recites*]: 'Gentle Jane was good as gold,
                She always did as she was told;
                She never spoke when her mouth was full,
                Or caught bluebottles their legs to pull,
                Or spilt plum jam on her nice new frock,
                Or put white mice in the eight-day clock,
                Or vivisected her last new doll,
                Or fostered a passion for alcohol.
        And when she grew up she was given in marriage
        To a first-class earl who keeps his carriage!'

I believe I am right in saying that there is not one word in that decalet which is calculated to bring the blush of shame to the cheek of modesty.

ANG.: Not one; it is purity itself.

GROS.: Here's another.

                'Teasing Tom was a very bad boy,
                A great big squirt was his favourite toy;
                He put live shrimps in his father's boots,

And sewed up the sleeves of his Sunday suits;
He punched his poor little sisters' heads,
And cayenne-peppered their four-post beds,
He plastered their hair with cobbler's wax,
And dropped hot halfpennies down their backs.
>   The consequence was he was lost totally,
>   And married a girl in the *corps de bally*!'

ANG.: Marked you how grandly – how relentlessly – the damning catalogue of crime strode on, till Retribution, like a poisèd hawk, came swooping down upon the Wrong-Doer? Oh, it was terrible!

ELLA: Oh, sir, you are indeed a true poet, for you touch our hearts, and they go out to you!

GROS. [*aside*]: This is simply cloying. [*Aloud*] Ladies, I am sorry to appear ungallant, but this is Saturday, and you have been following me about ever since Monday. I should like the usual half-holiday. I shall take it as a personal favour if you will kindly allow me to close early to-day.

SAPH.: Oh, sir, do not send us from you!

GROS.: Poor, poor girls! It is best to speak plainly. I know that I am loved by you, but I never can love you in return, for my heart is fixed elsewhere! Remember the fable of the Magnet and the Churn.

ANGELA [*wildly*]: But we don't know the fable of the Magnet and the Churn!

GROS.: Don't you? Then I will sing it to you.

SONG

GROS.:   A magnet hung in a hardware shop,
And all around was a loving crop
Of scissors and needles, nails and knives,
Offering love for all their lives;
But for iron the magnet felt no whim,
Though he charmed iron, it charmed not him;
From needles and nails and knives he'd turn,
For he'd set his love on a Silver Churn!

ALL: A Silver Churn?
GROS.:   A Silver Churn!

> His most aesthetic,
> Very magnetic
> Fancy took this turn –
>   'If I can wheedle
>   A knife or a needle,
> Why not a Silver Churn?'

CHORUS: His most aesthetic, etc.

GROS.:   And Iron and Steel expressed surprise,
          The needles opened their well-drilled eyes,
          The penknives felt 'shut up', no doubt,
          The scissors declared themselves 'cut out',
          The kettles they boiled with rage, 'tis said,
          While every nail went off its head,
          And hither and thither began to roam,
          Till a hammer came up – and drove them home.

ALL: It drove them home?
GROS.:   It drove them home!

> While this magnetic,
> Peripatetic
> Lover he lived to learn,
>   By no endeavour
>   Can magnet ever
> Attract a Silver Churn!

ALL: While this magnetic, etc.
   [They go off in low spirits, gazing back at him from time to time.]

GROS.: At last they are gone! What is this mysterious fascination that
  I seem to exercise over all I come across? A curse on my fatal beauty,
  for I am sick of conquests!

[PATIENCE *appears.*]

PA.: Archibald!

GROS. [*turns and sees her*]: Patience!

PA.: I have escaped with difficulty from my Reginald. I wanted to see you so much that I might ask you if you still love me as fondly as ever?

GROS.: Love you? If the devotion of a lifetime – [*Seizes her hand.*]

PA. [*indignantly*]: Hold! Unhand me, or I scream! [*He release her.*] If you are a gentleman, pray remember that I am another's! [*Very tenderly*] But you *do* love me, don't you?

GROS.: Madly, hopelessly, despairingly!

PA.: That's right! I never can be yours; but that's right!

GROS.: And you love this Bunthorne?

PA.: With a heart-whole ecstasy that withers, and scorches, and burns, and stings! [*Sadly*] It is my duty.

GROS.: Admirable girl! But you are not happy with him?

PA.: Happy? I am miserable beyond description!

GROS.: That's right! I never can be yours; but that's right!

PA.: But go now. I see dear Reginald approaching. Farewell, dear Archibald; I cannot tell you how happy it has made me to know that you still love me.

GROS.: Ah, if I only dared – [*Advances towards her.*]

PA.: Sir! this language to one who is promised to another! [*Tenderly*] Oh, Archibald, think of me sometimes, for my heart is breaking! He is so unkind to me, and you would be so loving!

GROS.: Loving! [*Advances towards her.*]

PA.: Advance one step, and as I am a good and pure woman, I scream! [*Tenderly*] Farewell, Archibald! [*Sternly*] Stop there! [*Tenderly*] Think of me sometimes! [*Angrily*] Advance at your peril! Once more, adieu!

> [GROSVENOR *sighs, gazes sorrowfully at her, sighs deeply, and exits. She bursts into tears.*]

[*Enter* BUNTHORNE, *followed by* JANE. *He is moody and pre-occupied.*]

JANE [*sings*]:   In a doleful train,
                    One and one I walk all day;
                    For I love in vain –

None so sorrowful as they
   Who can only sigh and say,
   Woe is me, alackaday!

BUN. [*seeing* PATIENCE]: Crying, eh? What are you crying about?

PA.: I've only been thinking how dearly I love you!

BUN.: Love me! Bah!

JANE: Love him! Bah!

BUN. [*to* JANE]: Don't you interfere.

JANE: He always crushes me!

PA. [*going to him*]: What is the matter, dear Reginald? If you have any sorrow, tell it to me, that I may share it with you. [*Sighing.*] It is my duty!

BUN. [*snappishly*]: Whom were you talking with just now?

PA.: With dear Archibald.

BUN. [*furiously*]: With dear Archibald! Upon my honour, this is too much!

JANE: A great deal too much!

BUN. [*angrily to* JANE]: Do be quiet!

JANE: Crushed again!

PA.: I think he is the noblest, purest and most perfect being I have ever met. But I don't love him. It is true that he is devotedly attached to me, but indeed I don't love *him*. Whenever he grows affectionate, I scream. It is my duty! [*Sighing.*]

BUN.: I dare say!

JANE: So do I! *I* dare say!

PA.: Why, how could I love him and love you too? You can't love two people at once!

BUN.: Oh, can't you, though!

PA.: No, you can't; I only wish you could.

BUN.: I don't believe you know what love is!

PA. [*sighing*]: Yes, I do. There was a happy time when I didn't, but a bitter experience has taught me.

[*Exeunt* BUNTHORNE *and* JANE.]

BALLAD

PA.:   Love is a plaintive song,
              Sung by a suffering maid,
         Telling a tale of wrong,
              Telling of hope betrayed;
         Tuned to each changing note,
              Sorry when *he* is sad,
         Blind to his every mote,
              Merry when he is glad!
                   Love that no wrong can cure,
                        Love that is always new,
                   That is the love that's pure,
                        That is the love that's true!

         Rendering good for ill,
              Smiling at every frown,
         Yielding your own self-will,
              Laughing your tear-drops down;
         Never a selfish whim,
              Trouble, or pain to stir;
         Everything for him,
              Nothing at all for her!
                   Love that will aye endure,
                        Though the rewards be few,
                   That is the love that's pure,
                        That is the love that's true!

                   [*At the end of ballad exit* PATIENCE, *weeping.*]
       [*Enter* BUNTHORNE *and* JANE.]

BUN.: Everything has gone wrong with me since that smug-faced idiot
     came here. Before that I was admired – I may say, loved.

JANE: Too mild – adored!

BUN.: Do let a poet soliloquize! The damozels used to follow me
     wherever I went; now they all follow him!

JANE: Not all! *I* am still faithful to you.

BUN.: Yes, and a pretty damozel *you* are!

JANE: No, not pretty. Massive. Cheer up! I will never leave you, I swear it!

BUN.: Oh, thank you! I know what it is; it's his confounded mildness. They find me too highly spiced, if you please! And no doubt I *am* highly spiced.

JANE: Not for my taste!

BUN. [*savagely*]: No, but I am for theirs. But I will show the world I can be as mild as he. If they want insipidity, they shall have it. I'll meet this fellow on his own ground and beat him on it.

JANE: You shall. And I will help you.

BUN.: You will? Jane, there's a good deal of good in you, after all!

DUET – BUNTHORNE *and* JANE

JANE: So go to him and say to him, with compliment ironical –

BUN.:   Sing 'Hey to you –
    Good day to you' –
    And that's what I shall say!

JANE: 'Your style is much too sanctified – your cut is too canonical' –

BUN.:   Sing 'Bah to you –
    Ha! ha! to you' –
    And that's what I shall say!

JANE: 'I was the beau ideal of the morbid young aesthetical –
To doubt my inspiration was regarded as heretical –
Until you cut me out with your placidity emetical.' –

BUN.:   Sing 'Booh to you –
    Pooh, pooh to you' –
    And that's what I shall say!

BOTH: Sing 'Hey to you – good day to you' –
Sing 'Bah to you – ha! ha! to you' –
Sing 'Booh to you – pooh, pooh to you' –
    And that's what $\begin{Bmatrix} \text{you} \\ \text{I} \end{Bmatrix}$ shall say!

BUN.: I'll tell him that unless he will consent to be more
jocular –

JANE: Sing 'Booh to you –
     Pooh, pooh to you' –
     And that's what you should say!

BUN.: To cut his curly hair, and stick an eyeglass in his
ocular –

JANE: Sing 'Bah to you –
     Ha! ha! to you' –
     And that's what you should say!

BUN.: To stuff his conversation full of quibble and of
quiddity[61] –
To dine on chops and roly-poly pudding with avidity –
He'd better clear away with all convenient rapidity.

JANE: Sing 'Hey to you –
     Good day to you' –
     And that's what you should say!

BOTH: Sing 'Booh to you – pooh, pooh to you' –
Sing 'Bah to you – ha! ha! to you' –
Sing 'Hey to you – good day to you' –

     And that's what $\left\{ \begin{array}{c} \text{I} \\ \text{you} \end{array} \right\}$ shall say!

          [*Exeunt* JANE *and* BUNTHORNE *together.*]
[*Enter* DUKE, COLONEL *and* MAJOR. *They have abandoned
their uniforms, and are dressed and made up in imitation of
Aesthetics. They have long hair, and other outward signs of
attachment to the brotherhood. As they sing they walk in stiff,
constrained and angular attitudes – a grotesque exaggeration of
the attitudes adopted by* BUNTHORNE *and the young Ladies in
Act I.*]

TRIO – DUKE, COLONEL *and* MAJOR

It's clear that mediaeval art alone retains its zest,
To charm and please its devotees we've done our little best.
We're not quite sure if all we do has the Early English ring;
But, as far as we can judge, it's something like this sort of
    thing:

    You hold yourself like this [*attitude*],
    You hold yourself like that [*attitude*],
By hook and crook you try to look both angular and flat
    [*attitude*].
        We venture to expect
        That what we recollect,
Though but a part of true High Art, will have its due effect.

If this is not exactly right, we hope you won't upbraid;
You can't get high Aesthetic tastes, like trousers, ready made.
True views on Mediaevalism Time alone will bring,
But, as far as we can judge, it's something like this sort of
    thing:

    You hold yourself like this [*attitude*],
    You hold yourself like that [*attitude*],
By hook and crook you try to look both angular and flat
    [*attitude*].
        To cultivate the trim
        Rigidity of limb,
You ought to get a Marionette, and form your style on him
    [*attitude*].

COL. [*attitude*]: Yes, it's quite clear that our only chance of making a
    lasting impression on these young ladies is to become as aesthetic
    as they are.
MAJ. [*attitude*]: No doubt. The only question is how far we've suc-
    ceeded in doing so. I don't know why, but I've an idea that this is
    not quite right.
DUKE [*attitude*]: *I* don't like it. I never did. I don't see what it means.
    I do it, but I don't like it.

COL.: My good friend, the question is not whether we like it, but whether they do. They understand these things – we don't. Now I shouldn't be surprised if this is effective enough – at a distance.

MAJ.: I can't help thinking we're a little stiff at it. It would be extremely awkward if we were to be 'struck' so!

COL.: I don't think we shall be struck so. Perhaps we're a little awkward at first – but everything must have a beginning. Oh, here they come! 'Tention!

[*They strike fresh attitudes, as* ANGELA *and* SAPHIR *enter.*]

ANG. [*seeing them*]: Oh, Saphir – see – see! The immortal fire has descended on them,[62] and they are of the Inner Brotherhood[63] – perceptively intense and consummately utter. [*The Officers have some difficulty in maintaining their constrained attitudes.*]

SAPH. [*in admiration*]: How Botticellian![64] How Fra Angelican![65] Oh, Art, we thank thee for this boon!

COL. [*apologetically*]: I'm afraid we're not quite right.

ANG.: Not supremely, perhaps, but oh, so all-but! [*To* SAPHIR] Oh, Saphir, are they not quite too all-but?

SAPH.: They are indeed jolly utter!

MAJ. [*in agony*]: I wonder what the Inner Brotherhood usually recommend for cramp?

COL.: Ladies, we will not deceive you. We are doing this at some personal inconvenience with a view of expressing the extremity of our devotion to you. We trust that it is not without its effect.

ANG.: We will not deny that we are much moved by this proof of your attachment.

SAPH.: Yes, your conversion to the principles of Aesthetic Art in its highest development has touched us deeply.

ANG.: And if Mr Grosvenor should remain obdurate –

SAPH.: Which we have every reason to believe he will –

MAJ. [*aside, in agony*]: I wish they'd make haste.

ANG.: We are not prepared to say that our yearning hearts will not go out to you.

COL. [*as giving a word of command*]: By sections of threes – Rapture! [*All strike a fresh attitude, expressive of aesthetic rapture.*]

SAPH.: Oh, it's extremely good – for beginners it's admirable.

MAJ.: The only question is, who will take who?

COL.: Oh, the Duke chooses first, as a matter of course.

DUKE: Oh, I couldn't think of it – you are really too good!

COL.: Nothing of the kind. You are a great matrimonial fish, and it's only fair that each of these ladies should have a chance of hooking you. It's perfectly simple. Observe, suppose you choose Angela, I take Saphir, Major takes nobody. Suppose you choose Saphir, Major takes Angela, I take nobody. Suppose you choose neither, I take Angela, Major takes Saphir. Clear as day!

QUINTET – DUKE, COLONEL, MAJOR, ANGELA, SAPHIR

DUKE [*taking* SAPHIR]:

> If Saphir I choose to marry,
>> I shall be fixed up for life;
> Then the Colonel need not tarry,
>> Angela can be his wife.

[DUKE *dances with* SAPHIR, COLONEL *with* ANGELA, MAJOR *dances alone.*]

MAJ. [*dancing alone*]:

> In that case unprecedented,
>> Single I shall live and die –
> I shall have to be contented
>> With their heartfelt sympathy!

ALL [*dancing as before*]:

> He will have to be contented
>> With our heartfelt sympathy!

DUKE [*taking* ANGELA]:

> If on Angy I determine,
>> At my wedding she'll appear
> Decked in diamonds and in ermine,
>> Major then can take Saphir!

[DUKE *dances with* ANGELA, MAJOR *with* SAPHIR, COLONEL *dances alone.*]

COL. [*dancing*]:

>> In that case unprecedented,
>> Single I shall live and die –
>> I shall have to be contented
>> With their heartfelt sympathy!

ALL [*dancing as before*]:

>> He will have to be contented
>> With our heartfelt sympathy!

DUKE [*taking both* ANGELA *and* SAPHIR]:

>> After some debate internal,
>> If on neither I decide,
>> Saphir then can take the Colonel,

[*Handing* SAPHIR *to* COLONEL.]

>> Angy be the Major's bride!

[*Handing* ANGELA *to* MAJOR.]

[COLONEL *dances with* SAPHIR, MAJOR *with* ANGELA, DUKE *dances alone.*]

DUKE [*dancing*]:

>> In that case unprecedented,
>> Single I must live and die –
>> I shall have to be contented
>> With their heartfelt sympathy!

ALL [*dancing as before*]:

>> He will have to be contented
>> With our heartfelt sympathy.

>> [*At the end,* DUKE, COLONEL *and* MAJOR, *and two girls dance off arm-in-arm.*]

[*Enter* GROSVENOR.]

GROS.: It is very pleasant to be alone. It is pleasant to be able to gaze at leisure upon those features which all others may gaze upon at their good will! [*Looking at his reflection in hand-mirror.*] Ah, I am a very Narcissus![66]

[*Enter* BUNTHORNE, *moodily.*]

BUN.: It's no use; I can't live without admiration. Since Grosvenor came here, insipidity has been at a premium. Ah, he is there!

GROS.: Ah, Bunthorne! come here – look! Very graceful, isn't it!

BUN. [*taking hand-mirror*]: Allow me; I haven't seen it. Yes, it is graceful.

GROS. [*re-taking hand-mirror*]: Oh, good gracious! not that – this –

BUN.: You don't mean that! Bah! I am in no mood for trifling.

GROS.: And what is amiss?

BUN.: Ever since you came here, you have entirely monopolized the attentions of the young ladies. I don't like it, sir!

GROS.: My dear sir, how can I help it? They are the plague of my life. My dear Mr Bunthorne, with your personal disadvantages, you can have no idea of the inconvenience of being madly loved, at first sight, by every woman you meet.

BUN.: Sir, until you came here I was adored!

GROS.: Exactly – until I came here. That's my grievance. I cut everybody out! I assure you, if you could only suggest some means whereby, consistently with my duty to society, I could escape these inconvenient attentions, you would earn my everlasting gratitude.

BUN.: I will do so at once. However popular it may be with the world at large, your personal appearance is highly objectionable to *me*.

GROS.: It is? [*Shaking his hand.*] Oh, thank you! thank you! How can I express my gratitude?

BUN.: By making a complete change at once. Your conversation must henceforth be perfectly matter-of-fact. You must cut your hair, and have a back parting. In appearance and costume you must be absolutely commonplace.

GROS. [*decidedly*]: No. Pardon me, that's impossible.

BUN.: Take care! When I am thwarted I am very terrible.

GROS.: I can't help that. I am a man with a mission. And that mission must be fulfilled.

BUN.: I don't think you quite appreciate the consequences of thwarting me.

GROS.: I don't care what they are.

BUN.: Suppose – I won't go so far as to say that I will do it – but suppose for one moment I were to curse you? [GROSVENOR *quails.*] Ah! Very well. Take care.

GROS.: But surely you would never do that? [*In great alarm.*]

BUN.: I don't know. It would be an extreme measure, no doubt. Still –

GROS. [*wildly*]: But you would not do it – I am sure you would not. [*Throwing himself at* BUNTHORNE'*s knees, and clinging to him.*] Oh, reflect, reflect! You had a mother once.

BUN.: Never!

GROS.: Then you had an aunt! [BUNTHORNE *affected.*] Ah! I see you had! By the memory of that aunt, I implore you to pause ere you resort to this last fearful expedient. Oh, Mr Bunthorne, reflect, reflect! [*Weeping.*]

BUN. [*aside, after a struggle with himself*]: I must not allow myself to be unmanned! [*Aloud*] It is useless. Consent at once, or may a nephew's curse –

GROS.: Hold! Are you absolutely resolved?

BUN.: Absolutely.

GROS.: Will nothing shake you?

BUN.: Nothing. I am adamant.

GROS.: Very good. [*Rising.*] Then I yield.

BUN.: Ha! You swear it?

GROS.: I do, cheerfully. I have long wished for a reasonable pretext for such a change as you suggest. It has come at last. I do it on compulsion!

BUN.: Victory! I triumph!

DUET – BUNTHORNE *and* GROSVENOR

BUN.:   When I go out of door,
          Of damozels a score
             (All sighing and burning,
              And clinging and yearning)
          Will follow me as before.
          I shall, with cultured taste,

    Distinguish gems from paste,
      And 'High diddle diddle'
      Will rank as an idyll,
    If I pronounce it chaste!

BOTH: A most intense young man,
      A soulful-eyed young man,
    An ultra-poetical, super-aesthetical,
      Out-of-the-way young man!

GROS.:   Conceive me, if you can,
    An every-day young man:
      A commonplace type,
      With a stick and a pipe,
    And a half-bred black-and-tan;[67]
      Who thinks suburban 'hops'
      More fun than 'Monday Pops',[68]
    Who's fond of his dinner,
    And doesn't get thinner
      On bottled beer and chops.

BOTH: A commonplace young man,
      A matter-of-fact young man,
    A steady and stolid-y, jolly Bank-holiday
      Every-day young man!

BUN.:   A Japanese young man,
      A blue-and-white young man,
    Francesca di Rimini,[69] miminy, piminy,
      Je-ne-sais-quoi young man!

GROS.:   A Chancery Lane[70] young man,
    A Somerset House,[71] young man,
    A very delectable, highly respectable,
      Threepenny-bus[72] young man!

BUN.: A pallid and thin young man,
A haggard and lank young man,
A greenery-yallery, Grosvenor Gallery,[73]
Foot-in-the-grave young man!

GROS.: A Sewell & Cross[74] young man,
A Howell & James[75] young man,
A pushing young particle – 'What's the next
    article?'[76] –
Waterloo House[77] young man!

ENSEMBLE

BUNTHORNE	GROSVENOR
Conceive me, if you can,	Conceive me, if you can,
A crotchety, cracked young man,	A matter-of-fact young man,
An ultra-poetical, super-aesthetical,	An alphabetical, arithmetical,
Out-of-the-way young man!	Every-day young man!

[*At the end,* GROSVENOR *dances off.* BUNTHORNE *remains.*]

BUN.: It is all right! I have committed my last act of ill-nature, and
henceforth I'm a changed character.

[*Dances about stage, humming refrain of last air.*]

[*Enter* PATIENCE. *She gazes in astonishment at him.*]

PA.: Reginald! Dancing! And – what in the world is the matter with
you?

BUN.: Patience, I'm a changed man. Hitherto I've been gloomy,
moody, fitful – uncertain in temper and selfish in disposition –

PA.: You have, indeed! [*Sighing.*]

BUN.: All that is changed. I have reformed. I have modelled myself
upon Mr Grosvenor. Henceforth I am mildly cheerful. My conversation will blend amusement with instruction. I shall still be aesthetic; but my aestheticism will be of the most pastoral kind.

PA.: Oh, Reginald! Is all this true?

BUN.: Quite true. Observe how amiable I am. [*Assuming a fixed
smile.*]

PA.: But, Reginald, how long will this last?

BUN.: With occasional intervals for rest and refreshment, as long as I do.

PA.: Oh, Reginald, I'm so happy! [*In his arms*] Oh, dear, dear Reginald, I cannot express the joy I feel at this change. It will no longer be a duty to love you, but a pleasure – a rapture – an ecstasy!

BUN.: My darling!

PA.: But – oh, horror! [*Recoiling from him.*]

BUN.: What's the matter?

PA.: Is it quite certain that you have absolutely reformed – that you are henceforth a perfect being – utterly free from defect of any kind?

BUN.: It is quite certain. I have sworn it.

PA.: Then I never can be yours!

BUN.: Why not?

PA.: Love, to be pure, must be absolutely unselfish, and there can be nothing unselfish in loving so perfect a being as you have now become!

BUN.: But, stop a bit! I don't want to change – I'll relapse – I'll be as I was – interrupted!

[*Enter* GROSVENOR, *followed by all the young Ladies, who are followed by Chorus of Dragoons. He has had his hair cut, and is dressed in an ordinary suit of dittoes and a pot hat.*[78] *They all dance cheerfully round the stage in marked contrast to their former languor.*]

CHORUS

GROSVENOR	GIRLS
I'm a Waterloo House young man,	We're Swears & Wells[79] young girls,
A Sewell & Cross young man,	We're Madame Louise[80] young girls,
A steady and stolid-y, jolly Bank-holiday, Every-day young man!	We're prettily pattering, cheerily chattering, Every-day young girls!

BUN.: Angela – Ella – Saphir – what – what does this mean?

ANG.: It means that Archibald the All-Right cannot be all-wrong; and if the All-Right chooses to discard aestheticism, it proves that aestheticism ought to be discarded.

PA.: Oh, Archibald! Archibald! I'm shocked – surprised – horrified!

GROS.: I can't help it. I'm not a free agent. I do it on compulsion.

PA.: This is terrible. Go! I shall never set eyes on you again. But – oh, joy!

GROS.: What is the matter?

PA.: Is it quite, quite certain that you will always be a commonplace young man?

GROS.: Always – I've sworn it.

PA.: Why, then, there's nothing to prevent my loving you with all the fervour at my command!

GROS.: Why, that's true.

PA.: My Archibald!

GROS.: My Patience! [*They embrace.*]

BUN.: Crushed again!

    [*Enter* JANE.]

JANE [*who is still aesthetic*]: Cheer up! I am still here. I have never left you, and I never will!

BUN.: Thank you, Jane. After all, there is no denying it, you're a fine figure of a woman!

JANE: My Reginald!

BUN.: My Jane!

    [*Flourish. Enter* COLONEL, DUKE *and* MAJOR.]

COL.: Ladies, the Duke has at length determined to select a bride! [*General excitement.*]

DUKE: I have a great gift to bestow. Approach, such of you as are truly lovely. [*All come forward, bashfully, except* JANE *and* PATIENCE.] In personal appearance you have all that is necessary to make a woman happy. In common fairness, I think I ought to choose the only one among you who has the misfortune to be distinctly plain. [*Girls retire disappointed.*] Jane!

JANE [*leaving* BUNTHORNE's *arms*]: Duke! [JANE *and* DUKE *embrace.* BUNTHORNE *is utterly disgusted.*]

BUN.: Crushed again!

FINALE

DUKE:
> After much debate internal,
> I on Lady Jane decide,
> Saphir now may take the Colonel,
> Angy be the Major's bride!

[SAPHIR *pairs off with* COLONEL, ANGELA *with* MAJOR, ELLA *with* SOLICITOR.]

BUN.:
> In that case unprecedented,
> Single I must live and die –
> I shall have to be contented
> With a tulip or li*ly*!

[*Takes a lily from button-hole and gazes affectionately at it.*]

ALL:
> He will have to be contented
> With a tulip or li*ly*!

> Greatly pleased with one another,
> To get married we decide.
> Each of us will wed the other,
> Nobody be Bunthorne's Bride!

DANCE

CURTAIN

IOLANTHE

OR

THE PEER AND THE PERI[1]

DRAMATIS PERSONAE

THE LORD CHANCELLOR
EARL OF MOUNTARARAT
EARL TOLLOLLER
PRIVATE WILLIS (*of the Grenadier Guards*)
STREPHON (*an Arcadian Shepherd*)
QUEEN OF THE FAIRIES
IOLANTHE (*a Fairy, Strephon's Mother*)
CELIA ⎫
LEILA ⎬ (*Fairies*)
FLETA ⎭
PHYLLIS (*an Arcadian Shepherdess and Ward in Chancery*)

Chorus of Dukes, Marquises, Earls, Viscounts, Barons and Fairies

ACT I – An Arcadian Landscape
ACT II – Palace Yard, Westminster

ACT I

SCENE – *An Arcadian Landscape.*[2] *A river runs around the back of the stage. A rustic bridge crosses the river.*

[*Enter Fairies, led by* LEILA, CELIA *and* FLETA. *They trip around the stage, singing as they dance.*]

CHORUS: Tripping hither, tripping thither,
                    Nobody knows why or whither;
                    We must dance and we must sing
                    Round about our fairy ring!

SOLO

CELIA: We are dainty little fairies,
                      Ever singing, ever dancing;
                    We indulge in our vagaries
                      In a fashion most entrancing.
                    If you ask the special function
                      Of our never-ceasing motion,
                    We reply, without compunction,
                      That we haven't any notion!

CHORUS: No, we haven't any notion!
                    Tripping hither, etc.

SOLO

LEILA: If you ask us how we live,
              Lovers all essentials give –
                   We can ride on lovers' sighs,
                   Warm ourselves in lovers' eyes,
                   Bathe ourselves in lovers' tears,
                   Clothe ourselves with lovers' fears,
                   Arm ourselves with lovers' darts,
                   Hide ourselves in lovers' hearts.
              When you know us, you'll discover
              That we almost live on lover!

CHORUS: Tripping hither, etc.
      [*At the end of Chorus, all sigh wearily.*]

CELIA: Ah, it's all very well, but since our Queen banished Iolanthe, fairy revels have not been what they were!

LEILA: Iolanthe was the life and soul of Fairyland. Why, she wrote all our songs and arranged all our dances! We sing her songs and we trip her measures, but we don't enjoy ourselves!

FLETA: To think that five-and-twenty years have elapsed since she was banished! What could she have done to have deserved so terrible a punishment?

LEILA: Something awful! She married a mortal!

FLETA: Oh! Is it injudicious to marry a mortal?

LEILA: Injudicious? It strikes at the root of the whole fairy system! By our laws, the fairy who marries a mortal dies!

CELIA: But Iolanthe didn't die!

      [*Enter* FAIRY QUEEN.]

QUEEN: No, because your Queen, who loved her with a surpassing love, commuted her sentence to penal servitude for life, on condition that she left her husband and never communicated with him again!

LEILA: That sentence of penal servitude she is now working out, on her head, at the bottom of that stream!

QUEEN: Yes, but when I banished her, I gave her all the pleasant places of the earth to dwell in. I'm sure I never intended that she should go and live at the bottom of a stream! It makes me perfectly wretched to think of the discomfort she must have undergone!

LEILA: Think of the damp! And her chest was always delicate.

QUEEN: And the frogs! Ugh! I never shall enjoy any peace of mind until I know why Iolanthe went to live among the frogs!

FLETA: Then why not summon her and ask her?

QUEEN: Why? Because if I set eyes on her I should forgive her at once!

CELIA: Then why not forgive her? Twenty-five years – it's a long time!

LEILA: Think how we loved her!

QUEEN: Loved her? What was your love to mine? Why, she was invaluable to me! Who taught me to curl myself inside a buttercup? Iolanthe! Who taught me to swing upon a cobweb? Iolanthe! Who taught me to dive into a dewdrop – to nestle in a nutshell – to gambol upon gossamer? Iolanthe!

LEILA: She certainly did surprising things!

FLETA: Oh, give her back to us, great Queen, for your sake if not for ours! [*All kneel in supplication.*]

QUEEN [*irresolute*]: Oh, I should be strong, but I am weak! I should be marble, but I am clay! Her punishment has been heavier than I intended. I did not mean that she should live among the frogs – and – well, well, well, it shall be as you wish – it shall be as you wish!

INVOCATION

QUEEN: Iolanthe!
                  From thy dark exile thou art summoned!
                            Come to our call –
                            Come, Iolanthe!

CELIA: Iolanthe!

LEILA: Iolanthe!

ALL: Come to our call,
                 Come, Iolanthe!

[IOLANTHE *rises from the water. She is clad in water-weeds. She approaches the* FAIRY QUEEN *with head bent and arms crossed.*]

IOL.:
> With humbled breast
>> And every hope laid low,
> To thy behest,
>> Offended Queen, I bow!

QUEEN:
> For a dark sin against our fairy laws
> We sent thee into life-long banishment;
> But mercy holds her sway within our hearts –
> Rise – thou art pardoned!

IOL.:   Pardoned!

ALL: Pardoned!

[*Her weeds fall from her, and she appears clothed as a fairy. The* FAIRY QUEEN *places a diamond coronet on her head, and embraces her. The others also embrace her.*]

CHORUS:
> Welcome to our hearts again,
>> Iolanthe! Iolanthe!
> We have shared thy bitter pain,
>> Iolanthe! Iolanthe!
>
> Every heart and every hand
> In our loving little band
> Welcomes thee to Fairyland,
>> Iolanthe!

QUEEN: And now, tell me, with all the world to choose from, why on earth did you decide to live at the bottom of that stream?

IOL.: To be near my son, Strephon.

QUEEN: Bless my heart, I didn't know you had a son.

IOL.: He was born soon after I left my husband by your royal command – but he does not even know of his father's existence.

FLETA: How old is he?

IOL.: Twenty-four.

LEILA: Twenty-four! No one, to look at you, would think you had a son of twenty-four! But that's one of the advantages of being immortal. We never grow old! Is he pretty?

IOL.: He's extremely pretty, but he's inclined to be stout.

ALL [*disappointed*]: Oh!

QUEEN: I see no objection to stoutness, in moderation.

CELIA: And what is he?

IOL.: He's an Arcadian shepherd – and he loves Phyllis, a Ward in Chancery.[3]

CELIA: A mere shepherd! and he half a fairy!

IOL.: He's a fairy down to the waist – but his legs are mortal.

ALL: Dear me!

QUEEN: I have no reason to suppose that I am more curious than other people, but I confess I should like to see a person who is a fairy down to the waist, but whose legs are mortal.

IOL.: Nothing easier, for here he comes!

[*Enter* STREPHON, *singing and dancing and playing on a flageolet. He does not see the Fairies, who retire up-stage as he enters.*]

SONG

STREPH.:   Good morrow, good mother!
        Good mother, good morrow!
       By some means or other,
        Pray banish your sorrow!
         With joy beyond telling
         My bosom is swelling,
         So join in a measure
         Expressive of pleasure,
       For I'm to be married to-day – to-day –
        Yes, I'm to be married to-day!

CHORUS [*aside*]: Yes, he's to be married to-day – to-day –
        Yes, he's to be married to-day!

IOL.: Then the Lord Chancellor[4] has at last given his consent to your marriage with his beautiful ward, Phyllis?

STREPH.: Not he, indeed. To all my tearful prayers he answers me, 'A shepherd lad is no fit helpmate for a Ward of Chancery.' I stood in court, and there I sang him songs of Arcadee, with flageolet accompaniment – in vain. At first he seemed amused, so did the Bar;[5] but quickly wearying of my song and pipe, bade me get out. A servile usher then, in crumpled bands and rusty bombazine,[6] led me, still singing, into Chancery Lane![7] I'll go no more; I'll marry her to-day, and brave the upshot, be it what it may! [*Sees Fairies.*] But who are these?

IOL.: Oh, Strephon! rejoice with me, my Queen has pardoned me!

STREPH.: Pardoned you, mother? This is good news indeed.

IOL.: And these ladies are my beloved sisters.

STREPH.: Your sisters! Then they are – my aunts!

QUEEN: A pleasant piece of news for your bride on her wedding day!

STREPH.: Hush! My bride knows nothing of my fairyhood. I dare not tell her, lest it frighten her. She thinks me mortal, and prefers me so.

LEILA: Your fairyhood doesn't seem to have done you much good.

STREPH.: Much good! My dear aunt! it's the curse of my existence! What's the use of being half a fairy? My body can creep through a keyhole, but what's the good of that when my legs are left kicking behind? I can make myself invisible down to the waist, but that's of no use when my legs remain exposed to view! My brain is a fairy brain, but from the waist downwards I'm a gibbering idiot. My upper half is immortal, but my lower half grows older every day, and some day or other must die of old age. What's to become of my upper half when I've buried my lower half I really don't know!

FAIRIES: Poor fellow!

QUEEN: I see your difficulty, but with a fairy brain you should seek an intellectual sphere of action. Let me see. I've a borough or two at my disposal.[8] Would you like to go into Parliament?

IOL.: A fairy Member! That would be delightful!

STREPH.: I'm afraid I should do no good there – you see, down to the waist, I'm a Tory of the most determined description, but my legs are a couple of confounded Radicals,[9] and, on a division, they'd be sure to take me into the wrong lobby.[10] You see, they're two to one, which is a strong working majority.

QUEEN: Don't let that distress you; you shall be returned as a Liberal-Unionist,[11] and your legs shall be our peculiar care.

STREPH. [*bowing*]: I see your Majesty does not do things by halves.

QUEEN: No, we are fairies down to the feet.

ENSEMBLE

QUEEN: Fare thee well, attractive stranger.
FAIRIES: Fare thee well, attractive stranger.
QUEEN: Shouldst thou be in doubt or danger,
Peril or perplexitee,
Call us, and we'll come to thee!
FAIRIES: Call us, and we'll come to thee!
Tripping hither, tripping thither,
Nobody knows why or whither;
We must now be taking wing
To another fairy ring!

[*Fairies and* FAIRY QUEEN *trip off,* IOLANTHE, *who takes an
affectionate farewell of her son, going off last.*]
[*Enter* PHYLLIS, *singing and dancing, and accompanying herself
on a flageolet.*]

SONG

PHYL.: Good morrow, good lover!
Good lover, good morrow!
I prithee discover,
Steal, purchase or borrow
Some means of concealing
The care you are feeling,
And join in a measure
Expressive of pleasure,
For we're to be married to-day – to-day!
For we're to be married to-day!

BOTH: Yes, we're to be married, etc.

STREPH. [*embracing her*]: My Phyllis! And to-day we are to be made
happy for ever.
PHYL.: Well, we're to be married.
STREPH.: It's the same thing.

PHYL.: I suppose it is. But oh, Strephon, I tremble at the step I'm taking! I believe it's penal servitude for life to marry a Ward of Court without the Lord Chancellor's consent! I shall be of age in two years. Don't you think you could wait two years?

STREPH.: Two years. Have you ever looked in the glass?

PHYL.: No, never.

STREPH.: Here, look at that [*showing her a pocket mirror*], and tell me if you think it rational to expect me to wait two years?

PHYL. [*looking at herself*]: No. You're quite right – it's asking too much. One must be reasonable.

STREPH.: Besides, who knows what will happen in two years? Why, you might fall in love with the Lord Chancellor himself by that time!

PHYL.: Yes. He's a clean old gentleman.

STREPH.: As it is, half the House of Lords are sighing at your feet.

PHYL.: The House of Lords are certainly extremely attentive.

STREPH.: Attentive? I should think they were! Why did five-and-twenty Liberal Peers come down to shoot over your grass-plot last autumn? It couldn't have been the sparrows. Why did five-and-twenty Conservative Peers come down to fish your pond? Don't tell me it was the gold-fish! No, no – delays are dangerous, and if we are to marry, the sooner the better.

DUET – STREPHON *and* PHYLLIS

PHYL.:   None shall part us from each other,
        One in life and death are we:
    All in all to one another –
        I to thee and thou to me!

BOTH: Thou the tree and I the flower –
        Thou the idol; I the throng –
    Thou the day and I the hour –
        Thou the singer; I the song!

STREPH.:   All in all since that fond meeting
        When, in joy, I woke to find
    Mine the heart within thee beating,
        Mine the love that heart enshrined!

BOTH: Thou the stream and I the willow –
  Thou the sculptor; I the clay –
 Thou the ocean; I the billow –
  Thou the sunrise; I the day!

   [*Exeunt* STREPHON *and* PHYLLIS *together.*]
 [*March. Enter Procession of Peers.*]

CHORUS: Loudly let the trumpet bray!
   Tantantara!
  Proudly bang the sounding brasses!
   Tzing! Boom!
 As upon its lordly way
  This unique procession passes,
   Tantantara! Tzing! Boom!
 Bow, bow, ye lower middle classes!
 Bow, bow, ye tradesmen, bow, ye masses!
 Blow the trumpets, bang the brasses!
  Tantantara! Tzing! Boom!
 We are peers of highest station,
 Paragons of legislation,
 Pillars of the British nation!
  Tantantara! Tzing! Boom!

[*Enter the* LORD CHANCELLOR, *followed by his train-bearer.*]

SONG

LORD CH.: The Law is the true embodiment
 Of everything that's excellent.
 It has no kind of fault or flaw,
 And I, my Lords, embody the Law.
 The constitutional guardian I
 Of pretty young Wards in Chancery,
 All very agreeable girls – and none
 Are over the age of twenty-one.
  A pleasant occupation for
  A rather susceptible Chancellor!

ALL: A pleasant, etc.

LORD CH.:   But though the compliment implied
            Inflates me with legitimate pride,
            It nevertheless can't be denied
            That it has its inconvenient side.
            For I'm not so old, and not so plain,
            And I'm quite prepared to marry again,
            But there'd be the deuce to pay in the Lords
            If I fell in love with one of my Wards!
                Which rather tries my temper, for
                I'm *such* a susceptible Chancellor!

ALL: Which rather, etc.

LORD CH.:   And every one who'd marry a Ward
            Must come to me for my accord,
            And in my court I sit all day,
            Giving agreeable girls away,
            With one for him – and one for he –
            And one for you – and one for ye –
            And one for thou – and one for thee –
            But never, oh, never a one for me!
                Which is exasperating for
                A highly susceptible Chancellor!

ALL: Which is, etc.
        [*Enter* LORD TOLLOLLER.]

LORD TOLL.: And now, my Lords, to the business of the day.

LORD CH.: By all means. Phyllis, who is a Ward of Court, has so
powerfully affected your Lordships, that you have appealed to
me in a body to give her to whichever one of you she may think
proper to select, and a noble Lord has just gone to her cottage
to request her immediate attendance. It would be idle to deny
that I, myself, have the misfortune to be singularly attracted by
this young person. My regard for her is rapidly undermining my
constitution. Three months ago I was a stout man. I need say no
more. If I could reconcile it with my duty, I should unhesitatingly

award her to myself, for I can conscientiously say that I know no man who is so well fitted to render her exceptionally happy. [*Peers:* Hear, hear!] But such an award would be open to misconstruction, and therefore, at whatever personal inconvenience, I waive my claim.

LORD TOLL.: My Lord, I desire, on the part of this House, to express its sincere sympathy with your Lordship's most painful position.

LORD CH.: I thank your Lordships. The feelings of a Lord Chancellor who is in love with a Ward of Court are not to be envied. What is his position? Can he give his own consent to his own marriage with his own Ward? Can he marry his own Ward without his own consent? And if he marries his own Ward without his own consent, can he commit himself for contempt of his own Court? And if he commit himself for contempt of his own Court, can he appear by counsel before himself, to move for arrest of his own judgement? Ah, my Lords, it is indeed painful to have to sit upon a woolsack[12] which is stuffed with such thorns as these!

[*Enter* LORD MOUNTARARAT.[13]]

LORD MOUNT.: My Lords, I have much pleasure in announcing that I have succeeded in inducing the young person to present herself at the Bar of this House.[14]

[*Enter* PHYLLIS.]

RECITATIVE

PHYL.:   My well-loved Lord and Guardian dear,
           You summoned me, and I am here!

CHORUS OF PEERS:
           Oh, rapture, how beautiful!
           How gentle – how dutiful!

SOLO

LORD TOLL.: Of all the young ladies I know
               This pretty young lady's the fairest;
            Her lips have the rosiest show,
               Her eyes are the richest and rarest.

Her origin's lowly, it's true,
 But of birth and position I've plenty;
I've grammar and spelling for two,
 And blood and behaviour for twenty!
  Her origin's lowly, it's true,
  I've grammar and spelling for two;

CHORUS: Of birth and position he's plenty,
    With blood and behaviour for twenty!

SOLO

LORD MOUNT.:

  Though the views of the House have diverged
   On every conceivable motion,
  All questions of Party are merged
   In a frenzy of love and devotion;
  If you ask us distinctly to say
   What Party we claim to belong to,
  We reply, without doubt or delay,
   The Party I'm singing this song to!

SOLO

PHYL.: I'm very much pained to refuse,
    But I'll stick to my pipes and my tabors;
   I can spell all the words that I use,
    And my grammar's as good as my neighbours'.
   As for birth – I was born like the rest,
    My behaviour is rustic but hearty,
   And I know where to turn for the best,
    When I want a particular Party!

CHORUS: Though her station is none of the best,
    I suppose she was born like the rest;
    And she knows where to look for her hearty,
    When she wants a particular Party!

RECITATIVE

PHYL.:   Nay, tempt me not.
        To rank I'll not be bound;
    In lowly cot
        Alone is virtue found!

CHORUS: No, no; indeed high rank will never hurt
        you,
    The Peerage is not destitute of virtue.

BALLAD

LORD TOLL.:   Spurn not the nobly born
        With love affected,
    Nor treat with virtuous scorn
        The well-connected.
    High rank involves no shame –
    We boast an equal claim
    With him of humble name
        To be respected!
    Blue blood! blue blood!
        When virtuous love is sought
        They power is naught,
    Though dating from the Flood,
    Blue blood!

CHORUS: Blue blood! blue blood! etc.

    Spare us the bitter pain
        Of stern denials,
    Nor with low-born disdain
        Augment our trials.
    Hearts just as pure and fair
    May beat in Belgrave Square[15]
    As in the lowly air
        Of Seven Dials![16]

Blue blood! Blue blood!
    Of what avail art thou
    To serve us now?
Though dating from the Flood,
Blue blood!

CHORUS: Blue blood! blue blood! etc.

RECITATIVE

PHYL.:   My Lords, it may not be.
                With grief my heart is riven!
            You waste your time on me,
                For ah! my heart is given!

ALL: Given!
PHYL.:   Yes, given!
ALL: Oh, horror!!!

RECITATIVE

LORD CH.:   And who has dared to brave our high displeasure,
                And thus defy our definite command?
    [*Enter* STREPHON.]
STREPH.:   'Tis I – young Strephon! mine this priceless treasure!
                Against the world I claim my darling's hand!
    [PHYLLIS *rushes to his arms.*]
            A shepherd I –
ALL: A shepherd he!
STREPH.:   Of Arcady –
ALL: Of Arcadee!
STREPH.:   Betrothed are we!
ALL: Betrothed are they –
STREPH.:   And mean to be –
ALL: Espoused to-day!

ENSEMBLE

STREPHON	THE OTHERS
A shepherd I	A shepherd he
Of Arcady,	Of Arcadee,
Betrothed are we,	Betrothed is he,
And mean to be	And means to be
Espoused to-day!	Espoused to-day!

DUET

LORD MOUNT. *and* LORD TOLL. [*aside to each other*]:
> 'Neath this blow,
>> Worse than stab of dagger –
>
> Though we mo-
>> Mentarily stagger,
>
> In each heart
>> Proud are we innately –
>
> Let's depart,
>> Dignified and stately!

ALL: Let's depart,
>> Dignified and stately!

CHORUS OF PEERS:
> Though our hearts she's badly bruising,
> In another suitor choosing,
> Let's pretend it's most amusing.
>> Ha! ha! ha! Tan-ta-ra!

[*Exeunt all the Peers, marching round stage with much dignity.*
LORD CHANCELLOR *separates* PHYLLIS *from* STREPHON
and orders her off. She follows Peers. Manent[17]
LORD CHANCELLOR *and* STREPHON.]

LORD CH.: Now, sir, what excuse have you to offer for having disobeyed an order of the Court of Chancery?[18]

STREPH.: My Lord, I know no Courts of Chancery; I go by Nature's

Acts of Parliament. The bees – the breeze – the seas – the rooks – the brooks – the gales – the vales – the fountains and the mountains cry, 'You love this maiden – take her, we command you!' 'Tis writ in heaven by the bright barbèd dart that leaps forth into lurid light from each grim thundercloud. The very rain pours forth her sad and sodden sympathy! When chorused Nature bids me take my love, shall I reply, 'Nay, but a certain Chancellor forbids it'? Sir, you are England's Lord High Chancellor, but are you Chancellor of birds and trees, King of the winds and Prince of thunderclouds?

LORD CH.: No. It's a nice point. I don't know that I ever met it before. But my difficulty is that at present there's no evidence before the Court that chorused Nature has interested herself in the matter.

STREPH.: No evidence! You have my word for it. I tell you that she bade me take my love.

LORD CH.: Ah! but, my good sir, you mustn't tell us what she told you – it's not evidence. Now an affidavit from a thunderstorm, or a few words on oath from a heavy shower, would meet with all the attention they deserve.

STREPH.: And have you the heart to apply the prosaic rules of evidence to a case which bubbles over with poetical emotion?

LORD CH.: Distinctly. I have always kept my duty strictly before my eyes, and it is to that fact that I owe my advancement to my present distinguished position.

SONG

LORD CH.: When I went to the Bar as a very young man,
      (Said I to myself – said I),
    I'll work on a new and original plan
      (Said I to myself – said I),
    I'll never assume that a rogue or a thief
    Is a gentleman worthy implicit belief,
    Because his attorney[19] has sent me a brief
      (Said I to myself – said I!).

Ere I go into court I will read my brief through
    (Said I to myself – said I),
And I'll never take work I'm unable to do
    (Said I to myself – said I),
My learned profession I'll never disgrace
By taking a fee with a grin on my face,
When I haven't been there to attend to the case
    (Said I to myself – said I!).

I'll never throw dust in a juryman's eyes
    (Said I to myself – said I),
Or hoodwink a judge who is not over-wise
    (Said I to myself – said I),
Or assume that the witnesses summoned in force
In Exchequer,[20] Queen's Bench,[21] Common Pleas[22] or
    Divorce,[23]
Have perjured themselves as a matter of course
    (Said I to myself – said I!).

In other professions in which men engage
    (Said I to myself – said I),
The Army, the Navy, the Church and the Stage
    (Said I to myself – said I),
Professional licence, if carried too far,
Your chance of promotion will certainly mar –
And I fancy the rule might apply to the Bar
    (Said I to myself – said I!).

                    [*Exit* LORD CHANCELLOR.]

[*Enter* IOLANTHE.]

STREPH.: Oh, Phyllis, Phyllis! To be taken from you just as I was on the point of making you my own! Oh, it's too much – it's too much!

IOL. [*to* STREPHON, *who is in tears*]: My son in tears – and on his wedding day!

STREPH.: My wedding day! Oh, mother, weep with me, for the Law has interposed between us, and the Lord Chancellor has separated us for ever!

IOL.: The Lord Chancellor! [*Aside*] Oh, if he did but know!

STREPH. [*overhearing her*]: If he did but know what?

IOL.: No matter! The Lord Chancellor has no power over you. Remember you are half a fairy. You can defy him – down to the waist.

STREPH.: Yes, but from the waist downwards he can commit me to prison for years! Of what avail is it that my body is free, if my legs are working out seven years' penal servitude?

IOL.: True. But take heart – our Queen has promised you her special protection. I'll go to her and lay your peculiar case before her.

STREPH.: My beloved mother! how can I repay the debt I owe you?

FINALE – QUARTET

[*As it commences, the Peers appear at the back, advancing unseen and on tiptoe.* LORD MOUNTARARAT *and* LORD TOLLOLLER *lead* PHYLLIS *between them, who listens in horror to what she hears.*]

STREPH. [*to* IOLANTHE]:

> When darkly looms the day,
> And all is dull and grey,
> To chase the gloom away,
>> On thee I'll call!

PHYL. [*speaking aside to* LORD MOUNTARARAT]: What was that?

LORD MOUNT. [*aside to* PHYLLIS]:

> I think I heard him say,
> That on a rainy day,
> To while the time away,
>> On her he'd call!

CHORUS: We think we heard him say, etc.

[PHYLLIS *much agitated at her lover's supposed faithlessness.*]

IOL. [*to* STREPHON]:

> When tempests wreck thy bark,[24]
> And all is drear and dark,
> If thou shouldst need an Ark,
>> I'll give thee one!

PHYL. [*speaking aside to* LORD TOLLOLLER]:
> What was that?

LORD TOLL. [*aside to* PHYLLIS]:

> I heard the minx remark,
> She'd meet him after dark,
> Inside St James's Park,[25]
>> And give him one!

PHYL.:

> The prospect's very bad,
> My heart so sore and sad
> Will never more be glad
>> As summer's sun.

IOL., LORD TOLL., STREPH., LORD MOUNT.:

> The prospect's not so bad,
> $\left.\begin{array}{l}\text{My}\\\text{Thy}\end{array}\right\}$ heart so sore and sad
> May very soon be glad
>> As summer's sun;

PHYL.,IOL., LORD TOLL., STREPH., LORD MOUNT.:

> For when the sky is dark
> And tempests wreck $\left\{\begin{array}{l}\text{my}\\\text{thy}\\\text{his}\end{array}\right\}$ bark,
> If $\left\{\begin{array}{l}\text{he should}\\\text{I should}\\\text{thou shouldst}\end{array}\right\}$ need an Ark,

$$\left.\begin{array}{c}\text{She'll}\\\text{I'll}\end{array}\right\}\ \text{give}\ \left\{\begin{array}{c}\text{him}\\\text{me}\\\text{thee}\end{array}\right\}\ \text{one!}$$

PHYL. [*revealing herself*]: Ah!
    [IOLANTHE *and* STREPHON *much confused.*]

PHYL.:	Oh, shameless one, tremble!
	Nay, do not endeavour
	Thy fault to dissemble,
	We part – and for ever!
	I worshipped him blindly,
	He worships another –
STREPH.:	Attend to me kindly,
	This lady's my mother!
LORD TOLL.:	This lady's his *what*?
STREPH.:	This lady's my mother!
TENORS:	This lady's his *what*?
BASSES:	He says she's his mother!

[*They point derisively to* IOLANTHE, *laughing heartily at her.
She goes for protection to* STREPHON.]
[*Enter* LORD CHANCELLOR. IOLANTHE *veils herself.*]

LORD CH.:	What means this mirth unseemly,
	That shakes the listening earth?
LORD TOLL.:	The joke is good extremely,
	And justifies our mirth.
LORD MOUNT.:	This gentleman is seen,
	With a maid of seventeen,
	A-taking of his *dolce far niente*;[26]
	And wonders he'd achieve,
	For he asks us to believe
	She's his mother – and he's nearly five-and-twenty!

LORD CH. [*sternly*]: Recollect yourself, I pray,
 And be careful what you say –
 As the ancient Romans said, *festina lente*.[27]
 For I really do not see
 How so young a girl could be
 The mother of a man of five-and-twenty.

ALL: Ha! ha! ha! ha! ha!

STREPH.: My Lord, of evidence I have no dearth –
 She is – has been – my mother from my birth!

BALLAD

 In babyhood
 Upon her lap I lay,
 With infant food
 She moistenèd my clay;
 Had she withheld
 The succour she supplied,
 By hunger quelled,
 Your Strephon might have died!

LORD CH. [*much moved*]:
 Had that refreshment been denied,
 Indeed our Strephon might have died!

ALL [*much affected*]:
 Had that refreshment been denied,
 Indeed our Strephon might have died!

LORD MOUNT.: But as she's not
 His mother, it appears,
 Why weep these hot
 Unnecessary tears?
 And by what laws
 Should we so joyously

> Rejoice, because
> > Our Strephon did not die!
> Oh, rather let us pipe our eye
> Because our Strephon did not die!

ALL: That's very true – let's pipe our eye
                  Because our Strephon did not die!

[*All weep.* IOLANTHE, *who has succeeded in hiding her face from* LORD CHANCELLOR, *escapes unnoticed.*]

PHYL.:   Go, traitorous one – for ever we must part:
                To one of you, my Lords, I give my heart!
ALL: Oh, rapture!
STREPH.: Hear me, Phyllis, ere you leave me.
PHYL.:   Not a word – you did deceive me.
ALL: Not a word – you did deceive her.

                            [*Exit* STREPHON.]

BALLAD

PHYL.:   For riches and rank I do not long –
                Their pleasures are false and vain;
            I gave up the love of a lordly throng
                For the love of a simple swain.
           But now that simple swain's untrue,
           With sorrowful heart I turn to you –
                A heart that's aching,
                Quaking, breaking,
           As sorrowful hearts are wont to do!

           The riches and rank that you befall
                Are the only baits you use,
           So the richest and rankiest of you all
                My sorrowful heart shall choose.
           As none are so noble – none so rich
           As this couple of lords, I'll find a niche

> In my heart that's aching,
> Quaking, breaking,
> For one of you two – and I don't care which!

ENSEMBLE

PHYL. [*to* MOUNTARARAT *and* TOLLOLLER]:
> To you I give my heart so rich!

ALL [*puzzled*]: To which?

PHYL.: I do not care!
> To you I yield – it is my doom!

ALL: To whom?

PHYL.: I'm not aware!
> I'm yours for life if you but choose.

ALL: She's whose?

PHYL.: That's your affair!
> I'll be a countess, shall I not?

ALL: Of what?

PHYL.: I do not care!

ALL: Lucky little lady!
> Strephon's lot is shady;
> Rank, it seems, is vital,
> 'Countess' is the title,
> But of what I'm not aware!

[*Enter* STREPHON.]

STREPH.: Can I inactive see my fortunes fade?
> No, no!
> Mighty protectress, hasten to my aid!

[*Enter Fairies, tripping, headed by* CELIA, LEILA *and* FLETA, *and followed by the* FAIRY QUEEN.]

CHORUS OF FAIRIES:
> Tripping hither, tripping thither,
> Nobody knows why or whither;
> Why you want us we don't know,

But you've summoned us, and so
    Enter all the little fairies
        To their usual tripping measure!
    To oblige you all our care is –
        Tell us, pray, what is your pleasure!

STREPH.: The lady of my love has caught me talking to
    another –

PEERS: Oh, fie! our Strephon is a rogue!

STREPH.: I tell her very plainly that the lady is my mother –

PEERS: Taradiddle, taradiddle, tol lol lay!

STREPH.: She won't believe my statement, and declares we
    must be parted,

Because on a career of double-dealing I have
    started,

Then gives her hand to one of these, and leaves me
    broken-hearted –

PEERS: Taradiddle, taradiddle, tol lol lay!

QUEEN: Ah, cruel ones, to separate two lovers from each
    other!

FAIRIES: Oh, fie! our Strephon's not a rogue!

QUEEN: You've done him an injustice, for the lady *is* his
    mother!

FAIRIES: Taradiddle, taradiddle, tol lol lay!

LORD CH.: That fable perhaps may serve his turn as well as any
    other.

[*Aside*] I didn't see her face, but if they fondled one
    another,

And she's but seventeen – I don't believe it was
    his mother!

    Taradiddle, taradiddle.

ALL: Tol lol lay!

LORD TOLL.: I have often had a use
    For a thorough-bred excuse
    Of a sudden (which is English for '*repente*'[28]),

But of all I ever heard
This is much the most absurd,
For she's seventeen, and he is five-and-twenty!

ALL: Though she is seventeen, and he's four or
five-and-twenty!
Oh, fie! our Strephon is a rogue!

LORD MOUNT.: Now, listen, pray, to me,
For this paradox will be
Carried, nobody at all *contradicente*.[29]
Her age, upon the date
Of his birth, was *minus* eight,
If she's seventeen, and he is five-and-twenty!

ALL: To say she is his mother is an utter bit of folly!
Oh, fie! our Strephon is a rogue!
Perhaps his brain is addled, and it's very melancholy!
Taradiddle, taradiddle, tol lol lay!
I wouldn't say a word that could be reckoned as
injurious,
But to find a mother younger than her son is very
curious,
And that's a kind of mother that is usually spurious.
Taradiddle, taradiddle, tol lol lay!

LORD CH.: Go away, madam;
I should say, madam,
You display, madam,
Shocking taste.

It is rude, madam,
To intrude, madam,
With your brood, madam,
Brazen-faced!

You come here, madam,
Interfere, madam,
With a peer, madam.
  (I am one.)

You're aware, madam,
What you dare, madam,
So take care, madam,
  And begone!

ENSEMBLE

FAIRIES [*to* QUEEN]

Let us stay, madam;
I should say, madam,
They display, madam,
  Shocking taste.

It is rude, madam,
To allude, madam,
To your brood, madam,
  Brazen-faced!

We don't fear, madam,
Any peer, madam,
Though, my dear madam,
  This is one.

They will stare, madam,
When aware, madam,
What they dare, madam –
  What they've done!

PEERS

Go away, madam;
I should say, madam,
You display, madam,
  Shocking taste.

It is rude, madam,
To intrude, madam,
With your brood, madam,
  Brazen-faced!

You come here, madam,
Interfere, madam,
With a peer, madam,
  (I am one.)

You're aware, madam,
What you dare, madam,
So take care, madam,
  And begone!

QUEEN [*furious*]:

Bearded by these puny mortals!
I will launch from fairy portals
All the most terrific thunders
In my armoury of wonders!

PHYL. [*aside*]: Should they launch terrific wonders,
All would then repent their blunders.
Surely these must be immortals.   [*Exit.*]

QUEEN: Oh! Chancellor unwary
It's highly necessary
   Your tongue to teach
   Respectful speech –
Your attitude to vary!

Your badinage so airy,
Your manner arbitrary,
   Are out of place
   When face to face
With an influential Fairy.

ALL THE PEERS [*aside*]:
   We never knew
   We were talking to
An influential Fairy!

LORD CH.: A plague on this vagary,
I'm in a nice quandary!
   Of hasty tone
   With dames unknown
I ought to be more chary;
It seems that she's a fairy
From Andersen's library,[30]
   And I took her for
   The proprietor
Of a Ladies' Seminary!

PEERS: We took her for
   The proprietor
Of a Ladies' Seminary!

QUEEN: When next your Houses do assemble,
   You may tremble!

CELIA: Our wrath, when gentlemen offend us,
    Is tremendous!

LEILA: They meet, who underrate our calling,
    Doom appalling!

QUEEN: Take down our sentence as we speak it,
    And *he* shall wreak it!
  [*Indicating* STREPHON.]

PEERS: Oh, spare us!

QUEEN: Henceforth, Strephon, cast away
    Crooks and pipes and ribbons so gay –
    Flocks and herds that bleat and low;
    Into Parliament you shall go!

ALL: Into Parliament he shall go!
    Backed by our supreme authority,
    He'll command a large majority;
    Into Parliament he shall go!

QUEEN: In the Parliamentary hive,
    Liberal or Conservative –
    Whig[31] or Tory[32] – I don't know –
    But into Parliament you shall go!

FAIRIES: Into Parliament, etc.

QUEEN [*speaking through music*]:
    Every bill and every measure,
    That may gratify his pleasure,
    Though your fury it arouses,
    Shall be passed by both your Houses!
PEERS: Oh!
QUEEN: You shall sit, if he sees reason,
    Through the grouse and salmon season;[33]

PEERS: No!

QUEEN: He shall end the cherished rights
            You enjoy on Friday nights:

PEERS: No!

QUEEN: He shall prick that annual blister,
            Marriage with deceased wife's sister:[34]

PEERS: Mercy!

QUEEN: Titles shall ennoble, then,
            All the Common Councilmen:

PEERS: Spare us!

QUEEN: Peers shall teem in Christendom,
            And a Duke's exalted station
            Be attainable by Com-
            Petitive Examination!

PEERS	FAIRIES *and* PHYLLIS
Oh, horror!	Their horror
	They can't dissemble
	Nor hide the fear that makes them
	tremble!

ENSEMBLE

PEERS	FAIRIES, PHYLLIS, STREPHON
Young Strephon is the kind of lout	With Strephon for your foe, no doubt,
We do not care a fig about!	A fearful prospect opens out,
We cannot say	And who shall say
What evils may	What evils may
Result in consequence.	Result in consequence?
But lordly vengeance will pursue	A hideous vengeance will pursue
All kinds of common people who	All noblemen who venture to
Oppose our views,	Oppose his views,
Or boldly choose	Or boldly choose
To offer us offence.	To offer him offence.

He'd better fly at humbler game,

Or our forbearance he must claim,
    If he'd escape
    In any shape
  A very painful wrench!

Your powers we dauntlessly pooh-
  pooh:
A dire revenge will fall on you,
    If you besiege
    Our high *prestige*
(The word '*prestige*' is French).

'Twill plunge them into grief and
  shame;
His kind forbearance they must claim,
    If they'd escape
    In any shape
  A very painful wrench.

Although our threats you now pooh-
  pooh,
A dire revenge will fall on you,
    Should he besiege
    Your high *prestige* –
(The word '*prestige*' is French).

PEERS: Our lordly style
               You shall not quench
               With base *canaille*![35]
FAIRIES: (That word is French.)
PEERS: Distinction ebbs
               Before a herd
               Of vulgar *plebs*!
FAIRIES: (A Latin word.)
PEERS: 'Twould fill with joy,
               And madness stark
               The *οἱ πολλοί*![36]
FAIRIES: (A Greek remark.)

PEERS: One Latin word, one Greek remark,
               And one that's French.

FAIRIES: Your lordly style
               We'll quickly quench
               With base *canaille*!
PEERS: (That word is French.)
FAIRIES: Distinction ebbs
               Before a herd
               Of vulgar *plebs*!

PEERS: (A Latin word.)
FAIRIES: 'Twill fill with joy
                                And madness stark
                                The οἱ πολλοί!
PEERS: (A Greek remark.)

FAIRIES: One Latin word, one Greek remark,
                                And one that's French.

PEERS	FAIRIES
You needn't wait:	We will not wait:
Away you fly!	We go sky-high!
Your threatened hate	Our threatened hate
We won't defy!	You won't defy!

[*Fairies threaten Peers with their wands. Peers kneel as begging for mercy.* PHYLLIS *implores* STREPHON *to relent. He casts her from him, and she falls fainting into the arms of* LORD MOUNTARARAT *and* LORD TOLLOLLER.]

END OF ACT I

ACT II

SCENE – *Palace Yard,*[37] *Westminster. Westminster Hall,*[38] *left. Clock tower up-stage, right centre.*

[PRIVATE WILLIS *discovered on sentry, right. Moonlight.*]

SONG

WILLIS: When all night long a chap remains
      On sentry-go, to chase monotony
He exercises of his brains,
    That is, assuming that he's got any.
Though never nurtured in the lap
    Of luxury, yet I admonish you,
I am an intellectual chap,
    And think of things that would astonish you.
        I often think it's comical – Fal, lal, la!
        How Nature always does contrive – Fal, lal, la!
          That every boy and every gal
            That's born into the world alive
          Is either a little Liberal
            Or else a little Conservative!
            Fal, lal, la!

When in that House MPs divide,
    If they've a brain and cerebellum, too,
They've got to leave that brain outside,
    And vote just as their leaders tell 'em to.

But then the prospect of a lot
Of dull MPs in close proximity,
All thinking for themselves, is what
No man can face with equanimity.
Then let's rejoice with loud Fal la – Fal lal la!
That Nature always does contrive – Fal lal la!
That every boy and every gal
That's born into the world alive
Is either a little Liberal
Or else a little Conservative!
Fal lal la!

[*Enter Fairies, with* CELIA, LEILA *and* FLETA. *They trip round stage.*]

CHORUS OF FAIRIES:

Strephon's a Member of Parliament!
Carries every Bill he chooses.
To his measures all assent –
Showing that fairies have their uses.
Whigs and Tories
Dim their glories,
Giving an ear to all his stories –
Lords and Commons are both in the blues!
Strephon makes them shake in their shoes!
Shake in their shoes!
Shake in their shoes!
Strephon makes them shake in their shoes!

[*Enter Peers from Westminster Hall.*]

CHORUS OF PEERS:

Strephon's a Member of Parliament!
Running a-muck of all abuses.
His unqualified assent
Somehow nobody now refuses.
Whigs and Tories
Dim their glories,

Giving an ear to all his stories –
Carrying every Bill he may wish:
Here's a pretty kettle of fish![39]
    Kettle of fish!
    Kettle of fish!
Here's a pretty kettle of fish!

[*Enter* LORD MOUNTARARAT *and* LORD TOLLOLLER *from Westminster Hall.*]

CELIA: You seem annoyed.

LORD MOUNT.: Annoyed! I should think so! Why, this ridiculous *protégé* of yours is playing the deuce with everything! To-night is the second reading of his Bill to throw the Peerage open to Competitive Examination!

LORD TOLL.: And he'll carry it, too!

LORD MOUNT.: Carry it? Of course he will! He's a Parliamentary Pickford[40] – he carries everything!

LEILA: Yes. If you please, that's our fault!

LORD MOUNT.: The deuce it is!

CELIA: Yes; we influence the members, and compel them to vote just as he wishes them to.

LEILA: It's our system. It shortens the debates.

LORD TOLL.: Well, but think what it all means. I don't so much mind for myself, but with a House of Peers[41] with no grandfathers worth mentioning, the country must go to the dogs!

LEILA: I suppose it must!

LORD MOUNT.: I don't want to say a word against brains – I've a great respect for brains – I often wish I had some myself – but with a House of Peers composed exclusively of people of intellect, what's to become of the House of Commons?

LEILA: I never thought of that!

LORD MOUNT.: This comes of women interfering in politics. It so happens that if there is an institution in Great Britain which is not susceptible of any improvement at all, it is the House of Peers!

SONG

LORD MOUNT.:　When Britain really ruled the waves –
　　　　　　　　(In good Queen Bess's time)
　　　　　　The House of Peers made no pretence
　　　　　　To intellectual eminence,
　　　　　　　　Or scholarship sublime;
　　　　　　Yet Britain won her proudest bays
　　　　　　In good Queen Bess's glorious days!

CHORUS:　　Yes, Britain won, etc.

LORD MOUNT.:　When Wellington thrashed Bonaparte,[42]
　　　　　　　　As every child can tell,
　　　　　　The House of Peers, throughout the war,
　　　　　　Did nothing in particular,
　　　　　　　　And did it very well:
　　　　　　Yet Britain set the world ablaze
　　　　　　In good King George's glorious days![43]

CHORUS:　　Yes, Britain set, etc.

LORD MOUNT.:　And while the House of Peers withholds
　　　　　　　　Its legislative hand,
　　　　　　And noble statesmen do not itch
　　　　　　To interfere with matters which
　　　　　　　　They do not understand,
　　　　　　As bright will shine Great Britain's rays
　　　　　　As in King George's glorious days!

CHORUS:　　As bright will shine, etc.

LEILA [*who has been much attracted by the Peers during this song*]:
　Charming persons, are they not?
CELIA: Distinctly. For self-contained dignity, combined with airy
　condescension, give me a British Representative Peer![44]

LORD TOLL.: Then pray stop this *protégé* of yours before it's too late. Think of the mischief you're doing!

LEILA [*crying*]: But we *can't* stop him now. [*Aside to* CELIA] Aren't they lovely! [*Aloud*] Oh, why did you go and defy us, you great geese!

DUET – LEILA *and* CELIA

LEILA:

In vain to us you plead –
　　　　Don't go!
Your prayers we do not heed –
　　　　Don't go!
　　It's true we sigh,
　　　　But don't suppose
　　A tearful eye
　　　　Forgiveness shows.
　　　　　　Oh, no!
We're very cross indeed –
　　　　Don't go!

FAIRIES:

It's true we sigh, etc.

CELIA:

Your disrespectful sneers –
　　　　Don't go!
Call forth indignant tears –
　　　　Don't go!
　　You break our laws –
　　　　You are our foe:
　　We cry because
　　　　We hate you so!
　　　　　You know!
You very wicked Peers!
　　　　Don't go!

FAIRIES	LORDS MOUNT. *and* TOLL.
You break our laws –	Our disrespectful sneers,
You are our foe:	Ha, ha!
We cry because	Call forth indignant tears,
We hate you so!	Ha, ha!
You know!	If that's the case, my dears –
You very wicked peers!	FAIRIES: Don't go!
Don't go!	PEERS: We'll go!

[*Exeunt* LORD MOUNTARARAT, LORD TOLLOLLER *and Peers. Fairies gaze wistfully after them.*]

[*Enter* FAIRY QUEEN.]

QUEEN: Oh, shame – shame upon you! Is this your fidelity to the laws you are bound to obey? Know ye not that it is death to marry a mortal?

LEILA: Yes, but it's not death to *wish* to marry a mortal!

FLETA: If it were, you'd have to execute us all!

QUEEN: Oh, this is weakness! Subdue it!

CELIA: We know it's weakness, but the weakness is so strong!

LEILA: We are not all as tough as you are!

QUEEN: Tough! Do you suppose that I am insensible to the effect of manly beauty? Look at that man! [*Referring to Sentry.*] A perfect picture! [*To Sentry*] Who are you, sir?

WILLIS [*coming to 'attention'*]: Private Willis, B Company, 1st Grenadier Guards.

QUEEN: You're a very fine fellow, sir.

WILLIS: I am generally admired.

QUEEN: I can quite understand it. [*To Fairies*] Now here is a man whose physical attributes are simply godlike. That man has a most extraordinary effect upon me. If I yielded to a natural impulse, I should fall down and worship that man. But I mortify this inclination; I wrestle with it, and it lies beneath my feet! That is how I treat my regard for that man!

SONG

QUEEN: Oh, foolish fay,
 Think you, because
His brave array
 My bosom thaws,
I'd disobey
 Our fairy laws?
Because I fly
 In realms above,
In tendency
 To fall in love,
Resemble I
 The amorous dove?

[*Aside*] Oh, amorous dove!
 Type of Ovidius Naso![45]
  This heart of mine
  Is soft as thine,
 Although I dare not say so!

CHORUS: Oh, amorous dove, etc.

QUEEN: On fire that glows
 With heat intense
I turn the hose
 Of common sense,
And out it goes
 At small expense!
We must maintain
 Our fairy law;
That is the main
 On which to draw –
In that we gain
 A Captain Shaw![46]

[*Aside*] Oh, Captain Shaw!
 Type of true love kept under!
 Could thy Brigade

With cold cascade
Quench my great love, I wonder!

CHORUS:　　　　　Oh, Captain Shaw! etc.
　　　　　　　　[*Exeunt Fairies and* FAIRY QUEEN, *sorrowfully.*]
　　[*Enter* PHYLLIS.]

PHYL. [*half crying*]: I can't think why I'm not in better spirits. I'm engaged to two noblemen at once. That ought to be enough to make any girl happy. But I'm miserable! Don't suppose it's because I care for Strephon, for I hate him! No girl *could* care for a man who goes about with a mother considerably younger than himself!
　　[*Enter* LORD MOUNTARARAT.]

LORD MOUNT.: Phyllis! My own! [*Embracing her.*]

PHYL.: Don't! How dare you! But perhaps you are the nobleman I'm engaged to?

LORD MOUNT.: I am one of them.

PHYL.: Oh! But how come *you* to have a peerage?

LORD MOUNT.: It's a prize for being born first.

PHYL.: A kind of Derby Cup?[47]

LORD MOUNT.: Not at all! I come of a very old and distinguished family.

PHYL.: And you're proud of your race? But of course you are – you won it! But why are people *made* peers?

LORD MOUNT.: The principle is not easy to explain. I'll give you an example.

SONG – LORD MOUNTARARAT

De Belville was regarded as the Crichton[48] of his age:
His tragedies were reckoned much too thoughtful for the
　　stage:
His poems held a noble rank – although it's very true
That, being very proper, they were read by very few.
He was a famous Painter, too, and shone upon the Line,
And even Mister Ruskin[49] came and worshipped at his
　　shrine:

But, alas, the school he followed was heroically high –
The kind of Art men rave about, but very seldom buy.
And everybody said,
'How can he be repaid –
This very great – this very good – this very gifted man?'
But nobody could hit upon a practicable plan!

He was a great Inventor, and discovered, all alone,
A plan for making everybody's fortune but his own;
For in business an Inventor's little better than a fool,
And my highly gifted friend was no exception to the rule.
His poems – people read 'em in the sixpenny Reviews;
His pictures – they engraved 'em in the *Illustrated News;*
His inventions – they perhaps might have enriched him by
degrees,
But all his little income went in Patent Office fees!
So everybody said
'How *can* he be repaid –
This *very* great – this *very* good – this *very* gifted man?'
But nobody could hit upon a practicable plan!

At last the point was given up in absolute despair,
When a distant cousin died, and he became a millionaire!
With a county seat in Parliament, a moor or two of grouse,
And a taste for making inconvenient speeches in the House.
Then, Government conferred on him the highest of
rewards –
They took him from the Commons and they put him in the
Lords!
And who so fit to sit in it, deny it if you can,
As this very great – this very good – this very gifted man?
Though I'm more than half afraid
That it sometimes may be said
That we never should have revelled in that source of proper
pride –
However great his merits – if his cousin hadn't died!
[*Enter* LORD TOLLOLLER.]

LORD TOLL.: Phyllis! My darling! [*Embraces her.*]

PHYL.: Here's the other! Well, have you settled which it's to be?

LORD TOLL.: Not altogether. It's a difficult position. It would be hardly delicate to toss up. On the whole we would rather leave it to you.

PHYL.: How can it possibly concern me? You are both Earls, and you are both rich, and you are both plain.

LORD MOUNT.: So we are. At least I am.

LORD TOLL.: So am I.

LORD MOUNT.: No, no!

LORD TOLL.: I am indeed. Very plain.

LORD MOUNT.: Well, well – perhaps you are.

PHYL.: There's really nothing to choose between you. If one of you would forgo his title, and distribute his estates among his Irish tenantry, why, then, I should then see a reason for accepting the other.

LORD MOUNT.: Tolloller, are you prepared to make this sacrifice?

LORD TOLL.: No!

LORD MOUNT.: Not even to oblige a lady?

LORD TOLL.: No! not even to oblige a lady.

LORD MOUNT.: Then, the only question is, which of us shall give way to the other? Perhaps, on the whole, she would be happier with me. I don't know. I may be wrong.

LORD TOLL.: No. I don't know that you are. I really believe she would. But the awkward part of the thing is that if you rob me of the girl of my heart, we must fight, and one of us must die. It's a family tradition that I have sworn to respect. It's a painful position, for I have a very strong regard for you, George.

LORD MOUNT. [*much affected*]: My dear Thomas!

LORD TOLL.: You are very dear to me, George. We were boys together – at least *I* was. If I were to survive you, my existence would be hopelessly embittered.

LORD MOUNT.: Then, my dear Thomas, you must not do it. I say it again and again – if it will have this effect upon you, you must not do it. No, no. If one of us is to destroy the other, let it be me!

LORD TOLL.: No, no!

LORD MOUNT.: Ah, yes! – by our boyish friendship I implore you!

LORD TOLL. [*much moved*]: Well, well, be it so. But, no – no! – I cannot consent to an act which would crush you with unavailing remorse.

LORD MOUNT.: But it would not do so. I should be very sad at first – oh, who would not be? – but it would wear off. I like you *very much* – but not, perhaps, as much as you like me.

LORD TOLL.: George, you're a noble fellow, but that tell-tale tear betrays you. No, George; you are very fond of me, and I cannot consent to give you a week's uneasiness on my account.

LORD MOUNT.: But, dear Thomas, it would not last a week! Remember, you lead the House of Lords! on your demise I shall take your place! Oh, Thomas, it would not last a day!

PHYL. [*coming down*]: Now, I do hope you're not going to fight about me, because it's really not worth while.

LORD TOLL. [*looking at her*]: Well, I don't believe it is!

LORD MOUNT.: Nor I. The sacred ties of Friendship are paramount.

QUARTETTE – LORD MOUNTARARAT, LORD TOLLOLLER, PHYLLIS, PRIVATE WILLIS

LORD TOLL.:   Though p'r'aps I may incur your blame,
                 The things are few
                 I would not do
            In Friendship's name!

LORD MOUNT.:   And I may say I think the same;
                 Not even love
                 Should rank above
            True Friendship's name!

PHYL.:   Then free me, pray; be mine the blame;
                 Forget your craze
                 And go your ways
            In Friendship's name!

ALL: Oh, many a man, in Friendship's name,[50]
 Has yielded fortune, rank and fame!
 But no one yet, in the world so wide,
 Has yielded up a promised bride!

WILLIS: Accept, O Friendship, all the same,
ALL: This sacrifice to thy dear name!
     [*Exeunt* LORD MOUNTARARAT *and* LORD
      TOLLOLLER, *lovingly, in one direction,*
      and PHYLLIS *in another. Exit Sentry.*]
  [*Enter* LORD CHANCELLOR, *very miserable.*]

RECITATIVE

LORD CH.: Love, unrequited, robs me of my rest:
 Love, hopeless love, my ardent soul encumbers:
 Love, nightmare-like, lies heavy on my chest,
 And weaves itself into my midnight slumbers!

SONG

LORD CH.: When you're lying awake with a dismal headache, and
 repose is taboo'd by anxiety,
 I conceive you may use any language you choose to
 indulge in, without impropriety;
 For your brain is on fire – the bedclothes conspire of
 usual slumber to plunder you:
 First your counterpane goes, and uncovers your toes,
 and your sheet slips demurely from under you;
 Then the blanketing tickles – you feel like mixed
 pickles – so terribly sharp is the pricking,
 And you're hot, and you're cross, and you tumble and
 toss till there's nothing 'twixt you and the ticking.
 Then the bedclothes all creep to the ground in a heap,
 and you pick 'em all up in a tangle;
 Next your pillow resigns and politely declines to
 remain at its usual angle!

Well, you get some repose in the form of a doze, with hot
    eye-balls and head ever aching,
But your slumbering teems with such horrible dreams that
    you'd very much better be waking;
For you dream you are crossing the Channel, and tossing
    about in a steamer from Harwich –
Which is sometimes between a large bathing machine and a
    very small second-class carriage –
And you're giving a treat (penny ice and cold meat) to a
    party of friends and relations –
They're a ravenous horde – and they all came on board at
    Sloane Square and South Kensington Stations.[51]
And bound on that journey you find your attorney (who
    started that morning from Devon);
He's a bit undersized, and you don't feel surprised when he
    tells you he's only eleven.
Well, you're driving like mad with this singular lad (by the
    by, the ship's now a four-wheeler),
And you're playing round games, and he calls you bad
    names when you tell him that 'ties pay the dealer';[52]
But this you can't stand, so you throw up your hand, and
    you find you're as cold as an icicle,
In your shirt and your socks (the black silk with gold
    clocks), crossing Salisbury Plain[53] on a bicycle:
And he and the crew are on bicycles too – which they've
    somehow or other invested in –
And he's telling the tars all the particu*lars* of a company he's
    interested in –
It's a scheme of devices, to get at low prices all goods from
    cough mixtures to cables
(Which tickled the sailors), by treating retailers as though
    they were all vegetables –
You get a good spadesman to plant a small tradesman (first
    take off his boots with a boot-tree),
And his legs will take root, and his fingers will shoot, and
    they'll blossom and bud like a fruit-tree –

From the greengrocer tree you get grapes and green pea,
    cauliflower, pineapple and cranberries,
While the pastrycook plant cherry brandy will grant, apple
    puffs, and three-corners, and Banburys –
The shares are a penny, and ever so many are taken by
    Rothschild and Baring,[54]
And just as a few are allotted to you, you awake with a
    shudder despairing –
You're a regular wreck, with a crick in your neck, and no
    wonder you snore, for your head's on the floor, and
    you've needles and pins from your soles to your shins,
    and your flesh is a-creep, for your left leg's asleep, and
    you've cramp in your toes, and a fly on your nose, and
    some fluff in your lung, and a feverish tongue, and a
    thirst that's intense, and a general sense that you haven't
    been sleeping in clover;
But the darkness has passed, and it's daylight at last, and the
    night has been long – ditto ditto my song – and thank
    goodness they're both of them over!

[LORD CHANCELLOR *falls exhausted on a seat.*]
[LORDS MOUNTARARAT *and* TOLLOLLER *come forward.*]

LORD MOUNT.: I am much distressed to see your Lordship in this condition.

LORD CH.: Ah, my Lords, it is seldom that a Lord Chancellor has reason to envy the position of another, but I am free to confess that I would rather be two Earls engaged to Phyllis than any other half-dozen noblemen upon the face of the globe.

LORD TOLL. [*without enthusiasm*]: Yes. It's an enviable position when you're the only one.

LORD MOUNT.: Oh yes, no doubt – most enviable. At the same time, seeing you thus, we naturally say to ourselves, 'This is very sad. His Lordship is constitutionally as blithe as a bird – he trills upon the bench like a thing of song and gladness. His series of judgements in F sharp minor, given *andante* in six-eight time, are among the most remarkable effects ever produced in a Court of Chancery. He is, perhaps, the only living instance of a judge whose decrees have received the honour of a double *encore*. How can we bring ourselves to do that which will deprive the Court of Chancery of one of its most attractive features?'

LORD CH.: I feel the force of your remarks, but I am here in two capacities, and they clash, my Lord, they clash! I deeply grieve to say that in declining to entertain my last application to myself, I presumed to address myself in terms which render it impossible for me ever to apply to myself again. It was a most painful scene, my Lord – most painful!

LORD TOLL.: This is what it is to have two capacities! Let us be thankful that we are persons of no capacity whatever.

LORD MOUNT.: Come, come. Remember you are a very just and kindly old gentleman, and you need have no hesitation in approaching yourself, so that you do so respectfully and with a proper show of deference.

LORD CH.: Do you really think so?

LORD MOUNT.: I do.

LORD CH.: Well, I will nerve myself to another effort, and, if that fails, I resign myself to my fate!

TRIO – LORD CHANCELLOR, LORDS MOUNTARARAT *and* TOLLOLLER

LORD MOUNT.:   If you go in
      You're sure to win –
  Yours will be the charming maidie:
      Be your law
      The ancient saw,
  'Faint heart never won fair lady!'[55]

ALL: Faint heart never won fair lady!
    Every journey has an end –
    When at the worst affairs will mend –
    Dark the dawn when day is nigh –
    Hustle your horse and don't say die!

LORD TOLL.:   He who shies
                        At such a prize
            Is not worth a maravedi,[56]
                        Be so kind
                        To bear in mind –
            Faint heart never won fair lady!

ALL: Faint heart never won fair lady!
                    While the sun shines make your hay[57] –
                Where a will is, there's a way[58] –
                Beard the lion in his lair[59] –
                None but the brave deserve the fair![60]

LORD CH.:   I'll take heart
                        And make a start –
            Though I fear the prospect's shady –
                        Much I'd spend
                        To gain my end –
            Faint heart never won fair lady!

ALL: Faint heart never won fair lady!
                    Nothing venture, nothing win[61] –
                Blood is thick, but water's thin[62] –
                In for a penny, in for a pound[63] –
                It's Love that makes the world go round![64]
                        [*Dance, and exeunt arm-in-arm together.*]
            [*Enter* STREPHON, *in very low spirits.*]

RECITATIVE

STREPH.:   My Bill has now been read a second time:
                His ready vote no Member now refuses;
            In verity I wield a power sublime,
                And one that I can turn to mighty uses!

What joy to carry, in the very teeth
    Of Ministry, Cross-Bench and Opposition,
Some rather urgent measures – quite beneath
    The ken of patriot and politician!

SONG

STREPH.:   Fold your flapping wings,
                Soaring Legislature!
            Stoop to little things –
                Stoop to Human Nature!
            Never need to roam,
                Members patriotic,
            Let's begin at home –
                Crime is no exotic!
                    Bitter is your bane –
                        Terrible your trials –
                    Dingy Drury Lane!⁶⁵
                        Soapless Seven Dials!

            Take a tipsy lout
                Gathered from the gutter –
            Hustle him about –
                Strap him to a shutter:
            What am I but he,
                Washed at hours stated –
            Fed on filagree –
                Clothed and educated?
                    He's a mark of scorn –
                        I might be another,
                    If I had been born
                        Of a tipsy mother!

            Take a wretched thief
                Through the city sneaking,
            Pocket handkerchief
                Ever, ever seeking:

What is he but I
  Robbed of all my chances –
Picking pockets by
  Force of circumstances?
  I might be as bad –
    As unlucky, rather –
  If I'd only had
    Fagin⁶⁶ for a father!

I suppose one ought to enjoy oneself in Parliament, when one leads both Parties, as I do! But I'm miserable, poor, broken-hearted fool that I am! Oh, Phyllis, Phyllis! –

[*Enter* PHYLLIS.]

PHYL.: Yes.

STREPH. [*surprised*]: Phyllis! But I suppose I should say 'My Lady'. I have not yet been informed which title your ladyship has pleased to select?

PHYL.: I – I haven't quite decided. You see *I* have no *mother* to advise *me*!

STREPH.: No. I have.

PHYL.: Yes; a *young* mother.

STREPH.: Not very – a couple of centuries or so.

PHYL.: Oh! She wears well.

STREPH.: She does. She's a fairy.

PHYL.: I beg your pardon – a what?

STREPH.: Oh, I've no longer any reason to conceal the fact – she's a fairy.

PHYL.: A fairy! Well, but – that would account for a good many things! Then – I suppose *you're* a fairy?

STREPH.: I'm half a fairy.

PHYL.: Which half?

STREPH.: The upper half – down to the waistcoat.

PHYL.: Dear me! [*Prodding him with her fingers.*] There is nothing to show it!

STREPH.: Don't do that.

PHYL.: But why didn't you tell me this before?

STREPH.: I thought you would take a dislike to me. But as it's all off, you may as well know the truth – I'm only half a mortal!

PHYL. [*crying*]: But I'd rather have half a mortal I do love, than half a dozen I don't!

STREPH.: Oh, I think not – go to your half-dozen.

PHYL. [*crying*]: It's only two! and I hate 'em! Please forgive me!

STREPH.: I don't think I ought to. Besides, all sorts of difficulties will arise. You know, my grandmother looks quite as young as my mother. So do all my aunts.

PHYL.: I quite understand. Whenever I see you kissing a very young lady, I shall know it's an elderly relative.

STREPH.: You will? Then, Phyllis, I think we shall be very happy! [*Embracing her.*]

PHYL.: We won't wait long.

STREPH.: No. We might change our minds. We'll get married first.

PHYL.: And change our minds afterwards?

STREPH.: That's the usual course.

DUET – STREPHON *and* PHYLLIS

STREPH.:
    If we're weak enough to tarry
      Ere we marry,
        You and I,
    Of the feeling I inspire
      You may tire
        By and by.
    For peers with flowing coffers
      Press their offers –
        That is why
    I am sure we should not tarry
      Ere we marry,
        You and I!

PHYL.:
    If we're weak enough to tarry
      Ere we marry,
        You and I,
    With a more attractive maiden,
      Jewel-laden,
        You may fly.

> If by chance we should be parted,
> Broken-hearted
> I should die –
> So I think we will not tarry
> Ere we marry,
> You and I.

PHYL.: But does your mother know you're – I mean, is she aware of our engagement?

[*Enter* IOLANTHE.]

IOL.: She is; and thus she welcomes her daughter-in-law! [*Kisses her.*]

PHYL.: She kisses just like other people! But the Lord Chancellor?

STREPH.: I forgot him! Mother, none can resist your fairy eloquence; you will go to him and plead for us?

IOL. [*much agitated*]: No, no; impossible!

STREPH.: But our happiness – our very lives – depend upon our obtaining his consent!

PHYL.: Oh, madam, you cannot refuse to do this!

IOL.: You know not what you ask! The Lord Chancellor is – my husband!

STREPH. *and* PHYL.: Your husband!

IOL.: My husband and your father! [*Addressing* STREPHON, *who is much moved.*]

PHYL.: Then our course is plain; on his learning that Strephon is his son, all objection to our marriage will be at once removed!

IOL.: No; he must never know! He believes me to have died childless, and, dearly as I love him, I am bound, under penalty of death, not to undeceive him. But see – he comes! Quick – my veil!

> [IOLANTHE *veils herself.* STREPHON *and* PHYLLIS *go
> off on tiptoe.*]

[*Enter* LORD CHANCELLOR.]

LORD CH.: Victory! Victory! Success has crowned my efforts, and I may consider myself engaged to Phyllis! At first I wouldn't hear of it – it was out of the question. But I took heart. I pointed out to myself that I was no stranger to myself; that, in point of fact, I had been personally acquainted with myself for some years. This had

its effect. I admitted that I had watched my professional advancement with considerable interest, and I handsomely added that I
yielded to no one in admiration for my private and professional
virtues. This was a great point gained. I then endeavoured to work
upon my feelings. Conceive my joy when I distinctly perceived a
tear glistening in my own eye! Eventually, after a severe struggle
with myself, I reluctantly – most reluctantly – consented.

[IOLANTHE *comes down veiled.*]

RECITATIVE

IOL.:   My lord, a suppliant at your feet I kneel,
     Oh, listen to a mother's fond appeal!
     Hear me to-night! I come in urgent need –
     'Tis for my son, young Strephon, that I plead!

BALLAD

IOL.:   He loves! If in the bygone years
     Thine eyes have ever shed
     Tears – bitter, unavailing tears,
      For one untimely dead –
     If, in the eventide of life,
      Sad thoughts of her arise,
     Then let the memory of thy wife
      Plead for my boy – he dies!

     He dies! If fondly laid aside
      In some old cabinet,
     Memorials of thy long-dead bride
      Lie, dearly treasured yet,
     Then let her hallowed bridal dress –
      Her little dainty gloves –
     Her withered flowers – her faded tress –
      Plead for my boy – he loves!

[*The* LORD CHANCELLOR *is moved by this appeal. After a
pause:*]

LORD CH.: It may not be – for so the fates decide!
     Learn thou that Phyllis is my promised bride.
IOL. [*in horror*]:
     Thy bride! No! no!
LORD CH.: It shall be so!
     Those who would separate us woe betide!
IOL.:   My doom thy lips have spoken –
         I plead in vain!
CHORUS OF FAIRIES [*without*]:
     Forbear! forbear!
IOL.:   A vow already broken
         I break again!

CHORUS OF FAIRIES [*without*]:
     Forbear! forbear!
IOL.:   For him – for her – for thee
         I yield my life.
     Behold – it may not be!
         I am thy wife.

CHORUS OF FAIRIES [*without*]:
     Aiaiah! Aiaiah! Willaloo!
LORD CH. [*recognizing her*]:
     Iolanthe! thou livest?
IOL.:   Aye!
     I live! Now let me die!
[*Enter* FAIRY QUEEN *and Fairies.* IOLANTHE *kneels to her.*]

QUEEN: Once again thy vows are broken:
     Thou thyself thy doom hast spoken!
CHORUS OF FAIRIES:
     Aiaiah! Aiaiah!
      Willahalah! Willaloo!
      Willahalah! Willaloo!
QUEEN: Bow thy head to Destiny:
     Death thy doom, and thou shalt die!

CHORUS OF FAIRIES:

Aiaiah! Aiaiah! etc.

[*Peers and Sentry enter. The* FAIRY QUEEN *raises her spear.*]

LEILA: Hold! If Iolanthe must die, so must we all; for, as she has sinned, so have we!

QUEEN: What?

CELIA: We are all fairy duchesses, marchionesses, countesses, viscountesses and baronesses.

LORD MOUNT.: It's our fault. They couldn't help themselves.

QUEEN: It seems they *have* helped themselves, and pretty freely, too! [*After a pause*] You have all incurred death; but I can't slaughter the whole company! And yet [*unfolding a scroll*] the law is clear – every fairy must die who marries a mortal!

LORD CH.: Allow me, as an old Equity draftsman,[67] to make a suggestion. The subtleties of the legal mind are equal to the emergency. The thing is really quite simple – the insertion of a single word will do it. Let it stand that every fairy shall die who *doesn't* marry a mortal, and there you are, out of your difficulty at once!

QUEEN: We like your humour. Very well! [*Altering the manuscript in pencil.*] Private Willis!

SENTRY [*coming forward*]: Ma'am!

QUEEN: To save my life, it is necessary that I marry at once. How should you like to be a fairy guardsman?

SENTRY: Well, ma'am, I don't think much of the British soldier who wouldn't ill-convenience himself to save a female in distress.

QUEEN: You are a brave fellow. You're a fairy from this moment. [*Wings spring from Sentry's shoulders.*] And you, my Lords, how say you, will you join our ranks?

[*Fairies kneel to Peers and implore them to do so.*]

[PHYLLIS *and* STREPHON *enter.*]

LORD MOUNT. [*to* LORD TOLLOLLER]: Well, now that the Peers are to be recruited entirely from persons of intelligence, I really don't see what use *we* are, down here, do you, Tolloller?

LORD TOLL.: None whatever.

QUEEN: Good! [*Wings spring from shoulders of Peers.*] Then away
we go to Fairyland.

FINALE

PHYL.:   Soon as we may,
                  Off and away!
              We'll commence our journey airy –
                  Happy are we –
                  As you can see,
              Every one is now a fairy!

ALL: Every one is now a fairy!

IOL., QUEEN, PHYL.:
              Though as a general rule we know
              Two strings go to every bow,
              Make up your minds that grief 'twill
                  bring,
              If you've two beaux to every string.

ALL: Though as a general rule, etc.

LORD CH.:   Up in the sky,
                  Ever so high,
              Pleasures come in endless series;
                  We will arrange
                  Happy exchange –
              House of Peers for House of Peris!

ALL: House of Peers for House of Peris!

LORDS CH., MOUNT., TOLL.:
              Up in the air, sky-high, sky-high,
              Free from Wards in Chancery,

$\left.\begin{array}{l} \text{I} \\ \text{He} \end{array}\right\}$ will be surely happier, for

$\left.\begin{array}{l} \text{I'm} \\ \text{He's} \end{array}\right\}$ such a susceptible Chancellor.

ALL: Up in the air, etc.

CURTAIN

PRINCESS IDA

OR

CASTLE ADAMANT

DRAMATIS PERSONAE

KING HILDEBRAND

HILARION (*his Son*)

CYRIL
FLORIAN } (*Hilarion's Friends*)

KING GAMA

ARAC
GURON } (*his Sons*)
SCYNTHIUS

PRINCESS IDA (*Gama's Daughter*)

LADY BLANCHE (*Professor of Abstract Science*)

LADY PSYCHE (*Professor of Humanities*)

MELISSA (*Lady Blanche's Daughter*)

SACHARISSA
CHLOE } (*Girl Graduates*)
ADA

Chorus of Soldiers, Courtiers, 'Girl Graduates', 'Daughters of the Plough', etc.

ACT I – Pavilion in King Hildebrand's Palace
ACT II – Gardens of Castle Adamant
ACT III – Courtyard of Castle Adamant

ACT I

SCENE – *Pavilion attached to* KING HILDEBRAND*'s Palace.*

[*Soldiers and Courtiers discovered looking out through opera-glasses, telescopes, etc.,* FLORIAN *leading.*]

CHORUS: Search throughout the panorama
For a sign of royal Gama,[1]
    Who to-day should cross the water
    With his fascinating daughter –
      Ida[2] is her name.

Some misfortune evidently
Has detained them – consequently
    Search throughout the panorama
    For the daughter of King Gama,
      Prince Hilarion's[3] flame!

SOLO

FLOR.:   Will Prince Hilarion's hopes be sadly blighted?
ALL: Who can tell?
FLOR.:   Will Ida break the vows that she has plighted?
ALL: Who can tell?
FLOR.:   Will she back out, and say she did not mean them?
ALL: Who can tell?
FLOR.:   If so, there'll be the deuce to pay between them!

ALL: No, no – we'll not despair,
               For Gama would not dare
               To make a deadly foe
               Of Hildebrand[4] and so,
                    Search throughout, etc.

[*Enter* KING HILDEBRAND, *with* CYRIL.]

HILD.:   See you no sign of Gama?

FLOR.:   None, my liege!

HILD.:   It's very odd indeed. If Gama fail
               To put in an appearance at our Court
               Before the sun has set in yonder west,
               And fail to bring the Princess Ida here
               To whom our son Hilarion was betrothed
               At the extremely early age of one,
               There's war between King Gama and ourselves!

[*Aside to* CYRIL]

               Oh, Cyril, how I dread this interview
               It's twenty years since he and I have met.
               He was a twisted monster – all awry –
               As though Dame Nature, angry with her work,
               Had crumpled it in fitful petulance!

CYR.:   But, sir, a twisted and ungainly trunk
               Often bears goodly fruit. Perhaps he was
               A kind, well-spoken gentleman?

HILD.:   Oh, no!
               For, adder-like, his sting lay in his tongue.
               (His 'sting' is present, though his 'stung' is past.)

FLOR. [*looking through glass*]:
               But stay, my liege; o'er yonder mountain's brow
               Comes a small body, bearing Gama's arms;
               And now I look more closely at it, sir,
               I see attached to it King Gama's legs;
               From which I gather this corollary
               That that small body must be Gama's own!

HILD.:   Ha! Is the Princess with him?

FLOR.:   Well, my liege,
               Unless her highness is full six feet high,

And wears mustachios too – and smokes cigars –
And rides *en cavalier*[5] in coat of steel –
I do not think she is.

HILD.:   One never knows.
She's a strange girl, I've heard, and does odd things!
Come, bustle there!
For Gama place the richest robes we own –
For Gama place the coarsest prison dress –
For Gama let our best spare bed be aired –
For Gama let our deepest dungeon yawn –
For Gama lay the costliest banquet out –
For Gama place cold water and dry bread!
For as King Gama brings the Princess here,
Or brings her not, so shall King Gama have
Much more than everything – much less than nothing!

SONG *and* CHORUS

HILD.: Now hearken to my strict command
  On every hand, on every hand –

CHORUS: To your command,
    On every hand,
    We dutifully bow!

HILD.: If Gama bring the Princess here,
  Give him good cheer, give him good cheer.

CHORUS: If she come here
    We'll give him a cheer,
   And we will show you how.
  Hip, hip, hurrah! hip, hip, hurrah!
  Hip, hip, hurrah! hurrah! hurrah!
    We'll shout and sing
    Long live the King,
   And his daughter, too, I trow!
  Then shout ha! ha! hip, hip, hurrah!

Hip, hip, hip, hip, hurrah!
For the fair Princess and her good papa,
            Hurrah! hurrah!

HILD.: But if he fail to keep his troth,
        Upon our oath, we'll trounce them both!

CHORUS: He'll trounce them both,
                Upon his oath,
              As sure as quarter-day![6]

HILD.: We'll shut him up in a dungeon cell,
        And toll his knell on a funeral bell.

CHORUS: From dungeon cell,
                His funeral knell
                Shall strike him with dismay!
        Hip, hip, hurrah! hip, hip, hurrah!
        Hip, hip, hurrah! hurrah! hurrah!
                As up we string
                The faithless King,
                In the old familiar way!
        We'll shout ha! ha! hip, hip, hurrah!
        Hip, hip, hip, hip, hurrah!
        As we make an end of her false papa,
                Hurrah! hurrah!

                                    [*Exeunt all.*]

[*Enter* HILARION.]

RECITATIVE

HIL.:   To-day we meet, my baby bride and I –
            But ah, my hopes are balanced by my fears!
        What transmutations have been conjured by
            The silent alchemy of twenty years!

BALLAD

HIL.: Ida was a twelvemonth old,
   Twenty years ago!
 I was twice her age, I'm told,
   Twenty years ago!
 Husband twice as old as wife
 Argues ill for married life
 Baleful prophecies were rife,
   Twenty years ago!

 Still, I was a tiny prince
   Twenty years ago.
 She has gained upon me, since
   Twenty years ago.
 Though she's twenty-one, it's true,
 I am barely twenty-two –
 False and foolish prophets you,
   Twenty years ago!

[*Enter* KING HILDEBRAND.]
 Well, father, is there news for me at last?
HILD.: King Gama is in sight, but much I fear
 With no Princess!
HIL.:   Alas, my liege, I've heard
 That Princess Ida has forsworn the world,
 And, with a band of women, shut herself
 Within a lonely country house, and there
 Devotes herself to stern philosophies!
HILD.: Then I should say the loss of such a wife
 Is one to which a reasonable man
 Would easily be reconciled.
HIL.:   Oh, no!
 Or I am not a reasonable man.
 She *is* my wife – has been for twenty years!
 [*Holding glass.*]
 I think I see her now.

HILD.:   Ha! let me look!

HIL.:   In my mind's eye, I mean – a blushing bride,
All bib and tucker, frill and furbelow![7]
How exquisite she looked as she was borne,
Recumbent, in her foster-mother's arms!
How the bride wept – nor would be comforted
Until the hireling mother-for-the-nonce
Administered refreshment in the vestry.
And I remember feeling much annoyed
That she should weep at marrying with me.
But then I thought, 'These brides are all alike.
You cry at marrying me? How much more cause
You'd have to cry if it were broken off!'
These were my thoughts; I kept them to myself,
For at that age I had not learnt to speak.

                                      [*Exeunt.*]

[*Enter Courtiers.*]

CHORUS: From the distant panorama
Come the sons of royal Gama.
     They are heralds evidently,
     And are sacred consequently,
        Sons of Gama, hail! oh, hail!
[*Enter* ARAC, GURON *and* SCYNTHIUS.]

SONG

ARAC: We are warriors three,
     Sons of Gama, Rex.
Like most sons are we,
     Masculine in sex.

ALL THREE: Yes, yes, yes,
     Masculine in sex.

ARAC: Politics we bar,
     They are not our bent;

On the whole we are
Not intelligent.

ALL THREE: No, no, no,
Not intelligent.

ARAC: But with doughty heart,
And with trusty blade
We can play our part –
Fighting is our trade.

ALL THREE: Yes, yes, yes,
Fighting is our trade.

ALL THREE: Bold, and fierce, and strong, ha! ha!
For a war we burn,
With its right or wrong, ha! ha!
We have no concern.
Order comes to fight, ha! ha!
Order is obeyed,
We are men of might, ha! ha!
Fighting is our trade.
Yes, yes, yes,
Fighting is our trade, ha! ha!

CHORUS: They are men of might, ha! ha!
Fighting is their trade.
Order comes to fight, ha! ha!
Order is obeyed, ha! ha!
Fighting is their trade!

[*Enter* KING GAMA.]

SONG[8]

GAMA: If you give me your attention, I will tell you what I am:
I'm a genuine philanthropist – all other kinds are sham,
Each little fault of temper and each social defect
In my erring fellow-creatures I endeavour to correct.
To all their little weaknesses I open people's eyes;
And little plans to snub the self-sufficient I devise;
I love my fellow-creatures – I do all the good I can –
Yet everybody says I'm such a disagreeable man!
    And I can't think why!

To compliments inflated I've a withering reply;
And vanity I always do my best to mortify;
A charitable action I can skilfully dissect;
And interested motives I'm delighted to detect;
I know everybody's income and what everybody earns;
And I carefully compare it with the income-tax returns;
But to benefit humanity however much I plan,
Yet everybody says I'm such a disagreeable man!
    And I can't think why!

I'm sure I'm no ascetic; I'm as pleasant as can be;
You'll always find me ready with a crushing repartee,
I've an irritating chuckle, I've a celebrated sneer,
I've an entertaining snigger, I've a fascinating leer.
To everybody's prejudice I know a thing or two;
I can tell a woman's age in half a minute – and I do.
But although I try to make myself as pleasant as I can,
Yet everybody says I am a disagreeable man!
    And I can't think why!

[*Enter* KING HILDEBRAND, HILARION, CYRIL *and* FLORIAN.]
So this is Castle Hildebrand? Well, well!
Dame Rumour whispered that the place was grand;
She told me that your taste was exquisite,
Superb, unparalleled!

HILD. [*gratified*]:   Oh, really, King!

GAMA: But she's a liar! Why, how old you've grown!
               Is this Hilarion? Why, you've changed too –
               You were a singularly handsome child!
     [*To* FLOR.] Are you a courtier? Come, then, ply your trade,
               Tell me some lies. How do you like your King?
               Vile rumour says he's all but imbecile.
               Now, that's not true?

FLOR.:   My lord, we love our King.
               His wise remarks are valued by his court
               As precious stones.

GAMA: And for the self-same cause.
               Like precious stones, his sensible remarks
               Derive their value from their scarcity!
               Come now, be honest, tell the truth for once!
               Tell it of me. Come, come, I'll harm you not.
               This leg is crooked – this foot is ill-designed –
               This shoulder wears a hump! Come, out with it!
               Look, here's my face! Now, am I not the worst
               Of Nature's blunders?

CYR.:   Nature never errs.
               To those who know the workings of your mind,
               Your face and figure, sir, suggest a book
               Appropriately bound.

GAMA [*enraged*]:   Why, harkye, sir,
               How dare you bandy words with me?

CYR.:   No need
               To bandy aught that appertains to you.

GAMA [*furiously*]:
               Do you permit this, King?

HILD.:   We are in doubt
               Whether to treat you as an honoured guest,
               Or as a traitor knave who plights his word
               And breaks it.

GAMA [*quickly*]:   If the casting vote's with me,
               I give it for the former!

HILD.:   We shall see.

313

By the terms of our contract, signed and sealed,
You're bound to bring the Princess here to-day:
Why is she not with you?

GAMA: Answer me this:
What think you of a wealthy purse-proud man,
Who, when he calls upon a starving friend,
Pulls out his gold and flourishes his notes,
And flashes diamonds in the pauper's eyes?
What name have you for such an one?

HILD.:   A snob.

GAMA: Just so. The girl has beauty, virtue, wit,
Grace, humour, wisdom, charity and pluck.
Would it be kindly, think you, to parade
These brilliant qualities before *your* eyes?
Oh no, King Hildebrand, I am no snob!

HILD. [*furiously*]:
                    Stop that tongue,
Or you shall lose the monkey head that holds it!

GAMA: Bravo! your King deprives me of my head,
That he and I may meet on equal terms!

HILD.: Where is she now?

GAMA: In Castle Adamant,
One of my many country houses. There
She rules a woman's University,[9]
With full a hundred girls, who learn of her.

CYR.: A hundred girls! A hundred ecstasies!

GAMA: But no mere girls, my good young gentleman;
With all the college learning that you boast,
The youngest there will prove a match for *you*.

CYR.: With all my heart, if she's the prettiest!
  [*To* FLOR.]Fancy, a hundred matches – all alight! –
That's if I strike them as I hope to do!

GAMA: Despair your hope; their hearts are dead to men.
He who desires to gain their favour must
Be qualified to strike their teeming brains,
And not their hearts. They're safety matches, sir,

And they light only on the knowledge box –
So *you've* no chance!

FLOR.: Are there no males whatever in those walls?

GAMA: None, gentlemen, excepting letter mails –
And they are driven (as males often are
In other large communities) by women.
Why, bless my heart, she's so particular
She'll scarcely suffer Dr Watts's hymns[10] –
And all the animals she owns are 'hers'!
The ladies rise at cockcrow every morn –

CYR.: Ah, then they have male poultry?

GAMA: Not at all,

[*confidentially*]

The crowing's done by an accomplished hen!

DUET – GAMA *and* HILDEBRAND

GAMA: Perhaps if you address the lady
    Most politely, most politely –
Flatter and impress the lady,
    Most politely, most politely –
Humbly beg and humbly sue –
She may deign to look on you,
But your doing you must do
    Most politely, most politely!

ALL: Humbly beg and humbly sue, etc.

HILD.: Go you, and inform the lady,
    Most politely, most politely,
If she don't, we'll storm the lady
    Most politely, most politely!
  [*To* GAMA] You'll remain as hostage here;
Should Hilarion disappear,
We will hang you, never fear,
    Most politely, most politely!

315

ALL: He'll
         I'll   } remain as hostage here, etc.
         You'll

[KING GAMA, ARAC, GURON *and* SCYNTHIUS *are marched off
in custody,* KING HILDEBRAND *following.*]

RECITATIVE

HIL.:   Come, Cyril, Florian, our course is plain,
        To-morrow morn fair Ida we'll engage;
    But we will use no force her love to gain,
        Nature has armed us for the war we wage!

TRIO – HILARION, CYRIL *and* FLORIAN

HIL.:   Expressive glances
    Shall be our lances,
        And pops of Sillery[11]
        Our light artillery.
    We'll storm their bowers
    With scented showers
    Of fairest flowers
        That we can buy!

CHORUS: Oh, dainty triolet![12]
        Oh, fragrant violet!
        Oh, gentle heigho-let
          (Or little sigh).
    On sweet urbanity,
    Though mere inanity,
    To touch their vanity
        We will rely!

CYR.:   When day is fading,
    With serenading
        And such frivolity
        We'll prove our quality.

A sweet profusion
Of soft allusion
This bold intrusion
 Shall justify.

CHORUS: Oh, dainty triolet, etc.

FLOR.:   We'll charm their senses
With verbal fences,
 With ballads amatory
 And declamatory.
Little heeding
Their pretty pleading,
Our love exceeding
 We'll justify!

CHORUS: Oh, dainty triolet, etc.

[*Re-enter* GAMA, ARAC, GURON *and* SCYNTHIUS *heavily ironed.*]

RECITATIVE

GAMA: Must we, till then, in prison cell be thrust?
HILD.:   You must!
GAMA: This seems unnecessarily severe!
ARAC, GURON *and* SCYNTHIUS:
      Hear, hear!

TRIO – ARAC, GURON *and* SCYNTHIUS

ALL: For a month to dwell
In a dungeon cell;
 Growing thin and wizen
 In a solitary prison,
Is a poor look-out
For a soldier stout,

Who is longing for the rattle
Of a complicated battle –
For the rum-tum-tum
Of the military drum,
And the guns that go boom! boom!

The rum-tum-tum
Of the military drum, etc.

HILD.: When Hilarion's bride
Has at length complied
With the just conditions
Of our requisitions,
You may go in haste
And indulge your taste
For the fascinating rattle
Of a complicated battle –
For the rum-tum-tum,
Of the military drum,
And the guns that go boom! boom!

ALL: For the rum-tum-tum
Of the military drum, etc.

But till that time $\left\{ \begin{array}{c} \text{we'll} \\ \text{you'll} \end{array} \right\}$ here remain,

And bail $\left\{ \begin{array}{c} \text{they} \\ \text{we} \end{array} \right\}$ will not entertain,

Should she $\left\{ \begin{array}{c} \text{his} \\ \text{our} \end{array} \right\}$ mandate disobey,

$\left. \begin{array}{c} \text{Our} \\ \text{Your} \end{array} \right\}$ lives the penalty will pay!

[KING GAMA, ARAC, GURON *and* SCYNTHIUS *are marched off.*]

END OF ACT I

ACT II

SCENE – *Gardens in Castle Adamant. A river runs across the back of the stage, crossed by a rustic bridge. Castle Adamant in the distance.*

[*Girl graduates discovered seated at the feet of* LADY PSYCHE.]

CHORUS: Towards the empyrean heights[13]
                  Of every kind of lore,
             We've taken several easy flights,
                  And mean to take some more.
             In trying to achieve success
                  No envy racks our heart,
             And all the knowledge we possess,
                  We mutually impart.

SONG

MEL.:   Pray, what authors should she read
             Who in Classics would succeed?

PSYCHE: If you'd climb the Helicon,[14]
             You should read Anacreon,[15]
             Ovid's *Metamorphoses*,[16]
             Likewise Aristophanes,[17]
             And the works of Juvenal:[18]
             These are worth attention, all;
             But, if you will be advised,
             You will get them Bowdlerized![19]

CHORUS: Ah! we will get them Bowdlerized!

SOLO

SACH.: Pray you, tell us, if you can,
What's the thing that's known as Man?

PSYCHE: Man will swear and Man will storm –
Man is not at all good form –
Man is of no kind of use –
Man's a donkey – Man's a goose –
Man is coarse and Man is plain –
Man is more or less insane –
Man's a ribald – Man's a rake,
Man is Nature's sole mistake!

CHORUS: We'll a memorandum make –
Man is Nature's sole mistake!

And thus to empyrean height
Of every kind of lore,
In search of wisdom's pure delight,
Ambitiously we soar.
In trying to achieve success
No envy racks our heart,
For all we know and all we guess,
We mutually impart!

[*Enter* LADY BLANCHE. *All stand up demurely.*]

BLA.: Attention, ladies, while I read to you
The Princess Ida's list of punishments.
The first is Sacharissa. She's expelled!

ALL: Expelled!

BLA.: Expelled, because although she knew
No man of any kind may pass our walls,
She dared to bring a set of chessmen here!

SACH. [*crying*]: I meant no harm; they're only men of wood!

BLA.: They're men with whom you give each other mate,
And that's enough! The next is Chloe.

CHLOE: Ah!

BLA.: Chloe will lose three terms, for yesterday,
When looking through her drawing-book, I found
A sketch of a perambulator!

ALL [*horrified*]: Oh!

BLA.: *Double* perambulator, shameless girl!
That's all at present. Now, attention, pray;
Your Principal the Princess comes to give
Her usual inaugural address
To those young ladies who joined yesterday.

CHORUS: Mighty maiden with a mission,
Paragon of common sense,
Running fount of erudition,
Miracle of eloquence,
We are blind, and we would see;
We are bound, and would be free;
We are dumb, and we would talk;
We are lame, and we would walk.

[*Enter* PRINCESS IDA.]

Mighty maiden with a mission –
Paragon of common sense;
Running fount of erudition –
Miracle of eloquence!

PRIN. [*recitative*]:
Minerva,[20] oh, hear me!

ARIA

PRIN.: Oh, goddess wise
That lovest light,
Endow with sight
Their unillumined eyes.

At this my call,
        A fervent few
        Have come to woo
The rays that from thee fall.
Let fervent words and fervent thoughts be mine,
That I may lead them to thy sacred shrine!

Women of Adamant, fair Neophytes –
Who thirst for such instruction as we give,
Attend, while I unfold a parable.
The elephant is mightier than Man,
Yet Man subdues him. Why? The elephant
Is elephantine everywhere but here [*tapping her forehead*],
And Man, whose brain is to the elephant's
As Woman's brain to Man's – (that's rule of three) –
Conquers the foolish giant of the woods,
As Woman, in her turn, shall conquer Man.
In Mathematics, Woman leads the way:
The narrow-minded pedant still believes
That two and two make four! Why, we can prove,
We women – household drudges as we are –
That two and two make five – or three – or seven;
Or five-and-twenty, if the case demands!
Diplomacy? The wiliest diplomat
Is absolutely helpless in our hands,
He wheedles monarchs – woman wheedles him!
Logic? Why, tyrant Man himself admits
It's waste of time to argue with a woman!
Then we excel in social qualities:
Though Man professes that he holds our sex
In utter scorn, I venture to believe
He'd rather pass the day with one of you,
Than with five hundred of his fellow-men!
In all things we excel. Believing this,
A hundred maidens here have sworn to place
Their feet upon his neck. If we succeed,
We'll treat him better than he treated us:
But if we fail, why, then let hope fail too!

Let no one care a penny how she looks –
Let red be worn with yellow – blue with green –
Crimson with scarlet – violet with blue!
Let all your things misfit, and you yourselves
At inconvenient moments come undone!
Let hair-pins lose their virtue: let the hook
Disdain the fascination of the eye –
The bashful button modestly evade
The soft embraces of the button-hole!
Let old associations all dissolve,
Let Swan secede from Edgar[21] – Gask from Gask,[22]
Sewell from Cross[23] – Lewis from Allenby![24]
In other words – let Chaos come again!

[*Coming down*]

  Who lectures in the Hall of Arts to-day?

BLA.: I, madam, on Abstract Philosophy.
  There I propose considering, at length,
  Three points – The Is, the Might Be and the Must.
  Whether the Is, from being actual fact,
  Is more important than the vague Might Be,
  Or the Might Be, from taking wider scope,
  Is for that reason greater than the Is:
  And lastly, how the Is and Might Be stand
  Compared with the inevitable Must!

PRIN.: The subject's deep – how do you treat it, pray?

BLA.: Madam, I take three possibilities,
  And strike a balance, then, between the three:
  As thus: The Princess Ida Is our head,
  The Lady Psyche Might Be – Lady Blanche,
  Neglected Blanche, inevitably Must.
  Given these three hypotheses – to find
  The actual betting against each of them!

PRIN.: Your theme's ambitious: pray you, bear in mind.
  Who highest soar fall farthest. Fare you well,
  You and your pupils! Maidens, follow me.

 [*Exeunt* PRINCESS *and Maidens singing refrain of chorus, 'And
  thus to empyrean heights', etc. Manet* LADY BLANCHE.]

BLA.:   I should command here – I was born to rule,
But do I rule? I don't. Why? I don't know.
I shall some day. Not yet. I bide my time.
I once was Some One – and the Was Will Be.
The Present as we speak becomes the Past,
The Past repeats itself, and so is Future!
This sounds involved. It's not. It's right enough.

SONG

BLA.:   Come, mighty Must!
    Inevitable Shall!
In thee I trust.
    Time weaves my coronal!
Go, mocking Is!
    Go, disappointing Was!
That I am this
    Ye are the cursed cause!
Yet humble second shall be first,
        I ween;
And dead and buried be the curst
        Has Been!

Oh, weak Might Be!
    Oh, May, Might, Could, Would, Should!
How powerless ye
    For evil or for good!
In every sense
    Your moods I cheerless call,
Whate'er your tense
    Ye are Imperfect, all!
Ye have deceived the trust I've shown
        In ye!
Away! The Mighty Must alone
        Shall be!

                    [*Exit* LADY BLANCHE.]

[*Enter* HILARION, CYRIL *and* FLORIAN, *climbing over wall, and creeping cautiously among the trees and rocks at the back of the stage.*]

TRIO – HILARION, CYRIL *and* FLORIAN

ALL: Gently, gently,
Evidently
  We are safe so far,
After scaling
Fence and paling,
  Here, at last, we are!
In this college
Useful knowledge
  Everywhere one finds,
And already,
Growing steady,
  We've enlarged our minds.

CYR.:   We've learnt that prickly cactus
Has the power to attract us
             When we fall.

ALL: When we fall!

HIL.:   That nothing man unsettles
Like a bed of stinging nettles,
             Short or tall.

ALL: Short or tall!

FLOR.:   That bull-dogs feed on throttles –
That we don't like broken bottles
             On a wall.

ALL: On a wall!

HIL.:   That spring-guns breathe defiance!
And that burglary's a science
             After all!

ALL: After all!

RECITATIVE

FLOR.:   A Woman's college! maddest folly going!
    What can girls learn within its walls worth knowing?
    I'll lay a crown (the Princess shall decide it)
    I'll teach them twice as much in half-an-hour outside it.

HIL.:   Hush, scoffer; ere you sound your puny thunder,
    List to their aims, and bow your head in wonder!

    They intend to send a wire
        To the moon – to the moon;
    And they'll set the Thames on fire
        Very soon – very soon;
    Then they learn to make silk purses
        With their rigs – with their rigs,
    From the ears of Lady Circe's
        Piggy-wigs[25] – piggy-wigs.
    And weasels at their slumbers
        They trepan[26] – they trepan;
    To get sunbeams from cu*cum*bers,[27]
        They've a plan – they've a plan.
    They've a firmly rooted notion
    They can cross the Polar Occan,
    And they'll find Perpetual Motion,
        If they can – if they can.

ALL: These are the phenomena
    That every pretty domina
        Is hoping we shall see
        At her Universitee!

CYR.:   As for fashion, they forswear it,
        So they say – so they say;
    And the circle – they will square it
        Some fine day – some fine day;

Then the little pigs they're teaching
    For to fly – for to fly;
And the niggers they'll be bleaching,[28]
    By and by – by and by!
Each newly-joined aspirant
    To the clan – to the clan –
Must repudiate the tyrant
    Known as Man – known as Man.
They mock at him and flout him,
For they do not care about him,
And they're 'going to do without him'
    If they can – if they can!

ALL: These are the phenomena, etc.

        In this college
        Useful knowledge
        Ev'rywhere one finds,
        And already growing steady
        We've enlarg'd our minds.

HIL.:   So that's the Princess Ida's castle! Well,
        They must be lovely girls, indeed, if it requires
        Such walls as those to keep intruders off!
CYR.:   To keep men off is only half their charge,
        And that the easier half. I much suspect
        The object of these walls is not so much
        To keep men off as keep the maidens in!
FLOR.:   But what are these? [*Examining some Collegiate robes.*]
HIL. [*looking at them*]:   Why, Academic robes,
        Worn by the lady undergraduates
        When they matriculate. Let's try them on. [*They do so.*]
        Why, see – we're covered to the very toes.
        Three lovely lady undergraduates
        Who, weary of the world and all its wooing –

FLOR.:	And penitent for deeds there's no undoing –
CYR.:	Looked at askance by well-conducted maids –
ALL:	Seek sanctuary in these classic shades!

TRIO – HILARION, CYRIL *and* FLORIAN

HIL.:
> I am a maiden, cold and stately,
>> Heartless I, with a face divine.
> What do I want with a heart, innately?
>> Every heart I meet is mine!

ALL:
>> Haughty, humble, coy or free,
>>> Little care I what maid may be.
>> So that a maid is fair to see,
>>> Every maid is the maid for me!
>>>> [*Dance.*]

CYR.:
> I am a maiden frank and simple,
>> Brimming with joyous roguery;
> Merriment lurks in every dimple,
>> Nobody breaks more hearts than I!

ALL:
>> Haughty, humble, coy or free,
>>> Little care I what maid may be.
>> So that a maid is fair to see,
>>> Every maid is the maid for me!
>>>> [*Dance.*]

FLOR.:
> I am a maiden coyly blushing,
>> Timid am I as a startled hind;
> Every suitor sets me flushing:
>> I am the maid that wins mankind!

ALL:
>> Haughty, humble, coy or free,
>>> Little care I what maid may be.
>> So that a maid is fair to see,
>>> Every maid is the maid for me!

[*Enter* PRINCESS IDA *reading. She does not see them.*]

FLOR.:   But who comes here? The Princess, as I live!
         What shall we do?

HIL. [*aside*]:   Why, we must brave it out!
   [*Aloud*]   Madam, accept our humblest reverence.
   [*They bow, then, suddenly recollecting themselves, curtsey.*]

PRIN. [*surprised*]:
         We greet you, ladies. What would you with us?

HIL. [*aside*]:
         What shall I say? [*Aloud*] We are three students,
            ma'am,
         Three well-born maids of liberal estate,
         Who wish to join this University.

   [HILARION *and* FLORIAN *curtsey again.* CYRIL *bows extravagantly, then, being recalled to himself by* FLORIAN, *curtseys.*]

PRIN.:   If, as you say, you wish to join our ranks,
         And will subscribe to all our rules, 'tis well.

FLOR.:   To all your rules we cheerfully subscribe.

PRIN.:   You say you're noblewomen. Well, you'll find
         No sham degrees for noblewomen here.
         You'll find no sizars here, or servitors,[29]
         Or other cruel distinctions, meant to draw
         A line 'twixt rich and poor: you'll find no tufts
         To mark nobility, except such tufts
         As indicate nobility of brain.
         As for your fellow-students, mark me well:
         There are a hundred maids within these walls,
         All good, all learned and all beautiful:
         They are prepared to love you: will you swear
         To give the fullness of your love to them?

HIL.:   Upon our words and honours, ma'am, we will!

PRIN.:   But we go further: will you undertake
         That you will never marry any man?

FLOR.:   Indeed we never will!

PRIN.:   Consider well,
         You must prefer our maids to all mankind!

HIL.:   To all mankind we much prefer your maids!
CYR.:   We should be dolts indeed, if we did not,
           Seeing how fair –
HIL. [*aside to* CYRIL]:
           Take care – that's rather strong!
PRIN.:   But have you left no lovers at your home
           Who may pursue you here?
HIL.:   No, madam, none.
           We're homely ladies, as no doubt you see,
           And we have never fished for lover's love.
           We smile at girls who deck themselves with gems,
           False hair and meretricious ornament,
           To chain the fleeting fancy of a man,
           But do not imitate them. What we have
           Of hair, is all our own. Our colour, too,
           Unladylike, but not unwomanly,
           Is Nature's handiwork, and man has learnt
           To reckon Nature an impertinence.
PRIN.:   Well, beauty counts for naught within these walls;
           If all you say is true, you'll pass with us
           A happy, happy time!
CYR.:   If, as you say,
           A hundred lovely maidens wait within,
           To welcome us with smiles and open arms,
           I think there's very little doubt we shall!

QUARTETTE – PRINCESS, HILARION, CYRIL, FLORIAN

PRIN.:   The world is but a broken toy,
           Its pleasure hollow – false its joy,
              Unreal its loveliest hue,
                            Alas!
              Its pains alone are true,
                            Alas!
              Its pains alone are true.
HIL.:   The world is everything you say,
           The world we think has had its day.

330

Its merriment is slow,
> Alas!
We've tried it, and we know,
> Alas!
We've tried it and we know.

PRINCESS	HILARION, CYRIL, FLORIAN
The world is but a broken toy,	*The world is but a broken toy*
Its pleasure hollow – false its joy,	*We freely give it up with joy,*
Unreal its loveliest hue,	*Unreal its loveliest hue,*
Alas!	*Alas!*
Its pains alone are true,	*Its pains alone are true,*
Alas!	*Alas!*
Its pains alone are true!	*Its pains alone are true!*

[*Exit* PRINCESS. *The three gentlemen watch her off.* LADY
PSYCHE *enters, and regards them with amazement.*]

HIL.:   I'faith, the plunge is taken, gentlemen!
               For, willy-nilly, we are maidens now,
               And maids against our will we must remain!
     [*All laugh heartily.*]
PSY. [*aside*]:   These ladies are unseemly in their mirth.
     [*The gentlemen see her, and, in confusion, resume their modest
     demeanour.*]
FLOR. [*aside*]: Here's a catastrophe, Hilarion!
               This is my sister! She'll remember me,
               Though years have passed since she and I have
                    met!
HIL. [*aside to* FLORIAN]:
               Then make a virtue of necessity,
               And trust our secret to her gentle care.
FLOR. [*to* PSYCHE, *who has watched* CYRIL *in amazement*]:
               Psyche!
                    Why, don't you know me? Florian!
PSY. [*amazed*]:
               Why, Florian!
FLOR.:   My sister! [*embraces her*].
PSY.:   Oh, my dear!

	What are you doing here – and who are these?
HIL.:	I am that Prince Hilarion to whom
	Your Princess is betrothed. I come to claim
	Her plighted love. Your brother Florian
	And Cyril come to see me safely through.
PSY.:	The Prince Hilarion? Cyril too? How strange!
	My earliest playfellows!
HIL.:	Why, let me look!

HIL.:

Are you that learned little Psyche who
At school alarmed her mates because she called
A buttercup 'ranunculus bulbosus'?

CYR.:

Are you indeed that Lady Psyche, who
At children's parties drove the conjuror wild,
Explaining all his tricks before he did them?

HIL.:

Are you that learned little Psyche, who
At dinner parties, brought in to dessert,
Would tackle visitors with 'You don't know
Who first determined longitude – I do –
Hipparchus[30] 'twas – BC one sixty-three!'
Are you indeed that small phenomenon?

PSY.:

That small phenomenon indeed am I!
But, gentlemen, 'tis death to enter here:
We have all promised to renounce mankind!

FLOR.:

Renounce mankind? On what ground do you base
This senseless resolution?

PSY.:

Senseless? No.
We are all taught, and, being taught, believe
That Man, sprung from an Ape, is Ape at heart.

CYR.:

That's rather strong.

PSY.:

The truth is always strong!

SONG

PSY.:

A Lady fair, of lineage high,
Was loved by an Ape, in the days gone by.
The Maid was radiant as the sun,
The Ape was a most unsightly one –

So it would not do –
His scheme fell through,
For the Maid, when his love took formal shape,
Expressed such terror
At his monstrous error,
That he stammered an apology and made his 'scape,
The picture of a disconcerted Ape.

With a view to rise in the social scale,
He shaved his bristles, and he docked his tail,
He grew moustachios, and he took his tub,
And he paid a guinea to a toilet club[31] –
But it would not do,
The scheme fell through –
For the Maid was Beauty's fairest Queen,
With golden tresses,
Like a real princess's,
While the Ape, despite his razor keen,
Was the apiest Ape that ever was seen!

He bought white ties, and he bought dress suits,
He crammed his feet into bright tight boots –
And to start in life on a brand-new plan,
He christened himself Darwinian Man![32]
But it would not do,
The scheme fell through –
For the Maiden fair, whom the monkey craved,
Was a radiant Being,
With a brain far-seeing –
While Darwinian Man, though well-behaved,
At best is only a monkey shaved!

ALL: While Darwinian Man, etc.

[*During this* MELISSA *has entered unobserved; she looks on in amazement.*]
MEL. [*coming down*]:
Oh, Lady Psyche!

333

PSY. [*terrified*]:   What! you heard us then?
           Oh, all is lost!

MEL.:   Not so! I'll breathe no word!
      [*Advancing in astonishment to* FLORIAN.]
           How marvellously strange! and are you then
           Indeed young men?

FLOR.:   Well, yes, just now we are –
           But hope by dint of study to become,
           In course of time, young women.

MEL. [*eagerly*]:   No, no, no –
           Oh, don't do that! Is this indeed a man?
           I've often heard of them, but, till to-day,
           Never set eyes on one. They told me men
           Were hideous, idiotic and deformed!
           They're quite as beautiful as women are!
           As beautiful, they're infinitely more so!
           Their cheeks have not that pulpy softness which
           One gets so weary of in womankind:
           Their features are more marked – and – oh, their chins!
           How curious! [*Feeling his chin.*]

FLOR.:   I fear it's rather rough.

MEL. [*eagerly*]:
           Oh, don't apologize – I like it so!

QUINTETTE – PSYCHE, MELISSA, HILARION, CYRIL,
                      FLORIAN

PSY.:   The woman of the wisest wit
                      May sometimes be mistaken, O!
                In Ida's views, I must admit,
                      My faith is somewhat shaken, O!

CYR.:   On every other point than this
                      Her learning is untainted, O!
                But Man's a theme with which she is
                      Entirely unacquainted, O!
                         – acquainted, O!

         – acquainted, O!
    Entirely unacquainted, O!

ALL: Then jump for joy and gaily bound,
        The truth is found – the truth is found!
        Set bells a-ringing through the air –
        Ring here and there and everywhere –
        And echo forth the joyous sound,
        The truth is found – the truth is found!

   [*Dance.*]

MEL.:   My natural instinct teaches me
        (And instinct is important, O!)
        You're everything you ought to be,
        And nothing that you oughtn't, O!

HIL.:   That fact was seen at once by you
        In casual conversation, O!
        Which is most creditable to
        Your powers of observation, O!
             – servation, O!
             – servation, O!
        Your powers of observation, O!

ALL: Then jump for joy, etc.
        [*Exeunt* PSYCHE, HILARION, CYRIL *and* FLORIAN.
                      MELISSA *going.*]
   [*Enter* LADY BLANCHE.]

BLA.:   Melissa!

MEL. [*returning*]:   Mother!

BLA.:   Here – a word with you.
        Those are the three new students?

MEL. [*confused*]:   Yes, they are.
        They're charming girls.

BLA.:   Particularly so.
        So graceful, and so very womanly!
        So skilled in all a girl's accomplishments!

MEL. [*confused*]:

Yes – very skilled.

BLA.: They sing so nicely too!

MEL.: They *do* sing nicely!

BLA.: Humph! It's very odd.

Two are tenors, one is a baritone!

MEL. [*much agitated.*]:

They've all got colds!

BLA.: Colds! Bah! D'ye think I'm blind?

These 'girls' are men disguised!

MEL.: Oh no – indeed!

You wrong these gentlemen – I mean – why, see,

Here is an *étui*[33] dropped by one of them [*picking up
  an étui*].

Containing scissors, needles and –

BLA. [*opening it*]: Cigars!

Why, these *are* men! And you knew this, you minx!

MEL.: Oh, spare them – they are gentlemen indeed.

The Prince Hilarion (married years ago

To Princess Ida) with two trusted friends!

Consider, mother, he's her husband now,

And has been, twenty years! Consider, too,

You're only second here – you should be first.

Assist the Prince's plan, and when he gains

The Princess Ida, why, you *will* be first.

You will design the fashions – think of that –

And always serve out all the punishments!

The scheme is harmless, mother – wink at it!

BLA. [*aside*]: The prospect's tempting! Well, well, well,

I'll try –

Though I've not winked at anything for years!

'Tis but one step towards my destiny –

The mighty Must! the inevitable Shall!

DUET – MELISSA *and* LADY BLANCHE

MEL.: Now wouldn't you like to rule the roast,

And guide this University?

BLA.:   I must agree
               'Twould pleasant be.
                    (Sing hey, a Proper Pride!)

MEL.:   And wouldn't you like to clear the coast
           Of malice and perversity?

BLA.:   Without a doubt
             I'll bundle 'em out,
              Sing hey, when I preside!

BOTH: Sing, hoity, toity! Sorry for some!
        Sing, marry come up and $\left\{ \begin{array}{c} \text{my} \\ \text{her} \end{array} \right\}$ day will come!
            Sing, Proper Pride
            Is the horse to ride,
              And Happy-go-lucky, my Lady, O!

BLA.:   For years I've writhed beneath her sneers,
           Although a born Plantagenet![34]

MEL.:   You're much too meek,
             Or you would speak.
              (Sing hey, I'll say no more!)

BLA.:   Her elder I, by several years,
           Although you'd ne'er imagine it.

MEL.:   Sing, so I've heard
             But never a word
              Have I e'er believed before!

BOTH: Sing, hoity toity! Sorry for some!
        Sing, marry come up and $\left\{ \begin{array}{c} \text{my} \\ \text{her} \end{array} \right\}$ day will come!
            Sing, she shall learn
            That a worm will turn.
          Sing Happy-go-lucky, my Lady, O!
                       [*Exit* LADY BLANCHE.]

MEL.:   Saved for a time, at least!
  [*Enter* FLORIAN, *on tiptoe.*]

FLOR. [*whispering*]:

    Melissa – come!

MEL.:   Oh, sir! you must away from this at once –
    My mother guessed your sex! It was my fault –
    I blushed and stammered so that she exclaimed,
    'Can these be men?' Then, seeing this, 'Why these –'
    '*Are men*', she would have added, but '*are men*'
    Stuck in her throat![35] She keeps your secret, sir,
    For reasons of her own – but fly from this
    And take me with you – that is – no – not that!

FLOR.:   I'll go, but not without you! [*Bell.*] Why, what's that?

MEL.:   The luncheon bell.

FLOR.:   I'll wait for luncheon then!

[*Enter* HILARION *with* PRINCESS, CYRIL *with* PSYCHE, LADY BLANCHE *and* LADIES. *Also '*Daughters of the Plough*'*[36] *bearing luncheon.*]

CHORUS

Merrily ring the luncheon bell!
Here in meadow of asphodel,[37]
Feast we body and mind as well,
So merrily ring the luncheon bell!

SOLO

BLA.:   Hunger, I beg to state,
     Is highly indelicate,
    This is a fact profoundly true,
    So learn your appetites to subdue.

ALL: Yes, yes,
    We'll learn our appetites to subdue!

SOLO

CYR. [*eating*]: Madam, your words so wise,
          Nobody should despise,

Cursed with an appetite keen I am
And I'll subdue it –
And I'll subdue it –
And I'll subdue it with cold roast lamb!

ALL: Yes – yes –
We'll subdue it with cold roast lamb!

CHORUS: Merrily ring, etc.

PRIN.:   You say you know the court of Hildebrand?
There is a Prince there – I forget his name –
HIL.:   Hilarion?
PRIN.:   Exactly – is he well?
HIL.:   If it be well to droop and pine and mope,
To sigh 'Oh, Ida! Ida!' all day long,
'Ida! my love! my life! Oh, come to me!'
If it be well, I say, to do all this,
Then Prince Hilarion is very well.
PRIN.:   He breathes *our* name? Well, it's a common one!
And is the booby comely?
HIL.:   Pretty well.
I've heard it said that if I dressed myself
In Prince Hilarion's clothes (supposing this
Consisted with my maiden modesty),
I might be taken for Hilarion's self.
But what is this to you or me, who think
Of all mankind with undisguised contempt?
PRIN.:   Contempt? Why, damsel, when I think of man,
Contempt is not the word.
CYR. [*getting tipsy*]:   I'm sure of that,
Or if it is, it surely should not be!
HIL. [*aside to* CYRIL]:
Be quiet, idiot, or they'll find us out.
CYR.:   The Prince Hilarion's a goodly lad!
PRIN.:   *You* know him then?
CYR. [*tipsily*]:   I rather think I do!

We are inseparables!

PRIN.:   Why, what's this?

You love him then?

CYR.:   We do indeed – all three!

HIL.: Madam, she jests! [*Aside to* CYRIL] Remember where
        you are!

CYR.: Jests? Not at all! Why, bless my heart alive,
       You and Hilarion, when at the Court,
       Rode the same horse!

PRIN. [*horrified*]:   Astride?

CYR.:   Of course! Why not?
       Wore the same clothes – and once or twice, I think,
       Got tipsy in the same good company!

PRIN.: Well, these are nice young ladies, on my word!

CYR. [*tipsy*]:
       Don't you remember that old kissing-song
       He'd sing to blushing Mistress Lalage,[38]
       The hostess of the Pigeons? Thus it ran:

SONG

[*During symphony* HILARION *and* FLORIAN *try to stop* CYRIL.
He shakes them off angrily.]

CYR.:   Would you know the kind of maid
      Sets my heart aflame-a?
  Eyes must be downcast and staid,
      Cheeks must flush for shame-a!
        She may neither dance nor sing,
        But, demure in everything,
        Hang her head in modest way,
        With pouting lips that seem to say,
  'Oh, kiss me, kiss me, kiss me, kiss me,
      Though I die of shame-a!'
  Please you, that's the kind of maid
      Sets my heart aflame-a!

When a maid is bold and gay
  With a tongue goes clang-a,
Flaunting it in brave array,
  Maiden may go hang-a!
      Sunflower gay and hollyhock
      Never shall my garden stock;
      Mine the blushing rose of May,
      With pouting lips that seem to say,
  'Oh, kiss me, kiss me, kiss me, kiss me,
    Though I die for shame-a!'
  Please you, that's the kind of maid
    Sets my heart aflame-a!

PRIN.:   Infamous creature, get you hence away!
   [HILARION, *who has been with difficulty restrained by* FLORIAN
   during this song, breaks from him and strikes CYRIL *furiously*
   on the breast.]
HIL.:   Dog! there is something more to sing about!
CYR. [*sobered*]:
        Hilarion, are you mad?
PRIN. [*horrified*]:   Hilarion? Help!
      Why, these are men! Lost! lost! betrayed! undone!
        [*Running on to bridge.*]
      Girls, get you hence! Man-monsters, if you dare
      Approach one step, I – Ah!
   [*Loses her balance, and falls into the stream.*]
PSY.:   Oh! save her, sir!
BLA.:   It's useless, sir, – you'll only catch your death!
   [HILARION *springs in.*]
SACH.:   He catches her!
MEL.:   And now he lets her go!
      Again she's in his grasp –
PSY.:   And now she's not.
      He seizes her back hair!
BLA. [*not looking*]:
         And it comes off!
PSY.:   No, no! She's saved! – she's saved! – she's saved! –
      she's saved!

FINALE

CHORUS OF LADIES:
> Oh! joy, our chief is saved,
>   And by Hilarion's hand;
> The torrent fierce he braved,
>   And brought her safe to land!
>   For his intrusion we must own
>   This doughty deed may well atone!

PRIN.:
>   Stand forth ye three,
>   Whoe'er ye be,
> And hearken to our stern decree!

HIL., CYR. *and* FLOR.:
> Have mercy, lady – disregard your oaths!

PRIN.: I know not mercy, men in women's clothes!
>   The man whose sacrilegious eyes
>   Invade our strict seclusion, dies.
>   Arrest these coarse intruding spies!
> [*They are arrested by the 'Daughters of the Plough'.*]

FLOR., CYR. *and* LADIES:
> Have mercy, lady – disregard your oaths!

PRIN.: I know not mercy, men in women's clothes!
> [CYRIL *and* FLORIAN *are bound.*]

SONG

HIL.: Whom thou hast chained must wear his chain,
>   Thou canst not set him free,
> He wrestles with his bonds in vain
>   Who lives by loving thee!
> If heart of stone for heart of fire,
>   Be all thou hast to give,

If dead to me my heart's desire,
    Why should I wish to live?

FLOR., CYR. *and* LADIES:
    Have mercy, O lady!

HIL.:   No word of thine – no stern command
        Can teach my heart to rove,
    Then rather perish by thy hand,
        Than live without thy love!
    A loveless life apart from thee
        Were hopeless slavery,
    If kindly death will set me free,
        Why should I fear to die?
        [*He is bound by two of the attendants, and the three
                gentlemen are marched off.*]

[*Enter* MELISSA.]

MEL.:   Madam, without the castle walls
        An armed band
    Demand admittance to our halls
        For Hildebrand!

ALL: Oh, horror!

PRIN.:   Deny them!
        We will defy them!

ALL: Too late – too late!
        The castle gate
        Is battered by them!
[*The gate yields.* SOLDIERS *rush in.* ARAC, GURON *and*
SCYNTHIUS *are with them, but with their hands handcuffed.*]

ENSEMBLE

GIRLS	MEN
Rend the air with wailing,	Walls and fences scaling,
Shed the shameful tear!	Promptly we appear;
Walls are unavailing,	Walls are unavailing,
Man has entered here!	We have entered here.
Shame and desecration	Female execration
Are his staunch allies,	Stifle if you're wise,
Let your lamentation	Stop your lamentation,
Echo to the skies!	Dry your pretty eyes!

[*Enter* HILDEBRAND.]

RECITATIVE

PRIN.:
Audacious tyrant, do you dare
To beard a maiden in her lair?

HILD.:
Since you inquire,
We've no desire
To beard a maiden here, or anywhere!

SOLDIERS:
No, no – we've no desire
To beard a maiden here, or anywhere!

SOLO

HILD.:
Some years ago
No doubt you know
(And if you don't I'll tell you so)
You gave your troth
Upon your oath
To Hilarion my son.
A vow you make
You must not break,
(If you think you may, it's a great mistake),

For a bride's a bride
Though the knot were tied
 At the early age of one!
  And I'm a peppery kind of King,
  Who's indisposed for parleying
  To fit the wit of a bit of a chit,
  And that's the long and the short of it!

SOLDIERS: For he's a peppery kind of King, etc.

HILD.:   If you decide
   To pocket your pride
  And let Hilarion claim his bride,
   Why, well and good,
   It's understood
  We'll let bygones go by –
   But if you choose
   To sulk in the blues
  I'll make the whole of you shake in your shoes.
   I'll storm your walls,
   And level your halls,
    In the twinkling of an eye!
     For I'm a peppery Potentate,
     Who's little inclined his claim to
      bate,
     To fit the wit of a bit of a chit,
     And that's the long and the short
      of it!

SOLDIERS: For he's a peppery kind of King, etc.

TRIO – ARAC, GURON *and* SCYNTHIUS

We may remark, though nothing can
   Dismay us,
That if you thwart this gentleman,
   He'll slay us.

We don't fear death, of course – we're taught
To shame it;
But still upon the whole we thought
We'd name it.

[*To each other*]
Yes, yes, yes, better perhaps to name it.
Our interests we would not press
With chatter,
Three hulking brothers more or less
Don't matter;
If you'd pooh-pooh this monarch's plan,
Pooh-pooh it,
But when he says he'll hang a man,
He'll do it.

[*To each other*]
Yes, yes, yes, devil doubt he'll do it.

PRIN. [*recitative*]:
Be reassured, nor fear his anger blind,
His menaces are idle as the wind.
He dares not kill you – vengeance lurks behind!

ARAC, GUR., SCYN.:
We rather think he dares, but never mind!
No, no, – never, never mind!

HILD.: I rather think I dare, but never, never mind!
Enough of parley – as a special boon,
We give you till to-morrow afternoon;
Release Hilarion, then, and be his bride,
Or you'll incur the guilt of fratricide!

ENSEMBLE

PRINCESS	THE OTHERS
To yield at once to such a foe	Oh! yield at once, 'twere better so
With shame were rife;	Than risk a strife!
So quick! away with him, although	And let the Prince Hilarion go –
He saved my life;	He saved thy life!
That he is fair, and strong, and tall,	Hilarion's fair, and strong, and tall –
Is very evident to all,	A worse misfortune might befall –
Yet I will die before I call	It's not so dreadful, after all,
Myself his wife!	To be his wife!

SOLO

PRIN.:
Though I am but a girl,
Defiance thus I hurl,
Our banners all
On outer wall
We fearlessly unfurl.

ALL:
Though she is but a girl, etc.

PRINCESS	THE OTHERS
That he is fair, etc.	Hilarion's fair, etc.

[*The* PRINCESS *stands, surrounded by girls kneeling,* HILDE-
BRAND *and soldiers stand on built rocks at back and sides of
stage. Picture.*]

END OF ACT II

ACT III

SCENE – *Outer Walls and Courtyard of Castle Adamant.*

[MELISSA, SACHARISSA *and ladies discovered, armed with battleaxes.*]

CHORUS:
　　Death to the invader!
　　　Strike a deadly blow,
　　As an old Crusader
　　　Struck his Paynim[39] foe!
　　Let our martial thunder
　　Fill his soul with wonder,
　　Tear his ranks asunder,
　　　Lay the tyrant low!

SOLO

MEL.:
　　Thus our courage, all untarnished,
　　　We're instructed to display:
　　But to tell the truth unvarnished,
　　　We are more inclined to say,
　　'Please you, do not hurt us.'

ALL:　　'Do not hurt us, if it please you!'
MEL.:　'Please you let us be.'
ALL:　　'Let us be – let us be!'
MEL.:　'Soldiers disconcert us.'
ALL:　　'Disconcert us, if it please you!'

348

MEL.:	'Frightened maids are we.'
ALL:	'Maids are we – maids are we!'
MEL.:	But 'twould be an error
	To confess our terror,
	So, in Ida's name,
	Boldly we exclaim:

CHORUS:	Death to the invader!
	Strike a deadly blow,
	As an old Crusader
	Struck his Paynim foe!

[*Flourish. Enter* PRINCESS, *armed, attended by* BLANCHE *and* PSYCHE.]

PRIN.:	I like your spirit, girls! We have to meet
	Stern bearded warriors in fight to-day:
	Wear naught but what is necessary to
	Preserve your dignity before their eyes,
	And give your limbs full play.
BLA.:	One moment, ma'am,
	Here is a paradox we should not pass
	Without inquiry. We are prone to say,
	'This thing is Needful – that, Superfluous' –
	Yet they invariably co-exist!
	We find the Needful comprehended in
	The circle of the grand Superfluous,
	Yet the Superfluous cannot be bought
	Unless you're amply furnished with the Needful.
	These singular considerations are –
PRIN.:	Superfluous, yet not Needful – so you see
	The terms may independently exist.
	[*To Ladies*] Women of Adamant, we have to show
	That Woman, educated to the task,
	Can meet Man, face to face, on his own ground,
	And beat him there. Now let us set to work:
	Where is our lady surgeon?
SACH.:	Madam, here!

PRIN.: We shall require your skill to heal the wounds
Of those that fall.

SACH. [*alarmed*]: What, heal the wounded?

PRIN.: Yes!

SACH.: And cut off real live legs and arms?

PRIN.: Of course!

SACH.: I wouldn't do it for a thousand pounds!

PRIN.: Why, how is this? Are you faint-hearted, girl?
You've often cut them off in theory!

SACH.: In theory I'll cut them off again
With pleasure, and as often as you like,
But not in practice.

PRIN.: Coward! get you hence,
I've craft enough for that, and courage too,
I'll do your work! My fusiliers, advance!
Why, you are armed with axes! Gilded toys!
Where are your rifles, pray?

CHLOE: Why, please you, ma'am,
We left them in the armoury, for fear
That in the heat and turmoil of the fight,
They might go off!

PRIN.: 'They might!' Oh, craven souls!
Go off yourselves! Thank heaven, I have a heart
That quails not at the thought of meeting men;
I will discharge your rifles! Off with you!
Where's my bandmistress?

ADA: Please you, ma'am, the band
Do not feel well, and can't come out to-day!

PRIN.: Why, this is flat rebellion! I've no time
To talk to them just now. But, happily,
I can play several instruments at once,
And I will drown the shrieks of those that fall
With trumpet music, such as soldiers love!
How stand we with respect to gunpowder?
My Lady Psyche – you who superintend
Our lab'ratory – are you well prepared
To blow these bearded rascals into shreds?

PSY.:   Why, madam –

PRIN.:   Well?

PSY.:   Let us try gentler means.

        We can dispense with fulminating grains

        While we have eyes with which to flash our rage!

        We can dispense with villainous saltpetre

        While we have tongues with which to blow them up!

        We can dispense, in short, with all the arts

        That brutalize the practical polemist!

PRIN. [*contemptuously*]:

        I never knew a more dispensing chemist!

        Away, away – I'll meet these men alone

        Since all my women have deserted me!

      [*Exeunt all but* PRINCESS, *singing refrain of 'Please you, do*

                       not hurt us', pianissimo.]

PRIN.:   So fail my cherished plans – so fails my faith –

        And with it hope, and all that comes of hope!

SONG

PRIN.:   I built upon a rock,

              But ere Destruction's hand

                Dealt equal lot

                To Court and cot,

              My rock had turned to sand!

            I leant upon an oak,

               But in the hour of need,

                Alack-a-day,

                My trusted stay

              Was but a bruisèd reed!

                Ah, faithless rock,

                My simple faith to mock!

                Ah, trait'rous oak,

                Thy worthlessness to cloak.

I drew a sword of steel,
 But when to home and hearth
  The battle's breath
  Bore fire and death,
 My sword was but a lath!
I lit a beacon fire,
 But on a stormy day
  Of frost and rime,
  In wintertime,
My fire had died away!
  Ah, coward steel,
  That fear can unanneal!
  False fire indeed,
  To fail me in my need!

[*She sinks on a seat. Enter* CHLOE *and all the ladies.*]

CHLOE: Madam, your father and your brothers claim
    An audience!

PRIN.:   What do they do here?

CHLOE: They come
    To fight for you!

PRIN.:   Admit them!

BLA.:   Infamous!
    One's brothers, ma'am, are men!

PRIN.:   So I have heard.
    But all my women seem to fail me when
    I need them most. In this emergency,
    Even one's brothers may be turned to use.

[*Enter* KING GAMA, *quite pale and unnerved.*]

GAMA: My daughter!

PRIN.:   Father! thou art free!

GAMA: Aye, free!
    Free as a tethered ass! I come to thee
    With words from Hildebrand. Those duly given
    I must return to blank captivity.
    I'm free so far.

PRIN.:   Your message.

GAMA: Hildebrand
Is loth to war with women. Pit my sons,
My three brave sons, against these popinjays,
These tufted jack-a-dandy featherheads,
And on the issue let thy hand depend!

PRIN.:   Insult on insult's head! Are we a stake
For fighting men? What fiend possesses thee,
That thou hast come with offers such as these
From such as he to such an one as I?

GAMA: I am possessed
By the pale devil of a shaking heart!
My stubborn will is bent. I dare not face
That devilish monarch's black malignity!
He tortures me with torments worse than
        death,
I haven't anything to grumble at!
He finds out what particular meats I love,
And gives me them. The very choicest wines,
The costliest robes – the richest rooms are mine:
He suffers none to thwart my simplest plan,
And gives strict orders none should contradict
        me!
He's made my life a curse! [weeps].

PRIN.:   My tortured father!

SONG

GAMA: Whene'er I poke
              Sarcastic joke
                   Replete with malice spiteful,
              This people mild
              Politely smiled,
                   And voted me delightful!
              Now when a wight
              Sits up all night
                   Ill-natured jokes devising,

And all his wiles
Are met with smiles,
    It's hard, there's no disguising!

Oh, don't the days seem lank and long
When all goes right and nothing goes wrong,
And isn't your life extremely flat
With nothing whatever to grumble at!

    When German bands[40]
    From music stands
Played Wagner imper*fect*ly –
    I bade them go –
    They didn't say no,
    But off they went directly!
    The organ boys
    They stopped their noise
With readiness surprising,
    And grinning herds
    Of hurdy-gurds[41]
Retired apologizing!
Oh, don't the days seem lank and long, etc.

    I offered gold
    In sums untold
To all who'd contradict me –
    I said I'd pay
    A pound a day
To any one who kicked me –
    I bribed with toys
    Great vulgar boys
To utter something spiteful,
    But, bless you, no!
    They *would* be so
Confoundedly politeful!

In short, these aggravating lads,
They tickle my tastes, they feed my fads,
They give me this and they give me that,
And I've nothing whatever to grumble at!

[*He bursts into tears, and falls sobbing on a seat.*]

PRIN.:   My poor old father! How he must have
                      suffered!
              Well, well, I yield!

GAMA [*hysterically*]:
              She yields! I'm saved, I'm saved!   [*Exits.*]

PRIN.:   Open the gates – admit these warriors,
              Then get you all within the castle walls.   [*Exits.*]

[*The gates are opened, and the girls mount the battlements as
soldiers enter. Also* ARAC, GURON *and* SCYNTHIUS.]

CHORUS OF SOLDIERS:
              When anger spreads his wing,
                  And all seems dark as night for it,
                  There's nothing but to fight for it,
              But ere you pitch your ring,
                  Select a pretty site for it,
                  (This spot is suited quite for it),
              And then you gaily sing,

              'Oh, I love the jolly rattle
              Of an ordeal by battle,
              There's an end of tittle-tattle,
                      When your enemy is dead.
              It's an arrant molly-coddle
              Fears a crack upon his noddle
              And he's only fit to swaddle
                      In a downy feather-bed!' –

ALL: For a fight's a kind of thing
        That I love to look upon,
            So let us sing,
            Long live the King,
        And his son Hilarion!

[*During this,* HILARION, FLORIAN *and* CYRIL *are brought out by the 'Daughters of the Plough'. They are still bound and wear the robes. Enter* KING GAMA.]

GAMA: Hilarion! Cyril! Florian! dressed as women!
        Is this indeed Hilarion?
HIL.:   Yes, it is!
GAMA: Why, you look handsome in your women's clothes!
        Stick to 'em! men's attire becomes you not!

   [*To* CYRIL *and* FLORIAN]

        And you, young ladies, will you please to pray
        King Hildebrand to set me free again?
        Hang on his neck and gaze into his eyes,
        He never could resist a pretty face!
HIL.:   You dog, you'll find, though I wear woman's garb,
        My sword is long and sharp!
GAMA: Hush, pretty one!
        Here's a virago! Here's a termagant!
        If length and sharpness go for anything,
        You'll want no sword while you can wag your tongue!
CYR.:   What need to waste your words on such as he?
        He's old and crippled.
GAMA: Aye, but I've three sons,
        Fine fellows, young, and muscular, and brave,
        They're well worth talking to! Come, what d'ye say?
ARAC: Aye, pretty ones, engage yourselves with us,
        If three rude warriors affright you not!
HIL.:   Old as you are, I'd wring your shrivelled neck
        If you were not the Princess Ida's father.
GAMA: If I were not the Princess Ida's father,
        And so had not her brothers for my sons,
        No doubt you'd wring my neck – in safety too!

Come, come, Hilarion, begin, begin!
Give them no quarter – they will give you none.
You've this advantage over warriors
Who kill their country's enemies for pay –
You know what you are fighting for – look there!
[*Pointing to Ladies on the battlements.*]

[*Exit* KING GAMA. HILARION, FLORIAN *and*
CYRIL *are led off.*]

SONG

ARAC: This helmet, I suppose,
Was meant to ward off blows,
         It's very hot,
         And weighs a lot,
As many a guardsman knows,
So off that helmet goes.

ALL: Yes, yes, yes,
So off that helmet goes!
[*Giving their helmets to attendants.*]

ARAC: This tight-fitting cuirass[42]
Is but a useless mass,
         It's made of steel,
         And weighs a deal,
A man is but an ass
Who fights in a cuirass,
So off goes that cuirass.

ALL: Yes, yes, yes,
So off goes that cuirass!
[*Removing cuirasses.*]

ARAC: These brassets,[43] truth to tell,
May look uncommon well,
         But in a fight

357

> They're much too tight,
> They're like a lobster shell!

ALL:
> Yes, yes, yes,
> They're like a lobster shell.
> [*Removing their brassets.*]

ARAC:
> These things I treat the same [*indicating leg
> pieces*].
> (I quite forget their name)
> They turn one's legs
> To cribbage pegs[44] –
> Their aid I thus disclaim,
> Though I forget their name!

ALL:
> Yes, yes, yes,
> Their aid $\left\{ \begin{array}{c} \text{we} \\ \text{they} \end{array} \right\}$ thus disclaim!

[*They remove their leg pieces and wear close-fitting shape suits.*]
[*Enter* HILARION, FLORIAN *and* CYRIL.]
[*Desperate fight between the three Princes and the three Knights, during which the Ladies on the battlements and the Soldiers on the stage sing the following chorus.*]

> This is our duty plain towards
> Our Princess all immaculate,
> We ought to bless her brothers' swords
> And piously ejaculate:
> Oh, Hungary![45]
> Oh, Hungary!
> Oh, doughty sons of Hungary!
> May all success
> Attend and bless
> Your warlike ironmongery!
> Hilarion! Hilarion! Hilarion!

[*By this time,* ARAC, GURON *and* SCYNTHIUS *are on the ground, wounded –* HILARION, CYRIL *and* FLORIAN *stand over them.*]

PRIN. [*entering through gate and followed by Ladies,* KINGS HILDE-BRAND *and* GAMA]: Hold! stay your hands! – we yield ourselves to you!

     Ladies, my brothers all lie bleeding there!
     Bind up their wounds – but look the other way.
  [*Coming down*]
     Is this the end? [*bitterly to* LADY BLANCHE]. How say
      you, Lady Blanche –
     Can I with dignity my post resign?
     And if I do, will you then take my place?
BLA.: To answer this, it's meet that we consult
     The great Potential Mysteries; I mean
     The five Subjunctive Possibilities –
     The May, the Might, the Would, the Could, the Should.
     Can you resign? The prince May claim you; if
     He Might, you Could – and if you Should, I Would!
PRIN.: I thought as much! Then, to my fate I yield –
     So ends my cherished scheme! Oh, I had hoped
     To band all women with my maiden throng,
     And make them all abjure tyrannic Man!
HILD.: A noble aim!
PRIN.:   You ridicule it now;
     But if I carried out this glorious scheme,
     At my exalted name Posterity
     Would bow in gratitude!
HILD.:   But pray reflect –
     If you enlist all women in your cause,
     And make them all abjure tyrannic Man,
     The obvious question then arises, 'How
     Is this Posterity to be provided?'
PRIN.: I never thought of that! My Lady Blanche,
     How do you solve the riddle?
BLA.:   Don't ask me –
     Abstract Philosophy won't answer it.

Take him – he is your Shall. Give in to Fate!

PRIN.: And you desert me. I alone am staunch!

HIL.: Madam, you placed your trust in Woman – well,
Woman has failed you utterly – try Man,
Give him one chance, it's only fair – besides,
Women are far too precious, too divine,
To try unproven theories upon.
Experiments, the proverb says, are made
On humble subjects – try our grosser clay,
And mould it as you will!

CYR.:   Remember, too,
Dear Madam, if at any time, you feel
A-weary of the Prince, you can return
To Castle Adamant, and rule your girls
As heretofore, you know.

PRIN.:   And shall I find
The Lady Psyche here?

PSY.:   If Cyril, ma'am,
Does not behave himself, I think you will.

PRIN.: And you, Melissa, shall I find *you* here?

MEL.: Madam, however Florian turns out,
Unhesitatingly I answer, No!

GAMA: Consider this, my love, if your mamma
Had looked on matters from your point of view
(I wish she had), why where would you have been?

BLA.: There's an unbounded field of speculation,
On which I could discourse for hours!

PRIN.:   No doubt!
We will not trouble you. Hilarion,
I have been wrong – I see my error now.
Take me, Hilarion – 'We will walk the world
Yoked in all exercise of noble end!
And so through those dark gates across the wild
That no man knows! Indeed, I love thee – Come!'

FINALE

PRIN.:

With joy abiding,
Together gliding
    Through life's variety,
    In sweet society,
And thus enthroning
The love I'm owning,
On this atoning
    I will rely!

CHORUS:

It were profanity
For poor humanity
To treat as vanity
    The sway of Love.
In no locality
Or principality
Is our mortality
    Its sway above!

HIL.:

When day is fading,
With serenading
    And such frivolity
    Of tender quality –
With scented showers
Of fairest flowers,
The happy hours
    Will gaily fly!

CHORUS:

It were profanity, etc.

CURTAIN

THE MIKADO[1]

OR

THE TOWN OF TITIPU

DRAMATIS PERSONAE

THE MIKADO OF JAPAN

NANKI-POO (*his Son, disguised as a wandering minstrel, and in love with* YUM-YUM)

KO-KO (*Lord High Executioner of Titipu*)

POOH-BAH (*Lord High Everything Else*)

PISH-TUSH (*a Noble Lord*)

YUM-YUM
PITTI-SING } (*Three Sisters – Wards of* KO-KO)
PEEP-BO

KATISHA (*an elderly Lady, in love with* NANKI-POO)

Chorus of School-girls, Nobles, Guards and Coolies

ACT I – Courtyard of Ko-Ko's Official Residence
ACT II – Ko-Ko's Garden

ACT I

[*Japanese nobles discovered standing and sitting in attitudes suggested by native drawings.*]

CHORUS OF NOBLES:

If you want to know who we are,
We are gentlemen of Japan:[3]
On many a vase and jar –
On many a screen and fan,
We figure in lively paint:
Our attitude's queer and quaint –
You're wrong if you think it ain't, oh!

If you think we are worked by strings,
Like a Japanese marionette,
You don't understand these things:
It is simply Court etiquette.
Perhaps you suppose this throng
Can't keep it up all day long?
If that's your idea, you're wrong, oh!

[*Enter* NANKI-POO[4] *in great excitement. He carries a native guitar on his back and a bundle of ballads in his hand.*]

RECITATIVE

NANK.:   Gentlemen, I pray you tell me
          Where a gentle maiden dwelleth,
          Named Yum-Yum,[5] the ward of Ko-Ko?[6]
          In pity speak – oh, speak, I pray you!

A NOBLE: Why, who are you who ask this question?
NANK.:   Come gather round me, and I'll tell you.

SONG *and* CHORUS

NANK.:   A wandering minstrel I –
              A thing of shreds and patches,[7]
              Of ballads, songs and snatches,
          And dreamy lullaby!

          My catalogue is long,
              Through every passion ranging,
              And to your humours changing
          I tune my supple song!

                  Are you in sentimental mood?
                      I'll sigh with you,
                          Oh, sorrow, sorrow!
                  On maiden's coldness do you brood?
                      I'll do so, too –
                          Oh, sorrow, sorrow!
                  I'll charm your willing ears
                  With songs of lovers' fears,
                  While sympathetic tears
                      My cheeks bedew –
                          Oh, sorrow, sorrow!

          But if patriotic sentiment is wanted,
              I've patriotic ballads cut and dried;
          For where'er our country's banner may be planted,
              All other local banners are defied!

Our warriors, in serried ranks assembled,
   Never quail – or they conceal it if they do –
And I shouldn't be surprised if nations trembled
   Before the mighty troops of Titipu!

CHORUS: We shouldn't be surprised, etc.

NANK.:   And if you call for a song of the sea,
     We'll heave the capstan round,
   With a yeo heave ho, for the wind is free,
   Her anchor's a-trip and her helm's a-lee,
     Hurrah for the homeward bound!

CHORUS: Yeo-ho – heave ho –
   Hurrah for the homeward bound!

NANK.:   To lay aloft in a howling breeze
     May tickle a landsman's taste,
   But the happiest hour a sailor sees
     Is when he's down
     At an inland town,
   With his Nancy on his knees, yeo ho!
     And his arm around her waist!

CHORUS: Then man the capstan – off we go,
     As the fiddler swings us round,
   With a yeo heave ho,
   And a rumbelow,
     Hurrah for the homeward bound!

NANK.:   A wandering minstrel I, etc.

[*Enter* PISH-TUSH.[8]]
PISH.: And what may be your business with Yum-Yum?
NANK.: I'll tell you. A year ago I was a member of the Titipu town
band. It was my duty to take the cap round for contributions. While
discharging this delicate office, I saw Yum-Yum. We loved each

other at once, but she was betrothed to her guardian Ko-Ko, a cheap tailor, and I saw that my suit was hopeless. Overwhelmed with despair, I quitted the town. Judge of my delight when I heard, a month ago, that Ko-Ko had been condemned to death for flirting! I hurried back at once, in the hope of finding Yum-Yum at liberty to listen to my protestations.

PISH.: It is true that Ko-Ko was condemned to death for flirting, but he was reprieved at the last moment, and raised to the exalted rank of Lord High Executioner under the following remarkable circumstances:

SONG *and* CHORUS

PISH.:
> Our great Mikado, virtuous man,
> When he to rule our land began,
> Resolved to try
> A plan whereby
> Young men might best be steadied.
> So he decreed, in words succinct,
> That all who flirted, leered or winked
> (Unless connubially linked),
> Should forthwith be beheaded.

> And I expect you'll all agree
> That he was right to so decree.
> And I am right,
> And you are right,
> And all is right as right can be!

CHORUS:
> And you are right,
> And we are right, etc.

PISH.:
> This stern decree, you'll understand,
> Caused great dismay throughout the land!
> For young and old
> And shy and bold
> Were equally affected.

368

The youth who winked a roving eye,
Or breathed a non-connubial sigh,
Was thereupon condemned to die –
　　He usually objected.

And you'll allow, as I expect,
That he was right to so object.
　　And I am right,
　　And you are right,
And everything is quite correct!

CHORUS:　　　　　　　And you are right,
　　　　　　　　　　And we are right, etc.

PISH.:　　And so we straight let out on bail
A convict from the county jail,
　　Whose head was next
　　　On some pretext
　　Condemnèd to be mown off,
And made *him* Headsman, for we said,
'Who's next to be decapited
Cannot cut off another's head
　　Until he's cut his own off.'

And we are right, I think you'll say,
To argue in this kind of way;
　　And I am right,
　　And you are right,
And all is right – too-looral-lay!

CHORUS:　　　　　　　And you are right,
　　　　　　　　　　And we are right, etc.

　　　　　　　　　　　　　　[*Exeunt* CHORUS.]

[*Enter* POOH-BAH.[9]]

NANK.: Ko-Ko, the cheap tailor, Lord High Executioner of Titipu! Why, that's the highest rank a citizen can attain!

POOH.: It is. Our logical Mikado, seeing no moral difference between the dignified judge who condemns a criminal to die, and the industrious mechanic who carries out the sentence, has rolled the two offices into one, and every judge is now his own executioner.

NANK.: But how good of you (for I see that you are a nobleman of the highest rank) to condescend to tell all this to me, a mere strolling minstrel!

POOH.: Don't mention it. I am, in point of fact, a particularly haughty and exclusive person, of pre-Adamite ancestral descent.[10] You will understand this when I tell you that I can trace my ancestry back to a protoplasmal primordial atomic globule. Consequently, my family pride is something inconceivable. I can't help it. I was born sneering. But I struggle hard to overcome this defect. I mortify my pride continually. When all the great officers of State resigned in a body, because they were too proud to serve under an ex-tailor,[11] did I not unhesitatingly accept all their posts at once?

PISH.: And the salaries attached to them? You did.

POOH.: It is consequently my degrading duty to serve this upstart as First Lord of the Treasury,[12] Lord Chief Justice, Commander-in-Chief, Lord High Admiral, Master of the Buckhounds,[13] Groom of the Back Stairs,[14] Archbishop of Titipu and Lord Mayor, both acting and elect, all rolled into one. And at a salary! A Pooh-Bah paid for his services! I a salaried minion! But I do it! It revolts me, but I do it!

NANK.: And it does you credit.

POOH.: But I don't stop at that. I go and dine with middle-class people on reasonable terms. I dance at cheap suburban parties for a moderate fee. I accept refreshment at any hands, however lowly. I also retail State secrets at a very low figure. For instance, any further information about Yum-Yum would come under the head of a State secret. [NANKI-POO *takes the hint, and gives him money.*] [*Aside*] Another insult, and, I think, a light one!

SONG – POOH-BAH *with* NANKI-POO *and* PISH-TUSH

Young man, despair,
Likewise go to,
Yum-Yum the fair
You must not woo.
It will not do:
I'm sorry for you,
You very imperfect ablutioner!
This very day
From school Yum-Yum
Will wend her way,
And homeward come,
With beat of drum
And a rum-tum-tum,
To wed the Lord High Executioner!
And the brass will crash,
And the trumpets bray,
And they'll cut a dash
On their wedding day.
She'll toddle away, as all aver,
With the Lord High Executioner!

NANK. *and* POOH.: And the brass will crash, etc.
It's a hopeless case,
As you may see,
And in your place
Away I'd flee;
But don't blame me –
I'm sorry to be
Of your pleasure a diminutioner.
They'll vow their pact
Extremely soon,
In point of fact
This afternoon.

Her honeymoon
With that buffoon
At seven commences, so *you* shun her!

ALL: And the brass will crash, etc.

[Exit PISH-TUSH.]

RECITATIVE

NANK.: And I have journeyed for a month, or nearly,
To learn that Yum-Yum, whom I love so dearly,
This day to Ko-Ko is to be united!
POOH.: The fact appears to be as you've recited:
But here he comes, equipped as suits his station;
He'll give you any further information.

[Exeunt POOH-BAH *and* NANKI-POO.]

[Enter CHORUS OF NOBLES.]

CHORUS: Behold the Lord High Executioner!
A personage of noble rank and title –
A dignified and potent officer,
Whose functions are particularly vital!
Defer, defer,
To the Lord High Executioner!

[Enter KO-KO *attended.]*

SOLO

KO.: Taken from the county jail
By a set of curious chances;
Liberated then on bail,
On my own recognizances;
Wafted by a favouring gale
As one sometimes is in trances,
To a height that few can scale,
Save by long and weary dances;

Surely, never had a male
    Under such like circumstances
So adventurous a tale,
    Which may rank with most romances.

CHORUS: Defer, defer,
      To the Lord High Executioner, etc.

KO.: Gentlemen, I'm much touched by this reception. I can only trust that by strict attention to duty I shall ensure a continuance of those favours which it will ever be my study to deserve. If I should ever be called upon to act professionally, I am happy to think that there will be no difficulty in finding plenty of people whose loss will be a distinct gain to society at large.

SONG – KO-KO *with* CHORUS OF MEN

KO.:   As some day it may happen that a victim must be found,
      I've got a little list[15] – I've got a little list
    Of society offenders who might well be underground,
      And who never would be missed – who never would be
        missed!
    There's the pestilential nuisances who write for
      autographs –
    All people who have flabby hands and irritating laughs –
    All children who are up in dates, and floor you with 'em
      flat –
    All persons who in shaking hands, shake hands with you
      like *that* –
    And all third persons who on spoiling *tête-à-têtes* insist –
      They'd none of 'em be missed – they'd none of 'em be
        missed!

CHORUS: He's got 'em on the list – he's got 'em on the list;
      And they'll none of 'em be missed – they'll none of 'em
        be missed.

KO.: There's the nigger serenader,[16] and the others of his
    race,
  And the piano-organist – I've got him on the list!
  And the people who eat peppermint and puff it in your
    face,
    They never would be missed – they never would be
      missed!
  Then the idiot who praises, with enthusiastic tone,
  All centuries but this, and every country but his own;
  And the lady from the provinces, who dresses like a guy,
  And who 'doesn't think she waltzes, but would rather like
    to try';
  And that singular anomaly, the lady novelist –
    I don't think she'd be missed – I'm *sure* she'd not be
      missed!

CHORUS: He's got her on the list – he's got her on the list;
    And I don't think she'll be missed – I'm *sure* she'll not
      be missed!

KO.: And that *Nisi Prius*[17] nuisance, who just now is rather
    rife,
  The Judicial humorist – I've got *him* on the list!
  All funny fellows, comic men and clowns of private
    life –
    They'd none of 'em be missed – they'd none of 'em be
      missed.
  And apologetic statesmen[18] of a compromising kind,
  Such as – What d'ye call him – Thing'em-bob, and
    likewise – Never-mind,
  And 'St-'st-'st- and What's-his-name, and also
    You-know-who –
  The task of filling up the blanks I'd rather leave to *you*.
  But it really doesn't matter whom you put upon the
    list,
    For they'd none of 'em be missed – they'd none of
      'em be missed!

CHORUS: You may put 'em on the list – you may put 'em on the
list;
And they'll none of 'em be missed – they'll none of 'em
be missed! [*Exeunt.*]
[*Enter* POOH-BAH.]

KO.: Pooh-Bah, it seems that the festivities in connection with my
approaching marriage must last a week. I should like to do it
handsomely, and I want to consult you as to the amount I ought to
spend upon them.

POOH.: Certainly. In which of my capacities? As First Lord of the
Treasury, Lord Chamberlain,[19] Attorney-General, Chancellor of the
Exchequer, Privy Purse or Private Secretary?

KO.: Suppose we say as Private Secretary.

POOH.: Speaking as your Private Secretary, I should say that, as the
city will have to pay for it, don't stint yourself, do it well.

KO.: Exactly – as the city will have to pay for it. That is your advice.

POOH.: As Private Secretary. Of course you will understand that, as
Chancellor of the Exchequer, I am bound to see that due economy
is observed.

KO.: Oh! But you said just now 'Don't stint yourself, do it well'.

POOH.: As Private Secretary.

KO.: And now you say that due economy must be observed.

POOH.: As Chancellor of the Exchequer.

KO.: I see. Come over here, where the Chancellor can't hear us. [*They
cross the stage.*] Now, as my Solicitor, how do you advise me to
deal with this difficulty?

POOH.: Oh, as your Solicitor, I should have no hesitation in saying
'Chance it –'

KO.: Thank you. [*Shaking his hand.*] I will.

POOH.: If it were not that, as Lord Chief Justice, I am bound to see
that the law isn't violated.

KO.: I see. Come over here where the Chief Justice can't hear us.
[*They cross the stage.*] Now, then, as First Lord of the Treasury?

POOH.: Of course, as First Lord of the Treasury, I could propose a
special vote that would cover all expenses, if it were not that, as
Leader of the Opposition, it would be my duty to resist it, tooth

and nail. Or, as Paymaster-General, I could so cook the accounts that, as Lord High Auditor, I should never discover the fraud. But then, as Archbishop of Titipu, it would be my duty to denounce my dishonesty and give myself into my own custody as First Commissioner of Police.

KO.: That's extremely awkward.

POOH.: I don't say that all these distinguished people couldn't be squared; but it is right to tell you that they wouldn't be sufficiently degraded in their own estimation unless they were insulted with a very considerable bribe.

KO.: The matter shall have my careful consideration. But my bride and her sisters approach, and any little compliment on your part, such as an abject grovel in a characteristic Japanese attitude, would be esteemed a favour. [*Exeunt together.*]

[*Enter procession of* YUM-YUM*'s schoolfellows, heralding* YUM-YUM, PEEP-BO[20] *and* PITTI-SING.]

CHORUS OF GIRLS:

> Comes a train of little ladies
>   From scholastic trammels free,
> Each a little bit afraid is,
>   Wondering what the world can be!
>
> Is it but a world of trouble –
>   Sadness set to song?
> Is its beauty but a bubble
>   Bound to break ere long?
>
> Are its palaces and pleasures
>   Fantasies that fade?
> And the glory of its treasures
>   Shadow of a shade?
>
> Schoolgirls we, eighteen and under,
>   From scholastic trammels free,
> And we wonder – how we wonder! –
>   What on earth the world can be!

TRIO – YUM-YUM, PEEP-BO *and* PITTI-SING,
with CHORUS OF GIRLS

THE THREE:	Three little maids[21] from school are we,
	Pert as a school-girl well can be,
	Filled to the brim with girlish glee,
	Three little maids from school!
YUM.:	Everything is a source of fun. [*Chuckle.*]
PEEP.:	Nobody's safe, for we care for none! [*Chuckle.*]
PITTI.:	Life is a joke that's just begun! [*Chuckle.*]
THE THREE:	Three little maids from school!
ALL [*dancing*]:	Three little maids who, all unwary,
	Come from a ladies' seminary,
	Freed from its genius tutelary[22]
THE THREE [*suddenly demure*]:	
	Three little maids from school!
YUM.:	One little maid is a bride, Yum-Yum –
PEEP.:	Two little maids in attendance come –
PITTI.:	Three little maids is the total sum.
THE THREE:	Three little maids from school!
YUM.:	From three little maids take one away.
PEEP.:	Two little maids remain, and they –
PITTI.:	Won't have to wait very long, they say –
THE THREE:	Three little maids from school!
ALL [*dancing*]:	Three little maids who, all unwary,
	Come from a ladies' seminary,
	Freed from its genius tutelary –
THE THREE [*suddenly demure*]:	
	Three little maids from school!

[*Enter* KO-KO *and* POOH-BAH.]

KO.: At last, my bride that is to be! [*About to embrace her.*]
YUM.: You're not going to kiss me before all these people?
KO.: Well, that was the idea.
YUM. [*aside to* PEEP-BO]: It seems odd, doesn't it?
PEEP.: It's rather peculiar.

PITTI.: Oh, I expect it's all right. Must have a beginning, you know.

YUM.: Well, of course I know nothing about these things; but I've no objection if it's usual.

KO.: Oh, it's quite usual, I think. Eh, Lord Chamberlain? [*Appealing to* POOH-BAH.]

POOH.: I have known it done. [KO-KO *embraces her.*]

YUM.: Thank goodness that's over! [*Sees* NANKI-POO, *and rushes to him.*] Why, that's never you?

[*The three Girls rush to him and shake his hands, all speaking at once.*]

YUM.: Oh, I'm so glad! I haven't seen you for ever so long, and I'm right at the top of the school, and I've got three prizes, and I've come home for good, and I'm not going back any more!

PEEP.: And have you got an engagement? – Yum-Yum's got one, but she doesn't like it, and she'd ever so much rather it was you! I've come home for good, and I'm not going back any more!

PITTI.: Now tell us all the news, because you go about everywhere, and we've been at school, but, thank goodness, that's all over now, and we've come home for good, and we're not going back any more!

[*These three speeches are spoken together in one breath.*]

KO.: I beg your pardon. Will you present me?

YUM.: Oh, this is the musician who used –

PEEP.: Oh, this is the gentleman who used –

PITTI.: Oh, it is only Nanki-Poo who used –

KO.: One at a time, if you please.

YUM.: Oh, if you please he's the gentleman who used to play so beautifully on the – on the –

PITTI.: On the Marine Parade.

YUM.: Yes, I think that was the name of the instrument.

NANK.: Sir, I have the misfortune to love your ward, Yum-Yum – oh, I know I deserve your anger!

KO.: Anger! not a bit, my boy. Why, I love her myself. Charming little girl, isn't she? Pretty eyes, nice hair. Taking little thing, altogether. Very glad to hear my opinion backed by a competent authority. Thank you very much. Good-bye. [*To* PISH-TUSH] Take him away. [PISH-TUSH *removes him.*]

PITTI. [*who has been examining* POOH-BAH]: I beg your pardon, but what is this? Customer come to try on?

KO.: That is a Tremendous Swell.[23]

PITTI.: Oh, it's alive. [*She starts back in alarm.*]

POOH.: Go away, little girls. Can't talk to little girls like you. Go away, there's dears.

KO.: Allow me to present you, Pooh-Bah. These are my three wards. The one in the middle is my bride elect.

POOH.: What do you want me to do to them? Mind, I *will not* kiss them.

KO.: No, no, you shan't kiss them; a little bow – a mere nothing – you needn't mean it, you know.

POOH.: It goes against the grain. They are not young ladies, they are young persons.

KO.: Come, come, make an effort, there's a good nobleman.

POOH. [*aside to* KO-KO]: Well, I shan't mean it. [*With a great effort*] How de do, little girls, how de do? [*Aside*] Oh, my protoplasmal ancestor!

KO.: That's very good. [*Girls indulge in suppressed laughter.*]

POOH.: I see nothing to laugh at. It is very painful to me to have to say 'How de do, little girls, how de do?' to young persons. I'm not in the habit of saying 'How de do, little girls, how de do?' to anybody under the rank of a Stockbroker.

KO. [*aside to girls*]: Don't laugh at him, he can't help it – he's under treatment for it. [*Aside to* POOH-BAH] Never mind them, they don't understand the delicacy of your position.

POOH.: We know how delicate it is, don't we?

KO.: I should think we did! How a nobleman of your importance can do it at all is a thing I never can, never shall understand.

[KO-KO *retires up-stage and goes off.*]

QUARTET *and* CHORUS – YUM-YUM, PEEP-BO,
PITTI-SING, POOH-BAH

YUM., PEEP., PITTI.:

   So please you, Sir, we much regret
   If we have failed in etiquette
   Towards a man of rank so high –
   We shall know better by and by.

YUM.:   But youth, of course, must have its fling,
     So pardon us,
     So pardon us,

PITTI.:   And don't, in girlhood's happy spring,
     Be hard on us,
     Be hard on us,
   If we're inclined to dance and sing.
     Tra la la, etc. [*Dancing.*]

CHORUS OF GIRLS:

   But youth, of course, etc.

POOH.:   I think you ought to recollect
   You cannot show too much respect
   Towards the highly titled few;
   But nobody does, and why should you?
   That youth at us should have its fling,
     Is hard on us,
     Is hard on us;
   To our prerogative we cling –
     So pardon us,
     So pardon us,
   If we decline to dance and sing.
     Tra la la, etc. [*Dancing.*]

CHORUS OF GIRLS:

   But youth, of course, must have its fling, etc.
       [*Exeunt all but* YUM-YUM.]

NANK.: Yum-Yum, at last we are alone! I have sought you night and day for three weeks, in the belief that your guardian was beheaded, and I find that you are about to be married to him this afternoon!

YUM.: Alas, yes!

NANK.: But you do not love him?

YUM.: Alas, no!

NANK.: Modified rapture! But why do you not refuse him?

YUM.: What good would that do? He's my guardian, and he wouldn't let me marry you!

NANK.: But I would wait until you were of age!

YUM.: You forget that in Japan girls do not arrive at years of discretion until they are fifty.

NANK.: True; from seventeen to forty-nine are considered years of indiscretion.

YUM.: Besides – a wandering minstrel, who plays a wind instrument outside tea-houses, is hardly a fitting husband for the ward of a Lord High Executioner.

NANK.: But – [*Aside*] Shall I tell her? Yes! She will not betray me! [*Aloud*] What if it should prove that, after all, I am no musician?

YUM.: There! I was certain of it, directly I heard you play!

NANK.: What if it should prove that I am no other than the son of his Majesty the Mikado?

YUM.: The son of the Mikado! But why is your Highness disguised? And what has your Highness done? And will your Highness promise never to do it again?

NANK.: Some years ago I had the misfortune to captivate Katisha, an elderly lady of my father's Court. She misconstrued my customary affability into expressions of affection, and claimed me in marriage, under my father's law. My father, the Lucius Junius Brutus[24] of his race, ordered me to marry her within a week, or perish ignominiously on the scaffold. That night I fled his Court, and, assuming the disguise of a Second Trombone, I joined the band in which you found me when I had the happiness of seeing you! [*Approaching her.*]

YUM. [*retreating*]: If you please, I think your Highness had better not come too near. The laws against flirting are excessively severe.

NANK.: But we are quite alone, and nobody can see us.

YUM.: Still, that doesn't make it right. To flirt is capital.

NANK.: It *is* capital!

YUM.: And we must obey the law.

NANK.: Deuce take the law!

YUM.: I wish it would, but it won't!

NANK.: If it were not for that, how happy we might be!

YUM.: Happy indeed!

NANK.: If it were not for the law, we should now be sitting side by side, like that. [*Sits by her.*]

YUM.: Instead of being obliged to sit half a mile off, like that. [*Crosses and sits at other side of stage.*]

NANK.: We should be gazing into each other's eyes, like that. [*Gazing at her sentimentally.*]

YUM.: Breathing sighs of unutterable love – like that. [*Sighing and gazing lovingly at him.*]

NANK.: With our arms round each other's waists, like that. [*Embracing her.*]

YUM.: Yes, if it wasn't for the law.

NANK.: If it wasn't for the law.

YUM.: As it is, of course we couldn't do anything of the kind.

NANK.: Not for worlds!

YUM.: Being engaged to Ko-Ko, you know!

NANK.: Being engaged to Ko-Ko!

DUET – YUM-YUM *and* NANKI-POO

YUM.:
    Were I not to Ko-Ko plighted,
      I would say in tender tone,
    'Loved one, let us be united –
      Let us be each other's own!'
    I would say 'Oh, gentle stranger,
      Press me closely to thy heart,
    Sharing every joy and danger,
      We will never part!'

BOTH:
    We will never part!
    We will never part!

YUM.:   But, as I'm to marry Ko-Ko,
        To express my love 'con fuoco'[25]
        Would distinctly be no gioco,[26]
        And for yam I should get toco![27]

BOTH: Toco, toco, toco, toco!

YUM.:   So I will not say, 'Oh, stranger,
            Press me closely to thy heart,
        Sharing every joy and danger,
            We will never, never part!'
        Clearly understand, I pray,
        This is what I never say –
            This – oh, this – oh, this – oh, this –
                This is what I'll never say.

NANK.: Were you not to Ko-Ko plighted
            I should thrill at words like those.
        Joy of joys is love requited,
            Love despised is woe of woes.
        I would merge all rank and station –
            Worldly sneers are nought to us –
        And, to mark my admiration,
            I would kiss you fondly thus – [*Kisses her.*]

BOTH: $\begin{Bmatrix} I \\ He \end{Bmatrix}$ would kiss $\begin{Bmatrix} you \\ me \end{Bmatrix}$ fondly thus –
                        [*kiss*].
        $\begin{Bmatrix} I \\ He \end{Bmatrix}$ would kiss $\begin{Bmatrix} you \\ me \end{Bmatrix}$ fondly thus –
                        [*kiss*].

NANK.: But as you're engaged to Ko-Ko,
        To embrace you thus, *con fuoco*,
        Would distinctly be no *gioco*,
        And for yam I should get toco –

BOTH: Toco, toco, toco, toco!

NANK.: So in spite of all temptation,
Such a theme I'll not discuss,
And on no consideration
Will I kiss you fondly thus – [*kissing her*].
Let me make it clear to you,
This, oh this, oh this, oh this [*kissing her*].
This is what I'll never do!

[*Exeunt in opposite directions.*]

[*Enter Ko-Ko.*]

KO. [*looking after* YUM-YUM]: There she goes! To think how entirely my future happiness is wrapped up in that little parcel! Really, it hardly seems worth while! Oh, matrimony! –

[*Enter* POOH-BAH *and* PISH-TUSH.]

Now then, what is it? Can't you see I'm soliloquizing? You have interrupted an apostrophe, sir!

PISH.: I am the bearer of a letter from his Majesty the Mikado.

KO. [*taking it from him reverentially*]: A letter from the Mikado! What in the world can he have to say to me? [*Reads letter.*] Ah, here it is at last! I thought it would come sooner or later! The Mikado is struck by the fact that no executions have taken place in Titipu for a year, and decrees that unless somebody is beheaded within one month the post of Lord High Executioner shall be abolished, and the city reduced to the rank of a village!

PISH.: But that will involve us all in irretrievable ruin!

KO.: Yes. There is no help for it, I shall have to execute somebody at once. The only question is, who shall it be?

POOH.: Well, it seems unkind to say so, but as you're already under sentence of death for flirting, everything seems to point to *you*.

KO.: To me? What are you talking about? I can't execute myself.

POOH.: Why not?

KO.: Why not? Because, in the first place, self-decapitation is an extremely difficult, not to say dangerous, thing to attempt; and, in the second, it's suicide, and suicide is a capital offence.

POOH.: That is so, no doubt.

PISH.: We might reserve that point.

POOH.: True, it could be argued six months hence, before the full Court.

KO.: Besides, I don't see how a man *can* cut off his own head.

POOH.: A man might try.

PISH.: Even if you only succeeded in cutting it half off, that would be something.

POOH.: It would be taken as an earnest of your desire to comply with the Imperial will.

KO.: No. Pardon me, but there I am adamant. As official Headsman, my reputation is at stake, and I can't consent to embark on a professional operation unless I see my way to a successful result.

POOH.: This professional conscientiousness is highly creditable to *you*, but it places us in a very awkward position.

KO.: My good sir, the awkwardness of your position is grace itself compared with that of a man engaged in the act of cutting off his own head.

PISH.: I am afraid that, unless you can obtain a substitute –

KO.: A substitute? Oh, certainly – nothing easier. [*To* POOH-BAH] Pooh-Bah, I appoint you Lord High Substitute.

POOH.: I should be delighted. Such an appointment would realize my fondest dreams. But no, at any sacrifice I must set bounds to my insatiable ambition!

TRIO

KO-KO	POOH-BAH	PISH-TUSH
My brain it teems	I am so proud,	I heard one day
With endless schemes	If I allowed	A gentleman say
Both good and new	My family pride	That criminals who
For Titipu;	To be my guide,	Are cut in two
But if I flit,	I'd volunteer	Can hardly feel
The benefit	To quit this sphere	The fatal steel,
That I'd diffuse	Instead of you,	And so are slain
The town would lose!	In a minute or two.	Without much pain.
Now every man	But family pride	If this is true,

To aid his clan	Must be denied,	It's jolly for you;
Should plot and plan	And set aside,	Your courage screw
As best he can,	And mortified.	To bid us adieu,
And so,	And so,	And go
Although	Although	And show
I'm ready to go,	I wish to go,	Both friend and foe
Yet recollect	And greatly pine	How much you dare.
'Twere disrespect	To brightly shine,	I'm quite aware
Did I neglect	And take the line	It's your affair,
To thus effect	Of a hero fine,	Yet I declare
This aim direct,	With grief condign	I'd take your share,
So I object –	I must decline –	But I don't much care –
So I object –	I must decline –	I don't much care –
So I object –	I must decline –	I don't much care –

ALL: To sit in solemn silence in a dull, dark dock,
In a pestilential prison, with a life-long lock,
Awaiting the sensation of a short, sharp shock,
From a cheap and chippy chopper on a big black block!

[*Exeunt* POOH. *and* PISH.]

KO.: This is simply appalling! I, who allowed myself to be respited at the last moment, simply in order to benefit my native town, am now required to die within a month, and that by a man whom I have loaded with honours! Is this public gratitude? Is this –

[*Enter* NANKI-POO, *with a rope in his hands.*]

                                               Go away, sir! How dare you? Am I never to be permitted to soliloquize?

NANK.: Oh, go on – don't mind me.

KO.: What are you going to do with that rope?

NANK.: I am about to terminate an unendurable existence.

KO.: Terminate your existence? Oh, nonsense! What for?

NANK.: Because you are going to marry the girl I adore.

KO.: And do you suppose that I am likely to stand quietly by while you deliberately take your life?

NANK.: Please yourself: you can withdraw if you prefer it.

KO.: Withdraw if I prefer it! Are you aware, sir, that I am Lord High

Executioner of this city, and that in that capacity, it is my duty to prevent unnecessary bloodshed?

NANK.: I know nothing about your capacity. I only know that I die to-day.

KO.: Nonsense, sir. I won't permit it. I am a humane man, and if you attempt anything of the kind I shall order your instant arrest. Come, sir, desist at once, or I summon my guard.

NANK.: That's absurd. If you attempt to raise an alarm, I instantly perform the Happy Despatch[28] with this dagger.

KO.: No, no, don't do that. This is horrible! [*Suddenly*] Why you cold-blooded scoundrel, are you aware that, in taking your life, you are committing a crime from which civilization recoils in horror? – a crime which is, in its essence, unmanly, cowardly, and impious? Are you aware that in depriving yourself of an existence which – which – which is – Oh! [*Struck by an idea.*]

NANK.: What's the matter?

KO.: Is it *absolutely certain* that you are resolved to die?

NANK.: Absolutely!

KO.: Will *nothing* shake your resolution?

NANK.: Nothing.

KO.: Threats, entreaties, prayers – all useless?

NANK.: All! My mind is made up.

KO.: Then, if you really mean what you say, and if you are absolutely resolved to die, and if nothing whatever will shake your determination – don't spoil yourself by committing suicide, but be beheaded handsomely at the hands of the Public Executioner!

NANK.: I don't see how that would benefit me.

KO.: You don't? Observe: you'll have a month to live, and you'll live like a fighting-cock at my expense. When the day comes there'll be a grand public ceremonial – you'll be the central figure – no one will attempt to deprive you of that distinction. There'll be a procession – bands – dead march – bells tolling – all the girls in tears – Yum-Yum distracted – then, when it's all over, general rejoicings, and a display of fireworks in the evening. *You* won't see them, but they'll be there all the same.

NANK.: Do you think Yum-Yum would really be distracted at my death?

KO.: I am convinced of it. Bless you, she's the most tender-hearted little creature alive.

NANK.: I should be sorry to cause her pain. Perhaps, after all, if I were to withdraw from Japan, and travel in Europe for a couple of years, I might contrive to forget her.

KO.: Oh, I don't think you could forget Yum-Yum so easily; and, after all, what is more miserable than a love-blighted life?

NANK.: True.

KO.: Life without Yum-Yum – why, it seems absurd!

NANK.: And yet there are a good many people in the world who have to endure it.

KO.: Poor devils, yes! You are quite right not to be of their number.

NANK. [*suddenly*]: I *won't* be of their number!

KO.: Noble fellow!

NANK.: I'll tell you how we'll manage it. Let me marry Yum-Yum to-morrow, and in a month you may behead me.

KO.: No, no. I draw the line at Yum-Yum.

NANK.: Very good. If you can draw the line, so can I. [*Preparing rope.*]

KO.: Stop, stop – listen one moment – be reasonable. How can I consent to your marrying Yum-Yum if I'm going to marry her myself?

NANK.: My good friend, she'll be a widow in a month, and you can marry her then.

KO.: That's true, of course. I quite see that. But, dear me! my position during the next month will be most unpleasant – most unpleasant.

NANK.: Not half so unpleasant as my position at the end of it.

KO.: But – dear me! – well – I agree – after all, it's only putting off my wedding for a month. But you won't prejudice her against me, will you? You see, I've educated her to be my wife; she's been taught to regard me as a wise and good man. Now I shouldn't like her views on that point disturbed.

NANK.: Trust me, she shall never learn the truth from me.

FINALE

[*Enter* CHORUS, POOH-BAH *and* PISH-TUSH.]

CHORUS: With aspect stern
               And gloomy stride,
           We come to learn
               How you decide.

           Don't hesitate
               Your choice to name,
           A dreadful fate
               You'll suffer all the same.

POOH.:   To ask you what you mean to do we punctually appear.

KO.:   Congratulate me, gentlemen, I've found a Volunteer!

ALL: The Japanese equivalent for Hear, Hear, Hear!

KO. [*presenting him*]:
               'Tis Nanki-Poo!

ALL: Hail, Nanki-Poo!

KO.:   I think he'll do?

ALL: Yes, yes, he'll do!

KO.:   He yields his life if I'll Yum-Yum surrender,
           Now I adore that girl with passion tender,
           And could not yield her with a ready will,
               Or her allot,
               If I did not
           Adore myself with passion tenderer still!

[*Enter* YUM-YUM, PEEP-BO *and* PITTI-SING.]

ALL: Ah, yes!
           He loves himself with passion tenderer still!

KO. [*to* NANKI-POO]:
               Take her – she's yours!   [*Exit.*]

ENSEMBLE

NANK.:   The threatened cloud has passed away,
YUM.:   And brightly shines the dawning day;
NANK.:   What though the night may come too soon,
YUM.:   There's yet a month of afternoon!

NANK., POOH., YUM., PITTI., PEEP.:
    Then let the throng
      Our joy advance,
    With laughing song
      And merry dance,

CHORUS: With joyous shout and ringing cheer,
    Inaugurate our brief career!

PITTI.:   A day, a week, a month, a year –
YUM.:   Or far or near, or far or near,
POOH.:   Life's eventime comes much too soon,
PITTI.:   You'll live at least a honeymoon!

ALL: Then let the throng, etc.

CHORUS: With joyous shout, etc.

SOLO

POOH.:   As in a month you've got to die,
      If Ko-Ko tells us true,
    'Twere empty compliment to cry
      'Long life to Nanki-Poo!'
    But as one month you have to live
      As fellow-citizen,
    This toast with three times three we'll give –
      'Long life to you – till then!'

[Exit.]

CHORUS: May all good fortune prosper you,
May you have health and riches too,
May you succeed in all you do!
    Long life to you – till then!

[*Dance.*]

[*Enter* KATISHA *melodramatically.*]

KAT.:   Your revels cease! Assist me, all of you!

CHORUS: Why, who is this whose evil eyes
Rain blight on our festivities?

KAT.:   I claim my perjured lover, Nanki-Poo!
Oh, fool! to shun delights that never cloy!

CHORUS: Go, leave thy deadly work undone!

KAT.:   Come back, oh, shallow fool! come back to joy!

CHORUS: Away, away! ill-favoured one!

NANK. [*aside to* YUM-YUM]:
    Ah!
    'Tis Katisha!
The maid of whom I told you. [*About to go.*]

KAT. [*detaining him*]:
    No!
    You shall not go,
These arms shall thus enfold you!

SONG

KAT. [*addressing* NANKI-POO]:
    Oh fool, that fleest
        My hallowed joys!
    Oh blind, that seest
        No equipoise!
    Oh rash, that judgest
        From half, the whole!
    Oh base, that grudgest
        Love's lightest dole![29]
        Thy heart unbind,
        Oh fool, oh blind!
        Give me my place,
        Oh rash, oh base!

CHORUS: If she's thy bride, restore her place,
               Oh fool, oh blind, oh rash, oh base!

KAT. [*addressing* YUM-YUM]:
               Pink cheek, that rulest
                   Where wisdom serves!
               Bright eye, that foolest
                   Heroic nerves!
               Rose lip, that scornest
                   Lore-laden years!
               Smooth tongue, that warnest
                   Who rightly hears!
                     Thy doom is nigh,
                     Pink cheek, bright eye!
                     Thy knell is rung,
                     Rose lip, smooth tongue!

CHORUS: If true her tale, thy knell is rung,
               Pink cheek, bright eye, rose lip, smooth tongue!

PITTI.:   Away, nor prosecute your quest –
               From our intention, well expressed,
                   You cannot turn us!
               The state of your connubial views
               Towards the person you accuse
                   Does not concern us!
               For he's going to marry Yum-Yum –
ALL: Yum-Yum!
PITTI.:   Your anger pray bury,
                   For all will be merry,
               I think you had better succumb –
ALL: Cumb – cumb!
PITTI.:   And join our expressions of glee.
               On this subject I pray you be dumb –
ALL: Dumb – dumb.
PITTI.:   You'll find there are many
                   Who'll wed for a penny –
               The word for your guidance is 'Mum' –

ALL: Mum – mum!
PITTI.:   There's lots of good fish in the sea!

ALL: On this subject we pray you be dumb, etc.

SOLO

KAT.:   The hour of gladness
                             Is dead and gone;
                         In silent sadness
                             I live alone!
                         The hope I cherished
                             All lifeless lies,
                         And all has perished
                             Save love, which never dies!
                  Oh, faithless one, this insult you shall rue!
                  In vain for mercy on your knees you'll sue.
                        I'll tear the mask from your disguising!

NANK. [*aside:*   Now comes the blow!
KAT.:   Prepare yourselves for new surprising!
NANK. [*aside*]:
                           How foil my foe?
KAT.:   No minstrel he, despite bravado!
YUM. [*aside, struck by an idea*]:
                           Ha! ha! I know!
KAT.:   He is the son of your –
        [NANKI-POO, YUM-YUM *and* CHORUS, *interrupting, sing
        Japanese words, to drown her voice.*]
                     O ni! bikkuri shakkuri to![30]
KAT.:   In vain you interrupt with this tornado!
           He is the only son of your –
ALL: O ni! bikkuri shakkuri to!
KAT.:   I'll spoil –
ALL: O ni! bikkuri shakkuri to!
KAT.:   Your gay gambado![31]
           He is the son –

ALL:	O ni! bikkuri shakkuri to!
KAT.:	Of your –
ALL:	O ni! bikkuri shakkuri to!
KAT.:	The son of your –
ALL:	O ni! bikkuri shakkuri to! oya! oya!

ENSEMBLE

KATISHA

Ye torrents roar!
Ye tempests howl!
Your wrath outpour
With angry growl!
Do ye your worst, my vengeance call
Shall rise triumphant over all!
Prepare for woe,
Ye haughty lords,
At once I go
Mikado-wards,
My wrongs with vengeance shall be
crowned!
My wrongs with vengeance shall be
crowned!

THE OTHERS

We'll hear no more,
Ill-omened owl,
To joy we soar,
Despite your scowl!
The echoes of our festival
Shall rise triumphant over all!
Away you go,
Collect your hordes;
Proclaim your woe
In dismal chords;
We do not heed their dismal sound,

For joy reigns everywhere around.

[KATISHA *rushes furiously up-stage, clearing the crowd away
right and left, finishing on steps at the back of stage.*]

END OF ACT I

ACT II

SCENE – KO-KO's *Garden.*

[YUM-YUM *discovered seated at her bridal toilet, surrounded by maidens, who are dressing her hair and painting her face and lips, as she judges of the effect in a mirror.*]

S O L O – PITTI-SING *and* CHORUS OF GIRLS

CHORUS: Braid the raven hair –
     Weave the supple tress –
Deck the maiden fair
     In her loveliness –
Paint the pretty face –
     Dye the coral lip –
Emphasize the grace
     Of her ladyship!
Art and nature, thus allied,
Go to make a pretty bride.

PITTI.:   Sit with downcast eye –
     Let it brim with dew –
Try if you can cry –
     We will do so, too.
When you're summoned, start
     Like a frightened roe –
Flutter, little heart,
     Colour, come and go!

	Modesty at marriage-tide
	Well becomes a pretty bride!
CHORUS:	Braid the raven hair, etc.
	[*Exeunt* PITTI-SING, PEEP-BO *and* CHORUS.]

YUM.: Yes, I am indeed beautiful! Sometimes I sit and wonder, in my artless Japanese way, why it is that I am so much more attractive than anybody else in the whole world. Can this be vanity? No! Nature is lovely and rejoices in her loveliness. I am a child of Nature, and take after my mother.

SONG

YUM.:

The sun, whose rays
Are all ablaze
　With ever-living glory,
Does not deny
His majesty –
　He scorns to tell a story!
He don't exclaim,
　'I blush for shame,
　So kindly be indulgent.'
But, fierce and bold,
In fiery gold,
　He glories all effulgent!

　　I mean to rule the earth,
　　　As he the sky –
　　We really know our worth,
　　　The sun and I!

Observe his flame,
That placid dame,
　The moon's Celestial Highness;
There's not a trace
Upon her face
　Of diffidence or shyness:
She borrows light

That, through the night,
  Mankind may all acclaim her!
And, truth to tell,
She lights up well,
  So I, for one, don't blame her!

  Ah, pray make no mistake,
    We are not shy;
  We're very wide awake,
    The moon and I!

[*Enter* PITTI-SING *and* PEEP-BO.]

Yes, everything seems to smile upon me. I am to be married to-day to the man I love best, and I believe I am the very happiest girl in Japan!

PEEP.: The happiest girl indeed, for she is indeed to be envied who has attained happiness in all but perfection.

YUM.: In 'all but' perfection?

PEEP.: Well, dear, it can't be denied that the fact that your husband is to be beheaded in a month is, in its way, a drawback. It does seem to take the top off it, you know.

PITTI.: I don't know about that. It all depends!

PEEP.: At all events, *he* will find it a drawback.

PITTI.: Not necessarily. Bless you, it all depends!

YUM. [*in tears*]: I think it very indelicate of you to refer to such a subject on such a day. If my married happiness *is* to be – to be –

PEEP.: Cut short.

YUM.: Well, cut short – in a month, can't you let me forget it? [*Weeping.*]

[*Enter* NANKI-POO, *followed by* PISH-TUSH.]

NANK.: Yum-Yum in tears – and on her wedding morn!

YUM. [*sobbing*]: They've been reminding me that in a month you're to be beheaded! [*Bursts into tears.*]

PITTI.: Yes, we've been reminding her that you're to be beheaded. [*Bursts into tears.*]

PEEP.: It's quite true, you know, you *are* to be beheaded! [*Bursts into tears.*]

NANK. [*aside*]: Humph! Now, some bridegrooms would be depressed by this sort of thing! [*Aloud*] A month? Well, what's a month? Bah! These divisions of time are purely arbitrary. Who says twenty-four hours make a day?

PITTI.: There's a popular impression to that effect.

NANK.: Then we'll efface it. We'll call each second a minute – each minute an hour – each hour a day – and each day a year. At that rate we've about thirty years of married happiness before us!

PEEP.: And, at that rate, this interview has already lasted four hours and three-quarters! [*Exit.*]

YUM. [*still sobbing*]: Yes. How time flies when one is thoroughly enjoying oneself!

NANK.: That's the way to look at it! Don't let's be downhearted! There's a silver lining to every cloud.

YUM.: Certainly. Let's – let's be perfectly happy! [*Almost in tears.*]

PISH.: [32]By all means. Let's – let's thoroughly enjoy ourselves.

PITTI.: It's – it's absurd to cry! [*Trying to force a laugh.*]

YUM.: Quite ridiculous! [*Trying to laugh.*]

[*All break into a forced and melancholy laugh.*]

MADRIGAL – YUM-YUM, PITTI-SING, NANKI-POO,
PISH-TUSH

> Brightly dawns our wedding day;
>> Joyous hour, we give thee greeting!
>> Whither, whither art thou fleeting?
> Fickle moment, prithee stay!
>> What though mortal joys be hollow?
>> Pleasures come, if sorrows follow:
> Though the tocsin[33] sound, ere long,
>> Ding dong! Ding dong!
> Yet until the shadows fall
> Over one and over all,
> Sing a merry madrigal –
>> A madrigal!
> Fal-la – fal-la! etc. [*Ending in tears.*]

Let us dry the ready tear,
   Though the hours are surely creeping
   Little need for woeful weeping,
Till the sad sundown is near.
   All must sip the cup of sorrow –
   I to-day and thou to-morrow;
This the close of every song –
   Ding dong! Ding dong!
What, though solemn shadows fall,
Sooner, later, over all?
Sing a merry madrigal –
           A madrigal!
Fal-la – fal-la! etc. [*Ending in tears.*]

             [*Exeunt* PITTI-SING *and* PISH-TUSH.]

[NANKI-POO *embraces* YUM-YUM. *Enter* KO-KO. NANKI-POO *releases* YUM-YUM.]

KO.: Go on – don't mind me.

NANK.: I'm afraid we're distressing you.

KO.: Never mind, I must get used to it. Only please do it by degrees. Begin by putting your arm round her waist. [NANKI-POO *does so.*] There; let me get used to that first.

YUM.: Oh, wouldn't you like to retire? It must pain you to see us so affectionate together!

KO.: No, I must learn to bear it! Now oblige me by allowing her head to rest on your shoulder.

NANK.: Like that? [*He does so.* KO-KO *much affected.*]

KO.: I am much obliged to you. Now – kiss her! [*He does so.* KO-KO *writhes with anguish.*] Thank you – it's simple torture!

YUM.: Come, come, bear up. After all, it's only for a month.

KO.: No. It's no use deluding oneself with false hopes.

NANK.:
YUM.: } What do you mean?

KO. [*to* YUM-YUM]: My child – my poor child! [*Aside*] How shall I break it to her? [*Aloud*] My little bride that was to have been –

YUM. [*delighted*]: *Was* to have been?

KO.: Yes, you never can be mine!

⎰ NANK.: *[in ecstasy]:* What!
⎱ YUM.: I'm so glad!

KO.: I've just ascertained that, by the Mikado's law, when a married man is beheaded his wife is buried alive.

NANK.: ⎫
YUM.: ⎭ Buried alive!

KO.: Buried alive. It's a most unpleasant death.

NANK.: But whom did you get that from?

KO.: Oh, from Pooh-Bah. He's my Solicitor.

YUM.: But he may be mistaken!

KO.: So I thought; so I consulted the Attorney-General,[34] the Lord Chief Justice,[35] the Master of the Rolls,[36] the Judge Ordinary[37] and the Lord Chancellor.[38] They're all of the same opinion. Never knew such unanimity on a point of law in my life!

NANK.: But stop a bit! This law has never been put in force.

KO.: Not yet. You see, flirting is the only crime punishable with decapitation, and married men never flirt.

NANK.: Of course, they don't. I quite forgot that! Well, I suppose I may take it that my dream of happiness is at an end!

YUM.: Darling – I don't want to appear selfish, and I love you with all my heart – I don't suppose I shall ever love anybody else half as much – but when I agreed to marry you – my own – I had no idea – pet – that I should have to be buried alive in a month!

NANK.: Nor I! It's the very first I've heard of it!

YUM.: It – it makes a difference, doesn't it?

NANK.: It *does* make a difference, of course.

YUM.: You see – burial alive – it's such a stuffy death!

NANK.: I call it a beast of a death.

YUM.: You see my difficulty, don't you?

NANK.: Yes, and I see my own. If I insist on your carrying out your promise, I doom you to a hideous death; if I release you, you marry Ko-Ko at once!

TRIO – YUM-YUM, NANKI-POO *and* KO-KO

YUM.:
    Here's a how-de-do!
    If I marry you,
When your time has come to perish,
Then the maiden whom you cherish
    Must be slaughtered, too!
    Here's a how-de-do!

NANK.:
    Here's a pretty mess!
    In a month, or less,
I must die without a wedding!
Let the bitter tears I'm shedding
    Witness my distress,
    Here's a pretty mess!

KO.:
    Here's a state of things!
    To her life she clings!
Matrimonial devotion
Doesn't seem to suit her notion –
    Burial it brings!
    Here's a state of things!

ENSEMBLE

YUM-YUM *and* NANKI-POO	KO-KO
With a passion that's intense	With a passion that's intense
I worship and adore,	You worship and adore,
But the laws of common sense	But the laws of common sense
We oughtn't to ignore.	You oughtn't to ignore.
If what he says is true,	If what I say is true,
'Tis death to marry you!	'Tis death to marry you!
Here's a pretty state of things!	Here's a pretty state of things!
Here's a pretty how-de-do!	Here's a pretty how-de-do!

[*Exit* YUM-YUM.]

KO. [*going up to* NANKI-POO]: My poor boy, I'm really very sorry for you.

NANK.: Thanks, old fellow. I'm sure you are.

KO.: You see I'm quite helpless.

NANK.: I quite see that.

KO.: I can't conceive anything more distressing than to have one's marriage broken off at the last moment. But you shan't be disappointed of a wedding – you shall come to mine.

NANK.: It's awfully kind of you, but that's impossible.

KO.: Why so?

NANK.: To-day I die.

KO.: What do you mean?

NANK.: I can't live without Yum-Yum. This afternoon I perform the Happy Despatch.

KO.: No, no – pardon me – I can't allow that.

NANK.: Why not?

KO.: Why, hang it all, you're under contract to die by the hand of the Public Executioner in a month's time! If you kill yourself, what's to become of me? Why, I shall have to be executed in your place!

NANK.: It would certainly seem so!

[*Enter* POOH-BAH.]

KO.: Now then, Lord Mayor, what is it?

POOH.: The Mikado and his suite are approaching the city, and will be here in ten minutes.

KO.: The Mikado! He's coming to see whether his orders have been carried out! [*To* NANKI-POO] Now look here, you know – this is getting serious – a bargain's a bargain, and you really mustn't frustrate the ends of justice by committing suicide. As a man of honour and a gentleman, you are bound to die ignominiously by the hands of the Public Executioner.

NANK.: Very well, then – behead me.

KO.: What, now?

NANK.: Certainly; at once.

POOH.: Chop it off! Chop it off!

KO.: My good sir, I don't go about prepared to execute gentlemen at a moment's notice. Why, I never even killed a blue-bottle!

POOH.: Still, as Lord High Executioner –

KO.: My good sir, as Lord High Executioner, I've got to behead him in a month. I'm not ready yet. I don't know how it's done. I'm going to take lessons. I mean to begin with a guinea pig, and work my way through the animal kingdom till I come to a Second Trombone. Why, you don't suppose that, as a humane man, I'd have accepted the post of Lord High Executioner if I hadn't thought the duties were purely nominal? I *can't* kill you – I can't kill anything! I can't kill anybody! [*Weeps.*]

NANK.: Come, my poor fellow, your feelings do you credit, but you must nerve yourself to this – you must, indeed. We all have unpleasant duties to discharge at times; and when these duties present themselves we must nerve ourselves to an effort. Come, now – after all, what is it? If I don't mind, why should you? Remember, sooner or later it must be done.

KO. [*springing up suddenly*]: *Must it?* I'm not so sure about that!

NANK.: What do you mean?

KO.: Why should I kill you when making an affidavit that you've been executed will do just as well? Here are plenty of witnesses – the Lord Chief Justice, Lord High Admiral, Commander-in-Chief, Secretary of State for the Home Department, First Lord of the Treasury and Chief Commissioner of Police.

NANK.: But where are they?

KO.: There they are. They'll all swear to it – [*to* POOH-BAH] won't you?

POOH.: Am I to understand that all of us high Officers of State are required to perjure ourselves to ensure your safety?

KO.: Why not? You'll be grossly insulted, as usual.

POOH.: Will the insult be cash down, or at a date?

KO.: It will be a ready-money transaction.

POOH. [*aside*]: Well, it will be a useful discipline. [*Aloud*] Very good. Choose your fiction, and I'll endorse it! [*Aside*] Ha! ha! Family Pride, how do you like *that*, my buck?

NANK.: But I tell you that life without Yum-Yum –

KO.: Oh, Yum-Yum, Yum-Yum! Bother Yum-Yum! Here, Commissionaire,[39] [*to* POOH-BAH] go and fetch Yum-Yum.

[*Exit* POOH-BAH.]
Take Yum-Yum

and marry Yum-Yum, only go away and never come back again.

[*Enter* POOH-BAH *with* YUM-YUM.]

Here she is. Yum-Yum, are you particularly busy?

YUM.: Not particularly.

KO.: You've five minutes to spare?

YUM.: Yes.

KO.: Then go along with his Grace the Archbishop of Titipu; he'll marry you at once.

YUM.: But if I'm to be buried alive?

KO.: Now, don't ask any questions, but do as I tell you, and Nanki-Poo will explain all.

NANK.: But one moment –

KO.: Not for worlds. Here comes the Mikado, no doubt to ascertain whether I've obeyed his decree, and if he finds you alive I shall have the greatest difficulty in persuading him that I've beheaded you.

[*Exeunt* NANKI-POO *and* YUM-YUM, *followed by* POOH-BAH.]

Close thing that, for here he comes!

[*Exit* KO-KO.]

[*March – Enter procession, heralding the* MIKADO OF JAPAN, *with* KATISHA.]

[*Entrance of* MIKADO *and* KATISHA.]

('*March of the Mikado's troops.*')

CHORUS:

Miya sama,[40] miya sama,
On n'm-ma no mayé ni
Pira-Pira suru no wa
Nan gia na
Toko tonyaré tonyaré na?

DUET – MIKADO *and* KATISHA

MIK.:

From every kind of man
    Obedience I expect;
I'm the Emperor of Japan –

KAT.:   And I'm his daughter-in-law elect!
 He'll marry his son
 (He's only got one)
To his daughter-in-law elect.

MIK.:   My morals have been declared
 Particularly correct;

KAT.:   But they're nothing at all, compared
 With those of his daughter-in-law elect!
  Bow – Bow –
 To his daughter-in-law elect!

ALL: Bow – Bow –
 To his daughter-in-law elect.

MIK.:   In a fatherly kind of way
 I govern each tribe and sect,
All cheerfully own my sway –

KAT.:   Except his daughter-in-law elect!
 As tough as a bone,
 With a will of her own,
Is his daughter-in-law elect!

MIK.:   My nature is love and light –
 My freedom from all defect –

KAT.:   Is insignificant quite,
 Compared with his daughter-in-law elect!
  Bow – Bow –
 To his daughter-in-law elect!

ALL: Bow – Bow –
 To his daughter-in-law elect!

SONG[41] – MIKADO *and* CHORUS

A more humane Mikado never
  Did in Japan exist,
    To nobody second,
    I'm certainly reckoned
  A true philanthropist.
It is my very humane endeavour
  To make, to some extent,
    Each evil liver
    A running river
  Of harmless merriment.

    My object all sublime
    I shall achieve in time –
  To let the punishment fit the crime –
      The punishment fit the crime;
    And make each prisoner pent
    Unwillingly represent
  A source of innocent merriment!
    Of innocent merriment!

All prosy dull society sinners,
  Who chatter and bleat and bore,
    Are sent to hear sermons
    From mystical Germans[42]
  Who preach from ten till four.
The amateur tenor, whose vocal villainies
  All desire to shirk,
    Shall, during off-hours,
    Exhibit his powers
  To Madame Tussaud's waxwork.[43]

The lady who dies a chemical yellow,
  Or stains her grey hair puce,
    Or pinches her figger,
    Is blacked like a nigger[44]

With permanent walnut juice.
The idiot who, in railway carriages,
    Scribbles on window-panes,
        We only suffer
        To ride on a buffer
    In Parliamentary trains.[45]

        My object all sublime, etc.

CHORUS: His object all sublime, etc.

The advertising quack who wearies
    With tales of countless cures,
        His teeth, I've enacted,
        Shall all be extracted
    By terrified amateurs.
The music-hall singer attends a series
    Of masses and fugues and 'ops'
        By Bach,[46] interwoven
        With Spohr[47] and Beethoven,
    At classical Monday Pops.[48]

The billiard sharp whom any one catches,
    His doom's extremely hard –
        He's made to dwell –
        In a dungeon cell
    On a spot that's always barred.
And there he plays extravagant matches
    In fitless finger-stalls[49]
        On a cloth untrue,
        With a twisted cue
    And elliptical billiard balls!

        My object all sublime, etc.

CHORUS: His object all sublime, etc.

[*Enter* POOH-BAH, KO-KO *and* PITTI-SING. *All kneel.* POOH-BAH *hands a paper to* KO-KO.]

KO.: I am honoured in being permitted to welcome your Majesty. I guess the object of your Majesty's visit – your wishes have been attended to. The execution has taken place.

MIK.: Oh, you've had an execution, have you?

KO.: Yes. The Coroner has just handed me his certificate.

POOH.: I am the Coroner. [KO-KO *hands certificate to* MIKADO.]

MIK.: And this is the certificate of his death. [*Reads*] 'At Titipu, in the presence of the Lord Chancellor, Lord Chief Justice, Attorney-General, Secretary of State for the Home Department, Lord Mayor and Groom of the Second Floor Front –'

POOH.: They were all present, your Majesty. I counted them myself.

MIK.: Very good house. I wish I'd been in time for the performance.

KO.: A tough fellow he was, too – a man of gigantic strength. His struggles were terrific. It was really a remarkable scene.

MIK.: Describe it.

TRIO *and* CHORUS – KO-KO, PITTI-SING, POOH-BAH, CHORUS

KO.:
The criminal cried, as he dropped him down,
   In a state of wild alarm –
With a frightful, frantic, fearful frown,
   I bared my big right arm.
I seized him by his little pig-tail,
   And on his knees fell he,
     As he squirmed and struggled,
     And gurgled and guggled,
   I drew my snickersnee![50]
      Oh, never shall I
      Forget the cry,
   Or the shriek that shriekèd he,
     As I gnashed my teeth,
     When from its sheath
   I drew my snickersnee!

CHORUS:
> We know him well,
>   He cannot tell
> Untrue or groundless tales –
>   He always tries
>   To utter lies,
> And every time he fails.

PITTI.:
> He shivered and shook as he gave the sign
>   For the stroke he didn't deserve;
> When all of a sudden his eye met mine,
>   And it seemed to brace his nerve;
> For he nodded his head and kissed his hand,
>   And he whistled an air,[51] did he,
>   As the sabre true
>   Cut cleanly through
>   His cervical vertebrae!
>
>   When a man's afraid,
>   A beautiful maid
>   Is a cheering sight to see;
>   And it's oh, I'm glad
>   That moment sad
>   Was soothed by sight of me!

CHORUS:
>   Her terrible tale
>   You can't assail,
>   With truth it quite agrees:
>   Her taste exact
>   For faultless fact
>   Amounts to a disease.

POOH.:
> Now though you'd have said that head was dead
>   (For its owner dead was he),
> It stood on its neck, with a smile well-bred,
>   And bowed three times to me!
> It was none of your impudent off-hand nods,
>   But as humble as could be;

> For it clearly knew
> The deference due
> To a man of pedigree!
> And it's oh, I vow,
> This deathly bow
> Was a touching sight to see;
> Though trunkless, yet
> It couldn't forget
> The deference due to me!

CHORUS:

> This haughty youth,
> He speaks the truth
> Whenever he finds it pays:
> And in this case
> It all took place
> Exactly as he says!   [*Exeunt.*]

MIK.: All this is very interesting, and I should like to have seen it. But we came about a totally different matter. A year ago my son, the heir to the throne of Japan, bolted from our Imperial Court.

KO.: Indeed! Had he any reason to be dissatisfied with his position?

KAT.: None whatever. On the contrary, I was going to marry him – yet he fled!

POOH.: I am surprised that he should have fled from one so lovely!

KAT.: That's not true.

POOH.: No!

KAT.: You hold that I am not beautiful because my face is plain. But you know nothing; you are still unenlightened. Learn, then, that it is not in the face alone that beauty is to be sought. My face is unattractive!

POOH.: It is.

KAT.: But I have a left shoulder-blade that is a miracle of loveliness. People come miles to see it. My right elbow has a fascination that few can resist.

POOH.: Allow me!

KAT.: It is on view Tuesdays and Fridays, on presentation of visiting card. As for my circulation, it is the largest in the world.

KO.: And yet he fled!

MIK.: And is now masquerading in this town, disguised as a Second Trombone.

KO., POOH. and PITTI.: A Second Trombone!

MIK.: Yes; would it be troubling you too much if I asked you to produce him? He goes by the name of –

KAT.: Nanki-Poo.

MIK.: Nanki-Poo.

KO.: It's quite easy. That is, it's rather difficult. In point of fact, he's gone abroad!

MIK.: Gone abroad! His address.

KO.: Knightsbridge![52]

KAT. [who is reading certificate of death]: Ha!

MIK.: What's the matter?

KAT.: See here – his name – Nanki-Poo – beheaded this morning. Oh, where shall I find another? Where shall I find another?

[KO-KO, POOH-BAH and PITTI-SING fall on their knees.]

MIK. [looking at paper]: Dear, dear, dear! this is very tiresome. [To KO-KO] My poor fellow, in your anxiety to carry out my wishes you have beheaded the heir to the throne of Japan!

KO.: I beg to offer an unqualified apology.

POOH.: I desire to associate myself with that expression of regret.

PITTI.: We really hadn't the least notion –

MIK.: Of course you hadn't. How could you? Come, come, my good fellow, don't distress yourself – it was no fault of yours. If a man of exalted rank chooses to disguise himself as a Second Trombone, he must take the consequences. It really distresses me to see you take on so. I've no doubt he thoroughly deserved all he got. [They rise.]

KO.: We are infinitely obliged to your Majesty –

PITTI.: Much obliged, your Majesty.

POOH.: Very much obliged, your Majesty.

MIK.: Obliged? not a bit. Don't mention it. How could you tell?

POOH.: No, of course we couldn't tell who the gentleman really was.

PITTI.: It wasn't written on his forehead, you know.

KO.: It might have been on his pocket-handkerchief, but Japanese don't use pocket-handkerchiefs! Ha! ha! ha!

MIK.: Ha! ha! ha! [*To* KATISHA] I forget the punishment for compassing the death of the Heir Apparent.

KO., POOH. *and* PITTI.: Punishment. [*They drop down on their knees again.*]

MIK.: Yes. Something lingering, with boiling oil in it, I fancy. Something of that sort. I think boiling oil occurs in it, but I'm not sure. I know it's something humorous, but lingering, with either boiling oil or melted lead. Come, come, don't fret – I'm not a bit angry.

KO. [*in abject terror*]: If your Majesty will accept our assurance, we had no idea –

MIK.: Of course –

PITTI.: I knew nothing about it.

POOH.: I wasn't there.

MIK.: That's the pathetic part of it. Unfortunately, the fool of an Act says 'compassing the death of the Heir Apparent'. There's not a word about a mistake –

KO., PITTI. *and* POOH.: No!

MIK.: Or not knowing –

KO.: No!

MIK.: Or having no notion –

PITTI.: No!

MIK.: Or not being there –

POOH.: No!

MIK.: There should be, of course –

KO., PITTI. *and* POOH.: Yes!

MIK.: But there isn't.

KO., PITTI. *and* POOH.: Oh!

MIK.: That's the slovenly way in which these Acts are always drawn. However, cheer up, it'll be all right. I'll have it altered next session. Now, let's see about your execution – will after luncheon suit you? Can you wait till then?

KO., PITTI. *and* POOH.: Oh, yes – we can wait till then!

MIK.: Then we'll make it after luncheon.

POOH.: I don't want any lunch.

MIK.: I'm really very sorry for you all, but it's an unjust world, and virtue is triumphant only in theatrical performances.

GLEE – PITTI-SING, KATISHA, KO-KO, POOH-BAH, MIKADO

MIK.: See how the Fates their gifts allot,
For A is happy – B is not.
Yet B is worthy, I dare say,
Of more prosperity than A!

KO., POOH. *and* PITTI.:
Is B more worthy?

KAT.: I should say
He's worth a great deal more than A.

ENSEMBLE: Yet A is happy!
Oh, so happy!
Laughing, Ha! ha!
Chaffing, Ha! ha!
Nectar quaffing, Ha! ha! ha!
Ever joyous, ever gay,
Happy, undeserving A!

KO., POOH *and* PITTI.:
If I were Fortune – which I'm not –
B should enjoy A's happy lot,
And A should die in miserie –
That is, assuming I am B.

MIK. *and* KAT.: But *should* A perish?

KO., POOH. *and* PITTI.: That should he
(Of course, assuming I am B).
B should be happy!
Oh, so happy!
Laughing, Ha! ha!
Chaffing, Ha! ha!
Nectar quaffing, Ha! ha! ha!
But condemned to die is he,
Wretched meritorious B!

[*Exeunt* MIKADO *and* KATISHA.]

KO.: Well, a nice mess you've got us into, with your nodding head and the deference due to a man of pedigree!

POOH:: Merely corroborative detail, intended to give artistic verisimilitude to an otherwise bald and unconvincing narrative.

PITTI.: Corroborative detail indeed! Corroborative fiddlestick!

KO.: And you're just as bad as he is with your cock-and-a-bull stories about catching his eye and his whistling an air. But that's so like you! You must put in your oar!

POOH.: But how about your big right arm?

PITTI.: Yes, and your snickersnee!

KO.: Well, well, never mind that now. There's only one thing to be done. Nanki-Poo hasn't started yet – he must come to life again at once.

[*Enter* NANKI-POO *and* YUM-YUM *prepared for journey.*]

Here he comes. Here, Nanki-Poo, I've good news for you – you're reprieved.

NANK.: Oh, but it's too late. I'm a dead man, and I'm off for my honeymoon.

KO.: Nonsense! A terrible thing has just happened. It seems you're the son of the Mikado.

NANK.: Yes, but that happened some time ago.

KO.: Is this a time for airy persiflage? Your father is here, and with Katisha!

NANK.: My father! And with Katisha!

KO.: Yes, he wants you particularly.

POOH.: So does she.

YUM.: Oh, but he's married now.

KO.: But, bless my heart! what has that to do with it?

NANK.: Katisha claims me in marriage, but I can't marry her because I'm married already – consequently she will insist on my execution, and if I'm executed, my wife will have to be buried alive.

YUM.: You see our difficulty.

KO.: Yes. I don't know what's to be done.

NANK.: There's one chance for you. If you could persuade Katisha to marry you, she would have no further claim on me, and in that case I could come to life without any fear of being put to death.

KO.: I marry Katisha!

YUM.: I really think it's the only course.

KO.: But, my good girl, have you seen her? She's something appalling!

PITTI.: Ah! that's only her face. She has a left elbow which people come miles to see!

POOH.: I am told that her right heel is much admired by connoisseurs.

KO.: My good sir, I decline to pin my heart upon any lady's right heel.

NANK.: It comes to this: While Katisha is single, I prefer to be a disembodied spirit. When Katisha is married, existence will be as welcome as the flowers in spring.

DUET[53] – NANKI-POO *and* KO-KO
[*with* YUM-YUM, PITTI-SING *and* POOH-BAH]

NANK.:   The flowers that bloom in the spring,
                Tra la,
        Breathe promise of merry sunshine –
      As we merrily dance and we sing,
                Tra la,
      We welcome the hope that they bring,
                Tra la,
        Of a summer of roses and wine.
          And that's what we mean when we say that a
            thing
          Is welcome as flowers that bloom in the spring.
                Tra la la la la la, etc.

ALL: Tra la la la, etc.

KO.:   The flowers that bloom in the spring,
                Tra la,
        Have nothing to do with the case.
      I've got to take under my wing,
                Tra la,
      A most unattractive old thing,
                Tra la,

With a caricature of a face
And that's what I mean when I say, or I sing,
'Oh, bother the flowers that bloom in the spring.'
Tra la la la la la, etc.

ALL: Tra la la la, Tra la la la, etc.

[*Dance and exeunt* NANKI-POO, YUM-YUM, POOH-BAH,
PITTI-SING *and* KO-KO.]

[*Enter* KATISHA.]

RECITATIVE *and* SONG

KAT.: Alone, and yet alive! Oh, sepulchre!
My soul is still my body's prisoner!
Remote the peace that Death alone can give –
My doom, to wait! my punishment, to live!

SONG

KAT.: Hearts do not break!
They sting and ache
For old love's sake,
But do not die,
Though with each breath
They long for death
As witnesseth
The living I!
Oh, living I!
Come, tell me why,
When hope is gone,
Dost thou stay on?
Why linger here,
Where all is drear?
Oh, living I!
Come, tell me why,
When hope is gone,
Dost thou stay on?
May not a cheated maiden die?

KO. [*entering and approaching her timidly*]: Katisha!

KAT.: The miscreant who robbed me of my love! But vengeance pursues – they are heating the cauldron!

KO.: Katisha – behold a suppliant at your feet! Katisha – mercy!

KAT.: Mercy? Had you mercy on him? See here, you! You have slain my love. He did not love *me*, but he would have loved me in time. I am an acquired taste – only the educated palate can appreciate *me*. I was educating *his* palate when he left me. Well, he is dead, and where shall I find another? It takes years to train a man to love me. Am I to go through the weary round again, and, at the same time, implore mercy for you who robbed me of my prey – I mean my pupil – just as his education was on the point of completion? Oh, where shall I find another?

KO. [*suddenly, and with great vehemence*]: Here! – Here!

KAT.: What!!!

KO. [*with intense passion*]: Katisha, for years I have loved you with a white-hot passion that is slowly but surely consuming my very vitals! Ah, shrink not from me! If there is aught of woman's mercy in your heart, turn not away from a love-sick suppliant whose every fibre thrills at your tiniest touch! True it is that, under a poor mask of disgust, I have endeavoured to conceal a passion whose inner fires are broiling the soul within me! But the fire will not be smothered – it defies all attempts at extinction, and, breaking forth, all the more eagerly for its long restraint, it declares itself in words that will not be weighed – that cannot be schooled – that should not be too severely criticized. Katisha, I dare not hope for your love – but I will not live without it! Darling!

KAT.: You, whose hands still reek with the blood of my betrothed, dare to address words of passion to the woman you have so foully wronged!

KO.: I do – accept my love, or I perish on the spot!

KAT.: Go to! Who knows so well as I that no one ever yet died of a broken heart!

KO.: You know not what you say. Listen!

SONG [54]

KO.:   On a tree by a river a little tom-tit
           Sang 'Willow, titwillow, titwillow!'
    And I said to him, 'Dicky-bird, why do you sit
           Singing "Willow, titwillow, titwillow"?'
    'Is it weakness of intellect, birdie?' I cried,
    'Or a rather tough worm in your little inside?'
    With a shake of his poor little head, he replied,
           'Oh, willow, titwillow, titwillow!'

    He slapped at his chest, as he sat on that bough,
           Singing 'Willow, titwillow, titwillow!'
    And a cold perspiration bespangled his brow,
           Oh, willow, titwillow, titwillow!
    He sobbed and he sighed, and a gurgle he gave,
    Then he plunged himself into the billowy wave,
    And an echo arose from the suicide's grave –
           'Oh, willow, titwillow, titwillow!'

    Now I feel just as sure as I'm sure that my name
           Isn't Willow, titwillow, titwillow,
    That 'twas blighted affection that made him exclaim,
           'Oh, willow, titwillow, titwillow!'
    And if you remain callous and obdurate, I
    Shall perish as he did, and you will know why,
    Though I probably shall not exclaim as I die,
           'Oh, willow, titwillow, titwillow!'

[*During this song* KATISHA *has been greatly affected, and at the end is almost in tears.*]

KAT. [*whimpering*]: Did he really die of love?
KO.: He really did.
KAT.: All on account of a cruel little hen?
KO.: Yes.
KAT.: Poor little chap!
KO.: It's an affecting tale, and quite true. I knew the bird intimately.

KAT.: Did you? He must have been very fond of her.

KO.: His devotion was something extraordinary.

KAT. [*still whimpering*]: Poor little chap! And – and if I refuse you, will you go and do the same?

KO.: At once.

KAT.: No, no – you mustn't! Anything but that! [*Falls on his breast.*] Oh, I'm a silly little goose!

KO. [*making a wry face*]: You are!

KAT.: And you won't hate me because I'm just a little teeny weeny wee bit bloodthirsty, will you?

KO.: Hate you? Oh, Katisha! is there not beauty even in blood-thirstiness?

KAT.: My idea exactly.

DUET – KATISHA *and* KO-KO

KAT.:   There is beauty in the bellow of the blast,
      There is grandeur in the growling of the gale,
          There is eloquent outpouring
          When the lion is a-roaring,
      And the tiger is a-lashing of his tail!

KO.:   Yes, I like to see a tiger
          From the Congo[55] or the Niger,
      And especially when lashing of his tail!

KAT.:   Volcanoes have a splendour that is grim,
      And earthquakes only terrify the dolts,
          But to him who's scientific
          There's nothing that's terrific
      In the falling of a flight of thunderbolts!

KO.:   Yes, in spite of all my meekness,
          If I have a little weakness,
      It's a passion for a flight of thunderbolts!

BOTH: If that is so,
          Sing derry down derry!
          It's evident, very,
             Our tastes are one.

Away we'll go,
And merrily marry,
Nor tardily tarry
Till day is done!

KO.: There is beauty in extreme old age –
Do you fancy you are elderly enough?
Information I'm requesting
On a subject interesting:
Is a maiden all the better when she's tough?

KAT.: Throughout this wide dominion
It's the general opinion
That she'll last a good deal longer when she's tough.

KO.: Are you old enough to marry, do you think?
Won't you wait till you are eighty in the shade?
There's a fascination frantic
In a ruin that's romantic;
Do you think you are sufficiently decayed?

KAT.: To the matter that you mention
I have given some attention,
And I think I am sufficiently decayed.

BOTH: If that is so,
Sing derry down derry!
It's evident, very,
Our tastes are one!
Away we'll go,
And merrily marry,
Nor tardily tarry
Till day is done!

[*Exeunt together.*]

[*Flourish. Enter the* MIKADO, *attended by* PISH-TUSH *and Court.*]

MIK.: Now then, we've had a capital lunch, and we're quite ready. Have all the painful preparations been made?

PISH.: Your Majesty, all is prepared.

MIK.: Then produce the unfortunate gentleman and his two well-meaning but misguided accomplices.

[*Enter* KO-KO, KATISHA, POOH-BAH *and* PITTI-SING. *They throw themselves at the* MIKADO's *feet.*]

KAT.: Mercy! Mercy for Ko-Ko! Mercy for Pitti-Sing! Mercy even for Pooh-Bah!

MIK.: I beg your pardon, I don't think I quite caught that remark.

POOH.: Mercy even for Pooh-Bah.

KAT.: Mercy! My husband that was to have been is dead, and I have just married this miserable object.

MIK.: Oh! You've not been long about it!

KO.: We were married before the Registrar.

POOH.: *I* am the Registrar.

MIK.: I see. But my difficulty is that, as you have slain the Heir Apparent –

[*Enter* NANKI-POO *and* YUM-YUM. *They kneel.*]

NANK.: The Heir Apparent is *not* slain.

MIK.: Bless my heart, my son!

YUM.: And your daughter-in-law elected!

KAT. [*seizing* KO-KO.]: Traitor, you have deceived me!

MIK.: Yes, you are entitled to a little explanation, but I think he will give it better whole than in pieces.

KO.: Your Majesty, it's like this: It is true that I stated that I had killed Nanki-Poo –

MIK.: Yes, with most affecting particulars.

POOH.: Merely corroborative detail intended to give artistic verisimilitude to a bald and –

KO.: *Will* you refrain from putting in your oar? [*To* MIKADO] It's like this: When your Majesty says, 'Let a thing be done,' it's as good as done – practically, it *is* done – because your Majesty's will is law. Your Majesty says, 'Kill a gentleman,' and a gentleman is told off to be killed. Consequently, that gentleman is as good as dead – practically, he *is* dead – and if he is dead, why not say so?

MIK.: I see. Nothing could possibly be more satisfactory!

FINALE

PITTI.:	For he's gone and married Yum-Yum –
ALL:	Yum-Yum!
PITTI.:	Your anger pray bury,
	For all will be merry,
	I think you had better succumb –
ALL:	Cumb – cumb!
PITTI.:	And join our expressions of glee!
KO.:	On this subject I pray you be dumb –
ALL:	Dumb – dumb!
KO.:	Your notions, though many,
	Are not worth a penny,
	The word for your guidance is 'Mum' –
ALL:	Mum – Mum!
KO.:	You've a very good bargain in me.
ALL:	On this subject we pray you be dumb –
	Dumb – dumb!
	We think you had better succumb –
	Cumb – cumb!
	You'll find there are many
	Who'll wed for a penny,
	There are lots of good fish in the sea.
YUM. *and* NANK.:	The threatened cloud has passed away,
	And brightly shines the dawning day;
	What though the night may come too soon,
	We've years and years of afternoon!
ALL:	Then let the throng
	Our joy advance,
	With laughing song
	And merry dance,
	With joyous shout and ringing cheer,
	Inaugurate our new career!

Then let the throng, etc.

CURTAIN

RUDDIGORE

OR
THE WITCH'S CURSE

DRAMATIS PERSONAE

MORTALS

SIR RUTHVEN MURGATROYD (*disguised as Robin Oakapple, a Young Farmer*)

RICHARD DAUNTLESS (*his Foster-Brother – a Man-o'-war's-man*)

SIR DESPARD MURGATROYD, OF RUDDIGORE (*a Wicked Baronet*)

OLD ADAM GOODHEART (*Robin's Faithful Servant*)

ROSE MAYBUD (*a Village Maiden*)

MAD MARGARET

DAME HANNAH (*Rose's Aunt*)

ZORAH ⎫
RUTH ⎭ (*Professional Bridesmaids*)

GHOSTS

SIR RUPERT MURGATROYD (*the First Baronet*)

SIR JASPER MURGATROYD (*the Third Baronet*)

SIR LIONEL MURGATROYD (*the Sixth Baronet*)

SIR CONRAD MURGATROYD (*the Twelfth Baronet*)

SIR DESMOND MURGATROYD (*the Sixteenth Baronet*)

SIR GILBERT MURGATROYD (*the Eighteenth Baronet*)

SIR MERVYN MURGATROYD (*the Twentieth Baronet*)

SIR RODERIC MURGATROYD (*the Twenty-first Baronet*)

Chorus of Officers, Ancestors, Professional Bridesmaids and Villagers

ACT I – The Fishing Village of Rederring, in Cornwall
ACT II – The Picture Gallery in Ruddigore Castle

Time – Early in the 19th century

ACT I

SCENE – *The Fishing Village of Rederring*[1] *in Cornwall.* ROSE MAYBUD*'s cottage is seen left.*

[*Enter Chorus of Bridesmaids. They range themselves in front of* ROSE*'s cottage.*]

CHORUS OF BRIDESMAIDS:
>Fair is Rose as the bright May-day;
>>Soft is Rose as the warm west-wind;
>Sweet is Rose as the new-mown hay –
>>Rose is the queen of maiden-kind!
>>>Rose, all glowing
>>>>With virgin blushes, say –
>>>Is anybody going
>>>>To marry you to-day?

SOLO

ZOR.:
>Every day, as the days roll on,
>Bridesmaids' garb we gaily don,
>Sure that a maid so fairly famed
>Can't long remain unclaimed.
>Hour by hour and day by day,
>Several months have passed away,
>Though she's the fairest flower that blows,
>No one has married Rose!

CHORUS: Rose, all glowing
                With virgin blushes, say –
            Is anybody, going
                To marry you to-day?
     [*Enter* DAME HANNAH, *from cottage.*]

HAN.: Nay, gentle maidens, you sing well but vainly, for Rose is still heart-free, and looks but coldly upon her many suitors.

ZOR.: It's very disappointing. Every young man in the village is in love with her, but they are appalled by her beauty and modesty, and won't declare themselves; so, until she makes her own choice, there's no chance for anybody else.

RUTH: This is, perhaps, the only village in the world that possesses an endowed corps of professional bridesmaids who are bound to be on duty every day from ten to four – and it is at least six months since our services were required. The pious charity by which we exist is practically wasted!

ZOR.: We shall be disendowed – that will be the end of it! Dame Hannah – you're a nice old person – *you* could marry if you liked. There's old Adam – Robin's faithful servant – he loves you with all the frenzy of a boy of fourteen.

HAN.: Nay – that may never be, for I am pledged!

ALL: To whom?

HAN.: To an eternal maidenhood! Many years ago I was betrothed to a god-like youth who woo'd me under an assumed name. But on the very day upon which our wedding was to have been celebrated, I discovered that he was no other than Sir Roderic Murgatroyd, one of the bad Baronets of Ruddigore, and the uncle of the man who now bears that title. As a son of that accursed race he was no husband for an honest girl, so, madly as I loved him, I left him then and there. He died but ten years since, but I never saw him again.

ZOR.: But why should you not marry a bad Baronet of Ruddigore?

RUTH: All baronets are bad; but was he worse than other baronets?

HAN.: My child, he was accursed.

ZOR.: But who cursed him? Not you, I trust!

HAN.: The curse is on all his line and has been, ever since the time of Sir Rupert, the first Baronet. Listen, and you shall hear the legend:

LEGEND

HAN.:
Sir Rupert Murgatroyd
  His leisure and his riches
He ruthlessly employed
  In persecuting witches.
With fear he'd make them quake –
He'd duck them in his lake –
    He'd break their bones
    With sticks and stones,
And burn them at the stake!

CHORUS:
This sport he much enjoyed,
Did Rupert Murgatroyd –
    No sense of shame
    Or pity came
To Rupert Murgatroyd!

HAN.:
Once, on the village green,
  A palsied hag he roasted,
And what took place, I ween,
  Shook his composure boasted;
For, as the torture grim
Seized on each withered limb,
    The writhing dame
    'Mid fire and flame
Yelled forth this curse on him:

'Each lord of Ruddigore,
  Despite his best endeavour,
Shall do one crime, or more,
  Once, every day, for ever!
This doom he can't defy,
However he may try,
    For should he stay
    His hand, that day
In torture he shall die!'

The prophecy came true:
  Each heir who held the title
Had, every day, to do
  Some crime of import vital;
Until, with guilt o'erplied,
'I'll sin no more!' he cried,
  And on the day
  He said that say,
In agony he died!

CHORUS: And thus, with sinning cloyed,
Has died each Murgatroyd,
  And so shall fall,
  Both one and all,
Each coming Murgatroyd!

[Exeunt Chorus of Bridesmaids.]
[Enter ROSE MAYBUD *from cottage, with small basket on her arm.]*

HAN.: Whither away, dear Rose? On some errand of charity, as is thy wont?

ROSE: A few gifts, dear aunt, for deserving villagers. Lo, here is some peppermint rock for old gaffer Gadderby, a set of false teeth for pretty little Ruth Rowbottom and a pound of snuff for the poor orphan girl on the hill.

HAN.: Ah, Rose, pity that so much goodness should not help to make some gallant youth happy for life! Rose, why dost thou harden that little heart of thine? Is there none hereaway whom thou couldst love?

ROSE: And if there were such an one, verily it would ill become me to tell him so.

HAN.: Nay, dear one, where true love is, there is little need of prim formality.

ROSE: Hush, dear aunt, for thy words pain me sorely. Hung in a plated dish-cover to the knocker of the workhouse door, with naught that I could call mine own, save a change of baby-linen and a book of etiquette, little wonder if I have always regarded that work as a voice from a parent's tomb. This hallowed volume [*producing a book of etiquette*], composed, if I may believe the title-page, by no less an authority than the wife of a Lord Mayor, has been, through life, my guide and monitor. By its solemn precepts I have learnt to test the moral worth of all who approach me. The man who bites his bread, or eats peas with a knife, I look upon as a lost creature, and he who has not acquired the proper way of entering and leaving a room is the object of my pitying horror. There are those in this village who bite their nails, dear aunt, and nearly all are wont to use their pocket combs in public places. In truth I could pursue this painful theme much further, but behold, I have said enough.

HAN.: But is there not one among them who is faultless, in thine eyes? For example – young Robin. He combines the manners of a Marquis with the morals of a Methodist. Couldst thou not love *him*?

ROSE: And even if I could, how should I confess it unto him? For lo, he is shy, and sayeth naught!

BALLAD

ROSE:

    If somebody there chanced to be
      Who loved me in a manner true,
    My heart would point him out to me,
      And I would point him out to you.
    But here it says of those who point,
        [*referring to book*]
    Their manners must be out of joint –
        You *may* not point –
        You *must* not point –
    It's manners out of joint, to point!
    Had I the love of such as he,
      Some quiet spot he'd take me to,
    Then he could whisper it to me,
      And I could whisper it to you.
    But whispering, I've somewhere met,
        [*referring to book*]

Is contrary to etiquette:
> Where can it be? [*Searching book*]
> Now let me see – [*finding reference*]
> Yes, yes!

It's contrary to etiquette!

> [*Showing it to* HANNAH.]

If any well-bred youth I knew,
  Polite and gentle, neat and trim,
Then I would hint as much to you,
  And you could hint as much to him.
But here it says, in plainest print,
> [*referring to book*]
  'It's most unladylike to hint'–
> You *may* not hint,
> You *must* not hint –
  It says you mustn't hint, in print!
And if I loved him through and through –
  (True love and not a passing whim),
Then I could speak of it to you,
  And you could speak of it to him.
But here I find it doesn't do
> [*referring to book*]
To speak until you're spoken to.
> Where can it be? [*Searching book*]
> Now let me see – [*finding reference*]
> Yes, yes!
  'Don't speak until you're spoken to!'
>   [*Exit* HANNAH.]

ROSE: Poor aunt! Little did the good soul think, when she breathed the hallowed name of Robin, that he would do even as well as another. But he resembleth all the youths in this village, in that he is unduly bashful in my presence, and lo, it is hard to bring him to the point. But soft, he is here!

  [ROSE *is about to go when* ROBIN *enters and calls her.*]
ROB.: Mistress Rose!

ROSE [*surprised*]: Master Robin!

ROB.: I wished to say that – it is fine.

ROSE: It is passing fine.

ROB.: But we do want rain.

ROSE: Aye, sorely! Is that all?

ROB. [*sighing*]: That is all.

ROSE: Good day, Master Robin!

ROB.: Good day, Mistress Rose! [*Both going – both stop.*]

ROSE: } I crave pardon, I –
ROB.: } I beg pardon, I –

ROSE: You were about to say? –

ROB.: I would fain consult you –

ROSE: Truly?

ROB.: It is about a friend.

ROSE: In truth I have a friend myself.

ROB.: Indeed? I mean, of course –

ROSE: And I would fain consult you –

ROB. [*anxiously*]: About him?

ROSE [*prudishly*]: About *her*.

ROB. [*relieved*]: Let us consult one another.

DUET – ROBIN *and* ROSE

ROB.:   I know a youth who loves a little maid –
        (Hey, but his face is a sight for to see!)
     Silent is he, for he's modest and afraid –
        (Hey, but he's timid as a youth can be!)

ROSE: I know a maid who loves a gallant youth,
        (Hey, but she sickens as the days go by!)
     She cannot tell him all the sad, sad truth –
        (Hey, but I think that little maid will die!)

ROB.:   Poor little man!
ROSE: Poor little maid!
ROB.:   Poor little man!
ROSE: Poor little maid!

BOTH: Now tell me pray, and tell me true,
         What in the world should the $\left\{\begin{array}{c}\text{young man}\\\text{maiden}\end{array}\right\}$ do?

ROB.:   He cannot eat and he cannot sleep –
             (Hey, but his face is a sight for to see!)
         Daily he goes for to wail – for to weep
             (Hey, but he's wretched as a youth can be!)

ROSE: She's very thin and she's very pale –
             (Hey, but she sickens as the days go by!)
         Daily she goes for to weep – for to wail –
             (Hey, but I think that little maid will die!)

ROB.:   Poor little maid!
ROSE: Poor little man!
ROB.:   Poor little maid!
ROSE: Poor little man!

BOTH: Now tell me pray, and tell me true,
         What in the world should the $\left\{\begin{array}{c}\text{young man}\\\text{maiden}\end{array}\right\}$ do?

ROSE: If I were the youth I should offer her my name –
             (Hey, but her face is a sight for to see!)
ROB.:   If I were the maid I should fan his honest flame –
             (Hey, but he's bashful as a youth can be!)
ROSE: If I were the youth I should speak to her to-day –
             (Hey, but she sickens as the days go by!)
ROB.:   If I were the maid I should meet the lad half way –
             (For I really do believe that timid youth will die!)

ROSE: Poor little man!
ROB.:   Poor little maid!
ROSE: Poor little man!
ROB.:   Poor little maid!

BOTH: I thank you, $\left\{\begin{array}{l}\text{miss,}\\\text{sir,}\end{array}\right\}$ for your counsel true;

I'll tell that $\left\{\begin{array}{l}\text{youth}\\\text{maid}\end{array}\right\}$ what $\left\{\begin{array}{l}\text{he}\\\text{she}\end{array}\right\}$ ought to do!

[*Exit* ROSE.]

ROB.: Poor child! I sometimes think that if she wasn't quite so particular I might venture – but no, no – even then I should be unworthy of her!

[*He sits desponding. Enter* OLD ADAM.]

ADAM:[2] My kind master is sad! Dear Sir Ruthven[3] Murgatroyd –

ROB.: Hush! As you love me, breathe not that hated name. Twenty years ago, in horror at the prospect of inheriting that hideous title, and with it the ban that compels all who succeed to the baronetcy to commit at least one deadly crime per day, for life, I fled my home, and concealed myself in this innocent village under the name of Robin Oakapple.[4] My younger brother, Despard, believing me to be dead, succeeded to the title and its attendant curse. For twenty years I have been dead and buried. Don't dig me up now.

ADAM: Dear master, it shall be as you wish, for have I not sworn to obey you for ever in all things? Yet, as we are here alone, and as I belong to that particular description of good old man to whom the truth is a refreshing novelty, let me call you by your own right title once more! [ROBIN *assents.*] Sir Ruthven Murgatroyd! Baronet! Of Ruddigore! Whew! It's like eight hours at the seaside!

ROB.: My poor old friend! Would there were more like you!

ADAM: Would there were indeed! But I bring you good tidings. Your foster-brother, Richard, has returned from sea – his ship the *Tom-Tit* rides yonder at anchor, and he himself is even now in this very village!

ROB.: My beloved foster-brother? No, no – it cannot be!

ADAM: It is even so – and see, he comes this way!

[*Exeunt together.*]

[*Enter Chorus of Bridesmaids.*]

CHORUS: From the briny sea

Comes young Richard, all victorious!

Valorous is he –

His achievements all are glorious!

Let the welkin ring[5]
With the news we bring
Sing it – shout it –
Tell about it –
Safe and sound returneth he.
All victorious from the sea!

[*Enter* RICHARD DAUNTLESS. *The girls welcome him as he greets old acquaintances.*]

BALLAD

RICH.: I shipped, d'ye see, in a Revenue sloop,[6]
And, off Cape Finistere,[7]
A merchantman we see,
A Frenchman, going free,
So we made for the bold Mounseer,
D'ye see?
We made for the bold Mounseer.
But she proved to be a Frigate – and she up with her ports,
And fires with a thirty-two![8]
It come uncommon near,
But we answered with a cheer,
Which paralysed the Parley-voo,
D'ye see?
Which paralysed the Parley-voo!

Then our Captain he up and he says, says he,
'That chap we need not fear –
We can take her, if we like,
She is sartin for to strike,
For she's only a darned Mounseer,
D'ye see?
She's only a darned Mounseer!
But to fight a French fal-lal – it's like hittin' of a gal –
It's a lubberly thing for to do;
For we, with all our faults,
Why we're sturdy British salts,

> While she's only a Parley-voo,
> > D'ye see?
> While she's only a Parley-voo!'

> So we up with our helm, and we scuds before the breeze
> > As we gives a compassionating cheer;
> > > Froggee answers with a shout
> > > As he sees us go about,
> > Which was grateful of the poor Mounseer,
> > > D'ye see?
> > Which was grateful of the poor Mounseer!
> And I'll wager in their joy they kissed each other's cheek
> > (Which is what them furriners do),
> > > And they blessed their lucky stars
> > > We were hardy British tars
> > Who had pity on a poor Parley-voo,
> > > D'ye see?
> > Who had pity on a poor Parley-voo!

[*Hornpipe.*]

[*Exeunt* CHORUS.]

[*Enter* ROBIN.]

ROB.: Richard!

RICH.: Robin!

ROB.: My beloved foster-brother, and very dearest friend, welcome home again after ten long years at sea! It is such deeds as yours that cause our flag to be loved and dreaded throughout the civilized world!

RICH.: Why, lord love ye, Rob, that's but a trifle to what we *have* done in the way of sparing life! I believe I may say, without exaggeration, that the marciful little *Tom-Tit* has spared more French frigates than any craft afloat! But 'taint for a British seaman to brag, so I'll just stow my jawin' tackle and belay. [ROBIN *sighs.*] But 'vast heavin', messmate, what's brought *you* all a-cockbill?[9]

ROB.: Alas, Dick, I love Rose Maybud, and love in vain!

RICH.: *You* love in vain? Come, that's too good! Why, you're a fine strapping muscular young fellow – tall and strong as a to'-gall'n'-m'st – taut as a fore-stay – aye, and a barrowknight[10] to boot, if all had their rights!

ROB.: Hush, Richard – not a word about my true rank, which none here suspect. Yes, I know well enough that few men are better calculated to win a woman's heart than I. I'm a fine fellow, Dick, and worthy any woman's love – happy the girl who gets me, say I. But I'm timid, Dick; shy – nervous – modest – retiring – diffident – and I cannot tell her, Dick, I cannot tell her! Ah, you've no idea what a poor opinion I have of myself, and how little I deserve it.

RICH.: Robin, do you call to mind how, years ago, we swore that, come what might, we would always act upon our hearts' dictates?

ROB.: Aye, Dick, and I've always kept that oath. In doubt, difficulty and danger I've always asked my heart what I should do, and it has never failed me.

RICH.: Right! Let your heart be your compass, with a clear conscience for your binnacle light, and you'll sail ten knots on a bowline, clear of shoals, rocks, and quicksands! Well, now, what does my heart say in this here difficult situation? Why, it says, 'Dick,' it says – (it calls me Dick acos it's known me from a babby) – 'Dick,' it says, '*you* ain't shy – *you* ain't modest – speak you up for him as is!' Robin, my lad, just you lay me alongside, and when she's becalmed under my lee, I'll spin her a yarn that shall sarve to fish you two together for life!

ROB.: Will you do this thing for me? Can you, do you think? Yes [*feeling his pulse*]. There's no false modesty about *you*. Your – what I would call bumptious self-assertiveness (I mean the expression in its complimentary sense) has already made you a bos'n's mate, and it will make an admiral of you in time, if you work it properly, you dear, incompetent old impostor! My dear fellow, I'd give my right arm for one tenth of your modest assurance!

SONG

ROB.:
My boy, you may take it from me,
That of all the afflictions accurst
With which a man's saddled
And hampered and addled,
A diffident nature's the worst.
Though clever as clever can be –
A Crichton[11] of early romance –
You must stir it and stump it,
And blow your own trumpet,
Or, trust me, you haven't a chance!

If you wish in the world to advance,
Your merits you're bound to enhance,
You must stir it and stump it,
And blow your own trumpet,
Or, trust me, you haven't a chance!

Now take, for example, *my* case:
I've a bright intellectual brain –
In all London city
There's no one so witty –
I've thought so again and again.
I've a highly intelligent face –
My features cannot be denied –
But, whatever I try, sir,
I fail in – and why, sir?
I'm modesty personified!

If you wish in the world to advance, etc.

As a poet, I'm tender and quaint –
I've passion and fervour and grace –
From Ovid[12] and Horace[13]
To Swinburne[14] and Morris,[15]
They all of them take a back place.

439

> Then I sing and I play and I paint:
> > Though none are accomplished as I,
> > > To say so were treason:
> > > You ask me the reason?
> > I'm diffident, modest and shy!
> > > If you wish in the world to advance, etc.

> > > > > *[Exit* ROBIN.]

RICH. [*looking after him*]: Ah, it's a thousand pities he's such a poor opinion of himself, for a finer fellow don't walk! Well, I'll do my best for him. 'Plead for him as though it was for your own father' – that's what my heart's a-remarkin' to me just now. But here she comes! Steady! Steady it is!

[*Enter* ROSE – *he is much struck by her.*]

> > > By the Port Admiral, but she's a tight little craft! Come, come, she's not for you, Dick, and yet – she's fit to marry Lord Nelson! By the Flag of Old England, I can't look at her unmoved.

ROSE: Sir, you are agitated –

RICH.: Aye, aye, my lass, well said! I am agitated, true enough! – took flat aback, my girl; but 'tis naught – 'twill pass. [*Aside*] This here heart of mine's a-dictatin' to me like anythink. Question is, Have I a right to disregard its promptings?

ROSE: Can I do aught to relieve thine anguish, for it seemeth to me that thou art in sore trouble? This apple – [*offering a damaged apple*].

RICH. [*looking at it and returning it*]: No, my lass, 'taint that: I'm – I'm took flat aback – I never see anything like you in all my born days. Parbuckle[16] me, if you ain't the loveliest gal I've ever set eyes on. There – I can't say fairer than that, can I?

ROSE: No. [*Aside*] The question is, Is it meet that an utter stranger should thus express himself? [*Refers to book.*] Yes – 'Always speak the truth.'

RICH.: I'd no thoughts of sayin' this here to you on my own account, for, truth to tell, I was chartered by another; but when I see you my heart it up and it says, says it, 'This is the very lass for *you*, Dick' – 'speak up to her, Dick,' it says – (it calls me Dick acos we was at school together) – 'tell her all, Dick,' it says, 'never sail under false colours[17] – it's mean!' *That's* what my heart tells me to say, and in my rough, common-sailor fashion, I've said it, and I'm a-waiting for your reply. I'm a-tremblin', miss. Lookye here – [*holding out his hand*]. That's narvousness!

ROSE [*aside*]: Now, how should a maiden deal with such an one? [*Consults book.*] 'Keep no one in unnecessary suspense.' [*Aloud*] Behold, I will not keep you in unnecessary suspense. [*Refers to book.*] 'In accepting an offer of marriage, do so with apparent hesitation.' [*Aloud*] I take you, but with a certain show of reluctance. [*Refers to book.*] 'Avoid any appearance of eagerness.' [*Aloud*] Though you will bear in mind that I am far from anxious to do so. [*Refers to book.*] 'A little show of emotion will not be misplaced!' [*Aloud*] Pardon this tear! [*Wipes her eye.*]

RICH.: Rose, you've made me the happiest blue-jacket[18] in England! I wouldn't change places with the Admiral of the Fleet, no matter who he's a-huggin' of at this present moment! But, axin' your pardon, miss [*wiping his lips with his hand*], might I be permitted to salute the flag I'm a-goin' to sail under?

ROSE [*referring to book*]: 'An engaged young lady should not permit too many familiarities.' [*Aloud*] Once! [RICHARD *kisses her.*]

DUET – RICHARD *and* ROSE

RICH.:

The battle's roar is over,
O my love!
Embrace thy tender lover,
O my love!
From tempests' welter,
From war's alarms,
O give me shelter
Within those arms!
Thy smile alluring,
All heart-ache curing,
Gives peace enduring,
O my love!

ROSE: If heart both true and tender,
      O my love!
A life-love can engender,
      O my love!
  A truce to sighing
      And tears of brine,
  For joy undying
      Shall aye be mine,
And thou and I, love,
Shall live and die, love,
Without a sigh, love –
    My own, my love!

[*Enter* ROBIN, *with Chorus of Bridesmaids.*]

CHORUS: If well his suit has sped,
Oh, may they soon be wed!
Oh, tell us, tell us, pray,
What doth the maiden say?
In singing are we justified,
  Hail the Bridegroom – hail the Bride!
  Let the nuptial knot be tied:
    In fair phrases
    Hymn their praises,
  Hail the Bridegroom – hail the Bride?

ROB.: Well – what news? Have you spoken to her?
RICH.: Aye, my lad, I have – so to speak – spoke her.
ROB.: And she refuses?
RICH.: Why, no, I can't truly say she do.
ROB.: Then she accepts! My darling! [*Embraces her.*]

BRIDESMAIDS: Hail the Bridegroom – hail the Bride! etc.

ROSE [*aside, referring to her book*]: Now, what should a maiden do
when she is embraced by the wrong gentleman?
RICH.: Belay,[19] my lad, belay. You don't understand.
ROSE: Oh, sir, belay, I beseech you!

RICH.: You see, it's like this: she accepts – but it's *me*!

ROB.: You! [RICHARD *embraces* ROSE.]

BRIDESMAIDS: Hail the Bridegroom – hail the Bride!
When the nuptial knot is tied –

ROB. [*interrupting angrily*]: Hold your tongues, will you! Now then,
what does this mean?

RICH.: My poor lad, my heart grieves for thee, but it's like this: the
moment I see her, and just as I was a-goin' to mention your name,
my heart it up and it says, says it – 'Dick, you've fell in love with
her yourself,' it says; 'Be honest and sailor-like – don't skulk under
false colours – speak up,' it says, 'take her, you dog, and with her
my blessin'!'

BRIDESMAIDS: Hail the Bridegroom – hail the Bride! –

ROB.: Will you be quiet! Go away!
[CHORUS *make faces at him and exeunt.*]
Vulgar girls!

RICH.: What could I do? I'm bound to obey my heart's dictates.

ROB.: Of course – no doubt. It's quite right – I don't mind – that is,
not particularly – only it's – it *is* disappointing, you know.

ROSE [*to* ROBIN]: Oh, but, sir, I knew not that thou didst seek me in
wedlock, or in very truth I should not have hearkened unto this
man, for behold, he is but a lowly mariner, and very poor withal,
whereas thou art a tiller of the land, and thou hast fat oxen, and
many sheep and swine, a considerable dairy farm and much corn
and oil!

RICH.: That's true, my lass, but it's done now, ain't it, Rob?

ROSE: Still it may be that I should not be happy in thy love. I am
passing young and little able to judge. Moreover, as to thy character
I know naught!

ROB.: Nay, Rose, I'll answer for that. Dick has won thy love fairly.
Broken-hearted as I am, I'll stand up for Dick through thick and thin!

RICH. [*with emotion*]: Thankye, messmate! that's well said. That's
spoken honest. Thankye, Rob! [*Grasps his hand.*]

ROSE: Yet methinks I have heard that sailors are but worldly men, and little prone to lead serious and thoughtful lives!

ROB.: And what then? Admit that Dick is *not* a steady character, and that when he's excited he uses language that would make your hair curl. Grant that – he does. It's the truth, and I'm not going to deny it. But look at his *good* qualities. He's as nimble as a pony, and his hornpipe is the talk of the Fleet!

RICH.: Thankye, Rob! That's well spoken. Thankye, Rob!

ROSE: But it may be that he drinketh strong waters which do bemuse a man, and make him even as the wild beasts of the desert!

ROB.: Well, suppose he does, and I don't say he don't, for rum's his bane, and ever has been. He *does* drink – I won't deny it. But what of that? Look at his arms – tattooed to the shoulder! [RICHARD *rolls up his sleeves.*] No, no – I won't hear a word against Dick!

ROSE: But they say that mariners are but rarely true to those whom they profess to love!

ROB.: Granted – granted – and I don't say that Dick isn't as bad as any of 'em. [RICHARD *chuckles.*] You are, you know you are, you dog! a devil of a fellow – a regular out-and-out Lothario![20] But what then? You can't have everything, and a better hand at turning-in a dead-eye[21] don't walk a deck! And what an accomplishment *that* is in a family man! No, no – not a word against Dick. I'll stick up for him through thick and thin!

RICH.: Thankye, Rob, thankye. You're a true friend. I've acted accordin' to my heart's dictates, and such orders as them no man should disobey.

ENSEMBLE

RICHARD, ROBIN, ROSE:

> In sailing o'er life's ocean wide
> Your heart should be your only guide;
> With summer sea and favouring wind,
> Yourself in port you'll surely find.

SOLO

RICH.: *My* heart says, 'To this maiden strike –
    She's captured you.
She's just the sort of girl you like –
    You know you do.
If other man her heart should gain,
    I shall resign.'
That's what it says to me quite plain,
    This heart of mine.

ROB.: *My* heart says, 'You've a prosperous lot,
    With acres wide;
You mean to settle all you've got
    Upon your bride.'
It don't pretend to shape my acts
    By word or sign;
It merely states these simple facts,
    This heart of mine!

ROSE: Ten minutes since my heart said 'white' –
    It now says 'black'.
It then said 'left' – it now says 'right' –
    Hearts often tack.[22]
I must obey its latest strain –
    You tell me so. [*To* RICHARD]
But should it change its mind again,
    I'll let you know.
[*Turning from* RICHARD *to* ROBIN, *who embraces her.*]

ENSEMBLE

In sailing o'er life's ocean wide
No doubt the heart should be your guide;
But it is awkward when you find
A heart that does not know its mind!
[*Exeunt* ROBIN *with* ROSE *left, and* RICHARD, *weeping, right.*]

[*Enter* MAD MARGARET. *She is wildly dressed in picturesque tatters, and is an obvious caricature of theatrical madness.*]

SCENA

MAR.:

Cheerily carols the lark
Over the cot.
Merrily whistles the clerk
Scratching a blot.
But the lark
And the clerk,
I remark,
Comfort me not!

Over the ripening peach
Buzzes the bee.
Splash on the billowy beach
Tumbles the sea.
But the peach
And the beach
They are each
Nothing to me!

And why?
Who am I?
Daft Madge! Crazy Meg!
Mad Margaret! Poor Peg!
He! he! he! he! he! [*chuckling*].

Mad, I?
Yes, very!
But why?
Mystery!
Don't call!
Whisht! whisht!

No crime –
'Tis only

That I'm
Love – lonely!
That's all!

BALLAD

MAR.:   To a garden full of posies
Cometh one to gather flowers,
And he wanders through its bowers
Toying with the wanton roses,
Who, uprising from their beds,
Hold on high their shameless heads
With their pretty lips a-pouting,
Never doubting – never doubting
That for Cytherean posies[23]
He would gather aught but roses!

In a nest of weeds and nettles
Lay a violet, half-hidden,
Hoping that his glance unbidden
Yet might fall upon her petals.
Though she lived alone, apart,
Hope lay nestling at her heart,
But, alas, the cruel awaking
Set her little heart a-breaking,
For he gathered for his posies
Only roses – only roses! [*Bursts into tears.*]
[*Enter* ROSE.]

ROSE: A maiden, and in tears? Can I do aught to soften thy sorrow?
This apple – [*offering apple*].
MAR. [*examines it and rejects it*]: No! [*Mysteriously*] Tell me, are you
mad?
ROSE: I? No! That is, I think not.
MAR.: That's well! Then you don't love Sir Despard Murgatroyd? All
mad girls love him. *I* love him. I'm poor Mad Margaret – Crazy
Meg – Poor Peg! He! he! he! he! [*chuckling*].

ROSE: Thou lovest the bad Baronet of Ruddigore? Oh, horrible – too horrible!

MAR.: You pity me? Then be my mother! The squirrel had a mother, but she drank and the squirrel fled! Hush! They sing a brave song in our parts – it runs somewhat thus [*sings*]:

> 'The cat and the dog and the little puppee
> Sat down in a – down in a – in a –'

I forget what they sat down in, but so the song goes! Listen – I've come to pinch her!

ROSE: Mercy, whom?

MAR.: You mean 'who'.

ROSE: Nay! it is the accusative after the verb.

MAR.: True. [*Whispers melodramatically*] I have come to pinch Rose Maybud!

ROSE [*aside, alarmed*]: Rose Maybud!

MAR.: Aye! I love him – he loved me once. But that's all gone, Fisht! He gave me an Italian glance[24] – thus – [*business*] – and made me his. He will give *her* an Italian glance, and make *her* his. But it shall not be, for I'll stamp on her – stamp on her – stamp on her! Did you ever kill anybody? No? Why not? Listen – I killed a fly this morning! It buzzed, and I wouldn't have it. So it died – pop! So shall she!

ROSE: But, behold, *I* am Rose Maybud, and I would fain not die 'pop'.

MAR.: You are Rose Maybud?

ROSE: Yes, sweet Rose Maybud!

MAR.: Strange! They told me she was beautiful! And *he* loves *you*! No, no! If I thought that, I would treat you as the auctioneer and land-agent treated the lady-bird – I would rend you asunder!

ROSE: Nay, be pacified, for behold I am pledged to another, and lo, we are to be wedded this very day!

MAR.: Swear me that! Come to a Commissioner and let me have it on affidavit! *I* once made an affidavit – but it died – it died – it died! But see, they come – Sir Despard and his evil crew! Hide, hide – they are all mad – quite mad!

ROSE: What makes you think that?

MAR.: Hush! They sing choruses in public. That's mad enough, I think! Go – hide away, or they will seize you! Hush! Quite softly – quite, quite softly! [*Exeunt together, on tiptoe.*]
[*Enter Chorus of Bucks and Blades,*[25] *heralded by Chorus of Bridesmaids.*]

CHORUS OF BRIDESMAIDS:

> Welcome, gentry,
> For your entry
> Sets our tender hearts a-beating.
> Men of station,
> Admiration
> Prompts this unaffected greeting.
> Hearty greeting offer we!

CHORUS OF BUCKS AND BLADES:

> When thoroughly tired
> Of being admired
> By ladies of gentle degree – degree,
> With flattery sated,
> High-flown and inflated,
> Away from the city we flee – we flee!

> From charms intramural
> To prettiness rural
> The sudden transition
> Is simply Elysian,[26]
> So come, Amaryllis,[27]
> Come, Chloe and Phyllis,[28]
> Your slaves, for the moment, are we!

ALL: From charms intramural, etc.

CHORUS OF BRIDESMAIDS:

> The sons of the tillage
> Who dwell in this village

Are people of lowly degree – degree.
    Though honest and active,
    They're most unattractive,
And awkward as awkward can be – can be.
    They're clumsy clodhoppers
    With axes and choppers,
    And shepherds and ploughmen
    And drovers and cowmen
    And hedgers and reapers
    And carters and keepers,
And never a lover for me!

So, welcome, gentry, etc.

When thoroughly tired, etc.

[*Enter* SIR DESPARD MURGATROYD.]

SONG *and* CHORUS

SIR D.:	Oh, why am I moody and sad?
CHORUS:	Can't guess!
SIR D.:	And why am I guiltily mad?
CHORUS:	Confess!
SIR D.:	Because I am thoroughly bad!
CHORUS:	Oh yes –
SIR D.:	You'll see it at once in my face.
	Oh, why am I husky and hoarse?
CHORUS:	Ah, why?
SIR D.:	It's the workings of conscience, of course.
CHORUS:	Fie, fie!
SIR D.:	And huskiness stands for remorse,
CHORUS:	Oh my!
SIR D.:	At least it does so in my case!
SIR D.:	When in crime one is fully employed –
CHORUS:	Like you –

SIR D.:   Your expression gets warped and destroyed:
CHORUS: It do.
SIR D.:   It's a penalty none can avoid;
CHORUS: How true!
SIR D.:   I once was a nice-looking youth;
           But like stone from a strong catapult –
CHORUS [*explaining to each other*]: A trice –
SIR D.:   I rushed at my terrible cult –
CHORUS [*explaining to each other*]: That's vice –
SIR D.:   Observe the unpleasant result!
CHORUS: Not nice.
SIR D.:   Indeed I am telling the truth!

SIR D.:   Oh, innocent, happy though poor!
CHORUS: That's we –
SIR D.:   If I had been virtuous, I'm sure –
CHORUS: Like me –
SIR D.:   I should be as nice-looking as you're!
CHORUS: May be.
SIR D.:   You are very nice-looking indeed!
           Oh, innocents, listen in time –
CHORUS: We *doe*,
SIR D.:   Avoid an existence of crime –
CHORUS: Just so –
SIR D.:   Or you'll be as ugly as I'm –
CHORUS [*loudly*]:   No! No!
SIR D.:   And now, if you please, we'll proceed.
      [*All the Girls express their horror of* SIR DESPARD. *As he
      approaches them they fly from him, terror-stricken, leaving him
      alone on the stage.*]

SIR D.: Poor children, how they loathe me – me whose hands are
   certainly steeped in infamy, but whose heart is as the heart of a
   little child! But what *is* a poor baronet to do, when a whole picture
   gallery of ancestors step down from their frames and threaten him
   with an excruciating death if he hesitate to commit his daily crime?
   But ha! ha! I am even with them! [*Mysteriously*] I get my crime

over the first thing in the morning, and then, ha! ha! for the rest of the day I do good – I do good – I do good! [*Melodramatically*] Two days since, I stole a child and built an orphan asylum. Yesterday I robbed a bank and endowed a bishopric. To-day I carry off Rose Maybud and atone with a cathedral! This is what it is to be the sport and toy of a Picture Gallery! But I will be bitterly revenged upon them! I will give them all to the Nation, and nobody shall ever look upon their faces again!

[*Enter* RICHARD.]

RICH.: Ax your honour's pardon, but –

SIR D.: Ha! observed! And by a mariner! What would you with me, fellow?

RICH.: Your honour, I'm a poor man-o'-war's man, becalmed in the doldrums –

SIR D.: I don't know them.

RICH.: And I make bold to ax your honour's advice. Does your honour know what it is to have a heart?

SIR D.: My honour knows what it is to have a complete apparatus for conducting the circulation of the blood through the veins and arteries of the human body.

RICH.: Aye, but has your honour a heart that ups and looks you in the face, and gives you quarter-deck orders that it's life and death to disobey?

SIR D.: I have not a heart of that description, but I have a Picture Gallery that presumes to take that liberty.

RICH.: Well, your honour, it's like this – Your honour had an elder brother –

SIR D.: It had.

RICH.: Who should have inherited your title and, with it, its cuss.

SIR D.: Aye, but he died. Oh, Ruthven! –

RICH.: He didn't.

SIR D.: He did *not*?

RICH.: He didn't. On the contrary, he lives in this here very village, under the name of Robin Oakapple, and he's a-going to marry Rose Maybud this very day.

SIR D.: Ruthven alive, and going to marry Rose Maybud! Can this be possible?

RICH.: Now the question I was going to ask your honour is – Ought I to tell your honour this?

SIR D.: I don't know. It's a delicate point. I think you ought. Mind, I'm not sure, but I think so.

RICH.: That's what my heart says. It says, 'Dick,' it says (it calls me Dick acos it's entitled to take that liberty), 'that there young gal would recoil from him if she knowed what he really were. Ought you to stand off and on, and let this young gal take this false step and never fire a shot across her bows to bring her to? No,' it says, 'you did *not* ought.' And I won't ought, accordin'.

SIR D.: Then you really feel yourself at liberty to tell me that my elder brother lives – that I may charge him with his cruel deceit, and transfer to his shoulders the hideous thraldom under which I have laboured for so many years! Free – free at last! Free to live a blameless life, and to die beloved and regretted by all who knew me!

DUET – SIR DESPARD *and* RICHARD

RICH.:	You understand?
SIR D.:	I think I do;
	With vigour unshaken
	This step shall be taken.
	It's neatly planned.
RICH.:	I think so too;
	I'll readily bet it
	You'll never regret it!
BOTH:	For duty, duty must be done;
	The rule applies to every one,
	And painful though that duty be,
	To shirk the task were fiddle-de-dee!
SIR D.:	The bridegroom comes –
RICH.:	Likewise the bride –
	The maidens are very
	Elated and merry;

They are her chums.

SIR D.: To lash their pride
Were almost a pity,
The pretty committee!

BOTH: But duty, duty must be done;
The rule applies to every one,
And painful though that duty be,
To shirk the task were fiddle-de-dee!

[*Exeunt* RICHARD *and* SIR DESPARD.]
[*Enter Chorus of Bridesmaids and Bucks.*]

CHORUS OF BRIDESMAIDS:

Hail the bride of seventeen summers:
In fair phrases
Hymn her praises;
Lift your song on high, all comers.
She rejoices
In your voices.
Smiling summer beams upon her,
Shedding every blessing on her:
Maidens greet her –
Kindly treat her –
You may all be brides some day!

CHORUS OF BUCKS:

Hail the bridegroom who advances,
Agitated,
Yet elated.
He's in easy circumstances,
Young and lusty,
True and trusty.

[*Enter* ROBIN, *attended by* RICHARD *and* OLD ADAM, *meeting* ROSE, *attended by* ZORAH *and* DAME HANNAH. ROSE *and* ROBIN *embrace.*]

MADRIGAL

ROSE: When the buds are blossoming,
Smiling welcome to the spring,
Lovers choose a wedding day –
Life is love in merry May!

GIRLS: Spring is green – Fal lal la!
Summer's rose – Fal lal la!

ALL: It is sad when summer goes,
Fal la!

MEN: Autumn's gold – Fal lal la!
Winter grey – Fal lal la!

ALL: Winter still is far away –
Fal la!

Leaves in autumn fade and fall,
Winter is the end of all.
Spring and summer teem with glee:
Spring and summer, then, for me!
Fal la!

HAN.:   In the spring-time seed is sown:
In the summer grass is mown:
In the autumn you may reap:
Winter is the time for sleep.

GIRLS: Spring is hope – Fal lal la!
Summer's joy – Fal lal la!

ALL: Spring and summer never cloy,
Fal la!

MEN: Autumn, toil – Fal lal la!
Winter, rest – Fal lal la!

ALL: Winter, after all, is best –
Fal la!

Spring and summer pleasure you,
Autumn, aye, and winter too –
Every season has its cheer,
Life is lovely all the year!
Fal la!

GAVOTTE[29]

[*After Gavotte, enter* SIR DESPARD.]

SIR D.:   Hold, bride and bridegroom, ere you wed each other,
I claim young Robin as my elder brother!
His rightful title I have long enjoyed:
I claim him as Sir Ruthven Murgatroyd!

ALL: O wonder!

ROSE [*wildly*]:

Deny the falsehood, Robin, as you should,
It is a plot!

ROB.:   I would, if conscientiously I could,
But I cannot!

ALL: Ah, base one!

SOLO

ROB.:   As pure and blameless peasant,
I cannot, I regret,
Deny a truth unpleasant,
I am that Baronet!

ALL: He is that Baronet!

ROB: But when completely rated
Bad Baronet am I,
That I am what he's stated
I'll recklessly deny!

ALL: He'll recklessly deny!

ROB.: When I'm a bad Bart. I will tell taradiddles!
ALL: He'll tell taradiddles when he's a bad Bart.
ROB.: I'll play a bad part on the falsest of fiddles.
ALL: On very false fiddles he'll play a bad part!
ROB.: But until that takes place I must be conscientious –
ALL: He'll be conscientious until that takes place.
ROB.: Then adieu with good grace to my morals sententious!
ALL: To morals sententious adieu with good grace!

ZOR.: Who is the wretch who hath betrayed thee?
                Let him stand forth!
RICH. [*coming forward*]:
      'Twas I!
ALL: Die, traitor!
RICH.:   Hold! my conscience made me! –
             Withhold your wrath!

SOLO

RICH.: Within this breast there beats a heart
      Whose voice can't be gainsaid.
It bade me thy true rank impart,
      And I at once obeyed.
I knew 'twould blight thy budding fate –
I knew 'twould cause thee anguish great –
But did I therefore hesitate?
      No! I at once obeyed!
ALL: Acclaim him who, when his true heart
Bade him young Robin's rank impart,
      Immediately obeyed!

SOLO

ROSE [*addressing* ROBIN: Farewell!
      Thou hadst my heart –
      'Twas quickly won!
      But now we part –

Thy face I shun!
Farewell!

Go bend the knee
At Vice's shrine,
Of life with me
All hope resign.
Farewell!

[*To* SIR DESPARD]: Take me – I am thy bride!

BRIDESMAIDS: Hail the Bridegroom – hail the Bride!
When the nuptial knot is tied;
Every day will bring some joy
That can never, never cloy!

[*Enter* MAD MARGARET, *who listens.*]

SIR D.:	Excuse me, I'm a virtuous person now –
ROSE:	That's why I wed you!
SIR D.:	And I to Margaret must keep my vow!
MAR.:	Have I misread you?
	Oh, joy! with newly kindled rapture warmed,
	I kneel before you! [*Kneels.*]
SIR D.:	I once disliked you; now that I've reformed,
	How I adore you! [*They embrace.*]

BRIDESMAIDS:

Hail the Bridegroom – hail the Bride!
When the nuptial knot is tied;
Every day will bring some joy
That can never, never cloy!

ROSE: Richard, of him I love bereft,
Through thy design,
Thou art the only one that's left,
So I am thine! [*They embrace.*]

BRIDESMAIDS:

> Hail the Bridegroom – hail the Bride!
> Let the nuptial knot be tied!

DUET – ROSE *and* RICHARD

Oh, happy the lily
> When kissed by the bee;
And, sipping tranquilly,
> Quite happy is he;
And happy the filly
> That neighs in her pride;
But happier than any,
A pound to a penny,
A lover is, when he
> Embraces his bride!

DUET – SIR DESPARD *and* MARGARET

Oh, happy the flowers
> That blossom in June,
And happy the bowers
> That gain by the boon,
But happier by hours
> The man of descent,
Who, folly regretting,
Is bent on forgetting
His bad baronetting,
> And means to repent!

TRIO – HANNAH, ADAM *and* ZORAH

Oh, happy the blossom
> That blooms on the lea,
Likewise the opossum
> That sits on a tree,

But when you come across 'em,
      They cannot compare
With those who are treading
The dance at a wedding,
While people are spreading
      The best of good fare!

SOLO

ROB.:

Oh, wretched the debtor
      Who's signing a deed!
And wretched the letter
      That no one can read!
But very much better
      Their lot it must be
Than that of the person
I'm making this verse on,
Whose head there's a curse on –
      Alluding to me!

[*Repeat ensemble with Chorus.*]

DANCE

[*At the end of the dance* ROBIN *falls senseless on the stage. Picture.*]

END OF ACT I

ACT II

SCENE – *Picture Gallery in Ruddigore Castle. The walls are covered with full-length portraits of the Baronets of Ruddigore from the time of James I – the first being that of* SIR RUPERT MURGATROYD, *alluded to in the legend; the last, that of the last deceased Baronet,* SIR RODERIC.

[*Enter* ROBIN *and* ADAM *melodramatically. They are greatly altered in appearance,* ROBIN *wearing the haggard aspect of a guilty roué;* ADAM, *that of the wicked steward to such a man.*]

DUET – ROBIN *and* ADAM

ROB.:   I once was as meek as a new-born lamb,
               I'm now Sir Murgatroyd – ha! ha!
                   With greater precision
                   (Without the elision[30]),
               Sir Ruthven Murgatroyd – ha! ha!

ADAM: And I, who was once his *valley-de-sham*,[31]
               As steward I'm now employed – ha! ha!
                   The dickens may take him –
                   I'll never forsake him!
               As steward I'm now employed – ha! ha!

BOTH: How dreadful when an innocent heart
               Becomes, perforce, a bad young Bart.,
               And still more hard on old Adam,
               His former faithful *valley-de-sham*!

ROB.:   My face is the index to my mind,
          All venom and spleen and gall – ha! ha!
              Or, properly speaking,
              It soon will be reeking
          With venom and spleen and gall – ha! ha!

ADAM: My name from Adam Goodheart you'll find
          I've changed to Gideon Crawle[32] – ha! ha!
              For a bad Bart.'s steward
              Whose heart is much *too* hard,
          Is always Gideon Crawle – ha! ha!

BOTH: How providential when you find
          The face an index to the mind,
          And evil men compelled to call
          Themselves by names like Gideon Crawle!

ROB.:   This is a painful state of things, Gideon Crawle!

ADAM: Painful, indeed! Ah, my poor master, when I swore that, come what would, I would serve you in all things for ever, I little thought to what a pass it would bring me! The confidential adviser to the greatest villain unhung! Now, sir, to business. What crime do you propose to commit to-day?

ROB.: How should I know? As my confidential adviser, it's your duty to suggest something.

ADAM: Sir, I loathe the life you are leading, but a good old man's oath is paramount, and I obey. Richard Dauntless is here with pretty Rose Maybud, to ask your consent to their marriage. Poison their beer.

ROB.: No – not that – I know I'm a bad Bart., but I'm not as bad a Bart. as all that.

ADAM: Well, there you are, you see! It's no use my making suggestions if you don't adopt them.

ROB. [*melodramatically*]: How would it be, do you think, were I to lure him here with cunning wile – bind him with good stout rope to yonder post – and then, by making hideous faces at him, curdle the heart-blood in his arteries, and freeze the very marrow in his bones? How say you, Gideon, is not the scheme well planned?

ADAM: It would be simply rude – nothing more. But soft – they come!

[ADAM *and* ROBIN *retire up-stage as* RICHARD *and* ROSE *enter, preceded by Chorus of Bridesmaids.*]

DUET – RICHARD *and* ROSE

RICH.:
Happily coupled are we,
  You see –
I am a jolly Jack Tar,
  My star,
 And you are the fairest,
 The richest and rarest
Of innocent lasses you are,
  By far –
Of innocent lasses you are!
Fanned by a favouring gale,
  You'll sail
Over life's treacherous sea
  With me,
 And as for bad weather,
 We'll brave it together,
And you shall creep under my lee,
  My wee!
And you shall creep under my lee!

For you are such a smart little craft –
Such a neat little, sweet little craft,
 Such a bright little, tight little,
 Slight little, light little,
Trim little, prim little craft!

CHORUS:
For she is such, etc.

ROSE:

My hopes will be blighted, I fear,
My dear;
In a month you'll be going to sea,
Quite free,
And all of my wishes
You'll throw to the fishes
As though they were never to be;
Poor me!
As though they were never to be.
And I shall be left all alone
To moan,
And weep at your cruel deceit,
Complete;
While you'll be asserting
Your freedom by flirting
With every woman you meet,
You cheat –
With every woman you meet!

Though I am such a smart little craft –
Such a neat little, sweet little craft,
Such a bright little, tight little,
Slight little, light little,
Trim little, prim little craft!

CHORUS:

Though she is such, etc.

[*Enter* ROBIN.]

ROB.: Soho![33] pretty one – in my power at last, eh? Know ye not that I have those within my call who, at my lightest bidding, would immure ye in an uncomfortable dungeon? [*Calling.*] What ho! within there!

RICH.: Hold – we are prepared for this [*producing a Union Jack*]. Here is a flag that none dare defy [*all kneel*], and while this glorious rag floats over Rose Maybud's head, the man does not live who would dare to lay unlicensed hand upon her!

ROB.: Foiled – and by a Union Jack! But a time will come, and then –

ROSE: Nay, let me plead with him. [*To* ROBIN] Sir Ruthven, have pity. In my book of etiquette the case of a maiden about to be wedded to one who unexpectedly turns out to be a baronet with a curse on him is not considered. Time was when you loved me madly. Prove that this was no selfish love by according your consent to my marriage with one who, if he be not you yourself, is the next best thing – your dearest friend!

BALLAD

ROSE: In bygone days I had thy love –
   Thou hadst my heart.
But Fate, all human vows above,
   Our lives did part!
By the old love thou hadst for me –
By the fond heart that beat for thee –
By joys that never now can be,
   Grant thou my prayer!

ALL [*kneeling*]: Grant thou her prayer!
ROB. [*recitative*]: Take her – I yield!
ALL [*recitative*]:   Oh, rapture!

CHORUS: Away to the parson we go –
   Say we're solicitous very
That he will turn two into one –
   Singing hey, derry down derry!

RICH.: For she *is* such a smart little craft –
ROSE: Such a neat little, sweet little craft –
RICH.:   Such a bright little –
ROSE: Tight little –
RICH.:   Slight little –
ROSE: Light little –
BOTH: Trim little, slim little craft!

CHORUS: For she *is* such a smart little craft, etc.
      [*Exeunt all but* ROBIN.]

ROB.: For a week I have fulfilled my accursed doom! I have duly committed a crime a day! Not a great crime, I trust, but still, in the eyes of one as strictly regulated as I used to be, a crime. But will my ghostly ancestors be satisfied with what I have done, or will they regard it as an unworthy subterfuge? [*Addressing Pictures*] Oh, my forefathers, wallowers in blood, there came at last a day when, sick of crime, you, each and every, vowed to sin no more, and so, in agony, called welcome Death to free you from your cloying guiltiness. Let the sweet psalm of that repentant hour soften your long-dead hearts, and tune your souls to mercy on your poor posterity! [*kneeling*].

[*The stage darkens for a moment. It becomes light again, and the Pictures are seen to have become animated.*]

CHORUS OF FAMILY PORTRAITS:
> Painted emblems of a race,
>> All accurst in days of yore,
> Each from his accustomed place
>> Steps into the world once more.

[*The Pictures step from their frames and march round the stage.*]

> Baronet of Ruddigore,
>> Last of our accursèd line,
> Down upon the oaken floor –
>> Down upon those knees of thine.

>> Coward, poltroon, shaker, squeamer,
>> Blockhead, sluggard, dullard, dreamer,
>> Shirker, shuffler, crawler, creeper,
>> Sniffler, snuffler, wailer, weeper,
>> Earthworm, maggot, tadpole, weevil!
>> Set upon thy course of evil,
>> Lest the King of Spectre-Land
>> Set on thee his grisly hand!

[*The Spectre of* SIR RODERIC MURGATROYD *descends from his frame.*]

SIR ROD.:	By the curse upon our race –
CHORUS:	Dead and hearsèd
	All accursèd!
SIR ROD.:	Each inheriting this place –
CHORUS:	Sorrows shake it!
	Devil take it!
SIR ROD.:	Must, perforce, or yea or nay –
CHORUS:	Yea or naying
	Be obeying!
SIR ROD.:	Do a deadly crime each day!
CHORUS:	Fire and thunder,
	We knocked under –
	Some atrocious crime committed
	Daily ere the world we quitted!
SIR ROD.:	Beware! beware! beware!
ROB.:	Gaunt vision, who art thou
	That thus, with icy glare
	And stern relentless brow,
	Appearest, who knows how?
SIR ROD.:	I am the spectre of the late
	Sir Roderic Murgatroyd,
	Who comes to warn thee that thy fate
	Thou canst not now avoid.
ROB.:	Alas, poor ghost![34]
SIR ROD.:	The pity you
	Express for nothing goes:
	We spectres are a jollier crew
	Than you, perhaps, suppose!
CHORUS:	We spectres are a jollier crew
	Than you, perhaps, suppose!

SONG

SIR ROD.: When the night wind howls in the chimney cowls, and
   the bat in the moonlight flies,
  And inky clouds, like funeral shrouds, sail over the
   midnight skies –
  When the footpads quail at the night-bird's wail, and
   black dogs bay at the moon,
  Then is the spectres' holiday – then is the ghosts'
   high-noon!

CHORUS: Ha! ha!
    Then is the ghosts' high-noon!

SIR ROD.: As the sob of the breeze sweeps over the trees, and the
   mists lie low on the fen,
  From grey tomb-stones are gathered the bones that
   once were women and men,
  And away they go, with a mop and a mow, to the revel
   that ends too soon,
  For cockcrow limits our holiday – the dead of the
   night's high-noon!

CHORUS: Ha! ha!
    The dead of the night's high-noon!

SIR ROD.: And then each ghost with his ladye-toast to their
   churchyard beds takes flight,
  With a kiss, perhaps, on her lantern chaps, and a grisly
   grim 'good-night';
  Till the welcome knell of the midnight bell rings forth
   its jolliest tune,
  And ushers in our next high holiday – the dead of the
   night's high-noon!

CHORUS: Ha! ha!
    The dead of the night's high-noon!

ROB.: I recognize you now – you are the picture that hangs at the end of the gallery.

SIR ROD.: In a bad light. I am.

ROB.: Are you considered a good likeness?

SIR ROD.: Pretty well. Flattering.

ROB.: Because as a work of art you are poor.

SIR ROD.: I am crude in colour, but I have only been painted ten years. In a couple of centuries I shall be an Old Master, and then you will be sorry you spoke lightly of me.

ROB.: And may I ask why you have left your frames?

SIR ROD.: It is our duty to see that our successors commit their daily crimes in a conscientious and workmanlike fashion. It is our duty to remind you that you are evading the conditions under which you are permitted to exist.

ROB.: Really, I don't know what you'd have. I've only been a bad baronet a week, and I've committed a crime punctually every day.

SIR ROD.: Let us inquire into this. Monday?

ROB.: Monday was a Bank Holiday.

SIR ROD.: True. Tuesday?

ROB.: On Tuesday I made a false income-tax return.

ALL: Ha! ha!

1ST GHOST: That's nothing.

2ND GHOST: Nothing at all.

3RD GHOST: Everybody does that.

4TH GHOST: It's expected of you.

SIR ROD.: Wednesday?

ROB. [*melodramatically*]: On Wednesday I forged a will.

SIR ROD.: Whose will?

ROB.: My own.

SIR ROD.: My good sir, you can't forge your own will!

ROB.: Can't I, though! I like that! I *did*! Besides, if a man can't forge his own will, whose will can he forge?

1ST GHOST: There's something in that.

2ND GHOST: Yes, it seems reasonable.

3RD GHOST: At first sight it does.

4TH GHOST: Fallacy somewhere, I fancy!

ROB.: A man can do what he likes with his own?

SIR ROD.: I suppose he can.

ROB.: Well, then, he can forge his own will, stoopid! On Thursday I shot a fox.

1ST GHOST: Hear, hear!

SIR ROD.: That's better [*addressing Ghosts*]. Pass the fox, I think? [*They assent.*] Yes, pass the fox. Friday?

ROB.: On Friday I forged a cheque.

SIR ROD.: Whose cheque?

ROB.: Old Adam's.

SIR ROD.: But Old Adam hasn't a banker.

ROB.: I didn't say I forged his banker – I said I forged his cheque. On Saturday I disinherited my only son.

SIR ROD.: But you haven't got a son.

ROB.: No – not yet. I disinherited him in advance, to save time. You see – by this arrangement – he'll be born ready disinherited.

SIR ROD.: I see. But I don't think you can do that.

ROB.: My good sir, if I can't disinherit my own unborn son, whose unborn son can I disinherit?

SIR ROD.: Humph! These arguments sound very well, but I can't help thinking that, if they were reduced to syllogistic form, they wouldn't hold water. Now quite understand us. We are foggy, but we don't permit our fogginess to be presumed upon. Unless you undertake to – well, suppose we say, carry off a lady? [*Addressing Ghosts*] Those who are in favour of his carrying off a lady? [*All hold up their hands except a Bishop.*] Those of the contrary opinion? [*Bishop holds up his hands.*] Oh, you're never satisfied! Yes, unless you undertake to carry off a lady at once – I don't care what lady – any lady – choose your lady – you perish in inconceivable agonies.

ROB.: Carry off a lady? Certainly not, on any account. I've the greatest respect for ladies, and I wouldn't do anything of the kind for worlds! No, no. I'm not that kind of baronet, I assure you! If that's all you've got to say, you'd better go back to your frames.

SIR ROD.: Very good – then let the agonies commence.

[*Ghosts make passes.* ROBIN *begins to writhe in agony.*]

ROB.: Oh! Oh! Don't do that! I can't stand it!

SIR ROD.: Painful, isn't it? It gets worse by degrees.

ROB.: Oh – Oh! Stop a bit! Stop it, will you? I want to speak.

    [SIR RODERIC *makes signs to Ghosts, who resume their attitudes.*]

SIR ROD.: Better?

ROB.: Yes – better now! Whew!

SIR ROD.: Well, do you consent?

ROB.: But it's such an ungentlemanly thing to do!

SIR ROD.: As you please. [*To Ghosts*] Carry on!

ROB.: Stop – I can't stand it! I agree! I promise! It shall be done!

SIR ROD.: To-day?

ROB.: To-day!

SIR ROD.: At once?

ROB.: At once! I retract! I apologize! I had no idea it was anything like that!

CHORUS: He yields! He answers to our call!
                  We do not ask for more.
            A sturdy fellow, after all,
                  This latest Ruddigore!
            All perish in unheard-of woe
                  Who dare our wills defy;
            We want your pardon, ere we go,
            For having agonized you so –
                  So pardon us –
                  So pardon us –
                  So pardon us –
                          Or die!

ROB.:   I pardon you!
                I pardon you!

ALL: He pardons us –
                    Hurrah!

    [*The Ghosts return to their frames.*]

CHORUS: Painted emblems of a race,
All accurst in days of yore,
Each to his accustomed place
Steps unwillingly once more!

[*By this time the Ghosts have changed to pictures again.* ROBIN *is overcome by emotion.*]

[*Enter* ADAM.]

ADAM: My poor master, you are not well –

ROB.: Gideon Crawle, it won't do – I've seen 'em – all my ancestors – they're just gone. They say that I must do something desperate at once, or perish in horrible agonies. Go – go to yonder village – carry off a maiden – bring her here at once – any one – I don't care which –

ADAM: But –

ROB.: Not a word, but obey! Fly!

[*Exit* ADAM.]

RECITATIVE AND SONG

ROB.: Away, Remorse!
Compunction, hence!
Go, Moral Force!
Go, Penitence!
To Virtue's plea
A long farewell –
Propriety,
I ring your knell!
Come, guiltiness of deadliest hue!
Come, desperate deeds of derring-do!

Henceforth all the crimes that I find in the *Times*,
I've promised to perpetrate daily;
To-morrow I start, with a petrified heart,
On a regular course of Old Bailey.
There's confidence tricking, bad coin, pocket-picking,
And several other disgraces –

There's postage-stamp prigging,[35] and then,
    thimble-rigging,[36]
      The three-card delusion[37] at races!
Oh! a baronet's rank is exceedingly nice,
But the title's uncommonly dear at the price!

Ye well-to-do squires, who live in the shires,
    Where petty distinctions are vital,
Who found Athenaeums[38] and local museums,
    With views to a baronet's title –
Ye butchers and bakers and candlestick makers
    Who sneer at all things that are tradey –
Whose middle-class lives are embarrassed by wives
    Who long to parade as 'My Lady',
Oh! allow me to offer a word of advice,
The title's uncommonly dear at the price!

Ye supple MPs, who go down on your knees,
    Your precious identity sinking,
And vote black or white as your leaders indite
    (Which saves you the trouble of thinking),
For your country's good fame, her repute, or her
    shame,
    You don't care the snuff of a candle –
But you're paid for your game when you're told that
    your name
    Will be graced by a baronet's handle –
Oh! allow me to give *you* a word of advice –
    The title's uncommonly dear at the price!   [*Exit.*]
[*Enter* DESPARD *and* MARGARET. *They are both dressed in sober black of formal cut, and present a strong contrast to their appearance in Act I.*]

DUET – DESPARD *and* MARGARET

DES.:	I once was a very abandoned person –
MAR.:	Making the most of evil chances.
DES.:	Nobody could conceive a worse 'un –
MAR.:	Even in all the old romances.
DES.:	I blush for my wild extravagances,
	But be so kind
	To bear in mind,
MAR.:	We were the victims of circumstances!
	[*Dance.*]
	That is one of our blameless dances.

MAR.:	I was once an exceedingly odd young lady –
DES.:	Suffering much from spleen and vapours.
MAR.:	Clergymen thought my conduct shady –
DES.:	She didn't spend much upon linen-drapers.
MAR.:	It certainly entertained the gapers.
	My ways were strange
	Beyond all range –
DES.:	Paragraphs got into all the papers.
	[*Dance.*]
DES.:	We only cut respectable capers.

DES.:	I've given up all my wild proceedings.
MAR.:	My taste for a wandering life is waning.
DES.:	Now I'm a dab at penny readings.
MAR.:	They are not remarkably entertaining.
DES.:	A moderate livelihood we're gaining.
MAR.:	In fact we rule
	A National School.[39]
DES.:	The duties are dull, but I'm not complaining.
	[*Dance.*]
	This sort of thing takes a deal of training!

DES.: We have been married a week.
MAR.: One happy, happy week!

DES.: Our new life –

MAR.: Is delightful indeed!

DES.: So calm!

MAR.: So unimpassioned! [*wildly*]. Master, all this I owe to you! See, I am no longer wild and untidy. My hair is combed. My face is washed. My boots fit!

DES.: Margaret, don't. Pray restrain yourself. Remember, you are now a district visitor.

MAR.: A gentle district visitor!

DES.: You are orderly, methodical, neat; you have your emotions well under control.

MAR.: I have! [*wildly*]. Master, when I think of all you have done for me, I fall at your feet. I embrace your ankles. I hug your knees! [*Doing so.*]

DES.: Hush. This is not well. This is calculated to provoke remark. Be composed, I beg!

MAR.: Ah! you are angry with poor little Mad Margaret!

DES.: No, not angry; but a district visitor should learn to eschew melodrama. Visit the poor, by all means, and give them tea and barley-water, but don't do it as if you were administering a bowl of deadly nightshade. It upsets them. Then when you nurse sick people, and find them not as well as could be expected, why go into hysterics?

MAR.: Why not?

DES.: Because it's too jumpy for a sick-room.

MAR.: How strange! Oh, Master! Master! – how shall I express the all-absorbing gratitude that – [*about to throw herself at his feet*].

DES.: Now! [*warningly*].

MAR.: Yes, I know, dear – it shan't occur again. [*He is seated – she sits on the ground by him.*] Shall I tell you one of poor Mad Margaret's odd thoughts? Well, then, when I am lying awake at night, and the pale moonlight streams through the latticed casement, strange fancies crowd upon my poor mad brain, and I sometimes think that if we could hit upon some word for you to use whenever I am about to relapse – some word that teems with hidden meaning – like 'Basingstoke'[40] – it might recall me to my saner self. For, after all, I am only Mad Margaret! Daft Meg! Poor Meg! He! he! he!

DES.: Poor child, she wanders! But soft – some one comes – Margaret – pray recollect yourself – Basingstoke, I beg! Margaret, if you don't Basingstoke at once, I shall be seriously angry.

MAR. [*recovering herself*]: Basingstoke it is!

DES.: Then make it so.

[*Enter* ROBIN. *He starts on seeing them.*]

ROB.: Despard! And his young wife! This visit is unexpected.

MAR.: Shall I fly at him? Shall I tear him limb from limb? Shall I rend him asunder? Say but the word and –

DES.: Basingstoke!

MAR. [*suddenly demure*]: Basingstoke it is!

DES. [*aside*]: Then make it so. [*Aloud*] My brother – I call you brother still, despite your horrible profligacy – we have come to urge you to abandon the evil courses to which you have committed yourself, and at any cost to become a pure and blameless ratepayer.

ROB.: But I've done no wrong yet.

MAR. [*wildly*]: No wrong! He has done no wrong! Did you hear that!

DES.: Basingstoke!

MAR. [*recovering herself*]: Basingstoke it is!

DES.: My brother – I still call you brother, you observe – you forget that you have been, in the eye of the law, a Bad Baronet of Ruddigore for ten years – and you are therefore responsible – in the eye of the law – for all the misdeeds committed by the unhappy gentleman who occupied your place.

ROB.: I see! Bless my heart, I never thought of that! Was I very bad?

DES.: Awful. Wasn't he? [*to* MARGARET].

ROB.: And I've been going on like this for how long?

DES.: Ten years! Think of all the atrocities you have committed – by attorney as it were – during that period. Remember how you trifled with this poor child's affections – how you raised her hopes on high (don't cry, my love – Basingstoke, you know), only to trample them in the dust when they were at the very zenith of their fullness. Oh fie, sir, fie – she trusted you!

ROB.: Did she? What a scoundrel I must have been! There, there – don't cry, my dear [*to* MARGARET, *who is sobbing on* ROBIN's *breast*], it's all right now. Birmingham, you know – Birmingham –

MAR. [*sobbing*]: It's Ba – Ba – Basingstoke!

ROB.: Basingstoke! of course it is – Basingstoke.

MAR.: Then make it so!

ROB.: There, there – it's all right – he's married you now – that is, *I've* married you [*turning to* DESPARD] – I say, which of us has married her?

DES.: Oh, *I've* married her.

ROB. [*aside*]: Oh, I'm glad of that. [*To* MARGARET] Yes, *he's* married you now [*passing her over to* DESPARD], and anything more disreputable than my conduct seems to have been I've never even heard of. But my mind is made up – I *will* defy my ancestors. I *will* refuse to obey their behests, thus, by courting death, atone in some degree for the infamy of my career!

MAR.: I knew it – I knew it – God bless you – [*hysterically*].

DES.: Basingstoke!

MAR.: Basingstoke it is! [*Recovers herself.*]

PATTER-TRIO[41] – ROBIN, DESPARD, MARGARET

ROB.:   My eyes are fully open to my awful situation –
        I shall go at once to Roderic and make him an oration.
        I shall tell him I've recovered my forgotten moral senses,
        And I don't care twopence-halfpenny for any
            consequences.
        Now I do not want to perish by the sword or by the
            dagger,
        But a martyr may indulge a little pardonable swagger,
        And a word or two of compliment my vanity would
            flatter,
        But I've got to die to-morrow, so it really doesn't matter!

DES.:   So it really doesn't matter –

MAR.:   So it really doesn't matter –

ALL: So it really doesn't matter, matter, matter, matter, matter!

MAR.:   If I were not a little mad and generally silly
        I should give you my advice upon the subject, willy-nilly;
        I should show you in a moment how to grapple with the
            question,

And you'd really be astonished at the force of my
    suggestion.
On the subject I shall write you a most valuable letter,
Full of excellent suggestions when I feel a little better,
But at present I'm afraid I am as mad as any hatter,
So I'll keep 'em to myself, for my opinion doesn't matter!

DES.:   Her opinion doesn't matter –
ROB.:   Her opinion doesn't matter –
ALL: Her opinion doesn't matter, matter, matter, matter,
    matter!

DES.:   If I had been so lucky as to have a steady brother
   Who could talk to me as we are talking now to one
       another –
   Who could give me good advice when he discovered I was
       erring
   (Which is just the very favour which on you I am
       conferring),
   My story would have made a rather interesting idyll,
   And I might have lived and died a very decent indiwiddle.
   This particularly rapid, unintelligible patter
   Isn't generally heard, and if it is it doesn't matter!

ROB.:   If it is it doesn't matter –
MAR.:   If it ain't it doesn't matter –
ALL: If it is it doesn't matter, matter, matter, matter, matter!

                [*Exeunt* DESPARD *and* MARGARET.]

  [*Enter* ADAM.]

ADAM [*guiltily*]: Master – the deed is done!

ROB.: What deed?

ADAM: She is here – alone, unprotected –

ROB.: Who?

ADAM: The maiden. I've carried her off – I had a hard task, for she
fought like a tiger-cat!

ROB.: Great heaven, I had forgotten her! I had hoped to have died
unspotted by crime, but I am foiled again – and by a tiger-cat!
Produce her – and leave us!

[ADAM *introduces* DAME HANNAH, *very much excited,*
and exit.]

ROB.: Dame Hannah! This is – this is not what I expected.

HAN.: Well, sir, and what would you with me? Oh, you have begun
bravely – bravely indeed! Unappalled by the calm dignity of blameless womanhood, your minion has torn me from my spotless home,
and dragged me, blindfold and shrieking, through hedges, over
stiles and across a very difficult country, and left me, helpless and
trembling, at your mercy! Yet not helpless, coward sir, for approach
one step – nay, but the twentieth part of one poor inch – and this
poniard [*produces a very small dagger*] shall teach ye what it is to
lay unholy hands on old Stephen Trusty's daughter!

ROB.: Madam, I am extremely sorry for this. It is not at all what I
intended – anything more correct – more deeply respectful than my
intentions towards you, it would be impossible for any one – however particular – to desire.

HAN.: Bah, I am not to be tricked by smooth words, hypocrite! But
be warned in time, for there are, without, a hundred gallant hearts
whose trusty blades would hack him limb from limb who dared to
lay unholy hands on old Stephen Trusty's daughter!

ROB.: And this is what it is to embark upon a career of unlicensed
pleasure!

[HANNAH, *who has taken a formidable dagger from one of the*
armed figures, throws her small dagger to ROBIN.]

HAN.: Harkye, miscreant, you have secured me, and I am your poor
prisoner; but if you think I cannot take care of myself you are very
much mistaken. Now then, it's one to one, and let the best man
win! [*Making for him.*]

ROB. [*in an agony of terror*]: Don't! don't look at me like that! I can't
bear it! Roderic! Uncle! Save me!

[RODERIC *enters, from his picture. He comes down the stage.*]

ROD.: What is the matter? Have you carried her off?

ROB.: I have – she is there – look at her – she terrifies me!

ROD. [*looking at* HANNAH]: Little Nannikin!

HAN. [*amazed*]: Roddy-doddy!

ROD.: My own old love! Why, how came *you* here?

HAN.: This brute – he carried me off! Bodily! But I'll show him!
[*about to rush at* ROBIN].

ROD.: Stop! [*To* ROB] What do you mean by carrying off this lady? Are you aware that once upon a time she was engaged to be married to me? I'm very angry – very angry indeed.

ROB.: Now I hope this will be a lesson to you in future not to –

ROD.: Hold your tongue, sir.

ROB.: Yes, uncle.

ROD.: Have you given him any encouragement?

HAN. [*to* ROB]: Have I given you any encouragement? Frankly now, have I?

ROB.: No. Frankly, you have not. Anything more scrupulously correct than your conduct, it would be impossible to desire.

ROD.: You go away.

ROB.: Yes, uncle.   [*Exit.*]

ROD.: This is a strange meeting after so many years!

HAN.: Very. I thought you were dead.

ROD.: I am. I died ten years ago.

HAN.: And are you pretty comfortable?

ROD.: Pretty well – that is – yes, pretty well.

HAN.: You don't deserve to be, for I loved you all the while, dear; and it made me dreadfully unhappy to hear of all your goings-on, you bad, bad boy!

BALLAD

HAN.:
> There grew a little flower
>   'Neath a great oak tree:
> When the tempest 'gan to lower
>   Little heeded she:
> No need had she to cower,
> For she dreaded not its power –
> She was happy in the bower
>   Of her great oak tree!
>   Sing hey,
>   Lackaday!
>   Let the tears fall free
> For the pretty little flower and the great oak tree!

HAN. *and* ROD.:   Sing hey,
        Lackaday, etc.

HAN.:   When she found that he was fickle,
       Was that great oak tree,
    She was in a pretty pickle,
       As she well might be –
    But his gallantries were mickle,[42]
    For Death followed with his sickle,
    And her tears began to trickle
       For her great oak tree!
BOTH: Sing hey,
        Lackaday! etc.

HAN.:   Said she, 'He loved me never,
       Did that great oak tree,
    But I'm neither rich nor clever,
       And so why should he?
    But though fate our fortunes sever,
    To be constant I'll endeavour,
    Aye, for ever and for ever,
       To my great oak tree!'
BOTH: Sing hey,
        Lackaday! etc.

[*Falls weeping on* SIR RODERIC's *bosom.*]
[*Enter* ROBIN, *excitedly, followed by all the characters and Chorus of Bridesmaids.*]

ROB.: Stop a bit – both of you.

ROD.: This intrusion is unmannerly.

HAN.: I'm surprised at you.

ROB.: I can't stop to apologize – an idea has just occurred to me. A Baronet of Ruddigore can only die through refusing to commit his daily crime.

ROD.: No doubt.

ROB.: Therefore, to refuse to commit a daily crime is tantamount to suicide!

ROD.: It would seem so.

ROB.: But suicide is, itself, a crime – and so, by your own showing, you ought never to have died at all!

ROD.: I see – I understand! Then I'm practically alive!

ROB.: Undoubtedly! [SIR RODERIC *embraces* HANNAH.] Rose, when you believed that I was a simple farmer, I believe you loved me?

ROSE: Madly, passionately!

ROB.: But when I became a bad baronet, you very properly loved Richard instead?

ROSE: Passionately, madly!

ROB.: But if I should turn out *not* to be a bad baronet after all, how would you love me then?

ROSE: Madly, passionately!

ROB.: As before?

ROSE: Why, of course!

ROB.: My darling! [*They embrace.*]

RICH.: Here, I say, belay!

ROSE: Oh sir, belay, if it's absolutely necessary!

ROB.: Belay! Certainly not!

FINALE

ROB.:
Having been a wicked baronet a week,
Once again a modest livelihood I seek,
Agricultural employment
Is to me a keen enjoyment,
For I'm naturally diffident and meek!

ROSE:
When a man has been a naughty baronet,
And expresses his repentance and regret,
You should help him, if you're able,
Like the mousie in the fable,
That's the teaching of my Book of Etiquette.

RICH.:
If you ask me why I do not pipe my eye,
Like an honest British sailor, I reply,
That with Zorah for my missis,

There'll be bread and cheese and kisses,
Which is just the sort of ration I enjye!

DES. *and* MAR.:

Prompted by a keen desire to evoke,
All the blessed calm of matrimony's yoke,
We shall toddle off to-morrow,
From this scene of sin and sorrow,
For to settle in the town of Basingstoke!

ALL:

For happy the lily
That's kissed by the bee;
And, sipping tranquilly,
Quite happy is he;
And happy the filly
That neighs in her pride;
But happier than any,
A pound to a penny,
A lover is, when he
Embraces his bride!

CURTAIN

THE YEOMEN OF THE GUARD[1]

OR

THE MERRYMAN AND HIS MAID

DRAMATIS PERSONAE

SIR RICHARD CHOLMONDELEY (*Lieutenant of the Tower*)
COLONEL FAIRFAX (*under sentence of death*)
SERGEANT MERYLL (*of the Yeomen of the Guard*)
LEONARD MERYLL (*his Son*)
JACK POINT (*a Strolling Jester*)
WILFRED SHADBOLT (*Head Jailer and Assistant Tormentor*)
THE HEADSMAN
FIRST YEOMAN
SECOND YEOMAN
FIRST CITIZEN
SECOND CITIZEN
ELSIE MAYNARD (*a Strolling Singer*)
PHOEBE MERYLL (*Sergeant Meryll's Daughter*)
DAME CARRUTHERS (*Housekeeper to the Tower*)
KATE (*her Niece*)

Chorus of Yeomen of the Guard, Gentlemen, Citizens, etc.

SCENE – Tower Green

Date, 16th Century

ACT I

SCENE – *Tower Green.*²

[PHOEBE *discovered spinning.*]

SONG

PHOE.:   When maiden loves, she sits and sighs,
        She wanders to and fro;
Unbidden tear-drops fill her eyes,
And to all questions she replies
      With a sad 'heigho!'
    'Tis but a little word – 'heigho!'
    So soft, 'tis scarcely heard – 'heigho!'
      An idle breath –
      Yet life and death
    May hang upon a maid's 'heigho!'

When maiden loves, she mopes apart,
      As owl mopes on a tree;
Although she keenly feels the smart,
She cannot tell what ails her heart,
      With its sad 'Ah me!'
    'Tis but a foolish sigh – 'Ah me!'
    Born but to droop and die – 'Ah me!'
      Yet all the sense
      Of eloquence
Lies hidden in a maid's 'Ah me!' [*weeps*].

[*Enter* WILFRED.]

WIL.: Mistress Meryll!

PHOE. [*looking up*]: Eh! Oh! it's you, is it? You may go away, if you like. Because I don't want you, you know.

WIL.: Haven't you anything to say to me?

PHOE.: Oh yes! Are the birds all caged? The wild beasts all littered down? All the locks, chains, bolts and bars in good order? Is the Little Ease[3] sufficiently uncomfortable? The racks, pincers and thumbscrews all ready for work? Ugh! you brute!

WIL.: These allusions to my professional duties are in doubtful taste. I didn't become a head-jailer because I like head-jailing. I didn't become an assistant-tormentor because I like assistant-tormenting. We can't *all* be sorcerers, you know. [PHOEBE *annoyed*.] Ah! you brought that upon yourself.

PHOE.: Colonel Fairfax[4] is *not* a sorcerer. He's a man of science and an alchemist.[5]

WIL.: Well, whatever he is, he won't be one long, for he's to be beheaded to-day for dealings with the devil. His master nearly had him last night, when the fire broke out in the Beauchamp Tower.[6]

PHOE.: Oh! how I wish he had escaped in the confusion! But take care; there's still time for a reply to his petition for mercy.

WIL.: Ah! I'm content to chance that. This evening at half-past seven – ah!

PHOE.: You're a cruel monster to speak so unfeelingly of the death of a young and handsome soldier.

WIL.: Young and handsome! How do *you* know he's young and handsome?

PHOE.: Because I've seen him every day for weeks past taking his exercise on the Beauchamp Tower.

WIL.: Curse him!

PHOE.: There, I believe you're jealous of *him*, now. Jealous of a man I've never spoken to! Jealous of a poor soul who's to die in an hour!

WIL.: I am! I'm jealous of everybody and everything. I'm jealous of the very words I speak to you – because they reach your ears – and I mustn't go near 'em!

PHOE.: How unjust you are! Jealous of the words you speak to me! Why, you know as well as I do that I don't even like them.

WIL.: You used to like 'em.

PHOE.: I used to *pretend* I liked them. It was mere politeness to comparative strangers.   [*Exit* PHOEBE, *with spinning wheel.*]

WIL.: I don't believe you know what jealousy is! I don't believe you know how it eats into a man's heart – and disorders his digestion – and turns his interior into boiling lead. Oh, you are a heartless jade to trifle with the delicate organization of the human interior!

[*Exit* WILFRED.]

[*Enter Crowd of Men and Women, followed by Yeomen of the Guard.*]

CHORUS [*as Yeomen march on*]:

Tower Warders,[7]
Under orders,
Gallant pikemen,[8] valiant sworders!
Brave in bearing,
Foemen scaring,
In their bygone days of daring!
Ne'er a stranger
There to danger –
Each was o'er the world a ranger;
To the story
Of our glory
Each a bold contributory!

CHORUS OF YEOMEN:

In the autumn of our life,
Here at rest in ample clover,
We rejoice in telling over
Our impetuous May and June.
In the evening of our day,
With the sun of life declining,
We recall without repining
All the heat of bygone noon.

SOLO

2ND YEO.:   This the autumn of our life,
  This the evening of our day;
Weary we of battle strife,
  Weary we of mortal fray.
But our year is not so spent,
  And our days are not so faded,
But that we with one consent,
  Were our lovèd land invaded,
   Still would face a foreign foe,
   As in days of long ago.

CHORUS: Still would face a foreign foe,
   As in days of long ago.

PEOPLE	YEOMEN
Tower Warders,	This the autumn of our life, etc.
Under orders, etc.	

[*Exeunt Crowd. Manent* YEOMEN.]

[*Enter* DAME CARRUTHERS.]

DAME: A good day to you!

2ND YEO.: Good day, Dame Carruthers. Busy to-day?

DAME: Busy, aye! the fire in the Beauchamp last night has given me work enough. A dozen poor prisoners – Richard Colfax, Sir Martin Byfleet, Colonel Fairfax, Warren the preacher-poet and half-a-score others – all packed into one small cell, not six feet square. Poor Colonel Fairfax, who's to die to-day, is to be removed to No. 14 in the Cold Harbour[9] that he may have his last hour alone with his confessor; and I've to see to that.

2ND YEO.: Poor gentleman! He'll die bravely. I fought under him two years since, and he valued his life as it were a feather!

PHOE.: He's the bravest, the handsomest and the best young gentleman in England! He twice saved my father's life; and it's a cruel thing, a wicked thing and a barbarous thing that so gallant a hero should lose his head – for it's the handsomest head in England!

DAME: For dealings with the devil. Aye! if all were beheaded who dealt with *him*, there'd be busy doings on Tower Green.

PHOE.: You know very well that Colonel Fairfax is a student of alchemy – nothing more, and nothing less; but this wicked Tower, like a cruel giant in a fairy-tale, must be fed with blood, and that blood must be the best and bravest in England, or it's not good enough for the old Blunderbore.[10] Ugh!

DAME: Silence, you silly girl; you know not what you say. I was born in the old keep, and I've grown grey in it, and, please God, I shall die and be buried in it; and there's not a stone in its walls that is not as dear to me as my own right hand.

SONG *and* CHORUS

DAME: When our gallant Norman foes
                 Made our merry land their own,
                    And the Saxons from the Conqueror were flying,
            At his bidding it arose,
                In its panoply of stone,
                    A sentinel unliving and undying.

            Insensible, I trow,
                As a sentinel should be,
                    Though a queen to save her head[11] should come
                         a-suing,
            There's a legend on its brow
                That is eloquent to me,
                    And it tells of duty done and duty doing.

                    'The screw may twist and the rack may turn,
                    And men may bleed and men may burn,
                    O'er London town and its golden hoard
                    I keep my silent watch and ward!'

YEOMEN CHORUS:
                    The screw may twist, etc.

DAME:
> Within its wall of rock
>> The flower of the brave
>>> Have perished with a constancy unshaken.
> From the dungeon to the block,
>> From the scaffold to the grave,
>>> Is a journey many gallant hearts have taken.
> And the wicked flames may hiss
>> Round the heroes who have fought
>>> For conscience and for home in all its beauty,
> But the grim old fortalice
>> Takes little heed of aught
>>> That comes not in the measure of its duty.

> 'The screw may twist and the rack may turn,
> And men may bleed and men may burn,
> O'er London town and its golden hoard
> I keep my silent watch and ward!'

YEOMEN CHORUS:
> The screw may twist, etc.

> *[Exeunt all but* PHOEBE.]

[*Enter* SERGEANT MERYLL.]

PHOE.: Father! Has no reprieve arrived for the poor gentleman?

MER.: No, my lass; but there's one hope yet. Thy brother Leonard, who, as a reward for his valour in saving his standard and cutting his way through fifty foes who would have hanged him, has been appointed a Yeoman of the Guard, will arrive to-day; and as he comes straight from Windsor, where the Court is, it may be – it *may* be – that he will bring the expected reprieve with him.

PHOE.: Oh, that he may!

MER.: Amen to that! For the Colonel twice saved my life, and I'd give the rest of my life to save his! And wilt thou not be glad to welcome thy brave brother, with the fame of whose exploits all England is a-ringing?

PHOE.: Aye, truly, if he brings the reprieve.

MER.: And not otherwise?

PHOE.: Well, he's a brave fellow indeed, and I love brave men.

MER.: *All* brave men?

PHOE.: Most of them, I verily believe! But I hope Leonard will not be too strict with me – they say he is a very dragon of virtue and circumspection! Now, my dear old father is kindness itself, and –

MER.: And leaves thee pretty well to thine own ways, eh? Well, I've no fears for thee; thou hast a feather-brain, but thou'rt a good lass.

PHOE.: Yes, that's all very well, but if Leonard is going to tell me that I may not do this and I may not do that, and I must not talk to this one, or walk with that one, but go through the world with my lips pursed up and my eyes cast down, like a poor nun who has renounced mankind – why, as I have *not* renounced mankind, and don't mean to renounce mankind, I won't have it – there!

MER.: Nay, he'll not check thee more than is good for thee, Phoebe! He's a brave fellow, and bravest among brave fellows, and yet it seems but yesterday that he robbed the Lieutenant's orchard.

SONG

MER.:
A laughing boy but yesterday,
A merry urchin, blithe and gay!
    Whose joyous shout
    Came ringing out,
  Unchecked by care or sorrow–
To-day, a warrior, all sun-brown,
Whose deeds of soldierly renown
Are all the boast of London Town:
    A veteran, to-morrow!

When at my Leonard's deeds sublime
A soldier's pulse beats double time,
    And brave hearts thrill,
    As brave hearts will,
    At tales of martial glory,
I burn with flush of pride and joy,
A pride unbittered by alloy,
To find my boy – my darling boy –
    The theme of song and story!

[*Enter* LEONARD MERYLL.]

LEON.: Father!

MER.: Leonard! my brave boy! I'm right glad to see thee, and so is Phoebe!

PHOE.: Aye – hast thou brought Colonel Fairfax's reprieve?

LEON.: Nay, I have here a despatch for the Lieutenant, but no reprieve for the Colonel!

PHOE.: Poor gentleman! poor gentleman!

LEON.: Aye, I would I had brought better news. I'd give my right hand – nay, my body – my life, to save his!

MER.: Dost thou speak in earnest, my lad?

LEON.: Aye, father – I'm no braggart. Did he not save thy life? and am I not his foster-brother?

MER.: Then hearken to me. Thou hast come to join the Yeomen of the Guard!

LEON.: Well?

MER.: None has seen thee but ourselves?

LEON.: And a sentry, who took but scant notice of me.

MER.: Now to prove thy words. Give me the despatch, and get thee hence at once! Here is money, and I'll send thee more. Lie hidden for a space, and let no one know. I'll convey a suit of Yeoman's uniform to the Colonel's cell – he shall shave off his beard, so that none shall know him, and I'll own him as my son, the brave Leonard Meryll, who saved his flag and cut his way through fifty foes who thirsted for his life. He will be welcomed without question by my brother-Yeomen, I'll warrant that. Now, how to get access to the Colonel's cell? [*To* PHOEBE.] The key is with thy sour-faced admirer, Wilfred Shadbolt.

PHOE. [*demurely*]: I think – I say, I *think* – I can get anything I want from Wilfred. I think – mind I say, I *think* – you may leave that to me.

MER.: Then get thee hence at once, lad – and bless thee for this sacrifice.

PHOE.: And take my blessing, too, dear, dear Leonard!

LEON.: And thine, eh? Humph! Thy love is new-born; wrap it up carefully, lest it take cold and die.

TRIO – PHOEBE, LEONARD, MERYLL

PHOE.:   Alas! I waver to and fro!
             Dark danger hangs upon the deed!

ALL: Dark danger hangs upon the deed!

LEON.:   The scheme is rash and well may fail,
          But ours are not the hearts that quail,
          The hands that shrink, the cheeks that pale
              In hours of need!

ALL: No, ours are not the hearts that quail,
          The hands that shrink, the cheeks that pale
              In hours of need!

MER.:   The air I breathe to him I owe:
          My life is his – I count it naught!

PHOE. *and* LEON.:
          That life is his – so count it naught!

MER.:   And shall I reckon risks I run
          When services are to be done
          To save the life of such an one?
              Unworthy thought!

PHOE. *and* LEON.:
          And shall we reckon risks we run
          To save the life of such an one?

ALL: Unworthy thought!
        We may succeed – who can foretell!
        May heaven help our hope – farewell!
    [LEONARD *embraces* MERYLL *and* PHOEBE, *and then exit,*
                  PHOEBE *weeping.*]

MER.: Nay, lass, be of good cheer, we may save him yet.

PHOE.: Oh! see, father – they bring the poor gentleman from the Beauchamp! Oh, father! his hour is not yet come?

MER.: No, no, – they lead him to the Cold Harbour Tower to await his end in solitude. But softly – the Lieutenant approaches! He should not see thee weep.

[*Enter* COLONEL FAIRFAX, *guarded. The* LIEUTENANT[12] *enters, meeting him.*]

LIEUT.: Halt! Colonel Fairfax, my old friend, we meet but sadly.

FAIR.: Sir, I greet you with all good-will; and I thank you for the zealous care with which you have guarded me from the pestilent dangers which threaten human life outside. In this happy little community, Death, when he comes, doth so in punctual and business-like fashion; and, like a courtly gentleman, giveth due notice of his advent, that one may not be taken unawares.

LIEUT.: Sir, you bear this bravely, as a brave man should.

FAIR.: Why, sir, it is no light boon to die swiftly and surely at a given hour and in a given fashion! Truth to tell, I would gladly have my life; but if that may not be, I have the next best thing to it, which is death. Believe me, sir, my lot is not so much amiss!

PHOE. [*aside to* MERYLL]: Oh, father, father, I cannot bear it!

MER.: My poor lass!

FAIR.: Nay, pretty one, why weepest thou? Come, be comforted. Such a life as mine is not worth weeping for. [*Sees* MERYLL.] Sergeant Meryll, is it not? [*To* LIEUT.] May I greet my old friend? [*Shakes* MERYLL'*s hand.*] Why, man, what's all this? Thou and I have faced the grim old king a dozen times, and never has his majesty come to me in such goodly fashion. Keep a stout heart, good fellow – we are soldiers, and we know how to die, thou and I. Take my word for it, it is easier to die well than to live well – for, in sooth, I have tried both.

BALLAD

FAIR.:

> Is life a boon?
> If so, it must befall
> That Death, whene'er he call,

Must call too soon.
>   Though fourscore years he give,
>   Yet one would pray to live
Another moon!
>   What kind of plaint have I,
>   Who perish in July?
>   I might have had to die,
Perchance, in June!

Is life a thorn?
>   Then count it not a whit!
>   Man is well done with it;
Soon as he's born
>   He should all means essay
>   To put the plague away;
And I, war-worn,
>   Poor captured fugitive,
>   My life most gladly give –
>   I might have had to live
Another morn!

[*At the end,* PHOEBE *is led off, weeping, by* MERYLL.]

And now, Sir Richard, I have a boon to beg. I am in this strait for no better reason than because my kinsman, Sir Clarence Poltwhistle,[13] one of the Secretaries of State, has charged me with sorcery, in order that he may succeed to my estate, which devolves to him provided I die unmarried.

LIEUT.: As thou wilt most surely do.

FAIR.: Nay, as I will most surely *not* do, by your worship's grace! I have a mind to thwart this good cousin of mine.

LIEUT.: How?

FAIR.: By marrying forthwith, to be sure!

LIEUT.: But heaven ha' mercy, whom wouldst thou marry?

FAIR.: Nay, I am indifferent on that score. Coming Death hath made of me a true and chivalrous knight, who holds all womankind in such esteem that the oldest, and the meanest, and the worst-favoured of them is good enough for him. So, my good Lieutenant, if thou wouldst serve a poor soldier who has but an hour to live, find me the first that comes – my confessor shall marry us, and her dower shall be my dishonoured name and an hundred crowns[14] to boot. No such poor dower for an hour of matrimony!

LIEUT.: A strange request. I doubt that I should be warranted in granting it.

FAIR.: There never was a marriage fraught with so little of evil to the contracting parties. In an hour she'll be a widow, and I – a bachelor again for aught I know!

LIEUT.: Well, I will see what can be done, for I hold thy kinsman in abhorrence for the scurvy trick[15] he has played thee.

FAIR.: A thousand thanks, good sir; we meet again on this spot in an hour or so. I shall be a bridegroom then, and your worship will wish me joy. Till then, farewell. [*To Guard*] I am ready, good fellows.   [*Exit with Guard into Cold Harbour Tower.*]

LIEUT.: He is a brave fellow, and it is a pity that he should die. Now, how to find him a bride at such short notice? Well, the task should be easy!   [*Exit.*]

[*Enter* JACK POINT *and* ELSIE MAYNARD, *pursued by a crowd of men and women.* POINT *and* ELSIE *are much terrified;* POINT, *however, assuming an appearance of self-possession.*]

CHORUS: Here's a man of jollity,
                       Jibe, joke, jollify!
              Give us of your quality,
                  Come, fool, follify![16]

              If you vapour vapidly,
              River runneth rapidly,
                  Into it we fling
                  Bird who doesn't sing!

              Give us an experiment
              In the art of merriment;
                  Into it we throw
                  Cock who doesn't crow!

Banish your timidity,
And with all rapidity
Give us quip and quiddity –
Willy-nilly, O!

River none can mollify; –
Into it we throw
Fool who doesn't follify,
Cock who doesn't crow!

POINT [*alarmed*]: My masters, I pray you bear with us, and we will satisfy you, for we are merry folk who would make all merry as ourselves. For, look you, there is humour in all things, and the truest philosophy is that which teaches us to find it and to make the most of it.

ELSIE [*struggling with one of the crowd*]: Hands off, I say, unmannerly fellow!

POINT [*to 1st Citizen*]: Ha! Didst thou hear her say, 'Hands off'?

1ST CIT.: Aye, I heard her say it, and I felt her do it! What then?

POINT: Thou dost not see the humour of that?

1ST CIT.: Nay, if I do, hang me!

POINT: Thou dost not? Now observe. She said, 'Hands off!' Whose hands? Thine. Off whom? Off *her*. Why? Because she is a woman. Now, had she *not* been a woman, thine hands had not been set upon her at all. So the reason for the laying on of hands is the reason for the taking off of hands, and herein is contradiction contradicted! It is the very marriage of *pro* with *con*; and no such lopsided union either, as times go, for *pro* is not more unlike *con* than man is unlike woman – yet men and women marry every day with none to say, 'Oh, the pity of it!' but I and fools like me! Now wherewithal shall we please you? We can rhyme you couplet, triolet, quatrain, sonnet, rondolet, ballade, what you will. Or we can dance you saraband, gondolet, carole, pimpernel or Jumping Joan.[17]

ELSIE: Let us give them the singing farce of the Merryman and his Maid – therein is song and dance too.

ALL: Aye, the Merryman and his Maid!

DUET – ELSIE *and* POINT

POINT: I have a song to sing, O!
ELSIE: Sing me your song, O!
POINT: It is sung to the moon
                           By a love-lorn loon,
        Who fled from the mocking throng, O!
It's a song of a merryman, moping mum,
Whose soul was sad, and whose glance was glum,
Who sipped no sup, and who craved no crumb,
        As he sighed for the love of a ladye.
              Heighdy! heighdy!
              Misery me, lackadaydee!
He sipped no sup, and he craved no crumb,
        As he sighed for the love of a ladye.

ELSIE: I have a song to sing, O!
POINT: What is your song, O?
ELSIE: It is sung with the ring
                           Of the songs maids sing
        Who love with a love life-long, O!
It's the song of a merrymaid, peerly proud,
Who loved a lord, and who laughed aloud
At the moan of the merryman, moping mum,
Whose soul was sad, and whose glance was glum,
Who sipped no sup, and who craved no crumb,
        As he sighed for the love of a ladye!
              Heighdy! heighdy!
               Misery me, lackadaydee!
               He sipped no sup, etc.

POINT: I have a song to sing, O!
ELSIE: Sing me your song, O!
POINT: It is sung to the knell
                           Of a churchyard bell,
        And a doleful dirge, ding dong, O!
It's a song of a popinjay, bravely born,

Who turned up his noble nose with scorn
At the humble merrymaid, peerly proud,
Who loved a lord, and who laughed aloud
At the moan of the merryman, moping mum,
Whose soul was sad, and whose glance was glum,
Who sipped no sup, and who craved no crumb,
　　As he sighed for the love of a ladye!

BOTH:　　　　　　　　Heighdy! heighdy!
　　　　　　　　　Misery me, lackadaydee!
　　　　　　　　　He sipped no sup, etc.

ELSIE:　　　　　　　I have a song to sing, O!
POINT:　　　　　　　Sing me your song, O!
ELSIE:　　　　　　　It is sung with a sigh
　　　　　　　　　And a tear in the eye,
　　　　For it tells of a righted wrong, O!
It's a song of the merrymaid, once so gay,
Who turned on her heel and tripped away
From the peacock popinjay, bravely born,
Who turned up his noble nose with scorn
At the humble heart that he did not prize:
So she begged on her knees, with downcast eyes,
For the love of the merryman, moping mum,
Whose soul was sad, and whose glance was glum,
Who sipped no sup, and who craved no crumb,
　　As he sighed for the love of a ladye!
BOTH:　　　　　　　Heighdy! heighdy!
　　　　　　　　　Misery me, lackadaydee!
His pains were o'er, and he sighed no more,
　　For he lived in the love of a ladye!

1ST CIT.: Well sung and well danced!
2ND CIT.: A kiss for that, pretty maid!
ALL: Aye, a kiss all round.
ELSIE [*drawing dagger*]: Best beware! I am armed!
POINT: Back, sirs – back! This is going too far.

2ND CIT.: Thou dost not see the humour of it, eh? Yet there is humour in all things – even in this. [*Trying to kiss her.*]

ELSIE: Help! help!

[*Enter* LIEUTENANT *with Guard. Crowd falls back.*]

LIEUT.: What is this pother?

ELSIE: Sir, we sang to these folk, and they would have repaid us with gross courtesy, but for your honour's coming.

LIEUT. [*to Mob*]: Away with ye! Clear the rabble.

[*Guards push Crowd off, and go off with them.*]

Now, my girl, who are you, and what do you here?

ELSIE: May it please you, sir, we are two strolling players, Jack Point and I, Elsie Maynard, at your worship's service. We go from fair to fair, singing, and dancing, and playing brief interludes; and so we make a poor living.

LIEUT.: You two, eh? Are ye man and wife?

POINT: No, sir; for though I'm a fool, there is a limit to my folly. Her mother, old Bridget Maynard, travels with us (for Elsie is a good girl), but the old woman is a-bed with fever, and we have come here to pick up some silver to buy an electuary[18] for her.

LIEUT.: Hark ye, my girl! Your mother is ill?

ELSIE: Sorely ill, sir.

LIEUT.: And needs good food, and many things that thou canst not buy?

ELSIE: Alas! sir, it is too true.

LIEUT.: Wouldst thou earn an hundred crowns?

ELSIE: An hundred crowns! They might save her life!

LIEUT.: Then listen! A worthy but unhappy gentleman is to be beheaded in an hour on this very spot. For sufficient reasons, he desires to marry before he dies, and he hath asked me to find him a wife. Wilt thou be that wife?

ELSIE: The wife of a man I have never seen!

POINT: Why, sir, look you, I am concerned in this; for though I am not yet wedded to Elsie Maynard, time works wonders, and there's no knowing what may be in store for us. Have we your worship's word for it that this gentleman will die to-day?

LIEUT.: Nothing is more certain, I grieve to say.

POINT: And that the maiden will be allowed to depart the very instant
the ceremony is at an end?

LIEUT.: The very instant. I pledge my honour that it shall be so.

POINT: An hundred crowns?

LIEUT.: An hundred crowns!

POINT: For my part, I consent. It is for Elsie to speak.

TRIO – ELSIE, POINT *and* LIEUTENANT

LIEUT.:   How say you, maiden, will you wed
               A man about to lose his head?
                   For half an hour
                     You'll be a wife,
                   And then the dower
                     Is yours for life.
          A headless bridegroom why refuse?
            If truth the poets tell,
          Most bridegrooms, ere they marry, lose
            Both head and heart as well!

ELSIE: A strange proposal you reveal,
               It almost makes my senses reel.
               Alas! I'm very poor indeed,
               And such a sum I sorely need.
           My mother, sir, is like to die,
            This money life may bring.
          Bear this in mind, I pray, if I
            Consent to do this thing!

POINT: Though as a general rule of life
               I don't allow my promised wife,
               My lovely bride that is to be,
               To marry any one but me,
           Yet if the fee is promptly paid,
            And he, in well-earned grave,
           Within the hour is duly laid,
            Objection I will waive!
            Yes, objection I will waive!

ALL: Temptation, oh, temptation,
                Were we, I pray, intended
                To shun, whate'er our station,
                Your fascinations splendid;
              Or fall, whene'er we view you,
              Head over heels into you?
                    Temptation, oh, temptation, etc.

[*During this, the* LIEUTENANT *has whispered to* WILFRED (*who has entered*). WILFRED *binds* ELSIE's *eyes with a kerchief, and leads her into the Cold Harbour Tower.*]

LIEUT.: And so, good fellow, you are a jester?

POINT: Aye, sir, and, like some of my jests, out of place.

LIEUT.: I have a vacancy for such an one. Tell me, what are your qualifications for such a post?

POINT: Marry, sir, I have a pretty wit. I can rhyme you extempore; I can convulse you with quip and conundrum; I have the lighter philosophies at my tongue's tip; I can be merry, wise, quaint, grim and sardonic, one by one, or all at once; I have a pretty turn for anecdote; I know all the jests – ancient and modern – past, present and to come; I can riddle you from dawn of day to set of sun, and, if that content you not, well on to midnight and the small hours. Oh, sir, a pretty wit, I warrant you – a pretty, pretty wit!

RECITATIVE *and* SONG

POINT: I've jibe and joke
                    And quip and crank
                  For lowly folk
                    And men of rank.
                  I ply my craft
                    And know no fear,
                  But aim my shaft
                    At prince or peer.
                At peer or prince – at prince or peer,
                I aim my shaft and know no fear!

I've wisdom from the East and from the West,[19]
    That's subject to no academic rule;
You may find it in the jeering of a jest,
    Or distil it from the folly of a fool.
I can teach you with a quip, if I've a mind;
    I can trick you into learning with a laugh;
Oh, winnow all my folly, and you'll find
    A grain or two of truth among the chaff!

I can set a braggart quailing with a quip,
    The upstart I can wither with a whim;
He may wear a merry laugh upon his lip,
    But his laughter has an echo that is grim!
When they're offered to the world in merry guise,
    Unpleasant truths are swallowed with a will –
For he who'd make his fellow-creatures wise
    Should always gild the philosphic pill![20]

LIEUT.: And how came you to leave your last employ?
POINT: Why, sir, it was in this wise. My Lord was the Archbishop of
Canterbury, and it was considered that one of my jokes was unsuited
to His Grace's family circle. In truth, I ventured to ask a poor riddle,
sir – Wherein lay the difference between His Grace and poor Jack
Point? His Grace was pleased to give it up, sir. And thereupon I
told him that whereas His Grace was paid £10,000 a year for being
good, poor Jack Point was good – for nothing. 'Twas but a harmless
jest, but it offended His Grace, who whipped me and set me in the
stocks for a scurril rogue, and so we parted. I had as lief not take
post again with the dignified clergy.
LIEUT.: But I trust you are very careful not to give offence. I have
daughters.
POINT: Sir, my jests are most carefully selected, and anything objectionable is expunged. If your honour pleases, I will try them first
on your honour's chaplain.
LIEUT.: Can you give me an example? Say that I had sat me down
hurriedly on something sharp?
POINT: Sir, I should say that you had sat down on the spur of the
moment.

LIEUT.: Humph! I don't think much of that. Is that the best you can do?

POINT: It has always been much admired, sir, but we will try again.

LIEUT.: Well, then, I am at dinner, and the joint of meat is but half cooked.

POINT: Why then, sir, I should say that what is *under*done cannot be helped.

LIEUT.: I see. I think that manner of thing would be somewhat irritating.

POINT: At first, sir, perhaps; but use is everything, and you would come in time to like it.

LIEUT.: We will suppose that I caught you kissing the kitchen wench under my very nose.

POINT: Under *her* very nose, good sir – not under yours! *That* is where *I* would kiss her. Do you take me? Oh, sir, a pretty wit – a pretty, pretty wit!

LIEUT.: The maiden comes. Follow me, friend, and we will discuss this matter at length in my library.

POINT: I am your worship's servant. That is to say, I trust I soon shall be. But, before proceeding to a more serious topic, can you tell me, sir, why a cook's brain-pan is like an overwound clock?

LIEUT.: A truce to this fooling – follow me.

POINT: Just my luck; my best conundrum wasted!

[*Exeunt.*]

[*Enter* ELSIE *from Tower, led by* WILFRED, *who removes the bandage from her eyes, and exit.*]

RECITATIVE *and* SONG

ELSIE: 'Tis done! I am a bride! Oh, little ring,
   That bearest in thy circlet all the gladness
That lovers hope for, and that poets sing,
   What bringest thou to me but gold and sadness?
A bridegroom all unknown, save in this wise,
To-day he dies! To-day, alas, he dies!

Though tear and long-drawn sigh
   Ill fit a bride,
No sadder wife than I
    The whole world wide!
      Ah me! Ah me!
      Yet maids there be
    Who would consent to lose
      The very rose of youth,
        The flower of life,
      To be, in honest truth,
        A wedded wife,
      No matter whose!

Ah me! what profit we,
   O maids that sigh,
Though gold, though gold should live
    If wedded love must die?
Ere half an hour has rung,
   A widow I!
Ah, heaven, he is too young,
    Too brave to die!
      Ah me! Ah me!
      Yet wives there be
    So weary worn, I trow,
      That they would scarce complain,
       So that they could
      In half an hour attain
       To widowhood,
        No matter how!

O weary wives
   Who widowhood would win,
Rejoice that ye have time
   To weary in.
   [*Exit* ELSIE *as* WILFRED *re-enters.*]

WIL. [*looking after* ELSIE]: 'Tis an odd freak, for a dying man and his confessor to be closeted alone with a strange singing girl. I would fain have espied them, but they stopped up the keyhole. *My* keyhole!

[*Enter* PHOEBE *with* MERYLL. MERYLL *remains in the background, unobserved by* WILFRED.]

PHOE. [*aside*]: Wilfred – and alone!

WIL.: Now what could he have wanted with her? That's what puzzles me!

PHOE. [*aside*]: Now to get the keys from him. [*Aloud*] Wilfred – has no reprieve arrived?

WIL.: None. Thine adored Fairfax is to die.

PHOE.: Nay, thou knowest that I have naught but pity for the poor condemned gentleman.

WIL.: I know that he who is about to die is more to thee than I, who am alive and well.

PHOE.: Why, that were out of reason, dear Wilfred. Do they not say that a live ass is better than a dead lion?[21] No, I don't mean that!

WIL.: Oh, they say that, do they?

PHOE.: It's unpardonably rude of them, but I believe they put it in that way. Not that it applies to thee, who art clever beyond all telling!

WIL.: Oh yes, as an assistant-tormentor.

PHOE.: Nay, as a wit, as a humorist, as a most philosophic commentator on the vanity of human resolution.

[PHOEBE *slyly takes bunch of keys from* WILFRED*'s waistband and hands them to* MERYLL, *who enters the Tower, unnoticed by* WILFRED.]

WIL.: Truly, I have seen great resolution give way under my persuasive methods [*working a small thumbscrew*]. In the nice regulation of a thumbscrew – in the hundredth part of a single revolution lieth all the difference between stony reticence and a torrent of impulsive unbosoming that the pen can scarcely follow. Ha! ha! I am a mad wag.

PHOE. [*with a grimace*]: Thou art a most light-hearted and delightful companion, Master Wilfred. Thine anecdotes of the torture-chamber are the prettiest hearing.

WIL.: I'm a pleasant fellow an I choose. I believe I am the merriest dog that barks. Ah, we might be passing happy together –

PHOE.: Perhaps. I do not know.

WIL.: For thou wouldst make a most tender and loving wife.

PHOE.: Aye, to one whom I really loved. For there is a wealth of love within this little heart – saving up for – I wonder whom? Now, of all the world of men, I wonder whom? To think that he whom I am to wed is now alive and somewhere! Perhaps far away, perhaps close at hand! And I know him not! It seemeth that I am wasting time in not knowing him.

WIL.: Now say that it is I – nay! suppose it for the nonce. Say that we are wed – suppose it only – say that thou art my very bride, and I thy cheery, joyous, bright, frolicsome husband – and that, the day's work being done, and the prisoners stored away for the night, thou and I are alone together – with a long, long evening before us!

PHOE. [*with a grimace*]: It is a pretty picture – but I scarcely know. It cometh so unexpectedly – and yet – and yet – *were* I thy bride –

WIL.: Aye! – wert thou my bride –?

PHOE.: Oh, how I would love thee!

SONG

PHOE.:

> Were I thy bride,
> Then all the world beside
> Were not too wide
>   To hold my wealth of love –
> Were I thy bride!

> Upon thy breast
> My loving head would rest,
>   As on her nest
>   The tender turtle dove –
> Were I thy bride!

> This heart of mine
> Would be one heart with thine,
>   And in that shrine
>   Our happiness would dwell –
> Were I thy bride!

And all day long
Our lives should be a song:
No grief, no wrong
Should make my heart rebel –
Were I thy bride!

The silvery flute,
The melancholy lute,
Were night-owl's hoot
To my low-whispered coo –
Were I thy bride!

The skylark's trill
Were but discordance shrill
To the soft thrill
Of wooing as I'd woo –
Were I thy bride!

[MERYLL *re-enters; gives keys to* PHOEBE, *who replaces them at* WILFRED's *girdle, unnoticed by him. Exit* MERYLL.]

The rose's sigh
Were as a carrion's cry
To lullaby
Such as I'd sing to thee,
Were I thy bride!

A feather's press
Were leaden heaviness
To my caress.
But then, of course, you see,
I'm not thy bride!   [*Exit* PHOEBE.]

WIL.: No, thou'rt not – not yet! But, Lord, how she woo'd! I should be no mean judge of wooing, seeing that I have been more hotly woo'd than most men. I have been woo'd by maid, widow and wife. I have been woo'd boldly, timidly, tearfully, shyly – by direct assault, by suggestion, by implication, by inference and by innuendo. But this wooing is not of the common order: it is the wooing of one who must needs woo me, if she die for it!

[*Exit* WILFRED.]

[*Enter* MERYLL, *cautiously, from Tower.*]

MER. [*looking after them*]: The deed is, so far, safely accomplished. The slyboots, how she wheedled him! What a helpless ninny is a love-sick man! He is but as a lute in a woman's hands – she plays upon him whatever tune she will. But the Colonel comes. I' faith, he's just in time, for the Yeomen parade here for his execution in two minutes!

[*Enter* FAIRFAX, *without beard and moustache, and dressed in Yeoman's uniform.*]

FAIR.: My good and kind friend, thou runnest a grave risk for me!

MER.: Tut, sir, no risk. I'll warrant none here will recognize you. You make a brave Yeoman, sir! So – this ruff is too high; so – and the sword should hang thus. Here is your halbert, sir; carry it thus. The Yeomen come. Now remember, you are my brave son, Leonard Meryll.

FAIR.: If I may not bear mine own name, there is none other I would bear so readily.

MER.: Now, sir, put a bold face on it, for they come.

FINALE

[*Enter Yeomen of the Guard.*]

CHORUS: Oh, Sergeant Meryll, is it true –
    The welcome news we read in orders?
Thy son, whose deeds of derring-do
Are echoed all the country through,
    Has come to join the Tower Warders?
If so, we come to meet him,
That we may fitly greet him,
And welcome his arrival here
With shout on shout and cheer on cheer.
    Hurrah! Hurrah! Hurrah!

RECITATIVE

MER.:   Ye Tower Warders, nursed in war's alarms,
          Suckled on gunpowder, and weaned on glory,
      Behold my son, whose all-subduing arms
          Have formed the theme of many a song and story!
          Forgive his aged father's pride; nor jeer
          His aged father's sympathetic tear!

[*Pretending to weep.*]

CHORUS: Leonard Meryll!
          Leonard Meryll!
      Dauntless he in time of peril!
          Man of power,
          Knighthood's flower,
      Welcome to the grim old Tower,
      To the Tower, welcome thou!

RECITATIVE

FAIR.:   Forbear, my friends, and spare me this ovation,
      I have small claim to such consideration;
      The tales that of my prowess are narrated
      Have been prodigiously exaggerated!

CHORUS: 'Tis ever thus!
      Wherever valour true is found,
      True modesty will there abound.

COUPLETS

1ST YEO.:   Didst thou not, oh, Leonard Meryll!
          Standard lost in last campaign,[22]
      Rescue it at deadly peril –
          Bear it safely back again?

CHORUS: Leonard Meryll, at his peril,
      Bore it safely back again!

2ND YEO.:   Didst thou not, when prisoner taken,
    And debarred from all escape,
  Face, with gallant heart unshaken,
    Death in most appalling shape?

CHORUS: Leonard Meryll faced his peril,
  Death in most appalling shape!

FAIR. [*aside*]:   Truly I was to be pitied,
    Having but an hour to live,
  I reluctantly submitted,
    I had no alternative!

 [*Aloud*]   Oh! the tales that are narrated
    Of my deeds of derring-do
  Have been much exaggerated,
  Very much exaggerated,
    Scarce a word of them is true!

3RD YEO.:   You, when brought to execution,
    Like a demigod of yore,
  With heroic resolution
    Snatched a sword and killed a score!

CHORUS: Leonard Meryll, Leonard Meryll
  Snatched a sword and killed a score!

4TH YEO.:   Then escaping from the foemen,
    Boltered with the blood you shed,
  You, defiant, fearing no men,
    Saved your honour and your head!

CHORUS: Leonard Meryll, Leonard Meryll
  Saved his honour and his head!

FAIR.:   True, my course with judgment shaping,
    Favoured, too, by lucky star,

> I succeeded in escaping
>   Prison bolt and prison bar!
> Oh! the tales that have been stated
>   Of my deeds of derring-do,
> Have been much exaggerated, etc.

CHORUS: They are not exaggerated,
          Not at all exaggerated,
          Could not be exaggerated!
              Every word of them is true!

[*Enter* PHOEBE. *She rushes to* FAIRFAX. *Enter* WILFRED.]

RECITATIVE

PHOE.:   Leonard!
FAIR. [*puzzled*]:   I beg your pardon?
PHOE.:   Don't you know me?
          I'm little Phoebe!
FAIR. [*still puzzled*]:   Phoebe? Is this Phoebe?
          What! little Phoebe? [*Aside*] Who the deuce may *she*
            be?
          It can't be Phoebe, surely?
WIL.:   Yes, 'tis Phoebe –
          Your sister Phoebe! Your own little sister!
ALL: Aye, he speaks the truth;
          'Tis Phoebe!
FAIR. [*pretending to recognize her*]:
              Sister Phoebe!
PHOE.:   Oh, my brother!
FAIR.:   Why, how you've grown! I did not recognize you!
PHOE.:   So many years! Oh, brother!
FAIR.:   Oh, my sister!
WIL.:   Aye, hug him, girl! There are three thou mayst
            hug –
          Thy father and thy brother and – myself!
FAIR.:   Thyself, forsooth? And who art thou thyself?

WIL.:   Good sir, we are betrothed.
[FAIRFAX *turns inquiringly to* PHOEBE.]
PHOE.:   Or more or less –
But rather less than more!
WIL.:   To thy fond care
I do commend thy sister. Be to her
An ever-watchful guardian – eagle-eyed!
And when she feels (as sometimes she does feel)
Disposed to indiscriminate caress,
Be thou at hand to take those favours from her!
ALL: Be thou at hand to take those favours from her!
PHOE.:   Yes, yes.
Be thou at hand to take those favours from me!

TRIO – WILFRED, FAIRFAX *and* PHOEBE

WIL.:   To thy fraternal care
                Thy sister I commend;
           From every lurking snare
                Thy lovely charge defend:
                And to achieve this end,
           Oh! grant, I pray, this boon –
                She shall not quit thy sight:
           From morn to afternoon –
                From afternoon to night –
           From seven o'clock to two –
                From two to eventide –
           From dim twilight to 'leven at night
                She shall not quit thy side!

ALL: From morn to afternoon, etc.

PHOE.:   So amiable I've grown,
                So innocent as well,
           That if I'm left alone
                The consequences fell
                No mortal can foretell.

So grant, I pray, this boon –
   I shall not quit thy sight:
From morn to afternoon –
   From afternoon to night –
From seven o'clock to two –
   From two to eventide –
From dim twilight to 'leven at night
   I shall not quit thy side.

ALL: From morn to afternoon, etc.

FAIR.:   With brotherly readiness,
   For my fair sister's sake,
At once I answer 'Yes' –
   That task I undertake –
   My word I never break.
I freely grant that boon,
   And I'll repeat my plight.
From morn to afternoon – [*kiss*]
   From afternoon to night – [*kiss*]
From seven o'clock to two – [*kiss*]
   From two to evening meal – [*kiss*]
From dim twilight to 'leven at night
   That compact I will seal. [*kiss*]

ALL: From morn to afternoon, etc.

[*The bell of St Peter's*[23] *begins to toll. The Crowd enters; the block is brought on to the stage, and the Headsman takes his place. The Yeomen of the Guard form up. The* LIEUTENANT *enters and takes his place, and tells off* FAIRFAX *and two others to bring the prisoner to execution.* WILFRED, FAIRFAX *and two Yeomen exeunt to Tower.*]

CHORUS [*to tolling accompaniment*]:
      The prisoner comes to meet his doom;
      The block, the headsman and the tomb.

The funeral bell begins to toll –
May Heaven have mercy on his soul!

SOLO

ELSIE *and* CHORUS:

Oh, Mercy, thou whose smile has shone
So many a captive heart upon;
Of all immured within these walls,
To-day the very worthiest falls!

[*Enter* FAIRFAX *and two other Yeomen from Tower in great excitement.*]

FAIR.:   My lord! I know not how to tell
The news I bear!
I and my comrades sought the prisoner's cell –
He is not there!

ALL: He is not there!
They sought the prisoner's cell – he is not there!

TRIO

FAIRFAX *and* TWO YEOMEN:

As escort for the prisoner
We sought his cell, in duty bound;
The double gratings open were,
No prisoner at all we found!

We hunted high, we hunted low,
We hunted here, we hunted there –
The man we sought with anxious care
Had vanished into empty air!

[*Exit* LIEUTENANT.]

GIRLS: Now, by my troth, the news is fair,
The man has vanished into air!

ALL: As escort for the prisoner
       They sought his cell in duty bound, etc.
   [*Enter* WILFRED, *followed by* LIEUTENANT.]

LIEUT.:   Astounding news! The prisoner fled!
  [*To* WILFRED] Thy life shall forfeit be instead!
   [WILFRED *is arrested.*]

WIL.:   My lord, I did not set him free,
      I hate the man – my rival he!
   [WILFRED *is taken away.*]

MER.:   The prisoner gone – I'm all agape!
      Who could have helped him to escape?

PHOE.:   Indeed I can't imagine who!
      I've no idea at all – have you?
   [*Enter* JACK POINT.]

DAME: Of his escape no traces lurk,
      Enchantment must have been at work!

ELSIE [*aside to* POINT]:
      What have I done! Oh, woe is me!
      I am his wife, and he is free!

POINT: Oh, woe is *you*? Your anguish sink!
      Oh, woe is *me*, I rather think!
      Oh, woe is *me*, I rather think!
      Yes, woe is *me*, I rather think!
       Whate'er betide
       You are his bride,
       And I am left
       Alone – bereft!
      Yes, woe is *me*, I rather think!
      Yes, woe is *me*, I rather think!

ENSEMBLE

LIEUTENANT *and* CHORUS:

> All frenzied with despair I rave,
>> The grave is cheated of its due.
> Who is the misbegotten knave
>> Who hath contrived this deed to do?
> Let search be made throughout the land,
>
> Or $\left\{ \begin{array}{c} \text{his} \\ \text{my} \end{array} \right\}$ vindictive anger dread –
>
> A thousand marks[24] to him $\left\{ \begin{array}{c} \text{he'll} \\ \text{I'll} \end{array} \right\}$ hand
>> Who brings him here, alive or dead.

[*At the end,* ELSIE *faints in* FAIRFAX'*s arms; all the Yeomen and populace rush off the stage in different directions, to hunt for the fugitive, leaving only the Headsman on the stage, and* ELSIE *insensible in* FAIRFAX'*s arms.*]

END OF ACT I

ACT II

SCENE – *The same – Moonlight. Two days have elapsed.*

[*Women and Yeomen of the Guard discovered.*]

CHORUS: Night has spread her pall once more,
                 And the prisoner still is free:
            Open is his dungeon door,
                 Useless now his dungeon key!
            He has shaken off his yoke –
                 How, no mortal man can tell!
            Shame on loutish jailer-folk –
                 Shame on sleepy sentinel!
[*Enter* DAME CARRUTHERS *and* KATE.]

SOLO

DAME: Warders are ye?
                          Whom do ye ward?
                    Bolt, bar and key,
                          Shackle and cord,
                    Fetter and chain,
                          Dungeon of stone,
                    All are in vain –
                          Prisoner's flown!
            Spite of ye all, he is free – he is free!
            Whom do ye ward? Pretty warders are ye!

CHORUS OF WOMEN:
> Pretty warders are ye, etc.

CHORUS

YEOMEN:
> Up and down, and in and out,
> Here and there, and round about;
> Every chamber, every house,
> Every chink that holds a mouse,
> Every crevice in the keep,
> Where a beetle black could creep,
> Every outlet, every drain,
> Have we searched, but all in vain.

CHORUS:
> Warders are ye?
>> Whom do ye ward? etc.

> *[Exeunt all.]*
> *[Enter* JACK POINT, *in low spirits, reading from a huge volume.]*

POINT [*reads*]: 'The Merrie Jestes of Hugh Ambrose. No. 7863. The Poor Wit and the Rich Councillor. A certayne poor wit, being an-hungered, did meet a well-fed councillor. "Marry, fool," quoth the councillor, "whither away?" "In truth," said the poor wag, "in that I have eaten naught these two dayes, I do wither away, and that right rapidly!" The councillor laughed hugely, and gave him a sausage.' Humph! The councillor was easier to please than my new master the Lieutenant. I would like to take post under that councillor. Ah! 'tis but melancholy mumming when poor heart-broken, jilted Jack Point must needs turn to Hugh Ambrose for original light humour!

> *[Enter* WILFRED, *also in low spirits.]*

WIL. [*sighing*]: Ah, Master Point!

POINT [*changing his manner*]: Ha! friend jailer! Jailer that wast – jailer that never shalt be more! Jailer that jailed not, or that jailed, if jail he did, so unjailerly that 'twas but jerry-jailing, or jailing in joke – though no joke to him who, by unjailerlike jailing, did so jeopardize his jailership. Come, take heart, smile, laugh, wink, twinkle, thou tormentor that tormentest none – thou racker that rackest not – thou pincher out of place – come, take heart and be merry, as I am! – [*aside, dolefully*] – as I am!

WIL.: Aye, it's well for thee to laugh. Thou hast a good post, and hast cause to be merry.

POINT [*bitterly*]: Cause? Have we not all cause? Is not the world a big butt of humour, into which all who will may drive a gimlet? See, I am a salaried wit; and is there aught in nature more ridiculous? A poor, dull, heart-broken man, who must needs be merry, or he will be whipped; who must rejoice, lest he starve; who must jest you, jibe you, quip you, crank you, wrack you, riddle you, from hour to hour, from day to day, from year to year, lest he dwindle, perish, starve, pine and die! Why, when there's naught else to laugh at, I laugh at myself till I ache for it!

WIL.: Yet I have often thought that a jester's calling would suit me to a hair.

POINT: Thee? Would suit *thee*, thou death's head and cross-bones?

WIL.: Aye, I have a pretty wit – a light, airy, joysome wit, spiced with anecdotes of prison cells and the torture chamber. Oh, a very delicate wit! I have tried it on many a prisoner, and there have been some who smiled. Now it is not easy to make a prisoner smile. And it should not be difficult to be a good jester, seeing that thou art one.

POINT: Difficult? Nothing easier. Nothing easier. Attend, and I will prove it to thee!

SONG

POINT: Oh! a private buffoon is a light-hearted loon,
    If you listen to popular rumour;
From the morn to the night he's so joyous and bright,
    And he bubbles with wit and good humour!
He's so quaint and so terse, both in prose and in verse;
    Yet though people forgive his transgression,
There are one or two rules that all family fools
    Must observe, if they love their profession.
      There are one or two rules,

Half a dozen, may be,
That all family fools,
Of whatever degree,
Must observe, if they love their profession.

If you wish to succeed as a jester, you'll need
To consider each person's auricular:
What is all right for B would quite scandalize C
(For C is so very particular);
And D may be dull, and E's very thick skull
Is as empty of brains as a ladle;
While F is F sharp, and will cry with a carp
That he's known your best joke from his cradle!
When your humour they flout,
You can't let yourself go;
And it *does* put you out
When a person says, 'Oh,
I have known that old joke from my cradle!'

If your master is surly, from getting up early
(And tempers are short in the morning),
An inopportune joke is enough to provoke
Him to give you, at once, a month's warning.
Then if you refrain, he is at you again,
For he likes to get value for money;
He'll ask then and there, with an insolent stare,
'If you know that you're paid to be funny?'
It adds to the tasks
Of a merryman's place,
When your principal asks,
With a scowl on his face,
If you know that you're paid to be funny?

Comes a Bishop, maybe, or a solemn D.D.[25] –
Oh, beware of his anger provoking!
Better not pull his hair – don't stick pins in his chair;
He don't understand practical joking.

If the jests that you crack have an orthodox smack,
 You may get a bland smile from these sages;
But should they, by chance, be imported from France,
 Half-a-crown is stopped out of your wages!
   It's a general rule,
    Though your zeal it may quench,
   If the family fool
    Tells a joke that's too French,
  Half-a-crown is stopped out of his wages!

Though your head it may rack with a bilious attack,
 And your senses with toothache you're losing,
Don't be mopy and flat – they don't fine you for that,
 If you're properly quaint and amusing!
Though your wife ran away with a soldier that day,
 And took with her your trifle of money;
Bless your heart, they don't mind – they're exceedingly
 kind –
 They don't blame you – as long as you're funny!
   It's a comfort to feel,
    If your partner should flit,
   Though *you* suffer a deal,
    They don't mind it a bit –
  They don't blame you – so long as you're funny!

And so thou wouldst be a jester, eh?

WIL.: Aye!

POINT: Now, listen! My sweetheart, Elsie Maynard, was secretly wed
to this Fairfax half an hour ere he escaped.

WIL.: She did well.

POINT: She did nothing of the kind, so hold thy peace and perpend.
Now, while he liveth she is dead to me and I to her, and so, my
jibes and jokes notwithstanding, I am the saddest and the sorriest
dog in England!

WIL.: Thou art a very dull dog indeed.

POINT: Now, if thou wilt swear that thou didst shoot this Fairfax
while he was trying to swim across the river – it needs but the

discharge of an arquebus[26] on a dark night – and that he sank and was seen no more, I'll make thee the very Archbishop of jesters, and that in two days' time! Now, what sayest thou?

WIL.: I am to lie?

POINT: Heartily. But thy lie must be a lie of circumstance, which I will support with the testimony of eyes, ears and tongue.

WIL.: And thou wilt qualify me as a jester?

POINT: As a jester among jesters. I will teach thee all my original songs, my self-constructed riddles, my own ingenious paradoxes; nay, more, I will reveal to thee the source whence I get them. Now, what sayest thou?

WIL.: Why, if it be but a lie thou wantest of me, I hold it cheap enough, and I say yes, it is a bargain!

DUET – POINT *and* WILFRED

BOTH: Hereupon we're both agreed,
All that we two
Do agree to
We'll secure by solemn deed,
To prevent all
Error mental.

POINT: I on Elsie am to call
With a story
Grim and gory;

WIL.: How this Fairfax died, and all
I declare to
You're to swear to.

BOTH: Tell a tale of cock and bull,[27]
Of convincing detail full
Tale tremendous,
Heaven defend us!
What a tale of cock and bull!

BOTH:
In return for $\left\{\begin{array}{l}\text{your}\\\text{my}\end{array}\right\}$ own part

$\left.\begin{array}{l}\text{You are}\\\text{I am}\end{array}\right\}$ making

Undertaking

To instruct $\left\{\begin{array}{l}\text{me}\\\text{you}\end{array}\right\}$ in the art

(Art amazing,
Wonder raising)

POINT:
Of a jester, jesting free.
Proud position –
High ambition!

WIL.:
And a lively one I'll be,
Wag-a-wagging,
Never flagging!

BOTH:
Tell a tale of cock and bull, etc.

[*Exeunt together.*]

[*Enter* FAIRFAX.]

FAIR.: Two days gone, and no news of poor Fairfax. The dolts! They seek him everywhere save within a dozen yards of his dungeon. So I am free! Free, but for the cursed haste with which I hurried headlong into the bonds of matrimony with – Heaven knows whom! As far as I remember, she should have been young; but even had not her face been concealed by her kerchief, I doubt whether, in my then plight, I should have taken much note of her. Free? Bah! The Tower bonds were but a thread of silk compared with these conjugal fetters which I, fool that I was, placed upon mine own hands. From the one I broke readily enough – how to break the other!

BALLAD

FAIR.:   Free from his fetters grim –
                  Free to depart;
              Free both in life and limb –
                  In all but heart!
              Bound to an unknown bride
                  For good and ill;
              Ah, is not one so tied
                  A prisoner still?

              Free, yet in fetters held
                  Till his last hour,
              Gyves[28] that no smith can weld,
                  No rust devour!
              Although a monarch's hand
                  Had set him free,
              Of all the captive band
                  The saddest he!

[*Enter* MERYLL.]

FAIR.: Well, Sergeant Meryll, and how fares thy pretty charge, Elsie Maynard?

MER.: Well enough, sir. She is quite strong again, and leaves us to-night.

FAIR.: Thanks to Dame Carruthers' kind nursing, eh?

MER.: Aye, deuce take the old witch! Ah, 'twas but a sorry trick you played me, sir, to bring the fainting girl to me. It gave the old lady an excuse for taking up her quarters in my house, and for the last two years I've shunned her like the plague. Another day of it and she would have married me!

[*Enter* DAME CARRUTHERS *and* KATE.]

                          Good Lord, here she is again! I'll e'en go.

[*Going.*]

DAME: Nay, Sergeant Meryll, don't go. I have something of grave import to say to thee.

MER. [*aside*]: It's coming.

527

FAIR. [*laughing*]: I'faith, I think I'm not wanted here. [*Going.*]

DAME: Nay, Master Leonard, I've naught to say to thy father that his son may not hear.

FAIR. [*aside*]: True. I'm one of the family; I had forgotten!

DAME: 'Tis about this Elsie Maynard. A pretty girl, Master Leonard.

FAIR.: Aye, fair as a peach blossom – what then?

DAME: She hath a liking for thee, or I mistake not.

FAIR.: With all my heart. She's as dainty a little maid as you'll find in a midsummer day's march.

DAME: Then be warned in time, and give not thy heart to her. Oh, *I* know what it is to give my heart to one who will have none of it!

MER. [*aside*]: Aye, *she* knows all about that. [*Aloud*] And why is my boy to take heed of her? She's a good girl, Dame Carruthers.

DAME: Good enough, for aught I know. But she's no girl. She's a married woman.

MER.: A married woman! Tush, old lady – she's promised to Jack Point, the Lieutenant's new jester.

DAME: Tush in thy teeth, old man! As my niece Kate sat by her bedside to-day, this Elsie slept, and as she slept she moaned and groaned, and turned this way and that way – and, 'How shall I marry one I have never seen?' quoth she – then, 'An hundred crowns!' quoth she – then, 'Is it certain he will die in an hour?' quoth she – then, 'I love him not, and yet I am his wife,' quoth she! Is it not so, Kate?

KATE: Aye, aunt, 'tis even so.

FAIR.: Art thou sure of all this?

KATE: Aye, sir, for I wrote it all down on my tablets.

DAME: Now, mark my words: it was of this Fairfax she spake, and he is her husband, or I'll swallow my kirtle!

MER. [*aside*]: Is it true, sir?

FAIR. [*aside to* MERYLL]: True? Why, the girl was raving! [*Aloud*] Why should she marry a man who had but an hour to live?

DAME: Marry? There be those who would marry but for a minute, rather than die old maids.

MER. [*aside*]: Aye, I know one of them!

QUARTET – FAIRFAX, SERGEANT MERYLL,
DAME CARRUTHERS, KATE

Strange adventure! Maiden wedded
To a groom she's never seen –
Never, never, never seen!
Groom about to be beheaded,
In an hour on Tower Green!
Tower, Tower, Tower Green!
Groom in dreary dungeon lying,
Groom as good as dead, or dying,
For a pretty maiden sighing –
Pretty maid of seventeen!
Seven – seven – seventeen!

Strange adventure that we're trolling:
Modest maid and gallant groom –
Gallant, gallant, gallant groom! –
While the funeral bell is tolling,
Tolling, tolling, Bim-a-boom!
Bim-a, Bim-a, Bim-a-boom!
Modest maiden will not tarry;
Though but sixteen years she carry,
She must marry, she must marry,
Though the altar be a tomb –
Tower – Tower – Tower tomb!

[*Exeunt* DAME CARRUTHERS, MERYLL *and* KATE.]

FAIR.: So my mysterious bride is no other than this winsome Elsie!
By my hand, 'tis no such ill plunge in Fortune's lucky bag! I might
have fared worse with my eyes open! But she comes. Now to test
her principles. 'Tis not every husband who has a chance of wooing
his own wife!

[*Enter* ELSIE.]

FAIR.: Mistress Elsie!

ELSIE: Master Leonard!

FAIR.: So thou leavest us to-night?

ELSIE: Yes, Master Leonard. I have been kindly tended, and I almost
fear I am loth to go.

FAIR.: And this Fairfax. Wast thou glad when he escaped?

ELSIE: Why, truly, Master Leonard, it is a sad thing that a young and
gallant gentleman should die in the very fullness of his life.

FAIR.: Then when thou didst faint in my arms, it was for joy at his
safety?

ELSIE: It may be so. I was highly wrought, Master Leonard, and I am
but a girl, and so, when I am highly wrought, I faint.

FAIR.: Now, dost thou know, I am consumed with a parlous jealousy?

ELSIE: Thou? And of whom?

FAIR.: Why, of this Fairfax, surely!

ELSIE: Of Colonel Fairfax?

FAIR.: Aye. Shall I be frank with thee? Elsie – I love thee, ardently,
passionately! [ELSIE *alarmed and surprised*.] Elsie, I have loved
thee these two days – which is a long time – and I would fain join
my life to thine!

ELSIE: Master Leonard! Thou art jesting!

FAIR.: Jesting? May I shrivel into raisins if I jest! I love thee with a
love that is a fever – with a love that is a frenzy – with a love that
eateth up my heart! What sayest thou? Thou wilt not let my heart
be eaten up?

ELSIE [*aside*]: Oh, mercy! What am I to say?

FAIR.: Dost thou love me, or hast thou been insensible these two
days?

ELSIE: I love all brave men.

FAIR.: Nay, there is love in excess. I thank heaven there are many
brave men in England; but if thou lovest them all, I withdraw my
thanks.

ELSIE: I love the bravest best. But, sir, I may not listen – I am not free
– I – I am a wife!

FAIR.: Thou a wife? Whose? His name? His hours are numbered –
nay, his grave is dug and his epitaph set up! Come, his name?

ELSIE: Oh, sir! keep my secret – it is the only barrier that Fate could
set up between us. My husband is none other than Colonel Fairfax!

FAIR.: The greatest villain unhung! The most ill-favoured, ill-
mannered, ill-natured, ill-omened, ill-tempered dog in Christendom!

ELSIE: It is very like. He is naught to me – for I never saw him. I was blindfolded, and he was to have died within the hour; and he did not die – and I am wedded to him, and my heart is broken!

FAIR.: He was to have died, and he did *not* die? The scoundrel! The perjured, traitorous villain! Thou shouldst have insisted on his dying first, to make sure. 'Tis the only way with these Fairfaxes.

ELSIE: I now wish I had!

FAIR. [*aside*]: Bloodthirsty little maiden! [*Aloud*] A fig for this Fairfax! Be mine – he will never know – he dares not show himself; and if he dare, what art thou to him? Fly with me, Elsie – we will be married tomorrow, and thou shalt be the happiest wife in England!

ELSIE: Master Leonard! I am amazed! Is it thus that brave soldiers speak to poor girls? Oh! for shame, for shame! I am wed – not the less because I love not my husband. I am a wife, sir, and I have a duty, and – oh, sir! thy words terrify me – they are not honest – they are wicked words, and unworthy thy great and brave heart! Oh, shame upon thee! shame upon thee!

FAIR.: Nay, Elsie, I did but jest. I spake but to try thee – [*Shot heard.*]
    [*Enter* MERYLL *hastily.*]

MER. [*recitative*]: Hark! What was that, sir?

FAIR.:   Why, an arquebus –
Fired from the wharf, unless I much mistake.

MER.: Strange – and at such an hour! What can it mean?
    [*Enter* CHORUS.]

CHORUS: Now what can that have been –
                        A shot so late at night,
                        Enough to cause a fright!
                  What can the portent mean?

                  Are foemen in the land?
                        Is London to be wrecked?
                        What are we to expect?
                  What danger is at hand?
                        Let us understand
                        What danger is at hand!
    [LIEUTENANT *enters, also* POINT *and* WILFRED.]

RECITATIVE

LIEUT.:	Who fired that shot? At once the truth declare!
WIL.:	My lord, 'twas I – to rashly judge forbear!
POINT:	My lord, 'twas he – to rashly judge forbear!

DUET *and* CHORUS – WILFRED *and* POINT

WIL.:   Like a ghost his vigil keeping –

POINT: Or a spectre all-appalling –

WIL.:   I beheld a figure creeping –

POINT: I should rather call it crawling –

WIL.:   He was creeping –

POINT: He was crawling –

WIL.:   He was creeping, creeping –

POINT: Crawling!

WIL.:   He was creeping –

POINT: He was crawling –

WIL.:   He was creeping, creeping –

POINT: Crawling!

WIL.:   Not a moment's hesitation –
        I myself upon him flung,
With a hurried exclamation
        To his draperies I hung;
Then we closed with one another
In a rough-and-tumble smother;
Colonel Fairfax and no other
        Was the man to whom I clung!

ALL: Colonel Fairfax and no other
        Was the man to whom he clung!

WIL.:   After mighty tug and tussle –

POINT: It resembled more a struggle –

WIL.:   He, by dint of stronger muscle –

POINT: Or by some infernal juggle –

WIL.: From my clutches quickly sliding –
POINT: I should rather call it slipping –
WIL.: With a view, no doubt, of hiding –
POINT: Or escaping to the shipping –
WIL.: With a gasp, and with a quiver –
POINT: I'd describe it as a shiver –
WIL.: Down he dived into the river,
        And, alas, I cannot swim.

ALL: It's enough to make one shiver –
     With a gasp and with a quiver,
     Down he dived into the river;
         It was very brave of him!

WIL.: Ingenuity is catching;
       With the view my king of pleasing,
     Arquebus from sentry snatching –
POINT: I should rather call it seizing –

WIL.:   With an ounce or two of lead
          I despatched him through the head!

ALL: With an ounce or two of lead
          He despatched him through the head!

WIL.: I discharged it without winking,
     Little time I lost in thinking,
     Like a stone I saw him sinking –
POINT: I should say a lump of lead.
ALL: He discharged it without winking,
     Little time he lost in thinking.
WIL.: Like a stone I saw him sinking –
POINT: I should say a lump of lead.
WIL.: Like a stone, my boy, I said –
POINT: Like a heavy lump of lead.
WIL.: Anyhow, the man is dead,
     Whether stone or lump of lead!

ALL: Anyhow, the man is dead,
                  Whether stone or lump of lead!
               Arquebus from sentry seizing,
               With the view his king of pleasing,
                  Wilfred shot him through the head,
                  And he's very, very dead.
               And it matters very little whether stone or lump of lead;
               It is very, very certain that he's very, very dead!

RECITATIVE

LIEUT.:   The river must be dragged – no time be lost;
               The body must be found, at any cost.
               To this attend without undue delay;
               So set to work with what despatch ye may!   [*Exit.*]

ALL: Yes, yes,
               We'll set to work with what despatch we may!
          [*Four men raise* WILFRED, *and carry him off on their shoulders.*]

CHORUS: Hail the valiant fellow who
               Did this deed of derring-do!
               Honours wait on such an one;
               By my head, 'twas bravely done!
               Now, by my head, 'twas bravely done!
               [*Exeunt all but* ELSIE, POINT, FAIRFAX *and* PHOEBE.]

POINT [*to* ELSIE, *who is weeping*]: Nay, sweetheart, be comforted.
   This Fairfax was but a pestilent fellow, and, as he had to die, he
   might as well die thus as any other way. 'Twas a good death.

ELSIE: Still, he was my husband, and had he not been, he was nevertheless a living man, and now he is dead; and so, by your leave, my
   tears may flow unchidden, Master Point.

FAIR.: And thou didst see all this?

POINT: Aye, with both eyes at once – this and that. The testimony of
   one eye is naught – he may lie. But when it is corroborated by the

other, it is good evidence that none may gainsay. Here are both present in court, ready to swear to him!

PHOE.: But art thou sure it was Colonel Fairfax? Saw you his face?

POINT: Aye, and a plaguey ill-favoured face too. A very hang-dog face – a felon face – a face to fright the headsman himself, and make him strike awry. Oh, a plaguey, bad face, take my word for 't. [PHOEBE *and* FAIRFAX *laugh.*] How they laugh! 'Tis ever thus with simple folk – an accepted wit has but to say 'Pass the mustard,' and they roar their ribs out!

FAIR. [*aside*]: If ever I come to life again, thou shalt pay for this, Master Point!

POINT: Now, Elsie, thou art free to choose again, so behold me: I am young and well-favoured. I have a pretty wit. I can jest you, jibe you, quip you, crank you, wrack you, riddle you –

FAIR.: Tush, man, thou knowest not how to woo. 'Tis not to be done with time-worn jests and thread-bare sophistries; with quips, conundrums, rhymes and paradoxes. 'Tis an art in itself, and must be studied gravely and conscientiously.

TRIO – ELSIE, PHOEBE *and* FAIRFAX

FAIR.:

A man who would woo a fair maid
Should 'prentice himself to the trade,
    And study all day,
    In methodical way,
How to flatter, cajole and persuade;
He should 'prentice himself at fourteen,
And practise from morning to e'en;
    And when he's of age,
    If he will, I'll engage,
He may capture the heart of a queen!

ALL:

It is purely a matter of skill,
Which all may attain if they will:
    But every Jack,
    He must study the knack
If he wants to make sure of his Jill!

ELSIE: If he's made the best use of his time,
     His twig he'll so carefully lime
       That every bird
       Will come down at his word,
     Whatever its plumage or clime.
     He must learn that the thrill of a touch
     May mean little, or nothing, or much:
       It's an instrument rare,
       To be handled with care,
     And ought to be treated as such.

ALL: It is purely a matter of skill, etc.

PHOE.: Then a glance may be timid or free,
     It will vary in mighty degree,
       From an impudent stare
       To a look of despair
     That no maid without pity can see!
     And a glance of despair is no guide –
     It may have its ridiculous side;
       It may draw you a tear
       Or a box on the ear;
     You can never be sure till you've tried!

ALL: It is purely a matter of skill, etc.

FAIR. [*aside to* POINT]: Now, listen to me – 'tis done thus – [*aloud*]
 – Mistress Elsie, there is one here who, as thou knowest, loves thee
 right well!

POINT [*aside*]: That he does – right well!

FAIR.: He is but a man of poor estate, but he hath a loving, honest
 heart. He will be a true and trusty husband to thee, and if thou wilt
 be his wife, thou shalt lie curled up in his heart, like a little squirrel
 in its nest!

POINT [*aside*]: 'Tis a pretty figure. A maggot in a nut lies closer, but
 a squirrel will do.

FAIR.: He knoweth that thou wast a wife – an unloved and unloving wife, and his poor heart was near to breaking. But now that thine unloving husband is dead, and thou art free, he would fain pray that thou wouldst hearken unto him, and give him hope that thou wouldst one day be his!

PHOE. [*alarmed*]: He presses her hands – and he whispers in her ear! Ods bodikins,[29] what does it mean?

FAIR.: Now, sweetheart, tell me – wilt thou be this poor good fellow's wife?

ELSIE: If the good, brave man – *is* he a brave man?

FAIR.: So men say.

POINT [*aside*]: That's not true, but let it pass.

ELSIE: If the brave man will be content with a poor, penniless, untaught maid –

POINT [*aside*]: Widow – but let *that* pass.

ELSIE: I will be his true and loving wife, and that with my heart of hearts!

FAIR.: My own dear love! [*Embracing her.*]

PHOE. [*in great agitation*]: Why, what's all this? Brother – brother – it is not seemly!

POINT [*also alarmed, aside*]: Oh, I can't let *that* pass! [*Aloud*] Hold, enough, Master Leonard! An advocate should have his fee, but methinks thou art over-paying thyself!

FAIR.: Nay, that is for Elsie to say. I promised thee I would show thee how to woo, and herein lies the proof of the virtue of my teaching. Go thou, and apply it elsewhere! [PHOEBE *bursts into tears.*]

QUARTET – ELSIE, PHOEBE, FAIRFAX, POINT

ELSIE *and* FAIR.:   When a wooer
                            Goes a-wooing,
                      Naught is truer
                            Than his joy.
                      Maiden hushing
                            All his suing –
                      Boldly blushing –
                            Bravely coy!

ALL:
 Oh, the happy days of doing!
 Oh, the sighing and the suing!
 When a wooer goes a-wooing,
  Oh, the sweets that never cloy!

PHOE. [*weeping*]:
 When a brother
  Leaves his sister
 For another,
  Sister weeps.
 Tears that trickle,
  Tears that blister –
 'Tis but mickle[30]
  Sister reaps!

ALL:
 Oh, the doing and undoing,
 Oh, the sighing and the suing,
 When a brother goes a-wooing,
  And a sobbing sister weeps!

POINT:
 When a jester
  Is outwitted,
 Feelings fester,
  Heart is lead!
 Food for fishes
  Only fitted,
 Jester wishes
  He was dead!

ALL:
 Oh, the doing and undoing,
 Oh, the sighing and the suing,
 When a jester goes a-wooing,
  And he wishes he was dead!
  [*Exeunt all but* PHOEBE, *who remains weeping.*]

PHOE.: And I helped that man to escape, and I've kept his secret, and pretended that I was his dearly loving sister, and done everything I could think of to make folk believe I *was* his loving sister, and this is his gratitude! Before I pretend to be sister to anybody again, I'll turn nun and be sister to everybody – one as much as another!

[*Enter* WILFRED.]

WIL.: In tears, eh? What a plague art thou grizzling for now?

PHOE.: Why am I grizzling? Thou hast often wept for jealousy – well, 'tis for jealousy I weep now. Aye, yellow, bilious, jaundiced jealousy. So make the most of that, Master Wilfred.

WIL.: But I have never given thee cause for jealousy. The Lieutenant's cook-maid and I are but the merest gossips!

PHOE.: Jealous of thee! Bah! I'm jealous of no craven cock-on-a-hill, who crows about what he'd do an he dared! I am jealous of another and a better man than thou – set that down, Master Wilfred. And he is to marry Elsie Maynard, the little pale fool – set that down, Master Wilfred – and my heart is wellnigh broken! There, thou hast it all! Make the most of it!

WIL.: The man thou lovest is to marry Elsie Maynard? Why, that is no other than thy brother, Leonard Meryll!

PHOE. [*aside*]: Oh, mercy! what have I said?

WIL.: Why, what manner of brother is this, thou lying little jade? Speak! Who is this man whom thou hast called brother, and fondled, and coddled, and kissed! – with my connivance, too! Oh Lord! with my connivance! Ha! should it be this Fairfax! [PHOEBE *starts*.] It is! It is this accursed Fairfax! It's Fairfax! Fairfax, who –

PHOE.: Whom thou hast just shot through the head, and who lies at the bottom of the river!

WIL.: A – I – I may have been mistaken. We are but fallible mortals, the best of us. But I'll make sure – I'll make sure. [*Going.*]

PHOE.: Stay – one word. I think it cannot be Fairfax – mind, I say I *think* – because thou hast just slain Fairfax. But whether he be Fairfax or no Fairfax, he is to marry Elsie – and – and – as thou hast shot him through the head, and he is dead, be content with that, and I will be thy wife!

WIL.: Is that sure?

PHOE.: Aye, sure enough, for there's no help for it! Thou art a very brute – but even brutes must marry, I suppose.

WIL.: My beloved! [*Embraces her.*]

PHOE. [*aside*]: Ugh!

[*Enter* LEONARD, *hastily.*]

LEON.: Phoebe, rejoice, for I bring glad tidings. Colonel Fairfax's reprieve was signed two days since, but it was foully and maliciously kept back by Secretary Poltwhistle, who designed that it should arrive after the Colonel's death. It hath just come to hand, and it is now in the Lieutenant's possession!

PHOE.: Then the Colonel is free? Oh, kiss me, kiss me, my dear! Kiss me, again, and again!

WIL. [*dancing with fury*]: Ods bobs, death o' my life! Art thou mad? Am *I* mad? Are we *all* mad?

PHOE.: Oh, my dear – my dear, I'm wellnigh crazed with joy! [*Kissing* LEONARD.]

WIL.: Come away from him, thou hussy – thou jade – thou kissing, clinging cockatrice![31] And as for thee, sir, devil take thee, I'll rip thee like a herring for this! I'll skin thee for it! I'll cleave thee to the chine! I'll – oh! Phoebe! Phoebe! Who is this man?

PHOE.: Peace, fool. He is my brother!

WIL.: Another brother! Are there any more of them? Produce them all at once, and let me know the worst!

PHOE.: This is the real Leonard, dolt; the other was but his substitute. The *real* Leonard, I say – my father's own son.

WIL.: How do I know this? Has he 'brother' writ large on his brow? I mistrust thy brothers! Thou art but a false jade!

[*Exit* LEONARD.]

PHOE.: Now, Wilfred, be just. Truly I did deceive thee before – but it was to save a precious life – and to save it, not for me, but for another. They are to be wed this very day. Is not this enough for thee? Come – I am thy Phoebe – thy very own – and we will be wed in a year – or two – or three, at the most. Is not that enough for thee?

[*Enter* MERYLL, *excitedly, followed by* DAME CARRUTHERS *who listens, unobserved.*]

MER.: Phoebe, hast thou heard the brave news?

PHOE. [*still in* WILFRED's *arms*]: Aye, father.

MER.: I'm nigh mad with joy! [*Seeing* WILFRED.] Why, what's all this?

PHOE.: Oh, father, he discovered our secret through my folly, and the price of his silence is –

WIL.: Phoebe's heart.

PHOE.: Oh dear, no – Phoebe's hand.

WIL.: It's the same thing!

PHOE.: *Is* it?

[*Exeunt* WILFRED *and* PHOEBE.]

MER. [*looking after them*]: 'Tis pity, but the Colonel had to be saved at any cost, and as thy folly revealed our secret, thy folly must e'en suffer for it! [DAME CARRUTHERS *comes down-stage.*] Dame Carruthers!

DAME: So this is a plot to shield this arch-fiend, and I have detected it. A word from me, and three heads besides his would roll from their shoulders!

MER.: Nay, Colonel Fairfax is reprieved. [*Aside*] Yet, if my complicity in his escape were known! Plague on the old meddler! There's nothing for it – [*aloud*] – Hush, pretty one! Such bloodthirsty words ill become those cherry lips! [*Aside*] Ugh!

DAME [*bashfully*]: Sergeant Meryll!

MER.: Why, look ye, chuck – for many a month I've – I've thought to myself – 'There's snug love saving up in that middle-aged bosom for some one, and why not for thee – that's me – so take heart and tell her – that's thee – that thou – that's me – lovest her – thee – and – and – well, I'm a miserable old man, and I've done it – and that's me!' But not a word about Fairfax! The price of thy silence is –

DAME: Meryll's heart?

MER.: No, Meryll's *hand*.

DAME: It's the same thing!

MER.: *Is* it!

DUET – DAME CARRUTHERS *and* SERGEANT MERYLL

DAME:

Rapture, rapture!
When love's votary,
Flushed with capture,
Seeks the notary,
Joy and jollity
Then is polity;
Reigns frivolity!
Rapture, rapture!

MER.:

Doleful, doleful!
When humanity,
With its soul full
Of satanity,
Courting privity,
Down declivity
Seeks captivity!
Doleful, doleful!

DAME:

Joyful, joyful!
When virginity
Seeks, all coyful,
Man's affinity;
Fate all flowery,
Bright and bowery,
Is her dowery!
Joyful, joyful!

MER.:

Ghastly, ghastly!
When man, sorrowful,
Firstly, lastly,
Of to-morrow full,
After tarrying,
Yields to harrying –
Goes a-marrying.
Ghastly, ghastly!

BOTH: Rapture, etc.

                              [*Exeunt* DAME *and* MERYLL.]

FINALE

[*Enter Yeomen and Women.*]

CHORUS OF WOMEN:

[ELEGIACS[32]]

Comes the pretty young bride, a-blushing, timidly
        shrinking –
    Set all thy fears aside – cheerily, pretty young bride!
Brave is the youth to whom thy lot thou art willingly
        linking!
    Flower of valour is he – loving as loving can be!
                Brightly thy summer is shining,
                Fair as the dawn of the day;
                    Take him, be true to him –
                    Tender his due to him –
                Honour him, love and obey!

[*Enter* DAME, PHOEBE *and* ELSIE *as Bride.*]

TRIO – PHOEBE, ELSIE, DAME CARRUTHERS

ALL: 'Tis said that joy in full perfection
            Comes only once to womankind –
        That, other times, on close inspection,
            Some lurking bitter we shall find.
        If this be so, and men say truly,
        My day of joy has broken duly.

        With happiness $\left\{ \begin{array}{c} \text{my} \\ \text{her} \end{array} \right\}$ soul is cloyed –

        This is $\left\{ \begin{array}{c} \text{my} \\ \text{her} \end{array} \right\}$ joy-day unalloyed!

        Yes, yes, with happiness her soul is cloyed!
        This is her joy-day unalloyed!

543

[*Flourish. Enter* LIEUTENANT.]

LIEUT.: Hold, pretty one! I bring to thee
　　　　　News – good or ill, it is for thee to say.
　　　　　Thy husband lives – and he is free,
　　　　　And comes to claim his bride this very day!

ELSIE: No! no! recall those words – it cannot be!

ENSEMBLE

KATE *and* CHORUS	DAME CARRUTHERS *and* PHOEBE
Oh, day of terror! Day of tears!	Oh, day of terror! Day of tears!
Who is the man who, in his pride,	The man to whom thou art allied
Claims thee as his bride?	Appears to claim thee as his bride.

LIEUT., MER., WIL.

	ELSIE
Come, dry these unbecoming,	Oh, Leonard, come thou to my side,
tears,	And claim me as thy loving bride!
Most joyful tidings greet thine	Oh, day of terror! Day of tears!
ears,	

The man to whom thou art allied
Appears to claim thee as his bride.

[*Flourish. Enter* COLONEL FAIRFAX, *handsomely dressed, and attended by other Gentlemen.*]

FAIR. [*sternly*]: All thought of Leonard Meryll set aside.
　　　　　　　Thou art mine own! I claim thee as my bride.

ALL: Thou art his own! Alas! he claims thee as his
　　　　　bride.

ELSIE: A suppliant at thy feet I fall;
　　　　Thine heart will yield to pity's call!

FAIR.: Mine is a heart of massive rock,
　　　　Unmoved by sentimental shock!

ALL: Thy husband he!

ELSIE [*aside*]:   Leonard, my loved one – come to me.
                            They bear me hence away!
                    But though they take me far from thee,
                            My heart is thine for aye!
                                My bruised heart,
                                My broken heart,
                    Is thine, my own, for aye!

[*To* FAIRFAX]
                            Sir, I obey!
                                I am thy bride;
                        But ere the fatal hour
                            I said the say
                    That placed me in thy power
                            Would I had died!
                        Sir, I obey!
                            I am thy bride!
            [*Looks up and recognizes* FAIRFAX.]
                        Leonard!
FAIR.:   My own!
ELSIE: Ah! [*Embrace.*]
ELSIE *and*   { With happiness my soul is cloyed,
    FAIR.:   { This is our joy-day unalloyed!

ALL: Yes, yes!
                    With happiness their souls are cloyed,
                    This is their joy-day unalloyed!
            [*Enter* JACK POINT.]

POINT: Oh, thoughtless crew!
                            Ye know not what ye do!
                    Attend to me, and shed a tear or two –
                        For I have a song to sing, O!

545

ALL: Sing me your song, O!

POINT: It is sung to the moon
By a love-lorn loon,
Who fled from the mocking throng, O!
It's the song of a merryman, moping mum,
Whose soul was sad, and whose glance was glum,
Who sipped no sup, and who craved no crumb,
As he sighed for the love of a ladye!

ALL: Heighdy! heighdy!
Misery me, lackadaydee!
He sipped no sup, and he craved no crumb,
As he sighed for the love of a ladye!

ELSIE: I have a song to sing, O!
ALL: What is your song, O?

ELSIE: It is sung with the ring
Of the songs maids sing
Who love with a love life-long, O!
It's the song of a merrymaid, nestling near,
Who loved her lord – but who dropped a tear
At the moan of the merryman, moping mum,
Whose soul was sad, and whose glance was glum,
Who sipped no sup, and who craved no crumb,
As he sighed for the love of a ladye!

ALL: Heighdy! heighdy!
Misery me, lackadaydee!
He sipped no sup, and he craved no crumb,
As he sighed for the love of a ladye!

[FAIRFAX *embraces* ELSIE *as* POINT *falls insensible at their feet.*]

CURTAIN

THE GONDOLIERS[1]

OR

THE KING OF BARATARIA

DRAMATIS PERSONAE

THE DUKE OF PLAZA-TORO (*a Grandee of Spain*)
LUIZ (*his Attendant*)
DON ALHAMBRA DEL BOLERO (*the Grand Inquisitor*)
MARCO PALMIERI ⎫
GIUSEPPE PALMIERI ⎪
ANTONIO ⎪
⎬ (*Venetian Gondoliers*)
FRANCESCO ⎪
GIORGIO ⎪
ANNIBALE ⎭
THE DUCHESS OF PLAZA-TORO
CASILDA (*her Daughter*)
GIANETTA ⎫
TESSA ⎪
FIAMETTA ⎬ (*Contadine*)
VITTORIA ⎪
GIULIA ⎭
INEZ (*the King's Foster-mother*)

Chorus of Gondoliers and Contadine, Men-at-Arms, Heralds and
 Pages

ACT I – The Piazzetta, Venice
ACT II – Pavilion in the Palace of Barataria
(*An interval of three months is supposed to elapse between Acts I*
and II)

Date 1750

ACT I

SCENE – *The Piazzetta,*[2] *Venice.*[3] *The Ducal Palace on the right.*

[FIAMETTA, GIULIA, VITTORIA *and other Contadine*[4] *discovered, each tying a bouquet of roses.*]

CHORUS OF CONTADINE:
    List and learn, ye dainty roses,
      Roses white and roses red,
    Why we bind you into posies
      Ere your morning bloom has fled.
    By a law of maiden's making,
    Accents of a heart that's aching,
    Even though that heart be breaking,
      Should by maiden be unsaid:
    Though they love with love exceeding,
    They must seem to be unheeding –
    Go ye then and do their pleading,
      Roses white and roses red!

FIA.:   Two there are for whom, in duty,
      Every maid in Venice sighs –
    Two so peerless in their beauty
      That they shame the summer skies.
    We have hearts for them, in plenty,
      They have hearts, but all too few,
    We, alas, are four-and-twenty!
      They, alas, are only two!

	We, alas!
CHORUS:	Alas!
FIA.:	Are four-and-twenty,
	They, alas!
CHORUS:	Alas!
FIA.:	Are only two.
CHORUS:	They, alas, are only two, alas!
	Now ye know, ye dainty roses,
	Why we bind you into posies,
	Ere your morning bloom has fled,
	Roses white and roses red!

[*During this chorus* ANTONIO, FRANCESCO, GIORGIO *and other Gondoliers have entered unobserved by the Girls – at first two, then two more, then four, then half a dozen, then the remainder of the Chorus.*]

SOLI

FRANC.:	Good morrow, pretty maids; for whom prepare ye
	These floral tributes extraordinary?
FIA.:	For Marco and Giuseppe Palmieri,
	The pink and flower of all the Gondolieri.[5]
GIULIA:	They're coming here, as we have heard but lately.
	To choose two brides from us who sit sedately.
ANT.:	Do all you maidens love them?
ALL:	Passionately!
ANT.:	These gondoliers are to be envied greatly!
GIOR.:	But what of us, who one and all adore you?
	Have pity on our passion, we implore you!
FIA.:	These gentlemen must make their choice before you;
VIT.:	In the meantime we tacitly ignore you.
GIULIA:	When they have chosen two that leaves you plenty –
	Two dozen we, and ye are four-and-twenty.
FIA. *and* VIT.:	Till then, enjoy your *dolce far niente*.[6]
ANT.:	With pleasure, nobody *contradicente*![7]

SONG – ANTONIO *and* CHORUS

For the merriest fellows are we, tra la,
That ply on the emerald sea, tra la;
  With loving and laughing,
  And quipping and quaffing,
We're happy as happy can be, tra la –
  As happy as happy can be!

With sorrow we've nothing to do, tra la,
And care is a thing to pooh-pooh, tra la;
  And Jealousy yellow,
  Unfortunate fellow,
We drown in the shimmering blue, tra la –
  We drown in the shimmering blue!

FIA. [*looking off*]:
  See, see, at last they come to make their choice –
  Let us acclaim them with united voice.
[MARCO *and* GIUSEPPE *appear in gondola at back.*]

CHORUS OF GIRLS:
  Hail, hail! gallant gondolieri, ben venuti![8]
  Accept our love, our homage and our duty.
[MARCO *and* GIUSEPPE *jump ashore – the Girls salute them.*]

DUET – MARCO *and* GIUSEPPE, *with* CHORUS OF GIRLS

MAR. *and* GIU.: Buon' giorno, signorine!
GIRLS: Gondolieri carissimi!
    Siamo contadine!

MAR. *and* GIU. [*bowing*]:
    Servitori umilissimi!
   Per chi questi fiori –
    Questi fiori bellissimi?

GIRLS: Per voi, bei signori
                        O eccellentissimi!

[*The Girls present their bouquets to* MARCO *and* GIUSEPPE,
who are overwhelmed with them, and carry them with difficulty.]

MAR. *and* GIU. [*their arms full of flowers*]:
                        O ciel'!
GIRLS: Buon' giorno, cavalieri!
MAR. *and* GIU. [*deprecatingly*]:
                        Siamo gondolieri.

   [*To* FIA. *and* VIT.]:
                        Signorina, io t'amo!
GIRLS [*deprecatingly*]:
                        Contadine siamo.
MAR. *and* GIU.:   Signorine!
GIRLS [*deprecatingly*]:
                        Contadine!
   [*Curtseying to* MAR. *and* GIU.]:
                        Cavalieri.
MAR. *and* GIU. [*deprecatingly*]:
                        Gondolieri!
                            Poveri gondolieri!

CHORUS: Buon' giorno, signorine, etc.[9]

DUET – MARCO *and* GIUSEPPE

We're called *gondolieri*,
But that's a vagary,
It's quite honorary
        The trade that we ply.
For gallantry noted
Since we were short-coated,
To beauty devoted,
        Guiseppe } and I;
        Are Marco }

When morning is breaking,
Our couches forsaking,
To greet their awaking
        With carols we come.
At summer day's nooning,
When weary lagooning,
Our mandolins tuning,
        We lazily thrum.
When vespers are ringing,
To hope ever clinging,
With songs of our singing
        A vigil we keep,
When daylight is fading,
Enwrapt in night's shading,
With soft serenading
        We sing them to sleep.

We're called *gondolieri*, etc.

RECITATIVE – MARCO *and* GIUSEPPE

MAR.:	And now to choose our brides!
GIU.:	As all are young and fair,
	And amiable besides,
BOTH:	We really do not care
	A preference to declare.
MAR.:	A bias to disclose
	Would be indelicate –
GIU.:	And therefore we propose
	To let impartial Fate
	Select for us a mate!
ALL:	Viva!
GIRLS:	A bias to disclose
	Would be indelicate –
MEN:	But how do they propose
	To let impartial Fate
	Select for them a mate?

GIU.: These handkerchiefs upon our eyes be good enough to bind,

MAR.: And take good care that both of us are absolutely blind;

BOTH: Then turn us round – and we, with all convenient despatch,
Will undertake to marry any two of you we catch!

ALL: Viva!

They undertake to marry any two of us $\begin{cases} \text{they catch} \\ \text{them they catch!} \end{cases}$

[*The Girls prepare to bind their eyes as directed.*]

FIA. [*to* MARCO]: Are you peeping?
Can you see me?

MAR.: Dark I'm keeping,
Dark and dreamy! [*slyly lifts bandage*].

VIT. [*to* GIUSEPPE]: If you're blinded
Truly, say so.

GIU.: All right-minded
Players play so! [*slyly lifts bandage*].

FIA. [*detecting* MARCO]:
Conduct shady!
They are cheating!
Surely they de-
Serve a beating! [*replaces bandage*].

VIT. [*detecting* GIUSEPPE]:
This too much is;
Maidens mocking –
Conduct such is
Truly shocking! [*replaces bandage*].

ALL: You can spy, sir!
Shut your eye, sir!
You may use it by and by, sir!
You can see, sir!
Don't tell me, sir!
That will do – now let it be, sir!

CHORUS OF GIRLS:

> My papa he keeps three horses,
>> Black, and white, and dapple grey, sir;
> Turn three times, then take your courses,
>> Catch whichever girl you may, sir!

CHORUS OF MEN:

> My papa, etc.

[MARCO *and* GIUSEPPE *turn round, as directed, and try to catch the girls. Business of blind-man's buff.*[10] *Eventually* MARCO *catches* GIANETTA, *and* GIUSEPPE *catches* TESSA. *The two girls try to escape, but in vain. The two men pass their hands over the girls' faces to discover their identity.*]

GIU.: I've at length achieved a capture!
 [*Guessing*] This is Tessa! [*removes bandage*]. Rapture, rapture!

MAR. [*guessing*]:

> To me Gianetta fate has granted! [*removes bandage*].
> Just the very girl I wanted!

GIU. [*politely to* MARCO]:

> If you'd rather change –

TESSA: My goodness!
> This indeed is simple rudeness.

MAR. [*politely to* GIUSEPPE]:

> I've no preference whatever –

GIA.: Listen to him! Well, I never!
 [*Each man kisses each girl.*]

GIA.:

> Thank you, gallant *gondolieri*!
>> In a set and formal measure
> It is scarcely necessary
>> To express our pleasure.
>> Each of us to prove a treasure,

Conjugal and monetary,
     Gladly will devote our leisure,
Gay and gallant *gondolieri*.
     Tra, la, la, la, la, la, etc.

TESSA: Gay and gallant *gondolieri*,
     Take us both and hold us tightly,
You have luck extraordinary;
     We might both have been unsightly!
     If we judge your conduct rightly,
'Twas a choice involuntary;
     Still we thank you most politely,
Gay and gallant *gondolieri*!
     Tra, la, la, la, la, la, etc.

CHORUS OF GIRLS:
Thank you, gallant *gondolieri*;
     In a set and formal measure,
It is scarcely necessary
     To express our pleasure.
     Each of us to prove a treasure
Gladly will devote our leisure,
Gay and gallant *gondolieri*!
     Tra, la, la, la, la, la, etc.

ALL: Fate in this has put his finger –
     Let us bow to Fate's decree,
Then no longer let us linger,
     To the altar hurry we!
          [*They all dance off two and two –* GIANETTA *with*
               MARCO, TESSA *with* GIUSEPPE.]
[*Flourish. A gondola arrives at the Piazzetta steps, from which
enter the* DUKE OF PLAZA-TORO, *the* DUCHESS, *their daughter*
CASILDA *and their attendant* LUIZ, *who carries a drum. All are
dressed in pompous but old and faded clothes.*]
[*Entrance of* DUKE,[11] DUCHESS, CASILDA *and* LUIZ.]

DUKE:	From the sunny Spanish shore,
	The Duke of Plaza-Tor' –
DUCH.:	And His Grace's Duchess true –
CAS.:	And His Grace's daughter, too –
LUIZ:	And His Grace's private drum
	To Venetia's shores have come:

ALL:
> If ever, ever, ever
>> They get back to Spain,
> They will never, never, never
>> Cross the sea again –

DUKE:	Neither that Grandee from the Spanish shore,
	The noble Duke of Plaza Tor' –
DUCH.:	Nor His Grace's Duchess, staunch and true –
CAS.:	You may add, His Grace's daughter, too –
LUIZ:	Nor His Grace's own particular drum
	To Venetia's shores will come:

ALL:
> If ever, ever, ever
>> They get back to Spain,
> They will never, never, never
>> Cross the sea again!

DUKE: At last we have arrived at our destination. This is the Ducal Palace, and it is here that the Grand Inquisitor[12] resides. As a Castilian hidalgo[13] of ninety-five quarterings,[14] I regret that I am unable to pay my state visit on a horse. As a Castilian hidalgo of that description, I should have preferred to ride through the streets of Venice; but owing, I presume, to an unusually wet season, the streets are in such a condition[15] that equestrian exercise is impracticable. No matter. Where is our suite?

LUIZ [*coming forward*]: Your Grace, I am here.

DUCH.: Why do you not do yourself the honour to kneel when you address His Grace?

DUKE: My love, it is so small a matter! [*To* LUIZ] Still, you may as well do it. [LUIZ *kneels.*]

559

CAS.: The young man seems to entertain but an imperfect appreciation of the respect due from a menial to a Castilian hidalgo.

DUKE: My child, you are hard upon our suite.

CAS.: Papa, I've no patience with the presumption of persons in his plebeian position. If he does not appreciate that position, let him be whipped until he does.

DUKE: Let us hope the omission was not intended as a slight. I should be much hurt if I thought it was. So would he. [*To* LUIZ] Where are the halberdiers[16] who were to have had the honour of meeting us here, that our visit to the Grand Inquisitor might be made in becoming state?

LUIZ: Your Grace, the halberdiers are mercenary people who stipulated for a trifle on account.

DUKE: How tiresome! Well, let us hope the Grand Inquisitor is a blind gentleman. And the band who were to have had the honour of escorting us? I see no band!

LUIZ: Your Grace, the band are sordid persons who required to be paid in advance.

DUCH.: That's so like a band!

DUKE [*annoyed*]: Insuperable difficulties meet me at every turn!

DUCH.: But surely they know His Grace?

LUIZ: Exactly – they know His Grace.

DUKE: Well, let us hope that the Grand Inquisitor is a deaf gentleman. A cornet-à-piston[17] would be something. You do not happen to possess the accomplishment of tootling like a cornet-à-piston?

LUIZ: Alas, no, Your Grace! But I can imitate a farmyard.

DUKE [*doubtfully*]: I don't see how that would help us. I don't see how we could bring it in.

CAS.: It would not help us in the least. We are not a parcel of graziers come to market, dolt!

DUKE: My love, our suite's feelings! [*To* LUIZ] Be so good as to ring the bell and inform the Grand Inquisitor that his Grace the Duke of Plaza-Toro,[18] Count Matadoro,[19] Baron Picadoro[20] –

DUCH.: And suite –

DUKE: And suite – have arrived at Venice, and seek –

CAS.: Desire –

DUCH.: Demand!

DUKE: And demand an audience.

LUIZ: Your Grace has but to command. [*Rising.*]

DUKE [*much moved*]: I felt sure of it – I felt sure of it!

[*Exit* LUIZ *into Ducal Palace.*]

And now, my love – [*aside to* DUCHESS] Shall we tell her? I think so – [*aloud to* CASILDA] And now, my love, prepare for a magnificent surprise. It is my agreeable duty to reveal to you a secret which should make you the happiest young lady in Venice!

CAS.: A secret?

DUCH.: A secret which, for State reasons, it has been necessary to preserve for twenty years.

DUKE: When you were a prattling babe of six months old you were married by proxy to no less a personage than the infant son and heir of His Majesty the immeasurably wealthy King of Barataria!

CAS.: Married to the infant son of the King of Barataria? Was I consulted? [DUKE *shakes his head.*] Then it was a most unpardonable liberty!

DUKE: Consider his extreme youth and forgive him. Shortly after the ceremony that misguided monarch abandoned the creed of his forefathers, and became a Wesleyan Methodist[21] of the most bigoted and persecuting type. The Grand Inquisitor, determined that the innovation should not be perpetuated in Barataria, caused your smiling and unconscious husband to be stolen and conveyed to Venice. A fortnight since the Methodist Monarch and all his Wesleyan Court were killed in an insurrection, and we are here to ascertain the whereabouts of your husband, and to hail you, our daughter, as Her Majesty, the reigning Queen of Barataria! [*Kneels.*]

[*During this speech* LUIZ *re-enters.*]

DUCH.: Your Majesty! [*Kneels.*]

DUKE: It is at such moments as these that one feels how necessary it is to travel with a full band.

CAS.: I, the Queen of Barataria! But I've nothing to wear! We are practically penniless!

DUKE: That point has not escaped me. Although I am unhappily in straitened circumstances at present, my social influence is something enormous; and a Company, to be called the Duke of Plaza-Toro,

Limited, is in course of formation to work me. An influential direc-torate[22] has been secured, and I shall myself join the Board after allotment.[23]

CAS.: Am I to understand that the Queen of Barataria may be called upon at any time to witness her honoured sire in process of liqui-dation?[24]

DUCH.: The speculation is not exempt from that drawback. If your father should stop, it will, of course, be necessary to wind him up.

CAS.: But it's so undignified – it's so degrading! A Grandee of Spain turned into a public company! Such a thing was never heard of!

DUKE: My child, the Duke of Plaza-Toro does not follow fashions – he leads them. He always leads everybody. When he was in the army he led his regiment. He occasionally led them into action. He invariably led them out of it.

SONG

DUKE:

In enterprise of martial kind,
    When there was any fighting,
He led his regiment from behind –
    He found it less exciting.
But when away his regiment ran,
    His place was at the fore, O –
        That celebrated,
        Cultivated,
        Underrated
          Nobleman,
    The Duke of Plaza-Toro!

ALL:

In the first and foremost flight, ha, ha!
You always found that knight, ha, ha!
        That celebrated,
        Cultivated,
        Underrated
          Nobleman,
    The Duke of Plaza-Toro!

DUKE:

When, to evade Destruction's hand,
    To hide they all proceeded,
No soldier in that gallant band
    Hid half as well as he did.
He lay concealed throughout the war,
    And so preserved his gore, O!
        That unaffected,
        Undetected,
        Well-connected
          Warrior,
    The Duke of Plaza-Toro!

ALL:

In every doughty deed, ha, ha!
He always took the lead, ha, ha!
        That unaffected,
        Undetected,
        Well-connected
          Warrior,
    The Duke of Plaza-Toro!

DUKE:

When told that they would all be shot
    Unless they left the service,
That hero hesitated not,
    So marvellous his nerve is.
He sent his resignation in,
    The first of all his corps, O!
        That very knowing,
        Overflowing,
        Easy-going
          Paladin,[25]
    The Duke of Plaza-Toro!

ALL:

To men of grosser clay, ha, ha!
He always showed the way, ha, ha!
        That very knowing,
        Overflowing,

Easy-going
Paladin,
The Duke of Plaza-Toro!
[*Exeunt* DUKE *and* DUCHESS *into Grand Ducal Palace. As soon as they have disappeared,* LUIZ *and* CASILDA *rush to each other's arms.*]

RECITATIVE AND DUET – CASILDA *and* LUIZ

BOTH: O rapture, when alone together
     Two loving hearts and those that bear them
May join in temporary tether,
     Though Fate apart should rudely tear them.

CAS.: Necessity, Invention's mother,
     Compelled me to a course of feigning –
But, left alone with one another,
     I will atone for my disdaining!

          Ah, well-beloved,
          Mine angry frown
          Is but a gown
          That serves to dress
          My gentleness!

LUIZ: Ah, well-beloved,
          Thy cold disdain,
          It gives no pain –
          'Tis mercy, played
          In masquerade!

BOTH: Ah, well-beloved, etc.

CAS.: O Luiz, Luiz – what have you said? What have I done? What have I allowed you to do?

LUIZ: Nothing, I trust, that you will ever have reason to repent. [*Offering to embrace her.*]

CAS. [*withdrawing from him*]: Nay, Luiz, it may not be. I have embraced you for the last time.

LUIZ [*amazed*]: Casilda!

CAS.: I have just learnt, to my surprise and indignation, that I was wed in babyhood to the infant son of the King of Barataria!

LUIZ: The son of the King of Barataria? The child who was stolen in infancy[26] by the Inquisition?[27]

CAS.: The same. But, of course, you know his story.

LUIZ: Know his story? Why, I have often told you that my mother was the nurse to whose charge he was entrusted!

CAS.: True. I had forgotten. Well, he has been discovered, and my father has brought me here to claim his hand.

LUIZ: But you will not recognize this marriage? It took place when you were too young to understand its import.

CAS.: Nay, Luiz, respect my principles and cease to torture me with vain entreaties. Henceforth my life is another's.

LUIZ: But stay – the present and the future – *they* are another's; but the past – that at least is ours, and none can take it from us. As we may revel in naught else, let us revel in that!

CAS.: I don't think I grasp your meaning.

LUIZ: Yet it is logical enough. You say you cease to love me?

CAS. [*demurely*]: I say I *may* not love you.

LUIZ: Ah, but you do not say you *did* not love me?

CAS.: I loved you with a frenzy that words are powerless to express – and that but ten brief minutes since!

LUIZ: Exactly. My own – that is, until ten minutes since, my own – my lately loved, my recently adored – tell me that until, say a quarter of an hour ago, I was all in all to thee! [*Embracing her.*]

CAS.: I see your idea. It's ingenious, but don't do that. [*Releasing herself.*]

LUIZ: There can be no harm in revelling in the past.

CAS.: None whatever, but an embrace cannot be taken to act retrospectively.

LUIZ: Perhaps not!

CAS.: We may recollect an embrace – I recollect many – but we must not repeat them.

LUIZ: Then let us, recollect a few! [*A moment's pause, as they recollect, then both heave a deep sigh.*]

LUIZ: Ah, Casilda, you were to me as the sun is to the earth!

CAS.: A quarter of an hour ago?

LUIZ: About that.

CAS.: And to think that, but for this miserable discovery, you would have been my own for life!

LUIZ: Through life to death – a quarter of an hour ago!

CAS.: How greedily my thirsty ears would have drunk the golden melody of those sweet words a quarter – well, it's now about twenty minutes since. [*Looking at her watch.*]

LUIZ: About that. In such a matter one cannot be too precise.

CAS.: And now our love, so full of life, is but a silent, solemn memory!

LUIZ: Must it be so, Casilda?

CAS.: Luiz, it must be so!

DUET – CASILDA *and* LUIZ

LUIZ:
There was a time –
  A time for ever gone – ah, woe is me!
It was no crime
  To love but thee alone – ah, woe is me!
One heart, one life, one soul,
  One aim, one goal –
Each in the other's thrall,
  Each all in all, ah, woe is me!

BOTH:
Oh, bury, bury – let the grave close o'er
The days that were – that never will be more!
Oh, bury, bury love that all condemn,
And let the whirlwind mourn its requiem!

CAS.:
Dead as the last year's leaves –
  As gathered flowers – ah, woe is me!
Dead as the garnered sheaves,
  That love of ours – ah, woe is me!

       Born but to fade and die
         When hope was high,
     Dead and as far away
         As yesterday! – ah, woe is me!

BOTH: Oh, bury, bury – let the grave close o'er, etc.

[*Re-enter from the Ducal Palace the* DUKE *and* DUCHESS, *followed by* DON ALHAMBRA DEL BOLERO, *the Grand Inquisitor.*]

DUKE: My child, allow me to present to you His Distinction Don Alhambra[28] del Bolero, the Grand Inquisitor of Spain. It was His Distinction who so thoughtfully abstracted your infant husband and brought him to Venice.

DON AL.: So this is the little lady who is so unexpectedly called upon to assume the functions of Royalty! And a very nice little lady, too!

DUKE: Jimp,[29] isn't she?

DON AL.: Distinctly jimp. Allow me! [*Offers his hand. She turns away scornfully.*] Naughty temper!

DUKE: You must make some allowance. Her Majesty's head is a little turned by her access of dignity.

DON AL.: I could have wished that Her Majesty's access of dignity had turned it in this direction.

DUCH.: Unfortunately, if I am not mistaken, there appears to be some little doubt as to His Majesty's whereabouts.

CAS. [*aside*]: A doubt as to his whereabouts? Then we may yet be saved!

DON AL.: A doubt? Oh dear, no – no doubt at all! He is here, in Venice, plying the modest but picturesque calling of a gondolier. I can give you his address – I see him every day! In the entire annals of our history there is absolutely no circumstance so entirely free from all manner of doubt of any kind whatever! Listen, and I'll tell you all about it.

SONG – DON ALHAMBRA *with* DUKE, DUCHESS,
CASILDA, LUIZ

I stole the Prince, and brought him here,
    And left him gaily prattling
With a highly respectable gondolier,
Who promised the Royal babe to rear,
And teach him the trade of a timoneer[30]
    With his own beloved bratling.[31]

    Both of the babes were strong and stout,
      And, considering all things, clever.
    Of that there is no manner of doubt –
    No probable, possible shadow of doubt –
      No possible doubt whatever.

But owing, I'm much disposed to fear,
    To his terrible taste for tippling,
That highly respectable gondolier
Could never declare with a mind sincere
Which of the two was his offspring dear,
    And which the Royal stripling!

    Which was which he could never make out
      Despite his best endeavour.
    Of *that* there is no manner of doubt –
    No probable, possible shadow of doubt –
      No possible doubt whatever.

Time sped, and when at the end of a year
    I sought that infant cherished,
That highly respectable gondolier
Was lying a corpse on his humble bier
I dropped a Grand Inquisitor's tear –
    That gondolier had perished.

A taste for drink, combined with gout,
   Had doubled him up for ever.
Of *that* there is no manner of doubt –
No probable, possible shadow of doubt –
   No possible doubt whatever.

The children followed his old career –
      (This statement can't be parried)
Of a highly respectable gondolier:
Well, one of the two (who will soon be here) –
But *which* of the two is not quite clear –
      Is the Royal Prince you married!

      Search in and out and round about,
         And you'll discover never
      A tale so free from every doubt –
      All probable, possible shadow of doubt –
         All possible doubt whatever!

CAS.: Then do you mean to say that I am married to one of two
   gondoliers, but it is impossible to say which?
DON AL.: Without any doubt of any kind whatever. But be reassured:
   the nurse to whom your husband was entrusted is the mother of
   the musical young man who is such a past-master of that delicately
   modulated instrument [*indicating the drum.*] She can, no doubt,
   establish the King's identity beyond all question.
LUIZ: Heavens, how did he know that?
DON AL.: My young friend, a Grand Inquisitor is always up to date.
   [*To* CAS.] His mother is at present the wife of a highly respectable
   and old-established brigand, who carries on an extensive practice
   in the mountains around Cordova.[32] Accompanied by two of my
   emissaries, he will set off at once for his mother's address. She will
   return with them, and if she finds any difficulty in making up her
   mind, the persuasive influence of the torture chamber will jog her
   memory.

RECITATIVE – CASILDA *and* DON ALHAMBRA

CAS.:   But, bless my heart, consider my position!
       I am the wife of one, that's very clear;
       But who can tell, except by intuition,
         Which is the Prince, and which the Gondolier?

DON AL.:   Submit to Fate without unseemly wrangle:
       Such complications frequently occur –
       Life is one closely complicated tangle:
       Death is the only true unraveller!

QUINTET – DUKE, DUCHESS, CASILDA, LUIZ, GRAND INQUISITOR

ALL: Try we life-long, we can never
       Straighten out life's tangled skein,
       Why should we, in vain endeavour,
       Guess and guess and guess again?

LUIZ: Life's a pudding full of plums,
DUCH.:   Care's canker that benumbs.
ALL: Life's a pudding full of plums,
       Care's a canker that benumbs.
       Wherefore waste our elocution
       On impossible solution?
       Life's a pleasant institution,
       Let us take it as it comes!

       Set aside the dull enigma,
       We shall guess it all too soon;
       Failure brings no kind of stigma –
       Dance we to another tune!

LUIZ: String the lyre and fill the cup,
DUCH.:   Lest on sorrow we should sup.
ALL: String the lyre and fill the cup,
       Lest on sorrow we should sup.

Hop and skip to Fancy's fiddle,
Hands across and down the middle –
Life's perhaps the only riddle
    That we shrink from giving up!
      [*Exeunt all into Ducal Palace except* LUIZ, *who*
                       goes off in gondola.]
[*Enter Gondoliers and Contadine, followed by* MARCO,
GIANETTA, GIUSEPPE *and* TESSA.]

CHORUS: Bridegroom and bride!
                  Knot that's insoluble,
                  Voices all voluble
              Hail it with pride.
              Bridegroom and bride!
                  Hail it with merriment;
                  It's an experiment
              Frequently tried.

              Bridegroom and bride!
                  Bridegrooms all joyfully,
                  Brides, rather coyfully,
               Stand at their side.
              Bridegroom and bride!
                  We in sincerity,
                  Wish you prosperity,
              Bridegroom and bride!

SONG

TESSA: When a merry maiden marries,
              Sorrow goes and pleasure tarries;
                  Every sound becomes a song,
                  All is right, and nothing's wrong!
              From to-day and ever after
              Let our tears be tears of laughter.
                  Every sigh that finds a vent
                  Be a sigh of sweet content!

When you marry, merry maiden,
Then the air with love is laden;
  Every flower is a rose,
    Every goose becomes a swan,
  Every kind of trouble goes
    Where the last year's snows have gone!

CHORUS: Sunlight takes the place of shade
           When you marry, merry maid!

TESSA: When a merry maiden marries,
           Sorrow goes and pleasure tarries;
             Every sound becomes a song,
             All is right, and nothing's wrong.
           Gnawing Care and aching Sorrow,
           Get ye gone until to-morrow;
             Jealousies in grim array,
             Ye are things of yesterday!
           When you marry, merry maiden,
           Then the air with joy is laden;
             All the corners of the earth
               Ring with music sweetly played,
             Worry is melodious mirth,
               Grief is joy in masquerade;

CHORUS: Sullen night is laughing day –
           All the year is merry May!
[*At the end of the song,* DON ALHAMBRA *enters at back. The Gondoliers and Contadine shrink from him, and gradually go off, much alarmed.*]

GIU.: And now our lives are going to begin in real earnest! What's a bachelor? A mere nothing – he's a chrysalis. He can't be said to live – he exists.

MAR.: What a delightful institution marriage is! Why have we wasted all this time? Why didn't we marry ten years ago?

TESSA: Because you couldn't find anybody nice enough.

GIA.: Because you were waiting for *us*.

MAR.: I suppose that *was* the reason. We were waiting for you without knowing it. [DON ALHAMBRA *comes forward.*] Hallo!

DON AL.: Good morning.

GIU.: If this gentleman is an undertaker, it's a bad omen.

DON AL.: Ceremony of some sort going on?

GIU. [*aside*]: He *is* an undertaker! [*Aloud*] No – a little unimportant family gathering. Nothing in *your* line.

DON AL.: Somebody's birthday, I suppose?

GIA.: Yes, mine!

TESSA: And mine!

MAR.: And mine!

GIU.: And mine!

DON AL.: Curious coincidence! And how old may you all be?

TESSA: It's a rude question – but about ten minutes.

DON AL.: Remarkably fine children! But surely you are jesting?

TESSA: In other words, we were married about ten minutes since.

DON AL.: Married! You don't mean to say you are married?

MAR.: Oh yes, we are married.

DON AL.: What, both of you?

ALL: All four of us.

DON AL. [*aside*]: Bless my heart, how extremely awkward!

GIA.: You don't mind, I suppose?

TESSA: You were not thinking of either of us for yourself, I presume? Oh, Giuseppe, look at him – he was. He's heart-broken!

DON AL.: No, no, I wasn't! I wasn't!

GIU.: Now, my man [*slapping him on the back*], we don't want anything in your line to-day, and if your curiosity's satisfied – you can go!

DON AL.: You mustn't call me your man. It's a liberty. I don't think you know who I am.

GIU.: Not we, indeed! We are jolly gondoliers, the sons of Baptisto Palmieri, who led the last revolution.[33] Republicans, heart and soul, we hold all men to be equal. As we abhor oppression, we abhor kings: as we detest vain-glory, we detest rank: as we despise effeminacy, we despise wealth. We are Venetian gondoliers – your equals in everything except our calling, and in that at once your masters and your servants.

DON AL.: Bless my heart, how unfortunate! One of you may be Baptisto's son, for anything I know to the contrary; but the other is no less a personage than the only son of the late King of Barataria.

ALL: What!

DON AL.: And I trust – I *trust* it was that one who slapped me on the shoulder and called me his man!

GIU.: One of us a king!

MAR.: Not brothers!

TESSA: The King of Barataria!   [*together*]

GIA.: Well, who'd have thought it!

MAR.: But which is it?

DON AL.: What does it matter? As you are both Republicans, and hold kings in detestation, of course you'll abdicate at once. Good morning! [*Going.*]

GIA. *and* TESSA: Oh, don't do that! [MARCO *and* GIUSEPPE *stop him.*]

GIU.: Well, as to that, of course there are kings and kings. When I say that I detest kings, I mean I detest *bad* kings.

DON AL.: I see. It's a delicate distinction.

GIU.: Quite so. Now I can conceive a kind of king – an ideal king – the creature of my fancy, you know – who would be absolutely unobjectionable. A king, for instance, who would abolish taxes and make everything cheap, except gondolas –

MAR.: And give a great many free entertainments to the gondoliers –

GIU.: And let off fireworks on the Grand Canal,[34] and engage all the gondolas for the occasion –

MAR.: And scramble money on the Rialto[35] among the gondoliers.

GIU.: Such a king would be a blessing to his people, and if I were a king, that is the sort of king I would be.

MAR.: And so would I!

DON AL.: Come, I'm glad to find your objections are not insuperable.

MAR. *and* GIU.: Oh, they're not insuperable.

GIA. *and* TESS.: No, they're not insuperable.

GIU.: Besides, we are open to conviction.

GIA.: Yes; they are open to conviction.

TESSA: Oh! they've often been convicted.

GIU.: Our views may have been hastily formed on insufficient grounds. They may be crude, ill-digested, erroneous. I've a very poor opinion of the politician who is not open to conviction.

TESSA [*to* GIA.]: Oh, he's a fine fellow!

GIA.: Yes, that's the sort of politician for *my* money!

DON AL.: Then we'll consider it settled. Now, as the country is in a state of insurrection, it is absolutely necessary that you should assume the reins of Government at once; and, until it is ascertained which of you is to be king, I have arranged that you will reign jointly, so that no question can arise hereafter as to the validity of any of your acts.

MAR.: As one individual?

DON AL.: As one individual.

GIU. [*linking himself with* MARCO]: Like this?

DON AL.: Something like that.

MAR.: And we may take our friends with us, and give them places about the Court?

DON AL.: Undoubtedly. That's always done!

MAR.: I'm convinced!

GIU.: So am I!

TESSA: Then the sooner we're off the better.

GIA.: We'll just run home and pack up a few things [*going*] –

DON AL.: Stop, stop – that won't do at all – ladies are not admitted.

ALL: What!

DON AL.: Not admitted. Not at present. Afterwards, perhaps. We'll see.

GIU.: Why, you don't mean to say you are going to separate us from our wives!

DON AL. [*aside*]: This is very awkward! [*Aloud*] Only for a time – a few months. After all, what is a few months?

TESSA: But we've only been married half an hour! [*Weeps.*]

FINALE

SONG

GIA.:
Kind sir, you cannot have the heart
　　　Our lives to part
　　From those to whom an hour ago
　　　　We were united!
Before our flowing hopes you stem,
　　　Ah, look at them,
　　And pause before you deal this blow,
　　　　All uninvited!
You men can never understand
　　　That heart and hand
　　Cannot be separated when
　　　　We go a-yearning;
You see, you've only women's eyes
　　　To idolize
　　And only women's hearts, poor men,
　　　　To set *you* burning!
Ah me, you men will never understand
That woman's heart is one with woman's hand!

Some kind of charm you seem to find
　　　In womankind –
　　Some source of unexplained delight
　　　　(Unless you're jesting),
But what attracts you, I confess,
　　　I cannot guess,
　　To me a woman's face is quite
　　　　Uninteresting!
If from my sister I were torn,
　　　It could be borne –
　　I should, no doubt, be horrified,
　　　　But I could bear it; –
But Marco's quite another thing –
　　　He is my King,

He has my heart and none beside
Shall ever share it!
Ah me, you men will never understand
That woman's heart is one with woman's hand!

RECITATIVE

DON AL.:   Do not give way to this uncalled-for grief,
Your separation will be very brief.
To ascertain which is the King
And which the other,
To Barataria's Court I'll bring
His foster-mother;
Her former nurseling to declare
She'll be delighted.
That settled, let each happy pair
Be reunited.

MAR., GIU., GIA., TESSA:
Viva! His argument is strong!
Viva! We'll not be parted long!
Viva! It will be settled soon!
Viva! Then comes our honeymoon!

[*Exit* DON ALHAMBRA.]

QUARTET – MARCO, GIUSEPPE, GIANETTA, TESSA

GIA.:   Then one of us will be a Queen,
And sit on a golden throne,
With a crown instead
Of a hat on her head,
And diamonds all her own!
With a beautiful robe of gold and green,
I've always understood;
I wonder whether
She'd wear a feather?
I rather think she should!

ALL: Oh, 'tis a glorious thing, I ween,
        To be a regular Royal Queen!
        No half-and-half affair, I mean,
        But a right-down regular Royal Queen!

MAR.:   She'll drive about in a carriage and pair,
            With the King on her left-hand side,
                And a milk-white horse,
                As a matter of course,
            Whenever she wants to ride!
        With beautiful silver shoes to wear
            Upon her dainty feet;
                With endless stocks
                Of beautiful frocks
            And as much as she wants to eat!

ALL: Oh, 'tis a glorious thing, I ween, etc.

TESSA: Whenever she condescends to walk,
            Be sure she'll shine at that,
                With her haughty stare
                And her nose in the air,
            Like a well-born aristocrat!
        At elegant high society talk
            She'll bear away the bell,
                With her 'How de do?'
                And her 'How are you?'
            And 'I trust I see you well!'

ALL: Oh, 'tis a glorious thing, I ween, etc.

GIU.:   And noble lords will scrape and bow,
            And double themselves in two,
                And open their eyes
                In blank surprise
            At whatever she likes to do.
        And everybody will roundly vow

>She's fair as flowers in May,
>>And say, 'How clever!'
>>At whatsoever
>>She condescends to say!

ALL:

>Oh, 'tis a glorious thing, I ween,
>To be a regular Royal Queen!
>No half-and-half affair, I mean,
>But a right-down regular Royal Queen!

[Enter Chorus of Gondoliers and Contadine.]

CHORUS:

>Now, pray, what is the cause of this remarkable hilarity?
>>This sudden ebullition of unmitigated jollity?
>Has anybody blessed you with a sample of his charity?
>>Or have you been adopted by a gentleman of quality?

MAR. *and* GIU.:

>Replying, we sing
>>As one individual,
>As I find I'm a king,
>>To my kingdom I bid you all.
>I'm aware you object
>>To pavilions and palaces,
>But you'll find I respect
>>Your Republican fallacies.

CHORUS:

>As they know we object
>>To pavilions and palaces,
>How can they respect
>>Our Republican fallacies?

MAR.:

>For every one who feels inclined,
>Some post we undertake to find
>Congenial with his frame of mind –
>>And all shall equal be.

GIU.:   The Chancellor in his peruke[36] –
    The Earl, the Marquis, and the Dook,
    The Groom, the Butler, and the Cook –
        They all shall equal be.

MAR.:   The Aristocrat who banks with Coutts[37] –
    The Aristocrat who hunts and shoots –
    The Aristocrat who cleans our boots –
        They all shall equal be!

GIU.:   The Noble Lord who rules the State –
    The Noble Lord who cleans the plate –

MAR.:   The Noble Lord who scrubs the grate –
        They all shall equal be!

GIU.:   The Lord High Bishop orthodox –
    The Lord High Coachman on the box –

MAR.:   The Lord High Vagabond in the stocks –
        They all shall equal be!

BOTH: For every one, etc.

        Sing high, sing low,
        Wherever they go,
            They all shall equal be!

CHORUS: Sing high, sing low,
        Wherever they go,
            They all shall equal be!

        The Earl, the Marquis and the Dook,
        The Groom, the Butler and the Cook,
        The Aristocrat who banks with Coutts,
        The Aristocrat who cleans the boots,

The Noble Lord who rules the State,
The Noble Lord who scrubs the grate,
The Lord High Bishop orthodox,
The Lord High Vagabond in the stocks –

For every one, etc.

Sing high, sing low,
Wherever they go,
They all shall equal be!

Then hail! O King,
Whichever you may be,
To you we sing,
But do not bend the knee.
It may be thou –
Likewise it may be thee –
So hail! O King,
Whichever you may be!

MAR. *and* GIU.:

Come, let's away – our island crown awaits me –
Conflicting feelings rend my soul apart!
The thought of Royal dignity elates me,
But leaving thee behind me breaks my heart!

[*Addressing* GIANETTA *and* TESSA.]
GIA. *and* TESSA:

Farewell, my love; on board you must be getting;
But while upon the sea you gaily roam,
Remember that a heart for thee is fretting –
The tender little heart you've left at home!

GIA.:

Now, Marco dear,
My wishes hear:
While you're away
It's understood

> You will be good,
>> And not too gay.
> To every trace
> Of maiden grace
>> You will be blind,
> And will not glance
> By any chance
>> On womankind!
>
> If you are wise,
> You'll shut your eyes
>> Till we arrive,
> And not address
> A lady less
>> Than forty-five.
> You'll please to frown
> On every gown
>> That you may see;
> And, O my pet,
> You won't forget
>> You've married me!

And O my darling, O my pet,
Whatever else you may forget,
In yonder isle beyond the sea,
Do not forget you've married me!

TESSA:
> You'll lay your head
> Upon your bed
>> At set of sun.
> You will not sing
> Of anything
>> To any one.
> You'll sit and mope
> All day, I hope,
>> And shed a tear

Upon the life
Your little wife
  Is passing here.

And if so be
You think of me,
  Please tell the moon!
I'll read it all
In rays that fall
  On the lagoon:
You'll be so kind
As tell the wind
  How you may be,
And send me words
By little birds
  To comfort me!

And O my darling, O my pet,
Whatever else you may forget,
In yonder isle beyond the sea,
Do not forget you've married me.

QUARTET: O my darling, O my pet, etc.

CHORUS [*during which a 'Xebeque'*[38] *is hauled, alongside the quay*]:
Then away we go to an island fair
  That lies in a Southern sea:
We know not where, and we don't much care,
  Wherever that isle may be.
THE MEN [*hauling on boat*]:
One, two, three,
  Haul!
One, two, three,
  Haul!
One, two, three,
  Haul!
With a will!

ALL: When the breezes are a-blowing
The ship will be going,
    When they don't we shall all stand still!
Then away we go to an island fair,
We know not where, and we don't much care,
    Wherever that isle may be.

SOLO

MAR.:   Away we go
    To a balmy isle,
Where the roses blow
    All the winter while.

ALL [*hoisting sail*]:
    Then away we go to an island fair
      That lies in a Southern sea:
    Then away we go to an island fair,
      Then away, then away, then away!

[*The men embark on the 'Xebeque'.* MARCO *and* GIUSEPPE
embracing GIANETTA *and* TESSA. *The girls wave a farewell to
the men as the curtain falls.*]

END OF ACT I

ACT II

SCENE – *Pavilion in the Court of Barataria.*

[MARCO *and* GIUSEPPE, *magnificently dressed, are seated on two thrones, occupied in cleaning the crown and the sceptre. The Gondoliers are discovered, dressed, some as courtiers, officers of rank, etc., and others as private soldiers and servants of various degrees. All are enjoying themselves without reference to social distinctions – some playing cards, others throwing dice, some reading, others playing cup and ball,[39] 'morra',[40] etc.*]

CHORUS OF MEN *with* MARCO *and* GIUSEPPE:
>   Of happiness the very pith
>   In Barataria you may see:
>   A monarchy that's tempered with
>   Republican Equality.
>   This form of government we find
>   The beau-ideal of its kind –
>   A despotism strict, combined
>   With absolute equality!

MAR. *and* GIU.:   Two kings, of undue pride bereft,
>   Who act in perfect unity,
>   Whom you can order right and left
>   With absolute impunity.
>   Who put their subjects at their ease
>   By doing all they can to please!
>   And thus, to earn their bread-and-cheese,
>   Seize every opportunity.

CHORUS: Of happiness the very pith, etc.

MAR.: Gentlemen, we are much obliged to you for your expressions
of satisfaction and good feeling – I say, we are much obliged to you
for your expressions of satisfaction and good feeling.

ALL: We heard you.

MAR.: We are delighted, at any time, to fall in with sentiments so
charmingly expressed.

ALL: That's all right.

GIU.: At the same time there is just one little grievance that we should
like to ventilate.

ALL [*angrily*]: What?

GIU.: Don't be alarmed – it's not serious. It is arranged that, until it
is decided which of us two is the actual King, we are to act as one
person.

GIOR.: Exactly.

GIU.: Now, although we act as *one* person, we are, in point of fact,
two persons.

ANNI.: Ah, I don't think we can go into that. It is a legal fiction, and
legal fictions are solemn things. Situated as we are, we can't recognize two independent responsibilities.

GIU.: No; but you can recognize two independent appetites. It's all
very well to say we act as one person, but when you supply us with
only one ration between us, I should describe it as a legal fiction
carried a little too far.

ANNI.: It's rather a nice point. I don't like to express an opinion
off-hand. Suppose we reserve it for argument before the full Court?

MAR.: Yes, but what are we to do in the meantime?

MAR. *and* GIU.: We want our tea.

ANNI.: I think we may make an interim order for double rations on
their Majesties entering into the usual undertaking to indemnify in
the event of an adverse decision?

GIOR.: That, I think, will meet the case. But you must work hard –
stick to it – nothing like work.

GIU.: Oh, certainly. We quite understand that a man who holds the
magnificent position of King should do something to justify it.
We are called 'Your Majesty', we are allowed to buy ourselves

magnificent clothes, our subjects frequently nod to us in the streets, the sentries always return our salutes, and we enjoy the inestimable privilege of heading the subscription lists to all the principal charities. In return for these advantages the least we can do is to make ourselves useful about the Palace.

SONG – GIUSEPPE *with* CHORUS

GIU.: Rising early in the morning,
   We proceed to light the fire,
  Then our Majesty adorning
    In its workaday attire,
     We embark without delay
     On the duties of the day.

  First, we polish off some batches
  Of political despatches,
   And foreign politicians circumvent;
  Then, if business isn't heavy,
  We may hold a Royal *levée*,
   Or ratify some Acts of Parliament.
  Then we probably review the household troops –
  With the usual 'Shalloo humps!' and 'Shalloo hoops!'
  Or receive with ceremonial and state
  An interesting Eastern potentate.
   After that we generally
   Go and dress our private *valet* –
  (It's a rather nervous duty – he's a touchy little man) –
   Write some letters literary
   For our private secretary –
  He is shaky in his spelling, so we help him if we can.
   Then, in view of cravings inner,
   We go down and order dinner;
  Then we polish the Regalia and the Coronation Plate –
   Spend an hour in titivating
   All our Gentlemen-in-Waiting;
  Or we run on little errands for the Ministers of State.

    Oh, philosophers may sing
    Of the troubles of a King;
Yet the duties are delightful, and the privileges great;
      But the privilege and pleasure
      That we treasure beyond measure
Is to run on little errands for the Ministers of State.

CHORUS: Oh, philosophers may sing, etc.

After luncheon (making merry
On a bun and glass of sherry),
    If we've nothing in particular to do,
We may make a Proclamation,
Or receive a deputation –
    Then we possibly create a Peer or two.
Then we help a fellow-creature on his path
With the Garter[41] or the Thistle[42] or the Bath,[43]
Or we dress and toddle off in semi-state
To a festival, a function, or a *fête*.
    Then we go and stand as sentry
    At the Palace (private entry),
Marching hither, marching thither, up and down and to
    and fro,
    While the warrior on duty
    Goes in search of beer and beauty
(And it generally happens that he hasn't far to go).
    He relieves us, if he's able,
    Just in time to lay the table,
Then we dine and serve the coffee, and at half-past twelve
    or one,
    With a pleasure that's emphatic,
    We retire to our attic
With the gratifying feeling that our duty has been done!

    Oh, philosophers may sing
    Of the troubles of a King,

But of pleasures there are many and of worries there are
  none;
  And the culminating pleasure
  That we treasure beyond measure
Is the gratifying feeling that our duty has been done!

CHORUS: Oh, philosophers may sing, etc.

[*Exeunt all but* MARCO *and* GIUSEPPE.]

GIU.: Yes, it really is a very pleasant existence. They're all so singularly kind and considerate. You don't find them wanting to do this, or wanting to do that, or saying 'It's my turn now.' No, they let us have all the fun to ourselves, and never seem to grudge it.

MAR.: It makes one feel quite selfish. It almost seems like taking advantage of their good nature.

GIU.: How nice they were about the double rations.

MAR.: Most considerate. Ah! there's only one thing wanting to make us thoroughly comfortable.

GIU.: And that is?

MAR.: The dear little wives we left behind us three months ago.

GIU.: Yes, it *is* dull without female society. We can do without everything else, but we can't do without that.

MAR.: And if we have that in perfection, we have everything. There is only one recipe for perfect happiness.

SONG

MAR.:   Take a pair of sparkling eyes,
                      Hidden, ever and anon,
                        In a merciful eclipse –
                  Do not heed their mild surprise –
                      Having passed the Rubicon,[44]
                        Take a pair of rosy lips;
                  Take a figure trimly planned –
                      Such as admiration whets
                        (Be particular in this);

Take a tender little hand,
      Fringed with dainty fingerettes,
            Press it – in parenthesis; –
Ah! Take all these, you lucky man –
Take and keep them, if you can!

Take a pretty little cot –
      Quite a miniature affair –
            Hung about with trellised vine,
Furnish it upon the spot
      With the treasures rich and rare
            I've endeavoured to define.
Live to love and love to live –
      You will ripen at your ease,
            Growing on the sunny side –
Fate has nothing more to give.
      You're a dainty man to please
            If you are not satisfied.
Ah! Take my counsel, happy man;
Act upon it, if you can!

[*Enter Chorus of Contadine, running in, led by* FIAMETTA *and*
VITTORIA. *They are met by all the Ex-Gondoliers, who welcome
them heartily.*]

SCENA – CHORUS OF GIRLS, QUARTET, DUET *and* CHORUS

      Here we are, at the risk of our lives,
      From ever so far, and we've brought your wives –
      And to that end we've crossed the main,
      And don't intend to return again!

FIA.:   Though obedience is strong,
                        Curiosity's stronger –
                  We waited for long,
                        Till we couldn't wait longer.

VIT.:   It's imprudent, we know,
                But without your society
          Existence was slow,
                And we wanted variety –

ALL: So here we are, at the risk of our lives,
          From ever so far, and we've brought your wives –
          And to that end we've crossed the main,
          And don't intend to return again!

[*Enter* GIANETTA *and* TESSA. *They rush to the arms of* MARCO
and GIUSEPPE.]

GIU.:   Tessa!
TESSA: Giuseppe!   [*Embrace.*]
GIA.:   Marco!
MAR.:   Gianetta!

TESSA: After sailing to this island –
GIA.:   Tossing in a manner frightful,
TESSA: We are all once more on dry land –
GIA.:   And we find the change delightful,
TESSA: As at home we've been remaining –
                We've not seen you both for ages,
GIA.:   Tell me, are you fond of reigning? –
                How's the food, and what's the wages?
TESSA: Does your new employment please ye? –
GIA.:   How does Royalizing strike you?
TESSA: Is it difficult or easy? –
GIA.:   Do you think your subjects like you?
TESSA: I am anxious to elicit,
                Is it plain and easy steering?
GIA.:   Take it altogether, is it –
                Better fun than gondoliering?
BOTH: We shall both go on requesting
                Till you tell us, never doubt it;
          Everything is interesting,
                Tell us, tell us all about it!

CHORUS: They will both go on requesting, etc.

TESSA: Is the populace exacting?
GIA.: Do they keep you at a distance?
TESSA: All unaided are you acting,
GIA.: Or do they provide assistance?
TESSA: When you're busy, have you got to
Get up early in the morning?
GIA.: If you do what you ought not to,
Do they give the usual warning?
TESSA: With a horse do they equip you?
GIA.: Lots of trumpeting and drumming?
TESSA: Do the Royal tradesmen tip you?
GIA.: Ain't the livery becoming!
TESSA: Does your human being inner
Feed on everything that nice is?
GIA.: Do they give you wine for dinner;
Peaches, sugar-plums and ices?
BOTH: We shall both go on requesting
Till you tell us, never doubt it;
Everything is interesting,
Tell us, tell us all about it!

CHORUS: They will both go on requesting, etc.

MAR.: This is indeed a most delightful surprise!
TESSA: Yes, we thought you'd like it. You see, it was like this. After you left we felt very dull and mopey, and the days crawled by, and you never wrote; so at last I said to Gianetta, 'I can't stand this any longer; those two poor Monarchs haven't got any one to mend their stockings or sew on their buttons or patch their clothes – at least, I hope they haven't – let us all pack up a change and go and see how they're getting on.' And she said, 'Done,' and they all said, 'Done'; and we asked old Giacopo to lend us his boat, and *he* said, 'Done'; and we've crossed the sea, and, thank goodness, *that's* done; and here we are, and – and – *I've* done!

GIA.: And now – which of you is King?

TESSA: And which of us is Queen?

GIU.: That we shan't know until Nurse turns up. But never mind that – the question is, how shall we celebrate the commencement of our honeymoon? Gentlemen, will you allow us to offer you a magnificent banquet?

ALL: We will!

GIU.: Thanks very much; and, ladies, what do you say to a dance?

TESSA: A banquet *and* a dance! Oh, it's too much happiness!

CHORUS *and* DANCE

Dance a cachucha,[45] fandango,[46] bolero,[47]
Xeres[48] we'll drink – Manzanilla,[49] Montero[50] –
Wine, when it runs in abundance, enhances
The reckless delight of that wildest of dances!
            To the pretty pitter-pitter-patter,
            And the clitter-clitter-clitter-clatter –
                    Clitter – clitter – clatter,
                    Pitter – pitter – patter,
            Patter, patter, patter, patter, we'll dance.
Old Xeres we'll drink – Manzanilla, Montero;
For wine, when it runs in abundance, enhances
The reckless delight of that wildest of dances!

CACHUCHA

[*The dance is interrupted by the unexpected appearance of* DON ALHAMBRA, *who looks on with astonishment.* MARCO *and* GIU-SEPPE *appear embarrassed. The others run off, except Drummer Boy, who is driven off by* DON ALHAMBRA.]

DON AL.: Good evening. Fancy ball?

GIU.: No, not exactly. A little friendly dance. That's all. Sorry you're late.

DON AL.: But I saw a groom dancing, and a footman!

MAR.: Yes. That's the Lord High Footman.

DON AL.: And, dear me, a common little drummer boy!

GIU.: Oh no! That's the Lord High Drummer Boy.

DON AL.: But surely, surely the servants'-hall is the place for these gentry?

GIU.: Oh dear no! *We* have appropriated the servants'-hall. It's the Royal Apartment, and accessible only by tickets obtainable at the Lord Chamberlain's office.

MAR.: We really must have some place that we can call our own.

DON AL. [*puzzled*]: I'm afraid I'm not quite equal to the intellectual pressure of the conversation.

GIU.: You see, the Monarchy has been re-modelled on Republican principles.

DON AL.: What!

GIU.: All departments rank equally, and everybody is at the head of his department.

DON AL.: I see.

MAR.: I'm afraid you're annoyed.

DON AL.: No. I won't say that. It's not quite what I expected.

GIU.: I'm awfully sorry.

MAR.: So am I.

GIU.: By the by, can I offer you anything after your voyage? A plate of macaroni and a rusk?

DON AL. [*preoccupied*]: No, no – nothing – nothing.

GIU.: Obliged to be careful?

DON AL.: Yes – gout. You see, in every Court there are distinctions that must be observed.

GIU. [*puzzled*]: There are, are there?

DON AL.: Why, of course. For instance, you wouldn't have a Lord High Chancellor play leapfrog with his own cook.

MAR.: Why not?

DON AL.: Why not! Because a Lord High Chancellor is a personage of great dignity, who should never, under any circumstances, place himself in the position of being told to tuck in his tuppenny,[51] except by noblemen of his own rank. A Lord High Archbishop, for instance, might tell a Lord High Chancellor to tuck in his tuppenny, but certainly not a cook, gentlemen, certainly not a cook.

GIU.: Not even a Lord High Cook?

DON AL.: My good friend, that is a rank that is not recognized at the Lord Chamberlain's office. No, no, it won't do. I'll give you an instance in which the experiment was tried.

SONG – DON ALHAMBRA, *with* MARCO *and* GIUSEPPE

DON AL.: There lived a King, as I've been told,
    In the wonder-working days of old,
    When hearts were twice as good as gold,
      And twenty times as mellow.
    Good-temper triumphed in his face,
    And in his heart he found a place
    For all the erring human race
      And every wretched fellow.
    When he had Rhenish wine to drink
    It made him very sad to think
    That some, at junket or at jink,
      Must be content with toddy.

MAR. *and* GIU.:
    With toddy, must be content with toddy.

DON AL.: He wished all men as rich as he
    (And he was rich as rich could be),
    So to the top of every tree
      Promoted everybody.

MAR. *and* GIU.:
    Now, that's the kind of King for me –
    He wished all men as rich as he,
    So to the top of every tree
      Promoted everybody!

DON AL.: Lord Chancellors were cheap as sprats,
    And Bishops in their shovel hats
    Were plentiful as tabby cats –
      In point of fact, too many.

Ambassadors cropped up like hay,
Prime Ministers and such as they
Grew like asparagus in May,
     And Dukes were three a penny.
On every side Field-Marshals gleamed,
Small beer were Lords-Lieutenant[52] deemed,
With Admirals the ocean teemed
     All round his wide dominions.

MAR. *and* GIU.:

     With Admirals all round his wide dominions.

DON AL.:   And Party Leaders you might meet
In twos and threes in every street
Maintaining, with no little heat,
     Their various opinions.

MAR. *and* GIU.:

     Now that's a sight you couldn't beat –
Two Party Leaders in each street
Maintaining, with no little heat,
     Their various opinions.

DON AL.:   That King, although no one denies
His heart was of abnormal size,
Yet he'd have acted otherwise
     If he had been acuter.
The end is easily foretold,
When every blessed thing you hold
Is made of silver, or of gold,
     You long for simple pewter.
When you have nothing else to wear
But cloth of gold and satins rare,
For cloth of gold you cease to care –
     Up goes the price of shoddy.

MAR. *and* GIU.:

     Of shoddy,[53] up goes the price of shoddy.

DON AL.:   In short, whoever you may be,
              To this conclusion you'll agree,
              When every one is somebodee,
                 Then no one's anybody!

MAR. *and* GIU.:

              Now that's as plain as plain can be,
              To this conclusion we agree –

ALL: When every one is somebodee,
                 Then no one's anybody!

[GIANETTA *and* TESSA *enter unobserved. The two girls, impelled by curiosity, remain listening at the back of the stage.*]

DON AL.: And now I have some important news to communicate. His Grace the Duke of Plaza-Toro, Her Grace the Duchess and their beautiful daughter Casilda – I say their beautiful daughter Casilda –

GIU.: We heard you.

DON AL.: Have arrived at Barataria, and may be here at any moment.

MAR.: The Duke and Duchess are nothing to us.

DON AL.: But the daughter – the beautiful daughter! Aha! Oh, you're a lucky dog, one of you!

GIU.: I think you're a very incomprehensible old gentleman.

DON AL.: Not a bit – I'll explain. Many years ago when you (whichever you are) were a baby, you (whichever you are) were married to a little girl who has grown up to be the most beautiful young lady in Spain. That beautiful young lady will be here to claim you (whichever you are) in half an hour, and I congratulate that one (whichever it is) with all my heart.

MAR.: Married when a baby!

GIU.: But we were married three months ago!

DON AL.: One of you – only one. The other (whichever it is) is an unintentional bigamist.

GIA. *and* TESSA [*coming forward*]: Well, upon my word!

DON AL.: Eh? Who are these young people?

TESSA: Who are we? Why, their wives, of course. We've just arrived.

DON AL.: Their wives! Oh dear, this is very unfortunate! Oh dear, this complicates matters! Dear, dear, what will Her Majesty say?

GIA.: And do you mean to say that one of these Monarchs was already married?

TESSA: And that neither of us will be a Queen?

DON AL.: That is the idea I intended to convey. [TESSA *and* GIANETTA *begin to cry.*]

GIU. [*to* TESSA]: Tessa, my dear, dear child –

TESSA: Get away! perhaps it's you!

MAR. [*to* GIA.]: My poor, poor little woman!

GIA.: Don't! Who knows whose husband you are?

TESSA: And pray, why didn't you tell us all about it before they left Venice?

DON AL.: Because, if I had, no earthly temptation would have induced these gentlemen to leave two such extremely fascinating and utterly irresistible little ladies!

TESSA: There's something in that.

DON AL.: I may mention that you will not be kept long in suspense, as the old lady who nursed the Royal child is at present in the torture chamber, waiting for me to interview her.

GIU.: Poor old girl. Hadn't you better go and put her out of her suspense?

DON AL.: Oh no – there's no hurry – she's all right. She has all the illustrated papers. However, I'll go and interrogate her, and, in the meantime, may I sugest the absolute propriety of your regarding yourselves as single young ladies. Good evening!   [*Exit.*]

GIA.: Well, here's a pleasant state of things!

MAR.: Delightful. One of us is married to two young ladies, and nobody knows which; and the other is married to one young lady whom nobody can identify!

GIA.: And one of us is married to one of you, and the other is married to nobody.

TESSA: But which of you is married to which of us, and what's to become of the other? [*About to cry.*]

GIU.: It's quite simple. Observe. Two husbands have managed to acquire three wives. Three wives – two husbands. [*Reckoning up.*] That's two-thirds of a husband to each wife.

TESSA: O Mount Vesuvius, here we are in arithmetic! My good sir, one can't marry a vulgar fraction![54]

GIU.: You've no right to call me a vulgar fraction.

MAR.: We are getting rather mixed. The situation entangled. Let's try and comb it out.

QUARTET – MARCO, GIUSEPPE, GIANETTA, TESSA

ALL:
In a contemplative fashion,
And a tranquil frame of mind,
Free from every kind of passion,
Some solution let us find.
Let us grasp the situation,
Solve the complicated plot –
Quiet, calm deliberation
Disentangles every knot.

TESSA	THE OTHERS
I, no doubt, Giuseppe wedded –	In a contemplative fashion, etc.
That's, of course, a slice of luck.	
He is rather dunder-headed,	
Still distinctly, he's a duck.	

GIANETTA	THE OTHERS
I, a victim, too, of Cupid,	Let us grasp the situation, etc.
Marco married – that is clear.	
He's particularly stupid,	
Still distinctly, he's a dear.	

MARCO	THE OTHERS
To Gianetta I was mated;	In a contemplative fashion, etc.
I can prove it in a trice:	
Though her charms are overrated,	
Still I own she's rather nice.	

599

GIUSEPPE
I to Tessa, willy-nilly,
  All at once a victim fell.
  She is what is called a silly,
    Still she answers pretty well.

THE OTHERS
Let us grasp the situation, etc.

MAR.:   Now when we were pretty babies
        Some one married us, that's clear –

GIA.:   And if I can catch her
            I'll pinch her and scratch her,
        And send her away with a flea in her ear.

GIU.:   He whom that young lady married,
        To receive her can't refuse.

TESSA: If I overtake her
           I'll warrant I'll make her
        To shake in her aristocratical shoes!

GIA. [*to* TESSA]:
        If she married your Giuseppe
        You and he will have to part –

TESSA [*to* GIA.]:   If I have to do it
           I'll warrant she'll rue it –
        I'll teach her to marry the man of my heart!

        If she married Messer[55] Marco
        You're a spinster, that is plain –

GIA. [*to* TESSA]:   No matter – no matter
           If I can get at her
        I doubt if her mother will know her again!

ALL: Quiet, calm deliberation
        Disentangles every knot!   [*Exeunt, pondering.*]

[MARCH. *Enter procession of Retainers, heralding approach of* DUKE, DUCHESS *and* CASILDA. *All three are now dressed with the utmost magnificence.*]

CHORUS OF MEN, *with* DUKE *and* DUCHESS:

With ducal pomp and ducal pride
(Announce these comers,
O ye kettle-drummers!)
Comes Barataria's high-born bride.
(Ye sounding cymbals clang!)
She comes to claim the Royal hand –
(Proclaim their Graces,
O ye double basses!)
Of the King who rules this goodly land.
(Ye brazen brasses bang!)

DUKE *and* DUCH.:

This polite attention touches
Heart of Duke and heart of Duchess,
Who resign their pet
With profound regret.
She of beauty was a model
When a tiny tiddle-toddle,
And at twenty-one
She's excelled by none!

CHORUS: With ducal pomp and ducal pride, etc.

DUKE [*to his attendants*]: Be good enough to inform His Majesty that
His Grace the Duke of Plaza-Toro, Limited, has arrived, and begs –
CAS.: Desires –
DUCH.: Demands –
DUKE: And demands an audience.

[*Exeunt attendants.*]
And now, my child, prepare to
receive the husband to whom you were united under such interesting
and romantic circumstances.

CAS.: But which is it? There are two of them!

DUKE: It is true that at present His Majesty is a double gentleman; but as soon as the circumstances of his marriage are ascertained, he will, *ipso facto*, boil down to a single gentleman – thus presenting a unique example of an individual who becomes a single man and a married man by the same operation.

DUCH. [*severely*]: I have known instances in which the characteristics of both conditions existed concurrently in the same individual.

DUKE: Ah, he couldn't have been a Plaza-Toro.

DUCH.: Oh! couldn't he, though!

CAS.: Well, whatever happens, I shall, of course, be a dutiful wife, but I can never love my husband.

DUKE: I don't know. It's extraordinary what unprepossessing people one can love if one gives one's mind to it.

DUCH.: I loved your father.

DUKE: My love – that remark is a little hard, I think? Rather cruel, perhaps? Somewhat uncalled-for, I venture to believe?

DUCH.: It was very difficult, my dear; but I said to myself, 'That man is a Duke, and I *will* love him.' Several of my relations bet me I couldn't, but I did – desperately!

SONG

DUCH.:

On the day when I was wedded
  To your admirable sire,
I acknowledge that I dreaded
  An explosion of his ire.
I was overcome with panic –
For his temper was volcanic,
  And I didn't dare revolt,
  For I feared a thunderbolt!
I was always very wary,
  For his fury was ecstatic –
His refined vocabulary
  Most unpleasantly emphatic.
    To the thunder
      Of this Tartar[56]

I knocked under
Like a martyr;
When intently
He was fuming,
I was gently
Unassuming –
When reviling
Me completely,
I was smiling
Very sweetly:
Giving him the very best, and getting back the very
worst –
That is how I tried to tame your great progenitor – at
first!

But I found that a reliance
On my threatening appearance,
And a resolute defiance
Of marital interference,
And a gentle intimation
Of my firm determination
To see what I could do
To be wife and husband too
Was the only thing required
For to make his temper supple,
And you couldn't have desired
A more reciprocating couple.
Ever willing
To be wooing,
We were billing –
We were cooing;
When I merely
From him parted,
We were nearly
Broken-hearted –
When in sequel
Reunited,

We were equal-
Ly delighted.
So with double-shotted guns and colours nailed unto the mast,
I tamed your insignificant progenitor – at last!

CAS.: My only hope is that when my husband sees what a shady family he has married into he will repudiate the contract altogether.

DUKE: Shady? A nobleman shady, who is blazing in the lustre of unaccustomed pocket-money? A nobleman shady, who can look back upon ninety-five quarterings? It is not every nobleman who is ninety-five quarters in arrear – I mean, who can look back upon ninety-five of them! And this, just as I have been floated at a premium![57] Oh fie!

DUCH.: Your Majesty is surely unaware that directly Your Majesty's father came before the public he was applied for over and over again.

DUKE: My dear, Her Majesty's father was in the habit of being applied for over and over again – and very urgently applied for, too – long before he was registered under the Limited Liability Act.[58]

RECITATIVE

DUKE: To help unhappy commoners, and add to their enjoyment,
Affords a man of noble rank congenial employment;
Of our attempts we offer you examples illustrative:
The work is light, and, I may add, it's most remunerative.

DUET – DUKE *and* DUCHESS

DUKE: Small titles and orders
For Mayors and Recorders[59]
I get – and they're highly delighted –
DUCH.:   They're highly delighted!

DUKE: MP's baronetted,[60]
Sham Colonels gazetted,[61]
And second-rate Aldermen[62] knighted –

DUCH.:   Yes, Aldermen knighted.

DUKE: Foundation-stone laying
               I find very paying:
                    It adds a large sum to my makings –

DUCH.:   Large sums to his makings.

DUKE: At charity dinners
               The best of speech-spinners,
                    I get ten per cent on the takings –

DUCH.:   One-tenth of the takings.

DUCH.:   I present any lady
               Whose conduct is shady
                    Or smacking of doubtful propriety –

DUKE: Doubtful propriety.

DUCH.:   When Virtue would quash her,
               I take and whitewash her,
                    And launch her in first-rate society –

DUKE: First-rate society!

DUCH.:   I recommend acres
               Of clumsy dressmakers –
                    Their fit and their finishing touches –

DUKE: Their finishing touches.

DUCH.:   A sum in addition
               They pay for permission
                    To say that they make for the Duchess –

DUKE: They make for the Duchess!

Those pressing prevailers,
The ready-made tailors,
   Quote me as their great double-barrel –

DUCH.:   Their great double-barrel.

DUKE: I allow them to do so,
Though Robinson Crusoe
   Would jib at their wearing apparel –

DUCH.:   Such wearing apparel!

DUKE: I sit, by selection,
Upon the direction
   Of several Companies bubble –

DUCH.:   All Companies bubble!

DUKE: As soon as they're floated
I'm freely bank-noted –
   I'm pretty well paid for my trouble –

DUCH.:   He's paid for his trouble!

At middle-class party
I play at *écarté*[63] –
   And I'm by no means a beginner –

DUKE [*significantly*]:
   She's not a beginner.

DUCH.:   To one of my station
The remuneration –
   Five guineas a night and my dinner –

DUKE: And wine with her dinner.

DUCH.: I write letters blatant
On medicines patent –
And use any other you mustn't –

DUKE: Believe me, you mustn't –

DUCH.: And vow my complexion
Derives its perfection
From somebody's soap – which it doesn't –

DUKE [*significantly*]:
It certainly doesn't.

We're ready as witness
To any one's fitness
To fill any place or preferment –

DUCH.: A place or preferment.

We're often in waiting
At junket or *fêting*,
And sometimes attend an interment –

DUKE: We enjoy an interment.

BOTH: In short, if you'd kindle
The spark of a swindle,
Lure simpletons into your clutches –
Yes; into your clutches.
Or hoodwink a debtor,
You cannot do better

DUCH.: Than trot out a Duke or a Duchess –

DUKE: A Duke or a Duchess!

[*Enter* MARCO *and* GIUSEPPE.]

Ah! Their Majesties. Your Majesty! [*Bows with great ceremony.*]

MAR.: The Duke of Plaza-Toro, I believe?

DUKE: The same. [MARCO *and* GIUSEPPE *offer to shake hands with him. The* DUKE *bows ceremoniously. They endeavour to imitate him.*] Allow me to present –

GIU.: The young lady one of us married?

[MARCO *and* GIUSEPPE *offer to shake hands with her.* CASILDA *curtsies formally. They endeavour to imitate her.*]

CAS.: Gentlemen, I am the most obedient servant of one of you. [*Aside*] Oh, Luiz!

DUKE: I am now about to address myself to the gentleman whom my daughter married; the other may allow his attention to wander if he likes, for what I am about to say does not concern him. Sir, you will find in this young lady a combination of excellences which you would search for in vain in any young lady who had not the good fortune to be my daughter. There is some little doubt as to which of you is the gentleman I am addressing, and which is the gentleman who is allowing his attention to wander; but when that doubt is solved, I shall say (still addressing the attentive gentleman), 'Take her, and may she make you happier than her mother has made me.'

DUCH.: Sir!

DUKE: If possible. And now there is a little matter to which I think I am entitled to take exception. I come here in state with Her Grace the Duchess and Her Majesty my daughter, and what do I find? Do I find, for instance, a guard of honour to receive me? No!

MAR. *and* GIU.: No.

DUKE: The town illuminated? No!

MAR. *and* GIU.: No.

DUKE: Refreshment provided? No!

MAR. *and* GIU.: No.

DUKE: A Royal salute fired? No!

MAR. *and* GIU.: No.

DUKE: Triumphal arches erected? No!

MAR. *and* GIU.: No.

DUKE: The bells set ringing?

MAR. *and* GIU.: No.

DUKE: Yes – one – the Visitors', and I rang it myself. It is not enough! It is not enough!

GIU.: Upon my honour, I'm very sorry; but you see, I was brought up in a gondola, and my ideas of politeness are confined to taking off my cap to my passengers when they tip me.

DUCH.: That's all very well in its way, but it is not enough.

GIU.: I'll take off anything else in reason.

DUKE: But a Royal Salute to my daughter – it costs so little.

CAS.: Papa, I don't want a salute.

GIU.: My dear sir, as soon as we know which of us is entitled to take that liberty she shall have as many salutes as she likes.

MAR.: As for guards of honour and triumphal arches, you don't know our people – they wouldn't stand it.

GIU.: They are very off-hand with us – very off-hand indeed.

DUKE: Oh, but you mustn't allow that – you must keep them in proper discipline, you must impress your Court with your importance. You want deportment – carriage –

GIU.: We've got a carriage.

DUKE: Manner – dignity. There must be a good deal of this sort of thing – [*business*] – and a little of this sort of thing – [*business*] – and possibly just a *soupçon* of this sort of thing! – [*business*] – and so on. Oh, it's very useful, and most effective. Just attend to me. You are a King – I am a subject. Very good –

GAVOTTE – DUKE, DUCHESS, CASILDA, MARCO, GIUSEPPE

DUKE: I am a courtier grave and serious
                      Who is about to kiss your hand:
                  Try to combine a pose imperious
                      With a demeanour nobly bland.

MAR. *and* GIU.:   Let us combine a pose imperious
                      With a demeanour nobly bland.

[MARCO *and* GIUSEPPE *endeavour to carry out his instructions.*]

DUKE: That's, if anything, *too* unbending –
                      Too aggressively stiff and grand;
          [*They suddenly modify their attitudes.*]

                      Now to the other extreme you're tending –
                      Don't be so deucedly condescending!

DUCH. *and* CAS.:

                      Now to the other extreme you're tending –
                      Don't be so dreadfully condescending!

MAR. *and* GIU.:   Oh, hard to please some noblemen seem!
                      At first, if anything, *too* unbending;
                   Off we go to the other extreme –
                      Too confoundedly condescending!

DUKE: Now a gavotte perform sedately –
                      Offer your hand with conscious pride;
                   Take an attitude not too stately,
                      Still sufficiently dignified.

MAR. *and* GIU.:   Now for an attitude not too stately,
                      Still sufficiently dignified.
          [*They endeavour to carry out his instructions.*]

DUKE [*beating time*]:
                      Oncely, twicely – oncely, twicely –
                         Bow impressively ere you glide. [*They do so.*]
                      Capital both – you've caught it nicely!
                      That is the style of thing precisely!

DUCH. *and* CAS.: Capital both – they've caught it nicely!
                      That is the style of thing precisely!

MAR. *and* GIU.:   Oh, sweet to earn a nobleman's praise!
                      Capital both – we've caught it nicely!

Supposing he's right in what he says,
This is the style of thing precisely!
[GAVOTTE. *At the end exeunt* DUKE *and* DUCHESS, *leaving*
CASILDA *with* MARCO *and* GIUSEPPE.]

GIU. [*to* MARCO]: The old birds have gone away and left the young chickens together. That's called tact.

MAR.: It's very awkward. We really ought to tell her how we are situated. It's not fair to the girl.

GIU.: Then why don't you do it?

MAR.: I'd rather not – you.

GIU.: I don't know how to begin. [*To* CASILDA] A – Madam – I – we, that is, several of us –

CAS.: Gentlemen, I am bound to listen to you; but it is right to tell you that, not knowing I was married in infancy, I am over head and ears in love with somebody else.

GIU.: Our case exactly! *We* are over head and ears in love with somebody else!

[*Enter* GIANETTA *and* TESSA.]

In point of fact, with our wives!

CAS.: Your wives! Then you are married?

TESSA: It's not our fault.

GIA.: We knew nothing about it.

BOTH: We are sisters in misfortune.

CAS.: My good girls, I don't blame you. Only before we go any further we must really arrive at some satisfactory arrangement, or we shall get hopelessly complicated.

QUINTET *and* FINALE – MARCO, GIUSEPPE, CASILDA, GIANETTA, TESSA

ALL: Here is a case unprecedented!
 Here are a King and Queen ill-starred!
 Ever since marriage was first invented
 Never was known a case so hard!

MAR. *and* GIU.:
>> I may be said to have been bisected,
>> By a profound catastrophe!

CAS., GIA., TESSA:
>> Through a calamity unexpected
>> I am divisible into three!

ALL:
>> O moralists all,
>>> How can you call
>> Marriage a state of unitee,
> When excellent husbands are bisected,
>> And wives divisible into three?
>>> O moralists all,
>>> How can you call
>> Marriage a state of union true?

CAS., GIA., TESSA:
>> One-third of myself is married to half of ye or you,

MAR. *and* GIU.:
>> When half of myself has married one-third of ye or
>>> you?
> [*Enter* DON ALHAMBRA, *followed by* DUKE, DUCHESS *and all the* CHORUS.]

FINALE

RECITATIVE

DON AL.: Now let the loyal lieges gather round –
>> The Prince's foster-mother has been found!
>> She will declare, to silver clarion's sound,
>> The rightful King – let him forthwith be crowned!

CHORUS: She will declare, etc.

[DON ALHAMBRA *brings forward* INEZ, *the Prince's foster-mother.*]

TESSA: Speak, woman, speak –
DUKE: We're all attention!
GIA.:   The news we seek –
DUCH.:   This moment mention.
CAS.:   To us they bring –
DON AL.:   His foster-mother.
MAR.:   Is he the King?
GIU.:   Or this my brother?

ALL: Speak, woman, speak, etc.

RECITATIVE

INEZ: The Royal Prince was by the King entrusted
           To my fond care, ere I grew old and crusted;
           When traitors came to steal his son reputed,
           My own small boy I deftly substituted!
           The villains fell into the trap completely –
           I hid the Prince away – still sleeping sweetly:
           I called him 'son' with pardonable slyness –
           His name, Luiz! Behold his Royal Highness!

[*Sensation.* LUIZ *ascends the throne, crowned and robed as King.*] ·

CAS. [*rushing to his arms*]: Luiz!
LUIZ: Casilda! [*Embrace.*]

ALL: Is this indeed the King?
                  Oh, wondrous revelation!
              Oh, unexpected thing!
                  Unlooked-for situation!

MAR., GIA., GIU., TESSA:
              This statement we receive
                  With sentiments conflicting;

> Our hearts rejoice and grieve,
>   Each other contradicting;
> To those whom we adore
>   We can be reunited –
> On one point rather sore,
>   But, on the whole, delighted!

LUIZ: When others claimed thy dainty hand,
                    I waited – waited – waited,

DUKE: As prudence (so I understand)
                    Dictated – tated – tated.

CAS.:   By virtue of our early vow
                    Recorded – corded – corded,

DUCH.:   Your pure and patient love is now
                    Rewarded – warded – warded.

ALL: Then hail, O King of a Golden Land,
            And the high-born bride who claims his
                    hand!
            The past is dead, and you gain your own,
            A royal crown and a golden throne!

[All kneel: LUIZ *crowns* CASILDA.]

ALL: Once more *gondolieri*,
                        Both skilful and wary,
                        Free from this quandary
                            Contented are we.
                        From Royalty flying,
                        Our gondolas plying,
                        And merrily crying
                            Our '*premé*,' '*stalì!*'[64]

So good-bye, cachucha, fandango, bolero –
We'll dance a farewell to that measure –
Old Xeres, adieu – Manzanilla – Montero –
We leave you with feelings of pleasure!

CURTAIN

UTOPIA[1] LIMITED

OR

THE FLOWERS OF PROGRESS

DRAMATIS PERSONAE

KING PARAMOUNT THE FIRST (*King of Utopia*)

SCAPHIO
PHANTIS } (*Judges of the Utopian Supreme Court*)

TARARA (*the Public Exploder*)

CALYNX (*the Utopian Vice-Chamberlain*)

IMPORTED FLOWERS OF PROGRESS

LORD DRAMALEIGH (*a British Lord Chamberlain*)

CAPTAIN FITZBATTLEAXE (*First Life Guards*)

CAPTAIN SIR EDWARD CORCORAN, KCB (*of the Royal Navy*)

MR GOLDBURY (*a Company Promoter; afterwards Comptroller of the Utopian Household*)

SIR BAILEY BARRE, QC, MP

MR BLUSHINGTON (*of the County Council*)

THE PRINCESS ZARA (*Eldest Daughter of King Paramount*)

THE PRINCESS NEKAYA
THE PRINCESS KALYBA } (*her Younger Sisters*)

THE LADY SOPHY (*their English Gouvernante*)

SALATA
MELENE } (*Utopian Maidens*)
PHYLLA

Chorus of Utopian Maidens, Nobles, Courtiers, Guards and English Troupers

ACT I – A Utopian Palm Grove
ACT II – Throne Room in King Paramount's Palace

ACT I

SCENE – *A Utopian Palm Grove in the gardens of* KING PARA-
MOUNT*'s Palace, showing a picturesque and luxuriant tropical
landscape,*[2] *with the sea in the distance.*

[SALATA, MELENE, PHYLLA *and other Maidens discovered,
lying lazily about the stage and thoroughly enjoying themselves
in lotus-eating fashion.*]

OPENING CHORUS

In lazy languor – motionless,
We lie and dream of nothingness;
  For visions come
  From Poppydom
    Direct at our command:
Or, delicate alternative,
In open idleness we live,
  With lyre and lute
  And silver flute,
    The life of Lazyland!

SOLO

PHYLLA: The song of birds
       In ivied towers;
         The rippling play
         Of waterway;

> The lowing herds;
>> The breath of flowers;
>>> The languid loves
>>> Of turtle doves –
> These simple joys are all at hand
> Upon thy shores, O Lazyland!

CHORUS: In lazy languor, etc.
      [*Enter* CALYNX.]

CAL.: Good news! Great news! His Majesty's eldest daughter, Princess Zara, who left our shores five years since to go to England – the greatest, the most powerful, the wisest country in the world – has taken a high degree at Girton,³ and is on her way home again, having achieved a complete mastery over all the elements that have tended to raise that glorious country to her present pre-eminent position among civilized nations!

SAL.: Then in a few months Utopia may hope to be completely Anglicized?

CAL.: Absolutely and without a doubt.

MEL. [*lazily*]: We are very well as we are. Life without a care – every want supplied by a kind and fatherly monarch, who, despot though he be, has no other thought than to make his people happy – what have we to gain by the great change that is in store for us?

SAL.: What have we to gain? English institutions, English tastes, and oh, English fashions!

CAL.: England has made herself what she is because, in that favoured land, every one has to think for himself. Here we have no need to think, because our monarch anticipates all our wants, and our political opinions are formed for us by the journals to which we subscribe. Oh, think how much more brilliant this dialogue would have been, if we had been accustomed to exercise our reflective powers! They say that in England the conversation of the very meanest is a coruscation of impromptu epigram!

      [*Enter* TARARA⁴ *in a great rage.*]

TAR.: Lalabalele talala! Callabale lalabalica falahle!

CAL. [*horrified*]: Stop – stop, I beg! [*All the ladies close their ears.*]

TAR.: Callamalala galalate! Caritalla lalabalee kallalale poo!

LADIES: Oh, stop him! stop him!

CAL.: My Lord, I'm surprised at you. Are you not aware that His Majesty, in his despotic acquiescence with the emphatic wish of his people, has ordered that the Utopian language shall be banished from his court, and that all communications shall henceforward be made in the English tongue?

TAR.: Yes, I'm perfectly aware of it, although – [*suddenly presenting an explosive 'cracker'*]. Stop – allow me.

CAL. [*pulls it*]: Now, what's that for?

TAR.: Why, I've recently been appointed Public Exploder to His Majesty, and as I'm constitutionally nervous, I must accustom myself by degrees to the startling nature of my duties. Thank you. I was about to say that although, as Public Exploder, I am next in succession to the throne, I nevertheless do my best to fall in with the royal decree. But when I am overmastered by an indignant sense of overwhelming wrong, as I am now, I slip into my native tongue without knowing it. I am told that in the language of that great and pure nation, strong expressions do not exist, consequently when I want to let off steam I have no alternative but to say, 'Lalabalele molola lililah kallalale poo!'

CAL.: But what is your grievance?

TAR.: This – by our Constitution we are governed by a Despot who, although in theory absolute – is, in practice, nothing of the kind – being watched day and night by two Wise Men whose duty it is, on his very first lapse from political or social propriety, to denounce him to me, the Public Exploder, and it then becomes my duty to blow up His Majesty with dynamite – allow me. [*Presenting a cracker which* CALYNX *pulls.*] Thank you – and, as some compensation to my wounded feelings, I reign in his stead.

CAL.: Yes. After many unhappy experiments in the direction of an ideal Republic, it was found that what may be described as a Despotism tempered by Dynamite provides, on the whole, the most satisfactory description of ruler – an autocrat who dares not abuse his autocratic power.

TAR.: That's the theory – but in practice, how does it act? Now, do you ever happen to see the *Palace Peeper*?[5] [*producing a 'Society' paper*].

CAL.: Never even heard of the journal.

TAR.: I'm not surprised, because His Majesty's agents always buy up the whole edition; but I have an aunt in the publishing department, and she has supplied me with a copy. Well, it actually teems with circumstantially convincing details of the King's abominable immoralities! If this high-class journal may be believed, His Majesty is one of the most Heliogabalian[6] profligates that ever disgraced an autocratic throne! And *do* these Wise Men denounce him to me? Not a bit of it! They wink at his immoralities! Under the circumstances I really think I am justified in exclaiming 'Lalabalele molola lililah kalabalele poo!' [*All horrified.*] I don't care – the occasion demands it. [*Exit.*]

[*March. Enter Guard, escorting* SCAPHIO *and* PHANTIS.]

CHORUS:
> O make way for the Wise Men!
> They are prizemen –
> Double-first in the world's university!
> For though lovely this island
> (Which is *my* land),
> She has no one to match them in *her* city.
> They're the pride of Utopia –
> Cornucopia
> Is each in his mental fertility.
> O they never make blunder,
> And no wonder,
> For they're triumphs of infallibility.

DUET – SCAPHIO *and* PHANTIS

> In every mental lore
> (The statement smacks of vanity)
> We claim to rank before
> The wisest of humanity.

As gifts of head and heart
   We wasted on 'utility',
We're 'cast' to play a part
   Of great responsibility.

Our duty is to spy
   Upon our King's illicities,
And keep a watchful eye
   On all his eccentricities.
If ever a trick he tries
   That savours of rascality,
At our decree he dies
   Without the least formality.

We fear no rude rebuff,
   Or newspaper publicity;
Our word is quite enough,
   The rest is electricity.
A pound of dynamite
   Explodes in his auriculars;
It's not a pleasant sight –
   We'll spare you the particulars.

Its force all men confess,
   The King needs no admonishing –
We may say its success
   Is something quite astonishing.
Our despot it imbues
   With virtues quite delectable,
He minds his P's and Q's, –
   And keeps himself respectable.

   Of a tyrant polite
   He's a paragon quite.
   He's as modest and mild
   In his ways as a child;

And no one ever met
With an autocrat, yet,
So delightfully bland
To the least in the land!

So make way for the wise men, etc.
[*Exeunt all but* SCAPHIO *and* PHANTIS. PHANTIS *is pensive.*]

SCA.: Phantis, you are not in your customary exuberant spirits. What is wrong?

PHAN.: Scaphio, I think you once told me that you have never loved?

SCA.: Never! I have often marvelled at the fairy influence which weaves its rosy web about the faculties of the greatest and wisest of our race; but I thank Heaven I have never been subjected to its singular fascination. For, oh, Phantis! there is that within me that tells me that when my time *does* come, the convulsion will be tremendous! When *I* love, it will be with the accumulated fervour of sixty-six years! But I have an ideal – a semi-transparent Being, filled with an inorganic pink jelly – and I have never yet seen the woman who approaches within measurable distance of it. All are opaque – opaque – opaque!

PHAN.: Keep that ideal firmly before you, and love not until you find her. Though but fifty-five, I am an old campaigner in the battle-fields of Love; and, believe me, it is better to be as you are, heart-free and happy, than as I am – eternally racked with doubting agonies! Scaphio, the Princess Zara returns from England to-day!

SCA.: My poor boy, I see it all.

PHAN.: Oh! Scaphio, she is so beautiful. Ah! you smile, for you have never seen her. She sailed for England three months before you took office.

SCA.: Now tell me, is your affection requited?

PHAN.: I do not know – I am not sure. Sometimes I think it is, and then come these torturing doubts! I feel sure that she does not regard me with absolute indifference, for she could never look at me without having to go to bed with a sick headache.

SCA.: That is surely something. Come, take heart, boy! you are young and beautiful. What more could maiden want?

PHAN.: Ah! Scaphio, remember she returns from a land where every youth is as a young Greek god, and where such poor beauty as I can boast is seen at every turn.

SCA.: Be of good cheer! Marry her, boy, if so your fancy wills, and be sure that love will come.

PHAN. [*overjoyed*]: Then you will assist me in this?

SCA.: Why, surely! Silly one, what have you to fear? We have but to say the word, and her father must consent. Is he not our very slave? Come, take heart. I cannot bear to see you sad.

PHAN.: Now I may hope, indeed! Scaphio, you have placed me on the very pinnacle of human joy!

DUET – SCAPHIO *and* PHANTIS

SCA.:
Let all your doubts take wing –
Our influence is great.
If Paramount our King
Presume to hesitate,
Put on the screw,
And caution him
That he will rue
Disaster grim
That must ensue
To life and limb,
Should he pooh-pooh
This harmless whim.

BOTH:
This harmless whim – this harmless whim,
It is, as $\left\{ \begin{array}{c} \text{I} \\ \text{you} \end{array} \right\}$ say, a harmless whim.

PHAN. [*dancing*]:
Observe this dance
Which I employ
When I, by chance,
Go mad with joy.

What sentiment
Does this express?
[PHANTIS *continues his dance while* SCAPHIO *vainly endeavours to discover its meaning.*]

Supreme content
And happiness!

BOTH: Of course it does! Of course it does!
Supreme content and happiness!

PHAN.:   Your friendly aid conferred,
I need no longer pine.
I've but to speak the word,
And lo! the maid is mine!

I do not choose
To be denied.
Or wish to lose
A lovely bride –
If to refuse
The King decide,
The Royal shoes
Then woe betide!

BOTH: Then woe betide – then woe betide!
The Royal shoes then woe betide!

SCA. [*dancing*]:   This step to use
I condescend
Whene'er I choose
To serve a friend.
What it implies
Now try to guess;
[SCAPHIO *continues his dance while* PHANTIS *is vainly endeavouring to discover its meaning.*]

It typifies
Unselfishness!

BOTH [*dancing*]:   Of course it does! Of course it does!
It typifies unselfishness!

[*Exeunt* SCAPHIO *and* PHANTIS.]
[*March. Enter* KING PARAMOUNT, *attended by guards and nobles, and preceded by girls dancing before him.*]

CHORUS: Quaff the nectar – cull the roses –
Gather fruit and flowers in plenty!
For our King no longer poses –
Sing the songs of *far niente*![7]
Wake the lute that sets us lilting,
Dance a welcome to each comer;
Day by day our year is wilting –
Sing the sunny songs of summer!
La, la, la, la!

SONG

KING: A King of autocratic power we –
A despot whose tyrannic will is law –
Whose rule is paramount o'er land and sea,
A presence of unutterable awe!
But though the awe that I inspire
Must shrivel with imperial fire
All foes whom it may chance to touch,
To judge by what I see and hear,
It does not seem to interfere
With popular enjoyment, much.

CHORUS: No, no – it does not interfere
With our enjoyment much.

KING: Stupendous when we rouse ourselves to strike,
Resistless when our tyrant thunder peals,

We often wonder what obstruction's like,
    And how a contradicted monarch feels.
But as it is our Royal whim
Our Royal sails to set and trim
    To suit whatever wind may blow –
What buffets contradiction deals
And how a thwarted monarch feels
    We probably shall never know.

CHORUS: No, no – what thwarted monarch feels
            You'll never, never know.

RECITATIVE

KING: My subjects all, it is your wish emphatic
    That all Utopia shall henceforth be modelled
    Upon that glorious country called Great Britain –
    To which some add – but others do not – Ireland.

ALL: It is!

KING: That being so, as you insist upon it,
    We have arranged that our two younger daughters
    Who have been 'finished' by an English Lady –
    [*tenderly*] A grave, and good, and gracious English Lady –
    Shall daily be exhibited in public,
    That all may learn what, from the English stand-point,
    Is looked upon as maidenly perfection!
    Come hither, daughters!

[*Enter* NEKAYA *and* KALYBA. *They are twins, about fifteen years old; they are very modest and demure in their appearance, dress and manner. They stand with their hands folded and their eyes cast down.*]

CHORUS: How fair! how modest! how discreet!
        How bashfully demure!
            See how they blush, as they've been taught,

At this publicity unsought!
How English and how pure!

DUET – NEKAYA *and* KALYBA

BOTH: Although of native maids the cream,
We're brought up on the English scheme –
  The best of all
  For great and small
   Who modesty adore.

NEK.: For English girls are good as gold,
Extremely modest (so we're told),
Demurely coy – divinely cold –

KAL.:   And we are that – and more.

To please papa, who argues thus –
All girls should mould themselves on us
  Because we are
  By furlongs far
   The best of all the bunch,
We show ourselves to loud applause
From ten to four without a pause –

NEK.: Which is an awkward time because
   It cuts into our lunch.

BOTH: Oh, maids of high and low degree,
Whose social code is rather free,
Please look at us and you will see
What good young ladies ought to be!

NEK.: And as we stand, like clockwork toys,
A lecturer whom papa employs
  Proceeds to praise
  Our modest ways
   And guileless character –

KAL.:   Our well-known blush – our downcast eyes –
        Our famous look of mild surprise
NEK.:   (Which competition still defies) –
KAL.:   Our celebrated 'Sir!!!'

        Then all the crowd take down our looks
        In pocket memorandum books.
            To diagnose
            Our modest pose
            The Kodaks[8] do their best:
NEK.:   If evidence you would possess
        Of what is maiden bashfulness,
        You only need a button press –
KAL.:   And *we* do all the rest.

[*Enter* LADY SOPHY – *an English lady of mature years and extreme gravity of demeanour and dress. She carries a lecturer's wand in her hand. She is led on by the* KING, *who expresses great regard and admiration for her.*]

RECITATIVE

LADY S.:   This morning we propose to illustrate
          A course of maiden courtship, from the start
          To the triumphant matrimonial finish.

[*Through the following song the two Princesses illustrate in gesture the description given by* LADY SOPHY.]

SONG

LADY S.:   Bold-faced ranger
           (Perfect stranger)
    Meets two well-behaved young ladies.
           He's attractive,
            Young and active –
    Each a little bit afraid is.
           Youth advances,
           At his glances

To their danger they awaken;
        They repel him
        As they tell him
He is very much mistaken.
Though they speak to him politely,
Please observe they're sneering slightly,
Just to show he's acting vainly.
This is Virtue saying plainly,
        'Go away, young bachelor,
        We are not what you take us for!'
When addressed impertinently,
English ladies answer gently,
        'Go away, young bachelor,
        We are not what you take us for!'

        As he gazes,
        Hat he raises,
Enters into conversation.
        Makes excuses –
        This produces
Interesting agitation.
        He, with daring,
        Undespairing,
Gives his card – his rank discloses.
        Little heeding
        This proceeding,
They turn up their little noses.
Pray observe this lesson vital –
When a man of rank and title
His position first discloses,
Always cock your little noses.
        When at home, let all the class
        Try this in the looking-glass.
English girls of well-bred notions
Shun all unrehearsed emotions.
        English girls of highest class
        Practise them before the glass.

His intentions
Then he mentions.
Something definite to go on –
Makes recitals
Of his titles,
Hints at settlements, and so on.
Smiling sweetly,
They, discreetly,
Ask for further evidences:
Thus invited,
He, delighted,
Gives the usual references.
This is business: Each is fluttered
When the offer's fairly uttered.
'Which of them has his affection?'
He declines to make selection.
Do they quarrel for his dross?
Not a bit of it – they toss!
Please observe this cogent moral –
English ladies never quarrel.
When a doubt they come across,
English ladies always toss.

RECITATIVE

LADY S.:   The lecture's ended. In ten minutes' space
'Twill be repeated in the market-place!
[*Exit* LADY SOPHY, *followed by* NEKAYA *and* KALYBA.]

CHORUS: Quaff the nectar – cull the roses –
Bashful girls will soon be plenty!
Maid who thus at fifteen poses
Ought to be divine at twenty!
[*Exit* CHORUS. *Manet* KING.]

KING: I requested Scaphio and Phantis to be so good as to favour me with an audience this morning. Oh, here they are!

[*Enter* SCAPHIO *and* PHANTIS.]

SCA.: Your Majesty wished to speak with us, I believe. You – you needn't keep your crown on, on our account, you know.

KING: I beg your pardon [*removes it*]. I always forget that! Odd, the notion of a King not being allowed to wear one of his own crowns in the presence of two of his own subjects.

PHAN.: Yes – bizarre, is it not?

KING: Most quaint. But then it's a quaint world.

PHAN.: Teems with quiet fun. I often think what a lucky thing it is that you are blessed with such a keen sense of humour!

KING: Do you know, I find it invaluable. Do what I will, I *cannot* help looking at the humorous side of things – for, properly considered, everything has its humorous side – even the *Palace Peeper* (*producing it*). See here – 'Another Royal Scandal', by Junius[9] Junior. 'How long is this to last?' by Senex[10] Senior. 'Ribald Royalty', by Mercury[11] Major. 'Where is the Public Exploder?' by Mephistopheles[12] Minor. When I reflect that all these outrageous attacks on my morality are written by me, at your command – well, it's one of the funniest things that have come within the scope of my experience.

SCA.: Besides, apart from that, they have a quiet humour of their own which is simply irresistible.

KING [*gratified*]: Not bad, I think. Biting, trenchant sarcasm – the rapier, not the bludgeon – that's my line. But then it's so easy – I'm such a good subject – a bad King but a good Subject – ha! ha! – a capital heading for next week's leading article! [*makes a note*]. And then the stinging little paragraphs about our Royal goings-on with our Royal Second Housemaid – delicately sub-acid, are they not?

SCA.: My dear King, in that kind of thing no one can hold a candle to you.

PHAN.: But the crowning joke is the Comic Opera you've written for us – 'King Tuppence, or A Good Deal Less than Half a Sovereign' – in which the celebrated English tenor, Mr Wilkinson, burlesques your personal appearance and gives grotesque imitations of your Royal peculiarities. It's immense!

KING: Ye-es – That's what I wanted to speak to you about. Now I've not the least doubt but that even *that* has its humorous side, too – if one could only see it. As a rule I'm pretty quick at detecting latent humour – but I confess I do *not* quite see where it comes in, in this particular instance. It's so horribly personal!

SCA.: Personal? Yes, of course it's personal – but consider the antithetical humour of the situation.

KING: Yes. I – I don't think I've quite grasped that.

SCA.: No? You surprise me. Why, consider. During the day thousands tremble at your frown, during the night (from 8 to 11) thousands roar at it. During the day your most arbitrary pronouncements are received by your subjects with abject submission – during the night, they shout with joy at your most terrible decrees. It's not every monarch who enjoys the privilege of undoing by night all the despotic absurdities he's committed during the day.

KING: Of course! Now I see it! Thank you very much. I was sure it had its humorous side, and it was very dull of me not to have seen it before. But, as I said just now, it's a quaint world.

PHAN.: Teems with quiet fun.

KING: Yes. Properly considered, what a farce life is, to be sure!

SONG

KING:
  First you're born – and I'll be bound you
  Find a dozen strangers round you.
  'Hallo,' cries the new-born baby,
  'Where's my parents? which may they be?'
   Awkward silence – no reply –
   Puzzled baby wonders why!
  Father rises, bows politely –
  Mother smiles (but not too brightly) –
  Doctor mumbles like a dumb thing –
  Nurse is busy mixing something. –
   Every symptom tends to show
   You're decidedly *de trop*[13] –

ALL: Ho! ho! ho! ho! ho! ho! ho! ho!
                     Time's teetotum,
                         If you spin it,
                     Gives its quotum
                         Once a minute.
                     I'll go bail
                     You hit the nail,
                     And if you fail
                         The deuce is in it!

KING: You grow up and you discover
         What it is to be a lover.
         Some young lady is selected –
         Poor, perhaps, but well-connected,
             Whom you hail (for Love is blind)
             As the Queen of fairy kind.
         Though she's plain – perhaps unsightly,
         Makes her face up – laces tightly,
         In her form your fancy traces
         All the gifts of all the graces.
             Rivals none the maiden woo,
             So you take her and she takes you!

ALL: Ho! ho! ho! ho! ho! ho! ho! ho!
                     Joke beginning,
                         Never ceases,
                     Till your inning
                         Time releases,
                     On your way
                     You blindly stray,
                     And day by day
                         The joke increases!

KING: Ten years later – Time progresses –
         Sours your temper – thins your tresses;
         Fancy, then, her chain relaxes;
         Rates are facts and so are taxes.

Fairy Queen's no longer young –
Fairy Queen has got a tongue.
Twins have probably intruded –
Quite unbidden – just as you did –
They're a source of care and trouble –
Just as you were – only double.
Comes at last the final stroke –
Time has had his little joke!

ALL: Ho! ho! ho! ho! ho! ho! ho! ho!
Daily driven
(Wife as drover)
Ill you've thriven –
Ne'er in clover;
Lastly, when
Three-score and ten
(And not till then),
The joke is over!
Ho! ho! ho! ho! ho! ho! ho! ho!
Then – and then
The joke is over!

[*Exeunt* SCAPHIO *and* PHANTIS. *Manet* KING.]

KING [*putting on his crown again*]: It's all very well. I always like to look on the humorous side of things; but I do *not* think I ought to be required to write libels on my own moral character. Naturally, I see the joke of it – anybody would – but Zara's coming home to-day; she's no longer a child, and I confess I should *not* like her to see my Opera – though it's uncommonly well written; and I should be sorry if the *Palace Peeper* got into her hands – though it's certainly smart – very smart indeed. It is almost a pity that I have to buy up the whole edition, because it's really too good to be lost. And Lady Sophy – that blameless type of perfect womanhood! Great Heavens, what would *she* say if the Second Housemaid business happened to meet *her* pure blue eye!

[*Enter* LADY SOPHY.]

LADY S.: My monarch is soliloquizing. I will withdraw [*going*].

KING: No – pray don't go. Now I'll give you fifty chances, and you won't guess whom I was thinking of.

LADY S.: Alas, sir, I know too well. Ah! King, it's an old, old story, and I'm wellnigh weary of it! Be warned in time – from my heart I pity you, but I am not for you! [*going*].

KING: But hear what I have to say.

LADY S.: It is useless. Listen. In the course of a long and adventurous career in the principal European Courts, it has been revealed to me that I unconsciously exercise a weird and supernatural fascination over all Crowned Heads. So irresistible is this singular property, that there is not a European Monarch who has not implored me, with tears in his eyes, to quit his kingdom, and take my fatal charms elsewhere. As time was getting on it occurred to me that by descending several pegs in the scale of Respectability I might qualify your Majesty for my hand. Actuated by this humane motive and happening to possess Respectability enough for Six, I consented to confer Respectability enough for Four upon your two younger daughters – but although I have, alas, only Respectability enough for Two left, there is still, as I gather from the public press of this country [*producing the 'Palace Peeper'*], a considerable balance in my favour.

KING [*aside*]: Da –! [*Aloud*] May I ask how you came by this?

LADY S.: It was handed to me by the officer who holds the position of Public Exploder to your Imperial Majesty.

KING: And surely, Lady Sophy, surely you are not so unjust as to place any faith in the irresponsible gabble of the Society press!

LADY S. [*referring to paper*]: I read on the authority of Senex Senior that your Majesty was seen dancing with your Second House-maid on the Oriental Platform of the Tivoli Gardens.[14] That is untrue?

KING: Absolutely. Our Second Housemaid has only one leg.

LADY S. [*suspiciously*]: How do you know that?

KING: Common report, I give you my honour.

LADY S.: It may be so. I further read – and the statement is vouched for by no less an authority than Mephistopheles Minor – that your

Majesty indulges in a bath of hot rum-punch every morning. I trust I do not lay myself open to the charge of displaying an indelicate curiosity as to the mysteries of the royal dressing-room when I ask if there is any foundation for this statement?

KING: None whatever. When our medical adviser exhibits rum-punch it is as a draught, not as a fomentation. As to our bath, our valet plays the garden hose upon us every morning.

LADY S. [*shocked*]: Oh, pray – pray spare me these unseemly details. Well, you are a Despot – have you taken steps to slay this scribbler?

KING: Well, no – I have *not* gone so far as that. After all, it's the poor devil's living, you know.

LADY S.: It is the poor devil's living that surprises me. If this man lies, there is no recognized punishment that is sufficiently terrible for him.

KING: That's precisely it. I – I am waiting until a punishment is discovered that will exactly meet the enormity of the case. I am in constant communication with the Mikado of Japan,[15] who is a leading authority on such points; and, moreover, I have the ground plans and sectional elevations of several capital punishments in my desk at this moment. Oh, Lady Sophy, as you are powerful, be merciful!

DUET – KING *and* LADY SOPHY

KING:

Subjected to your heavenly gaze
(Poetical phrase),
My brain is turned completely.
Observe me now,
No Monarch, I vow,
Was ever so far afflicted!

LADY S.:

I'm pleased with that poetical phrase,
'A heavenly gaze',
But though you put it neatly,
Say what you will,
These paragraphs still
Remain uncontradicted.

Come, crush me this contemptible worm
(A forcible term),
If he's assailed you wrongly.
The rage display,
Which, as you say,
Has moved your Majesty lately.

KING: Though I admit that forcible term,
'Contemptible worm',
Appeals to me most strongly,
To treat this pest
As you suggest
Would pain my Majesty greatly.

LADY S.: This writer lies!
KING: Yes, bother his eyes!
LADY S.: He lives, you say?
KING: In a sort of a way.
LADY S.: Then have him shot.
KING: Decidedly not.
LADY S.: Or crush him flat.
KING: I cannot do that.
BOTH: O royal Rex,

My ⎫
Her ⎭ blameless sex

  Abhors such conduct shady.

You ⎫
I ⎭ plead in vain,

You ⎫
I ⎭ never will gain

  Respectable English lady!

[*Dance of repudiation by* LADY SOPHY. *Exit,
followed by* KING.]

[*March. Enter all the Court, heralding the arrival of the* PRIN-
CESS ZARA, *who enters, escorted by* CAPTAIN FITZBATTLEAXE
*and four Troopers, all in the full uniform of the First Life
Guards.*]

CHORUS: Oh, maiden, rich
    In Girton lore,
That wisdom which
    We prized before,
We do confess
Is nothingness,
And rather less,
    Perhaps, than more.
On each of us
    Thy learning shed.
On calculus[16]
    May we be fed.
And teach us, please,
To speak with ease
All languages,
    Alive and dead!

SOLO – PRINCESS *and* CHORUS

ZARA: Five years have flown since I took wing –
    Time flies, and his footstep ne'er retards –
I'm the eldest daughter of your king.
TROOPERS: And we are her escort – First Life Guards![17]
On the royal yacht,
    When the waves were white,
In a helmet hot
    And a tunic tight,
And our great big boots,
    We defied the storm:
For we're not recruits,
    And his uniform
A well-drilled trooper ne'er discards –
And we are her escort – First Life Guards!

ZARA: These gentlemen I present to you,
    The pride and boast of their barrack-yards;
They've taken, O! such care of me!

TROOPERS: For we are her escort – First Life Guards!
When the tempest rose,
    And the ship went *so* –
Do you suppose
    We were ill? No, no!
Though a qualmish lot
    In a tunic tight,
And a helmet hot,
    And a breastplate bright
(Which a well-drilled trooper ne'er discards),
We stood as her escort – First Life Guards!

FULL CHORUS:
Knightsbridge[18] nursemaids – serving fairies –
Stars of proud Belgravian[19] airies;
At stern duty's call you leave them,
Though you know how that must grieve them!

ZARA., CAPT. FITZ., *and* CHORUS:
Tantantarara-rara-rara!
Trumpet-call of Princess Zara!
That's trump-call, and they're all trump cards –
They are her escort – First Life Guards!

ENSEMBLE

LADIES	ZARA *and* FITZBATTLEAXE [*aside*]
Knightsbridge nursemaids, etc.	Oh! the hours are gold,
	And the joys untold,
	When my eyes behold
MEN	My beloved Princess;
When the tempest rose, etc.	And the years will seem
	But a brief day-dream,
	In the joy extreme
	Of our happiness!

FULL CHORUS:

Knightsbridge nursemaids, serving fairies, etc.

[*Enter* KING, PRINCESSES NEKAYA *and* KALYBA *and* LADY SOPHY. *As the* KING *enters the escort present arms.*]

KING: Zara! my beloved daughter! Why, how well you look and how lovely you have grown! [*embraces her*].

ZARA: My dear father! [*embracing him.*] And my two beautiful little sisters! [*embracing them*].

NEK.: Not beautiful.

KAL.: Nice-looking.

ZARA: But first let me present to you the English warrior who commands my escort, and who has taken, O! such care of me during the voyage – Captain Fitzbattleaxe!

TROOPERS:

The First Life Guards.
When the tempest rose,
And the ship went *so* –

[CAPTAIN FITZBATTLEAXE *motions them to be silent. The Troopers place themselves in the four corners of the stage, standing at ease, immovably, as if on sentry. Each is surrounded by an admiring group of young ladies, of whom they take no notice.*]

KING [*to* CAPT. FITZ.]: Sir, you come from a country where every virtue flourishes. We trust that you will not criticize too severely such shortcomings as you may detect in our semi-barbarous society.

FITZ. [*looking at* ZARA]: Sir, I have eyes for nothing but the blameless and the beautiful.

KING: We thank you – he is really very polite! [LADY SOPHY, *who has been greatly scandalized by the attentions paid to the Lifeguardsmen by the young ladies, marches the* PRINCESSES NEKAYA *and* KALYBA *towards an exit.*] Lady Sophy, do not leave us.

LADY S.: Sir, your children are young, and, so far, innocent. If they are to remain so, it is necessary that they be at once removed from the contamination of their present disgraceful surroundings. [*She marches them off.*]

KING [*whose attention has thus been called to the proceedings of the young ladies – aside*]: Dear, dear! They really shouldn't. [*Aloud*] Captain Fitzbattleaxe –

FITZ.: Sir.

KING: Your Troopers appear to be receiving a troublesome amount of attention from those young ladies. I know how strict you English soldiers are, and I should be extremely distressed if anything occurred to shock their puritanical British sensitiveness.

FITZ.: Oh, I don't think there's any chance of that.

KING: You think not? They won't be offended?

FITZ.: Oh no! They are quite hardened to it. They get a good deal of that sort of thing, standing sentry at the Horse Guards.[20]

KING: It's English, is it?

FITZ.: It's particularly English.

KING: Then, of course, it's all right. Pray proceed, ladies, it's particularly English. Come, my daughter, for we have much to say to each other.

ZARA: Farewell, Captain Fitzbattleaxe! I cannot thank you too emphatically for the devoted care with which you have watched over me during our long and eventful voyage.

DUET – ZARA *and* CAPTAIN FITZBATTLEAXE

ZARA:
    Ah! gallant soldier, brave and true
        In tented field and tourney,
    I grieve to have occasioned you
        So very long a journey.
    A British warrior gives up all –
        His home and island beauty –
    When summoned by the trumpet-call
        Of Regimental Duty!

ALL:
    Tantantarara-rara-rara!
    Trumpet-call of Princess Zara!

ENSEMBLE

MEN	FITZBATTLEAXE *and* ZARA [*aside*]
A British warrior gives up all, etc.	Oh, my joy, my pride,
	My delight to hide,
LADIES	Let us sing, aside,
Knightsbridge nursemaids, etc.	What in truth we feel.
	Let us whisper low
	Of our love's glad glow,
	Lest the truth we show
	We would fain conceal.

FITZ.:

Such escort duty, as his due,
　　To young Lifeguardsman falling
Completely reconciles him to
　　His uneventful calling.
When soldier seeks Utopian glades
　　In charge of Youth and Beauty,
Then pleasure merely masquerades
　　As Regimental Duty!

ALL:

Tantantarara-rara-rara!
Trumpet-call of Princess Zara!

ENSEMBLE

MEN	FITZBATTLEAXE *and* ZARA [*aside*]
A British warrior, etc.	Oh! the hours are gold,
	And the joys untold,
	When my eyes behold
WOMEN	My beloved Princess;
Knightsbridge nursemaids, etc.	And the years will seem
	But a brief day-dream,
	In the joy extreme
	Of our happiness!

[*Exeunt* KING *and* PRINCESS *in one direction, Lifeguardsmen and crowd in opposite direction. Enter, at back,* SCAPHIO *and* PHANTIS, *who watch the* PRINCESS *as she goes off.* SCAPHIO *is seated, shaking violently, and obviously under the influence of some strong emotion.*]

PHAN.: There – tell me, Scaphio, is she not beautiful? Can you wonder that I love her so passionately?

SCA.: No. She is extraordinarily – miraculously lovely! Good heavens, what a singularly beautiful girl!

PHAN.: I knew you would say so!

SCA.: What exquisite charm of manner! What surprising delicacy of gesture! Why, she's a goddess! a very goddess!

PHAN. [*rather taken aback*]: Yes – she's – she's an attractive girl.

SCA.: Attractive? Why, you must be blind! – She's entrancing – enthralling! – intoxicating! [*Aside*] God bless my heart, what's the matter with me?

PHAN. [*alarmed*]: Yes. You – you promised to help me to get her father's consent, you know.

SCA.: Promised! Yes, but the convulsion has come, my good boy! It is she – my ideal! Why, what's this? [*staggering*]. Phantis! Stop me – I'm going mad – mad with the love of her!

PHAN.: Scaphio, compose yourself, I beg. The girl is perfectly opaque! Besides, remember – each of us is helpless without the other. You can't succeed without my consent, you know.

SCA.: And you dare to threaten? Oh, ungrateful! When you came to me, palsied with love for this girl, and implored my assistance, did I not unhesitatingly promise it? And this is the return you make? Out of my sight, ingrate! [*Aside*] Dear! dear! what is the matter with me?

[*Enter* CAPTAIN FITZBATTLEAXE *and* ZARA.]

ZARA: Dear me. I'm afraid we are interrupting a *tête-à-tête*.

SCA. [*breathlessly*]: No, no. You come very appropriately. To be brief, we – we love you – this man and I – madly – passionately!

ZARA: Sir!

SCA.: And we don't know how we are to settle which of us is to marry you.

FITZ.: Zara, this is very awkward.

SCA. [*very much overcome*]: I – I am paralysed by the singular radiance of your extraordinary loveliness. I know I am incoherent. I never was like this before – it shall not occur again. I – shall be fluent, presently.

ZARA [*aside*]: Oh, dear, Captain Fitzbattleaxe, what *is* to be done?

FITZ. [*aside*]: Leave it to me – I'll manage it. [*Aloud*] It's a common situation. Why not settle it in the English fashion?

BOTH: The English fashion? What is that?

FITZ.: It's very simple. In England, when two gentlemen are in love with the same lady, and until it is settled which gentleman is to blow out the brains of the other, it is provided, by the Rival Admirers' Clauses Consolidation Act, that the lady shall be entrusted to an officer of Household Cavalry as stakeholder, who is bound to hand her over to the survivor (on the Tontine principle[21]) in a good condition of substantial and decorative repair.

SCA.: Reasonable wear and tear and damages by fire excepted?

FITZ.: Exactly.

PHAN.: Well, that seems very reasonable. [*To* SCAPHIO] What do you say – Shall we entrust her to this officer of Household Cavalry? It will give us time.

SCA. [*trembling violently*]: I – I am not at present in a condition to think it out coolly – but if he *is* an officer of Household Cavalry, and if the Princess consents –

ZARA: Alas, dear sirs, I have no alternative – under the Rival Admirers' Clauses Consolidation Act!

FITZ.: Good – then that's settled.

QUARTET – FITZBATTLEAXE, ZARA, SCAPHIO, PHANTIS

FITZ.:   It's understood, I think, all round
               That, by the English custom bound
               I hold the lady safe and sound
                    In trust for either rival,
               Until you clearly testify
               By sword or pistol, by and by,
               Which gentleman prefers to die,
                    And which prefers survival.

ENSEMBLE

SCAPHIO *and* PHANTIS
It's clearly understood, all round,
That, by your English custom bound,
He holds the lady safe and sound
    In trust for either rival,
Until we clearly testify
By sword or pistol, by and by,
Which gentleman prefers to die,
    And which prefers survival.

ZARA *and* FITZBATTLEAXE [*aside*]
We stand, I think, on safish ground,
Our senses weak it will astound
If either gentleman is found
    Prepared to meet his rival.
Their machinations we defy;
We won't be parted, you and I –
Of bloodshed each is rather shy –
    They both prefer survival.

PHAN. [*aside to* FITZ.]:
    If I should die and he should live,
    To you, without reserve, I give
    Her heart so young and sensitive,
        And all her predilections.

SCA. [*aside to* FITZ.]:
    If he should live and I should die,
    I see no kind of reason why
    You should not, if you wish it, try
        To gain her young affections.

ENSEMBLE

SCAPHIO *and* PHANTIS [*angrily to
each other*]
If I should die and you should live,
To this young officer I give
Her heart so soft and sensitive,
    And all her predilections.
If you should live and I should die,
I see no kind of reason why
He should not, if he chooses, try
    To win her young affections.

FITZBATTLEAXE *and* ZARA [*aside*]
As both of us are positive
That both of them intend to live,
There's nothing in the case to give
    Us cause for grave reflections.
As both will live and neither die
I see no kind of reason why
I should not, if I wish it, try
    To gain your young affections!

[*Exeunt* SCAPHIO *and* PHANTIS *together.*]

DUET – ZARA *and* FITZBATTLEAXE

BOTH:

Oh, admirable art!
   Oh, neatly-planned intention!
   Oh, happy intervention –
      Oh, well-constructed plot!
When sages try to part
   Two loving hearts in fusion,
   Their wisdom's a delusion,
      And learning serves them not!

FITZ.:

Until quite plain
   Is their intent,
These sages twain
   I represent.
Now please infer
   That, nothing loth,
You're henceforth, as it were,
   Engaged to marry both –
Then take it that I represent the two –
On that hypothesis, what would you do?

ZARA [*aside*]:
[*To* FITZ]

What would I do? what would I do?
In such a case,
   Upon your breast,
My blushing face
   I think I'd rest – [*doing so*].
Then perhaps I might
   Demurely say –
'I find this breastplate bright
   Is sorely in the way!'

FITZ.:

Our mortal race
   Is never blest –
There's no such case
   As perfect rest;

Some petty blight
  Asserts its sway –
Some crumpled roseleaf light
Is always in the way!

[*Exit* FITZBATTLEAXE. *Manet* ZARA.]

ZARA [*looking off, in the direction in which* SCAPHIO *and* PHANTIS *have gone*]: Poor, trusting, simple-minded and affectionate old gentlemen! I'm really sorry for them! How strange it is that when the flower of a man's youth has faded, he seems to lose all charm in a woman's eyes; and how true are the words of my expurgated Juvenal:

'*– Festinat decurrere velox*
Flosculus, angustae, miseraeque brevissima vitae
Portio!'[22]

Ah, if we could only make up our minds to invest our stock of youth on commercial principles instead of squandering it at the outset, old age would be as extinct as the Dodo!

SONG

ZARA:

Youth is a boon avowed –
  A gift of priceless worth
To rich and poor allowed –
  With which all men at birth –
    The lowly and the proud –
    Are equally endowed.
But sorrow comes anon,
  For Man's a prodigal
Who madly lives upon
  His little capital.
    And this, alas, goes on
    Till every penny's gone:
He finds himself, at Life's concluding stage,
With no Youth left to comfort his old age!

Ah, dame improvident,
   If you, in very sooth
In infancy had lent
    Your Capital of Youth
      At four or five per cent –
      (As Nature doubtless meant),
Resolved, within your breast,
   To do as others do
Who Capital invest,
   And live a lifetime through,
     With modest comfort blest,
     Upon the interest –
You might be still in girlhood's mid-career
A merry madcap maid of fourscore year!

[*Enter* KING.]

KING: My daughter! At last we are alone together.

ZARA: Yes, and I'm glad we are, for I want to speak to you very seriously. Do you know this paper?

KING [*aside*]: Da –! [*Aloud*] Oh yes – I've – I've seen it. Where in the world did you get this from?

ZARA: It was given to me by Lady Sophy – my sisters' governess.

KING [*aside*]: Lady Sophy's an angel, but I do sometimes wish she'd mind her own business! [*Aloud*] It's – ha! ha! – it's rather humorous.

ZARA: I see nothing humorous in it. I only see that you, the despotic King of this country, are made the subject of the most scandalous insinuations. Why do you permit these things?

KING: Well, they appeal to my sense of humour. It's the only really comic paper in Utopia, and I wouldn't be without it for the world.

ZARA: If it had any literary merit I could understand it.

KING: Oh, it *has* literary merit. Oh, distinctly, it has literary merit.

ZARA: My dear father, it's mere ungrammatical twaddle.

KING: Oh, it's not ungrammatical. I can't allow that. Unpleasantly personal, perhaps, but written with an epigrammatical point that is very rare nowadays – very rare indeed.

ZARA [*looking at cartoon*]: Why do they represent you with such a big nose?

KING [*looking at cartoon*]: Eh? Yes, it *is* a big one! Why, the fact is that, in the cartoons of a comic paper, the size of your nose always varies inversely as the square of your popularity. It's the rule.

ZARA: Then you must be at a tremendous discount just now! I see a notice of a new piece called 'King Tuppence', in which an English tenor has the audacity to personate you on a public stage. I can only say that I am surprised that any English tenor should lend himself to such degrading personalities.

KING: Oh, he's not really English. As it happens he's a Utopian, but he calls himself English.

ZARA: Calls himself English?

KING: Yes. Bless you, they wouldn't listen to any tenor who didn't call himself English.

ZARA: And you permit this insolent buffoon to caricature you in a pointless burlesque! My dear father – if you were a free agent, you would never permit these outrages.

KING [*almost in tears*]: Zara – I – I admit I am not altogether a free agent. I – I am controlled. I try to make the best of it, but sometimes I find it very difficult – very difficult indeed. Nominally a Despot, I am, between ourselves, the helpless tool of two unscrupulous Wise Men, who insist on my falling in with all their wishes and threaten to denounce me for immediate explosion if I remonstrate! [*Breaks down completely.*]

ZARA: My poor father! Now listen to me. With a view to remodelling the political and social institutions of Utopia, I have brought with me six Representatives of the principal causes that have tended to make England the powerful, happy and blameless country which the consensus of European civilization has declared it to be. Place yourself unreservedly in the hands of these gentlemen, and they will reorganize your country on a footing that will enable you to defy your persecutors. They are all now washing their hands after their journey. Shall I introduce them?

KING: My dear Zara, how can I thank you? I will consent to anything that will release me from the abominable tyranny of these two men. [*Calling*] What ho! Without there!

[*Enter* CALYNX.]

Summon my Court without an instant's delay!

[*Exit* CALYNX.]

FINALE

[*Enter every one, except the Flowers of Progress.*]

CHORUS: Although your Royal summons to appear
        From courtesy was singularly free,
        Obedient to that summons we are here –
            What would your Majesty?

RECITATIVE

KING: My worthy people, my beloved daughter
      Most thoughtfully has brought with her from England
      The types of all the causes that have made
      That great and glorious country what it is.

CHORUS: Oh, joy unbounded!
SCA., TAR., *and* PHAN. [*aside*]:
      Why, what *does* this mean?

RECITATIVE

ZARA: Attend to me, Utopian populace,
      Ye South Pacific Island viviparians;[23]
      All, in the abstract, types of courtly grace,
      Yet, when compared with Britain's glorious race,
      But little better than half-clothed barbarians!

CHORUS

      Yes! Contrasted when
      With Englishmen,
Are little better than half-clothed barbarians!
[*Enter all the Flowers of Progress, led by* CAPTAIN FITZ-BATTLEAXE.]

SOLO

ZARA [*presenting* FITZBATTLEAXE]:

> When Britain sounds the trump of war
> > (And Europe trembles),
> The army of that conqueror
> > In serried ranks assembles;
> 'Tis then this warrior's eyes and sabre gleam
> > For our protection –
> He represents a military scheme
> > In all its proud perfection!

CHORUS:

> > Yes – yes –
> He represents a military scheme
> > In all its proud perfection!
> > Ulahlica! Ulahlica! Ulahlica!

SOLO

ZARA [*presenting* SIR BAILEY BARRE]:

> A complicated gentleman allow me to present,
> Of all the arts and faculties the terse embodiment,
> He's a great Arithmetician who can demonstrate with ease
> That two and two are three, or five, or anything you please;
> An eminent Logician who can make it clear to you
> That black is white – when looked at from the proper point
> > of view;
> A marvellous Philologist who'll undertake to show
> That 'yes' is but another and a neater form of 'no'.

SIR B. BAR.:

> > Yes – yes – yes –
> 'Yes' is but another and a neater form of 'no'.
> All preconceived ideas on any subject I can scout,
> And demonstrate beyond all possibility of doubt,
> That whether you're an honest man or whether you're a thief
> Depends on whose solicitor has given me my brief.

CHORUS: Yes – yes – yes –
                  That whether you're an honest man, etc.
                     Ulahlica! Ulahlica! Ulahlica!

SOLO

ZARA [*presenting* LORD DRAMALEIGH *and County Councillor*]:
                  What these may be, Utopians all,
                     Perhaps you'll hardly guess –
                  They're types of England's physical
                     And moral cleanliness.
                  This is a Lord High Chamberlain,[24]
                     Of purity the gauge –
                  He'll cleanse our Court from moral stain
                     And purify our Stage.

LORD D.:   Yes – yes – yes –
                  Court reputations I revise,
                  And presentations scrutinize,
                  New plays I read with jealous eyes,
                     And purify the Stage.

CHORUS: Court reputations, etc.

ZARA: This County Councillor acclaim,
                     Great Britain's latest toy –
                  On anything you like to name
                     His talents he'll employ –
                  All streets and squares he'll purify
                     Within your city walls,
                  And keep meanwhile a modest eye
                     On wicked music halls.

C. C.:   Yes – yes – yes –
                  In towns I make improvements great,
                  Which go to swell the County Rate –
                  I dwelling-houses sanitate,
                     And purify the Halls!

CHORUS: In towns he makes improvements great, etc.
            Ulahlica! Ulahlica! Ulahlica!

SOLO

ZARA [*presenting* MR GOLDBURY]:
     A Company Promoter this, with special education,
     Which teaches what Contango[25] means and also
        Backwardation[26] –
     To speculators he supplies a grand financial leaven,
     Time was when *two* were company – but now it must be
        seven.

MR GOLD.:   Yes – yes – yes –
     Stupendous loans to foreign thrones
        I've largely advocated;
     In ginger-pops and peppermint-drops
        I've freely speculated;
     Then mines of gold, of wealth untold,
        Successfully I've floated,
     And sudden falls in apple-stalls
        Occasionally quoted:
     And soon or late I always call
        For Stock Exchange quotation –
     No schemes too great and none too small
        For Companification!

CHORUS: Yes! Yes! Yes! No schemes too great, etc.
        Ulahlica! Ulahlica! Ulahlica!

ZARA [*presenting* CAPTAIN CORCORAN]:
     And lastly I present
        Great Britain's proudest boast,
     Who from the blows
     Of foreign foes
        Protects her sea-girt coast –
     And if you ask him in respectful tone,
     He'll show you how you may protect your own!

SOLO

CAPT. COR.: I'm Captain Corcoran, KCB,[27]
I'll teach you how we rule the sea,
    And terrify the simple Gauls;
And how the Saxon and the Celt
Their Europe-shaking blows have dealt
With Maxim gun[28] and Nordenfelt[29]
    (Or will, when the occasion calls).
If sailor-like you'd play your cards,
Unbend your sails and lower your yards,
    Unstep your masts – you'll never want 'em more.
Though we're no longer hearts of oak,
Yet we can steer and we can stoke,
And, thanks to coal, and thanks to coke,
    We never run a ship ashore!

ALL: What never?

CAPT. COR.:   No, never!

ALL: What *never*?

CAPT. COR.:   Hardly ever![30]

ALL: Hardly ever run a ship ashore!
    Then give three cheers, and three cheers more,
    For the tar who never runs his ship ashore;
    Then give three cheers, and three cheers more,
        For he never runs his ship ashore!

CHORUS

All hail, ye types of England's power –
    Ye heaven-enlightened band!
We bless the day, and bless the hour
    That brought you to our land.

QUARTET – LORD DRAMALEIGH, CAPTAINS FITZBATTLEAXE
and CORCORAN, SIR BAILEY BARRE

ALL: Ye wanderers from a mighty State,
        Oh, teach us how to legislate –
        Your lightest word will carry weight
                In our attentive ears.
        Oh, teach the natives of this land
        (Who are not quick to understand)
        How to work off their social and
                Political arrears!

CAPT. FITZ.: Increase your army!
LORD D.:   Purify your Court!
CAPT. COR.: Get up your steam and cut your canvas short!
SIR B. BAR.: To speak on both sides teach your sluggish brains!
CAPT. COR.: Widen your thoroughfares, and flush your drains!
MR GOLD.:   Utopia's much too big for one small head –
            I'll float it as a Company Limited!

KING: A Company Limited? What may that be?
        The term, I rather think, is new to me.

CHORUS: A Company Limited? etc.

SCA., PHAN. *and* TAR. [*aside*]:
        What does he mean? What does he mean?
                Give us a kind of clue!
        What does he mean? What does he mean?
                What is he going to do?

SONG

MR GOLD.:   Some seven men form an Association
                (If possible, all Peers and Baronets),
            They start off with a public declaration
                To what extent they mean to pay their debts.

That's called their Capital: if they are wary
    They will not quote it at a sum immense.
The figure's immaterial – it may vary
    From eighteen million down to eighteenpence.
        I should put it rather low;
        The good sense of doing so
    Will be evident at once to any debtor.
        When it's left to you to say
        What amount you mean to pay,
    Why, the lower you can put it at, the better.

CHORUS: When it's left to you to say, etc.

MR GOLD.: They then proceed to trade with all who'll trust 'em,
    Quite irrespective of their capital
(It's shady, but it's sanctified by custom);
    Bank, Railway, Loan or Panama Canal.[31]
You can't embark on trading too tremendous –
    It's strictly fair, and based on common sense –
If you succeed, your profits are stupendous –
    And if you fail, pop goes your eighteenpence.
        Make the money-spinner spin!
        For you only stand to win,
    And you'll never with dishonesty be twitted,
        For nobody can know,
        To a million or so,
    To what extent your capital's committed!

CHORUS: No, nobody can know, etc.

MR GOLD.: If you come to grief, and creditors are craving
    (For nothing that is planned by mortal head
Is certain in this Vale of Sorrow – saving
    That one's Liability is Limited), –
Do you suppose that signifies perdition?
    If so you're but a monetary dunce –

You merely file a Winding-Up Petition,[32]
 And start another Company at once!
  Though a Rothschild[33] you may be
  In your own capacity,
 As a Company you've come to utter sorrow –
  But the Liquidators say,
   'Never mind – you needn't pay,'
 So you start another Company to-morrow!

CHORUS: But the Liquidators say, etc.

RECITATIVE

KING: Well, at first sight it strikes us as dishonest,
     But if it's good enough for virtuous England –
     The first commercial country in the world –
     It's good enough for us.

SCA., PHAN. *and* TAR. [*aside to* KING]:
        You'd best take care –
     Please recollect *we* have not been consulted.

KING [*not heeding them*]:
     And do I understand you that Great Britain
     Upon this Joint Stock principle is governed?

MR GOLD.: We haven't come to that, exactly – but
     We're tending rapidly in that direction.
     The date's not distant.

KING [*enthusiastically*]:
     We will be before you!
     We'll go down to Posterity renowned
     As the First Sovereign in Christendom
     Who registered his Crown and Country under
     The Joint Stock Company's Act of Sixty-Two.[34]

ALL: Ulahlica!

SOLO

KING: Henceforward, of a verity,
  With Fame ourselves we link –
We'll go down to Posterity
  Of sovereigns all the pink!

SCA., PHAN. *and* TAR. [*aside to* KING]:
  If you've the mad temerity
   Our wishes thus to blink,
  You'll go down to Posterity
   Much earlier than you think!

TAR. [*correcting them*]:
  He'll go *up* to Posterity,
   If *I* inflict the blow!

SCA. *and* PHAN. [*angrily*]:
  He'll go *down* to Posterity –
   We think we ought to know!

TAR. [*explaining*]:
  He'll go *up* to Posterity,
   Blown up with dynamite!

SCA. *and* PHAN. [*apologetically*]:
  He'll go *up* to Posterity,
   Of course he will, you're right!

ENSEMBLE

KING, LADY SOPHY, NEK., KAL., CALYNX *and* CHORUS	SCAPHIO, PHANTIS *and* TARARA [*aside*]	FITZBATTLEAXE *and* ZARA [*aside*]
Henceforward, of a verity, With fame ourselves we link –	If he has the temerity Our wishes thus to blink,	Who love with all sincerity, Their lives may safely link;

| And go down to Posterity, | He'll go up to Posterity | And as for our Posterity – |
| Of sovereigns all the pink! | Much earlier than they think! | We don't care what they think! |

CHORUS: Let's seal this mercantile pact –
                     The step we ne'er shall rue –
              It gives whatever we lacked –
                     The statement's strictly true,
              All hail, astonishing Fact!
                     All hail, Invention new –
              The Joint Stock Company's Act –
                     The Act of Sixty-Two!

END OF ACT I

ACT II

SCENE – *Throne Room in the Palace. Night.*

[CAPTAIN FITZBATTLEAXE *discovered, singing to* ZARA.]

RECITATIVE

FITZ.:   Oh, Zara, my beloved one, bear with me!
Ah, do not laugh at my attempted C!
Repent not, mocking maid, thy girlhood's choice –
The fervour of my love affects my voice!

SONG

FITZ.:   A tenor, all singers above
(This doesn't admit of a question),
Should keep himself quiet,
Attend to his diet
And carefully nurse his digestion;
But when he is madly in love
It's certain to tell on his singing –
You can't do chromatics
With proper emphatics
When anguish your bosom is wringing!
When distracted with worries in plenty,
And his pulse is a hundred and twenty,
And his fluttering bosom the slave of mistrust is,
A tenor can't do himself justice.

Now observe – [*sings a high note*],
You see, I can't do myself justice!

I could sing if my fervour were mock,
It's easy enough if you're acting –
But when one's emotion
Is born of devotion
You mustn't be over-exacting.
One ought to be firm as a rock
To venture a shake in *vibrato*,[35]
When fervour's expected
Keep cool and collected
Or never attempt *agitato*.[36]
But, of course, when his tongue is of leather,
And his lips appear pasted together,
And his sensitive palate as dry as a crust is,
A tenor can't do himself justice.
Now observe – [*sings a cadence*],
It's no use – I can't do myself justice!

ZARA: Why, Arthur, what *does* it matter? When the higher qualities of the heart are all that can be desired, the higher notes of the voice are matters of comparative insignificance. Who thinks slightingly of the cocoanut because it is husky? Besides [*demurely*], you are not singing for an engagement [*putting her hand in his*], you have that already!

FITZ.: How good and wise you are! How unerringly your practised brain winnows the wheat from the chaff – the material from the merely incidental!

ZARA: My Girton training, Arthur. At Girton all is wheat, and idle chaff is never heard within its walls! But tell me, is not all working marvellously well? Have not our Flowers of Progress more than justified their name?

FITZ.: We have indeed done our best. Captain Corcoran and I have, in concert, thoroughly remodelled the sister-services – and upon so sound a basis that the South Pacific trembles at the name of Utopia!

ZARA: How clever of you!

FITZ.: Clever? Not a bit. It's as easy as possible when the Admiralty and Horse Guards are not there to interfere. And so with the others. Freed from the trammels imposed upon them by idle Acts of Parliament, all have given their natural talents full play and introduced reforms which, even in England, were never dreamt of!

ZARA: But perhaps the most beneficent change of all has been effected by Mr Goldbury, who, discarding the exploded theory that some strange magic lies hidden in the number Seven, has applied the Limited Liability principle to individuals, and every man, woman and child is now a Company Limited with liability restricted to the amount of his declared Capital! There is not a christened baby in. Utopia who has not already issued his little Prospectus!

FITZ.: Marvellous is the power of a Civilization which can transmute, by a word, a Limited Income into an Income Limited.

ZARA: Reform has not stopped here – it has been applied even to the costume of our people. Discarding their own barbaric dress, the natives of our land have unanimously adopted the tasteful fashions of England in all their rich entirety. Scaphio and Phantis have undertaken a contract to supply the whole of Utopia with clothing designed upon the most approved English models – and the first Drawing-Room under the new state of things is to be held here this evening.

FITZ.: But Drawing-Rooms are always held in the afternoon.

ZARA: Ah, we've improved upon that. We all look so much better by candle-light! And when I tell you, dearest, that my Court train has just arrived, you will understand that I am longing to go and try it on.

FITZ.: Then we must part?

ZARA: Necessarily, for a time.

FITZ.: Just as I wanted to tell you, with all the passionate enthusiasm of my nature, how deeply, how devotedly I love you!

ZARA: Hush! Are these the accents of a heart that really feels? True love does not indulge in declamation – its voice is sweet, and soft, and low. The west wind whispers when he woos the poplars!

DUET – ZARA *and* FITZBATTLEAXE

ZARA: Words of love too loudly spoken
      Ring their own untimely knell;
Noisy vows are rudely broken,
      Soft the song of Philomel.[37]
Whisper sweetly, whisper slowly,
      Hour by hour and day by day;
Sweet and low[38] as accents holy
      Are the notes of lover's lay!

BOTH: Sweet and low, etc.

FITZ.:   Let the conqueror, flushed with glory,
      Bid his noisy clarions bray;
Lovers tell their artless story
      In a whispered virelay.[39]
False is he whose vows alluring
      Make the listening echoes ring;
Sweet and low when all-enduring
      Are the songs that lovers sing!

BOTH: Sweet and low, etc.

[Exit ZARA.*]*

[Enter KING, *dressed as Field-Marshal.]*

KING: To a Monarch who has been accustomed to the uncontrolled use of his limbs, the costume of a British Field-Marshal is, perhaps, at first, a little cramping. Are you sure that this is all right? It's not a practical joke, is it? No one has a keener sense of humour than I have, but the First Statutory Cabinet Council of Utopia Limited must be conducted with dignity and impressiveness. Now, where are the other five who signed the Articles of Association?

FITZ.: Sir, they are here.

[Enter LORD DRAMALEIGH, CAPTAIN CORCORAN, SIR BAILEY BARRE, MR BLUSHINGTON *and* MR GOLDBURY *from different entrances.]*

KING: Oh! [*Addressing them*] Gentlemen, our daughter holds her first Drawing-Room in half an hour, and we shall have time to make our half-yearly report in the interval. I am necessarily unfamiliar with the forms of an English Cabinet Council – perhaps the Lord Chamberlain will kindly put us in the way of doing the thing properly, and with due regard to the solemnity of the occasion.

LORD D.: Certainly – nothing simpler. Kindly bring your chairs forward – His Majesty will, of course, preside.

[*They range their chairs across stage like Christy Minstrels.*[40] KING *sits centre,* LORD DRAMALEIGH *on his left,* MR GOLDBURY *on his right,* CAPT. CORCORAN *left of* LORD DRAMALEIGH, CAPTAIN FITZBATTLEAXE *right of* MR GOLDBURY, MR BLUSHINGTON *extreme right,* SIR BAILEY BARRE *extreme left.*]

KING: Like this?

LORD D.: Like this.

KING: We take your word for it that this is all right. You are not making fun of us? This is in accordance with the practice at the Court of St James's?[41]

LORD D.: Well, it is in accordance with the practice at the Court of St James's Hall.[42]

KING: Oh! it seems odd, but never mind.

SONG

KING:	Society has quite forsaken all her wicked courses,
	Which empties our police courts, and abolishes divorces.
CHORUS:	Divorce is nearly obsolete in England.
KING:	No tolerance we show to undeserving rank and splendour;
	For the higher his position is, the greater the offender.
CHORUS:	That's a maxim that is prevalent in England.

KING: No peeress at our Drawing-room before the Presence
      passes
Who wouldn't be accepted by the lower-middle classes.
Each shady dame, whatever be her rank, is bowed out
      neatly.

CHORUS: In short, this happy country has been Anglicized
      completely!
        It really is surprising
        What a thorough Anglicizing
We have brought about – Utopia's quite another land;
      In her enterprising movements,
      She is England – with improvements,
Which we dutifully offer to our mother-land!

KING: Our city we have beautified – we've done it willy-nilly –
And all that isn't Belgrave Square is Strand and
      Piccadilly.

CHORUS: We haven't any slummeries in England!

KING: We have solved the labour question with discrimination
      polished,
So poverty is obsolete and hunger is abolished –

CHORUS: We are going to abolish it in England.

KING: The Chamberlain our native stage has purged, beyond a
      question,
Of 'risky' situation and indelicate suggestion;
No piece is tolerated if it's costumed indiscreetly –

CHORUS: In short, this happy country has been Anglicized
      completely!
      It really is surprising, etc.

KING: Our Peerage we've remodelled on an intellectual basis,
Which certainly is rough on our hereditary races –

CHORUS: We are going to remodel it in England.

KING: The Brewers[43] and the Cotton Lords[44] no longer seek
             admission,
         And Literary Merit meets with proper recognition –
CHORUS: As Literary Merit does in England!

KING: Who knows but we may count among our intellectual
             chickens,
         Like you, an Earl of Thackeray and p'r'aps a Duke of
             Dickens –
         Lord Fildes[45] and Viscount Millais[46] (when they come)
             we'll welcome sweetly –
CHORUS: In short, this happy country has been Anglicized
             completely!
             It really is surprising, etc.
    [*At the end all rise and replace their chairs.*]

KING: Now, then, for our first Drawing-Room. Where are the
    Princesses? What an extraordinary thing it is that since European
    looking-glasses have been supplied to the Royal bedrooms my
    daughters are invariably late!
LORD D.: Sir, their Royal Highnesses await your pleasure in the
    Ante-room.
KING: Oh. Then request them to do us the favour to enter at once.
    [*March. Enter all the Royal Household, including (besides the
    Lord Chamberlain) the Vice-Chamberlain, the Master of the
    Horse, the Master of the Buckhounds,*[47] *the Lord High Treasurer,
    the Lord Steward,*[48] *the Comptroller of the Household,*[49] *the
    Lord-in-Waiting, the Groom-in-Waiting, the Field Officer in
    Brigade Waiting, the Gold and Silver Stick*[50] *and the Gentlemen
    Ushers. Then enter the three Princesses (their trains carried by
    Pages of Honour),* LADY SOPHY *and the Ladies-in-Waiting.*]

KING: My daughters, we are about to attempt a very solemn cer-
    emonial, so no giggling, if you please. Now, my Lord Chamberlain,
    we are ready.
LORD D.: Then, ladies and gentlemen, places, if you please. His
    Majesty will take his place in front of the throne, and will be so

obliging as to embrace all the *débutantes*. [LADY SOPHY *much shocked*.]

KING: What – must I really?

LORD D.: Absolutely indispensable.

KING: More jam for the *Palace Peeper*!

[*The* KING *takes his place in front of the throne, the* PRINCESS ZARA *on his left, the two younger Princesses on the left of* ZARA.]

KING: Now, is every one in his place?

LORD D.: Every one is in his place.

KING: Then let the revels commence.

[*Enter the ladies attending the Drawing-Room. They give their cards to the Groom-in-Waiting, who passes them to the Lord-in-Waiting, who passes them to the Vice-Chamberlain, who passes them to the Lord Chamberlain, who reads the names to the* KING *as each lady approaches. The ladies curtsey in succession to the* KING *and the three Princesses, and pass out. When all the presentations have been accomplished, the* KING, *Princesses and* LADY SOPHY *come forward, and all the ladies re-enter*.]

RECITATIVE

KING:
This ceremonial our wish displays
To copy all Great Britain's courtly ways.
Though lofty aims catastrophe entail,
We'll gloriously succeed or nobly fail!

UNACCOMPANIED CHORUS:
Eagle high in cloudland soaring –
    Sparrow twittering on a reed –
Tiger in the jungle roaring –
    Frightened fawn in grassy mead –
Let the eagle, not the sparrow,
Be the object of your arrow –
    Fox the tiger with your eye –
    Pass the fawn in pity by.
    Glory then will crown the day –
    Glory, glory, anyway!

[*Then exeunt all*.]

[*Enter* SCAPHIO *and* PHANTIS, *now dressed as judges in red and ermine robes and undress wigs. They come down-stage melo-dramatically – working together.*]

DUET – SCAPHIO *and* PHANTIS

SCA.: With fury deep we burn –
PHAN.:   We do –
SCA.: We fume with smothered rage –
PHAN.:   We do –
SCA.: These Englishmen who rule supreme,
Their undertaking they redeem
By stifling every harmless scheme
    In which we both engage –
PHAN.:   They do –
SCA.:   In which we both engage.
PHAN.: We think it is our turn –
SCA.:   We do –
PHAN.: We think our turn has come –
SCA.:   We do.
PHAN.: These Englishmen, they must prepare
To seek at once their native air.
The King as heretofore, we swear,
Shall be beneath our thumb –
SCA.:   He shall –
PHAN.: Shall be beneath our thumb –
SCA.:   He shall.
BOTH [*with great energy*]:
        For this mustn't be, and this won't do,
        If you'll back me, then I'll back you,
                No, this won't do,
                No, this mustn't be.

    [*Enter the* KING.]

KING: Gentlemen, gentlemen – really! This unseemly display of energy within the Royal Precincts is altogether unpardonable. Pray, what do you complain of?

SCA. [*furiously*]: What do we complain of? Why, through the innovations introduced by the Flowers of Progress all our harmless
schemes for making a provision for our old age are ruined. Our
Matriomonial Agency is at a standstill, our Cheap Sherry business
is in bankruptcy, our Army Clothing contracts are paralysed and
even our Society paper, the *Palace Peeper*, is practically defunct!

KING: Defunct? Is that so? Dear, dear, I am truly sorry.

SCA.: Are you aware that Sir Bailey Barre has introduced a law of
libel by which all editors of scurrilous newspapers are publicly
flogged – as in England? And six of our editors have resigned in
succession! Now, the editor of a scurrilous paper can stand a good
deal – he takes a private thrashing as a matter of course – it's
considered in his salary – but no gentleman likes to be publicly
flogged.

KING: Naturally. I shouldn't like it myself.

PHAN.: Then our Burlesque Theatre is absolutely ruined!

KING: Dear me. Well, theatrical property is not what it was.

PHAN.: Are you aware that the Lord Chamberlain, who has his own
views as to the best means of elevating the national drama, has
declined to license any play that is not in blank verse and three
hundred years old – as in England?

SCA.: And as if that wasn't enough, the County Councillor has ordered
a four-foot wall to be built up right across the proscenium, in case
of fire – as in England.

PHAN.: It's so hard on the company – who are liable to be roasted
alive – and this has to be met by enormously increased salaries – as
in England.

SCA.: You probably know that we've contracted to supply the entire
nation with a complete English outfit. But perhaps you do *not* know
that, when we send in our bills, our customers plead liability limited
to a declared capital of eighteenpence, and apply to be dealt with
under the Winding-up Act – as in England?

KING: Really, gentlemen, this is very irregular. If you will be so
good as to formulate a detailed list of your grievances in writing,
addressed to the Secretary of Utopia Limited, they will be laid
before the Board, in due course, at their next monthly meeting.

SCA.: Are we to understand that we are defied?

KING: That is the idea I intended to convey.

PHAN.: Defied! We are defied!

SCA. [*furiously*]: Take care – you know our powers. Trifle with us, and you die!

TRIO – SCAPHIO, PHANTIS *and* KING

SCA.:   If you think that, when banded in unity,
We may both be defied with impunity,
      You are sadly misled of a verity!

PHAN.:   If you value repose and tranquillity,
You'll revert to a state of docility,
      Or prepare to regret your temerity!

KING: If my speech is unduly refractory
You will find it a course satisfactory
      At an early Board meeting to show it up.
Though if proper excuse you can trump any,
You may *wind* up a Limited Company,
      You cannot conveniently *blow* it up!

[SCAPHIO *and* PHANTIS *thoroughly baffled.*]

KING [*dancing quietly*]:
      Whene'er I chance to baffle you
      I, also, dance a step or two –
      Of this now guess the hidden sense:

[SCAPHIO *and* PHANTIS *consider the question as* KING *continues dancing quietly – then give it up.*]
      It means – complete indifference.

SCA. *and* PHAN.:
      Of course it does – indifference!
      It means complete indifference!

[KING *dancing quietly.* SCAPHIO *and* PHANTIS *dancing furiously.*]

SCA. *and* PHAN.:   As we've a dance for every mood
      With *pas de trois*[51] we will conclude.

What this may mean you all may guess –
It typifies remorselessness!

KING: It means unruffled cheerfulness!
[KING *dances off placidly as* SCAPHIO *and* PHANTIS *dance furiously.*]

PHAN. [*breathless*]: He's right – we are helpless! He's no longer a human being – he's a Corporation, and so long as he confines himself to his Articles of Association we can't touch him! What are we to do?

SCA.: Do? Raise a Revolution, repeal the Act of Sixty-Two, reconvert him into an individual and insist on his immediate explosion!
    [TARARA *enters.*]
Tarara, come here; you're the very man we want.

TAR.: Certainly, allow me. [*Offers a cracker to each; they snatch them away impatiently.*] That's rude.

SCA.: We have no time for idle forms. You wish to succeed to the throne?

TAR.: Naturally.

SCA.: Then you won't unless you join us. The King has defied us, and, as matters stand, we are helpless. So are you. We must devise some plot at once to bring the people about his ears.

TAR.: A plot?

PHAN.: Yes, a plot of superhuman subtlety. Have you such a thing about you?

TAR. [*feeling*]: No, I think not. No. There's one on my dressing-table.

SCA.: We can't wait – we must concoct one at once, and put it into execution without delay. There is not a moment to spare!

TRIO – SCAPHIO, PHANTIS *and* TARARA

ENSEMBLE: With wily brain upon the spot
                        A private plot we'll plan,
                The most ingenious private plot
                    Since private plots began.

That's understood. So far we've got.
And, striking while the iron's hot,
We'll now determine like a shot
The details of this private plot.

SCA.: I think we ought – [*whispers*].

PHAN. *and* TAR.: Such bosh I never heard!

PHAN.: Ah! happy thought! – [*whispers*].

SCA. *and* TAR.: How utterly dashed absurd!

TAR.: *I'll* tell you how – [*whispers*].

SCA. *and* PHAN.: Why, what put that in your head?

SCA.: I've got it now – [*whispers*].

PHAN. *and* TAR.: Oh, take him away to bed!

PHAN.: Oh, put him to bed!

TAR.: Oh, put him to bed!

SCA.: What! put *me* to bed?

PHAN. *and* TAR.: Yes, certainly put him to bed!

SCA.: But, bless me, don't you see –

PHAN.: Do listen to me, I pray –

TAR.: It certainly seems to me –

SCA.: Bah – this is the only way!

PHAN.: It's rubbish absurd you growl!

TAR.: You talk ridiculous stuff!

SCA.: You're a drivelling barndoor owl!

PHAN.: You're a vapid and vain old muff!

[*All, coming down to audience*]

So far we haven't quite solved the plot –
They're not a very ingenious lot –
But don't be unhappy,
It's still on the *tapis*,[52]
We'll presently hit on a capital plot!

SCA.: Suppose we all – [*whispers*].

PHAN.: Now *there* I think you're right.
Then we might all – [*whispers*].

TAR.: That's true – we certainly might.
I'll tell you what – [*whispers*].

SCA.:   We will if we possibly can.
                        Then on the spot – [*whispers*].
PHAN. *and* TAR.:   Bravo! a capital plan!
SCA.:   That's exceedingly neat and new!
PHAN.:   Exceedingly new and neat.
TAR.:   I fancy that that will do.
SCA.:   It's certainly very complete.
PHAN.:   Well done, you sly old sap!
TAR.:   Bravo, you cunning old mole!
SCA.:   You very ingenious chap!
PHAN.:   You intellectual soul!
    [*All, coming down and addressing audience*]

          At last a capital plan we've got;
          We won't say how and we won't say what:
             It's safe in my noddle –
             Now off we will toddle,
          And slyly develop this capital plot!
        [*Business. Exeunt* SCAPHIO *and* PHANTIS *in one
              direction, and* TARARA *in the other.*]
   [*Enter* LORD DRAMALEIGH *and* MR GOLDBURY.]

LORD D.: Well, what do you think of our first South Pacific Drawing-
room? Allowing for a slight difficulty with the trains, and a little
want of familiarity with the use of the rouge-pot, it was, on the
whole, a meritorious affair?
GOLD.: My dear Dramaleigh, it redounds infinitely to your credit.
LORD D.: One or two judicious innovations, I think?
GOLD.: Admirable. The cup of tea and the plate of mixed biscuits
were a cheap and effective inspiration.
LORD D.: Yes – my idea entirely. Never been done before.
GOLD.: Pretty little maids, the King's youngest daughters, but timid.
LORD D.: That'll wear off. Young.
GOLD.: *That'll* wear off. Ha! here they come, by George! And without
the Dragon! What can they have done with her?
    [*Enter* NEKAYA *and* KALYBA, *timidly.*]
NEK.: Oh, if you please, Lady Sophy has sent us in here, because Zara

and Captain Fitzbattleaxe are going on, in the garden, in a manner which no well-conducted young ladies ought to witness.

LORD D.: Indeed, we are very much obliged to her Ladyship.

KAL.: Are you? I wonder why.

NEK.: Don't tell us if it's rude.

LORD D.: Rude? Not at all. We are obliged to Lady Sophy because she has afforded us the pleasure of seeing you.

NEK.: I don't think you ought to talk to us like that.

KAL.: It's calculated to turn our heads.

NEK.: Attractive girls cannot be too particular.

KAL.: Oh pray, pray do not take advantage of our unprotected innocence.

GOLD.: Pray be reassured – you are in no danger whatever.

LORD D.: But may I ask – is this extreme delicacy – this shrinking sensitiveness – a general characteristic of Utopian young ladies?

NEK.: Oh no; we are crack specimens.

KAL.: We are the pick of the basket. *Would* you mind not coming quite so near? Thank you.

NEK.: And please don't look at us like that; it unsettles us.

KAL.: And we don't like it. At least, we *do* like it; but it's wrong.

NEK.: *We* have enjoyed the inestimable privilege of being educated by a most refined and easily shocked English lady, on the very strictest English principles.

GOLD.: But, my dear young ladies –

KAL.: Oh, don't! You mustn't. It's too affectionate.

NEK.: It really does unsettle us.

GOLD.: Are you really under the impression that English girls are so ridiculously demure? Why, an English girl of the highest type is the best, the most beautiful, the bravest and the brightest creature that Heaven has conferred upon this world of ours. She is frank, open-hearted and fearless, and never shows in so favourable a light as when she gives her own blameless impulses full play!

NEK. *and* KAL.: Oh, you shocking story!

GOLD.: Not at all. I'm speaking the strict truth. I'll tell you all about her.

SONG

MR GOLD.:   A wonderful joy our eyes to bless,
In her magnificent comeliness,
Is an English girl of eleven stone two,
And five foot ten in her dancing shoe!
She follows the hounds, and on she pounds –
The 'field' tails off and the muffs
diminish –
Over the hedges and brooks she bounds
Straight as a crow, from find to finish.
At cricket,[53] her kin will lose or win –
She and her maids, on grass and clover,
Eleven maids out – eleven maids in –
And perhaps an occasional 'maiden over!'

Go search the world and search the sea,
Then come you home and sing with me
There's no such gold and no such pearl
As a bright and beautiful English girl!

With a ten-mile spin she stretches her limbs,
She golfs, she punts, she rows, she swims –
She plays, she sings, she dances, too,
From ten or eleven till all is blue!
At ball or drum, till small hours come
(Chaperon's fan conceals her yawning)
She'll waltz away like a teetotum,
And never go home till daylight's
dawning.
Lawn-tennis may share her favours fair –
Her eyes a-dance and her cheeks
a-glowing –
Down comes her hair, but what does she care?
It's all her own and it's worth the showing!
Go search the world, etc.

Her soul is sweet as the ocean air,
For prudery knows no haven there;
To find mock-modesty, please apply
To the conscious blush and the downcast eye.
    Rich in the things contentment brings,
      In every pure enjoyment wealthy,
    Blithe as a beautiful bird she sings,
      For body and mind are hale and healthy.
    Her eyes they thrill with right goodwill –
      Her heart is light as a floating feather –
    As pure and bright as the mountain rill
      That leaps and laughs in the Highland
        heather!
      Go search the world, etc.

QUARTET – NEKAYA, LORD DRAMALEIGH, KALYBA,
MR GOLDBURY

NEK.:	Then I may sing and play?
LORD D.:	You may!
KAL.:	And I may laugh and shout?
GOLD.:	No doubt!
NEK.:	These maxims you endorse?
LORD D.:	Of course!
KAL.:	You won't exclaim 'Oh fie!'
GOLD.:	Not I!

Whatever you are – be that:
    Whatever you say – be true:
      Straightforwardly act –
      Be honest – in fact,
    Be nobody else but *you*.

LORD D.:   Give every answer pat –
      Your character true unfurl;
        And when it is ripe,
        You'll then be a type
      Of a capital English girl.

ALL: Oh, sweet surprise – oh, dear delight,
                To find it undisputed quite,
                All musty, fusty rules despite,
                That Art is wrong and Nature right!

NEK.:   When happy I,
                   With laughter glad
                         I'll wake the echoes fairly,
                And only sigh
                   When I am sad –
                         And that will be but rarely!

KAL.:   I'll row and fish,
                   And gallop, soon –
                         No longer be a prim one –
                And when I wish
                   To hum a tune,
                         It needn't be a hymn one?

GOLD. *and* LORD D.:
                   No, no!
                   It needn't be a hymn one!

ALL [*dancing*]:
                   Oh, sweet surprise and dear delight
                   To find it undisputed quite –
                   All musty, fusty rules despite –
                   That Art is wrong and Nature right!

                                    [*Dance, and off.*]

[*Enter* LADY SOPHY.]

RECITATIVE

LADY S.:   Oh, would some demon power the gift impart
                To quell my over-conscientious heart –
                Unspeak the oaths that never had been spoken,
                And break the vows that never should be broken!

SONG

LADY S.:   When but a maid of fifteen year,
                  Unsought – unplighted –
          Short-petticoated – and, I fear,
                  Still shorter-sighted –
          I made a vow, one early spring,
          That only to some spotless King
          Who proof of blameless life could bring
                  I'd be united.
          For I had read, not long before,
          Of blameless kings in fairy lore,
          And thought the race still flourished here –
                  Well, well –
             I was a maid of fifteen year!

[*The* KING *enters and overhears this verse.*]

          Each morning I pursued my game
                  (An early riser);
          For spotless monarchs I became
                  An advertiser:
          But all in vain I searched each land,
          So, kingless, to my native strand
          Returned, a little older, and
                  A good deal wiser!
          I learnt that spotless King and Prince
          Have disappeared some ages since –
          Even Paramount's angelic grace –
                  Ah, me! –
          Is but a mask on Nature's face!

[KING *comes forward.*]

RECITATIVE

KING: Ah, Lady Sophy – then you love me!
                 For so you sing –

LADY S. [*indignant and surprised, producing 'Palace Peeper'*]:

No, by the stars that shine above me,
Degraded King!

For while these rumours, through the city bruited,
Remain uncontradicted, unrefuted,
The object thou of my aversion rooted,
Repulsive thing!

KING: Be just – the time is now at hand
When truth may published be.
These paragraphs were written and
Contributed by me!

LADY S.:   By you? No, no!

KING: Yes, yes, I swear, by me!
I, caught in Scaphio's ruthless toil,
Contributed the lot!

LADY S.:   And *that* is why you did not boil
The author on the spot!

KING: And *that* is why I did not boil
The author on the spot!

LADY S.:   I *couldn't* think why you did not boil!

KING: But *I* know why I did not boil
The author on the spot!

DUET – LADY SOPHY *and* KING

LADY S.:   Oh, the rapture unrestrained
Of a candid retractation!
For my sovereign has deigned
A convincing explanation –
And the clouds that gathered o'er,
All have vanished in the distance,
And of Kings of fairy lore
One, at least, is in existence!

KING: Oh, the skies are blue above,
And the earth is red and rosal,

Now the lady of my love
    Has accepted my proposal!
For that *asinorum pons*[54]
    I have crossed without assistance,
And of prudish paragons
    One, at least, is in existence!

[KING *and* LADY SOPHY *dance gracefully. While this is going on* LORD DRAMALEIGH *enters unobserved with* NEKAYA *and* MR GOLDBURY *with* KALYBA. *Then enter* ZARA *and* CAPTAIN FITZBATTLEAXE. *The two girls direct* ZARA's *attention to the* KING *and* LADY SOPHY, *who are still dancing affectionately together. At this point the* KING *kisses* LADY SOPHY, *which causes the Princesses to make an exclamation. The* KING *and* LADY SOPHY *are at first much confused at being detected, but eventually throw off all reserve, and the four couples break into a wild Tarantella,[55] and at the end exeunt severally.*]

[*Enter all the male Chorus, in great excitement, from various entrances, led by* SCAPHIO, PHANTIS *and* TARARA, *and followed by the female Chorus.*]

CHORUS: Upon our sea-girt land
    At our enforced command
    Reform has laid her hand
        Like some remorseless ogress –
    And made us darkly rue
    The deeds she dared to do –
    And all is owing to
        Those hated Flowers of Progress!
        So down with them!
        So down with them!
    Reform's a hated ogress.
        So down with them!
        So down with them!
    Down with the Flowers of Progress!
[*Flourish. Enter* KING, *his three daughters,* LADY SOPHY, *and the Flowers of Progress.*]

KING: What means this most unmannerly irruption?
Is this your gratitude for boons conferred?

SCA.: Boons? Bah! A fico[56] for such boons, say we!
These boons have brought Utopia to a standstill!
Our pride and boast – the Army and the Navy –
Have both been reconstructed and remodelled
Upon so irresistible a basis
That all the neighbouring nations have disarmed –
And War's impossible! Your County Councillor
Has passed such drastic Sanitary laws
That all the doctors dwindle, starve and die!
The laws, remodelled by Sir Bailey Barre,
Have quite extinguished crime and litigation:
The lawyers starve, and all the jails are let
As model lodgings for the working-classes!
In short –
Utopia, swamped by dull Prosperity,
Demands that these detested Flowers of Progress
Be sent about their business, and affairs
Restored to their original complexion!

KING [to ZARA]: My daughter, this is a very unpleasant state of things. What is to be done?

ZARA: I don't know – I don't understand it. We must have omitted something.

KING: Omitted something? Yes, that's all very well, but –

[SIR BAILEY BARRE whispers to ZARA.]

ZARA [suddenly]: Of course! Now I remember! Why, I had forgotten the most essential element of all!

KING: And that is? –

ZARA: Government by Party! Introduce that great and glorious element – at once the bulwark and foundation of England's greatness – and all will be well! No political measures will endure, because one Party will assuredly undo all that the other Party has done; inexperienced civilians will govern your Army and your Navy; no social reforms will be attempted, because out of vice, squalor and drunkenness no political capital is to be made; and while grouse is to be shot, and foxes worried to death, the legislative action of the country will be at a standstill. Then there will be sickness in plenty, endless lawsuits, crowded jails, interminable confusion in the Army and Navy, and, in short, general and unexampled prosperity!

ALL: Ulahlica! Ulahlica!

PHAN. [*aside*]: Baffled!

SCA.: But an hour *will* come!

KING: Your hour has come already – away with them, and let them wait my will! [SCAPHIO *and* PHANTIS *are led off in custody*]. From this moment Government by Party is adopted, with all its attendant blessings; and henceforward Utopia will no longer be a Monarchy Limited, but, what is a great deal better, a Limited Monarchy!

FINALE

ZARA: There's a little group of isles beyond the wave –
   So tiny, you might almost wonder where it is –
That nation is the bravest of the brave,
   And cowards are the rarest of all rarities.
The proudest nations kneel at her command;
   She terrifies all foreign-born rapscallions;
And holds the peace of Europe in her hand
   With half a score invincible battalions!
      Such, at least, is the tale
      Which is borne on the gale,
        From the island which dwells in the sea.
      Let us hope, for her sake,
      That she makes no mistake –
        That she's all she professes to be!

KING: Oh, may we copy all her maxims wise,
   And imitate her virtues and her charities;
And may we, by degrees, acclimatize
   Her Parliamentary peculiarities!
By doing so, we shall, in course of time,
   Regenerate completely our entire land –

Great Britain is that monarchy sublime,
 To which some add (but others do not) Ireland.
  Such, at least, is the tale, etc.

When Monarch of barbaric land,
 For self-improvement burning,
Foregathers with a glorious band
 Of sweetness, light, and learning –
A group incalculably wise –
 Unequalled in their beauty –
Their customs to acclimatize
 Becomes a moral duty.

ZARA [*to* FITZBATTLEAXE]:
 Oh gallant soldier,
   brave and true
 In tented field and tourney,
 I trust you'll ne'er regret that you
  Embarked upon this journey.

FITZ.: To warriors all may it befall
  To gain so pure a beauty,
 When they obey the trumpet call
  Of Regimental Duty!

CURTAIN

685

THE GRAND DUKE

OR

THE STATUTORY DUEL

DRAMATIS PERSONAE

RUDOLPH (*Grand Duke of Pfennig Halbpfennig*)
ERNEST DUMMKOPF (*a Theatrical Manager*)
LUDWIG (*his Leading Comedian*)
DR TANNHÄUSER (*a Notary*)
THE PRINCE OF MONTE CARLO
VISCOUNT MENTONE
BEN HASHBAZ (*a Costumier*)
HERALD
THE PRINCESS OF MONTE CARLO (*betrothed to* RUDOLPH)
THE BARONESS VON KRAKENFELDT (*betrothed to* RUDOLPH)
JULIA JELLICOE (*an English Comédienne*)
LISA (*a Soubrette*)

OLGA
GRETCHEN
BERTHA   } (*Members of Ernest Dummkopf's Company*)
ELSA
MARTHA

Chorus of Chamberlains, Nobles, Actors, Actresses, Citizens, etc.

ACT I – Scene. Public Square of Speisesaal
ACT II – Scene. Hall in the Grand Ducal Palace
Date 1750

ACT I

SCENE – *Market-place of Speisesaal, in the Grand Duchy*[1] *of Pfennig Halbpfennig.*[2] *A well, with decorated iron-work, up-stage left centre.*

[GRETCHEN, BERTHA, OLGA, MARTHA *and other members of* ERNEST DUMMKOPF's[3] *theatrical company are discovered, seated at several small tables, enjoying a repast in honour of the nuptials of* LUDWIG, *his leading comedian, and* LISA, *his soubrette.*]

CHORUS:	Won't it be a pretty wedding?
	Will not Lisa look delightful?
	Smiles and tears in plenty shedding –
	Which in brides of course is rightful.
	One could say, if one were spiteful,
	Contradiction little dreading,
	Her bouquet is simply frightful –
	Still, 'twill be a pretty wedding!
	Oh, it is a pretty wedding!
	Such a pretty, pretty wedding!

ELSA:	If her dress *is* badly fitting,
	Theirs the fault who made her *trousseau*.

BERTHA:	If her gloves *are* always splitting,
	Cheap kid gloves, we know, will do so.

OLGA: If upon her train she stumbled,
                On one's train one's always treading.

GRET.:   If her hair *is* rather tumbled,
                Still, 'twill be a pretty wedding!

CHORUS: Such a pretty, pretty wedding!

Here they come, the couple plighted –
        On life's journey gaily start them.
Soon to be for aye united,
        Till divorce or death shall part them.
[LUDWIG *and* LISA *come forward.*]

DUET – LUDWIG *and* LISA

LUD.:   Pretty Lisa, fair and tasty,
           Tell me now, and tell me truly,
Haven't you been rather hasty?
           Haven't you been rash unduly?
Am I quite the dashing *sposo*[4]
           That your fancy could depict you?
Perhaps you think I'm only so-so?
[*She expresses admiration.*]
           Well, I will not contradict you!

CHORUS: No, he will not contradict you!

LISA: Who am I to raise objection?
           I'm a child, untaught and homely –
When you tell me you're perfection,
           Tender, truthful, true and comely –
That in quarrel no one's bolder,
           Though dissensions always grieve you –
Why, my love, you're so much older
           That, of course, I must believe you!

CHORUS: Yes, of course, she must believe you!

If he ever acts unkindly,
Shut your eyes and love him blindly –
Should he call you names uncomely,
Shut your mouth and love him dumbly –
Should he rate you, rightly – leftly –
Shut your ears and love him deafly.
　　Ha! ha! ha! ha! ha! ha! ha!
　　　　Thus and thus and thus alone
　　　　Ludwig's wife may hold her own!
[LUDWIG and LISA sit at table.]
[Enter NOTARY TANNHÄUSER.[5]]

NOT.: Hallo! Surely I'm not late? [All chatter unintelligibly in reply.] But, dear me, you're all at breakfast! Has the wedding taken place? [All chatter unintelligibly in reply.] My good girls, one at a time, I beg. Let me understand the situation. As solicitor to the conspiracy to dethrone the Grand Duke – a conspiracy in which the members of this company are deeply involved – I am invited to the marriage of two of its members. I present myself in due course, and I find, not only that the ceremony has taken place – which is not of the least consequence – but the wedding breakfast is half eaten – which is a consideration of the most serious importance.

[LUDWIG and LISA come down.]

LUD.: But the ceremony has *not* taken place. We can't get a parson!
NOT.: Can't get a parson! Why, how's that? They're three a penny!
LUD.: Oh, it's the old story – the Grand Duke!
ALL: Ugh!
LUD.: It seems that the little imp has selected this, our wedding day, for a convocation of all the clergy in the town to settle the details of his approaching marriage with the enormously wealthy Baroness von Krakenfeldt,[6] and there won't be a parson to be had for love or money until six o'clock this evening!
LISA: And as we produce our magnificent classical revival of *Troilus and Cressida*[7] to-night at seven, we have no alternative but to eat our wedding breakfast before we've earned it. So sit down, and make the best of it.
GRET.: Oh, I should like to pull his Grand Ducal ears for him, that I

should! He's the meanest, the cruellest, the most spiteful little ape in Christendom!

OLGA: Well, we shall soon be freed from his tyranny. To-morrow the Despot is to be dethroned!

LUD.: Hush, rash girl! You know not what you say.

OLGA: Don't be absurd! We're all in it – we're all tiled, here.

LUD.: That has nothing to do with it. Know ye not that in alluding to our conspiracy without having first given and received the secret sign, you are violating a fundamental principle of our Association?

SONG

LUD.:
By the mystic regulation
Of our dark Association,
Ere you open conversation
    With another kindred soul,
    You must eat a sausage-roll![8] [*Producing one.*]

ALL:
You must eat a sausage-roll!

LUD.:
If, in turn, he eats another,
That's a sign that he's a brother –
Each may fully trust the other.
    It is quaint and it is droll,
    But it's bilious on the whole.

ALL:
Very bilious on the whole.

LUD.:
It's a greasy kind of pasty,
Which, perhaps, a judgement hasty
Might consider rather tasty:
    Once (to speak without disguise)
    It found favour in our eyes.

ALL:
It found favour in our eyes.

LUD.:　　　　　　But when you've been six months feeding
　　　　　　　　(As we have) on this exceeding
　　　　　　　　Bilious food, it's no ill-breeding
　　　　　　　　　　If at these repulsive pies
　　　　　　　　　　Our offended gorges rise!

ALL:　　　　　　　　Our offended gorges rise!

MARTHA: Oh, bother the secret sign! I've eaten it until I'm quite uncomfortable! I've given it six times already to-day – and [*whimpering*] I can't eat any breakfast!

BERTHA: And it's so unwholesome. Why, we should all be as yellow as frogs if it wasn't for the make-up!

LUD.: All this is rank treason to the cause. I suffer as much as any of you. I loathe the repulsive thing – I can't contemplate it without a shudder – but I'm a conscientious conspirator, and if you won't give the sign I will. [*Eats sausage-roll with an effort.*]

LISA: Poor martyr! He's always at it, and it's a wonder where he puts it!

NOT.: Well now, about *Troilus and Cressida*. What do *you* play?

LUD. [*struggling with his feelings*]: If you'll be so obliging as to wait until I've got rid of this feeling of warm oil at the bottom of my throat, I'll tell you all about it. [LISA *gives him some brandy.*] Thank you, my love; it's gone. Well, the piece will be produced upon a scale of unexampled magnificence. It is confidently predicted that my appearance as King Agamemnon,[9] in a Louis Quatorze[10] wig, will mark an epoch in the theatrical annals of Pfennig Halbpfennig. I endeavoured to persuade Ernest Dummkopf, our manager, to lend us the classical dresses for our marriage. Think of the effect of a real Athenian wedding procession cavorting through the streets of Speisesaal! Torches burning – cymbals banging – flutes tootling – citharae twanging – and a throng of fifty lovely Spartan virgins capering before us, all down the High Street, singing 'Eloia! Eloia! Opoponax,[11] Eloia!' It would have been tremendous!

NOT.: And he declined?

LUD.: He did, on the prosaic ground that it might rain, and the ancient Greeks didn't carry umbrellas! If, as is confidently expected, Ernest

Dummkopf is elected to succeed the dethroned one, mark my words, he will make a mess of it.

[*Exit* LUDWIG *with* LISA.]

OLGA: He's sure to be elected. His entire company has promised to plump for him on the understanding that all the places about the Court are filled by members of his troupe, according to professional precedence.

[ERNEST DUMMKOPF *enters in great excitement.*]

BERTHA [*looking off*]: Here comes Ernest Dummkopf. Now we shall know all about it!

ALL: Well – what's the news? How is the election going?

ERN.: Oh, it's a certainty – a practical certainty! Two of the candidates have been arrested for debt, and the third is a baby in arms – so, if you keep your promises, and vote solid, I'm cocksure of election!

OLGA: Trust to us. But you remember the conditions?

ERN.: Yes – all of you shall be provided for, for life. Every man shall be ennobled – every lady shall have unlimited credit at the Court Milliner's, and all salaries shall be paid weekly in advance!

GRET.: Oh, it's quite clear he knows how to rule a Grand Duchy!

ERN.: Rule a Grand Duchy? Why, my good girl, for ten years past I've ruled a theatrical company! A man who can do that can rule anything!

SONG

ERN.:
Were I a king in very truth,
And had a son – a guileless youth –
    In probable succession;
To teach him patience, teach him tact,
How promptly in a fix to act,
He should adopt, in point of fact,
    A manager's profession.
To that condition he should stoop
    (Despite a too fond mother),
With eight or ten 'stars' in his troupe,
    All jealous of each other!

694

Oh, the man who can rule a theatrical crew,
Each member a genius (and some of them two),
And manage to humour them, little and great,
    Can govern this tuppenny State!

ALL: Oh, the man, etc.

ERN.:   Both A and B rehearsal slight –
    They say they'll be 'all right at night'
        (They've both to go to school yet);
    C in each act *must* change her dress,
    D *will* attempt to 'square the press';
    E won't play Romeo unless
        His grandmother plays Juliet;
    F claims all hoydens[12] as her rights
        (She's played them thirty seasons);
    And G must show herself in tights
        For two convincing reasons –
        Two very well-shaped reasons!
Oh, the man who can drive a theatrical team,
With wheelers and leaders in order supreme,
Can govern and rule, with a wave of his fin,
    All Europe – with Ireland thrown in!

ALL: Oh, the man, etc.

                [Exeunt all but ERNEST.]

ERN.: Elected by my fellow-conspirators to be Grand Duke of Pfennig
Halbpfennig as soon as the contemptible little occupant of the
historical throne is deposed – here is promotion indeed! Why,
instead of playing Troilus of Troy for a month, I shall play Grand
Duke of Pfennig Halbpfennig for a lifetime! Yet, am I happy? No
– far from happy! The lovely English *comédienne* – the beautiful
Julia, whose dramatic ability is so overwhelming that our audiences
forgive even her strong English accent – that rare and radiant being
treats my respectful advances with disdain unutterable! And yet,
who knows? She is haughty and ambitious, and it may be that the

splendid change in my fortunes may work a corresponding change in her feelings towards me!

[*Enter* JULIA JELLICOE.]

JULIA: Herr Dummkopf, a word with you, if you please.

ERN.: Beautiful English maiden –

JULIA: No compliments, I beg. I desire to speak with you on a purely professional matter, so we will, if you please, dispense with allusions to my personal appearance, which can only tend to widen the breach which already exists between us.

ERN. [*aside*]: My only hope shattered! The haughty Londoner still despises me! [*Aloud*] It shall be as you will.

JULIA: I understand that the conspiracy in which we are all concerned is to develop to-morrow, and that the company is likely to elect you to the throne on the understanding that the posts about the Court are to be filled by members of your theatrical troupe, according to their professional importance.

ERN.: That is so.

JULIA: Then all I can say is that it places me in an extremely awkward position.

ERN. [*very depressed*]: I don't see how it concerns you.

JULIA: Why, bless my heart, don't you see that, as your leading lady, I am bound under a serious penalty to play the leading part in all your productions?

ERN.: Well?

JULIA: Why, of course, the leading part in this production will be the Grand Duchess!

ERN.: My wife?

JULIA: That is another way of expressing the same idea.

ERN. [*aside – delighted*]: I scarcely dared even to hope for this!

JULIA: Of course, as your leading lady, you'll be mean enough to hold me to the terms of my agreement. Oh, that's so like a man! Well, I suppose there's no help for it – I shall have to do it!

ERN. [*aside*]: She's mine! [*Aloud*] But – do you really think you would care to play that part? [*Taking her hand.*]

JULIA [*withdrawing it*]: Care to play it? Certainly not – but what am I to do? Business is business, and I am bound by the terms of my agreement.

ERN.: It's for a long run, mind – a run that may last many, many years – no understudy – and once embarked upon there's no throwing it up.

JULIA: Oh, we're used to these long runs in England: they are the curse of the stage – but, you see, I've no option.

ERN.: You think the part of Grand Duchess will be good enough for you?

JULIA: Oh, I think so. It's a very good part in Gerolstein,[13] and oughtn't to be a bad one in Pfennig Halbpfennig. Why, what did you suppose I was going to play?

ERN. [*keeping up a show of reluctance*]: But, considering your strong personal dislike to me and your persistent rejection of my repeated offers, won't you find it difficult to throw yourself into the part with all the impassioned enthusiasm that the character seems to demand? Remember, it's a strongly emotional part, involving long and repeated scenes of rapture, tenderness, adoration, devotion – all in luxuriant excess, and all of the most demonstrative description.

JULIA: My good sir, throughout my career I have made it a rule never to allow private feeling to interfere with my professional duties. You may be quite sure that (however distasteful the part may be) if I undertake it, I shall consider myself professionally bound to throw myself into it with all the ardour at my command.

ERN. [*aside – with effusion*]: I'm the happiest fellow alive! [*Aloud*] Now – would you have any objection – to – to give me some idea – if it's only a mere sketch – as to how you would play it? It would be really interesting – to me – to know your conception of – of – the part of my wife.

JULIA: How would I play it? Now, let me see – let me see. [*Considering*] Ah, I have it!

BALLAD

JULIA: How would I play this part –
                    The Grand Duke's Bride?
              All rancour in my heart
                    I'd duly hide –

I'd drive it from my recollection
And 'whelm you with a mock affection,
Well calculated to defy detection –
That's how I'd play this part –
    The Grand Duke's Bride.

With many a winsome smile
    I'd witch and woo;
With gay and girlish guile
    I'd frenzy you –
    I'd madden you with my caressing,
    Like turtle, her first love confessing –
    That it was 'mock', no mortal would be guessing,
With so much winsome wile
    I'd witch and woo!

Did any other maid
    With you succeed,
I'd pinch the forward jade –
    I would indeed!
    With jealous frenzy agitated
    (Which would, of course, be simulated),
    I'd make her wish she'd never been created –
Did any other maid
    With you succeed!
And should there come to me,
    Some summers hence,
In all the childish glee
    Of innocence,
    Fair babes, aglow with beauty vernal,
    My heart would bound with joy diurnal!
    This sweet display of sympathy maternal,
Well, that would also be
    A mere pretence!
My histrionic art
    Though you deride,
That's how I'd play that part –
    The Grand Duke's Bride!

ENSEMBLE

ERNEST	JULIA
Oh joy! when two glowing young hearts,	My boy, when two glowing young hearts,
From the rise of the curtain,	From the rise of the curtain,
Thus throw themselves into their parts,	Thus throw themselves into their parts,
Success is most certain!	Success is most certain!
If the *rôle* you're prepared to endow	The *rôle* I'm prepared to endow
With such delicate touches,	With most delicate touches,
By the heaven above us, I vow	By the heaven above us, I vow
You shall be my Grand Duchess!	I will be your Grand Duchess!
[*Dance.*]	

[*Enter all the Chorus with* LUDWIG, NOTARY *and* LISA – *all greatly agitated.*]

CHORUS [*excited*]:

My goodness me! what shall we do? Why, what a dreadful
situation!

[*To* LUDWIG]

It's all your fault, you booby you – you lump of
indiscrimination!
I'm sure I don't know where to go – it's put me into
such a tetter –
But this at all events I know – the sooner we are off, the
better!

ERN.:   What means this *agitato*?[14] What d'ye seek?
As your Grand Duke elect I bid you speak!

SONG

LUD.:   Ten minutes since I met a chap
                         Who bowed an easy salutation –
                 Thinks I, 'This gentleman, mayhap,
                         Belongs to our Association.'
                                 But, on the whole,
                                     Uncertain yet,
                                 A sausage-roll
                                     I took and eat –
                 That chap replied (I don't embellish)
                 By eating *three* with obvious relish.

CHORUS [*angrily*]:

                         Why, gracious powers,
                         No chum of ours
                 Could eat three sausage-rolls with relish!

LUD.:   Quite reassured, I let him know
                         Our plot – each incident explaining;
                 That stranger chuckled much, as though
                         He thought me highly entertaining.
                                 I told him all,
                                     Both bad and good;
                                 I bade him call –
                                     He said he would:
                 I added much – the more I muckled,
                 The more that chuckling chummy chuckled!

ALL [*angrily*]:

                         A bat could see
                         He couldn't be
                 A chum of ours if he chuckled!

LUD.:   Well, as I bowed to his applause,
                         Down dropped he with hysteric bellow –
                 And *that* seemed right enough, because
                         I *am* a devilish funny fellow.

Then suddenly,
　　As still he squealed,
　It flashed on me
　　That I'd revealed
Our plot, with all details effective,
To Grand Duke Rudolph's own detective!

ALL: 　　　　What folly fell,
　　　　　To go and tell
　　　Our plot to any one's detective!

CHORUS [*attacking* LUDWIG]:
　　　　　　You booby dense –
　　　　　　You oaf immense,
　　　　　　With no pretence
　　　　　　To common sense!
　　　　　　A stupid muff
　　　　　　Who's made of stuff
　　　　　　Not worth a puff
　　　　　　Of candle-snuff!
Pack up at once and off we go, unless we're anxious to exhibit
Our fairy forms all in a row, strung up upon the Castle gibbet!

　　　　　[*Exeunt Chorus. Manent* LUDWIG, LISA, ERNEST,
　　　　　　　　　　　　　　JULIA *and* NOTARY.]

JULIA: Well, a nice mess you've got us into! There's an end of our precious plot! All up – pop – fizzle – bang – done for!

LUD.: Yes, but – ha! ha! – fancy my choosing the Grand Duke's private detective, of all men, to make a confidant of! When you come to think of it, it's really devilish funny!

ERN. [*angrily*]: When you come to think of it, it's extremely injudicious to admit into a conspiracy every pudding-headed baboon who presents himself!

LUD.: Yes – I should never do that. If I were chairman of this gang, I should hesitate to enrol *any* baboon who couldn't produce satisfactory credentials from his last Zoological Gardens.

LISA: Ludwig is far from being a baboon. Poor boy, he could not help giving us away – it's his trusting nature – he was deceived.

JULIA [*furiously*]: His trusting nature! [*To* LUDWIG] Oh, I should like to talk to you in my own language for five minutes – only five minutes! I know some good, strong, energetic English remarks that would shrivel your trusting nature into raisins – only you wouldn't understand them!

LUD.: Here we perceive one of the disadvantages of a neglected education!

ERN. [*to* JULIA]: And I suppose you'll never be my Grand Duchess now!

JULIA: Grand Duchess? My good friend, if you don't produce the piece how can I play the part?

ERN.: True. [*To* LUDWIG] You see what you've done.

LUD.: But, my dear sir, you don't seem to understand that the man ate three sausage-rolls. Keep that fact steadily before you. Three large sausage-rolls.

JULIA: Bah! – Lots of people eat sausage-rolls who are not conspirators.

LUD.: Then they shouldn't. It's bad form. It's not the game. When one of the Human Family proposes to eat a sausage-roll, it is his duty to ask himself, 'Am I a conspirator?' And if, on examination, he finds that he is *not* a conspirator, he is bound in honour to select some other form of refreshment.

LISA: Of course he is. One should always play the game. [*To* NOTARY, *who has been smiling placidly through this*] What are you grinning at, you greedy old man?

NOT.: Nothing – don't mind me. It is always amusing to the legal mind to see a parcel of laymen bothering themselves about a matter which to a trained lawyer presents no difficulty whatever.

ALL: No difficulty!

NOT.: None whatever! The way out of it is quite simple.

ALL: Simple?

NOT.: Certainly! Now attend. In the first place, you two men fight a Statutory Duel.[15]

ERN.: A Statutory Duel?

JULIA: A Stat-tat-tatutory Duel! Ach! what a crack-jaw[16] language this German is!

LUD.: Never heard of such a thing.

NOT.: It is true that the practice has fallen into abeyance through disuse. But all the laws of Pfennig Halbpfennig run for a hundred years, when they die a natural death, unless, in the meantime, they have been revived for another century. The Act that institutes the Statutory Duel was passed a hundred years ago, and as it has never been revived, it expires to-morrow. So you're just in time.

JULIA: But what is the use of talking to us about Statutory Duels when we none of us know what a Statutory Duel is?

NOT.: Don't you? Then I'll explain.

SONG

NOT.:   About a century since,
       The code of the duello
         To sudden death
         For want of breath
       Sent many a strapping fellow.
    The then presiding Prince
       (Who useless bloodshed hated),
         He passed an Act,
         Short and compact,
       Which may be briefly stated.
    Unlike the complicated laws
    A Parliamentary draftsman draws,
       It may be briefly stated.

ALL: We know that complicated laws,
    Such as a legal draftsman draws,
       Cannot be briefly stated.

NOT.:   By this ingenious law,
       If any two shall quarrel,
         They may not fight
         With falchions[17] bright
       (Which seemed to him immoral);
    But each a card shall draw,

And he who draws the lowest
    Shall (so 'twas said)
    Be thenceforth dead –
In fact, a legal 'ghoest'
(When exigence of rhyme compels,
Orthography forgoes her spells,
    And 'ghost' is written 'ghoest').

ALL [*aside*]: With what an emphasis he dwells
Upon 'orthography' and 'spells'!
    That kind of fun's the lowest.

NOT.: When off the loser's popped
    (By pleasing legal fiction),
        And friend and foe
        Have wept their woe
    In counterfeit affliction,
The winner must adopt
    The loser's poor relations –
        Discharge his debts,
        Pay all his bets,
    And take his obligations.
In short, to briefly sum the case,
The winner takes the loser's place,
    With all its obligations.

ALL: How neatly lawyers state a case!
The winner takes the loser's place,
    With all its obligations!

LUD.: I see. The man who draws the lowest card –

NOT.: Dies, *ipso facto*, a social death. He loses all his civil rights – his identity disappears – the Revising Barrister[18] expunges his name from the list of voters, and the winner takes his place, whatever it may be, discharges all his functions, and adopts all his responsibilities.

ERN.: This is all very well, as far as it goes, but it only protects one of us. What's to become of the survivor?

LUD.: Yes, that's an interesting point, because *I* might be the survivor.

NOT.: The survivor goes at once to the Grand Duke, and, in a burst of remorse, denounces the dead man as the moving spirit of the plot. He is accepted as King's evidence,[19] and, as a matter of course, receives a free pardon. To-morrow, when the law expires, the dead man will, *ipso facto*, come to life again – the Revising Barrister will restore his name to the list of voters, and he will resume all his obligations as though nothing unusual had happened.

JULIA: When he will be at once arrested, tried and executed on the evidence of the informer! Candidly, my friend, I don't think much of your plot!

NOT.: Dear, dear, dear, the ignorance of the laity! My good young lady, it is a beautiful maxim of our glorious Constitution that a man can only die once. Death expunges crime, and when he comes to life again, it will be with a clean slate.

ERN.: It's really very ingenious.

LUD. [*to* NOTARY]: My dear sir, we owe you our lives!

LISA [*aside to* LUDWIG]: May I kiss him?

LUD.: Certainly not: you're a big girl now. [*To* ERNEST] Well, miscreant, are you prepared to meet me on the field of honour?

ERN.: At once. By Jove, what a couple of fire-eaters we are!

LISA: Ludwig doesn't know what fear is.

LUD.: Oh, I don't mind this sort of duel!

ERN.: It's not like a duel with swords. I hate a duel with swords. It's not the blade I mind – it's the blood.

LUD.: And I hate a duel with pistols. It's not the ball I mind – it's the bang.

NOT.: Altogether it is a great improvement on the old method of giving satisfaction.

QUINTET – LUDWIG, LISA, NOTARY, ERNEST, JULIA

> Strange the views some people hold!
> Two young fellows quarrel –
> Then they fight, for both are bold –
> Rage of both is uncontrolled –
> Both are stretched out, stark and cold!

Prithee, where's the moral?
Ding dong! Ding dong!
There's an end to further action,
And this barbarous transaction
Is described as 'satisfaction'!
Ha! ha! ha! ha! satisfaction!
Ding dong! Ding dong!
Each is laid in churchyard mould –
Strange the views some people hold!

Better than the method old,
Which was coarse and cruel,
Is the plan that we've extolled.
Sing thy virtues manifold
(Better than refinèd gold),
Statutory Duel!
Sing song! Sing song!
Sword or pistol neither uses –
Playing card he lightly chooses,
And the loser simply loses!
Ha! ha! ha! ha! simply loses.
Sing song! Sing song!
Some prefer the churchyard mould!
Strange the views some people hold!

NOT. [*offering a card to* ERNEST]:
Now take a card and gaily sing
How little you care for Fortune's rubs –

ERN. [*drawing a card*]:
Hurrah, hurrah! – I've drawn a King!

ALL:
He's drawn a King!
He's drawn a King!
Sing Hearts and Diamonds, Spades and Clubs!

ALL [*dancing*]:   He's drawn a King!
       How strange a thing!
  An excellent card – his chance it aids –
  Sing Hearts and Diamonds, Spades and Clubs –
  Sing Diamonds, Hearts and Clubs and Spades!

NOT. [*to* LUDWIG]:
   Now take a card with heart of grace –
   (Whatever our fate, let's play our parts).

LUD. [*drawing card*]:
   Hurrah, hurrah! – I've drawn an Ace!

ALL: He's drawn an Ace!
      He's drawn an Ace!
  Sing Clubs and Diamonds, Spades and Hearts!

ALL [*dancing*]:   He's drawn an Ace!
      Observe his face –
  Such very good fortune falls to few –
  Sing Clubs and Diamonds, Spades and Hearts –
  Sing Clubs, Spades, Hearts and Diamonds too!

NOT.: That both these maids may keep their troth,
   And never misfortune them befall,
  I'll hold 'em as trustee for both –

ALL: He'll hold 'em both!
      He'll hold 'em both!
  Sing Hearts, Clubs, Diamonds, Spades and all!

[*Dancing*]:   By joint decree
     As $\left\{ \begin{array}{c} \text{our} \\ \text{your} \end{array} \right\}$ trustee
  This Notary $\left\{ \begin{array}{c} \text{we} \\ \text{you} \end{array} \right\}$ will now instal –

In custody let him keep $\left\{ \begin{array}{l} \text{their} \\ \text{our} \end{array} \right\}$ hearts,

Sing Hearts, Clubs, Diamonds, Spades and all!

[*Dance and exeunt* LUDWIG, ERNEST *and*
NOTARY *with the two Girls.*]
[*March. Enter the seven Chamberlains of the* GRAND DUKE
RUDOLPH.]

CHORUS OF CHAMBERLAINS:

The good Grand Duke of Pfenning Halbpfennig,
Though, in his own opinion, very very big,
In point of fact he's nothing but a miserable prig
Is the good Grand Duke of Pfennig Halbpfennig!

Though quite contemptible, as every one agrees,
We must dissemble if we want our bread and cheese,
So hail him in a chorus, with enthusiasm big,
The good Grand Duke of Pfennig Halbpfennig!

[*Enter the* GRAND DUKE RUDOLPH. *He is meanly and miserably
dressed in old and patched clothes, but blazes with a profusion
of orders and decorations. He is very weak and ill, from low
living.*]

SONG

RUD.:   A pattern to professors of monarchical autonomy,
I don't indulge in levity or compromising *bonhomie*,
But dignified formality, consistent with economy,
Above all other virtues I particularly prize.
I never join in merriment – I don't see joke or jape any –
I never tolerate familiarity in shape any –
This, joined with an extravagant respect for
tuppence-ha'penny,
A keynote to my character sufficiently supplies.
[*Speaking*]
Observe. [*To Chamberlains*] My snuff-box!

[The snuff-box is passed with much ceremony from the Junior Chamberlain, through all the others, until it is presented by the Senior Chamberlain to RUDOLPH, *who uses it.]*

That incident a keynote to my character supplies.

I weigh out tea and sugar with precision mathematical –
Instead of beer, a penny each – my orders are emphatical –
(Extravagance unpardonable, any more than that I call),
    But, on the other hand, my Ducal dignity to keep –
All Courtly ceremonial – to put it comprehensively –
I rigidly insist upon (but not, I hope, offensively)
Whenever ceremonial can be practised inexpensively –
    And, when you come to think of it, it's really very cheap!
[Speaking]
    Observe. *[To Chamberlains]* My handkerchief!
[Handkerchief is handed by Junior Chamberlain to the next in order, and so on until it reaches RUDOLPH, *who is much inconvenienced by the delay.]*

It's sometimes inconvenient, but it's always very cheap!

My Lord Chamberlain, as you are aware, my marriage with the wealthy Baroness von Krakenfeldt will take place to-morrow, and you will be good enough to see that the rejoicings are on a scale of unusual liberality. Pass that on. *[Chamberlain whispers to Vice-Chamberlain, who whispers to the next, and so on.]* The sports will begin with a Wedding Breakfast Bee. The leading pastry-cooks of the town will be invited to compete, and the winner will not only enjoy the satisfaction of seeing his breakfast devoured by the Grand Ducal pair, but he will also be entitled to have the Arms of Pfennig Halbpfennig tattoo'd between his shoulder-blades. The Vice-Chamberlain will see to this. All the public fountains of Speisesaal[20] will run with Gingerbierheim and Currantweinmilch at the public expense. The Assistant Vice-Chamberlain will see to this. At night, everybody will illuminate; and as I have no desire to tax the public funds unduly, this will be done at the inhabitants' private expense.

The Deputy Assistant Vice-Chamberlain will see to this. All my Grand Ducal subjects will wear new clothes, and the Sub-Deputy Assistant Vice-Chamberlain will collect the usual commission on all sales. Wedding presents (which, on this occasion, should be on a scale of extraordinary magnificence) will be received at the Palace at any hour of the twenty-four, and the Temporary Sub-Deputy Assistant Vice-Chamberlain will sit up all night for this purpose. The entire population will be commanded to enjoy themselves, and with this view the Acting Temporary Sub-Deputy Assistant Vice-Chamberlain will sing comic songs in the Market-place from noon to nightfall. Finally, we have composed a Wedding Anthem, with which the entire population are required to provide themselves. It can be obtained from our Grand Ducal publishers at the usual discount price, and all the Chamberlains will be expected to push the sale.   [*Chamberlains bow and exeunt.*]

I don't feel at all comfortable. I hope I'm not doing a foolish thing in getting married. After all, it's a poor heart that never rejoices, and this wedding of mine is the first little treat I've allowed myself since my christening. Besides, Caroline's income is very considerable, and as her ideas of economy are quite on a par with mine, it ought to turn out well. Bless her tough old heart, she's a mean little darling! Oh, here she is, punctual to her appointment!

[*Enter* BARONESS VON KRAKENFELDT.]

BAR.: Rudolph! Why, what's the matter?

RUD.: Why, I'm not quite myself, my pet. I'm a little worried and upset. I want a tonic. It's the low diet, I think. I am afraid, after all, I shall have to take the bull by the horns and have an egg with my breakfast.

BAR.: I shouldn't do anything rash, dear. Begin with a jujube.[21] [*Gives him one.*]

RUD. [*about to eat it, but changes his mind*]: I'll keep it for supper. [*He sits by her and tries to put his arm round her waist.*]

BAR.: Rudolph, don't! What in the world are you thinking of?

RUD.: I was thinking of embracing you, my sugar-plum. Just as a little cheap treat.

BAR.: What, here? In public? Really, you appear to have no sense of delicacy.

RUD.: No sense of delicacy, Bon-bon!

BAR.: No. I can't make you out. When you courted me, all your courting was done publicly in the Market-place. When you proposed to me, you proposed in the Market-place. And now that we're engaged you seem to desire that our first *tête-à-tête* shall occur in the Market-place! Surely you've a room in your Palace – with blinds – that would do?

RUD.: But, my own, I can't help myself. I'm bound by my own decree.

BAR.: Your own decree?

RUD.: Yes. You see, all the houses that give on the Market-place belong to me, but the drains (which date back to the reign of Charlemagne[22]) want attending to, and the houses wouldn't let – so, with a view to increasing the value of the property, I decreed that all love-episodes between affectionate couples should take place, in public, on this spot, every Monday, Wednesday and Friday, when the band doesn't play.

BAR.: Bless me, what a happy idea! So moral too! And have you found it answer?

RUD.: Answer? The rents have gone up fifty per cent, and the sale of opera-glasses (which is a Grand Ducal monopoly) has received an extraordinary stimulus! So, under the circumstances, *would* you allow me to put my arm round your waist? As a source of income. Just once!

BAR.: But it's so very embarrassing. Think of the opera-glasses!

RUD.: My good girl, that's just what I *am* thinking of. Hang it all, we must give them *something* for their money! What's that?

BAR. [*unfolding paper, which contains a large letter, which she hands to him*]: It's a letter which your detective asked me to hand to you. I wrapped it up in yesterday's paper to keep it clean.

RUD.: Oh, it's only his report! That'll keep. But, I say, you've never been and bought a newspaper?

BAR.: My dear Rudolph, do you think I'm mad? It came wrapped round my breakfast.

RUD. [*relieved*]: I thought you were not the sort of girl to go and buy a newspaper! Well, as we've got it, we may as well read it. What does it say?

BAR.: Why – dear me – here's your biography! 'Our Detested Despot!'

RUD.: Yes – I fancy that refers to me.

BAR.: And it says – Oh, it can't be!

RUD.: What can't be?

BAR.: Why, it says that although you're going to marry me to-morrow, you were betrothed in infancy to the Princess of Monte Carlo!

RUD.: Oh yes – that's quite right. Didn't I mention it?

BAR.: Mention it! You never said a word about it!

RUD.: Well, it doesn't matter, because, you see, it's practically off.

BAR.: Practically off?

RUD.: Yes. By the terms of the contract the betrothal is void unless the Princess marries before she is of age. Now, her father, the Prince, is stony-broke, and hasn't left his house for years for fear of arrest. Over and over again he has implored me to come to him to be married – but in vain. Over and over again he has implored me to advance him the money to enable the Princess to come to me – but in vain. I am very young, but not as young as that; and as the Princess comes of age at two to-morrow, why at two to-morrow I'm a free man, so I appointed that hour for our wedding, as I shall like to have as much marriage as I can get for my money.

BAR.: I see. Of course, if the married state is a happy state, it's a pity to waste any of it.

RUD.: Why, every hour we delayed I should lose a lot of you and you'd lose a lot of me!

BAR.: My thoughtful darling! Oh, Rudolph, we ought to be very happy!

RUD.: If I'm not, it'll be my first bad investment. Still, there *is* such a thing as a slump even in Matrimonials.

BAR.: I often picture us in the long, cold, dark December evenings, sitting close to each other and singing impassioned duets to keep us warm, and thinking of all the lovely things we could afford to buy if we chose, and, at the same time, planning out our lives in a spirit of the most rigid and exacting economy!

RUD.: It's a most beautiful and touching picture of connubial bliss in its highest and most rarefied development!

DUET – BARONESS *and* RUDOLPH

BAR.: As o'er our penny roll we sing,
It is not reprehensive
To think what joys our wealth would bring
Were we disposed to do the thing
Upon a scale extensive.
There's rich mock-turtle – thick and clear –

RUD. [*confidentially*]:
Perhaps we'll have it once a year!

BAR. [*delighted*]:
You *are* an open-handed dear!

RUD.: Though, mind you, it's expensive.

BAR.: No doubt it *is* expensive.

BOTH: How fleeting are the glutton's joys!
With fish and fowl he lightly toys,

RUD.: And pays for such expensive tricks
Sometimes as much as two-and-six!

BAR.: As two-and-six?

RUD.: As two-and-six –

BOTH: Sometimes as much as two-and-six!

BAR.: It gives him no advantage, mind –
For you and he have only dined,
And you remain when once it's down
A better man by half-a-crown.

RUD.: By half-a-crown?

BAR.: By half-a-crown.

BOTH: Yes, two-and-six is half-a-crown.
Then let us be modestly merry,
And rejoice with a derry down derry.
For to laugh and to sing
No extravagance bring –
It's a joy economical, very!

BAR.:   Although as you're of course aware
(I never tried to hide it)
I moisten my insipid fare
With water – which I can't abear –

RUD.:   Nor I – I can't abide it.

BAR.:   This pleasing fact our souls will cheer,
With fifty thousand pounds a year
We *could* indulge in table beer!

RUD.:   Get out!

BAR.:   We could – I've tried it!

RUD.:   Yes, yes, of course you've tried it!

BOTH: Oh, he who has an income clear
Of fifty thousand pounds a year –

BAR.:   Can purchase all his fancy loves
Conspicuous hats –

RUD.:   Two-shilling gloves –

BAR. [*doubtfully*]:
                      Two-shilling gloves?

RUD. [*positively*]:
                      Two-shilling gloves –

BOTH: Yes, think of that, two-shilling gloves!

BAR.:   Cheap shoes and ties of gaudy hue,
And Waterbury watches, too –
And think that he could buy the lot
Were he a donkey –

RUD.:   Which he's *not*!

BAR.:   Oh no, he's *not*!

RUD.:   Oh no, he's *not*!

BOTH [*dancing*]:
           That kind of donkey he is *not*!
             Then let us be modestly merry,
             And rejoice with a derry down derry.

For to laugh and to sing
Is a rational thing –
It's a joy economical, very!

[*Exit* BARONESS.]

RUD.: Oh, now for my detective's report. [*Opens letter.*] What's this!
Another conspiracy! A conspiracy to depose *me*! And my private
detective was so convulsed with laughter at the notion of a conspirator selecting him for a confidant that he was physically unable to
arrest the malefactor! Why, it'll come off! This comes of engaging
a detective with a keen sense of the ridiculous! For the future I'll
employ none but Scotchmen. And the plot is to explode to-morrow!
My wedding day! Oh, Caroline, Caroline! [*Weeps.*] This is perfectly
frightful! What's to be done? I don't know! I ought to keep cool
and think, but you *can't* think when your veins are full of hot
soda-water, and your brain's fizzing like a firework, and all your
faculties are jumbled in a perfect whirlpool of tumblication! And
I'm going to be ill! I know I am! I've been living too low, and I'm
going to be very ill indeed!

SONG

RUD.:   When you find you're a broken-down critter,
          Who is all of a trimmle and twitter,
          With your palate unpleasantly bitter,
              As if you'd just eaten a pill –
          When your legs are as thin as dividers,
          And you're plagued with unruly insiders,
          And your spine is all creepy with spiders,
              And you're highly gamboge in the gill –
          When you've got a beehive in your head,
              And a sewing machine in each ear,
          And you feel that you've eaten your bed,
              And you've got a bad headache *down here* –
                  When such facts are about,
                      And these symptoms you find
                          In your body or crown –

> Well, you'd better look out,
>   You may make up your mind
>   You had better lie down!
>
> When your lips are all smeary – like tallow,
> And your tongue is decidedly yallow,
> With a pint of warm oil in your swallow,
>   And a pound of tin-tacks in your chest –
> When you're down in the mouth with the vapours,
> And all over your Morris wall-papers[23]
> Black-beetles are cutting their capers,
>   And crawly things never at rest –
> When you doubt if your head is your own,
>   And you jump when an open door slams –
> Then you've got to a state which is known
>   To the medical world as 'jim-jams'.
>   If such symptoms you find
>   In your body or head,
>   They're not easy to quell –
>   You may make up your mind
>   You are better in bed,
>   For you're not at all well!

[*Sinks exhausted and weeping at foot of well.*]
[*Enter* LUDWIG.]

LUD.: Now for my confession and full pardon. They told me the
Grand Duke was dancing duets in the Market-place, but I don't see
him. [*Sees* RUDOLPH.] Hallo! Who's this? [*Aside*] Why, it *is* the
Grand Duke!

RUD. [*sobbing*]: Who are you, sir, who presume to address me in
person? If you've anything to communicate, you must fling yourself
at the feet of my Acting Temporary Sub-Deputy Assistant Vice-
Chamberlain, who will fling himself at the feet of his immediate
superior, and so on, with successive foot-flingings through the
various grades – your communication will, in course of time, come
to my august knowledge.

LUD.: But when I inform your Highness that in me you see the most unhappy, the most unfortunate, the most completely miserable man in your whole dominion –

RUD. [*still sobbing*]: *You* the most miserable man in my whole dominion? How can you have the face to stand there and say such a thing? Why, look at me! Look at me! [*Bursts into tears.*]

LUD.: Well, I wouldn't be a cry-baby.

RUD.: A cry-baby? If you had just been told that you were going to be deposed to-morrow, and perhaps blown up with dynamite for all I know, wouldn't *you* be a cry-baby? I do declare if I could only hit upon some cheap and painless method of putting an end to an existence which has become insupportable, I would unhesitatingly adopt it!

LUD.: You would? [*Aside*] I see a magnificent way out of this! By Jupiter, I'll try it! [*Aloud*] Are you, by any chance, in earnest?

RUD.: In earnest? Why, look at me!

LUD.: If you are really in earnest – if you really desire to escape scot-free from this impending – this unspeakably horrible catastrophe – without trouble, danger, pain or expense – why not resort to a Statutory Duel?

RUD.: A Statutory Duel?

LUD.: Yes. The Act is still in force, but it will expire to-morrow afternoon. You fight – you lose – you are dead for a day. To-morrow, when the Act expires, you will come to life again and resume your Grand Duchy as though nothing had happened. In the meantime, the explosion will have taken place and the survivor will have had to bear the brunt of it.

RUD.: Yes, that's all very well, but who'll be fool enough to *be* the survivor?

LUD. [*kneeling*]: Actuated by an overwhelming sense of attachment to your Grand Ducal person, I unhesitatingly offer myself as the victim of your subjects' fury.

RUD.: You do? Well, really that's very handsome. I daresay being blown up is not nearly as unpleasant as one would think.

LUD.: Oh, yes it is. It mixes one up, awfully!

RUD.: But suppose I were to lose?

LUD.: Oh, that's easily arranged. [*Producing cards.*] I'll put an Ace up my sleeve – you'll put a King up yours. When the drawing takes place, I shall seem to draw the higher card and you the lower. And there you are!

RUD.: Oh, but that's cheating.

LUD.: So it is. I never thought of that. [*Going.*]

RUD. [*hastily*]: Not that I mind. But I say – you won't take an unfair advantage of your day of office? You won't go tipping people, or squandering my little savings in fireworks, or any nonsense of that sort?

LUD.: I am hurt – really hurt – by the suggestion.

RUD.: You – you wouldn't like to put down a deposit, perhaps?

LUD.: No. I don't think I should like to put down a deposit.

RUD.: Or give a guarantee?

LUD.: A guarantee would be equally open to objection.

RUD.: It would be more regular. Very well, I suppose you must have your own way.

LUD.: Good. I say – we must have a devil of a quarrel!

RUD.: Oh, a devil of a quarrel!

LUD.: Just to give colour to the thing. Shall I give you a sound thrashing before all the people? Say the word – it's no trouble.

RUD.: No, I think not, though it would be very convincing and it's extremely good and thoughtful of you to suggest it. Still, a devil of a quarrel!

LUD.: Oh, a devil of a quarrel!

RUD.: No half measures. Big words – strong language – rude remarks. Oh, a devil of a quarrel!

LUD.: Now the question is, how shall we summon the people?

RUD.: Oh, there's no difficulty about that. Bless your heart, they've been staring at us through those windows for the last half-hour!

FINALE

RUD.:   Come hither, all you people –
        When you hear the fearful news,
    All the pretty women weep'll,
        Men will shiver in their shoes.

LUD.: And they'll all cry 'Lord, defend us!'
When they learn the fact tremendous
   That to give this man his gruel
   In a Statutory Duel –

BOTH: This plebeian man of shoddy –
This contemptible nobody –
   Your Grand Duke does not refuse!
[*During this, Chorus of men and women have entered, all trembling with apprehension under the impression that they are to be arrested for their complicity in the conspiracy.*]

CHORUS: With faltering feet,
            And our muscles in a quiver,
      Our fate we meet
            With our feelings all unstrung!
      If our plot complete
            He has managed to diskiver,
      There is no retreat –
            We shall certainly be hung!

RUD. [*aside to* LUDWIG]:
      Now *you* begin and pitch it strong – walk into me
         abusively –
LUD. [*aside to* RUDOLPH]:
      I've several epithets that I've reserved for you exclusively.
      A choice selection I have here when you are ready *to*
         begin.

RUD.: Now *you* begin –
LUD.:   No, *you* begin –
RUD.:   No, *you* begin –
LUD.:   No, *you* begin!
CHORUS [*trembling*]:
      Has it happed as we expected?
      Is our little plot detected?

DUET – RUDOLPH *and* LUDWIG

RUD. [*furiously*]:

> Big bombs, small bombs, great guns and little ones!
>> Put him in a pillory!
>> Rack him with artillery!

LUD. [*furiously*]:

> Long swords, short swords, tough swords and brittle
> ones!
>> Fright him into fits!
>> Blow him into bits!

RUD.:	You muff, sir!
LUD.:	You lout, sir!
RUD.:	Enough, sir!
LUD.:	Get out, sir! [*Pushes him.*]
RUD.:	A hit, sir?
LUD.:	Take that, sir! [*Slaps him.*]
RUD.:	It's tit, sir,
LUD.:	For tat, sir!

CHORUS [*appalled*]:

> When two doughty heroes thunder,
> All the world is lost in wonder;
>> When such men their temper lose,
>> Awful are the words they use!

LUD.: Tall snobs, small snobs, rich snobs and needy ones!

RUD. [*jostling him*]:

> Whom are you alluding to?

LUD. [*jostling him.*]:

> Where are you intruding to?

RUD.: Fat snobs, thin snobs, swell snobs and seedy ones!

LUD.: I rather think you err.

> To whom do you refer?

RUD.:   To you, sir!
LUD.:   To me, sir?
RUD.:   I do, sir!
LUD.:   We'll see, sir!
RUD.:   I jeer, sir!
   [*Makes a face at* LUDWIG]   Grimace, sir!
LUD.:   Look here, sir –
   [*Makes a face at* RUDOLPH] A face, sir!

CHORUS [*appalled*]:
            When two heroes, once pacific,
            Quarrel, the effect's terrific!
               What a horrible grimace!
               What a paralysing face!

ALL: Big bombs, small bombs, etc.

LUD. *and* RUD. [*recitative*]:
            He has insulted me, and, in a breath,
            This day we fight a duel to the death!
NOT. [*checking them*]:
            You mean, of course, by duel (*verbum sat.*[24]),
            A Statutory Duel.
ALL: Why, what's that?
NOT.:   According to established legal uses,
            A card apiece each bold disputant chooses –
            Dead as a doornail is the dog who loses –
            The winner steps into the dead man's shoeses!

ALL: The winner steps into the dead man's shoeses!

RUD. *and* LUD.:
            Agreed! Agreed!
RUD.:   Come, come – the pack!
LUD. [*producing one*]:   Behold it here!
RUD.:   I'm on the rack!

LUD.: I quake with fear!

[NOTARY *offers card to* LUDWIG.]

LUD.: First draw to you!

RUD.: If that's the case,
Behold the King! [*Drawing card from his sleeve.*]

LUD. [*same business*]: Behold the Ace!

CHORUS: Hurrah, hurrah! Our Ludwig's won.
And wicked Rudolph's course is run –
So Ludwig will as Grand Duke reign
Till Rudolph comes to life again –

RUD.: Which will occur to-morrow!
I come to life to-morrow!

GRET. [*with mocking curtsey*]:
My Lord Grand Duke, farewell!
A pleasant journey, very,
To your convenient cell
In yonder cemetery!

LISA [*curtseying*]:
Though malcontents abuse you,
We're much distressed to lose you!
You were, when you were living,
So liberal, so forgiving!

BERTHA: So merciful, so gentle!
So highly ornamental!

OLGA: And now that you've departed,
You leave us broken-hearted!

ALL [*pretending to weep*]:
Yes, truly, truly, truly, truly –
Truly broken-hearted!
Ha! ha! ha! ha! ha! ha! [*Mocking him.*]

RUD. [*furious*]:
Rapscallions,[25] in penitential fires,
You'll rue the ribaldry that from you falls!

> To-morrow afternoon the law expires.
> And then – look out for squalls!
> > [*Exit* RUDOLPH, *amid general ridicule.*]

CHORUS: Give thanks, give thanks to wayward fate –
> By mystic fortune's sway,
> Our Ludwig guides the helm of State
> For one delightful day!

[*To* LUDWIG] We hail you, sir!
> We greet you, sir!
> Regale you, sir!
> We treat you, sir!
> Our ruler be
> By fate's decree
> For one delightful day!

NOT.: You've done it neatly! Pity that your powers
> Are limited to four-and-twenty hours!

LUD.: No matter, though the time will quickly run,
> In hours twenty-four much may be done!

SONG

LUD.: Oh, a Monarch who boasts intellectual graces
> Can do, if he likes, a good deal in a day –
> He can put all his friends in conspicuous places,
> With plenty to eat and with nothing to pay!
> You'll tell me, no doubt, with unpleasant grimaces,
> To-morrow, deprived of your ribbons and laces,
> You'll get your dismissal – with very long faces –
> But wait! on that topic I've something to say!
> > [*Dancing*]:
> I've something to say – I've something to say – I've
> something to say!
> Oh, our rule shall be merry – I'm not an ascetic –
> And while the sun shines we will get up our hay –

> By a pushing young Monarch, of turn energetic,
> A very great deal may be done in a day!

CHORUS: Oh, his rule will be merry, etc.
> [*During this,* LUDWIG *whispers to* NOTARY, *who writes.*]
> For instance, this measure (his ancestor drew it),
> [*alluding to* NOTARY]
>> This law against duels – to-morrow will die –
>> The Duke will revive, and you'll certainly rue it –
>>> He'll give you 'what for' and he'll let you know
>>> why!
>> But in twenty-four hours there's time to renew it –
>> With a century's life I've the right to imbue it –
>> It's easy to do – and, by Jingo,[26] I'll do it!
> [*Signing paper, which* NOTARY *presents.*]

>> It's done! Till I perish your Monarch am I!
>> Your Monarch am I – your Monarch am I – your
>> Monarch am I!
>>> Though I do not pretend to be very prophetic,
>>> I fancy I know what you're going to say –
>>> By a pushing young Monarch, of turn energetic,
>>> A very great deal may be done in a day!

ALL [*astonished*]:
>> Oh, it's simply uncanny, his power prophetic –
>> It's perfectly right – we *were* going to say,
>> By a pushing, etc.
> [*Enter* JULIA, *at back.*]

LUD. [*recitative*]:
>> This very afternoon – at two (about) –
>> The Court appointments will be given out.
>> To each and all (for that was the condition)
>> According to professional position!

ALL: Hurrah!

JULIA [*coming forward*]:
>> According to professional position?

LUD.:   According to professional position!

JULIA: Then, horror!

ALL: Why, what's the matter? What's the matter?
         What's the matter?

SONG

JULIA [LISA *clinging to her*]:
         Ah, pity me, my comrades true,
         Who love, as well I know you do,
             This gentle child,
                 To me so fondly dear!

ALL: Why, what's the matter?

JULIA: Our sister love so true and deep
         From many an eye unused to weep
             Hath oft beguiled
                 The coy reluctant tear!

ALL: Why, what's the matter?

JULIA: Each sympathetic heart 'twill bruise
         When you have heard the frightful news
             (O will it not?)
                 That I must now impart!

ALL: Why, what's the matter?

JULIA: Her love for him is all in all!
         Ah, cursed fate! that it should fall
             Unto *my* lot
                 To break my darling's heart!

ALL: Why, what's the matter?

LUD.: What means our Julia by those fateful looks?
Please do not keep us all on tenter-hooks –
Now, what's the matter?

JULIA: Our duty, if we're wise,
We never shun.
This Spartan rule applies
To every one.
In theatres, as in life,
Each has her line –
This part – the Grand Duke's wife
(Oh agony!) is mine!
A maxim new I do not start –
The canons of dramatic art
Decree that this repulsive part
(The Grand Duke's wife)
Is mine!

ALL: Oh, *that's* the matter!

LISA [*appalled, to* LUDWIG]:
Can that be so?

LUD.: I do not know –
But time will show
If that be so.

CHORUS: Can that be so? etc.

LISA [*recitative*]:

Be merciful!

DUET – LISA *and* JULIA

LISA: Oh, listen to me, dear –
          I love him only, darling!
            Remember, oh, my pet,
            On him my heart is set!
      This kindness do me, dear –
          Nor leave me lonely, darling!
            Be merciful, my pet,
            Our love do not forget!

JULIA: Now don't be foolish, dear –
          You couldn't play it, darling!
            It's 'leading business', pet.
            And you're but a soubrette.[27]
      So don't be mulish, dear –
          Although I say it, darling,
            It's not your line, my pet –
            I play that part, you bet!
            I play that part –
            I play that part, you bet!
  [LISA *overwhelmed with grief.*]

NOT.:   The lady's right. Though Julia's engagement
                Was for the stage meant –
      It certainly frees Ludwig from his
                Connubial promise.
      Though marriage contracts – or whate'er you call
      'em –
                Are very solemn,
      Dramatic contracts (which you all adore so)
                Are even more so!

ALL: That's very true!
      Though marriage contracts, etc.

SONG

LISA:
>The die is cast,
>My hope has perished!
>Farewell, O Past,
>Too bright to last,
>Yet fondly cherished!
>My light has fled,
>My hope is dead,
>Its doom is spoken –
>My day is night,
>My wrong is right
>In all men's sight –
>My heart is broken!

>[*Exit weeping.*]

LUD. [*recitative*]:
>Poor child, where will she go? What will she do?

JULIA:
>*That* isn't in your part, you know.

LUD. [*sighing*]:   Quite true!

[*With an effort*]

>Depressing topics we'll not touch upon –
>Let us begin as we are going on!
>For this will be a jolly Court, for little and for big!

ALL:
>Sing hey, the jolly jinks of Pfennig Halbpfennig!

LUD.:
>From morn to night our lives shall be as merry as a
>grig![28]

ALL:
>Sing hey, the jolly jinks of Pfennig Halbpfennig!

LUD.:
>All state and ceremony we'll eternally abolish –
>We don't mean to insist upon unnecessary polish –
>And, on the whole, I rather think you'll find our rule
>tollolish![29]

ALL:
>Sing hey, the jolly jinks of Pfennig Halbpfennig!

JULIA: But stay – your new-made Court
   Without a courtly coat is –
    We shall require
    Some Court attire,
   And at a moment's notice.
  In clothes of common sort
   Your courtiers must not grovel –
    Your new *noblesse*
    Must have a dress
   Original and novel!

LUD.: Old Athens we'll exhume!
   The necessary dresses,
    Correct and true
    And all brand-new,
   The company possesses:
  Henceforth our Court costume
   Shall live in song and story,
    For we'll upraise
    The dead old days
   Of Athens in her glory!

ALL: Yes, let's upraise
    The dead old days
   Of Athens in her glory!

ALL: Agreed! Agreed!
  For this will be a jolly Court for little and for big! etc.
[*They carry* LUDWIG *round stage and deposit him on the iron-work of well.* JULIA *stands by him, and the rest group round them.*]

END OF ACT I

ACT II

[*The next morning*]

SCENE – *Entrance Hall of the Grand Ducal Palace.*

[*Enter a procession of the members of the theatrical company* (*now dressed in the costumes of* Troilus and Cressida), *carrying garlands, playing on pipes, citharae*[30] *and cymbals, and heralding the return of* LUDWIG *and* JULIA *from the marriage ceremony, which has just taken place.*]

CHORUS: As before you we defile,
                    Eloia! Eloia!
       Pray you, gentles, do not smile
       If we shout, in classic style,
                    Eloia!
       Ludwig and his Julia true
       Wedded are each other to –
       So we sing, till all is blue,
                    Eloia! Eloia!
                    Opoponax! Eloia!

       Wreaths of bay and ivy twine,
                    Eloia! Eloia!
       Fill the bowl with Lesbian wine,[31]
       And to revelry incline –
                    Eloia!

For as gaily we pass on
Probably we shall, anon,
Sing a Diergeticon –
        Eloia! Eloia!
        Opoponax! Eloia!

RECITATIVE

LUD.:   Your loyalty our Ducal heartstrings touches:
           Allow me to present your new Grand Duchess.
           Should she offend, you'll graciously excuse her –
           And kindly recollect *I* didn't choose her!

SONG

LUD.: At the outset I may mention it's my sovereign intention
    To revive the classic memories of Athens at its best,
For the company possesses all the necessary dresses
    And a course of quiet cramming will supply us with the
        rest.
We've a choir hyporchematic[32] (that is, ballet-operatic)
    Who respond to the *choreutae*[33] of that cultivated age,
And our clever chorus-master, all but captious
        criticaster[34]
    Would accept as the *choregus*[35] of the early Attic stage.
This return to classic ages is considered in their wages,
    Which are always calculated by the day or by the week –
And I'll pay 'em (if they'll back me) all in *oboloi*[36] and
    drachmae,
Which they'll get (if they prefer it) at the Kalends[37] that are
    Greek!
[*Confidentially to audience*]
    At this juncture I may mention
      That this erudition sham
    Is but classical pretension,
      The result of steady 'cram.':
    Periphrastic[38] methods spurning,

> To this audience discerning
> I admit this show of learning
>   Is the fruit of steady 'cram.'!

CHORUS: Periphrastic methods, etc.

LUD.: In the period Socratic[39] every dining-room was Attic
      (Which suggests an architecture of a topsy-turvy kind),
    There they'd satisfy their thirst on a *recherché* cold
        ἄριστον,[40]
      Which is what they called their lunch – and so may you, if
        you're inclined.
    As they gradually got on, they'd τρέπεσθαι πρὸς τὸν
      πότον[41] (Which is Attic for a steady and a conscientious
      drink).
    But they mixed their wine with water – which I'm sure they
        didn't oughter –
      And we modern Saxons know a trick worth two of that, I
        think!
    Then came rather risky dances (under certain circumstances)
      Which would shock that worthy gentleman, the Licenser
        of Plays,
    Corybantian[42] mani*ac* kick – Dionysiac[43] or Bacchic[44] –
    And the Dithyrambic[45] revels of those undecorous days.
  [*Confidentially to audience*]
>   And perhaps I'd better mention,
>   Lest alarming you I am,
>   That it isn't our intention
>   To perform a Dithyramb –
>   It displays a lot of stocking,
>   Which is always very shocking,
>   And of course I'm only mocking
>   At the prevalence of 'cram.'!

CHORUS: It displays a lot, etc.

LUD.: Yes, on reconsideration, there are customs of that nation
　　　Which are not in strict accordance with the habits of our
　　　　　day,
　　And when I come to codify, their rules I mean to modify,
　　　Or Mrs Grundy,[46] p'r'aps, may have a word or two to
　　　　　say.
　　For they hadn't macintoshes or umbrellas or goloshes –
　　　And a shower with their dresses must have played the
　　　　　very deuce,
　　And it must have been unpleasing when they caught a fit of
　　　　sneezing,
　　　For, it seems, of pocket-handkerchiefs they didn't know
　　　　　the use.
　　They wore little underclothing – scarcely anything – or
　　　　nothing –
　　　And their dress of Coan silk[47] was quite transparent in
　　　　　design –
　　Well, in fact, in summer weather, something like the
　　　　'altogether'.
　　　And it's *there*, I rather fancy, I shall have to draw the line!
[*Confidentially to audience*]
　　　　　　　And again I wish to mention
　　　　　　　　That this erudition sham
　　　　　　　Is but classical pretension,
　　　　　　　　The result of steady 'cram.'
　　　　　　　Yet my classic lore aggressive
　　　　　　　(If you'll pardon the possessive)
　　　　　　　Is exceedingly impressive
　　　　　　　　When you're passing an exam.

CHORUS:　　　　　　Yet his classic lore, etc.
　　　　　　[*Exeunt Chorus. Manent* LUDWIG, JULIA *and* LISA.]

LUD. [*recitative*]:
　　　　　Yes, Ludwig and his Julia are mated!
　　　　　For when an obscure comedian, whom the law backs,

To sovereign rank is promptly elevated,
He takes it with its incidental drawbacks!
So Julia and I are duly mated!
[LISA, *through this, has expressed intense distress at having to
surrender* LUDWIG.]

SONG

LISA: Take care of him – he's much too good to live,
        With him you must be very gentle:
  Poor fellow, he's so highly sensitive,
        And O, so sentimental!
  Be sure you never let him sit up late
        In chilly open air conversing –
  Poor darling, he's extremely delicate,
        And wants a deal of nursing!

LUD.:   I want a deal of nursing!

LISA: And O, remember this –
        When he is cross with pain,
        A flower and a kiss –
        A simple flower – a tender kiss
        Will bring him round again!

  His moods you must assiduously watch:
        When he succumbs to sorrow tragic,
  Some hardbake[48] or a bit of butter-scotch
        Will work on him like magic.
  To contradict a character so rich
        In trusting love were simple blindness –
  He's one of those exalted natures which
        Will only yield to kindness!

LUD.:   I only yield to kindness!

LISA: And O, the bygone bliss!
          And O, the present pain!
      That flower and that kiss –
      That simple flower – that tender kiss
      I ne'er shall give again!

                                     [Exit, weeping.]

JULIA: And now that everybody has gone, and we're happily and comfortably married, I want to have a few words with my new-born husband.

LUD. [*aside*]: Yes, I expect you'll often have a few words with your new-born husband! [*Aloud*] Well, what is it?

JULIA: Why, I've been thinking that as you and I have to play our parts for life, it is most essential that we should come to a definite understanding as to how they shall be rendered. Now, I've been considering how I can make the most of the Grand Duchess.

LUD.: Have you? Well, if you'll take my advice, you'll make a very fine part of it.

JULIA: Why, that's quite *my* idea.

LUD.: I shouldn't make it one of your hoity-toity vixenish viragoes.[49]

JULIA: You think not?

LUD.: Oh, I'm quite clear about that. I should make her a tender, gentle, submissive, affectionate (but not too affectionate) child-wife – timidly anxious to coil herself into her husband's heart, but kept in check by an awestruck reverence for his exalted intellectual qualities and his majestic personal appearance.

JULIA: Oh, that is your idea of a good part?

LUD.: Yes – a wife who regards her husband's slightest wish as an inflexible law, and who ventures but rarely into his august presence, unless (which would happen seldom) he should summon her to appear before him. A crushed, despairing violet, whose blighted existence would culminate (all too soon) in a lonely and pathetic death-scene! A fine part, my dear.

JULIA: Yes. There's a good deal to be said for your view of it. Now there are some actresses whom it would fit like a glove.

LUD. [*aside*]: I wish I'd married one of 'em!

JULIA: But, you see, I *must* consider my temperament. For instance, my temperament would demand some strong scenes of justifiable jealousy.

LUD.: Oh, there's no difficulty about that. You shall have *them*.

JULIA: With a lovely but detested rival –

LUD.: Oh, *I'll* provide the rival.

JULIA: Whom I should stab – stab – stab!

LUD.: Oh, I wouldn't stab her. It's been done to death. I should treat her with a silent and contemptuous disdain, and delicately withdraw from a position which, to one of your sensitive nature, would be absolutely untenable. Dear me, I can see you delicately withdrawing, up centre and off!

JULIA: *Can* you?

LUD.: Yes. It's a fine situation – and in your hands, full of quiet pathos!

DUET – LUDWIG *and* JULIA

LUD.:   Now Julia, come,
Consider it from
      This dainty point of view –
A timid tender
Feminine gender,
      Prompt to coyly coo –
Yet silence seeking,
Seldom speaking
      Till she's spoken to –
A comfy, cosy,
Rosy-posy
      Innocent *ingenoo*!
        The part you're suited to –
        (To give the deuce her due)
      A sweet (O, jiminy!)
      Miminy-piminy,
        Innocent inge*noo*!

ENSEMBLE

LUDWIG	JULIA
The part you're suited to –	I'm much obliged to you,
(To give the deuce her due)	I don't think that would do –
A sweet (O, jiminy!)	To play (O, jiminy!)
Miminy-piminy,	Miminy-piminy,
Innocent inge*noo*!	Innocent inge*noo*!

JULIA: You forget my special magic
                    (In a high dramatic sense)
            Lies in situations tragic –
                    Undeniably intense.
            As I've justified promotion
                    In the histrionic art,
            I'll submit to you my notion
                    Of a first-rate part.

LUD.:   Well, let us see your notion
                    Of a first-rate part.

JULIA [*dramatically*]:
        I have a rival! Frenzy-thrilled,
            I find you both together!
        My heart stands still – with horror chilled –
            Hard as the millstone nether!
        Then softly, slyly, snaily, snaky –
        Crawly, creepy, quaily, quaky –
            I track her on her homeward way,
            As panther tracks her fated prey!
[*Furiously*]   I fly at her soft white throat –
            The lily-white laughing leman![50]
        On her agonized gaze I gloat
            With the glee of a dancing demon!
        My rival she – I have no doubt of her –
        So I hold on – till the breath is out of her!
               – till the breath is out of her!

And then – Remorse! Remorse!
O cold unpleasant corse,
            Avaunt! Avaunt!
        That lifeless form
            I gaze upon –
        That face, still warm
            But weirdly wan –
        Those eyes of glass
            I contemplate –
        And then, alas,
            Too late – too late!
        I find she is – your Aunt!

[*Shuddering*]

        Remorse! Remorse!
    Then, mad – mad – mad!
        With fancies wild – chimerical –
    Now sorrowful – silent – sad –
        Now hullaballoo hysterical!
            Ha! ha! ha! ha!
    But whether I'm sad or whether I'm glad,
        Mad! mad! mad! mad!

    This calls for the resources of a high-class art,
    And satisfies my notion of a first-rate part!   [*Exit.*]
[*Enter all the Chorus, hurriedly, and in great excitement.*]

CHORUS: Your Highness, there's a party at the door –
            Your Highness, at the door there is a party –
                She says that we expect her,
                But we do not recollect her,
            For we never saw her countenance before!

            With rage and indignation she is rife,
                Because our welcome wasn't very hearty –
                She's as sulky as a super,
                And she's swearing like a trooper,
            O, you never heard such language in your life!

[*Enter* BARONESS VON KRAKENFELDT, *in a fury.*]

BAR.:   With fury indescribable I burn!
      With rage I'm nearly ready to explode!
      There'll be grief and tribulation when I learn
        To whom this slight unbearable is owed!
          For whatever may be due I'll pay it double –
          There'll be terror indescribable and trouble!
        With a hurly-burly and a hubble-bubble
        I'll pay you for this pretty episode!

ALL: Oh, whatever may be due she'll pay it double –
      It's very good of her to take the trouble –
      But we don't know what she means by
        'hubble-bubble' –
      No doubt it's an expression *à la mode*.

BAR. [*to* LUDWIG]:
      Do you know who I am?
LUD. [*examining her*]:   I don't;
      Your countenance I can't fix, my dear.
BAR.:   This proves I'm not a sham.
    [*Showing pocket-handkerchief.*]
LUD. [*examining it*]:   It won't;
      It only says 'Krakenfeldt, Six', my dear.

BAR.:   Express your grief profound!
LUD.:   I shan't!
      This tone I never allow, my love.
BAR.:   Rudolph at once produce!
LUD.:   I can't;
      He isn't at home just now, my love.

BAR. [*astonished*]:
      He isn't at home just now!

ALL: He isn't at home just now,
    [*Dancing derisively.*]

He has an appointment particular, very –
You'll find him, I think, in the town cemetery;
And that's how we come to be making so merry,
For he isn't at home just now!

BAR.:   But bless my heart and soul alive, it's impudence
        personified!
    I've come here to be matrimonially matrimonified!

LUD.:   For any disappointment I am sorry unaffectedly,
    But yesterday that nobleman expired quite
        unexpectedly –

ALL [*sobbing*]:   Tol the riddle lol!
        Tol the riddle lol!
    Tol the riddle, lol the riddle, lol lol lay!
  [*Then laughing wildly*]
    Tol the riddle, lol the riddle, lol lol lay!

BAR.: But this is most unexpected. He was well enough at a quarter
to twelve yesterday.

LUD.: Yes. He died at half-past eleven.

BAR.: Bless me, how very sudden!

LUD.: It *was* sudden.

BAR.: But what in the world am I to do? I was to have been married
to him to-day!

ALL [*singing and dancing*]:
    For any disappointment we are sorry
        unaffectedly,
    But yesterday that nobleman expired quite
        unexpectedly –
        Tol the riddle lol!

BAR.: Is this Court Mourning or a Fancy Ball?

LUD.: Well, it's a delicate combination of both effects. It is intended
to express inconsolable grief for the decease of the late Duke and

ebullient joy at the accession of his successor. *I* am his successor. Permit me to present you to my Grand Duchess. [*Indicating* JULIA.]

BAR.: Your Grand Duchess? Oh, your Highness! [*Curtseying profoundly.*]

JULIA [*sneering at her*]: Old frump!

BAR.: Humph! A recent creation, probably?

LUD.: We were married only half an hour ago.

BAR.: Exactly. I thought she seemed new to the position.

JULIA: Ma'am, I don't know who you are, but I flatter myself I can do justice to *any* part on the very shortest notice.

BAR.: My dear, under the circumstances you are doing admirably – and you'll improve with practice. It's so difficult to be a lady when one isn't born to it.

JULIA [*in a rage, to* LUDWIG]: Am I to stand this? Am I not to be allowed to pull her to pieces?

LUD. [*aside to* JULIA]: No, no – it isn't Greek. Be a violet, I beg.

BAR.: And now tell me all about this distressing circumstance. How did the Grand Duke die?

LUD.: He perished nobly – in a Statutory Duel.

BAR.: In a Statutory Duel? But that's only a civil death! – and the Act expires to-night, and then he will come to life again!

LUD.: Well, no. Anxious to inaugurate my reign by conferring some inestimable boon on my people, I signalized this occasion by reviving the law for another hundred years.

BAR.: For another hundred years? Then set the merry joybells ringing! Let festive epithalamia[51] resound through these ancient halls! Cut the satisfying sandwich – broach the exhilarating Marsala[52] – and let us rejoice to-day, if we never rejoice again!

LUD.: But I don't think I quite understand. We have already rejoiced a good deal.

BAR.: Happy man, you little reck of the extent of the good things you are in for. When you killed Rudolph you adopted all his overwhelming responsibilities. Know then that I, Caroline von Krakenfeldt, am the most overwhelming of them all!

LUD.: But stop, stop – I've just been married to somebody else!

JULIA: Yes, ma'am, to somebody else, ma'am! Do you understand, ma'am? To somebody else!

BAR.: Do keep this young woman quiet; she fidgets me!

JULIA: Fidgets you!

LUD. [*aside to* JULIA]: Be a violet – a crushed, despairing violet.

JULIA: Do you suppose I intend to give up a magnificent part without a struggle?

LUD.: My good girl, she has the law on her side. Let us both bear this calamity with resignation. If you must struggle, go away and struggle in the seclusion of your chamber.

SONG

BAR.: Now away to the wedding we go,
    So summon the charioteers –
No kind of reluctance they show
    To embark on their married careers.
Though Julia's emotion may flow
    For the rest of her maidenly years,

CHORUS: To the wedding we eagerly go,
    So summon the charioteers!

Now away, etc.
[*All dance off to wedding except* JULIA.]

RECITATIVE

JULIA: So ends my dream – so fades my vision fair!
Of hope no gleam – distraction and despair!
My cherished dream, the Ducal throne to share,
That aim supreme has vanished into air!

SONG

JULIA: Broken every promise plighted –
    All is darksome – all is dreary.[53]
Every new-born hope is blighted!
    Sad and sorry – weak and weary!

Death the Friend or Death the Foe,
Shall I call upon thee? No!
I will go on living, though
    Sad and sorry – weak and weary!

No, no! Let the bygone go by!
    No good ever came of repining:
If to-day there are clouds o'er the sky,
    To-morrow the sun may be shining!
        To-morrow, be kind,
        To-morrow, to me!
        With loyalty blind
        I curtsey to thee!
To-day is a day of illusion and sorrow,
So *viva* To-morrow, To-morrow, To-morrow!
    God save you, To-morrow!
    Your servant, To-morrow!
God save you, To-morrow, To-morrow,
    To-morrow!   *[Exit.]*

[*Enter* ERNEST.]

ERN.: It's of no use – I can't wait any longer. At any risk I must gratify my urgent desire to know what is going on. [*Looking off.*] Why, what's that? Surely I see a wedding procession winding down the hill, dressed in my *Troilus and Cressida* costumes! That's Ludwig's doing! I see how it is – he found the time hang heavy on his hands, and is amusing himself by getting married to Lisa. No – it can't be to Lisa, for here she is!

[*Enter* LISA.]

LISA [*not seeing him*]: I really cannot stand seeing my Ludwig married twice in one day to somebody else!

ERN.: Lisa!

[LISA *sees him, and stands as if transfixed with horror.*]

ERN.: Come here – don't be a little fool – I want you.

[LISA *suddenly turns and bolts off.*]

ERN.: Why, what's the matter with the little donkey? One would think she saw a ghost! But if he's not marrying Lisa, whom *is* he marrying? [*Suddenly*] Julia! [*Much overcome.*] I see it all! The scoundrel! He had to adopt all my responsibilities, and he's shabbily taken advantage of the situation to marry the girl I'm engaged to! But no, it can't be Julia, for here *she* is!

[*Enter* JULIA.]

JULIA [*not seeing him*]: I've made up my mind. I won't stand it! I'll send in my notice at once!

ERN.: Julia! Oh, what a relief!

[JULIA *gazes at him as if transfixed.*]

ERN.: Then you've not married Ludwig? You are still true to me?

[JULIA *turns and bolts in grotesque horror.* ERNEST *follows and stops her.*]

ERN.: Don't run away! Listen to me. Are you all crazy?

JULIA [*in affected terror*]: What would you with me, spectre? Oh, ain't his eyes sepulchral! And ain't his voice hollow! What are you doing out of your tomb at this time of day – apparition?

ERN.: I do wish I could make you girls understand that I'm only technically dead, and that physically I'm as much alive as ever I was in my life!

JULIA: Oh, but it's an awful thing to be haunted by a technical bogy!

ERN.: You won't be haunted much longer. The law must be on its last legs, and in a few hours I shall come to life again – resume all my social and civil functions, and claim my darling as my blushing bride!

JULIA: Oh – then you haven't heard?

ERN.: My love, I've heard nothing. How could I? There are no daily papers where I come from.

JULIA: Why, Ludwig challenged Rudolph and won, and now *he's* Grand Duke, and he's revived the law for another century!

ERN.: What! But you're not serious – you're only joking!

JULIA: My good sir, I'm a light-hearted girl, but I don't chaff bogies.

ERN.: Well, that's the meanest dodge I ever heard of!

JULIA: Shabby trick, *I* call it.

ERN.: But you don't mean to say that you're going to cry off!

JULIA: I really can't afford to wait until your time is up. You know, I've always set my face against long engagements.

ERN.: Then defy the law and marry me now. We will fly to your native country, and I'll play broken-English in London as you play broken-German here!

JULIA: No. These legal technicalities cannot be defied. Situated as you are, you have no power to make me your wife. At best you could only make me your widow.

ERN.: Then be my widow – my little, dainty, winning, winsome widow!

JULIA: Now what would be the good of that? Why, you goose, I should marry again within a month!

DUET – ERNEST *and* JULIA

ERN.:
> If the light of love's lingering ember
> Has faded in gloom,
> You cannot neglect, O remember,
> A voice from the tomb!
> That stern supernatural diction
> Should act as a solemn restriction,
> Although by a mere legal fiction
> A voice from the tomb!

JULIA [*in affected terror*]:
> I own that that utterance chills me –
> It withers my bloom!
> With awful emotion it thrills me –
> That voice from the tomb!
> Oh, spectre, won't anything lay thee?
> Though pained to deny or gainsay thee,
> In this case I cannot obey thee,
> Thou voice from the tomb!

[*Dancing*]
> So, spectre appalling,
> I bid you good-day –
> Perhaps you'll be calling
> When passing this way.
> Your bogydom scorning,

And all your love-lorning,
   I bid you good-morning,
      I bid you good-day.

ERN. [*furious*]:   My offer recalling,
   Your words I obey –
Your fate is appalling,
   And full of dismay.
To pay for this scorning
I give you fair warning
I'll haunt you each morning,
   Each night, and each day!

[*Repeat Ensemble, and exeunt in opposite directions.*]
[*Re-enter the Wedding Procession dancing.*]

CHORUS: Now bridegroom and bride let us toast
   In a magnum of merry champagne –
Let us make of this moment the most,
   We may not be so lucky again.
So drink to our sovereign host
   And his highly intelligent reign –
His health and his bride's let us toast
   In a magnum of merry champagne!

SONG

BAR.:   I once gave an evening party
   (A sandwich and cut-orange ball),
But my guests had such appetites hearty
   That I couldn't enjoy it, enjoy it at all!
I made a heroic endeavour
   To look unconcerned, but in vain,
And I vow'd that I never – oh never –
   Would ask anybody again!
But there's a distinction decided –
   A difference truly immense –
When the wine that you drink is provided, provided,
   At somebody else's expense.

So bumpers – aye, ever so many –
　　The cost we may safely ignore!
For the wine doesn't cost us a penny,
　　Tho' it's Pomméry seventy-four![54]

CHORUS:　　　　　So bumpers – aye, ever so many – etc.

BAR.:　　Come, bumpers – aye, ever so many –
　　And then, if you will, many more!
This wine doesn't cost us a penny,
　　Tho' it's Pomméry, Pomméry seventy-four!
Old wine is a true panacea
　　For ev'ry conceivable ill,
When you cherish the soothing idea
　　That somebody else pays the bill!
Old wine is a pleasure that's hollow
　　When at your own table you sit,
For you're thinking each mouthful you swallow
　　Has cost you, has cost you a threepenny-bit!
So bumpers – aye, ever so many –
　　And then, if you will, many more!
This wine doesn't cost us a penny,
　　Tho's it's Pomméry seventy-four!

CHORUS:　　　　So, bumpers – aye, ever so many – etc.
　　[*March heard.*]

LUD. [*recitative*]:
　　　　Why, who is this approaching,
　　　　Upon our joy encroaching?
　　　　Some rascal come a-poaching
　　　　Who's heard that wine we're broaching?

ALL:　　　　　Who may this be?
　　　　　Who may this be?
　　　　Who is he? Who is he? Who is he?
　　[*Enter* HERALD.]

747

HERALD: The Prince of Monte Car*lo*,
        From Mediterranean water,
Has come here to bestow
        On you his beautiful daughter.
They've paid off all they owe,
        As every statesman oughter –
That Prince of Monte Car*lo*
        And his be-eautiful daughter!

CHORUS: The Prince of Monte Car*lo*, etc.

HERALD: The Prince of Monte Car*lo*,
        Who is so very partickler,
Has heard that you're also
        For ceremony a stickler –
Therefore he lets you know
        By word of mouth auric'lar –
(That Prince of Monte Car*lo*
        Who is so very particklar) –

CHORUS: The Prince of Monte Car*lo*, etc.

HERALD: That Prince of Monte Car*lo*,
        From Mediterranean water,
Has come here to bestow
        On you his be-eautiful daughter!

LUD. [*recitative*]:
        His Highness we know not – nor the locality
        In which is situate his Principality;[55]
        But, as he guesses by some odd fatality,
        This *is* the shop for cut and dried formality!
           Let him appear –
           He'll find that we're
        Remarkable for cut and dried formality.
[*Reprise of March. Exit* HERALD. LUDWIG *beckons his Court.*]

LUD.:   I have a plan – I'll tell you all the plot of it –
    He wants formality – he shall have a lot of it!

[*Whispers to them, through symphony.*]

> Conceal yourselves, and when I give the cue,
> Spring out on him – you all know what to do!

[*All conceal themselves behind the draperies that enclose the stage.*]

[*Pompous March. Enter the* PRINCE *and* PRINCESS OF MONTE CARLO, *attended by six theatrical-looking Nobles and the Court Costumier.*]

DUET – PRINCE *and* PRINCESS

PRINCE: We're rigged out in magnificent array
        (Our own clothes are much gloomier)
    In costumes which we've hired by the day
        From a very well-known costumier.

COST. [*bowing*]:   *I* am the well-known costumier.

PRINCESS: With a brilliant staff a Prince should make a show
        (It's a rule that never varies),
    So we've engaged from the Theatre Monaco
        Six supernumeraries.

NOBLES: We're the supernumeraries.

ALL: At a salary immense,
        Quite regardless of expense,
    Six supernumeraries!

PRINCE: They do not speak, for they break our grammar's laws,
        And their language is lamentable –
    And they never take off their gloves, because
        Their nails are not presentable.

NOBLES: Our nails are not presentable!

PRINCESS: To account for their shortcomings manifest
        We explain, in a whisper bated,
    They are wealthy members of the brewing interest
        To the Peerage elevated.

NOBLES: To the Peerage elevated.

ALL: They're ⎱
               We're ⎰ very, very rich,
                   And accordingly, as sich,
               To the Peerage elevated.

PRINCE: Well, my dear, here we are at last – just in time to compel Duke Rudolph to fulfil the terms of his marriage contract. Another hour and we should have been too late.

PRINCESS: Yes, papa, and if you hadn't fortunately discovered a means of making an income by honest industry, we should never have got here at all.

PRINCE: Very true. Confined for the last two years within the precincts of my palace by an obdurate bootmaker who held a warrant for my arrest, I devoted my enforced leisure to a study of the doctrine of chances – mainly with the view of ascertaining whether there was the remotest chance of my ever going out for a walk again – and this led to the discovery of a singularly fascinating little round game which I have called Roulette, and by which, in one sitting, I won no less than five thousand francs! My first act was to pay my bootmaker – my second, to engage a good useful working set of second-hand nobles – and my third, to hurry you off to Pfenning Halbpfennig as fast as a *train de luxe* could carry us!

PRINCESS: Yes, and a pretty job-lot of second-hand nobles you've scraped together!

PRINCE [*doubtfully*]: Pretty, you think? Humph! I don't know. I should say tol-lol, my love – only tol-lol. They are not wholly satisfactory. There is a certain air of unreality about them – they are not convincing.

COST.: But, my goot friend, vhat can you expect for eighteenpence a day!

PRINCE: Now take this Peer, for instance. What the deuce do you call *him*?

COST.: Him? Oh, he's a swell – he's the Duke of Riviera.

PRINCE: Oh, he's a Duke, is he? Well, that's no reason why he should look so confoundedly haughty. [*To Noble*] Be affable, sir! [*Noble takes attitude of affability.*] That's better. Now [*passing to another*] here's a nobleman's coat all in holes!

COST. [*to Noble*]: Vhat a careless chap you are! Vhy don't you take care of the clo's? These cost money, these do! D'ye think I stole 'em?

PRINCE: It's not the poor devil's fault – it's yours. I don't wish you to end our House of Peers, but you might at least mend them. [*Passing to another.*] Now, who's this with his moustache coming off?

COST.: Why, you're Viscount Mentone,[56] ain't you?

NOBLE: Blest if I know. [*Turning up sword belt.*] It's wrote here – yes, Viscount Mentone.

COST.: Then vhy don't you say so? 'Old yerself up – you ain't carryin' sandwich boards now. [*Adjusts his moustache and hat – a handkerchief falls out.*]

PRINCE: And we may be permitted to hint to the Noble Viscount, in the most delicate manner imaginable, that it is not the practice among the higher nobility to carry their handkerchiefs in their hats.

NOBLE: I ain't got no pockets.

PRINCE: Then tuck it in here. [*Sticks it in his breast.*] Now, once for all, you Peers – when His Highness arrives, don't stand like sticks, but appear to take an intelligent and sympathetic interest in what is going on. You needn't say anything, but let your gestures be in accordance with the spirit of the conversation. Now take the word from me. Affability! [*Attitude.*] Submission! [*Attitude.*] Surprise! [*Attitude.*] Shame! [*Attitude.*] Grief! [*Attitude.*] Joy! [*Attitude.*] That's better! You can do it if you like!

PRINCESS: But, papa, where in the world is the Court? There is positively no one here to receive us!

PRINCE: Well, my love, you must remember that we have taken Duke Rudolph somewhat by surprise. These small German potentates are famous for their scrupulous adherence to ceremonial observances, and it may be that the etiquette of this Court demands that we should be received with a certain elaboration of processional pomp – which Rudolph may, at this moment, be preparing.

PRINCESS: I can't help feeling that he wants to get out of it. First of all you implored him to come to Monte Carlo and marry me there, and he refused on account of the expense. Then you implored him to advance us the money to enable us to go to him – and again he refused, on account of the expense. He's a miserly little wretch – that's what he is.

PRINCE: Well, I shouldn't go so far as to say that. I should rather describe him as an enthusiastic collector of coins – of the realm – and we must not be too hard upon a numismatist if he feels a certain disinclination to part with some of his really very valuable specimens. It's a pretty hobby: I've often thought I should like to collect some coins myself.

PRINCESS: Papa, I'm sure there's some one behind that curtain. I saw it move!

PRINCE: Then no doubt they are coming. Now mind, you Peers – haughty affability combined with a sense of what is due to your exalted ranks, or I'll fine you half a franc each – upon my soul I will!

[*Gong. The curtains fly back and the Court are discovered. They give a wild yell and rush on to the stage dancing wildly, with* PRINCE, PRINCESS *and Nobles, who are taken by surprise at first, but eventually join in a reckless dance. At the end all fall down exhausted.*]

LUD.: There, what do you think of that? That's our official ceremonial for the reception of visitors of the very highest distinction.

PRINCE [*puzzled*]: It's very quaint – very curious indeed. Prettily footed, too. Prettily footed.

LUD.: Would you like to see how we say 'good-bye' to visitors of distinction? That ceremony is also performed with the foot.

PRINCE: Really, this tone – ah, but perhaps you have not completely grasped the situation?

LUD.: Not altogether.

PRINCE: Ah, then I'll give you a lead over. [*Significantly*] I am the father of the Princess of Monte Carlo. Doesn't that convey any idea to the Grand Ducal mind?

LUD. [*stolidly*]: Nothing definite.

PRINCE [*aside*]: H'm – very odd! Never mind – try again! [*Aloud*] This is the daughter of the Prince of Monte Carlo. Do you take?

LUD. [*still puzzled*]: No – not yet. Go on – don't give it up – I daresay it will come presently.

PRINCE: Very odd – never mind – try again. [*With sly significance*] Twenty years ago! Little doddle doddle! *Two* little doddle doddles! Happy father – hers and yours. Proud mother – yours and hers! Hah! *Now* you take? I see you do! I see you do!

LUD.: Nothing is more annoying than to feel that you're not equal to the intellectual pressure of the conversation. I wish he'd say something intelligible.

PRINCE: You didn't expect me?

LUD. [*jumping at it*]: No, no. I grasp that – thank you very much. [*Shaking hands with him*] No, I did *not* expect you!

PRINCE: I thought not. But ha! ha! at last I have escaped from my enforced restraint. [*General movement of alarm.*] [*To crowd, who are stealing off*] No, no – you misunderstand me. I mean I've paid my debts! And how d'you think I did it? Through the medium of Roulette!

ALL: Roulette?

LUD.: Now you're getting obscure again. The lucid interval has expired.

PRINCE: I'll explain. It's an invention of my own – the simplest thing in the world – and what is most remarkable, it comes just in time to supply a distinct and long-felt want! I'll tell you all about it.

[*Nobles bring forward a double Roulette table, which they unfold.*]

SONG

PRINCE:
> Take my advice – when deep in debt,
> Set up a bank and play Roulette!
> At once distrust you surely lull,
> And rook the pigeon and the gull.
> The bird will stake his every franc
> In wild attempt to break the bank –
> But you may stake your life and limb
> The bank will end by breaking him!

[*All crowd round and eagerly stake gold on the board.*]

> *Allons, encore*[57] –
>> *Garçons, fillettes* –
> *Vos louis d'or*
>> *Vos roues d'charette!*
>> *Holà! holà!*
> *Mais faites vos jeux* –
>> *Allons, la classe* –
>> *Le temps se passe* –
>> *La banque se casse* –
>> *Rien n'va plus! Rien n'va plus! Rien n'va plus!*
>> *Le dix-sept noir, impair et manque!*
>> *Holà! holà! vive la banque!*
> For every time the board you spin,
> Be sure the bank is bound to win!

CHORUS: For every time, etc.

[*During Chorus,* PRINCESS *and* COSTUMIER *rake in all the stakes.*]

PRINCE: A cosmic game is this Roulette!
        The little ball's a true coquette –
        A maiden coy whom 'numbers' woo –
        Whom six-and-thirty suitors sue!
        Of all complexions, too, good lack!
        For some are red and some are black,
        And some must be extremely green,
        For half of them are not nineteen!

[*All stake again.*]

> *Allons, encore* –
>> *Garçons, fillettes* –
> *Vos louis d'or* –
>> *Vos roues d'charette!*
>> *Holà! holà!*
> *Mais faites vos jeux* –
>> *Allons, la foule!*
>> *Ça roule – ça roule*
>> *Le temps s'écoule* –

Rien n'va plus! Rien n'va plus! Rien n'va plus!
Le trente-cinq rouge – impair et passe!
Très bien, étudiants de la classe –
The moral's safe – when you begin
Be sure the bank is bound to win!

CHORUS: The moral's safe, etc.
    [PRINCE *rakes in all the stakes.*]

PRINCE: The little ball's a flirt inbred –
                    She flirts with black – she flirts with red;
                    From this to that she hops about
                    Then back to this as if in doubt.
                    To call her thoughtless were unkind –
                    The child is making up her mind,
                    For all the world like all the rest,
                    Which *prétendant*[58] will pay the best!

                        Allons, encore –
                          Garçons, fillettes –
                        Vos louis d'or –
                          Vos roues d'charette!
                            Holà! holà!
                          Mais faites vos jeux –
                            Qui perte fit
                            Au temps jadis
                            Gagne aujourd' hui!
                    Rien n'va plus! Rien n'va plus! Rien n'va plus!
                    Tra, la, la, la! le double zéro!
                    Vous perdez tout, mes nobles héros –
                    Where'er at last the ball pops in,
                    Be sure the bank is bound to win!

CHORUS.:   *Tra, la, la, la! le double zéro, etc.*
    [PRINCE *gathers in the stakes. Nobles fold up table and take it
    away.*]

LUD.: Capital game. – Haven't a penny left!

PRINCE: Pretty toy, isn't it? Have another turn?

LUD.: Thanks, no. I should only be robbing you.

PRINCESS [*affectionately*]: Do, dearest – it's such fun!

BAR.: Why, you forward little hussy, how dare you? [*Takes her away from* LUDWIG.]

LUD.: You mustn't do that, my dear – never in the presence of the Grand Duchess, I beg!

PRINCESS [*weeping*]: Oh, papa, he's got a Grand Duchess!

LUD.: *A* Grand Duchess! My good girl, I've got three Grand Duchesses!

PRINCESS: *Three* Grand Duchesses! But let us understand each other. Am I not addressing the Grand Duke Rudolph?

LUD.: Not at all. You're addressing another-guess sort of Grand Duke altogether.

PRINCESS: This comes of not asking the way. We've mistaken the turning and got into the wrong Grand Duchy.

PRINCE: But – let us know where we are. Who the deuce is this gentleman?

LISA: He's the gentleman I married yesterday –

JULIA: He's the gentleman I married this morning –

BAR.: He's the gentleman I married this afternoon –

PRINCESS: Well, I'm sure! Papa, let's go away – this is not a respectable Court.

PRINCE: All these Grand Dukes have their little fancies, my love. This Potentate appears to be collecting wives. It's a pretty hobby – I should like to collect a few myself. This [*admiring* BARONESS] is a charming specimen – an antique, I should say – of the early Merovingian period,[59] if I'm not mistaken; and here's another – a Scotch lady, I think [*alluding to* JULIA], and [*alluding to* LISA] a little one thrown in. Two half-quarters and a make-weight! [*To* LUDWIG] Have you such a thing as a catalogue of the Museum?

PRINCESS: But this is getting serious. If this is not Rudolph, the question is, where in the world is he?

LUD.: No – the question is, where *out* of the world is he? And *that's* a very curious question, too!

PRINCE *and* PRINCESS: What do you mean?

LUD. [*pretending to weep*]: The Grand Duke Rudolph died yesterday!

PRINCE *and* PRINCESS: What!

LUD.: Quite suddenly – of – of – a cardiac affection.

PRINCE *and* PRINCESS: Of a cardiac affection?

LUD.: Yes, a pack-of-cardiac affection. He fought a Statutory Duel with me and lost, and I took over all his engagements – including this imperfectly preserved old lady, to whom he has been engaged for the last three weeks.

PRINCESS: Three weeks! But I've been engaged to him for the last twenty years!

BARONESS, LISA *and* JULIA: Twenty years!

PRINCE [*aside*]: It's all right, my love – they can't get over that. [*Aloud*] He's yours – take him, and hold him as tight as you can!

PRINCESS: My own! [*Embracing* LUDWIG.]

LUD.: Here's another! – the fourth in four-and-twenty hours! Would anybody else like to marry me? You, ma'am – or you – anybody! I'm getting used to it!

BAR.: But let me tell you, ma'am –

JULIA: Why, you impudent little hussy –

LISA: Oh, here's another – here's another! [*Weeping.*]

PRINCESS: Poor ladies, I'm very sorry for you all; but, you see, I've a prior claim. Come, away we go – there's not a moment to be lost!

CHORUS [*as they dance towards exit*]:

> Away to the wedding we'll go
>> To summon the charioteers,
> Though her rival's emotion may flow
>> In the form of impetuous tears –

[*At this moment* RUDOLPH, ERNEST *and* NOTARY *appear. All kneel in astonishment.*]

RECITATIVE – RUDOLPH, ERNEST *and* NOTARY

Forbear! This may not be!
Frustrated are your plans!
With paramount decree
The Law forbids the banns!

ALL: The Law forbids the banns!

SONG

RUD. [*furiously*]:

Well, you're a pretty kind of fellow, thus my life to
   shatter, O!
My dainty bride – my bride elect – you wheedle and you
   flatter, O!
You fascinate her tough old heart with vain and vulgar
   patter, O!
And eat my food and drink my wine – especially the
   latter, O!

ALL: The latter, O!
                    The latter, O!
           Especially the latter, O!

RUD.: But when compared with other crimes, for which your head
       I'll batter, O!

                    This flibberty gibberty
                    Kind of a liberty
             Scarcely seems to matter, O!

       For O, you vulgar vagabond, you fount of idle chatter, O!
       You've done a deed on which I vow you won't get any
          fatter, O!
       You fancy you've revived the Law – mere empty brag and
          chatter, O!
       You can't – you shan't – you don't – you won't – you thing
          of rag and tatter, O!

ALL: Of tatter, O!
                     Of tatter, O!
            You thing of rag and tatter, O!

RUD.: For this you'll suffer agonies like rat in clutch of ratter, O!
                   This flibberty gibberty
                   Kind of a liberty
                   's quite another matter, O!

ALL: This flibberty gibberty
                     Kind of a liberty
              's quite another matter, O!

[RUDOLPH *sinks exhausted into* NOTARY's *arms.*]

LUD.: My good sir, it's no use your saying that I can't revive the Law, in face of the fact that I *have* revived it.

RUD.: You didn't revive it! You couldn't revive it! You – you are an impostor, sir – a tuppenny rogue, sir! You – you never were, and in all human probability never will be – Grand Duke of Pfennig Anything!

ALL: What!!!

RUD.: Never – never, never! [*Aside*] Oh, my internal economy!

LUD.: That's absurd, you know. I fought the Grand Duke. He drew a King, and I drew an Ace. He perished in inconceivable agonies on the spot. Now, as that's settled, we'll go on with the wedding.

RUD.: It – it isn't settled. You – you can't. I – I – [*To* NOTARY] Oh, tell him – tell him! I can't!

NOT.: Well, the fact is, there's been a little mistake here. On reference to the Act that regulates Statutory Duels, I find it is expressly laid down that Ace shall count invariably as lowest!

ALL: As lowest!

RUD. [*breathlessly*]: As lowest – lowest – lowest! So *you're* the ghoest – ghoest – ghoest! [*Aside*] Oh, what *is* the matter with me inside here!

ERN.: Well, Julia, as it seems that the Law hasn't been revived – and as, consequently, I shall come to life in about three minutes – [*consulting his watch*] –

JULIA: My objection falls to the ground. [*Resignedly*] Very well. But will you promise to give me some strong scenes of justifiable jealousy?

ERN.: Justifiable jealousy! My love, I couldn't do it!

JULIA: Then I won't play.

ERN.: Well, well, I'll do my best! [*They retire up-stage together.*]

LUD.: And am I to understand that, all this time, I've been a dead man without knowing it?

BAR.: And that I married a dead man without knowing it?

PRINCESS: And that I was on the point of marrying a dead man without knowing it? [*To* RUDOLPH, *who revives*] Oh, my love, what a narrow escape I've had!

RUD.: Oh – you are the Princess of Monte Carlo, and you've turned up just in time! Well, you're an attractive little girl, you know, but you're as poor as a rat!

PRINCE: Pardon me – there you mistake. Accept her dowry – with a father's blessing! [*Gives him a small Roulette board, then flirts with* BARONESS.]

RUD.: Why, what do you call this?

PRINCESS: It's my little Wheel of Fortune. I'll tell you all about it. [*They retire up-stage, conversing.*]

LISA: That's all very well, but what is to become of *me*? [*To* LUDWIG] If you're a dead man – [*Clock strikes three.*]

LUD.: But I'm not. Time's up – the Act has expired – I've come to life – the parson is still in attendance, and we'll all be married directly.

ALL: Hurrah!

FINALE

CHORUS:
    Happy couples, lightly treading,
      Castle chapel will be quite full!
    Each shall have a pretty wedding,
      As, of course, is only rightful,
      Though the bride be fair or frightful.
    Contradiction little dreading,
      This will be a day delightful –

Each shall have a pretty wedding!
Such a pretty, pretty wedding!
Such a pretty wedding!

[*All dance off to get married as the curtain falls.*]

THE END

A Note on the Text

There is no definitive text for the Gilbert and Sullivan operas, and if one were to publish the original libretto of each work the text would differ wildly from the versions usually performed. This problem has arisen because W. S. Gilbert was a serial dabbler. No sooner had a production been premiered than the author was hard at work with his scalpel and scissors, snipping here, shearing there; removing this song, reworking that speech. For instance with *Trial by Jury*, three songs were soon cut and the ending of Act I revised. With *HMS Pinafore* there is the added confusion of one of the ballads, 'Reflect My Child', being cut prior to the first night, yet being rediscovered in 1998. Some companies use it; many don't. Another example involves *The Pirates of Penzance*. The opera opened in New York three months before it was premiered in London, and many changes occurred between the two 'first' nights. Experts now argue about which was the definitive first night: the very first in New York (as Americans suggest) or the London night (which Englanders argue for)?

And so it goes on throughout the canon. Include everything that Gilbert ever (once) favoured and readers using this book in conjunction with a production they are watching will be comparing like with unlike. Be too spruce and purists will complain of heavy-handedness. So why not turn to the supposedly definitive texts which Gilbert created in publishing the opera libretti in his series of Original Plays (1879; 1881; 1895; 1911)? Remarkably, these have glaring errors, such as the omission of Ko-Ko's little list song in *The Mikado*.

With this in mind, the editor has chosen the 1926 Macmillan edition (sub-titled 'Being the complete text ... produced in the years 1875–1896') as the bedrock for this first Penguin Classics version, it being one of a number of relatively 'faithful' editions from which most production companies take their libretti. Even so, some changes have been made at Mike Leigh's suggestion. A number of songs included on the opening nights, taken from the 1958 *First Night Gilbert and Sullivan*, published by the Heritage Press of New

York, have been added, as has the latter's complete libretto of *Thespis*, the first Gilbert and Sullivan collaboration, which was not included in Macmillan's version. See the Appendix for lists of emendations and alternative versions.

The illustrations have been taken from W. S. Gilbert's *The Bab's Ballads*, ed. James Ellis (Cambridge, Mass.: Belknap Press, 1970).

The operas are presented in chronological order, and there are explanatory notes, each with a headnote which, it is hoped, illuminates the text and clarifies any mystery arising out of Gilbert's esoteric choice of allusion.

Small Penguin house-style changes have been made to the Macmillan and *First Night* texts: surplus commas (comma in a series before 'and') have been removed; 'Mr', 'Mrs', 'St', 'Dr', 'M.P.', 'K.C.B.' and 'H.M.S.' are printed without full stops; spelling of words ending 'ise/ize' are made consistent; speech prefixes have been rearranged for clarity and a few missing ones added; and unspaced em-rules have been replaced by spaced en-rules.

EG

Alternative versions from *The First Night Gilbert and Sullivan*

The Pirates of Penzance

FINALE

RUTH: At length we are provided, with unusual facility,
To change piratic crime for dignified respectability.

KING: Combined, I needn't say, with the unparalleled felicity
Of what we have been longing for – unbounded domesticity.

MABEL: To-morrow morning early we will quickly be parsonified –
Hymeneally coupled, conjugally matrimonified.

SERG.: And this shall be accomplished by that doctor of divinity
Who happily resides in the immediate vicinity.

CHORUS: Who happily resides in the immediate vicinity.

GEN.: My military knowledge, though I'm plucky and adventury,
Has only been brought down to the beginning of the century;
But still, in getting off my daughters – eight or nine or ten in all –
I've shown myself the model of a modern Major-General.

ALL: His military knowledge, etc.

DANCE

This is an alternative Finale, see p. 191.

The Mikado

KO-KO:
> As a victim must be found,
> If you'll only look around,
> There are criminals at large
> (And enough to fill a barge),
> > Whose swift decapitation
> > Whould be hailed with acclamation,
> > If accomplished by the nation
> At a reasonable charge.

This verse was sung on the first night in 1885, but was cut by Gilbert and replaced by the Men's Chorus immediately afterwards. The verse followed each stanza of the song 'As some day it may happen', sung by Ko-Ko with the Chorus of Noblemen, see p. 373.

Ruddigore

ROBIN:
> For thirty-five years I've been sober and wary –
> My favourite tipple came straight from a dairy –
> I kept guinea-pigs and a Belgian canary –
> > A squirrel, white mice, and a small black-and-tan.
> I played on the flute, and I drank lemon squashes –
> I wore chamois leather, thick boots, and macintoshes,
> And things that will some day be known as galoshes,
> > The type of a highly respectable man!
>
> For the rest of my life I abandon propriety –
> Visit the haunts of Bohemian society,
> Wax-works, and other resorts of impiety,
> > Placed by the moralist under a ban.
> My ways must be those of a regular satyr,
> At carryings-on I must be a first-rater –
> Go night after night to a wicked theayter –
> > It's hard on a highly respectable man!

Well, the man who has spent the first half of his tether,
On all the bad deeds you can bracket together,
Then goes and repents – in his cap it's a feather –
  Society pets him as much as it can.
It's a comfort to think, if I now go a cropper,
I sha'n't, on the whole, have done more that's improper
Than he who was once an abandoned tip-topper,
  But now is a highly respectable man!

This is an alternative song to 'Henceforth all the crimes' sung by Robin, in the standard libretto and D'Oyly Carte productions, see p. 472. It can be heard on the 1987 centenary recording of the New Sadler's Wells Opera production (CDTER 2 1128).

SIR RODERIC: I see – I understand! We are all practically alive!

ROBIN: Every man jack of you!

SIR RODERIC: My brother ancestors! Down from your frames! [*The Ancestors descend.*] You believe yourselves to be dead – you may take it from me that you're not, and an application to the Supreme Court is all that is necessary to prove that you never ought to have died at all!

 [*The Ancestors embrance the Bridesmaids.*]

 [*Enter* RICHARD *and* ROSE, *also* SIR DESPARD *and* MARGARET.]

ROBIN: Rose, when you believed that I was a simple farmer, I believe you loved me?

ROSE: Madly, passionately!

ROBIN: But when I became a bad baronet, you very properly loved Richard instead?

ROSE: Passionately, madly!

ROBIN: But if I should turn out *not* to be a bad baronet after all, how would you love me then?

ROSE: Madly, passionately!

ROBIN: As before!

ROSE: Why, of course!

ROBIN: My darling! [*They embrace.*]

CHORUS: Hail the Bridegroom – hail the Bride! –

RICHARD [*interrupting them*]: Will you be quiet? [*To* ROBIN] Belay, my lad, belay, you don't understand!

ROSE: Oh, sir belay, if it's absolutely necessary.

ROBIN: Belay? Certainly not. [*To* RICHARD] You see, it's like this – as all

my ancestors are alive, it follows, as a matter of course, that the eldest of
them is the family baronet, and I revert to my former condition.

RICHARD [*going to* ZORAH]: Well, I think it's exceedingly unfair!

ROBIN [*To* FIRST GHOST]: Here, great uncle, allow me to present you. [*To
the others*] Sir Ruthven Murgatroyd, Baronet, of Ruddygore!

ALL: Hurrah!

FIRST GHOST: Fallacy somewhere!

Gilbert cut the Chorus of Ghosts all coming back to life. The passage followed
'But suicide is, itself, a crime . . . died at all', p. 482.

The Yeomen of the Guard

ELSIE: It's the song of a merrymaid, peerly proud,
     Who loved a lord, and who laughed aloud
     At the moan of the merryman moping mum,
     Whose soul was sad and whose glance was glum,

This earlier hard-edged version sung by Elsie was replaced by a soppy,
sentimental effort later, which is in the standard text, see p. 501.

The Grand Duke

RUDOLPH: When your clothes, from your hat to your socks,
     Have tickled and scrubbed you all day;
    When your brain is a musical box
     With a barrel that turns the wrong way;
    When you find you're too big for your coat,
     And a great deal too small for your vest,
    With a pint of warm oil in your throat,
     And a pound of tin-tacks in your chest;
    When you've got a beehive in your head,
     And a sewing machine in each ear;
    And you feel that you've eaten your bed,
     And you've got a bad headache down here;
    When your lips are like underdone paste,
     And you're highly gamboge in the gill;
    And your mouth has a coppery taste,
     As if you'd just bitten a pill;
     And whatever you tread,
      From a yawning abyss

You recoil with a yell, –
You are better in bed,
For, depend upon this,
You are not at all well.

When everything spins like a top
And your stock of endurance gives out;
If some miscreant proposes a chop
(Mutton-chop, with potatoes and stout),
When your mouth is of flannel – like mine –
And your teeth not on terms with their stumps,
And spiders crawl over your spine,
And your muscles have all got the mumps;
When you're bad with the creeps and the crawls,
And the shivers, and shudders, and shakes,
And the pattern that covers the walls
Is alive with black-beetles and snakes;
When you doubt if your head is your own,
And you jump when an open door slams,
And you've got to a state which is known
To the medical world as 'jim-jams', –
If such symptoms you find
In your body or head
They're not easy to quell
You may make up your mind
That you're better in bed,
For you're not at all well!

This is an alternative version of Rudolph's song, 'When you find you're a broken-down critter', see p. 715.

Additional verses, replaced and emended text from *The First Night Gilbert and Sullivan*

Trial by Jury

p. 60: added as a final stanza 'Though defendant is a snob ... And a good job too!'

The Sorcerer

p. 64: following 'no hope, no solace, no alloy!' added 'When I rejoice . . . My life is very sad and drear!'

p. 71: added Lady Sangazure's Ballad.

p. 86: 'But stay' emended to 'But soft'.

p. 96: added Mr Wells's Recitative and Aline's speech.

The Pirates of Penzance

p. 182: following 'Till we are wed, and even after.' added 'What joy to know . . . He is my foe.'

p. 185: following 'For General Stanley's story.' added 'They come in force . . . Is to conceal ourselves.'

Patience

p. 212: following 'spite of all my/your pains, etc.' added 'Time fled, and one unhappy day . . . all my pains, etc.'

p. 223: at the end of Act I, Tutti Ensemble replaces the Macmillan version.

Iolanthe

p. 287: 'Phyllis! My darling! . . . which it's to be?' replaced by 'Phyllis! My own! . . . Well, have you settled which it's to be?'

p. 293: added Strephon's Recitative and Song.

The Mikado

p. 382: Yum-Yum and Nanki-Poo's Duet replaces the Macmillan version.

pp. 386–7: 'Nonsense, sir . . . Substitute!' replaced by 'And do you suppose . . . [*Struck by an idea.*]'

p. 403: 'We all have unpleasant duties to discharge at times' replaced by 'your feelings do you credit . . . Come now –'

Ruddigore

pp. 462: following '*valley-de-sham*!' added 'My face is the index to my mind . . . by names like Gideon Crawle!' Subsequently, 'old Adam' replaced by 'Gideon Crawle' and 'Adam' with 'Gideon'.

p. 467: following '[*The Spectre of* SIR RODERIC MURGATROTD *descends from his frame.*]' added 'By the curse upon our race . . . the world we quitted!'

The Yeomen of the Guard

p. 493: added Meryll's Song.
p. 513: following 'Scarce a word of them is true!' added 'You, when brought to execution . . . Every word of them is true!'

The Gondoliers

p. 571: two stanzas have replaced the one stanza starting 'Bridegroom and bride!'
p. 581: 'Then hail! Oh king.' replaced by 'It may be thou . . . Whichever you may be!'

Utopia Limited

p. 649: added Zara's speech and Song.
pp. 683–4: following 'the other Party has done' inserted '; inexperienced civilians . . . no political capital is to be made'.

The Grand Duke

pp. 751–60: '[*Passing to another.*] . . . [*They retire up-stage together.*]' replaced by 'Now [*passing to another*] . . . [*They retire up-stage, conversing.*]'

Notes

Abbreviations

Baily: 1973	Leslie Baily, *Gilbert and Sullivan and Their World* (1973)
Bradley: 1996	Ian Bradley (ed.), *The Complete Annotated Gilbert and Sullivan* (1996)
Dark: 1923	Sidney Dark, *Gilbert, His Life and Letters* (1923)
MacGeorge: 1930	Ethel MacGeorge, *The Life and Reminiscences of Jessie Bond, the Old Savoyard, As Told By Herself* (1930)
Sullivan–Flower: 1927	Herbert Sullivan and Walter Flower, *Sir Arthur Sullivan, His Life, Letters and Diaries* (1927)
Walbrook: 1922	H. M. Walbrook, *Gilbert and Sullivan Opera: A History and a Comment* (1922)

Biblical references are from the King James Version.

Thespis; or, The Gods Grown Old

First performed 26 December 1871 at the Gaiety Theatre, Strand, London.

Original Cast

Jupiter	John Maclean
Apollo	Fred Sullivan
Mars	Frank Wood
Diana	Mrs Henry Leigh
Mercury	Ellen Farren

Thespis	J. L. Toole
Sillimon	J. G. Taylor
Timidon	Mr Marshall
Tipseion	Robert Soutar
Preposteros	Henry Payne
Stupidas	Fred Payne
Sparkeion	Mlle Clary
Nicemis	Constance Loseby
Pretteia	Rose Berend
Daphne	Annie Tremaine
Cymon	Miss L. Wilson

Thespis was not the most auspicious of debuts for a partnership as fruitful and fecund as Gilbert and Sullivan's. Its subject matter – the gods on Mount Olympus taking a rest while a group of travelling actors take their place – was never likely to appeal to any but a small section of the public. Its creation was rushed (it enjoyed only three weeks' gestation), and its premiere under-rehearsed (one week). Its libretto was published in what many Gilbert and Sullivan experts deem an imperfect form, and, worse still, the full score of the music, though well received, soon became lost, with only minimal survival, namely the songs 'Little Maid of Arcadee' and 'Climbing Over Rocky Mountain', the latter re-appearing in *The Pirates of Penzance*.

Consequently, *Thespis* is rarely performed and is now the most neglected work in the canon. Yet such has been the ingenuity of Savoyards worldwide over the years that a number of full scores have been presented alongside productions of the work. Some have set Gilbert's words to compositions from other Sullivan works; others, like Quade Winter, have gone to the lengths of composing original music in best Sullivan style. Winter's version was enthusiastically received at its world premiere by the Ohio Light Opera in 1996.

The most inspired devotees have been Roderick Spencer and Selwyn Tillett of the Sir Arthur Sullivan Society, who during rehearsals for Sullivan's 1864 ballet *L'Île Enchantée* found while rummaging through the score several numbers in a different handwriting, with a different pagination from the rest of the work, two of these pieces being captioned 'Act 2', even though *L'Île Enchantée* has only one act. Deciding that the three numbers were from another Sullivan work, they matched the handwriting and pagination with the only surviving manuscript from *Thespis* – the score of 'Climbing Over Rocky Mountain' – to Sullivan's hand. Now there was what they claim was the original ballet music as well.

As for Gilbert's contribution, it is clear the librettist had considerable fun with the names for his characters. There are many gods, mostly presented with the Latin versions of their names (Jupiter, Mars, Venus), which would have been better known to Victorian audiences than the Greek alternative (Zeus, Ares and Aphrodite), and there are Greek-styled participants based on some flippant characteristic: Preposteros (preposterous), Nicemis (nice miss) and Stupidas (stupid ass), a technique later used with similar humorous effect by many comic writers, including the creators of the mid-twentieth-century musical *A Funny Thing Happened on the Way to the Forum*, which includes a nervous slave called Hysterium.

Press reviews of *Thespis* were mixed. While the *Illustrated London News* spoke of how 'the result was quite satisfactory, and the audience had reason to be pleased', the *Sporting Life* of 1871 complained that the opera was above people's heads, and *Punch* moaned how 'it was past midnight when the curtain descended, the audience in a fidgety state to get away'. Yet *Thespis* was not a complete failure. The Gaiety was filled to capacity of around 1,500 for the opening night and the show ran for 64 performances. Also, Sullivan was pleased. He told his mother: 'I have rarely seen anything more beautiful put upon the stage' (Audrey Williamson, *Gilbert and Sullivan Opera: An Assessment* (1982)). Yet it must also be said that there wasn't much competition at the time. English theatre was in the doldrums. No one had come forward to match the work of Sheridan, dead fifty years, bowdlerized versions of Shakespeare were rife and the next masters, such as Shaw and Wilde, were in their adolescence.

What draws Gilbert and Sullivan lovers to *Thespis* now is its status as the partnership's first collaboration. Its existence brings with it a tingle of excitement at the thought of these two extraordinary talents meeting for the first time, and with it the fear that if such an event had never occurred, or more likely had occurred later, when they were more set into alternative career paths, how much poorer British musical theatre would have been. When they met, Gilbert was thirty-three and Sullivan twenty-seven. Both were reasonably well known to the public, Gilbert as a dramatist and author of *Bab Ballads*, with its doggerel verse about characters such as Captain Reece, whose 'sisters, cousins, aunts and niece' sailed on the HMS *Mantelpiece*; Sullivan more so after composing his orchestral suite to Shakespeare's *The Tempest* and his Symphony in E flat (the 'Irish Symphony').

Gilbert later recalled the first meeting as 'rather amusing', if also rather perplexing to anyone not experienced in trenchant musical analysis. He approached the composer and told him:

I am very pleased to meet you, Mr Sullivan, because you will be able to settle a question which has just arisen between Mr Clay and myself. My contention is that when a musician who is master of many instruments has a musical theme to express, he can express it as perfectly upon the simple tetrachord of Mercury (in which there are, as we all know, no diatonic intervals whatever) as upon the more elaborate disdiapason (with the familiar four tetrachords and the redundant note) which (I need not remind you) embraces in its simple consonance all the single, double, and inverted chords.

Sullivan was a little nonplussed and, according to Gilbert, 'reflected for a moment, and asked me to oblige him by repeating my question'. In agreeing to work together the two men decided they were on a crusade. 'The burlesque stage was in a very unclean state,' Gilbert later recalled; 'We made up our minds to do all in our power to wipe out the grosser element, never to let an offending word escape our characters' (*Strand Magazine*, 1891). There was no mention of topsy-turvydom.

1. *Thespis*: Greek poet of the sixth century BC, known as the Father of Tragedy, who is believed to have introduced the idea of dramatic performances with actors rather than just dancers and singers. Actors have since been known in elevated circles as 'thespians'.
2. *Mount Olympus*: The heavenly dwelling place of the chief Greek gods. The name Olympus was later ascribed to the tallest peak in the range of Greek mountains located some 65 miles south-west of Salonika.
3. DIANA: Diana to the Romans (Artemis to the Greeks), daughter of Zeus and Leto, twin to Apollo and goddess of the hunt and the moon.
4. *Apollo*: God of the sun, son of Leto and Zeus. According to Homer's *Iliad*, he shot arrows of plague into the Greek camp.
5. *Mercury*: Messenger to the gods (Hermes to the Greeks), son of Zeus and Maia; he presided over commerce, good luck, wealth, trickery, roads and fertility.
6. *Jupiter*: Chief of the gods (Zeus to the Greeks), also known as Jove, whose progeny include some 90 per cent of the characters in Greek mythology.
7. *peruke*: A wig.
8. *Cupid*: Roman god of love (Eros to the Greeks), also known as Amor, son of Venus and Mars and depicted in painting as a nude winged boy or male youth armed with a bow and a quiver of arrows. Some goddesses, including Vesta, Minerva and Diana were believed to be immune to Cupid's arrows.
9. *auricomous fluid*: A treatment for golden hair.
    hare's foot: In the Victorian theatre, real hares' feet were used as stage make-up brushes.

10. *Venus*: Goddess of love and beauty, known to the Greeks as Aphrodite. Occasionally she is portrayed as Zeus's daughter; at other times she rises from the sea from the blood of the slaughtered Uranus.

11. *Mars*: God of war (Ares to the Greeks) and most powerful god after Jupiter.

12. *Hymen*: Greek god of marriage.

13. *Phoebus*: An alternative name for Apollo, meaning 'bright'.

14. *Bacchus*: The Roman god of wine (Dionysus to the Greeks). Bacchanalia, orgies in honour of Dionysus, began in Rome around 200 BC but were banned by the Senate in 186 BC after the celebrations became too excessive.

15. *Minerva*: Roman goddess of arts and crafts (Athena to the Greeks), later became the goddess of war and victory.

16. *plate-powder*: A polishing material for silver and plate.

17. *Tartarus*: The lowest region of the world, located as far below earth as earth is below heaven, according to classical mythology. The Greek poet Hesiod claimed that a bronze anvil would take nine days to fall from heaven to earth, and another nine days to reach Tartarus.

18. *Cook's Excursion*: Tours managed by Thomas Cook (1808–92), the Derbyshire temperance campaigner, who began arranging excursions on the Midland Railway in 1841 and later founded the well-known travel firm bearing his name.

19. *Daphne*: A nymph who metamorphosed into a laurel tree in order to escape Apollo's clutches.

20. *burrage*: Borage, which was made into a cordial, and added to claret cup.

21. *Diddlesex*: Gilbert took the name, evidently a play on Middlesex, the county in which much of London resides, from Thackeray's *Vanity Fair* (1847), which features a Diddlesex Bank Western Branch.

22. *Bath-bun*: A cake invented by Dr W. Oliver, an eighteenth-century physician, in Bath, which was originally liberally sprinkled with crushed caraway seed comfits.

23. *Tooting*: A south London suburb; in Gilbert's day it enjoyed respectable middle-class aspirations.

24. *Barking*: A stretch of east London by the Thames with a long history dating back to the founding of Barking Abbey in 666. In late Victorian times Barking still had a separate identity from London.

25. *Regent Circus*: The original name for Piccadilly Circus (built 1819) was Regent Circle South, while that of Oxford Circus was Regent Circus North.

26. *Thessalian*: Thessaly is a region of northern Greece which in antiquity supplied most of the horses for Athens.

27. *Iliads and Odysseys*: Homer's *Iliad*, an epic poem written *c.* 700 BC, tells the story of the Trojan War. His *Odyssey* continues the story with the ten-year homeward voyage of Odysseus after the fall of Troy.

28. *Calliope*: The Muse who presides over epic poetry, she is sometimes seen holding a writing tablet and at other times with a roll of paper or a book. She was the mother of Orpheus and Linus, who was slain by Hercules.

29. *symposia*: Plural of Symposium, the word denotes a conference and interestingly derives from the Greek 'to drink together'. *Symposium* is also the title of a work by Plato (*c.* 360 BC), which recounts a drinking party attended by the poet Aristophanes, Alcibiades and Socrates.

30. *Ambrosia*: The food of the gods, consumption of which was supposed to bring about immortality. It derives from the Greek for 'immortal'.

31. *Vulcan*: Roman fire god, son of Jupiter and Juno (Hera), associated with the Greek god Hephaestus.

32. *Arcadee*: Arcadee or properly, Arcadia, is a region in central Peloponnesus, Greece, whose inhabitants, isolated from the bustle of Mediterranean society, traditionally lived a simple pastoral life. The Arcadian theme is one of the most widely used and enticing in the arts, usually as part of the enigmatic and subtly morbid Latin phrase 'Et in Arcadia Ego (Sum)' ('Even in Arcadia there am I').

33. *Pluto*: Roman god of the underworld, the name being given to the planet furthest from the sun, discovered in 1930.

34. *Lemprière's Classical Dictionary*: A seminal work on Classical mythology published in 1788.

35. *Issa*: Princess of Dryopia in Greece who was seduced by Apollo in the disguise of a shepherd.

36. *Bolina*: A mortal maiden of the town of Bolina in Achaia, southern Greece, who leapt into the sea to escape Apollo; the god transformed her into an immortal nymph.

37. *Coronis*: She gave birth to Asclepius, the father being Apollo, who killed her after a raven told him of her infidelity.

38. *Chymene*: A mistake, for the name should be Clymene, who appears in Ovid's *Metamorphoses* (*c.* AD 1).

39. *Cyrene*: Daughter of Creusa and Hypseus.

40. *Chione*: According to some the daughter of Boreas and Orithya, according to others the daughter of Daedalion and a remarkable beauty.

41. *Acacallis*: A daughter of the Cretan king, Minos, who was Apollo's first love.

42. *Mytilene*: The main town of the Greek island Lesbos.

43. *BALLET DIVERTISSEMENT*: A short ballet given as an entertainment between acts, or as here, at the end of the opera.

Trial by Jury

First performed 25 March 1875 at the Royalty Theatre, 73 Dean Street, Soho, London.

Original Cast

The Learned Judge	Fred Sullivan
The Plaintiff	Nellie Bromley
The Defendant	Walter Fisher
Counsel for the Plaintiff	John Hollingshead
Usher	Belville R. Pepper
Foreman of the Jury	Charles Kelleher

Trial by Jury stands as a triumphant introduction to the regularly performed Savoy Operas. Many have hailed it as a masterpiece. David Eden, long-time chairman of the Sir Arthur Sullivan Society, has cited it as 'the finest work of Gilbert and Sullivan'.

After *Thespis*'s run the two men went their separate ways without any plans to collaborate further. Gilbert continued to write plays, Sullivan mostly church music. Three years later D'Oyly Carte, manager of the Royalty Theatre, looking for a two-act opera to precede the staging of Offenbach's comic opera, *La Périchole*, met Gilbert by chance and persuaded him to produce a piece suitable for the slot. Gilbert turned to *Trial by Jury*, a primitive version of which had been published in the April 1868 edition of *Fun* magazine. Gilbert had first expanded the work into a full libretto in 1873, at the behest of the impresario Carl Rosa, but had abandoned it when Rosa's wife suddenly died. Now he rewrote it as a one-act farce, sung throughout with no spoken dialogue.

Gilbert and D'Oyly Carte discussed a suitable composer for the revived piece and soon settled on Sullivan. The librettist trudged through the snow with the complete text to Sullivan's Victoria Street flat. By the time he arrived he was in a foul mood. As the composer later recalled: 'He read it through, as it seemed to me, in a perturbed sort of way, with a gradual crescendo of indignation, in the manner of a man considerably disappointed with what he had written. As soon as he had come to the last word he closed the manuscript violently, apparently unconscious of the fact that he had achieved his purpose so far as I was concerned, inasmuch as I was screaming with laughter the whole time' (Sullivan–Flower: 1927).

Trial by Jury tells the story of a jilted bride who sues for breach of promise of marriage. It satirizes the legal system with which Gilbert, as a former trainee for the Bar at the Temple, was familiar, and he based the court on the Clerkenwell Sessions House where he had briefly appeared. The opera set the scene for what was to follow in the Gilbert and Sullivan canon: absurd plot, heart-warming comedy and sympathetic characters acting as conduits for universal truths about human weakness.

There is much farce. The judge and jury side with the Plaintiff, while the ladies in the Public Gallery are enamoured with the Defendant, who has a new love. As an unusual solution the Defendant suggests marrying 'this lady to-day' and marrying 'the other to-morrow'. Throughout, Gilbert reminds us of the hypocrisy of the legal system and the tendency for those who participate in it to succumb to moral weakness rather than embrace justice.

Trial by Jury joined a bill that included the romantic extravaganza *Crypto-conchoid Syphonostomata* as well as *La Périchole*. It stole the show. 'Both Mr Words and Mr Music have worked together,' wrote *Punch*, 'and for the first quarter of an hour the Cantata (as they've called it) is the funniest bit of nonsense your representative has seen for a considerable time.' The public warmed to this mockery of an English court in which the Usher, while urging the case to be tried 'from bias free of every kind', refers to the '*broken-hearted* bride' and the '*ruffianly* defendant'; in which jurymen scrutinize the morning papers while the Defendant's case is submitted; in which the judge outlines his own moral conduct before turning to the business of the day and later casts his roving eye over the Plaintiff.

Playing the part of the Learned Judge – 'Yes, now I am a Judge! / Though all my law is fudge, / Yet I'll never, never budge, / But I'll live and die a Judge!' – was Fred Sullivan, elder brother of the composer, made up to look like the Lord Chief Justice, Sir Alexander Cockburn, who attended the performance once and vowed to stay away in future lest he be ridiculed. Fred Sullivan did not live long enough to become a Savoyard stalwart à la George Grossmith and Durward Lely. He died of liver disease and tuberculosis two years later at the age of thirty-nine, a tragedy which Sullivan attempted to assuage by composing *The Lost Chord*.

To D'Oyly Carte, Sullivan not Gilbert was the potential cash cow in this partnership. Indeed, the first announcement of the new work in *The Times* omitted Gilbert's name. Worse still, the programme on the opening night incorrectly listed the latter as 'W. C. Gilbert'. But Sullivan was barely able to bathe in the luxury of top billing, for there was shock and even dismay from some quarters that Britain's leading composer of serious oratorios had contributed to a comic opera and resorted to burlesquing Handel, Bellini and Donizetti.

Trial by Jury's producers initially felt the show might run only a few weeks, and at that time the idea of a lasting Gilbert–Sullivan partnership seemed remote. However it continued till the end of the year, longer than *La Périchole*, to which it was only supposed to be a supplement, after all, and its success enabled D'Oyly Carte to secure a lease on the Opéra Comique Theatre, in the Strand, to which the show moved in January 1876.

1. *Edwin, sued by Angelina*: The line is based on the following verse from 'The Hermit' (1764) by Oliver Goldsmith:

> Turn, Angelina, ever dear,
> My charmer, turn to see
> Thy own, thy long-lost Edwin here,
> Restored to love and thee.

2. *Court of the Exchequer*: Henry I (ruled 1100–1135) formed the Court of the Exchequer to handle his financial affairs, its name being taken from the checkered cloth or table on which the accounts were calculated. The court's remit was gradually extended to include civil matters, and it occasionally dealt with breach of promise cases (see note 4). It was subsumed into the newly created High Court in 1873.

3. *in banc*: French, *in* or *en banc*, a legal term meaning 'in the bench' or 'full bench'. It refers to sessions using the entire membership of a court.

4. *Breach of Promise*: Failure to fulfil a promise, particularly a promise of marriage made by a man who having abandoned his fiancée left himself liable to be sued. This was the position until the law was changed in 1970. The most famous 'breach of promise' case is a fictitious one, that of Mr Pickwick vs. Mrs Bardell in Dickens's *Pickwick Papers* (1836).

5. *Westminster Hall*: The most visible survival of a medieval Palace of Westminster, built by William Rufus in 1097 to house the royal treasure; now used as the vestibule of the House of Commons.

6. *the Bailey*: The Old Bailey, the Central Criminal Court of England and Wales, setting for many of the most famous trials in British legal history.

7. *Middlesex Sessions*: Gilbert himself practised at the Middlesex Sessions, a predecessor to the Crown Court, which were held four times a year in the counties and were then based in Clerkenwell Green, half a mile north of the Old Bailey. In 1923 the courts moved to the Middlesex Guildhall building in Parliament Square, Westminster.

8. *the Gurneys*: A firm of East Anglian bankers. The London branch went bankrupt in 1866 and was taken over by Barclays.

9. *incubus*: An evil spirit that has sexual intercourse with women as they sleep.

10. *Camberwell*: South-east London suburb which enjoyed genteel aspirations in Gilbert's day.

11. *Peckham*: South-east London suburb near Camberwell, where in the 1760s the young William Blake saw a vision of angels in a tree, only to be beaten by his father when he returned home and recounted the incident.

12. *Arcadian Vale*: See *Thespis* note 32.

13. *otto*: From attar of roses, i.e. perfume made of rose petals.

14. *Watteau*: Jean-Antoine Watteau (1684–1721), French rococo artist with an enthusiasm for theatre and ballet.

15. *Oh! fetch some water / From far Cologne*: A couplet whose comedic slant would be regularly echoed some hundred years later in the unswervingly British Carry On films, worthy 1960s heirs to the Savoy Operas. Eau de Cologne, a blend of extracts, alcohol and water, is the oldest and probably the most famous of perfumes. It was invented as Aqua Admirabilis in 1709 by Gian Paolo Feminis, an Italian barber who settled in Cologne. Napoleon Bonaparte supposedly used eight quarts of violet cologne every month.

16. *James the Second*: British king whose fraught reign (1685–9) was curtailed when he was forced off the throne for excessive sympathy towards Catholicism, and replaced jointly by his daughter, Mary Stuart, and her husband, William III, in what is now known as 'the Glorious Revolution'.

The Sorcerer

First performed 17 November 1877 at the Opéra Comique, 299 Strand, London.

Original Cast

Sir Marmaduke Pointdextre	Richard Temple
Alexis	George Bentham
Dr Daly	Rutland Barrington
Notary	Fred Clifton
John Wellington Wells	George Grossmith
Lady Sangazure	Isabelle Paul
Aline	Alice May

Mrs Partlet   Harriett Everard
Constance   Giulia Warwick

The success of *Trial by Jury* enthused D'Oyly Carte into urging Gilbert and Sullivan to provide a comic opera follow-up. Gilbert was heartened but wanted to see the colour of D'Oyly's money first. 'It's astonishing how quickly these capitalists dry up under the magical influence of the words "cash down",' he wrote to Sullivan (Dark: 1923). By late 1876 D'Oyly Carte had complied with Gilbert's wishes. After all, D'Oyly Carte was himself keen to create a theatre devoted to the genre. 'English comic opera had practically ceased to exist,' Sullivan later explained; 'Such musical entertainments as held the stage were adaptations of the plots of the operas of Offenbach, Audran and Lecocq. The plots had generally been bowdlerised out of intelligibility, and when they had not been subjected to this treatment they were frankly improper' (Sullivan–Flower: 1927).

D'Oyly Carte's new Comedy Opera company was bankrolled by four men, including Frank Chappell, the music publisher, and Edward Hodgson Bayley, chief entrepreneur of London's street cleaning, known popularly as 'Watercart Bayley'. Despite the grand intentions behind the new company, it had no permanent venue and with some irony found itself leasing the Gallic-sounding Opéra Comique Theatre on the Strand, a venue lost when the maze of pokey streets it nestled amongst were cleared for road improvements in the early twentieth century.

Gilbert and Sullivan complemented the management's aspirations with their own recipe for success. They knew that no matter how ridiculous the plot, it should be coherent, that there should be no cross-dressing by the cast – at least not on stage – and no unrealistic costumes for the ladies. Their first work for the Comedy Opera company was *The Sorcerer*, a charming magic romp satirizing old-fashioned manners, working-class insobriety and dozy curates. The story centres around Gilbert's perennially favourite plot idea, which he had already used in the play *Dulcamara* (1866) and the short story 'An Elixir of Love' (1876), that of a device – a 'magic lozenge' – that can suddenly transform the lives or nature of its users. In this case it is a love potion – a 'philtre' – administered from a teapot that can make people fall in love, much in the same way that the flower love-in-idleness works in Shakespeare's *A Midsummer Night's Dream* (II.1.168).

The philtre is the invention of John Wellington Wells of the firm of J. W. Wells & Co., Family Sorcerers of St Mary Axe, which can be bought in 'four-and-a-half and nine gallon casks'. Its powers create romantic upheaval which in typically Gilbertian fashion are smoothed over during the denouement when Wells, possessed with demoniac powers and clothed in black frock-coat, top hat and grey trousers, descends to hell through the trapdoor 'amid red fire' while carefully drawing on his gloves, respectable to the last.

Casting *The Sorcerer* caused considerable delay. Neither Gilbert nor Sullivan wanted to use star names or experienced opera performers. They were particularly suspicious of the temperament of the typical tenor. They wanted fresh talents, chosen for the strength of their personality, who would be willing to work hard and whom they could mould. Inspired inspection of the world of sub-standard melodramas unearthed Rutland Barrington and George Grossmith who had been performing comic song and dance routines in the provinces. 'I should have thought you required a fine man with a fine voice,' Grossmith mused after reading through his intended part. 'That's exactly what we don't want,' snorted Gilbert (Bradley: 1996).

Grossmith was worried that appearing on the professional stage might dissuade genteel Christian institutes from hiring him again. He also rejected D'Oyly Carte's initial offer on financial grounds, and asked for more money. D'Oyly Carte suggested they discuss the matter over lunch. There, with the help of oysters and champagne, he convinced a relaxed Grossmith into signing a contract worth three guineas *less* a week. The performer later calculated that D'Oyly Carte's epicurean seduction cost him some £1,800.

A cast hired on the cheap or no, Gilbert would soon create roles with these regular ensemble figures in mind, Barrington smoothly assuming the persona of King Paramount in *Utopia Limited* sixteen years later, for instance.

The Sorcerer wasn't initially successful even though it showed that the previously derided idea of the English comic opera could stand up to its French rivals. The *Monthly Musical Record* (January 1878) was most put out by Gilbert's decision to mock a man of the cloth: 'The earnest, hard-working and serious Clergy should not be made the subject of sneering caricature upon the stage. It is necessary that some relic of our ancient respect for dignity, position, or learning should be maintained.' Other elements of the British press commended Gilbert for finding a fresh way of enlivening an age-old theme. 'Messrs. W. S. Gilbert and Arthur Sullivan have once again combined their efforts with the happiest result,' wrote *The Times*; 'The Sorcerer*, produced at the Opéra Comique on Saturday Night before an audience that crowded the theatre in every part, achieved a genuine success, and moreover, a success in every respect deserved.' *Figaro*, unsympathetic to the company's aim of instigating an English comic opera in a French-styled venue, was as damning about the music as the *Monthly Musical Record* was about the blasphemy: 'There is nothing whatever in Mr Sullivan's score which any theatrical conductor engaged at a few pounds a week could not have written equally well ... The music is neither that of opera nor of *opéra* *bouffe*, but it misses the dramatic feeling of the one and the sparkle of the other, while it preserves the dull respectability of the former and the triviality of the latter.'

The Sorcerer eventually gained wider acceptance not on its own terms but on the coat-tails of the more substantial Savoy products such as *Patience* and *Iolanthe*. When it was revived again in 1898, Gilbert and Sullivan took their last curtain call together ... without speaking to each other, such was the strength of their mutual animus. *The Sorcerer* dropped out of the Savoy Opera repertoire after the Second World War – the scenery and costumes had been destroyed during a bombing raid – and it wasn't performed again by the company until 1971. Nowadays it is among the least performed Savoy Operas. One would like to think it was because no one has been found to fill adequately the shoes of Grossmith as John Wellington Wells and Barrington as Dr Daly.

1. *Pointdextre*: A heraldic surname of French origin. 'Point' is to pierce or prick; 'dexter' refers to the right-hand side.
2. *Sangazure*: French, 'blue blood'. Lady Sangazure has the only non-speaking principal part in the Savoy Operas.
3. PARTLET: A neck ruff. The word was applied to hen-like women.
4. DR DALY: The only traditional clergyman in the Savoy Operas, although it is worth mentioning that Pooh-Bah counts being Archbishop of Titipu among his manifold activities. The role was created by Barrington whose father was a clergyman. One first-night reviewer wrote how 'Mr Barrington is wonderful. He always manages to sing one-sixteenth of a tone flat; it's so like a vicar.'
5. *gilded dukes and belted earls*: The House of Lords, of which dukes are the most elevated group and earls third, is occasionally referred to as the 'gilded chamber'.
6. *Helen of Troy*: According to Greek mythology, Helen of Troy, who was half divine (her father was Zeus), was the most beautiful woman of her age. When the time came for her to marry she chose as a husband Menelaus, King of Sparta and brother of the mightiest Greek king, Agamemnon, even though Aphrodite, goddess of love, had promised her to Paris, Prince of Troy. Aphrodite later made Helen fall for Paris and the couple eloped to Troy. On discovering this, Menelaus declared war on the city and eventually won Helen back.
7. *the lucid lake of liquid love*: Typical Gilbertian alliteration, but with a nod to Milton's *Paradise Lost* (1667): 'He lights – if it were land that ever burned / With solid, as the lake with liquid fire' (Book I, lines 228–9).

8. *Aurora*: Roman goddess of dawn, famously satirized by William Hogarth in his painting *Four Times of the Day: Morning* (1738), in which a pock-marked Aurora, her appearance based on a relative of the painter who subsequently cut him out of her will, makes her way across Covent Garden Piazza to prayers at St Paul's.

9. NOTARY: A legal officer who certifies deeds and other writings with his official seal.

10. *Mechanics' Institutes*: Early nineteenth-century institutions aimed at workers (mechanics) featured reading-rooms, a lecture hall for debating societies and a library at a time when there were no public libraries in Britain. The scheme was adopted throughout the country and thrived during the Victorian era. The best-known surviving Mechanics' Institute building, at Burnley in Lancashire, is now an entertainments venue; few others remain.

11. *Noble fellows*: The recurring Victorian theme of the nobility of manual work reached its apogee with Ford Madox Brown's monumental painting *Work* (1852–65) which depicts a group of navvies laying a sewage system under The Mount in Hampstead, north-west London.

12. *St Mary Axe*: A street in the City of London (properly pronounced 'Simmery Axe'), named after a church, officially known as St Mary the Virgin and St Ursula and the Eleven Thousand Virgins, which was demolished in the late sixteenth century. The church's unusual name came from the legend of an English princess who went to Germany with 11,000 handmaidens but met a bloody end from axes wielded by Attila the Hun and his troops; one axe, supposedly, was later stored in the church.

13. *philtre*: A love potion. In the American short-story writer O'Henry's 'The Love-Philtre of Ikey Schoenstein' (1906), the hero administers to his intended 'two soluble tablets, each containing a quarter of a grain of morphia . . . a little sugar of milk to increase the bulk, the mixture [folded] neatly in a white paper'.

14. *Hercules*: Properly Heracles in Greek mythology, son of Zeus and Alcmene, he was known for the twelve labours he was obliged to undertake. He was nearly murdered in his infancy by his jealous stepmother, Hera, who put a serpent in his cradle, but which he killed using his great strength.

15. *Abudah chests, each containing a patent hag*: Abudah, in James Ridley's *Tales of the Genii* (1764), is a Baghdad merchant haunted by a hag. His stories were republished in 1820 by Sir Charles Morell and had considerable influence on the young Charles Dickens who incorporated ideas from them into *Great Expectations* (1861).

16. *Unified*: Government stock.

17. *John Wellington Wells*: One of the greatest comic roles in the Savoy Operas' canon, he has been played in a variety of ways. On the opening night of *The Sorcerer*, Grossmith appeared in frock-coat and top hat, and during the tea-pot scene staged an impromptu shuffle clutching the pot, imitating the hissing of a steam train. Fortunately Gilbert approved of the unauthorized experiment. Henry Lytton's Wells was a grotesque drunkard with bottle nose and mottled cheeks, described by A. H. Godwin in *Gilbert and Sullivan, A Critical Appreciation of the Savoy Operas* (1926) as 'a crude, unmannerly creature in a ludicrous garb'.

18. *melt a rich uncle in wax*: Make a waxen effigy to be melted down, an act which supposedly inflicts considerable pain on the target. In 'Sister Helen' (1881), Dante Gabriel Rossetti asks:

> Why did you melt your waxen man, Sister Helen?
> Today is the third since you began . . .
> Oh the waxen knave was plump today . . .
> How like dead folk he has dropped away! (lines 1–2, 22, 24)

19. *Djinn*: Genies who, according to Persian mythology, were made of fire two thousand years before the creation of Adam but who after sinning against God were demoted in rank. Their chief was Eblis, whom Allah cast out for refusing to worship Adam.

20. *Number seventy, Simmery Axe*: There was no 70 St Mary Axe at that time, which was why Gilbert deliberately chose the number.

21. *mirrors so magical*: According to St Augustine in *De Civitate Dei* (*The City of God*, 413–27), magic mirrors were used by the witches of Thessaly who wrote their oracles on them in human blood.

22. *Tetrapods*: Greek, 'four feet'. In this case it refers not to animals but to a verse form of four metrical feet popular with writers of Greek tragedy.

23. *'Lectro-biology*: An early term for hypnosis.

24. *nosology*: The study of disease classification.

25. *philology*: Study of language.

26. *Army and Navy Stores*: A London department store founded as a co-operative in 1871 by a group of military men who wanted to provide cheap provisions for colleagues and their families. After the First World War the store opened to the public on Victoria Street, Westminster.

27. *Incantation*: Based on a scene from the Weber opera *Der Freischütz* (1821) in which Max, the young huntsman, meets Caspar, servant of the Devil, at midnight to witness the forging of seven magic bullets.

28. *Fiends of flame and fire*: Compare Shelley's 'The Revolt of Islam' (1817):

'Give sanction from thine hell of fiends and flame / That we will kill with fire and torments slow' (X.xxix).

29. *Sally Lunn*: A young French refugee of the eighteenth century who settled in Bath, where she began to bake a bun that became a delicacy in Georgian times and was later named after her.

30. *Brindisi*: An Italian toast named after the Adriatic port.

31. *jorum*: A large drinking bowl named after the biblical character who according to the Book of Samuel brought King David vessels of silver, gold and brass.

32. *dark lantern*: A lantern with a sliding shutter, much loved by burglars, featured by Dickens in *Oliver Twist* (1838): 'We, being men, took a dark lantern that was standing on Brittle's hob, and groped our way downstairs in the pitch dark' (ch. 28).

33. *Baronet*: A hereditary British title ranking above all orders of knighthood except the Garter.

34. *KCB*: Knight Commander of the Bath, the second of the three classes of the Most Honourable Order of the Bath, is a chivalric order instituted by George I in May 1725. The name derives from an ancient ceremony whereby would-be knights bathed to purify themselves.

35. *Doctor of Divinity*: A holder of the highest theology degree.

36. *QC*: Queen's Counsel, i.e. a senior barrister appointed on the recommendation of the Lord Chancellor. QCs are often known as 'silks' after the fabric of their gowns.

37. *oi*: Gilbert is trying to denote a West Country accent. In 'An Elixir of Love', Ploverleigh, the setting for *The Sorcerer*, is 'a picturesque little village in Dorsetshire'.

38. *Rosherville*: Victorian pleasure gardens located in an old chalk quarry near Gravesend in Kent.

39. *One Tree Hill*: There are various south London possibilities for One Tree Hill but it is most likely to be the hill at Honor Oak, the site of Boadicea's defeat to Suetonius Paulinus in the year AD 61, where Elizabeth I is believed to have rested whilst picnicking in 1602, bestowing on the area its elevated title.

40. *mésalliances*: French, mismatched marriages.

41. *Ahrimanes*: The Zoroastrian god of evil and darkness. Gilbert may have been thinking at this point of the Thackeray line: 'I recognise the evil spirit, sir, and do honour to Ahrimanes in this young man.'

HMS Pinafore; or, The Lass that loved a Sailor

First performed 25 May 1878 at the Opéra Comique, London.

Original Cast

The Rt Hon. Sir Joseph Porter, KCB	George Grossmith
Captain Corcoran	Rutland Barrington
Ralph Rackstraw	George Power
Dick Deadeye	Richard Temple
Bill Bobstay	Fred Clifton
Bob Becket	Mr Dymott
Josephine	Emma Howson
Hebe	Jessie Bond
Mrs Cripps (Little Buttercup)	Harriett Everard

HMS Pinafore is a delicious comedy that satirizes the snobbery and hypocrisy of the English social system. It tells the tale of a lowly able seaman, Ralph Rackstraw, who has fallen in love with Josephine, his Captain's daughter, in turn 'sought in marriage' by Sir Joseph Porter, First Lord of the Admiralty, 'Ruler of the Queen's Navee'.

The plot rests on a typically Gilbertian topsy-turvy notion – mistaken identity at birth – a position outlined by Little Buttercup, who explains that many years before, when practising baby-farming, she had two children in her care, one high born, one of low birth, whom she mixed up. He who became Ralph Rackstraw should have been Captain Corcoran and vice versa. At the end of the play, the two swap stations; the world is righted.

The Victorian establishment was not initially amused. Benjamin Disraeli, Prime Minister, proclaimed that he had 'never seen anything so bad as *Pinafore*' (Baily: 1973), while the *Daily Telegraph* not only thought the 'music trite and the plot too thin' but dismissed *Pinafore* as 'a frothy production, destined soon to subside into nothingness'. Indeed, Gilbert and Sullivan's fourth collaboration nearly did fade into oblivion. But this was not due to any inadequacies of the libretto, plot or score. The summer of 1878 turned London into an inferno that made theatrical performance near impossible. Crowds dwindled as London wilted. Expenses surpassed receipts. The board of directors posed closure notices six times while the cast gallantly agreed to accept a pay cut of one-third. Then came salvation. Not solely through a break in the weather but mostly through Sullivan's inspired decision to incorporate melodies from the show in the Promenade concerts he was then conducting at the Royal Opera House. Sophisticated concert-goers marvelled at the ingenious marriage of melody and metre that could be found in this 'frothy nothingness'. (They would have marvelled more had they known that the songs had been composed by a man wracked with the pain of kidney-stones.) The promenaders decided to slum it down the Strand to see if the production merited equal refinement. It did. The crowds returned, the sun dipped and *Pinafore* was saved from being wrecked.

Only a few weeks elapsed before those damned directors chanced upon a new agitation. They had bankrolled the show, now they would prosper. Rather than pay the authors an increased rate, they mused, why should they not shift the production to another theatre and save a royalty or two? In fact, why not shift the scenery to the new venue as well? A band of hired thugs entered the Opéra Comique en masse on 31 July 1879, brushed their way past the hapless doorman and raided the stage. Invaders and stalwarts fought for the props and their pride, while George Grossmith gallantly explained the nature of the impromptu drama to the bemused audience on the other side of the 'safety' curtain. Eventually D'Oyly Carte's stalwart marines saw off the roughs. Not to be outdone, the impostors launched a rival *Pinafore* nearby. Both productions played side by side while m'learned friends extricated the rivals from their mess. This time victory to the authors and D'Oyly Carte was final. D'Oyly Carte paid off the recalcitrant directors and a new company was formed, with the impresario, Gilbert and Sullivan meeting on equal terms. *Pinafore* continued successfully for nearly two years, running for 571 performances in all.

Outside the theatre, beyond the turmoil of production ownership, Britain was asserting its imperial majesty on the seas. The authorities could afford to laugh at *HMS Pinafore* and at the real-life Porter – W. H. Smith (see note 9) – for Britain's power was peerless. A week after *Pinafore* opened the Ottoman Empire ceded Cyprus to Britain, and even when Britain endured a diplomatic crisis with Russia over the Navy's presence in the Balkans, the disagreement ended in Britain's favour. This coup was zealously commemorated by the music-hall performer G. H. Macdermott in his 'War Song' (written by G. W. Hunt), introduced at the London Pavilion in 1878, which gave the country a suitable neologism:

> We don't want to fight but by jingo if we do . . .
> We've got the ships, we've got the men, and got the money too!
> We've fought the Bear before . . . and while we're Britons true,
> The Russians shall not have Constantinople.

(See also *The Grand Duke* note 26.)

Britain was also establishing its might retrospectively. At the beginning of 1878 Cleopatra's Needle, an Egyptian granite obelisk dating back to 1475 BC, arrived in London after a stormier passage than that experienced aboard *HMS* Pinafore and was erected on Victoria Embankment near the Opéra Comique. Gilbert admirably captured the euphoric spirit of the times:

> He is an Englishman!
>   For he himself has said it,
>   And it's greatly to his credit,
> That he is an Englishman!

HMS Pinafore even managed to cross the Atlantic in style. Eight New York companies began performing the work, as did another six in Philadelphia. The streets of these cities were soon awash with barrel-organists and bandsters airing its tunes. *The Times*'s US correspondent reported that it had taken 'our leading cities by storm'. *Pinafore* mania was everywhere. Alas, neither Gilbert, Sullivan nor D'Oyly Carte were profiting from this. The American enthusiasts had pirated the work and few were bothering to remain faithful to the text or music. D'Oyly Carte made a Stateside visit and surmised that if America was to reproduce the work as it had been intended, with some English cast members, they would be able to recoup some of the lost revenue.

Gilbert and Sullivan and Co. crossed the Atlantic to set up a new production. Their trip westwards in October 1879 was so rough Gilbert must have wondered whether Neptune was seeking revenge for some perceived slight, perhaps his fanciful claim that he was descended from Sir Humphrey Gilbert, the pioneering Elizabethan explorer. But when the vessel neared New Jersey, and Gilbert and Sullivan saw steamers decorated with Union Jacks alongside the stars and stripes, and heard the bands playing *Pinafore* melodies, they realized the hard voyage had been worthwhile. Lip-licking interviewers gathered round the startled writer and told him he would make a fortune if he changed 'HMS' to 'USS' and introduced the Stars and Stripes for the British ensign, but Gilbert refused to compromise. Yet despite reviews lavish with praise, the rogue versions had sated the public's appetite for *HMS Pinafore* and sales of seats for the real deal were low. 'We shall reduce our expenses by not paying the postage on our letters home,' Sullivan joked to his mother (Sullivan–Flower: 1927).

The partnership and D'Oyly Carte were, however, to reap the reward for their labours with the next production, *The Pirates of Penzance*, which also allowed Gilbert to capitalize handsomely on his sea-born profits and buy himself a yacht.

1. *HMS Pinafore*: Gilbert chose the name of the ship for its rhyming quality: it resonated with 'one cheer more'. He modelled *Pinafore* on Nelson's HMS *Victory* and ensured authenticity by visiting Nelson's vessel in Portsmouth, where he sketched details of the quarterdeck, taking care with the smallest ring, bolt and halyard. Gilbert had a stone model of the ship mounted on the gable of his Kensington home, but when a visitor asked if it was HMS *Pinafore* he replied: 'Sir, I don't put my trade mark on my house' (Dark: 1923).

2. *Portsmouth*: English south-coast port; birthplace of Dickens and known in naval and football circles as 'Pompey'.

3. *jacky*: Twists of tobacco soaked in rum for chewing.

4. *Soft tommy*: Type of bread.

5. *polonies*: A corruption of the word 'Bologna', the Italian city where polony sausages were first made.

6. *Spithead*: Body of water in the Solent off Portsmouth.

7. *Dick Deadeye*: A suitably nautical name as a deadeye is a large wooden block connected to the shrouds of a ship.

8. *What, never? / Hardly ever*: The phrase became one of the most hackneyed of the era, seeping into the public consciousness much in the same way that 'Don't mention the war' and 'This parrot is deceased' did a hundred years later. Legend has it that one American newspaper editor, after counting the phrase twenty times in the latest edition, summoned his staff and ordered them to desist immediately from using the phrase again. 'What never?' asked a young reporter, only to be fired on the spot.

9. *Sir Joseph Porter*: Based on William Henry Smith, son of the founder of the W. H. Smith newsagency business, who was Conservative MP for Westminster at the time of *Pinafore*'s premiere and more pertinently as First Lord of the Admiralty the minister in charge of the Navy (1877–80), during which time he never went to sea.

   In writing to Sullivan in 1878 Gilbert noted impishly 'the fact that the First Lord in the opera is a Radical of the most pronounced type will do away with any suspicion that W. H. Smith is intended' (Dark: 1923). It was not that Gilbert intended there to be no link between Porter and Smith, but rather that he was anxious to protect Sullivan who mixed in elevated social circles. He shouldn't have been so neurotic. Disraeli himself was soon describing the minister as *Pinafore Smith*.

   By the time Gilbert came to pen *The Story of H.M.S. Pinafore* (1908), a guide for children, he was less circumspect about Smith, who had died seventeen years previously:

One of the most important personages in the Government of that day was Sir Joseph Porter, First Lord of the Admiralty. You would naturally think that a person who commanded the entire Navy would be the most accomplished sailor who could be found, but that is not the way in which such things are managed in England. Sir Joseph Porter . . . knew nothing whatever about ships. Now as England is a great maritime country it is very important that all Englishmen should understand something about men-of-war. So as soon as it was discovered that his ignorance of a ship was so complete that he did not know one end of it from the other, some important person said: 'Let us set this poor ignorant gentleman to command the British Fleet, and by that means give him an opportunity of ascertaining what a ship really is.'

Grossmith played the role on the opening night in the guise of Lord Nelson, and later captured some of the essence of the name Porter by dubbing his great comic creation, hero of *The Diary of a Nobody* (1892), Charles Pooter.

10. *KCB*: See *The Sorcerer* note 34.
11. *BARCAROLLE*: A song imitating those sung by Venetian gondoliers.
12. *loud nine-pounders*: The smallest of the canons carried by the Royal Navy in the nineteenth century.
13. *articled clerk*: One who is training to be a fully qualified solicitor.
14. *pocket borough*: Also called a rotten borough; a parliamentary constituency where votes were controlled by a local dignitary, who could therefore nominate the local Members of Parliament. Those who opposed the system and favoured reform were obliged to participate in this sham in order to change it, which was why in 1812 the reformist Henry Brougham was obliged to buy the parliamentary seat of Camelford and its thirty-one voters from the Whig peer the Duke of Bedford for £32,000. Pocket boroughs were abolished in the 1832 Reform Act.
15. *hornpipe*: A wind instrument with a single reed, finger holes and bell, which gave its name to a British folk dance.
16. *grog*: Alcoholic drink, long associated with the Navy, consisting of one shot of rum, one teaspoon of sugar, a squeeze of lime juice, a cinnamon stick and enough boiling water to fill the glass. Grog was introduced by the eighteenth-century naval leader Admiral Vernon, whose nickname was 'Old Grog', the name taken from the grogram coat of thick silk he wore. Parliament abolished the Navy's daily grog ration in July 1970.
17. *seven bells*: On board ship the day is divided into six watches, each of four hours. A bell is rung every half-hour to remind the crew of the time.

18. *GLEE*: Eighteenth-century English song sung by three or more unaccompanied voices.

19. *Cimmerian darkness*: The Cimmerians were a nomadic race that moved from Mesopotamia into central Asia. According to Homer's *Odyssey* they dwelt in a dark land beyond the ocean.

20. *ganglion*: A tumour.

21. *Jove's armoury*: The armoury of Jove (see *Thespis* note 6) was thunder and lightning.

22. *bumboat*: A small boat used for selling groceries to ships in port.

23. *Highlows*: Laced women's ankle boots popular in Victorian times.

24. *Jackdaws strut in peacock's feathers*: In Aesop's 'The Vain Jackdaw', the bird covers himself in gaudy feathers dropped by other birds to try and win a beauty contest but only succeeds in becoming a figure of fun.

25. *All that glitters is not gold*: Adapted from the line 'All that glisters is not gold' from Shakespeare's *The Merchant of Venice* (II.7). Gilbert often adapted Shakespeare even though he was not particularly enamoured of the bard, as he once revealed to Grossmith: 'Promise me faithfully not to mention this to a single person, not even to your dearest friend. I don't think Shakespeare rollicking.' He also once told a friend: 'Shakespeare is a very obscure writer. Explain this passage. "I would as lief be thrust through a quicket hedge as cry Pooh to a callow throstle." ' 'Aah, that's easy,' replied the friend. 'A great lover of feathered songsters, rather than disturb the little warbler, would prefer to go through a thorny hedge. I can't recall the passage. Where does it occur?' 'It doesn't,' Gilbert explained. 'I have just invented it, and jolly good Shakespeare too!' (Dark: 1923).

26. *Storks turn out to be but logs*: The frogs in Aesop's 'The Frogs Desiring a King', having voted to be ruled by a king, are sent a log by Jove. After being frightened they realize it is lifeless and petition for another ruler, only to be sent a stork which gobbles them up, the moral being 'Better no rule than cruel rule'.

27. *Bulls are but inflated frogs*: 'The Frog and the Ox', also from *Aesop's Fables*, tells the story of a frog that tries to make itself as big as an ox but only succeeds in puffing itself up to bursting point.

28. *farthing*: British coin, worth a quarter of a pre-decimal penny, abolished in 1961.

29. *Only brave deserve the fair*: Adapted from John Dryden's 'None but the brave deserve the fair', line 15 from *Alexander's Feast* (1697).

30. *Wink is often good as nod*: Originally 'A nod is as good as a wink to a blind horse'; the first known use was by William Godwin in *The Adventures of Caleb Williams* (1794).

31. *spoils the child who spares the rod*: Based on Proverbs 23:13: 'Withhold not correction from the child: for if thou beatest him with the rod, he shall not die.'

32. *Thirsty lambs run foxy dangers*: A hybrid of various tales from *Aesop's Fables*, in particular 'The Fox, the Lamb and the Dog'.

33. *Dogs are found in many mangers*: Also taken from *Aesop's Fables*, in this case 'The Dog in the Manger'. The phrase relates to a selfish person who won't let another use something he or she does not want.

34. *Paw of cat the chestnut snatches*: Pope Julius II, the early sixteenth-century pontiff, supposedly owned a cat that could pull chestnuts from the fire.

35. *Worn-out garments show new patches*: Adapted from Mark 2:21: 'No man also seweth a piece of new cloth on an old garment: else the new piece that filled it up taketh away from the old, and the rent is made worse.'

36. *Only count the chick that hatches*: This is taken from the famous English saying 'Don't count your chickens before they are hatched.'

37. *SCENA*: An elaborate dramatic solo.

38. *Rare 'blue and white'*: Blue and white Chinese ceramics, particularly Blue Willow pattern, have long captivated not just the genteel British middle classes but wealthy Europeans as well. Augustus the Strong, seventeenth-century King of Poland and elector of Saxony, supposedly swapped an entire regiment of soldiers for forty-eight Chinese vases. In 1867 there was a special sale of blue and white Chinese pottery at Christie's auction house in London. Dante Gabriel Rossetti and Whistler were particular fans of such pieces, and Oscar Wilde's college rooms at Oxford were renowned for his collection of 'blue'. 'Oh, would that I could live up to my blue china,' he was heard to wax, a line which the cartoonist George du Maurier happily borrowed for one of his captions. In *Patience*, Reginald Bunthorne describes himself as a 'blue-and-white young man'.

39. *Gillow's*: Furniture shop originally based in Oxford Street and later Brompton Road.

40. *Elysian*: Idyllic, as in the Elysian fields of Greek mythology, where the souls of the virtuous were placed after death.

41. *cat-o'-nine-tails*: An instrument of punishment consisting of nine pieces of cord fastened to a handle.

42. *Hymen*: See *Thespis* note 12.

43. *telephone*: Perhaps the first literary reference to a device that had been patented only two years previously. The first London telephone exchange was set up in June 1878, a month after *Pinafore* opened.

44. *baby-farming*: Such was the stigma attached to procreation out of wedlock that the bizarre practice of baby farming developed in the Victorian era. It involved women offering fostering and adoption services to unmarried mothers for a price, usually around £10. The practice faded once suitable welfare agencies were established towards the end of the century.

The Pirates of Penzance; or, The Slave of Duty

First performed 30 December 1879 at the Royal Bijou Theatre, Paignton, Devon.

Original Cast

	New York	London
Major-General Stanley	J. H. Ryley	George Grossmith
The Pirate King	'Signor Brocolini'	Richard Temple
Samuel	Furneaux Cook	George Temple
Frederic	Hugh Talbot	George Power
Sergeant of Police (Edward)	F. Clifton	Rutland Barrington
Mabel	Blanche Roosevelt	Marion Hood
Edith	Jessie Bond	Julia Gwynne
Kate	Rosina Brandram	Lilian La Rue
Isabel	Billie Barlow	Neva Bond
Ruth	Alice Barnett	Emily Cross

Uniquely among the Savoy Operas, and despite its ancient British setting, *The Pirates of Penzance* was given its official premiere overseas: in New York. D'Oyly Carte, Gilbert and Sullivan carefully chose the location at a time when the lack of copyright laws between Britain and America was causing them considerable financial privation. As soon as a song was heard on one side of the Atlantic it could be performed on the other side, with no payment owing to the publishers. By launching a new work in America they could beat the pirates to the spoils. 'I will not have another libretto of mine produced if the Americans are going to steal it,' Gilbert thundered, adding: 'not that I need the money so much but it upsets my digestion' (MacGeorge: 1930).

Unfortunately their grand plan soon began to fall apart. Sullivan, about to begin rehearsals, discovered he had left his material for the first act in Britain, and so the performers had to work on Act II instead while he rewrote the previous section. Then, only a few days before *Pirates'* premiere, the band went on strike. The new work was grand opera, they asserted, and therefore they deserved more money. 'Very well,' Sullivan responded, 'if you strike I shall bring over the Covent Garden orchestra to take your place and in the meantime run the show with myself at piano.' The bluff worked, the strikers relented, but he only just finished the music in time; his overture was not ready for the dress rehearsal, and once again he overworked himself, often staying up to 5.30 in the morning. By the opening night, unable to eat or sleep and fuelled by the popular drugs of the day – champagne and oysters, a dozen of the latter – he struggled to the conductor's podium 'more dead than alive', he later explained (Sullivan–Flower: 1927).

Fortunately *The Pirates of Penzance* was rapturously received. The cast – J. H. Ryley, Furneaux Cook and the grandly Italianate sounding 'Signor Brocolini', prosaically born as John Clark in Cork, Ireland – was sufficiently experienced in topsy-turvydom and overcame the absence of Grossmith, Barrington and Temple. New York loved the wild but essentially British setting of the remote rocky Cornish cove. It instantly warmed to the group of pirates drinking and playing cards, sympathized with Frederic, the unhappy Pirate apprentice, who had been wrongly apprenticed as a pirate instead of a *pilot*, and swooned to the work's joyous romance, particularly scenes such as the opening of Act II, set in a ruined Gothic chapel by moonlight.

Meanwhile D'Oyly Carte's team, low on sentiment, were taking no chances with artistic security. Rehearsals had been held with guards on the door. Now, after every show, they locked up the music in a safe until the next performance. Nevertheless potential pirates tried to bribe members of the orchestra for the score. Expert music readers sat in the stalls desperately trying to write down the main melodies by ear. To protect themselves back home, Gilbert and Sullivan made plans for a copyright performance to be held almost simultaneously in Britain. This took place not at the Opéra Comique, where *Pirates* later enjoyed its first London run, but well away from the London theatrical world at the Royal Bijou Theatre, Paignton, in Devon. There, the *Pinafore* touring company, still carrying their scripts and with handkerchiefs tied around their heads to denote their picaresque qualifications, played before one 'paying' customer, whose one guinea fee was returned after the final curtain came down. *Pirates* transferred to London in April 1880 and ran for 363 performances, by which time it had practically overrun not just the Eastern Seaboard cities of the United States but parts of the Wild West (wilder and wester than Cornwall) as well.

Despite initial complaints that the new opera was the previous opera, *HMS Pinafore* Mark Two, or rather Act III (there are many similarities), *The Pirates of Penzance* has remained one of the most successful and most repeated of the series. Not because of the timeliness of its satire (what shocked the Victorians amuses us), or the severity of Gilbert's wit, but because of the contrary: the warmth with which Gilbert ridicules the snobbery of the nouveau riche, bourgeois respectability and police bumptiousness, the latter encapsulated in what is probably the Savoy series' best-known song, 'A Policeman's Lot'.

Contemporary versions have boldly changed the format with some success, despite severe and understandable criticism from Savoyards, not least of all Joseph Papp's flamboyant 1980s rock production, released as a film in 1982 starring Kevin Kline (a perfect choice) and somewhat incongruously AOR chanteuse Linda Ronstadt. A version which opened at London's revamped Coliseum Theatre in Covent Garden in December 2004 was low on satire but high on sartorial dazzle, the cast looking more like punks than pirates, with their tattoos, mohican haircuts and piercings. It was a long way from Sullivan's grand opera aspirations but perfectly in keeping with Gilbert's view that 'Every moment brings a treasure / Of its own especial pleasure' (Dark: 1923).

1. *Cornwall*: Two of the Savoy Operas take place in this far western outpost of England as *Ruddigore* is set in the fictitious Cornish village of Rederring. The sea around Cornwall, the English county most surrounded by water, was for centuries at the mercy of pirates, the most famous of whom were the seventeenth-century Killigrews. Sir John Killigrew of the same family built the first lighthouse at the Lizard in 1619.

2. *scuttling a Cunarder*: I.e the sinking of a ship of the Cunard line, the company founded by the Canadian-born Samuel Cunard in 1839. The company's first steamship, the *Britannia*, sailed from Liverpool to Boston the following year, and soon Cunard was running regular mail and passenger services to the United States. The company's heyday came in the early twentieth century with vessels such as the *Carpathia* and the *Mauretania*. The former rescued survivors from the *Titanic* in 1912, while the latter, then the biggest liner the world had ever seen, operated under the slogan: 'Getting there is half the fun.' Cunard now runs two of the world's best-known luxury liners: *Queen Elizabeth* 2 and *Queen Mary* 2.

3. *cutting out a P&O*: Separating a P&O ship to capture it. P&O is the Peninsula and Oriental Steam Navigation Company, founded in 1822 by Brodie McGhie Willcox, a London shipbroker, and Arthur Anderson, a Royal Navy clerk who worked in Willcox's office.

4. *As a child I was regularly apprenticed to your band*: The infant Gilbert,

aged two, was stolen in Naples by a couple of 'ingratiating brigands', as Leslie Baily (1973) called them, while being pushed by his nurse. His father paid a £25 ransom to recover the child.

5. *black flag*: Pirates began to use a black flag in the seventeenth century. Better known is the flag sported by the nastier pirates, the Jolly Roger, the name a corruption of the French *joli rouge* – 'pretty red' – which were blood-red flags emblazoned with a graphic of two human thigh bones laid across one another.

6. *Custom House*: Waterside office for the Department of Customs and Excise.

7. *climbing over rocky mountain*: Gilbert based the girls' chorus on lines from *Thespis*.

8. *doctor of divinity*: See *The Sorcerer* note 35.

9. *caravanserai*: A rather incongruous word for Cornwall, as it is the Persian word for a desert inn where caravans draw up.

10. *Wards in Chancery*: A young person under the care of a guardian, answerable in the nineteenth century to the Court of Chancery, as depicted by Dickens in *Bleak House* (1853): ' "More wiglomeration," said [Mr Jarndyce]. "It's the only name I know for the thing. He is a ward in Chancery, my dear" ' (ch. 8).

11. *Major-General*: Major-General Stanley was partly based on Sir Garnet Wolseley, who led the British Army in the Ashanti wars of 1873, and who in 1885 was sent to relieve General Gordon in Khartoum.

12. *Marathon to Waterloo*: After the Battle of Marathon, fought between the Persians and the Greeks in September 490 BC, a messenger ran the twenty-two miles from the battle scene to Attica to deliver news of the Greek victory, only to die the moment he had conveyed the message. The Olympic movement later purloined the name for its race of similar length and endurance. Waterloo, in Belgium, was where Napoleon surrendered in 1815 after the battle between the victorious British and Prussian forces, and the defeated French.

13. *equations, both the simple and the quadratical*: Simple equations are of the form $ax + b = 0$, where a and b are real numbers and x is a variable, and denote straight lines. Quadratic, rather than quadratical, equations take the form $ax^2 + bx + c = 0$ and denote curves.

14. *binomial theorem*: The theorem, first outlined by Isaac Newton in a letter to Henry Oldenburg dated 13 June 1676, states that for numbers a, b and n

$$(a + b)^n = a^n + \frac{na^{n-1} b}{1!} + \frac{n(n-1)a^{n-2} b^2}{2!} + \ldots b^n$$

Despite its daunting nature, the binomial theorem is used regularly, albeit in a watered down form, by bridge players in calculating the likelihood of how the opponents' cards might be distributed and by gamblers when calculating their winnings from multiple bets such as 'Yankees'.

15. *square of the hypotenuse*: A reference to perhaps the most famous mathematical rule of all – Pythagoras's Theorem – which states that for a right angled triangle of lengths x, y and z where z is the longest side (the hypotenuse), $x^2 + y^2 = z^2$.

16. *integral and differential calculus*: Isaac Newton (1643–1727) and Gottfried Leibniz (1646–1716) are both credited with originating calculus, the mathematics of rates of change, simultaneously *c.* 1674.

17. *animalculous*: A microscopic animal.

18. *King Arthur's and Sir Caradoc's*: No British story is more laden down in legend than that of King Arthur, the alleged sixth-century warlord, who led the English forces against the Saxons with his Knights of the Round Table, of whom Sir Caradoc was said to be one of the most valiant.

19. *acrostics*: Puzzles in which the first letter of each line spells out a word or message. There are several Hebrew acrostics in the Bible, for example in Psalm 119.

20. *elegiacs*: Types of epic Classical poetry with alternate hexameters and pentameters.

21. *Heliogabalus*: Third-century Roman emperor, born Varius Avitus Bassianus, also known as Caesar Marcus Aurelius Antonius Augustus. His short reign was coloured by animated homosexual orgies and the promotion of the pagan god Baal. He adopted the name Heliogabalus after being appointed priest of the sun-god, Elagabal.

22. *In conics I can floor peculiarities parabulous*: Shapes such as circles, ellipses and parabolae are made when a cone is cut by a plane.

23. *Raphaels ... Gerard Dows ... Zoffanies*: Italian Renaissance artist Raffaello Sanzio (1483–1520); Gerard Dou (1613–75), Dutch portrait painter and pupil of Rembrandt; and Johannes Josephus Zauffaly (1725–1810), German neoclassical portrait painter who settled in England where he made his name with commissions of actors on stage.

24. *croaking chorus from the Frogs of Aristophanes*: The infamous 'berke-kekex koax koax' chorus from the Aristophanes comedy *The Frogs*, written 406 BC.

25. *fugue*: Musical composition in which a theme or themes is extended and developed through counterpoint.

26. *Babylonic cuneiform*: Babylonian form of writing dating back to the

fourth millennium BC, in which wedge-shaped characters were pressed into clay.

27. *Caractacus*: Leader of the rebel Britons during the Roman invasion of 43 AD. After nine years he was defeated and taken to Rome, where, after being made to take part in a triumphal parade, the Emperor Claudius pardoned him and his family.

28. *mamelon*: A mound used in fortifications.

29. *ravelin*: A ridge.

30. *chassepôt rifle*: A bolt gun that fires a cartridge, named after Antoine A. Chassepot, first used by the French Army in 1870.

31. *commissariat*: Army department in charge of providing food and supplies.

32. *sat a gee*: Ridden a horse.

33. *A ruined chapel*: David Eden of the Sir Arthur Sullivan Society has argued that Gilbert made a poor choice in trying to satirize the romance of the Gothic ruin, for this was more than fifty years after the cult, inspired by Horace Walpole's Strawberry Hill, had run its course.

34. *emeutes*: French, 'brawls'. Bradley (1996) suggests that Gilbert was thinking of using the word 'brawls', in which case the next line would have needed to end with the Victorianly incorrect 'balls'.

35. *Astronomer Royal*: Official title of the royally appointed head of the Greenwich Observatory, a post established in 1675, first awarded to John Flamsteed. The observatory, through which the 0° Meridian runs, is now a museum.

36. *leap-year*: The plot hinges on the notion that as Frederic was born on 29 February in a leap year he has not yet reached his twenty-first birthday, only a quarter of that. Leap years exist because the earth takes not 365 days but nearly 365 and a quarter days to complete its orbit around the sun. Therefore an extra day is needed, mostly every four years, to correct any anomalies in the calendar.

37. *General Stanley*: A name very much in the news around the time of *Pirates*' opening. There was a Sir Frederick Stanley, Secretary of State for War 1878–80, and the better-known Henry Morton Stanley (1841–1904), intrepid explorer of deepest Africa and 'discoverer' of David Livingstone in 1871.

38. *centrebit*: An instrument for boring cylindrical holes that turns on a projecting centrepoint; a burglar's tool.

39. *silent matches*: Invented in 1836 by the Hungarian János Irinyi who used a mixture of phosphorous mixed with lead dioxide, instead of calcium chlorate, for the heads.

40. *Central Criminal Court*: See *Trial by Jury* note 6.

Patience; or, Bunthorne's Bride

First performed 23 April 1881 at the Opéra Comique, London.

Original Cast

Colonel Calverley	Richard Temple
Major Murgatroyd	Frank Thornton
Lieut. the Duke of Dunstable	Durward Lely
Reginald Bunthorne	George Grossmith
Archibald Grosvenor	Rutland Barrington
Mr Bunthorne's solicitor	George Bowley
The Lady Angela	Jessie Bond
The Lady Saphir	Julia Gwynne
The Lady Ella	May Fortescue
The Lady Jane	Alice Barnett
Patience	Leonora Braham

How ironic that Oscar Wilde should condemn satire for being as 'sterile as it is shameful and as impotent as it is insolent', for being the 'homage which mediocrity pays to genius' (*The English Renaissance of Art*, a lecture given in New York in 1882), as Gilbert and Sullivan's 1881 opera, *Patience*, while lampooning Wilde and the Aesthetic Movement which enclosed him and his ilk like a cloak of crushed velvet in the late nineteenth century, also had the probably unintended but nevertheless unmistakable outcome of enthusing later generations into admiring the very characters and characteristics it mocks.

Aestheticism was central to the reaction against the gross industrialization of society which characterized the Victorian era. For every tub-thumping capitalist there was a nostalgic romantic advocating handicrafts rather than mass production, traditional decoration not metallic brutality. Within the arts this was manifested in the revival of English vernacular architecture from the 1850s, embodied by William Morris's Red House at Bexley Heath and the later proto-suburban work of Norman Shaw, and the arrival of the Pre-Raphaelite school of artists headed by Dante Gabriel Rossetti and John Everett Millais.

By the 1870s, the Pre-Raphaelites had been supplanted by the Aesthetes, who extended their predecessors' romanticism into a manifesto that trumpeted *l'art pour l'art* – art for art's sake. Oscar Wilde's dynamic arrival in London in 1878 gave the Aesthetes a suitably heroic and flamboyant figure, and galvanized the sceptics, for Wilde, describing himself as Professor of Aesthetics, seemed more concerned with fashion than cultural output.

And it is Wilde's shadow that towers over *Patience*, refracted through its two chief characters: the poets Reginald Bunthorne and Archibald Grosvenor. Bunthorne, described as 'fleshly', and Grosvenor 'idyllic', are composites of several late nineteenth-century figures, not just Wilde but the artist James Whistler, the poet Algernon Charles Swinburne, his lesser-known contemporary Coventry Patmore, and the design guru, proto-socialist and epic poet William Morris. The two poets are rivals for the village milkmaid, the 'Patience' of the title. It is Grosvenor who wins her hand, and though the opera is alternatively titled *Bunthorne's Bride*, Bunthorne is the only man left bride-less at the end.

Satirizing the movement wasn't a new theme in 1881, for the *Contemporary Review* had savaged the Aesthetes more than ten years before and the cartoons of George du Maurier in *Punch* kept the jokes in the public eye; nor is it a dated one – witness the current cynicism afforded to those who now extol so-called New Age philosophies in opposition to mass, rootless culture or globalization. But it is Gilbert who has provided the most memorable satirical touches. It is hard not to marvel at Bunthorne's poem, a masterpiece of labyrinthine lexical long-windedness in lines such as: 'What time the poet hath hymned / The writhing maid, lithe-limbed, / Quivering on amaranthine asphodel'. It is hard not to feel a touch of self-satisfaction when, soon after, 'alone' and 'unobserved', Bunthorne admits to being a pseud (and this after musing on shallowness): 'Then let me own / I'm an aesthetic sham!'; even worse, admits that his 'languid love for lilies' and his affectation for medievalism has been contrived for no other reason than to quell his fear of not being loved. In other words, that it's all a show to attract the ladies.

Was Wilde mortified? Perhaps if he had been a sham, an impostor, a false prophet, he might have buckled under the weight of ridicule. Instead, Wilde had nothing to fear. He bought a box seat for the opening night and declared the show a success. Alongside him was Whistler, flattered that a member of the cast had adopted his trademark white tuft of hair. Cynics pointed out that Wilde had refused to see an earlier send-up, *The Colonel* (1881), by Francis Burnand, editor of *Punch*, a magazine which had pioneered mockery of the Aesthetes, which he wrote off as 'poor', and may have embraced *Patience* because he knew the show would be successful. 'Dear Grossmith, I should like to go to the first night of your new opera,' he wrote to the Gilbert and Sullivan stalwart who played Bunthorne on the opening night; 'With Gilbert and Sullivan I am sure we will have something better than the dull farce of *The Colonel*. I am looking forward to being greatly amused' (Richard Ellman, *Oscar Wilde* (1987)).

Wilde made a wise choice in running with the winners, for *Patience*'s success had the paradoxical effect of widening the Aesthetes' popularity, perhaps even aiding their most fruitful period, which was to include the work of Aubrey Beardsley and the plays for which Wilde is still best known. And to underline the irony, D'Oyly Carte promoted both *Patience* and Wilde's 1881 tour of the United States, where Wilde was able to explain Aestheticism and simultaneously stimulate American interest in a new opera which lampooned him, a paradox which may explain why he began lacing his earlier support of the opera with a dose of scepticism and a withering quip, describing *Patience* as the tribute which mediocrity pays to genius.

Aesthetes weren't the initial target in *Patience*. In devising the opera Gilbert first aired one of his Bab Ballads, 'The Rival Curates', about two timid priests, one the wonderfully named the Rev Lawn Tennison (sic), but then decided that an opera attacking the clergy might not be in good taste: 'I do not feel happy about it,' he wrote to Sullivan; 'I mistrust the clerical element. I feel hampered by the restrictions which the nature of the subject places upon my freedom of action' (Dark: 1923). So Gilbert forsook the Church for the Word. Not the Word of God, but the florid, decorative, serifed Word, probably cast in Troy or Golden, the Word as it might have appeared in a Morris woodcut. It wasn't an improbable switch. Many of the era's most decorative talents were strongly allied with a romanticized vision of Christianity. They peddled an idealized view of a suffering saintly church and a pastoral medievalism that eschewed the stock images of nineteenth-century Protestant Britain, with its smoking metal machines, money mania and industrial work ethic, for a mystical spirituality and love of ceremony, a belief in a deeper beauty at the expense of reason and logic.

Patience was premiered at the Opéra Comique, on 23 April 1881 and transferred to the new Savoy Theatre, where it ran for a year and a half (578 performances), its initial run being second in length only to *The Mikado* among the canon. Interestingly, it was the first Gilbert and Sullivan opera to be performed in a building – the Savoy Theatre – which in being expressively modern and progressive was everything the Aesthetes abjured. When D'Oyly Carte went on the stage on the opening night at the new venue, held a bulb covered with muslin in his hand, smashed it with a hammer and brandished a cloth absent of scorch marks to reassure the public that there was no danger from the hundreds of electric lamps bathing the auditorium in a rich yellow light, he ushered in the new technological era and knocked another nail in the coffin of the medievalists.

1. *Twenty*: A customer once threatened the D'Oyly Carte company with legal action under the Trades Description Act for not fielding twenty

maidens in a production of *Patience*. The management responded by claiming that there was nothing in the text to say that all twenty maidens had to be on the stage at the same time.

2.   *love will die*: When Jessie Bond, who played Angela in the original production, received a love letter from some members of the audience, Gilbert became unreasonably possessive and angrily confronted the protagonists. 'There are three ways of dealing with you,' he thundered. 'I will go before the curtain, if you like, explain what has happened, and say that Miss Bond refuses to continue whilst you are here, or you can go of your own accord, or I can send a couple of commissionaires to carry you' (MacGeorge: 1930). After Bond married (her husband wasn't one of the *Patience* suitors), Gilbert called her a fool and refused to send a present.

3.   *Reginald*: Bunthorne, billed in the cast list as a 'fleshly poet', is often likened to Wilde or Whistler, but a fitting comparison would be the incorrigible Algernon Swinburne, the 'libidinous laureate of a pack of satyrs' according to the *Saturday Review*'s John Morley, whom Robert Buchanan included in 1866 as part of the 'Fleshly School of Poetry'. In 1880, a year before *Patience*'s appearance, du Maurier, the *Punch* cartoonist, introduced two characters, the poet Jellaby Postlethwaite and his painter friend Maudle, both of whom spoke with sub-Wildean flourishes.

4.   *cynosure*: Shining star. The word has a strange etymology. The Greek *kunosoura* means dog's tail, which was the ancient name for the constellation Ursa Minor.

5.   *Dragoon Guards*: Mounted infantrymen armed with light rifles.

6.   *Lord Nelson on board of the Victory*: *Victory*, Nelson's flagship at the 1805 Battle of Trafalgar, and now the oldest surviving warship in the world, can be found in dry dock at Portsmouth naval base. Gilbert used the ship as the model for HMS *Pinafore* in the opera of the same name.

7.   *Bismarck*: Otto von Bismarck, first Chancellor of Prussia (1866–90).

8.   *humour of Fielding*: Henry Fielding's *Tom Jones* (1749) is one of the first great comic novels in English literature.

9.   *Paget*: Sir James Paget (1814–99), one-time President of the Royal College of Surgeons and sergeant-surgeon to Queen Victoria.

10.   *Jullien*: Louis Antoine Jullien (1812–60), conductor of the Promenade concerts, toyed with the idea of setting 'The Lord's Prayer' to music so that he could witness the publication of a manuscript bearing the legend: ' "The Lord's Prayer". Words by Jesus Christ. Music by Jullien'.

11.   *Macaulay*: Thomas Babington Macaulay (1800–59), the greatest historian of the age.

12. *Boucicault*: Anglo-Irish playwright Dionysius Lardner Boucicault (1822–90).

13. *Bishop of Sodor and Man*: Sodor and Man is the diocese of the Church of England that includes the Isle of Man and originally the Hebrides. Since the isle is not part of the United Kingdom the Bishop cannot sit in the House of Lords. *Sodor*, Norse for 'southern isles'.

14. *D'Orsay*: Count Alfred Guillaume Gabriel d'Orsay (1801–52), friend of Lord Byron, known as the Count of France, a title bought by his family.

15. *Victor Emmanuel*: First king of a united Italy (reigned 1861–78).

16. *peak-haunting Peveril*: Sir Walter Scott's 1823 novel, *Peveril of the Peak*, set around the time of the Popish Plot of 1678 when Catholics were supposedly planning to assassinate Charles II and replace him with his Roman Catholic brother, the Duke of York (later King James II), features the Derbyshire landowner Sir Geoffrey Peveril. 'Peveril of the Peak' was also the name of the early nineteenth-century Manchester to London stagecoach which took twenty-two hours to complete the journey, a time occasionally beaten in the modern era by the 'express' train.

17. *Thomas Aquinas*: Catholic saint (1225–74) whom Rome claims as its greatest theologian.

18. *Doctor Sacheverell*: Henry Sacheverell (*c.* 1674–1724), English clergyman who criticized the Whig government and was convicted of seditious libel, which saw him given a three-year suspension from preaching.

19. *Tupper*: Martin Tupper, Victorian poet (1810–89) and author of the best seller *Proverbial Philosophy* (3 series: 1838–76). He was expected to be appointed Poet Laureate but was beaten to it by Tennyson.

20. *Mr Guizot*: François Guizot (1787–1874), French historian and statesman castigated by Marx and Engels in an 1850 review which noted how 'even the ablest men of the *ancien regime*, as well as men who cannot be denied certain historical talents, have become so confused . . . they have lost all sense of history'.

21. *Mephisto*: Mephistopheles, common medieval form of the devil (the name first appeared in the German *Faustbuch* in 1587), to whom Faust sold his soul.

22. *Lord Waterford*: Henry de la Poer, 3rd Marquis of Waterford (1811–59), was known as the Mad Marquis, thanks to his reckless lifestyle. He died in a hunting accident.

23. *Roderick*: An ambiguous reference to one of two characters featured by Sir Walter Scott. Roderick Dhu, a Scottish warrior, features in 'The Lady of the Lake', while another Scott poem, 'The Vision of Don

Roderick', refers to Roderic, the last Visigoth king of Spain, who reigned in the eighth century.

24. *Paddington Pollaky*: Ignatius Paul Pollaky, a well-known detective of the 1870s (died 1918).

25. *Odalisque*: A harem girl, especially in Turkey. Erotic paintings of the time often feature undraped odalisques reclining on divans.

26. *Sir Garnet*: Sir Garnet Wolseley, British military leader (1833–1913), who distinguished himself during the relief of Lucknow of 1857. He became Commander-in-Chief of the British Army in 1895.

27. *the Stranger*: A late eighteenth-century Benjamin Thompson tragedy, adapted from the German story *Menschenhass und Reue* (*Misanthropy and Remorse*), about a German count who leaves home and roams the world known simply as 'The Stranger'.

28. *Manfred*: The hero of Byron's eponymous dramatic poem of 1817. Given that Byron's work is prefaced by the quote from *Hamlet* ('There are more things in heaven and earth, Horatio, / Than are dreamt of in your philosophy'), it is likely that Gilbert decided to acknowledge *Manfred* first and then thought of including a reference to Hamlet, placed a few lines earlier in the *Patience* text.

29. *Beadle of Burlington*: Uniformed official who patrolled Burlington Arcade, a covered passageway of luxury shops off London's Piccadilly.

30. *Richardson's show*: Dramatic show first performed by John Richardson (1767–1837) at Bartholomew Fair.

31. *Mr Micawber*: A leading character in Dickens's *David Copperfield* (1850), infamous for his hope that 'something will turn up' and partly based on the author's father.

32. *Madame Tussaud*: The now world-famous waxworks exhibition devised by the Strasbourg-born Marie Tussaud and first brought to Britain in 1795. It has been situated on Marylebone Road by Baker Street station since 1884.

33. *fleshly thing*: A reference to the so-called 'Fleshly School of Poetry' (see note 3 above), a phrase coined by Robert Buchanan in a withering 1866 review for the group which was headed by Dante Gabriel Rossetti. After Rossetti responded animatedly in a letter to the *Athenaeum* Buchanan began to regret the violence of his attack.

34. *Hollow! Hollow! Hollow*: 'And I am blown along a wandering wind, / And hollow, hollow, hollow all delight', from *Idylls of the King* ('The Passing of Arthur', lines 36–7) (1859) by Tennyson.

35. *faint lilies*: A favourite flower of the Pre-Raphaelites, used as a symbol of purity by Dante Gabriel Rossetti in his painting *Ecce Ancilla Domine* (1849) and Wilde, see note 50.

36. *amaranthine asphodel*: Amaranthine means everlasting, and was applied by the Greeks to evergreen flowers. Asphodel is the lexical ancestor of daffodil, but is also associated with lilies, the flowers which according to Greek mythology cover the Elysian Fields. With this line Gilbert was probably thinking of the lines (in verse 5) of Alexander Pope's 'Ode for Music on St Cecilia's Day' (1713): 'By those happy souls who dwell / In yellow meads of Asphodel, / Or Amaranthine bow'rs'.

37. *calomel*: Mercurous chloride, used as a purgative.

38. *colocynth*: A tropical plant of the gourd family, also called bitter apple. Another purgative drug.

39. *Empyrean*: According to Classical mythology the highest heavenly sphere. Milton used the name for heaven in *Paradise Lost*.

40. *Della Cruscan*: The Della Cruscan Academy was a late eighteenth-century school of sentimental English poets, mostly based in Florence. Robert Merry, a member of the school, used the pseudonym 'Della Crusca'.

41. *Early English*: The first of the three periods of English Gothic architecture, lasting from the late twelfth to the late thirteenth century, which was characterized by elongated windows (lancets) often grouped in threes, fives or sevens, pointed arches and dog-tooth ornament. Salisbury Cathedral, begun in 1220, is one of the best-known buildings in this style.

42. *Red and Yellow! Primary colours*: Red, yellow and blue are primary colours as they cannot be made by mixing other colours together. The Pre-Raphaelites attained a powerful luminosity in their work by painting primary colours onto canvasses laden with white paint.

43. *South Kensington*: Stylish, mostly residential district of south-west London, which in 1857 became home to what was then the Museum of Ornamental Art, a repository of lady art students devoted to the Aesthetic cult, and is now the Victoria and Albert Museum, a world-renowned collection devoted to design and the applied arts. The Pre-Raphaelite John Millais (1829–96) lived at 7 Cromwell Place, South Kensington in the 1860s, and it was there that he retouched one of his major works, *Ophelia*, in 1873 after noticing that some of the yellow had faded while it was being shown at a South Kensington exhibition. The success of *Patience* enabled Gilbert to buy himself a luxurious new house, in Harrington Gardens, South Kensington.

44. *something Japanese*: The Victorian fascination with Japanese culture, which formed the thinking behind *The Mikado* (see headnote), stemmed partly from displays of Japanese craftsmanship at South Kensington in 1862 and was satisfied by ceramics decorated with Japanese motifs,

such as prunus blossom, pine branches and storks. In *The Decay of Living* (1889), Wilde noted: 'If you desire to see a Japanese effect ... you will stay at home ... and sit in the park or stroll down Piccadilly, and if you can not see a Japanese effect there you will not see it anywhere.'

45. *Hessians*: High tasselled boots, as originally worn by the Hessians, German mercenaries who served in the British Army during the American Civil War.

46. *peripatetics*: Those who go from place to place on their business, the word deriving from the Greek *peripatein*, 'to walk about'. The term was first applied to Aristotle, who believed in teaching while ambulating.

47. *Empress Josephine*: Marie Joséphine Rose Tascher de la Pagerie (1763–1814), Parisian socialite who married Napoleon Bonaparte and held a glittering court.

48. *Piccadilly*: One of two traditional routes leading west from central London. Piccadilly takes its name from the 'picadil', a stiff collar made by a local seventeenth-century tailor, Robert Baker. It was at the Haymarket Theatre, just off Piccadilly, that a rare recorded meeting between Gilbert and Wilde took place. After Wilde had captivated the dinner guests with his conversation for half an hour, Gilbert interrupted to announce: 'I wish I could talk like you [pause] I'd keep my mouth shut and claim it as a virtue,' to which Wilde responded: 'Ah, that would be selfish! I could deny myself the pleasure of talking, but not to others the pleasure of listening' (Ellman, *Oscar Wilde*).

49. *poppy*: Another Pre-Raphaelite favourite. In Dante Gabriel Rossetti's *Dante's Dream* (1871), the ground is scattered with poppies.

50. *lily*: Lily Langtry, the actress and companion of Edward, Prince of Wales (later Edward VII), claimed that as Wilde at the outset of his career could not afford elaborate bouquets he used to buy a single lily and carry this solitary bloom along Piccadilly.

51. *mediaeval hand*: The Pre-Raphaelites were obsessed with the purity and simplicity of the medieval period. The most lasting connection between the two eras, however, was the Gothic revival in architecture, which saw hundreds of towering medieval-styled public buildings and churches erected, particularly in northern cities like Manchester and Leeds.

52. *Elysian Fields*: See *HMS Pinafore* note 40.

53. *Aceldama*: Potter's field, mentioned in Matthew 27:7, bought as a burial place for strangers with the thirty pieces of silver Judas Iscariot took for betraying Christ.

54. *Enter ARCHIBALD GROSVENOR*: Grosvenor, named after London's

Grosvenor Gallery (see next note), is a combination of William Morris, one of the towering figures of the Victorian era, and Coventry Patmore, poet and passionate supporter of the Pre-Raphaelites. Patmore received one star on the Brotherhood's 'List of Immortals' (only Jesus Christ received as many as four stars) and was described by the critic Edmund Gosse as the 'laureate of the tea-table, with his hum-drum stories of girls that smell of bread and butter' (*Athenaeum*, 12 June 1886).

55. *a man of propertee*: Another indication that Grosvenor must be at least partly modelled on Morris (1834–96), for he famously lived in Britain's most exquisite domestic building, the Red House at Bexley Heath, designed in a fundamentalist medieval style by Philip Webb in 1859, with Morris himself providing its furniture.

56. *Chronos*: The personification of time in Greek mythology.

57. *Pandaean pleasure*: Pleasure associated with Pan, god of shepherds and huntsmen.

58. *Daphnephoric*: In Classical mythology Daphne, daughter of a river god, was turned into a laurel tree to escape the clutches of Apollo.

59. *blue-and-white*: See *HMS Pinafore* note 38.

60. *decalet*: A 10-line poem.

61. *quiddity*: An oddity in argument, from the Latin for 'what'.

62. *The immortal fire has descended on them*: Compare Byron's 'The Giaour' (1813):

> Yes, Love indeed is light from heaven;
> A spark of that immortal fire
> With angels shared, by Alla given,
> To lift from earth our low desire. (lines 1121–4)

63. *The Inner Brotherhood*: The Pre-Raphaelite Brotherhood, Britain's best-known art movement, was founded in 1848 by the painters Dante Gabriel Rossetti, William Holman Hunt and John Everett Millais to create a body of work similar in brightness of colour, attention to detail, and moral purity to the period of Italian painting prior to Raphael Sanzio (1483–1520). Rossetti wanted the group's name to include the then fashionable term 'Early Christian', but when Hunt objected he proposed the phrase 'Pre-Raphaelite' instead. Rossetti added the word 'Brotherhood' as he wanted the society to be secret, like the Italian political group the Carbonari.

In the summer of 1849 the Pre-Raphaelites staged their first exhibition, in which Dante Gabriel Rossetti's *The Girlhood of Mary Virgin* was signed 'PRB' to maintain the society's air of mystery. The Brotherhood fell apart when Millais, whom the leading critic John Ruskin had taken under his wing, was elected to be an associate of the previously despised Royal Academy, and Holman Hunt left for Palestine.

64. *Botticellian*: In the manner of Sandro Botticelli (1445–1510), one of the leading Renaissance artists, who spent much of his career painting portraits for the great families of Florence, particularly the Medicis. The Pre-Raphaelites revived his notion of an ideal of feminine beauty – pouting lips, graceful neck, mass of black hair, elegant loose clothes – using William Morris's wife, Jane, as their model.

65. *Fra Angelican*: After Fra Angelico (*c.* 1400–1455), Italian painter of the Florentine school.

66. *Narcissus*: Handsome youth of Classical mythology, son of the river god Cephissus and the nymph Liriope, whom Nemesis made fall in love with his own reflection. Narcissus's inability to touch this beautiful object provoked him to desperation and he died of unrequited passion, at which point he was changed into the flower narcissus.

67. *black-and-tan*: A type of terrier dog.

68. *Monday Pops*: The predecessors to London's Promenade concerts which began in 1859 at St James's Hall, near Piccadilly, and transferred to the Queen's Hall, Oxford Circus, in 1901.

69. *Francesca di Rimini*: Subject of Dante's *Inferno* (*c.* 1307), she was the daughter of a thirteenth-century Italian aristocrat and was killed by her husband for having an affair with his brother.

70. *Chancery Lane*: Street just to the west of the City of London, associated with the legal profession since Edward III took possession of one of its buildings, the House for Converted Jews, in 1377 and handed it to the Keeper of the Rolls of Chancery, the court of public records and archives. The building of the Royal Courts of Justice at the south-west end of the street in the 1870s emphasized Chancery Lane's central position in the English legal world.

71. *Somerset House*: A monumental riverside complex on the Strand which is the only surviving medieval palace of the many that used to line the river between Blackfriars and Westminster. In 1771 the Royal Academy, founded by leading artists of the time, took rooms in Somerset House, and it was there in 1779 that the twenty-one-year-old William Blake passed his interview for the Academy. By the nineteenth century, Somerset House was being used solely as offices for the civil service. It was partly converted into a tourist attraction in the 1990s.

72. *Threepenny-bus*: Intense competition among the bus companies of London saw the standard fare drop to threepence by the time *Patience* was premiered.

73. *Grosvenor Gallery*: London's first independent art gallery, which opened in 1877, soon came to be associated with the Aesthetic Movement. It was painted in green and yellow, colours the Victorians thought not only unmanly, but a sure sign of sexual depravity, especially once Aesthetic Movement members began appearing in public carrying colour-coordinated flowers. The gallery's opening ceremony was attended by Ruskin, the critic and mentor of British art, and Wilde, who wore a frock-coat designed at the back in the shape of a cello, a feat which ensured he made the papers and advanced his status as a celebrity. By this time there was a schism among the new romantics, with the original Pre-Raphaelites (Rossetti, Ruskin) on one side and the Aesthetes (Wilde, Whistler) on the other. Reviewing Whistler's *Nocturne in Black and Gold: The Falling Rocket* when it was first exhibited (1877), Ruskin declared that he had 'seen and heard much of Cockney impudence before now but never expected to hear a coxcomb ask two hundred guineas for flinging a pot of paint in the public's face'. Whistler sued for libel and won damages – of a farthing – but was ruined financially by the trial. The Grosvenor Gallery reopened as the Aeolian Hall to stage concerts in 1903. It was taken over by the BBC in 1941 and is now used by Sotheby's, the auctioneers.

74. *Sewell & Cross*: Linen drapers of Old Compton Street, Soho, also mentioned in *Princess Ida*.

75. *Howell & James*: Drapers of Regent Street, half a mile west of Sewell and Cross.

76. *What's the next article*: A common catchphrase among sales assistants of the period.

77. *Waterloo House*: A building on Cockspur Street, by Trafalgar Square, then occupied by Halling, Pearce and Stone, mercers and drapers, and since demolished.

78. *suit of dittoes . . . pot hat*: A matching jacket and trousers and a bowler hat.

79. *Swears & Wells*: Furrier in Regent Street.

80. *Madame Louise*: Well-known milliner of Regent Street.

Iolanthe; or, The Peer and the Peri

First performed 25 November 1882 at the Savoy Theatre, Savoy Court, London.

Original Cast

The Lord Chancellor	George Grossmith
Earl of Mountararat	Rutland Barrington
Earl Tolloller	Durward Lely
Private Willis	Charles Manners
Strephon	Richard Temple
Queen of the Fairies	Alice Barnett
Iolanthe	Jessie Bond
Celia	May Fortescue
Leila	Julia Gwynne
Fleta	Sybil Grey
Phyllis	Leonora Braham

Iolanthe, the first theatrical work to open on the same night in London and New York, and the first true Savoy Opera (its predecessors were premiered elsewhere), is partly set in a fanciful, rarefied dream world far removed from the mundane and prosaic responsibilities of real life: the House of Lords. In 1882, the year of *Iolanthe*'s opening, the status of the House of Lords was a major political issue. Public mood was stacked against the peers and their enthusiasm for rejecting elements of William Gladstone's Liberal agenda. Reformers were calling for a change to parliamentary rules; some were even suggesting the abolition of the lords' veto.

It satisfied Gilbert's absurdist humour that only Britain could tolerate a political structure in which membership of the upper house of government was limited to those born to it, while the existence of an upper chamber arranged along hereditary lines particularly irked those mindful of the struggles of reformists and radicals earlier in the century that had succeeded in loosening the aristocracy's hold on the state.

While work on *Iolanthe* proceeded, Gilbert, who was rightly paranoid about being pirated, freely revealed the news that the title of his new opera would be *Perola*. Only at the final rehearsal did he unveil its true title, *Iolanthe*, a name deriving from a translation of Henrik Hertz's *King Rene's Daughter*. When one chorus member complained that she would not be able to remember the new name at the premiere, Sullivan replied: 'Never mind, so long as you sing the music. Use any name that happens to come first to you. Nobody in the audience will be any the wiser, except Mr Gilbert and he won't be there', referring to how the author would pace the streets of the surrounding Savoy neighbourhood on nervous first nights rather than watch the performance (Leslie Baily, *The Gilbert and Sullivan Book* (1952)).

As with *Patience*, *Iolanthe*'s title gives no indication as to the nature of the tale within. Gilbert raided his *Bab Ballads* – the 'Fairy Curate' this time – in relating the story of Strephon, a half fairy / half mortal shepherd, whose mother, Iolanthe, a fairy and the driving force of Fairyland, had married a mortal. Although the Queen of Fairies has banished Iolanthe, she begins to miss her and soon accepts the fairies' request that Iolanthe be pardoned and summoned back to Fairyland. Strephon, meanwhile, intends to marry Phyllis, an Arcadian shepherdess, despite the Lord Chancellor's refusal to give his consent . . . the same Lord Chancellor who is Strephon's own father. In the second act Gilbert takes us to the equally fantastic setting of Palace Yard, Westminster, where Parliament carries all the bills proposed by Strephon with the greatest of ease – 'To his measures all assent'.

Sullivan's score, which turns to Mendelssohn's fairy music from *A Midsummer Night's Dream*, to Wagnerian leitmotif, and features a fugue to accompany the Lord Chancellor's entrance, was crafted at a taxing time for the composer, whose mother had recently died. It was first conducted at another stressful moment. With an hour to go before the premiere, Sullivan learned that his investment brokers had gone bust, wiping out savings of some £7,000. At least the initial run of 398 performances meant that the composer did not remain poor for long.

Savoyards have long enjoyed matching the opera's characters with real-life contemporary figures. The Queen of the Fairies is of course Queen Victoria, who knighted Sullivan, but not Gilbert, the following year. Private Willis can be taken as John Brown, Victoria's personal servant and 'close companion'. Strephon might well be Lord Randolph Churchill, a reformist Conservative and father of Winston. For the Lord Chancellor read not Lord Selborne, the Lord Chancellor in Gladstone's Liberal government of the time, but Gladstone himself, recently returned as Prime Minister. And if that seems improbable, it is worth considering that the Lord Chancellor – Speaker of the House of Lords, head of the Judiciary, Cabinet Minister, custodian of the Great Seal, no less – is in some ways the most powerful figure in the country, the politician who wields the most direct power, especially when compared to the Prime Minister.

So is *Iolanthe* a repudiation or a ratification of an arcane system? The Victorians were more enthusiastic about the British constitution than cynical modern-day Britons. They could openly admire the longevity of the country's governing traditions, the mostly impassive way it had adapted and readapted itself over the centuries, through consent than coercion, and could happily appreciate the lack of corruption within rather than carping constantly about occasional lapses in probity. They could admire the marriage of logic and pageantry, the justice of it all, despite the flaws. Gilbert could mock the office of Lord Chancellor and the absurdity of the House of Lords while realizing that no country had ever devised a fairer legal or governmental system. His critique is refined rather than rabid. *Iolanthe* is a gentle satire, dominated by fairies, not revolutionaries. In arranging the intricate layers of dialogue, story and melody that comprise the work, the collaborators were concerned more with entertainment than rhetoric. Not that Gilbert would be drawn politically. When in 1909, twenty-seven years after he had written *Iolanthe*, the Liberal Party were campaigning against the Upper House, and asked his permission to use verses from the opera in their propaganda, he responded curtly: 'I cannot permit the verses from *Iolanthe* to be used for electioneering purposes. They do not all express my own views. They are supposed to be the views of the wrong-headed donkey who sings them' (Bradley: 1996).

1. *PERI*: In Persian folklore, a supernatural being descended from fallen angels and barred from paradise until a term of penance was completed.
2. *Arcadian Landscape*: See *Thespis* note 32.
3. *A Ward in Chancery*: See *Pirates of Penzance* note 10.
4. *Lord Chancellor*: Gilbert probably chose to target this great office of state due to its long history (it predates the Prime Minister's office by several centuries) and powerful status. Although in medieval times the Lord Chancellor was a comparatively lowly figure, being simply the chief domestic chaplain of the King, who carried out the monarch's secretarial work and issued his writs, its powers gradually increased. During Edward III's fourteenth-century reign the duties became judicial, and by the time Henry VIII came to the throne in the sixteenth century the Chancellor had become the most important figure in the legal system. Later the Lord Chancellor's remit expanded (see headnote). Indeed, no British politician, not even the PM, wields such wide-reaching power.

    Gilbert and Sullivan scholars have correctly identified the Lord Chancellor's role as being the very pinnacle of Gilbertian topsy-turvydom. For clearly if there is one legal figure whose role should be separate from the executive government it is the Lord Chancellor, on whose advice, for instance, the Crown appoints judges. Yet not only is the Lord Chancellor one of the most influential men in the cabinet (there has never been a Lady Chancellor), but when the government is defeated he resigns with it. 'Was there ever such an illogical absurdity?' Guy H.

and Claude A. Walmisley ask in their undated treatise on *Iolanthe* ('Tit-Willow; or Notes and Jottings on Gilbert and Sullivan Operas'). No wonder the idea took Gilbert's fancy.

If Gilbert had one Lord Chancellor in mind, it is likely to have been John Scott (Lord Eldon), Lord Chancellor 1801–6 and 1807–27, his twenty-five years being the longest for any incumbent. Eldon is best known for suspending habeas corpus in 1817 at a time of considerable political repression in Britain, and he was targeted by Shelley in the poet's barbed 'The Mask of Anarchy' (1819). As a Lord Chancellor was only allowed to turn to ex-Lord Chancellors to help him with the legalities of the House of Lords at that time, once Lord Eldon had outlived all the previous incumbents, he had no one with whom he could share key responsibilities other than Lord Redesdale, ex-Lord Chancellor of Ireland. Indeed Eldon, as the United Kingdom's final Appeal Court, often appeared with one or two non-legal peers as 'dummies', just so that he didn't have to talk to himself.

Britain's most celebrated Lord Chancellors have been Thomas More, the sixteenth-century radical who defied Henry VIII's plans to break with Rome and was beheaded for his pains, and the sixteenth-century polymath Francis Bacon: author, philosopher, Rosicrucian, pioneering scientist and, according to some theories, author of the plays attributed to William Shakespeare.

5. *the Bar*: Collective term for barristers, those who argue the merits of cases in a court of law; so called from the barrier which once separated seats in the legal Inns of Court, to which newly qualified barristers would be called. Gilbert trained for the Bar at the Temple.

6. *crumpled bands . . . rusty bombazine*: Bands are wide collars worn with legal and academic robes. Bombazine is a twilled material made of silk, cotton and wool.

7. *Chancery Lane*: See *Patience* note 70.

8. *I've a borough or two at my disposal*: See *HMS Pinafore* note 14.

9. *Radicals*: Those wishing to instigate political change by uprooting the foundations of society are usually described as radicals, a term which has come to be seen as having mostly left-wing connotations, but need not. The nineteenth century was *the* century for radicalism in English politics, particularly in its early years, when fervent speakers railing mostly against the restrictive suffrage laws addressed a series of infamous rallies, the best known being Manchester's Peterloo Massacre of 1819, at which the Yeomanry massacred eleven demonstrators and injured hundreds more. By the time *Iolanthe* was premiered, Radicals had aligned themselves with the Liberal Party, to the chagrin of free spirits

such as William Morris, who realized that any worthwhile radical poli-
cies would henceforth be diluted to the point of insipidity. The following
year the Radicals had a new and more suitable party to join – the Social
Democratic Foundation – which bookended the last days of Victorian
radicalism and the nascent Labour Party.

10. *lobby*: A room in the House of Commons where Members go to vote.
    Those wishing to say 'Aye' head to the right of the Speaker's chair, those
    'No' to the left.

11. *Liberal-Unionist*: The original production had 'Liberal-Conservative', a
    difficult notion given the polarity between what were then the two main
    British political parties. This was soon replaced with 'Liberal-Unionist',
    a reference to the splinter group that broke away from the Liberal Party
    to support continued British presence in Ireland and ironically joined
    the Conservatives just before the First World War.

12. *woolsack*: The wool-stuffed seat upon which the Lord Chancellor sits
    in the House of Lords.

13. LORD MOUNTARARAT: A contraction of Mount Ararat, the peak on
    which Noah's Ark supposedly came to rest after the flood.

14. *Bar of this House*: These were two rods placed against the benches in
    the House of Lords. Those appealing to the Lords as the highest court
    in the land would have to kneel against them.

15. *Belgrave Square*: A large square near Buckingham Palace lined with
    immense stucco properties, a number of which are now embassies. At
    No. 24 is Downshire House, the Spanish Embassy, where businessmen
    at a dinner party in 1907 conceived the ill-fated *Titanic* liner. No. 5 was
    home from 1935 to 1958 to Henry 'Chips' Channon, who wrote the
    best-known social diary of the era. At the time of *Iolanthe*'s creation,
    Belgrave Square still had an aristocratic cachet. It is now mostly com-
    mercial.

16. *Seven Dials*: Tightly packed central London territory between St Giles
    and Covent Garden where seven small streets meet, named after a 1693
    monument that was torn down in 1773 by a mob who believed a horde
    of treasure was buried at its base but found nothing. By the nineteenth
    century Seven Dials was a slum – Dickens raged against its 'wild visions
    of prodigies of wickedness, want and beggary' in *Sketches by Boz* (1839)
    – but it was cleaned up and commercialized at the beginning of the
    twentieth century and the monument was reconstructed to the original
    design in the late 1980s.

17. *Manent*: Latin, 'they remain', a stage direction requiring some of the
    cast to stay on-stage as others leave (singular: *manet*).

18. *Courts of Chancery*: The courts, now part of the High Court, tradition-

ally dealt with disputes not easily settled by law, such as wardship of infants, wills, land ownership, debts and marriage settlements. The most famous Chancery case is a fictitious one, that of Jarndyce vs. Jarndyce in Dickens's *Bleak House* (1853).

19. *attorney*: Lawyers who dealt with common law in Britain were known as attorneys until the Judicature Act of 1873. The word is still used for lawyers in the United States.

20. *Exchequer*: The Court of the Exchequer collected the monarch's debts and ruled on revenue matters, also until 1873. The word 'Exchequer' is now used to denote the British treasury, the head of which is known as the Chancellor of the Exchequer, rather than as with most countries the Minister of Finance. This suitably esoteric term, one of many similar in the British Constitution, reinforces Britain's reputation as a repository for the politically arcane.

21. *Queen's Bench*: The court that adjudicates on matters involving the state vs. British subjects when the monarch is a queen.

22. *Common Pleas*: This court dealt with cases between private individuals. The Judicature Act of 1873 merged these last three courts into the newly formed High Court.

23. *Divorce*: Before 1857 only the rich were able to indulge in divorce, as the husband was obliged to obtain damages against a man who had begun a relationship with his wife.

24. *When tempests wreck thy bark*: Gilbert was probably reading *The Biblical Treasury* (1873):

> Fear not the windy tempests wild,
> Thy bark they shall not wreck;
> Lie down and sleep, O helpless child!
> Thy Father's on the deck.

25. *St James's Park*: London's first royal park was created in 1532 by Henry VIII and opened to the public by Charles II in 1660. As late as the eighteenth century there were no powers of arrest within, even though the park had by then become a haven for robbers and in particular a gang known as the Mohocks whose members roamed it brandishing swords.

26. *dolce far niente*: Italian, 'sweet doing nothing'. *Dolce far Niente* is the title of an 1879 John William Waterhouse painting, also known as *The White Feather Fan*, which can be seen in Kirkcaldy Art Gallery, Scotland.

27. *festina lente*: Latin, 'hurry slowly'.

28. *repente*: Italian or Latin, 'suddenly'.

29. *contradicente*: Italian, 'contradicting'.

30. *Andersen's library*: A reference to the works of Hans Christian Andersen (1805–75), well-known Danish creator of fairy tales such as *Thumbelina* and *The Emperor's New Suit*.

31. *Whig*: Political party formed in the seventeenth century, the strange name deriving from the Scots word 'Whiggamore', the name of a Presbyterian group that marched on Edinburgh in 1648. The Whigs came to prominence in the 1680s when they supported moves to unseat James II from the British throne on account of his fondness for Catholicism. They were the most powerful force in British politics for the next hundred and fifty years and could be differentiated from the Conservatives or Tories through their (limited) support for social reform. In the 1860s they metamorphosed into the Liberal Party.

32. *Tory*: Members of the seventeenth-century Court Party, which believed in the divine right of kings and supported James II's bid to remain on the throne, were given the nickname 'Tories', an Irish word for outlaw, by the Whigs, who suspected them of latent Catholicism. The Court Party later brazenly adopted the name, and even though by the 1830s the term 'Conservative' had supplanted 'Tory', the latter is still popularly used, particularly by opponents.

33. *grouse and salmon season*: Grouse can only be hunted between 12 August (the Glorious Twelfth) and 10 December. Salmon fishing officially begins on 1 February and ends on 31 August.

34. *Marriage with deceased wife's sister*: The Liberals supported the idea of a man marrying his deceased wife's sister and legalized it in 1907. Holman Hunt (see *Patience* note 63) defied the law in 1875 to marry Edith Waugh, his late wife's sister. The theme appears in Thomas Hardy's *Tess of the d'Urbervilles* (1891), in which Tess reassures Angel Clare that 'people marry their sisters-in-law continually around Marlott' (ch. 58).

35. *canaille*: French, 'mob'.

36. *οἱ πολλοί*: Hoi polloi, Greek, literally, 'the many' or 'masses'.

37. *Palace Yard*: The land outside the Houses of Parliament, to the south of Westminster Hall, takes its name from a yard in Canute's eleventh-century Palace of Westminster. Much of the 1606 Gunpowder Plot to blow up Parliament was hatched at the Palace Yard house of Thomas Percy, cousin of the Earl of Northumberland, which stood where the southern section of the Parliament buildings are now.

38. *Westminster Hall*: See *Trial by Jury* note 5.

39. *kettle of fish*: A muddle.

40. *Pickford*: Famous removal firm whose slogan at that time was: 'We carry everything.'

41. *House of Peers*: Alternative name for the House of Lords, the upper chamber of the Houses of Parliament, which ratifies all legislation passed to it by the House of Commons. Originally comprising only members of the aristocracy, whose qualification was by accident of birth – as was mostly the case when *Iolanthe* was written – the House of Lords has long been the target of abolitionists. In 1886, two years after *Iolanthe*'s premiere, the great Liberal MP John Bright asked the Commons during a debate on the Reform Bill: 'Shall the policy of a great and free country be thwarted by men, sitting in the hereditary chamber, who are not there by right of votes given them, and through whom the voice of the millions of the United Kingdom is not heard?'

    Iolanthe was originally to be set in the House of Commons until Gilbert realized the comic potential afforded by the other chamber.

42. *When Wellington thrashed Bonaparte*: At the Battle of Waterloo in 1815.

43. *King George*: George III (1760–1820).

44. *British Representative Peer*: Twenty-eight peers representing Ireland were elected by their fellows to sit in the House of Lords until 1922 when the Irish Free State was established. A similar system was used for Scotland until 1963.

45. *Oh, amorous dove . . . Ovidius Naso*: Publius Ovidius Naso, Ovid, was a Roman love poet who lived from 43 BC to *c.* AD 17. The Emperor Augustus exiled him to Tomis on the Black Sea, possibly for carousing with the Emperess Livia or because he had witnessed the emperor committing incest with his daughter, Julia. He is best known for *Metamorphoses*, in which he refers to the 'tim'rous' rather than the 'amorous' dove (of Philomela in Book 6). The 'naso' appellation referred to his big nose.

46. *Captain Shaw*: Captain Eyre Massey Shaw was chief of the Metropolitan Fire Brigade (1861–91) and was infamous for attending opening nights, such as that for *Iolanthe*.

47. *Derby Cup*: The Derby, one of Britain's great horse races, founded by the Earl of Derby, was first staged in 1780. It takes place at Epsom, 15 miles south of London. The term Derby is also used to describe a sporting contest between two teams from the same locality.

48. *Crichton*: James Crichton (1560–82), Scottish polyglot known as 'the Admirable Crichton'. *The Admirable Crichton* was also a play (1902) by J. M. Barrie.

49. *Ruskin*: John Ruskin (1819–1900), the greatest art and architecture

critic of the nineteenth century, championed Turner in *Modern Painters I* (1843) and the Pre-Raphaelites in *Modern Painters II* (1846). His *The Seven Lamps of Architecture* (1848) and *The Stones of Venice* (1851–3) are landmark works in evaluating architecture. Ruskin was also a supporter of socialism, and taught at the Working Men's College in London in the 1850s.

50. *Oh, many a man, in Friendship's name*: Adapted from Alexander Pope's 'Eloisa to Abelard' (1717): 'Thou know'st how guiltless first I met thy flame,/When Love approach'd me under Friendship's name' (lines 57–8).

51. *Sloane Square and South Kensington Stations*: Consecutive underground stations on the Circle and District lines. South Kensington, along with Gloucester Road, became Gilbert's local tube station when he moved to Harrington Gardens in 1883.

52. *ties pay the dealer*: In some card games a tie between the player and dealer sees the dealer win.

53. *Salisbury Plain*: An unrelenting and mostly barren chalk plateau, some 300 square miles in size, in England's West Country, which includes a number of ancient monuments, most notably Stonehenge.

54. *Rothschild and Baring*: Two major banking firms. Rothschild's at the time *Iolanthe* was created was run by Nathan Meyer Rothschild, who had helped Disraeli secure the Suez Canal for Britain in 1875. Baring's was less well known. The two banks were linked by Lord Byron in the twelfth Canto of *Don Juan* (1822):

> Who keeps the world, both old and new, in pain
> Or pleasure? Who make politics run glibber all?
> The shade of Bonaparte's noble daring,
> Jew Rothschild, and his fellow Christian Baring.

55. *Faint heart never won fair lady*: From Part III, Book 10, of Cervantes's *Don Quixote* (1605).

56. *maravedi*: Spanish copper coin worth about a twelfth of a British penny.

57. *While the sun shines make your hay*: A sixteenth-century saying.

58. *Where a will is, there's a way*: A saying first aired in the 1830s.

59. *Beard the lion in his lair*: Referring to the biblical story of Daniel braving the lions (Daniel, ch. 6).

60. *None but the brave deserve the fair*: From John Dryden's 'Alexander's Feast' (1697).

61. *Nothing venture, nothing win*: A seventeenth-century saying; used by

Everest conqueror Sir Edmund Hillary for the title of his autobiography (1975).

62. *Blood is thick, but water's thin*: Compare Sir Walter Scott's 'Weel! Blude's thicker than water. She's welcome to the cheeses and the hams just the same' (ch. 38) of *Guy Mannering* (1815), the first recorded usage.

63. *In for a penny, in for a pound*: Of unknown origin, believed to date no earlier than the seventeenth century.

64. *It's Love that makes the world go round*: Translation of an early eighteenth-century French song. Not for the first time, Gilbert seems to have Dickens's *Our Mutual Friend* (1865) in mind: 'And O there are days in this life, worth life and worth death. And O what a bright old song it is, that O 'tis love, 'tis love, 'tis love that makes the world go round!' (ch. 54).

65. *Drury Lane*: Central London street close to many of the major theatres although the Theatre Royal Drury Lane is actually on Catherine Street. By the nineteenth century, Dickens described how 'the filthy and miserable appearance of this part of London can hardly be imagined by those who have not witnessed it' in 'A Gin Shop' from *Sketches By Boz* (1837). The area was cleaned up towards the end of the century.

66. *Fagin*: A major character in Dickens's *Oliver Twist* (1838).

67. *Equity draftsman*: A barrister skilled in drawing up contracts and wills, particularly those involving equity law, i.e. the system of jurisprudence which modifies common law.

Princess Ida; or, Castle Adamant

First performed 5 January 1884 at the Savoy Theatre, London.

Original Cast

King Hildebrand	Rutland Barrington
Hilarion	H. Bracy
Cyril	Durward Lely
Florian	Charles Ryley
King Gama	George Grossmith
Arac	Richard Temple
Guron	William Lugg
Scynthius	Warwick Grey
Princess Ida	Leonora Braham
Lady Blanche	Rosina Brandram

Lady Psyche	Kate Chard
Melissa	Jessie Bond
Sacharissa	Sybil Grey
Chloe	Miss Heathcote
Ada	Miss Twyman

Gilbert and Sullivan's stock had never been higher than in 1883. *Iolanthe* was captivating London at the new Savoy Theatre. *Patience* had just finished its own equally successful run there. The world of entertainment was agog for the partnership's next move. Something of suitable stature was needed. A voracious satire on one of the great issues of the day surely awaited the public. Instead Gilbert delivered an unexpected anti-climax. *Princess Ida* did not smoothly follow the previous two works. Despite being rich in humour, it was clearly not a jolly romp. For pity's sake, it was in blank verse! As a piece of literature it wasn't even entirely new, Gilbert having cannibalized his 1870 play *The Princess*. Worse still, it wasn't even a Gilbert original, for *The Princess* was itself an adaptation of Tennyson's lengthy 1847 poem of the same name about the founding of a college for women, which in turn was derived from two oriental stories related by Henry Weber in *Tales of the East* (1812).

Sullivan, at least, was not entirely upset with this odd manoeuvre. He had already shown impatience with Gilbert's 'topsy-turvy plots', and had argued zealously with Gilbert over *Iolanthe*'s follow-up, once again rubbishing Gilbert's indefatigable magic-lozenge storyline. Why, he, Arthur Sullivan, was now a knight of the realm. He couldn't be seen trifling with such frivolity. But a collaboration based on a serious work from the pen of the Poet Laureate; that was more his *métier*. Sullivan consequently produced one of his greatest scores, lush with complex harmonies, the songs of Act II earning the epithet 'Sullivan's string of pearls'.

The cast found life more difficult, not least of all in the learning of blank verse. Gilbert also tussled wittily with George Grossmith who, obliged to repeat one scene some twenty times, moaned: 'I've rehearsed this confounded business until I feel a perfect fool', only to be told by Gilbert: 'Ah, now we can talk on equal terms' (Dark: 1923).

Princess Ida relates the story of a prince whose hand has been promised to Ida, an advocate of women's rights who has opened an all-female university – 'A women's college! modest folly going!' – but is upstaged by her father, King Gama, monarch of a country 'across the water', famed for his biting sarcasm.

Gilbert's satire was contemporary, even if the format wasn't as vivacious as usual, for women's education was a newsworthy topic, and Oxford and

Cambridge had just established their first female colleges. Gilbert's own views on the subject were not only nowhere near as progressive as Tennyson's, but were reactionary even by Victorian standards. Commentators schooled in post-Gilbertian, Freudian analysis aver that the author's wretched relationship with his own mother (his parents were separated) can be blamed for his refusal to accept that women might object to his notions of a fairer sex screened from society's horrors by his protectiveness. And it is this that has handicapped *Princess Ida*'s longevity, especially when compared with the universality of the targets in *The Mikado* or *Iolanthe*.

As with *The Pirates of Penzance*, Sullivan was not in peak physical condition on the opening night. He had worked through New Year's Eve on the score, spent the next day rehearsing and then walked home in a snowstorm. Overwork and under-performing kidneys combined to render the composer almost incapable. He made plans for François Cellier to take his place and for the public to be told that he was suffering from 'muscular affliction of the neck'. As for medicinal aids, this time it was morphine and black coffee. In his diary Sullivan recorded: 'At 7 p.m. had another strong hypodermic injection to ease the pain, and a strong cup of black coffee to keep me awake. Managed to get up and dress, and drove to the theatre more dead than alive' (Sullivan–Flower: 1927). Even then the composer could only proceed with lengthier than usual intervals between acts. He collapsed just after taking his bow.

Gilbert enjoyed a more light-hearted moment on the opening night. For once he remained in the theatre. As Act III proceeded he was sitting in the green room, reading the evening paper, when in burst the Frenchman who had supplied the suits of armour worn by the principal ladies during the battle scene. 'Mais, monsieur, savez vous que vous avez là un succès solide?' ('But, sir, do you know you have a great success?') the Gaul cried in his excitement. 'Oh! it seems to be going very well,' replied Gilbert. 'Mais vous êtes si calme!' ('But you are so calm!') exclaimed the visitor, unused to such British reserve. Gilbert, on retelling the story later, added: 'I suppose he expected to see me kissing all the carpenters' (Bradley: 1996).

Princess Ida received an unfavourable first-night press. Critics called it 'desperately dull', 'tedious' and 'clumsy', although the *Sunday Times* described the score as 'the best thing in every way that Sir Arthur Sullivan has produced', with the notable rider, 'apart from his serious works'. Unsurprisingly, *Princess Ida* ran for only 246 performances and is amongst the least revived Savoy Operas. A 1992 English National Opera production at the London Coliseum directed by Ken Russell, the *enfant terrible* of cinematic iconoclasm, set King Hildebrand's residency in London as Buck and Yen Palace, a Japanese theme-park built after the sale of Buckingham Palace.

Sullivan, despite his initial enthusiasm for the work, soon had second thoughts. Only three weeks into production he announced he would not work on any more comic operas. D'Oyly Carte believed that the composer would reconsider after a holiday, and reminded him of their contract, which stipulated that he, D'Oyly Carte, was complying with the requirement that he give the two men six months' notice that a new opera was required. Sullivan quickly wrote back, explaining that with *Princess Ida* he had 'come to the end of my tether', his tunes being in danger of becoming 'mere repetitions of my former pieces', and he would not be able to provide another work 'of the character of those already written by Gilbert and myself' (Sullivan–Flower: 1927). D'Oyly Carte was nonplussed and reminded Sullivan that if they broke their contract they would be responsible for any losses that might accrue as a result. Although Gilbert revealed that he had already started work on a new piece, Sullivan was insistent that this was the end. And so the communications went back and forth, with composer becoming increasingly frustrated and librettist increasingly anguished. When *Princess Ida* closed there was no new piece to replace it. Was the partnership at an end? On the contrary it was about to enter a newly fruitful period.

1. *Gama*: Gilbert made some embellishments to Tennyson's original, and presented King Gama as a 'twisted monster – all awry', usually played 'grim and ghastly', as Sir Henry Lytton described it when cast in the role at the end of the nineteenth century (Bradley: 1996).

2. *Ida*: A mountain near Troy from which the gods of Classical mythology watched the Trojan War. It was on another Mount Ida, in Crete, that Zeus himself was raised.

3. *Hilarion*: St Hilarion (291–371) was a hermit who lived most of his life in the desert, according to the example set by St Anthony of Egypt.

4. *Hildebrand*: Gilbert has taken the name from one of his favourite writers – Walter Scott – in this case from Scott's *Rob Roy* (1817), which features a Sir Hildebrand Osbaldistone.

5. *en cavalier*: French, 'like a knight'.

6. *quarter-day*: Any of four days in the year when ground rents are due. In England these are 25 March (Lady Day), 24 June (Midsummer Day), 29 September (Michaelmas) and 25 December (Christmas Day).

7. *bib and tucker, frill and furbelow*: Best clothes, beautification and adornment.

8. *SONG*: Gama's solipsistic song with its memorable refrain, 'everybody

says I'm such a disagreeable man! / And I can't think why!', is one of the choral high points of the canon.

9. *A woman's University*: Newnham college, opened for women in Cambridge in 1871, followed two years later by Girton (founded in Hitchin in 1869).

10. *Dr Watts's hymns*: Isaac Watts (1674–1748), one of Britain's greatest hymn writers, responsible for 'O God, our help in ages past'.

11. *Sillery*: A champagne-producing district in France.

12. *triolet*: An eight-line stanza based on French verse form with a rhyming pattern *abcadeab*.

13. *empyrean heights*: Heaven.

14. *Helicon*: Mountain range near the Gulf of Corinth in Greece, which in Classical mythology was home to the Muses.

15. *Anacreon*: Sixth-century BC Greek poet who at the age of eighty-five was choked to death by a grape pip.

16. *Ovid's Metamorphoses*: Ovid's most famous work was *Metamorphoses*, which in fifteen books traces the story of the world from its origins to the era of Julius Caesar. For Ovid, see *Iolanthe* note 45.

17. *Aristophanes*: Greek comic playwright of the fifth century BC, best known for *The Frogs* and *The Birds*.

18. *Juvenal*: Roman satirist of the first century AD.

19. *Bowdlerized*: A passage of text censored of supposed immoral leanings and obscenities is said to have been bowdlerized, the word deriving from Dr Thomas Bowdler, an English physician who published an expurgated edition of Shakespeare in 1818.

20. *Minerva*: See *Thespis* note 15.

21. *Swan secede from Edgar*: Swan and Edgar, noted Victorian and twentieth-century drapers and milliners based at 49 Regent Street, which closed in 1982.

22. *Gask from Gask*: Gask and Gask were Victorian silk retailers in Oxford Street.

23. *Sewell from Cross*: Sewell and Cross, another well-known Soho drapery firm of that era. It stood at the corner of Frith Street and Old Compton Street, and is also mentioned in *Patience*.

24. *Lewis from Allenby*: Lewis and Allenby, silk retailers of Regent Street. Because most of these firms had ceased trading by the mid twentieth century, recent productions have tended to cut their names from the text.

25. *Circe's / Piggy-wigs*: In Greek mythology Circe was a sorceress who lived on the island of Aeaea and who turned Odysseus's companions into pigs.

26. *trepan*: Catch in a trap.

27. *sunbeams from cucumbers*: Compare Jonathan Swift's *Gulliver's Travels* (1726):

   'Eight years upon a project for extracting sunbeams out of cucumbers, which were to be put into phials hermetically sealed, and let out to warm the air in raw inclement summers' (ch. 21).

28. *And the niggers they'll be bleaching*: The notion of inter-race procreation over several generations so that descendants had eventually lost their Negroid features, becoming, as far as the state was concerned, 'legally white'. The line was changed to the less controversial 'And they'll practise what they're preaching' in the 1950s. See also *The Mikado* notes 16 and 43.

29. *sizars . . . servitors*: Students who worked as servants in exchange for free board and lodging and the waiving of their college fees were known as sizars at Cambridge and servitors at Oxford.

30. *Hipparchus*: Greek astronomer and mathematician (190–120 BC), who pioneered basic work on trigonometry and introduced to Greece the idea of a circle being divided into 360 degrees.

31. *toilet club*: A barbershop which charged an annual subscription.

32. *Darwinian Man*: Charles Darwin (1809–82) claimed in *The Origin of Species* (1859) that man, rather than being created directly by God, had developed from apes through natural selection.

33. *étui*: French, needle case.

34. *Plantagenet*: Alternative name afforded to the British Angevin kings from the reign of Henry II (1154–89) to that of Richard III (1483–5). The name came courtesy of Geoffrey, Count of Anjou, husband of Matilda, daughter of Henry I, who wore a sprig of the *Planta genista* shrub.

35. *but 'are men' / Stuck in her throat*: Compare Shakespeare's *Macbeth*: 'But wherefore could I not pronounce "Amen? / I had most need of blessing, and Amen / Stuck in my throat' (II.2.31–3).

36. *Daughters of the Plough*: The fourth section of Tennyson's *Princess* describes these Amazonians thus: 'Eight daughters of the plough, stronger than men, / Huge women blowzed with health, and wind, and rain, / And labour. Each was like a Druid rock' (lines 227–9).

37. *asphodel*: See *Patience* note 36.

38. *Mistress Lalage*: A cryptic reference to one of Horace's *Odes*, Lalage being one of the poet's mistresses to whom no harm can come as she walks through the woods.

> In Sabine woods, and fancy-free
> A wolf observed my wandering tread;
> Unarmed, I sang of Lalage;
> He saw, and fled.

39. *Paynim*: Archaic English word for pagan.
40. *German bands*: A regular feature of Victorian London were itinerant German bands playing so-called 'oompah music', as recalled in the famous 1903 music-hall song 'Down at the Old Bull and Bush'.

> Come, come, come drink port wine with me,
> Down at the Old Bull and Bush,
> You can hear the German Band,
> Da da da-da, da-da-da.

41. *hurdy-gurds*: The hurdy-gurdy is a bowed stringed instrument, which is strapped to the midriff of the player who uses the right hand to turn a crank and producing a droning sound.
42. *cuirass*: Armour containing a breastplate and backplate.
43. *brassets*: Archaic English word for upper-arm armour.
44. *cribbage pegs*: When points are scored in the card game of cribbage, players move pegs along a board.
45. *Hungary*: The fact that Hungary has not previously occurred in the text as the location of Castle Adamant suggests that Gilbert was simply desperate to find something to rhyme with 'ironmongery'.

The Mikado; or, The Town of Titipu

First performed 14 March 1885 at the Savoy Theatre, London.

Original Cast

The Mikado of Japan	Richard Temple
Nanki-Poo	Durward Lely
Ko-Ko	George Grossmith
Pooh-Bah	Rutland Barrington
Pish-Tush	Frederick Bovill
Yum-Yum	Leonora Braham
Pitti-Sing	Jessie Bond

| Peep-Bo | Sybil Grey |
| Katisha | Rosina Brandram |

The Mikado is Gilbert and Sullivan's pièce de résistance, a magnificent mix of moods, manners and music, cascading with hummable melodies and memorable couplets, and populated by some of the librettist's finest-drawn characters. It is the most popular and most performed work in the canon, and was the first to be filmed. From the plaintive beauty of 'A Wandering Minstrel I' to the delightful verbal interplay of 'Three Little Maids', from the lexical dexterity of Ko-Ko's county jail solo to the lachrymose tenderness of 'Tit Willow', Gilbert and Sullivan created a triumph that no British musical composer would equal until Lionel Bart with *Oliver* some eighty years later.

Despite the Japanese theme, the opera's main target is not the land of the rising sun but the land of warm beer. Titipu is Britain, disguised as a strange and distant country, a place overrun with Pooh-Bahs, the character who as 'Lord High Everything Else' – First Lord of the Treasury, Lord Chief Justice, Commander-in-Chief, Lord High Admiral, Master of the Buckhounds, Groom of the Backstairs, Archbishop of Titipu and Lord Mayor – is the epitome of every jumped-up petty town-hall or Whitehall bureaucrat obstructing the smooth passage of human endeavour, symbolic of a country where the Prime Minister, whose position has no constitutional authority, is also the First Lord of the Treasury, while the head of the treasury is known mystifyingly as the Chancellor of the Exchequer; of a country where the senior offices of government include positions of arcane nomenclature, such as Lord Privy Seal and Lord President of the Council, who have no particular or useful function.

Gilbert had to surmount a number of difficulties to produce *The Mikado*. His partnership with Sullivan was threatened by their first serious disagreement following the relatively unsuccessful *Princess Ida* and pressure from D'Oyly Carte about deriving a suitable follow-up. Gilbert felt insulted by Sullivan's gripe that the music was 'never allowed to rise and speak for itself' (Sullivan–Flower: 1927) and did himself no favours when for their new collaboration he insisted on polishing up an old chestnut: the magic-lozenge plot.

For Sullivan the perennial lozenge was too much to swallow, and he wrote to Gilbert in May 1884 informing him that 'further discussion was useless', he'd had enough of 'topsy-turvy plots' and wanted to devote his energies to more serious endeavours. Despite being contractually obliged to deliver one more work he would write no more Savoy Operas. The partnership seemed to be at its end. Then, one day that May, legend has it, a Japanese sword fell from its fixture on Gilbert's wall and triggered in the librettist thoughts of the Far East. Gilbert devised an outline for *The Mikado* and received a favourable response from Sullivan, who told him: 'If you will construct a plot without the supernatural and impromptu elements I gladly undertake to set it without further discussing the matter or asking what the subject is to be' (Sullivan–Flower: 1927).

Much work was needed to realize *The Mikado*. 'A Japanese piece would afford opportunities for picturesque scenery and costumes,' Gilbert later recalled, but nothing of the kind had ever been attempted in England. 'Could a sufficient number of genuine Japanese dresses in good condition be procured in London? How would the ladies of our chorus look in black wigs? Could they be taught to wear the Japanese costume effectively?' (Williamson, *Gilbert and Sullivan Opera: An Assessment* (1982)). Fortunately, during rehearsals, a Japanese-styled village opened near Hyde Park (in a building called Humphry's Hall, on the site now occupied by Imperial College), allowing Gilbert a rich new source of information, but in rehearsals the librettist remained a hard taskmaster. Preparation fitted into the pattern outlined by Weedon Grossmith, who in contrasting Gilbert's regime at the Savoy with that of Henry Irving at the nearby Lyceum noted that whereas at every Lyceum rehearsal Irving 'groped for perfection' Gilbert arrived every day with 'perfection in his pocket' (Weedon Grossmith, *From Studio to Stage: Reminiscences of Weedon Grossmith* (1913)).

Yet tension grew between Gilbert and the main performers. At one point George Grossmith fell over and rolled on the floor, leading Gilbert to bark: 'Kindly omit that,' and Grossmith to retort: 'Certainly, if you wish it, but I get an enormous laugh by it.' Gilbert snapped back: 'So you would if you sat on a pork pie' (Baily: 1973), which may have contributed to Grossmith's opening-night nerves and the fluffing of his lines during 'I've Got A Little List'. At one of the auditions, a young Australian lady who asked Gilbert if he had any preference for the song she should sing was curtly told that one thing was as good as another. After she delivered an aria from *La Traviata*, Gilbert announced: 'Yes, Mrs. Armstrong, that is alright, and if you go on studying for another year, there might be a chance that we could give you a small part in *The Mikado*' (source: internet). The auditioner was the prospective Nellie Melba. The episode may explain why Gilbert would proudly admit that he knew only two songs: 'One is "God Save the Queen", the other isn't' (source: internet).

The original players for *The Mikado* contained the usual suspects. Grossmith was cast as Ko-Ko, Lord High Executioner, the part being written specifically for the thespian-humorist as an 'exceptionally tender-hearted person whose natural instincts were in direct opposition to the nature of his official duties' (*New-York Daily Tribune*, 1885), and who on the opening night brought on stage with him the sword which had fallen from Gilbert's wall and inspired the genesis of *The Mikado*. Barrington devised much of the role of Pooh-Bah, 'the most remarkable man in ancient or modern history', as Gilbert himself explained in *The Story of 'The Mikado' for Children*. Richard Temple took the part of the eponymous Mikado, who doesn't appear until late in the opera. The three little maids were Leonora Braham, Jessie Bond and Sybil Grey who, as Gilbert explained, being 'short in stature and all of a height suggested the advisability of grouping them as three Japanese school-girls who should work together throughout the piece' (*New-York Daily Tribune*, 1885).

To the critics *The Mikado* was 'magnificent' . . . an 'unbounded success'. For one ecstatic reviewer it was subject to 'one disadvantage, and only one' – the difficulty of getting to see it. 'Such is the anxiety of the public to witness it, that, though the theatre were twice as large as it is, it would not suffice for the accommodation of all comers' (source: internet). The painter James Whistler, evidently not dissuaded from the canon by the lampooning he had endured in *Patience*, attended the premiere and 'vibrated symphoniously from stall to gangway and back', according to one witness (Walbrook: 1922).

The Mikado initially ran for 672 performances, the longest opening stint of any of the Savoy Operas. In America it was rapturously received, and Mikado rooms became a must for any society house. Back in London in 1907, during a state visit by a Japanese prince, the dreaded censorious Lord Chamberlain withdrew *The Mikado*'s performance licence for six weeks. Gilbert believed, wrongly, that the Japanese government had requested the ban, and ordered the company to proceed with its performances regardless. The author was probably right to do so. One of the Japanese journalists covering the visit attended a performance of *The Mikado* and announced he was 'deeply and pleasingly disappointed' (source: internet). Expecting to see his country insulted, he found instead that he had thoroughly enjoyed 'the bright music and much fun'.

1.   *MIKADO*: The Imperial ruler of Japan. He should not be seen as a political figure but rather as a high priest, although not quite as glorified as the military samurai class or shoguns (Grand Generals). Etymologically the word derives from *mi* ('august' or 'sublime') and *kado* ('gate'), and can be read as meaning 'Gate of Heaven'. The Japanese considered the Mikado to be the direct descendant of the sun goddess, Amaterasu-Omikami, until 1945. Some Japanese productions have presented the opera as a light-hearted gangster story, with the Mikado as a godfather.

2.   *Titipu*: Based on the Japanese town of Chichibu, located in the moun-

tains north-west of Tokyo. Although a poor farming community in the nineteenth century, it is now known as 'the cement capital of Japan'.

3. *Japan*: Nipponese influence arrived in Britain around the middle of the nineteenth century after the Japanese were allowed to travel outside their own land for the first time. At the International Exhibition of 1862 a display of Japanese arts and crafts further whetted Britons' appetite for the Far East, and the painters Whistler and Rossetti later helped to foster a taste for Japanese prints and pots. By the time *The Mikado* was produced in 1885, Liberty's, the fashionable department store near Oxford Circus, was successfully selling Japanese-styled fabrics. That year thousands of people, including Gilbert himself, visited the Japanese Village located near Hyde Park.

4. NANKI-POO: The name is more Sinological than Nipponese. Gilbert may have confused Japanese and Chinese, subsuming the sound of Nanking, the Chinese city, into this Japanese name.

5. *Yum-Yum*: Long a term to signify something delicious, it has no Japanese connections.

6. *Ko-Ko*: A rare *Mikado* name with some Japanese relevance, having some thirty-seven meanings in that language, including pickles, prince or pithead, depending on pronunciation and context.

7. *shreds and patches*: The phrase comes from Shakespeare's *Hamlet*, after the ghost of Hamlet's father has entered the Queen's chamber: 'A king of shreds and patches – / Save me, and hover o'er me with your wings, / You heavenly guards! What would your gracious figure?' (III.4.103–5).

8. *Pish-Tush*: Pish is 'a natural exclamation', according to the *Oxford English Dictionary*, and has a literary precedent in Thomas Nashe's *Pierce Pennilesse* (1592): 'Pish, pish, what talke you of old age or balde pates?' Tush contains similar sentiments and dates back to the fifteenth century.

9. POOH-BAH: The word Pooh, historically, has been used as a childish word for faeces or as an ejaculation to express impatience. In *Beppo* (1817), Lord Byron waxes about 'A thing which causes many "poohs" and "pishes"' (verse 7).

10. *pre-Adamite ancestral descent*: A nod to the inexhaustible public and private debates over Charles Darwin's Theory of Evolution (see *Princess Ida* note 31) which were raging at the end of the nineteenth century.

11. *ex-tailor*: That an ex-tailor should reach the highest offices of state is not as fanciful as might first appear. Jacob Peters, who worked as a tailor's assistant in a shop on London's Holloway Road a few years after *The Mikado* opened, rose through the ranks of the early Soviet

bureaucracy to become Stalin's Number Two in the Cheka, the USSR's secret police.

12. *First Lord of the Treasury*: In Britain, a role that has been taken up nominally by the Prime Minister since the eighteenth century.

13. *Master of the Buckhounds*: The official in control of the royal hounds, who heads the royal procession along the racecourse at Ascot every year.

14. *Groom of the Back Stairs*: An invented title based on several members of Her Majesty's Lord Chamberlain's department: Groom of the Chamber, Groom of the Privy Chamber, Groom of the Great Chamber, Groom of the Stole, Groom of the Beds, Groom of the Crossbows and Groom in waiting. 'Back Stairs' refers to the servants' quarters.

15. *I've got a little list*: There have been innumerable pastiches of this piece, mostly attuned to events and mores with which the audience would be familiar. A typically erudite example comes from Andrew Crowther of the internet Gilbert and Sullivan magazine, *Babliophile*:

> As it seems to be essential that I sing you an encore,
> I've got *another* list – that's right, another list –
> Of present-day offenders whose behaviour I deplore –
> And who never would be missed – who never would be missed –
> There's the omnipresent pundit who is always asked his views
> On 'sleaze', taxation, Grobbelaar – whatever's in the news –
> The one who dislikes *Frasier*, or the one who does like *Friends*,
> And the fellow who assiduously follows last year's trends,
> And on slightest provocation will complain that he's been 'dissed' –
> I don't think he'd be missed – I'm *sure* he'd not be missed!

16. *nigger serenader*: The text was changed to 'banjo serenader' in 1948 after American audiences found it offensive. See also note 43.

17. *Nisi Prius*: A term in English law based on the Latin 'unless before', i.e. 'unless heard before', to denote cases tried in the Assize Court which should have been civil cases.

18. *apologetic statesmen*: On *The Mikado*'s opening night, Grossmith mocked Gladstone by wearing a high collar, a Lord Salisbury beard and the monocle of Joseph Chamberlain. Since then, a long list of leading politicians have been lampooned at this point of the opera including David Lloyd George, Ted Heath and Tony Blair.

19. *Lord Chamberlain*: Chief official of the royal household, responsible for royal weddings etc., and until 1968 for vetting all plays produced on the British stage. For decades the Lord Chamberlain locked British

theatre in a stranglehold of constraint and restriction. When the Chamberlain briefly withdrew *The Mikado*'s licence in 1907, one MP asked the House whether *Hamlet* would be banned during a visit by Danish dignitaries, given that the play portrayed the King of Denmark as a murderer.

20. PEEP-BO: Similar to the name of the childish game 'peekaboo' which involves momentarily covering the face.

21. *Three little maids*: To ensure verisimilitude in the women's movements Gilbert hired a girl from the Japanese Village, who was soon given the nickname 'Miss Sixpence Please' as her only words of English were 'sixpence, please'. The song was rapturously received on the opening night, as Sullivan noted in his diary for 14 March 1885: 'New opera "The Mikado, or the Town of Titipu" produced at the Savoy Theatre with every sign of success. A most brilliant house. Tremendous reception. A *treble* encore for "Three Little Maids" and for "The Flowers that Bloom in the Spring". Seven encores taken – might have taken twelve' (Sullivan–Flower: 1927). Indeed, those present on the opening night talked for years of the roar from the whole audience that followed the above song, 'it being twice renewed with undiminished volume, until two more repetitions had been granted' (Walbrook: 1922).

22. *tutelary*: Appertaining to a guardian.

23. *Swell*: A stylish person, the term 'swell' is mostly associated with mid-twentieth-century American songs and was famously distorted syntactically in the 1956 Cole Porter song, 'Did You Ever', in the line, 'What a swelegant, elegant party this is'.

24. *Lucius Junius Brutus*: Military leader of the sixth century BC, who ousted the despotic Etruscan king Lucius Tarquinius Superbus, *c.* 509 BC and founded the Roman Republic with himself as the first Consul. He supposedly sentenced his own sons to death when they joined in a conspiracy to restore the previous rulers.

25. *con fuoco*: Italian, 'with fire'.

26. *gioco*: Italian, 'joke'.

27. *for yam I should get toco*: Instead of a ration of yam I get corporal punishment. (Toco is also a Japanese name.)

28. *the Happy Despatch*: Suicide enforced on Japanese officials, committed ritualistically by disembowelling – *hara-kiri* in Japanese; it was revoked as a requirement in 1868.

29. *dole*: One's lot or destiny.

30. *O ni! bikkuri shakkuri to*: Japanese, roughly translatable as 'Oh no, what a surprise and shock'.

31. *gambado*: Spanish, 'surprise action'.

32. *PISH*: For this scene, Gilbert and Sullivan invented an alternative character, Go-To, to be sung by a bass, replacing Pish-Tush, a baritone.

33. *tocsin*: An alarm bell or signal; or here, a funeral bell.

34. *Attorney-General*: The Government's main legal adviser, usually a Member of Parliament.

35. *Lord Chief Justice*: The judge who presides over the Queen's Bench Division of the High Court.

36. *Master of the Rolls*: The judge ranking immediately below the Lord Chief Justice, who presides over the Court of Appeal in the House of Lords.

37. *Judge Ordinary*: A judge in the Court of Probate overseeing wills, trusts and the administration of estates.

38. *Lord Chancellor*: See *Iolanthe* note 4.

39. *Commissionaire*: During the 1975 D'Oyly Carte season, Pooh-Bah made his entrance at this point wearing the cap of a Savoy Hotel commissionaire.

40. *Miya sama*: The song is authentically Japanese, having been composed in the 1860s by Masujiro Omura and Yajiro Shinagawa as a war song for the Japanese Imperial Army, and sung in 1877 by troops suppressing a rebellion. It can be translated thus:

> *Miya sama* – Noble Prince
> *On n'm-ma no maye ni* – In front of your Highness's horse
> *Pira-Pira suru no wa* – the thing which is fluttering.
> *Nan gia na?* – What is it?
> *Toko tonyare tonyare na* – [the sound of musical instruments]

41. *SONG*: Prior to the opening night, Gilbert made the absurd decision to cut this number, usually referred to as the 'Punishment Fit the Crime' song, from the refrain. It was reinstated after the chorus objected in the sternest manner and won the argument.

42. *mystical Germans*: An obscure reference to a group of Lutheran evangelists who had recently been touring England.

43. *Madame Tussaud's waxwork*: See *Patience* note 32.

44. *Is blacked like a nigger*: Changed in 1948 by A. P. Herbert to 'Is painted with vigour'.

45. *Parliamentary trains*: Trains which were required under the 1844 Railway Regulation Act to stop at every station with fares priced at 1p per mile.

46. *By Bach*: The score moves into the first twelve notes of Bach's Fugue in G Minor at this point.

47. *Spohr*: The German violinist and composer Louis Spohr (1784–1859), who was considered to be one of the best conductors of his time.

48. *Monday Pops*: See *Patience* note 68.

49. *The billiard sharp ... finger-stalls*: Gilbert was trained in billiards by Jack Mannock who pioneered the 'finger-stall' position that uses a device clenched in the bridge hand.

50. *snickersnee*: Dutch, 'knife'.

51. *whistled an air*: Originally the orchestra would now play a few bars of the 'Cotillion Waltz'.

52. *Knightsbridge*: The Japanese Village was near Hyde Park, just off Knightsbridge. Once the village had closed it no longer seemed necessary to cite the street at this point in the libretto and subsequent productions have changed it at will, often to a location local to the theatre.

53. *DUET*: The always nervous Grossmith accidentally fell in the middle of this song on the opening night, to the amusement of the audience and even Gilbert, who told him to repeat the 'accident' every night.

54. *SONG*: Gilbert based this song on the poem 'Colin's Complaint' by Nicholas Rowe (1674–1718), which included the stanza:

> Despairing beside a clear stream,
> A shepherd forsaken was laid,
> And while a false nymph was his theme,
> A willow supported his head.
> The wind that blew over the Plain,
> With a sigh to his sigh did reply,
> And the brook in return to his pain,
> Ran mournfully murmuring by.

55. *a tiger / From the Congo*: There are of course no tigers in Africa, but Gilbert had evidently been following the news in which the Congo area, then being colonized by a private company headed by the Belgian king Leopold, featured regularly.

Ruddigore; or, The Witch's Curse

First performed 22 January 1887 at the Savoy Theatre, London.

Original Cast

Sir Ruthven Murgatroyd (Robin Oak-apple)	George Grossmith
Richard Daunt-less	Durward Lely
Sir Despard Murgatroyd	Rutland Barrington
Old Adam Good-heart	Rudolph Lewis
Rose Maybud	Leonora Braham
Mad Margaret	Jessie Bond
Dame Hannah	Rosina Brandram
Zorah	Josephine Findlay
Ruth	Miss Lindsay
Sir Rupert Murgatroyd	Sydney Price
Sir Jasper Murgatroyd	Harold Charles
Sir Lionel Murgatroyd	Harris Trevor
Sir Conrad Murgatroyd	Percy Burbank
Sir Desmond Murgatroyd	Mr Tuer
Sir Gilbert Murgatroyd	James Wilbraham
Sir Mervyn Murgatroyd	Mr Cox
Sir Roderick Murgatroyd	Richard Temple

There is no disguising the fact that *Ruddigore* was a major anticlimax after the euphoria of *The Mikado* and that the public was disappointed at this somewhat out-dated take-off of drawing-room melodrama, filled with the stock characters of the genre: the passionate sailor, the ruddy-faced farmer, the hero in disguise, the wicked baronet and the virtuous heroine.

Ruddygore, as it was first spelt, premiered just three days after the closure of *The Mikado*, for which the crowds were thinning out. It used most of the same performers, who rehearsed almost to the point of collapse, which was of course the normal physical condition of Sullivan. He had been composing the music at an extraordinarily busy time in his life, the 1886 Leeds Festival having premiered his new work, *The Golden Legend*, damned with the faintest of praise by *The Times* whose critic wrote how it would do 'until our long-expected English Beethoven appears on the scene'.

Early rehearsals were conducted amid strict secrecy. The librettist and composer were both unwilling to let the press reveal details of the plot, mostly because of the fear of piracy. Gilbert told the *Pall Mall Gazette*: 'Even the actors themselves do not know the name of the play, nor the characters they are severally engaged to represent. The name of the play is at present unknown to myself and I shall be much obliged to anyone who will tell it to me.' When the name did emerge, tender Victorian dispositions were horrified to discover that it contained the coarse phoneme 'ruddy'. Given that 'ruddy' was then a polite word for 'bloody', and gore an obscure term for blood, *Ruddygore* effectively meant 'bloody blood'. Indeed, when a member of Gilbert's club complained that using the term 'ruddy' was tantamount to using the word 'bloody' Gilbert retorted: 'I suppose you'll take it that if I say "I admire your ruddy countenance" (which I do) I mean I like your bloody cheek (which I don't)' (Bradley: 1996). He also responded to complainers in typical fashion by suggesting he would change the title to either *Kensington Gore (Not Half So Good as The Mikado)* or *Kensington Gore (Robin and Richard Were Two Pretty Men)*, before settling for a cosmetic change, converting the 'y' to an 'i' and *Ruddigore*.

The opening night of the new work was beset by misfortune. George Grossmith as Robin Oakapple fluffed some of his lines, while Leonora Braham (Rose Maybud) sang poorly amid several prompts. The Prince and Princess of Wales (the future Edward VII and Queen Alexandra), who were due to attend, were unexpectedly called away at the last minute and replaced by the Lord Mayor and Lady Mayoress, from whose box an opera glass fell during the interval, missing the head of one the distinguished singers in the audience, Madame Albani, by a few inches. And this only one night after an empty soda water bottle had dropped from the gallery of Drury Lane Theatre and narrowly missed the head of a High Court judge, a coincidence worthy of Gilbert's pen itself. Gilbert thought Sullivan's music too grand, in particular the song 'When the night wind howls in the chimney cowls', claiming that it was like inserting fifty lines of *Paradise Lost* into a farcical comedy. One critic slammed Sullivan's music for being 'pitched in the wrong key' during the ghost scene, 'as if the ancestral ghosts were a dread reality coming straight from the charnel house'. Sullivan thought that *Ruddigore* was more a play with musical interludes than an opera, and jokily left the score to Gilbert in his will.

Ruddigore, which Gilbert based on his play *Ages Ago* and several of his Bab Ballads, with occasional nods to *Hamlet*, tells of how the girls of the Cornish fishing village of Rederring have little chance of finding a suitor as all the young men love Rose Maybud. Alas none of them can match her requirements of a husband. Nevertheless the village's professional bridesmaids stand by on duty every day from ten to four in case their services are required. When they tire of this ('Every day, as the days roll on / Bridesmaids' garb we daily don'), they try to persuade Dame Hannah, Rose's aunt, to marry Old Adam, Robin's faithful servant, who loves her. Unfortunately she cannot; she is pledged to 'eternal maidenhood'. Many years previously she had fallen in love with a 'god-like youth' who wooed her under an assumed name, but on the morning of the wedding she discovered her intended was Sir Roderic Murgatroyd, one of the 'bad baronets of Ruddigore'. Alas the Murgatroyds are cursed, the spell cast by a witch the first baronet burnt on the village green, and they must commit one crime a day or die in torment.

Although Act I was a success, the curtain rising repeatedly to recall the players, Act II, with its spectral ensemble of deceased Murgatroyds, was less so. The technical wizardry was not as spellbinding as the newspapers had promised. Two painting frames crashed to the stage, some members of the audience hissed and the fall of the curtain witnessed the first 'boo' for a Gilbert and Sullivan opera, something *The Times* attributed to the 'feebleness of the second act and the downright stupidity of its dénouement'. Then there was Richard Dauntless's entrance song, 'I Shipped, D'ye See, in a Revenue sloop'. It nearly created an international incident as *Le Figaro*'s London correspondent objected to the 'Mounseers' and 'Parley-voos' in the text and mistook the lampoon on British cowardice under fire as an insult to the French. There was even talk of Gilbert himself being challenged to a duel. Fortunately the contretemps was settled around an evening's cigar-fuelled banter.

Ruddigore ran for 288 performances, which took less than a year. As it closed before the next opera was ready, D'Oyly Carte was obliged to revive *HMS Pinafore*, *The Pirates of Penzance* and *The Mikado* to keep the duo's work in the public eye. Nineteen years later Gilbert, in a speech before Savoy artistes, recalled the problems with the original run: 'We were credited, or discredited, with one conspicuous failure, *Ruddigore, or The Witch's Curse*. Well, it ran eight months and, with the sale of the libretto, put £7,000 into my pocket' (Walbrook: 1922).

Although *Ruddigore* was a personal favourite of the author, it was never revived in his lifetime. A 1910 production was curtailed after the elderly Gilbert rowed with C. Herbert Workman, manager of the Savoy, and thus the world never witnessed the new version revised by the librettist himself. In 1964 an animated version of *Ruddigore*, created by Halas and Batchelor, was released to a mixed reception.

1. *Rederring*: An obvious but still amusing pun. The Cornish location is fictitious; the period the early nineteenth century.
2. ADAM: Based on Adam, the servant in Shakespeare's *As You Like It*, who enters the Forest of Arden and announces: 'Dear master, I can go

no further. O, I die for food! Here lie I down and measure out my grave. Farewell, kind master' (II.6.1–3).

3. *Ruthven*: A name of great Caledonian significance, see also note 30. It was the family name of the Earls of Gowrie, whose 1600 incumbent kidnapped James VI of Scotland (later James I of England), an incident that led the Scots to pass a law banning the use of the name Ruthven in perpetuity. The law was later relaxed.

4. *Oakapple*: The brownish gall that parasites form on oak leaves. Oakapple Day – 29 May – was the day on which Royalists celebrated the 1660 restoration of the throne, chosen as it was Charles II's birthday, 'to be for ever kept as a day of thanksgiving for our redemption from tyranny and the King's return to his Government', as Samuel Pepys noted in his Diary for 1 June 1660. The fruit was chosen to commemorate Charles's hiding in an oak tree following the 1651 Battle of Worcester. A dying custom in parts of England sees people wearing sprigs of oak on the day to commemorate the occasion.

5. *Let the welkin ring*: Welkin is an old Saxon word for sky. Here Gilbert may have been thinking of the passage in Mark Twain's *Tom Sawyer* (1876): 'But I was aggravated about that welkin. I wanted to know. I got the subject up again, and then Tom explained, the best he could. He said when a person made a big speech the newspapers said the shouts of the people made the welkin ring' (ch. 25).

6. *Revenue sloop*: A customs officer's boat that patrols the shore to deter smugglers.

7. *Cape Finistere*: The westernmost point of Spain, known locally as Cabo Finisterre.

8. *fires with a thirty-two*: Fires a 32-pound cannon shot.

9. *a-cockbill*: A nautical term meaning having one yardarm higher than the other. In non-nautical parlance it could mean being out of shape.

10. *barrowknight*: Slang for 'baronet'.

11. *Crichton*: See *Iolanthe* note 48.

12. *Ovid*: See *Iolanthe* note 45.

13. *Horace*: Roman poet and satirist Quintus Horatius Flaccus (65 BC–AD 8), whose greatest works were the three books of *Odes* dating from 19 BC.

14. *Swinburne*: See headnote to *Patience*. Of course Robin Oakapple in his eighteenth-century setting should not be mentioning a figure from a future time.

15. *Morris*: The same anachronism applies with William Morris; see *Patience* notes 54 and 55.

16. *Parbuckle*: A rope sling used for lifting heavy cylindrical objects.

17. *sail under false colours*: Pretend to be something one's not to cheat

others, a term originating from the pirate's practice of sailing under false colours to trap potential victims.

18. *blue-jacket*: A term for a sailor, which also refers to the waistcoat-like garment lined with cork that could act as a life preserver.

19. *Belay*: In nautical terms, to secure or make fast a rope.

20. *Lothario*: A womanizer, as in the name of the principal character of Nicholas Rowe's play *The Fair Penitent* (1703).

21. *dead-eye*: Block and tackle for tightening the shrouds of a mast.

22. *tack*: Several nautical meanings but in this sense refers to the idea of changing from one position to another.

23. *Cytherean posies*: Cythera is the south-easternmost of the Ionian Islands, off the southern Peloponnesus, where Aphrodite – goddess of love and beauty, the Romans' Venus – rose from the sea. In modern Greece it is known as Kíthira.

24. *Italian glance*: An elaborately furtive glance. Compare Henry James's *Roderick Hudson* (1876): 'But the Cavaliere only looked out at him keenly from among his wrinkles, and seemed to say, with all the vividness of the Italian glance, "Oh, I say nothing more. I am not so shallow as to complain!" ' (ch. 5).

25. *Bucks and Blades*: A 'buck' is a smart young man, a 'blade' a sharp young soldier. For *Ruddigore*'s opening night, £6,000 was spent on replica Napoleonic uniforms for the chorus of bucks and blades.

26. *Elysian*: See *HMS Pinafore* note 40.

27. *Amaryllis*: A fair shepherdess in Virgil's *Eclogues* (37 BC).

28. *Chloe and Phyllis*: Like Amaryllis these are poetic names for rustic Arcadian maidens. Compare Dickens's *Little Dorrit* (1857): 'The poor little old man knew some pale and vapid little songs, long out of date, about Chloe, and Phyllis' (ch. 31).

29. *GAVOTTE*: French folk dance named after the Gavot people of the Pays de Gap region.

30. *elision*: The omission of a sound in pronunciation – in this instance 'Ruthven' is pronounced 'Rivven'.

31. *valley-de-sham*: A corruption of the French *valet de chambre* ('personal servant') or what Bertie Wooster might call a gentleman's gentleman.

32. *Gideon Crawle*: Old Adam has changed his name to 'Gideon Crawle' to go with his master's wicked new identity.

33. *Soho*: As in the Duke of Monmouth's hunting cry which gave rise to the London place name.

34. *Alas, poor ghost*: From Shakespeare's *Hamlet* (I.5), and to which Hamlet's father's ghost replies: 'Pity me not.'

35. *prigging:* Thieving.

36. *thimble-rigging*: Cheating using sleight of hand, after the game 'Thimblerig', which used three thimbles and a pea, and was similar to the three-card trick (see next note).

37. *three-card delusion*: A street game in which a conman manipulates playing cards and takes bets on their supposed location.

38. *Athenaeums*: Victorian cultural clubs found in big cities.

39. *National School*: Church-run school for the poor, set up following the 1870 Education Act.

40. *Basingstoke*: Bland Hampshire town, long the butt of jokes from stand-up comedians.

41. *PATTER-TRIO*: Humorous song for three, where a large number of words are sung rapidly to a few notes.

42. *mickle*: Middle English word meaning 'great' or 'greatly', nowadays mostly used in northern or Scottish dialect. It was used comically by the hero in the film version of Keith Waterhouse's *Billy Liar* (1959): 'I'm just about thraped with this place, it's neither mickling nor muckling.'

The Yeomen of the Guard;
or, The Merryman and his Maid

First performed 3 October 1888 at the Savoy Theatre, London.

Original Cast

Sir Richard Cholmondeley	Wallace Brownlow
Colonel Fairfax	Courtice Pounds
Sergeant Meryll	Richard Temple
Leonard Meryll	W. R. Shirley
Jack Point	George Grossmith
Wilfred Shadbolt	W. H. Denny
The Headsman	Mr H. Richards
First Yeoman	James Wilbraham
Second Yeoman	Antonio Medcalf
Third Yeoman	Mr Merton
Fourth Yeoman	Rudolf Lewis
First Citizen	Tom Redmond
Second Citizen	Mr Boyd
Elsie Maynard	Geraldine Ulmar
Phoebe Meryll	Jessie Bond

Dame Carruthers   Rosina Brandram
Kate   Rose Hervey

The Tower of London, with its thousand-plus years of history as prison, fortress, mint and royal seat, was always a prime setting for a Gilbert and Sullivan treatment. Yet it was Gilbert's chance sighting of a poster advertising the Tower Furnishing Company, complete with a picture of its namesake, while he was waiting for a train at Uxbridge station in late 1887, that caused the idea of a 'human story' about the Tower to germinate. And how lucky Gilbert was to make that connection, for the new work came at an uninspired time for the librettist. *Ruddigore* had ended its initial run, and with no new opera ready D'Oyly Carte was once again reviving old stalwarts such as *HMS Pinafore*, *The Pirates of Penzance* and *The Mikado*, with Gilbert once again reduced to his old standby – the magic-lozenge plot.

Reinvigorated by thoughts of the Tower, Gilbert decided the new opera, to be called simply *The Tower of London*, would be staffed with grand figures dressed in traditional costume, always a Gilbert favourite. He outlined a synopsis of the plot to Sullivan and D'Oyly Carte on Christmas Day 1887. The setting would be the Tower in the sixteenth century. Colonel Fairfax, under sentence of death on a false charge of sorcery, not wishing to leave his estate to his accuser, secretly marries Elsie Maynard, a strolling singer. With help he escapes, to the chagrin of the Tower authorities and his intended.

Sullivan pronounced himself delighted with Gilbert's outline. Here was a story that required no magic of any sort, a story that was 'very human and funny also; no topsy-turvydom' (Sullivan–Flower: 1927). In reality there was some measure of these everyday Gilbertian devices, but not as many as usual. To research the new work Gilbert visited and revisited the Tower at length. However, in changing the title first to *The Tower Warders*, then *The Beefeaters* and finally *The Yeomen of the Guard*, he made a curious mistake: the Yeomen of the Guard (see note 1) are stationed at St James's Palace, not the Tower, which is the home of the Yeomen *Warders* or Beefeaters.

Pedantry aside, Gilbert and Sullivan did well to create a historical opera set in the Tower. Victoria had just celebrated her fiftieth year as Queen, the Tower of London ranked then and now as the most powerful symbol of British might and heritage, and the Tudor period was the time when Britain first ventured into the world with grand imperialist designs.

The Yeomen of the Guard is by Savoy standards a serious work. The plot does indeed eschew the usual seasoning of topsy-turvydom. The music is tinged with pathos. It has a tragic ending; a form resembling standard opera. There is rich depth to the characters and atmosphere. Dark themes such as greed, revenge, opportunism, obsession and cruelty vie with the more virtuous concepts of duty, honour, love, courage and bravery. Gilbert needed inspiration in choosing a cast. After ten years' service, Barrington, his 'staid, stolid swine', had quit to take over at the St James's Theatre, Piccadilly. His replacement was W. H. Denny, whose face was his fortune, as H. M. Walbrook (1922) once explained: 'Made up with long, forbidding black locks and an ill-shaven chin and cheeks, [Denny] was certainly as unprepossessing a lover as ever a maiden shivered before or an audience laughed at' (Walbrook: 1922).

As the first night neared, the librettist was at his most nervous. He changed some of the finale to Act I minutes before the curtain rose and fretted in front of Jessie Bond to such an extent that she was moved to implore him to leave: 'For heaven's sake, Mr Gilbert, Go away and leave me alone or I shan't be able to sing a note!' (MacGeorge: 1930). Gilbert left and went to the Drury Lane Theatre to see *The Armada*, returning to find Sullivan receiving warm applause. Indeed, the composer had excelled himself. Inspired by Mozart's 'Deh Vieni' from *Don Giovanni* for the Jester's song, 'I've Wisdom From the East and From the West', he gave the singer one melody and the orchestra another. Punters marvelled at numbers such as 'I Have a Song to Sing, O', joyful on its original airing, sad on its reprise, despite the identical harmonization. Enthused, the composer noted in his diary: 'Crammed house – usual enthusiastic reception. I was awfully nervous and continued so until the duet "Heighday" which settled the fate of the opera. Its success was tremendous, three times encored! After that everything went on wheels, and I think its success is even greater than *The Mikado*. Nine encores' (Sullivan–Flowers: 1927). Gilbert was not so euphoric. *The Times*'s review of the premiere caused him concern. 'It should be acknowledged that Mr Gilbert has earnestly endeavoured to leave familiar grooves and rise to higher things on his abandoned self as on stepping stones,' wrote The Thunderer. 'Whether the move in the new direction will be altogether a successful one is a different question, which at present it would be premature to decide.' Other critics pointed out that Gilbert was now plagiarizing earlier Savoy operas (Jack Point's love for Elsie parallels Bunthorne's for Patience; the preoccupation with execution and torture features in *The Mikado*) and other contemporary operas (the marriage scene in which the prisoner is prevented from knowing the identity of the bride can be found in Vincent Wallace's 1845 opera, *Maritana*), sending the librettist into even blacker moods.

1. *YEOMEN OF THE GUARD*: Britain's oldest military body, set up by Henry VII in 1485 as his personal bodyguard. One of their first tasks was to make the king's bed, which no one else was allowed to touch. The Yeomen's uniform consists of a royal red tunic with purple facings

and stripes, gold lace ornaments, red knee-breeches and red stockings. Today they have a permanent room in St James's Palace and still take part in ceremonial duties such as searching the Houses of Parliament, distributing Maundy Money in Westminster Abbey the day before Good Friday, and offering gold, frankincense and myrrh during Epiphany.

2. *Tower Green*: A flat, lawned area by the south-west corner of the Tower complex where the scaffold was erected when public figures were to be beheaded. Seven people are known to have been executed here including Anne Boleyn, the second wife of Henry VIII (in 1536), and Lady Jane Grey, the nine-day queen (1554).

3. *the Little Ease*: A four-foot square four-foot high prison cell in the Tower, which was probably located underneath the Chapel of St John and was built specifically so that the captive could never find a comfortable position.

4. *Colonel Fairfax*: The name probably comes from Thomas Fairfax, Lord General in Oliver Cromwell's mid-seventeenth-century New Model Army. The most famous colonel connected with the Tower is Colonel Blood, who attempted to steal the Crown Jewels in 1671 but was arrested as he tried to leave by the Iron Gate.

5. *alchemist*: Raymond Lully, the revered thirteenth-century Italian alchemist, was granted a room in the Tower by Edward II so that he could work on transmuting base metals into gold. When the king tired of Lully, he held him prisoner therein, but with the help of John Cremer, Abbot of Westminster, Lully eventually escaped, fleeing to the continent.

6. *Beauchamp Tower*: A tower on the west side of Tower Green, built 1275–81 at the behest of Edward I, and later named after Thomas Beauchamp (pronounced 'Beecham'), a fourteenth-century inmate. It was often used to hold prisoners of high rank such as Thomas More, Henry VIII's Lord Chancellor, the Elizabethan explorer Sir Walter Ralegh and the diarist Samuel Pepys.

7. *Tower Warders*: Officially the Corps of Yeoman Warders, established in 1548, and better known as the Beefeaters, a name which may be derived from the French *buffetier*, 'food taster'. Their uniform is similar to the Yeomen of the Guard, and their role is also ceremonial. Every day for the past 700 years or so the Yeoman Warders have taken part in the Ceremony of the Keys, during which the gates of the Tower of London are secured shortly before 10 p.m. by the Chief Yeoman Warder, who is escorted by four armed guards. After locking the gates, the Chief Yeoman Warder is challenged by a sentry who 'recognizes' him as the bearer of the monarch's keys and announces: 'Pass, Queen Elizabeth's

keys, and all's well.' At coronations the Yeoman Warders form a guard of honour inside Westminster Abbey.

8. *pikemen*: The Yeomen Warders carry a halberd or pike known as a partisan. The Chief Warder carries a staff topped by a silver model of the White Tower.

9. *Cold Harbour*: Henry III built the Coldharbour Gate in the mid thirteenth century next to the White Tower. It was demolished in the late seventeenth century and its remains can still be seen jutting out from the White Tower.

10. *old Blunderbore*: The name of a giant in Richard Doyle's midnineteenth-century tale *Jack the Giant Killer*.

11. *save her head*: Two queens were beheaded at the Tower, see note 2.

12. *LIEUTENANT*: The Lieutenant of the Tower in the opera, Sir Richard Cholmondeley, was based on a real life figure of the same name, who filled the position in the sixteenth century, during the reign of Queen Mary.

13. *Clarence Poltwhistle*: The name probably comes from Geoffrey Poltwhistle, a contemporary of Sir Richard Cholmondeley (see previous note).

14. *hundred crowns*: A sum of £25. A crown was worth 5 shillings, a quarter of a pound.

15. *scurvy trick*: A naval term meaning dirty trick.

16. *follify*: A Gilbertian neologism meaning be foolish.

17. *saraband . . . Jumping Joan*: Various European dances.

18. *electuary*: Medicine powder with added honey or syrup to disguise the repellent taste.

19. *I've wisdom from the East and from the West*: Compare Psalm 107:3: 'And gathered them out of the lands, from the east, and from the west'.

20. *gild the philosophic pill*: Add a spoonful of sugar to make the medicine go down.

21. *a live ass is better than a dead lion*: Based on the line from Ecclesiastes 9:4: 'for a living dog is better than a dead lion'.

22. *last campaign*: Leonard Meryll's last campaign was probably the Scottish borders battle near Jedburgh of September 1523, when the Earl of Surrey beat off the Scottish challenger to the throne, the Duke of Albany.

23. *bell of St Peter's*: The bell of the church of St Peter ad Vincula, which stands in the precincts of the Tower, was rung during a Tower execution. During the early run of *The Yeomen of the Guard*, the stage manager, J. M. Gordon, provided a two-hundredweight bell which he positioned so that the percussionist could see the conductor at all times. Gilbert later took the bell to furnish the billiard room of his Grim's Dyke mansion. In the 1960s and 70s, the real St Peter's bell was sounded

during a number of productions of the opera held in the moat of the Tower. Tommy Steele player the Jester in 1978.

24. *thousand marks*: A mark was worth two-thirds of a pound – thirteen shillings and fourpence.

25. *D. D.*: Doctor of Divinity, see *The Sorcerer* note 35.

26. *arquebus*: A portable gun.

27. *tale of cock and bull*: Rambling, barely believable story.

28. *Gyves*: Leg irons. Given that Gilbert had been devouring Shakespeare prior to writing *The Yeomen of the Guard*, he may have been thinking of 'A Lover's Complaint' (1609):

> But, O my sweet, what labour is't to leave
> The thing we have not, mastering what not strives?
> Paling the place which did no form receive,
> Playing patient sports in unconstrained gyves? (lines 239–42)

29. *Ods bodikins*: An antiquated cuss meaning 'God's little body'.

30. *mickle*: See *Ruddigore* note 42.

31. *cockatrice*: A mythical beast that was a mixture of a rooster and a serpent. Compare Isaiah 14:29: 'Rejoice not thou, whole Palestina, because the rod of him that smote thee is broken: for out of the serpent's root shall come forth a cockatrice, and his fruit shall be a fiery flying serpent.'

32. *ELEGIACS*: Poems written in alternate lines of hexameter and pentameter, originally as a lament.

The Gondoliers; or, The King of Barataria

First performed 7 December 1889 at the Savoy Theatre, London.

Original Cast

The Duke of Plaza-Toro	Frank Wyatt
Luiz, his attendant	Wallace Brownlow
Don Alhambra del Bolero	W. H. Denny
Marco Palmieri	Courtice Pounds
Giuseppe Palmieri	Rutland Barrington
Antonio	Mr Metcalf
Francesco	Charles Rose
Giorgio	George de Pledge

Annibale	James Wilbraham
Ottavio	Charles Gilbert
The Duchess of Plaza-Toro	Rosina Brandram
Casilda	Decima Moore
Gianetta	Geraldine Ulmar
Tessa	Jessie Bond
Fiametta	Nellie Lawrence
Vittoria	Annie Cole
Giulia	Norah Phyllis
Inez	Annie Bernard

The Gondoliers, with its sparkling music, frivolity and archly romantic Venetian setting, was Gilbert's topsy-turvical revenge on Sullivan. 'I thought *The Yeomen of the Guard* the best thing we had done,' he told a newspaper reporter, 'but I am told that the public like the topsy-turvy best, so this time they are going to get it' (Walbrook: 1922). Consequently *The Gondoliers* involves typically Gilbertian mistaken identities and a deus ex machina last-minute resolution of plot. It also satirizes snobbery, republicanism and those who profess egalitarianism while behaving with self-interest, something which a Venetian gondolier can be as guilty of as a Doge. 'As we abhor oppression, we abhor kings,' Giuseppe reveals early in the story. Later, when he learns that he may himself be heir to a throne, he explains: 'of course there are kings and kings. When I say I detest kings, I mean I detest *bad* kings.'

After the longest opening musical stretch in any of the Savoy Operas, two gondoliers, Marco and Giuseppe, discover that one of them is no less a figure than the only son of the late King of Barataria. Which of the two is uncertain, as the gondolier to whom the royal babe was entrusted mixed up the child with his own baby son. Because of his 'terrible taste for tippling, that highly respectable gondolier could never declare with a mind sincere which of the two was his offspring dear, and which the Royal stripling'. But no fears. Until it can be ascertained who is the rightful royal heir, they can reign jointly.

The success of Gilbert and Sullivan's previous venture, *The Yeomen of the Guard*, further crystallized Sullivan's wish to compose a truly serious opera. Gilbert would not accept such a departure. He was willing to contemplate another *Yeomen*, but nothing more. 'I think we should be risking everything in writing more seriously still,' he wrote to Sullivan. When Sullivan talked of the music being supreme, Gilbert wrote back that 'if we meet, it must be as master and master, not as master and servant' (Dark: 1923). Sullivan's ire increased. In a letter to D'Oyly Carte he complained how Gilbert dominated and time-wasted at rehearsals, reducing him, Sullivan, to a 'cipher in the theatre' (Sullivan–Flower: 1927). It needed all D'Oyly Carte's and his wife Helen's diplomatic skills to appease Sullivan.

Once things had cooled, charm replaced conflict. Hearing from D'Oyly Carte that Gilbert was contemplating an opera set in Venice, Sullivan declared that this was something they could both work on 'with warmth and enthusiasm' (Sullivan–Flower: 1927). Relations between the two men then proceeded with rare cordiality. Gilbert even provided alternative versions of lyrics, allowed lines to be omitted and offered to write new material to please the composer. Notably, the ratio of music to words is greater in *The Gondoliers* than in any other of the operas. But Gilbert constrained his own creativity with his perennial niggardliness. Because he felt that some members of the Savoy cast were becoming too conceited, he decided to have no star parts and creates the characters accordingly, with more ensemble and chorus numbers than solos. Or as the Grand Inquisitor himself puts it in the libretto: 'When everybody's somebody, then no one's anybody.'

Although Gilbert's decision to play down the star roles was made easier by the departure of Grossmith, who returned to the stand-up comic circuit, Barrington had returned to the team and Jessie Bond refused to appear unless her money was increased from £20 to £30 a week. Gilbert stood his ground on Bond's wage but Sullivan and D'Oyly Carte supported the singer, and Gilbert was forced to accede. After that he never spoke to Bond again other than to acknowledge her arrival on stage with the words: 'Make way for the high-salaried artiste' (Baily, *Gilbert and Sullivan Book*, 1952).

How he enjoyed dealing with the newly arrived Decima Moore (Casilda) instead. As Moore had no previous acting experience she had 'nothing to unlearn'. Gilbert moulded her furiously, rehearsing with trenchant rhythmic clapping to ram home the metre: 'I've no patience [clap] with the presumption [clap] of persons [clap] . . .' (MacGeorge: 1930). Nevertheless, Gilbert's attempt at in-house egalitarianism mostly succeeded in uniting the members for what became the partnership's last great hurrah. Sullivan, having declared Gilbert's libretto 'bright, interesting, funny, and very pretty' (Sullivan–Flower: 1927), steeped himself in Italian opera, and journeyed to Venice to soak up the city's atmosphere and its inhabitants' mores before setting to work. He filled his score with splashes of bright Mediterranean colour and authentic Latin dances – the saltarello, tarantella and cachucha.

This perfect marriage of engaging plot, songs and music saw excellent reviews greet *The Gondoliers*. 'A verdict of emphatic and unanimous approval was passed last night by a brilliant house upon Mr W. S. Gilbert and Sir Arthur Sullivan's new comic opera,' wrote the *Sunday Times*. 'That verdict was never for a moment in doubt. From the time the curtain rose . . .

there reigned in the Savoy Theatre but one steady, undisturbed atmosphere of contentment – contentment with the music, the dances, the piece, the scenery, the dresses, and not the least of all, with the talented and loyal members of Mr D'Oyly Carte's company.' After hearing the near twenty-minute opening music-only scene, Frank Burnand, editor of *Punch* and librettist of *Cox and Box*, wrote to Sullivan: 'Place some of it, costumes and all, on the stage as an extract without saying from what, and they'd say Grand Opera.' Gilbert was so enchanted by the music of *The Gondoliers* that he wrote to Sullivan delighted that he would have 'the chance of shining right through to the twentieth century with a reflected light', to which the composer gallantly replied that Gilbert should not talk of reflected light because his words 'shine with an individual brilliancy which no other writer can hope to attain' (Sullivan–Flower: 1927).

The Gondoliers wasn't so well received Stateside. It was premiered at the Park Theatre, New York, a month after its Savoy opening, but failed to captivate American audiences, and critics soon mockingly renamed it *The Gone-Dollars*. D'Oyly Carte himself journeyed over to boost the production, but found himself vying with a pirate company presenting a camped-up version. At the Savoy the initial production of *The Gondoliers* ran for 554 performances – almost as many as *The Mikado* – and when the number of performances had surpassed Sullivan's dramatic opera *Ivanhoe* playing at D'Oyly Carte's latest new theatre, the Royal English Opera House (now the Palace Theatre at Cambridge Circus), some reviewers suggested that light opera was more Sullivan's forte, a claim that stunned the composer, who was so used to being chastised for supposedly throwing away his talents on frivolous works.

In March 1891 *The Gondoliers* achieved the rare and considerable feat of being chosen for a royal command performance. The entire company – all 170 of them – journeyed on a chartered train to Windsor to play in front of Queen Victoria at the castle, where the monarch particularly enjoyed the lines,

> Oh, philosophers may sing
> Of the troubles of a King;
> Yet the duties are delightful, and the privileges great;
> But the privilege and pleasure
> That we treasure beyond measure
> Is to run on little errands for the Ministers of State!

The Gondoliers continues to be produced regularly even though staging the work is not cheap as it requires a gondola that can move across the stage and a costume change for the second act involving almost every male member of the cast.

1. *BARATARIA*: Gilbert took the name from Cervantes's *Don Quixote*, in which Barataria is the island of which Sancho Panza becomes governor.

2. *PIAZZETTA*: One of the world's most famous tourist sights between St Mark's and the Canale di San Marco, Venice. Although the setting is instantly identifiable, not least of all through the paintings of Canaletto, Guardi and Turner, the glory that awaited so many visitors arriving by boat has been lost to the modern-day rail or air traveller.

3. *Venice*: With its archly romantic setting – Lord Byron called Venice 'a fairy city of the heart' – graceful palazzo architecture, buildings that appear to float magically on water and twenty-eight miles of canals, Venice was always a likely choice for a Gilbert and Sullivan setting. By the time of *The Gondoliers*' opening, Thomas Cook was running an affordable package tour to the city, complemented by Baedeker's guidebook. But even those members of the audience who had not taken up Cook's offer would have been familiar with various aspects of Venice: the canals, the gondolas and their gondoliers, St Mark's, the Doge's Palace, the city's fierce sense of independence – perhaps even its equally fierce medieval imperialist history which saw the banner of St Mark flying over much of the eastern Mediterranean until the Turks captured Constantinople in 1453.

    British fascination with Venice had increased since 1851 when the art critic John Ruskin published his paean to the city's architecture, *The Stones of Venice*, citing buildings such as the Ducal Palace as not only embodying an architectural ideal, but acting as a metaphor of an ideal society.

4. *Contadine*: Italian, 'peasant girls'.

5. *Gondolieri*: Italian, 'gondola oarsmen'. As Venice is so dominated by water, and cars are banned, movement around the city is still best conducted by the gondola, the flat long boat, used since the eleventh century, exquisitely captured in the fifteenth-century paintings of Carpaccio and Bellini. Gondolas, which have no keel, making them easy to manipulate in shallow water, were originally the limousines of nobility and not the taxi cabs of the public, but in the seventeenth century the Doge of Venice decreed that all gondolas be painted black to avoid the glorification of wealth, as captured by Canaletto in his painting *The Reception of the Ambassador in the Doge's Palace* (1703). After Napoleon conquered Venice in 1797, the gondoliers began ferrying patrons

to make money. They also started singing, to extend the vessels' romantic appeal. During this period, when Venice reached its greatest power as a city state, there were around 10,000 gondolas in use. Nowadays their number is down to some five hundred. Nevertheless their ornamental ironwork (*ferro*), curved at both ends, is the official symbol of the city.

6. *dolce far niente*: Italian, 'sweet doing nothing'.

7. *contradicente*: Italian, 'contradicting'.

8. *ben venuti*: Italian, 'welcome'.

9. *Buon' giorno, signorine . . . signorine, etc.*: This section can be translated as follows:

MAR. *and* GIU.:	Good morning, young ladies!
GIRLS:	Dearest Gondoliers!
	We are country girls!
MAR. *and* GIU.:	Your humble servants!
	For whom are these flowers –
	These most beautiful flowers?
GIRLS:	For you, good gentlemen,
	O, most excellent!
MAR. *and* GIU.:	O heaven!
GIRLS:	Good morning, cavaliers!
MAR. *and* GIU.:	We are gondoliers.
	Young lady, I love you!
GIRLS:	Country girls are we.
MAR. *and* GIU.:	Young ladies!
GIRLS:	Country girls!
	Cavaliers.
MAR. *and* GIU.:	Gondoliers!
	Poor gondoliers!
	Good morning, young ladies etc.

10. *blind-man's buff*: Children's game in which one person is blindfolded and stands in the middle of the room while the others try to approach as close as possible without being touched.

11. DUKE: It tickled Gilbert's sense of irony that while the Venetians made a big play of egalitarianism and democracy, the city was for so long ruled by a despotic duke (elected, of course).

12. *Grand Inquisitor*: Would the Spanish Grand Inquisitor really be ensconced in the Doge's Palace? Although much of Italy was under Spanish rule in the mid eighteenth century, Venice remained independent.

13. *Castilian hidalgo*: A Spanish noble.

14. *quarterings*: Parts of a heraldic shield.

15. *the streets are in such a condition*: Robert Benchley, the early twentieth-century American theatre critic, once arrived in Venice and wired back to New York: 'Streets full of water. Please advise.'

16. *halberdiers*: Soldiers carrying halberds, a weapon that consists of a long shaft topped with an axe or pick.

17. *cornet-à-piston*: Musical instrument usually referred to simply as a cornet.

18. *Plaza-Toro*: Place of the bull.

19. *Count Matadoro*: At a Spanish bullfight, the matador waves a red handkerchief in front of the bull to provoke it.

20. *Baron Picadoro*: The picador, mounted on a horse, annoys the beast further by attacking it with a lance.

21. *Wesleyan Methodist*: A follower of John Wesley, who started the Wesleyan Methodist Society in the 1730s. The line is of course farcical, for it is extremely unlikely that Methodism would have reached Venice by the date the work is set – 1750 – or that the King of Barataria would have been a convert to this English affiliation.

22. *influential directorate*: New companies often appoint dignitaries to the board, their nominal role garnering confidence among the shareholders. Such figures used to be known as guinea pigs: they drew their guineas as director's fees but provided little tangible in return.

23. *allotment*: A company allotting shares after it is formed.

24. *liquidation*: The winding up of a company when all the assets are turned into liquid, i.e. cash, form.

25. *Paladin*: A knight in shining armour. The term is derived from the Emperor Charlemagne's eighth-century court and the Latin word *palatinus* ('attached to the palace').

26. *stolen in infancy*: See *The Pirates of Penzance* note 4.

27. *the Inquisition*: Notorious Spanish courts set up in the fifteenth century by Queen Isabella and empowered by her General Inquisitor, Tomas de Torquemada, to prosecute religious heretics, mostly Jews. In the mid sixteenth century, the Inquisition turned its ire on Protestants in order to keep Spain Catholic. It died away in the early nineteenth century.

28. *Don Alhambra*: The name is taken from the Alhambra, the thirteenth-century palace of the Moorish kings in Granada, Spain.

29. *Jimp*: Of unknown etymology, possibly old Norse, meaning 'neat'.

30. *timoneer*: Helmsman.

31. *bratling*: Similar to brat – an annoying child.

32. *Cordova*: City in southern Spain, usually spelt Cordoba.

33. *the last revolution*: Gilbert probably had in mind the events of 1848, when Daniele Manin staged an unsuccessful mini-revolution during

which Venice became the first city to be attacked from the air – by hot-air balloons containing time bombs. The conflict had been likely since 1815 when Venice, despite its long proud history of autonomy, became part of Austria, whose leaders believed they could win over the Venetians by promising home rule, not realizing that the natives would settle for nothing less than independence. Resentment built up, and on 22 March 1848 Manin and a group of supporters broke into the Venice arsenal to challenge the Austrian authorities. Although the Austrians eventually took back the city, Venice became part of the newly unified Italy in 1866.

34. *Grand Canal*: The main Venetian waterway, which divides the city in two.

35. *Rialto*: The Rialto Bridge, which connects the two parts of Venice bisected by the Grand Canal, was built 1588–91 to the designs of Antonio da Ponte (Anthony of the Bridge). It has a twenty-four-foot high arch, rests on 12,000 wooden pilings and until the nineteenth century was the only bridge crossing the Grand Canal. Ruskin, in *The Stones of Venice*, called it 'very noble in its simplicity, in its proportions, and in its masonry'.

36. *peruke*: A wig.

37. *Coutts*: London's most prestigious bank, patronized by many royal clients, was founded by Scottish goldsmith John Campbell at the sign of the Three Crowns in the Strand in 1692. In 1755 James Coutts, member of a Scottish banking family married into the business. By 1775 the bank was known as Coutts & Co, and James's younger brother, Thomas, was the Senior Partner. It was under Thomas Coutts that the bank flourished. In 1739, the bank took premises at 59 Strand. In 1904 it moved to 440 Strand and is now independently operated as part of the Royal Bank of Scotland.

38. *Xebeque*: A small, three-masted Mediterranean vessel popular with Algerian pirates. Compare 'By the time Philip was on deck the vessel had been distinctly made out to be a three-masted xebeque, very low in the water', from Captain Frederick Marryat's *The Phantom Ship* (1839).

39. *cup and ball*: Children's game involving a wooden cup on a stem, with a ball attached by a cord.

40. *morra*: An Italian finger game.

41. *Garter*: Knights of the Order of the Garter, the highest Order of the English Knighthood, founded by Edward III in 1348, encircle their escutcheon with a representation of the Garter on which is written the motto of the Order: 'Honi soit qui mal y pense' ('Evil be to him who evil thinks'). These were the words, tradition has it, which Edward spoke

when he picked up the Countess of Salisbury's garter after it had fallen at a Ball. Knights of the Garter include the monarch and those honoured for serving the monarch personally.

42. *Thistle*: The Order of the Thistle, the Scottish equivalent to the Order of the Garter, was founded in 1540, restored by James II in 1687 and now comprises sixteen Scottish nobles as well as Royalty. Their arms are surrounded with a green circle edged with gold, bearing the motto: 'Nemo me impune lacessit' ('No man provokes me with impunity').

43. *Bath*: The Order of the Bath is an elevated post which dates back to the eve of Henry IV's Coronation in 1399, when some forty-six baths filled with warm water and draped with clean sheets were laid out in the White Tower for new knights. As the knights bathed, the King entered and approached each man, dipping his finger in the water and making the sign of the cross on the knight's bare back. The ceremony later fell into disuse, but was revived by George I in 1725 as an additional source of political reward for Sir Robert Walpole, the first Prime Minister. Gilbert would have done better, perhaps, to include the reference in *The Yeomen of the Guard*, for the Order has very close connections with the Tower of London.

44. *Rubicon*: A river between Italy and France that was used as a boundary. When Caesar crossed it with his army in 49 BC it was considered an act of war. The word has since come to be used to mean a point of no return. Compare Byron, *The Age of Bronze* (1823): 'Thou Rome, who saw'st thy Caesar's deeds outdone! / Alas! Why pass'd he too the Rubicon / The Rubicon of man's awaken'd rights' (lines 137–9).

45. *cachucha*: Andalusian solo dance in 3/4 time closely resembling the bolero (see below).

46. *fandango*: Spanish and Latin-American dance in 6/8 time.

47. *bolero*: Spanish dance in 3/4 time.

48. *Xeres*: Sherry, the fortified wine. The name comes from the Spanish city of Jerez de la Frontera, near Cadiz, where the white grapes used in sherry grow.

49. *Manzanilla*: Pale dry sherry from Spain, made and kept at San Lucar de Barrameda. Experts claim its strong character comes from being matured so near the sea.

50. *Montero*: Wine from the Pyrenees region.

51. *tuck in his tuppenny*: Tuck in his head, a saying not used until 1859.

52. *Lords-Lieutenant*: Nowadays the monarch's representatives in each county. The post was created in 1549 and assumed the duties formerly charged to the sheriff.

53. *shoddy*: A cheap cloth made from woollen rags.

54. *vulgar fraction*: A ratio of two numbers in the form *a*/*b*, where *a* and *b* are both integers, for instance $1/2$, $3/4$ and $5/8$.

55. *Messer*: Italian, 'master'.

56. *Tartar*: A native of the area to the east of the Caspian Sea, traditionally cast as ferocious.

57. *floated at a premium*: A company which, following a successful inauguration, floats its shares at a higher price.

58. *Limited Liability Act*: Company law was amended in 1855 so that investors were only liable for the amount of capital they invested and not for their personal assets.

59. *Recorders*: Judges who preside over the courts in a city.

60. *baronetted*: Raised to the rank of baronet with a hereditary knighthood.

61. *gazetted*: Mentioned in the *London Gazette* along with other army promotions.

62. *Aldermen*: Senior members of a borough council in England and Ireland who before 1974 were elected for six rather than three years. Their role now is mostly nominal as appointments are made to community elders.

63. *écarté*: A card game for two players where cards are discarded (*écarter*, French, 'discard') and replaced from the pack.

64. *premé, stalì*: Gondolier cries: 'push down on your pole, stop'.

Utopia Limited; or, The Flowers of Progress

First performed 7 October 1893 at the Savoy Theatre, London.

Original Cast

King Paramount the First	Rutland Barrington
Scaphio	W. H. Denny
Phantis	John le Hay
Tarara	Walter Passmore
Calynx	J. Bowden Haswell
Lord Dramaleigh	Scott Russell
Captain Fitz-battleaxe	Charles Kenningham
Captain Sir Edward Corcoran, KCB	Lawrence Gridley
Mr Goldbury	R. Scott Fishe
Sir Bailey Barre, QC, MP	H. Enes Blackmore
Mr Blushington	Herbert Ralland
Princess Zara	Nancy McIntosh
Princess Nekaya	Emmie Owen

Princess Kalyba	Florence Perry
Lady Sophy	Rosina Brandram
Salata	Edith Johnson
Melene	May Bell
Phylla	Miss Horwell-Hersee

The genesis of *Utopia Limited*, the penultimate Savoy Opera, was over-shadowed by the notorious Great Carpet Quarrel. This dramatic fall-out, a defining moment in the partnership's history, has been succinctly summed up as 'the almost inevitable culmination of years of strain and tension in the partnership' by Andrew Crowther (source: internet), secretary of the W. S. Gilbert Society, and occurred four months after the glorious spectacle that was *The Gondoliers*. The latter's success had induced an unprecedented bout of mutual praise between the two men, but when Gilbert asked D'Oyly Carte for detailed accounts of the cost of putting it on, he was surprised to find that he had charged him and Sullivan £500 'for new carpets for the front of the house' at the theatre as part of production expenses.

The author felt strongly that he and Sullivan should not have to pay for others to tread the boards. Sullivan, initially sympathetic to Gilbert, was anxious to keep on good terms with D'Oyly Carte, for whom he was about to write the opera *Ivanhoe*. He was also suffering with his kidneys to care too much about what he called 'a few miserable pounds', and he could not be bothered to study the company's accounts with the intensity Gilbert would have wished and failed to support him. Gilbert however was adamant. It was the principle of the thing. He had long suspected D'Oyly Carte of not being entirely honest in his business dealings, and he vowed not to write for him again nor to allow his existing works to be performed at the Savoy after Christmas unless D'Oyly Carte withdrew the charge. The matter went to court and Gilbert won, thus further souring the various relationships. However, when Gilbert later learned that Sullivan was seriously ill in Monte Carlo he sought reconciliation, which occurred after a fashion.

In some respects it was lucky for Gilbert that Sullivan's *Ivanhoe* was only a moderate success. Had it been a resounding hit the composer might have felt that a Savoy Opera was beneath him. Had it been a flop, Sullivan would probably have been so mortified he wouldn't have been able to consider a new Savoy Opera. Similarly, with Gilbert, there had been just moderate success for *The Mountebanks*, his collaboration with Alfred Cellier in which, at last, he had managed to use the infamous 'magic-lozenge' idea. Suitably chastened, the two men re-formed their partnership.

The result, after a gap of nearly four years, was *Utopia Limited*, a healthy satire on English institutions and mores. Its targets are party politics, the law and the monarchy, and it is set not in Albion, of course, but on a tropical Polynesian island, Utopia. The island is ruled over by King Paramount, a monarch of the absolute school, his power held in check by two Wise Men who can report him to the Public Exploder for any lapse in judgement, which may result in the King being exploded on the spot. The King, long an admirer of British institutions, decides his people should adopt the latter's customs and institutions, even going as far as converting each inhabitant into a 'company limited', as in the British Companies Act (see note 34). Ultimately, the King of Utopia converts his realm into a limited monarchy run alongside a two-party parliamentary system. Some could argue that he ruins the tropical paradise with Anglicization. Others might aver that Gilbert's satire is double-edged; that so-called tropical paradises are not all they're cracked up to be, and that a little bit of British bureaucracy and bumptiousness might help them survive and progress.

Gilbert's decision to borrow the name of Thomas More's island (see note 1) may reveal a dwindling of inspiration, but his use of a 'limited monarchy' model for the ending was prescient, as was the theme of exotic overseas regimes desperately trying to adopt western European political systems. Sullivan was delighted with Gilbert's libretto which he pronounced to be the writer's best yet. The reason why is obvious: in his eyes there was no topsy-turvydom! As Howard Dicus of the Washington Savoyards has noted: 'This is one of the least convoluted of all the G&S plots. No babies are switched at birth. No legal fine print or leap year technicalities are required. The "solution" to the dilemma of the plot is nothing but a sardonic observation about politics' (source: internet).

With the greatest of irony, given the row over the costly carpet, spending on *Utopia Limited* was the Savoy's most lavish yet. The Drawing-Room Scene in Act II, in which the members of the Utopian Court are presented to King Paramount, called for a parquet floor to cover the Savoy stage. No wonder the cost of staging *Utopia Limited* at £7,200 was almost double that for *The Gondoliers*. At least the cantankerous librettist could humorize his parsimony. When Helen D'Oyly Carte asked Gilbert for a donation for an orchestral charity, he replied: 'I hate the orchestra. They take up a lot of paying stalls and they play so loud that my words can't be heard. They are the first to come begging, cap in hand, when they are in difficulties. Having thus blown off steam, I have much pleasure in sending five guineas for the fund' (Baily: 1973).

While *Utopia*'s first night was the usual success – George Bernard Shaw claimed he enjoyed the score 'more than that of any of the previous Savoy operas', and it remained one of Gilbert's own favourites – it ran for only 245 performances and ranks as one of the least performed since. Rupert D'Oyly

Carte abandoned plans to revive the piece in the 1920s due to the cost, and Savoyards had to wait until the D'Oyly Carte Centenary Season in 1975. This, however, was a well-received revival. Queues snaked along the Strand, such was the public demand.

Nevertheless, it is hard to make a case for *Utopia* ranking alongside *The Mikado*, *Iolanthe* or *Patience* in the loftier eyries of the canon. There are too few memorable songs, too few sympathetic characters, too much plagiarizing of earlier Savoy Operas and what *The Times* on the opening night called 'the almost complete absence of anything in the shape of plot'. The text suffers from Gilbert's endless cutting and rewriting; it is too clever by half. Indeed, these were dark days for the world of light entertainment.

1. *UTOPIA*: Although normally used when referring to an ideal place, the word is derived from the Greek for 'no place'. It came into popular use after the 1516 publication in Latin of Thomas More's *Utopia*, a radical critique of European civil life which advocates the abolition of property, set on the imaginary island of the same name.

2. *luxuriant tropical landscape*: Gilbert had two well-known precedents for the idea of Westerners bringing European ideas to the Far East. In 1862 Anna Leonowens arrived in Siam (now Thailand) to teach English to the king's children, experiences later romantically relived in Rodgers' and Hammerstein's *The King and I*. In 1891 Paul Gauguin, a disillusioned French Stock Exchange financier, journeyed to the paradisical Pacific island of Tahiti, looking to immerse himself in primitive native culture, purify himself through nature and capture the results in paint.

   Gilbert probably had Hawaii in mind for Utopia, given the historic links between Britain and the island, which has the Union Jack in its flag, and the regular visits the nineteenth-century Hawaiian court made to London. (By 1893 Hawaii's Princess Kaiulani was being educated at a private school in England and was being featured regularly in the society pages of the popular press, alongside speculation about the effect her spell in England would have on her homeland.) Some theatre companies have performed *Utopia Limited* with *South Pacific* in mind, playing it as Rogers and Hammerstein meets Gilbert and Sullivan.

3. *Girton*: See *Princess Ida* note 9.

4. TARARA: 'Tarara Boomdeay' was the name of a joyous music-hall song made famous in 1891 by Lottie Collins, who while singing it at London's Tivoli Theatre would high-kick her legs in a vibrant manner that sent the crowd into paroxysms of excitement.

5. *Palace Peeper*: The Gilbert and Sullivan Society of New York has used the title of Gilbert's scurrilous royal rag as the name of its newsletter.

6. *Heliogabalian*: See *The Pirates of Penzance* note 21.

7. *far niente*: Italian, 'doing nothing'.

8. *Kodaks*: George Eastman introduced the Kodak box camera in 1888. He invented the name, which has no particular meaning.

9. *Junius*: Marcus Junius Brutus (85–42 BC), one of the conspirators who assassinated Julius Caesar on 44 BC.

10. *Senex*: Latin, 'old man'.

11. *Mercury*: See *Thespis* note 5.

12. *Mephistopheles*: See *Patience* note 21.

13. *de trop*: French, 'too much', 'superfluous'.

14. *Tivoli Gardens*: Well-known amusement park in Copenhagen which opened in 1843 as Tivoli and Vauxhall in honour of London's Vauxhall Gardens, the prototype for many similar establishments.

15. *Mikado of Japan*: See *The Mikado* note 1.

16. *calculus*: The branch of mathematics concerned with infinitesimally small change. See *The Pirates of Penzance* note 16.

17. *First Life Guards*: Senior regiment of the British Army, founded after the restoration of the throne in 1660 by a group of Royalists who had gone into exile with Charles II.

18. *Knightsbridge*: Exclusive south-west London thoroughfare south of Hyde Park.

19. *Belgravian*: See *Iolanthe* note 15.

20. *Horse Guards*: A courtyard off Whitehall which was once the main entrance to Buckingham Palace and is surrounded by elegant mid-eighteenth-century buildings designed by William Kent.

21. *Tontine principle*: Whereby individuals contribute money to a central fund which is handed to the last contributor to remain alive.

22. *Festinat . . . Portio*: Taken from Juvenal's *Sixteen Satires* (IX.127), it should read:

> Festinat enim decurrere velox
> Flosculus angustae miseraeque brevissima vitae
> Portio; dum bibimus dum sera unguenta puellas
> Poscimus obrepit non intellecta senectus.

(The short bloom of our brief and narrow life flies fast away. While we are calling for flowers and wine and women, old age is upon us.)

23. *viviparians*: Viviparous animals are those who give birth to living creatures and include mammals.

24. *Lord High Chamberlain*: See *The Mikado* note 19.

25. *Contango*: The percentage which a buyer of stock pays the seller to postpone transfer to a future settling day.

26. *Backwardation*: The opposite of contango in finance (see above), i.e. the state when the futures price is lower than the spot price. The seller then postpones delivery with the consent of the buyer upon payment of a premium.

27. *KCB*: See *The Sorcerer* note 34.

28. *Maxim gun*: Invented by the American Hiram Maxim in 1881.

29. *Nordenfelt*: The Nordenfelt machine-gun, developed between 1873 and 1878.

30. *What never . . . Hardly ever*: See *HMS Pinafore* (note 8).

31. *Panama Canal*: The ship-going canal in Central America linking the Pacific and Atlantic oceans was still being built at the time of *Utopia Limited*'s premiere and officially opened in 1914.

32. *Winding-Up Petition*: In 1893 the Companies (Winding-Up) Act came into force for folding companies.

33. *Rothschild*: See *Iolanthe* note 54.

34. *Joint Stock Company's Act of Sixty-Two*: The 1862 Act made it easier for small investors to set up companies without risking their personal money.

35. *vibrato*: Musical effect whereby a singer or instrumentalist creates a throbbing quality to a note by oscillating between it and a pitch slightly below.

36. *agitato*: Musical term, meaning in a restless, agitated style.

37. *Philomel*: In Classical mythology, a daughter of King Pandion; she was turned into a nightingale.

38. *Sweet and low*: As in the opening of Tennyson's *The Princess* (1847): 'Sweet and low, sweet and low, / Wind of the western sea'.

39. *virelay*: A short French poem with two rhymes to a stanza, variously arranged.

40. *Christy Minstrels*: White singers who 'blacked up' to look like African-Americans were popular in America in the mid nineteenth century. One of the best-known such troupes was the Christy Minstrels, started by Edwin P. Christy in 1846.

41. *Court of St James's*: To which ambassadors to the UK are officially designated. The palace of the same name, which can be found only a few hundred yards from Buckingham Palace, is still a royal residence.

42. *St James's Hall*: Concert hall by Piccadilly Circus built in 1858 and replaced in 1905 by the Piccadilly Hotel.

43. *Brewers*: The brewing industry's influence on government is a long one,

and as many a radical speaker has explained over the last few centuries, the near permanent inebriation of vast sections of the British working class, cleverly engineered by politicians, has consistently obstructed the route to socialism. Many factory owners would pay their workers in the nearby pub, which they also owned.

44. *Cotton Lords*: The epitome of the new breed of capitalists who symbolized nineteenth-century society. Politically they tended to espouse laissez-faire liberalism, advocating free trade as being beneficial to all countries.

45. *Lord Fildes*: Samuel Luke Fildes (1844–1927), establishment painter commissioned at the end of the century for official royal portraits.

46. *Viscount Millais*: See *Patience* note 63.

47. *Master of the Buckhounds*: See *The Mikado* note 13.

48. *Lord Steward*: Member of the government, often a peer, nominally in charge of the royal household's domestic duties. In Tudor and Stuart times the office had political importance. It carried Cabinet rank until the eighteenth century.

49. *Comptroller of the Household*: Member of the government just below the rank of the Lord Steward in the royal household.

50. *Gold and Silver Stick*: Two attendants to the royal family, first appointed in Tudor times, who carried gold and silver sticks and protected the monarch.

51. *pas de trois*: Corruption of the well-known ballet term *pas-de-deux*, French for 'step for two', referring to a partnership.

52. *tapis*: French, 'carpet'.

53. *cricket*: Gilbert was not an aficionado and this is the only mention in the canon. A 2005 production of *The Mikado* at the Orange Tree Theatre, Richmond, ingeniously cast Titipu around a cricket pitch.

54. *asinorum pons*: Latin for 'asses' bridge', a term which refers to a problem that tests the ability of an inexperienced person. In geometry, *pons asinorum* is used for the Euclidian notion that the angles at the base of an isosceles triangle are equal.

55. *Tarantella*: A fast whirling dance from southern Italian (after the town of Taranto).

56. *fico*: Italian, 'fig'.

The Grand Duke; or, The Statutory Duel

First performed 7 March 1896 at the Savoy Theatre, London.

Original Cast

Rudolph	Walter Passmore
Ernest Dummkopf	Charles Kenningham
Ludwig	Rutland Barrington
Dr Tannhäuser	Scott Russell
The Prince of Monte Carlo	R. Scott Fishe
Viscount Mentone	E. Carleton
Ben Hashbaz	C. Herbert Workman
Herald	Jones Hewson
The Princess of Monte Carlo	Emmie Owen
The Baroness von Krakenfeldt	Rosina Brandram
Julia Jellicoe	Ilka von Palmay
Lisa	Florence Perry
Olga	Mildred Baker
Gretchen	Ruth Vincent
Bertha	Jessie Rose
Elsa	Ethel Wilson
Martha	Beatrice Perry

The Grand Duke was an anticlimatic send off for Britain's greatest ever theatrical partnership. When asked about the work, Gilbert admitted: 'I'm not at all a proud Mother, and I never want to see the ugly misshapen little brat again' (Baily: 1973) The opera had the shortest run – 123 performances – of any Gilbert and Sullivan work save for *Thespis*; it is rarely mentioned by Savoyards, and less performed. The fault is mainly Gilbert's, whose contribution was either mostly formulaic or prolix to the point of incomprehensibility. While the names of the characters and places are wonderfully ridiculous, while the scenery was rich and vivid, and the costumes sparkled, the text reads like a parody of Gilbert, like the work of a tired man.

Sullivan scored the music in Berlin while working on the European premiere of *Ivanhoe*, which was not a great success. To whet the public's appetite back in London, D'Oyly Carte revived *The Mikado*, to which the crowds flocked. But Gilbert found work on a new opera laborious. He constantly altered the original plot, drew too many ideas from other sources and became too absorbed in topics which, though for him were of historic interest (duelling, for instance), had long passed out of the public eye, a state of affairs which some critics blame, perhaps unfairly, on his age.

Because Gilbert and Sullivan no longer enjoyed a good working relationship (see headnote to *Utopia Limited*), *The Grand Duke* suffers from lack of suitable editing. Neither man was confident of providing the constructive criticism that had sharpened earlier collaborations, and Gilbert had succumbed to a carelessness that failed to eschew sub-standard lyrics. It is also likely that each man in himself knew that this would be their last joint venture and was happy to get it out the way with the minimum of fuss.

The critics were nonplussed. They railed against the long and rambling libretto, the complex plot, the inordinate amount of plumbing jokes and the sausage-roll gag (shades of Gilbert and Sullivan's comedic alter egos, the Carry On team). They pronounced themselves displeased with lyrics that looked as if they had been hastily cobbled together, with the text's pretentiousness (Ludwig's Act II tribute to the Greeks is partly *in* Greek) and the contrived final twist. The laughs directed at Ilka von Palmay's heavily Teutonic English (she is supposed to be an 'English *comédienne*') were at her accent not at Gilbert's witty decision to have the English lady unable to speak natively.

It wasn't enough that the Savoy team had delivered again. *The Times* noted how 'the libretto is very conspicuously inferior to the music', pointing out that 'the dialogue seems to have lost much of its crispness, the turning-point of what plot there is requires considerable intellectual application before it can be thoroughly grasped, and some of the jests are beaten out terribly thin'. Sullivan's diary entry on the night of the premiere makes interesting reading alongside those for the earlier sure-fire successes. The composer noted that parts of *The Grand Duke* 'dragged a little', that the dialogue was 'redundant'. He also seemed quite pleased that the opening night meant that he could take a break from working with Gilbert: 'Another week's rehearsal with W.S.G. and I should have gone raving mad. I had already ordered some straw for my hair' (Baily: 1973).

The setting for *The Grand Duke* is the Grand Duchy of Pfennig-Halbpfennig, where Ernest Dummkopf, leader of a band of actors, is planning a conspiracy to overthrow the monarchy, and install himself as the new duke and his fellow thespians in roles that accord with their position in the company. Although this sounds plausible in a Gilbertian universe, the creator lets himself down when providing the rebels with their secret sign. They know of each other not by a password or by a secret handshake but by eating a sausage-roll. At least there's an element of closure in the Grand Duke's story of a theatrical troupe who begin to act out the roles they are meant to be performing, a similarity with *Thespis*, but that too was a disappointment.

After working on *The Grand Duke* Gilbert and Sullivan never spoke again even though Gilbert, to his credit, offered a reconciliation during the November 1900 revival of *Patience*. By then Sullivan was too ill to accept the invitation. He had been spending his time in the casinos of Monte Carlo in agony from his perpetual kidney stones, his face lined through overuse of morphine. After catching bronchitis in Switzerland, the composer struggled back to London and died a lonely death on 22 November 1900. D'Oyly Carte, gravely ill himself, was spared the news; he died four months later.

Gilbert outlived them both, playing the role of the country squire at his Grim's Dyke mansion in Harrow Weald, north-west London. When asked whether he would ever write another opera, he could only sadly reply: 'I should like to very much, but what is the use of Gilbert without a Sullivan?' (Dark: 1923). A wittier story tells of a fellow Garrick Club member, who had not heard of Sullivan's death, asking Gilbert if the former was still composing, only to be told in response: 'Why, on the contrary, I believe he is decomposing.'

Gilbert was belatedly knighted in 1907. Four years later, on 29 May 1911, he tried to rescue a girl swimming in his lake but suffered heart failure in the attempt. A generation of theatre-goers then grew up without regular performances of the Gilbert and Sullivan works, and it was not till after the First World War that Rupert D'Oyly Carte, Richard's son, began to stage triumphant revivals. Ironically, *The Grand Duke* is far better received now than it was at the time of its conception. Many have enjoyed the music as a piece of light orchestral Victoriana in its own right, and revivals at the end of the twentieth century by the City of Durham Light Opera Group and the Oxford Sullivan Society were greeted well. But there's no disguising the fact that this was an unsatisfactory end to a remarkable partnership.

1. *Grand Duchy*: The most famous Grand Duchy is that of Luxembourg, the independent state of 999 square miles tucked between Belgium, France and Germany. For 'Speisesaal', see note 20.

2. *Pfennig Halbpfennig*: German, literally 'penny half-penny'. It would have been too rude for Gilbert to have used the phrase 'tuppenny ha'penny', slang for something worthless.

3. *DUMMKOPF*: German, 'blundering fool'.

4. *sposo*: Italian, 'bridegroom'.

5. *TANNHÄUSER*: The name of Wagner's third opera, first staged in 1845.

6. *Krakenfeldt*: A literal translation from the German would render this as 'Octopuses' field'.

7. *Troilus and Cressida*: Shakespeare's play, a doomed love story between the couple of the title, set against the siege of Troy. Troilus was the son

of Trojan King Priam and Queen Hecuba. Cressida was also a Trojan whose father defected to the Greeks.

8. *sausage-roll*: Foreign audiences have struggled to appreciate the sheer low-brow Britishness of this rather feeble gag about a notoriously dismal foodstuff.

9. *Agamemnon*: King of Mycenae in Classical mythology and the leader of the Greek forces during the Trojan War.

10. *Louis Quatorze*: Louis XIV, also known as the Sun King, ruler of France 1643–1715.

11. *Eloia ... Opoponax*: Gilbert fills this section with a number of cod Greek words. For 'Eloia' he may have had in mind the Eloi, H. G. Wells's childlike creatures of the future, introduced in his science fiction novel *The Time Machine* (1895). 'Opoponax' is a Somalian gum resin known as sweet myrrh, which King Solomon regarded as one of the noblest of all incense gums.

12. *hoydens*: High-spirited or boisterous girls. The word is of Dutch origin.

13. *Gerolstein*: A German spa resort.

14. *agitato*: A musical term, meaning in a restless, agitated styles.

15. *Statutory Duel*: Duels stopped taking place in Britain after 1852, the last one to the death being held between two Frenchmen in Windsor.

16. *crack-jaw*: Difficult to pronounce.

17. *falchions*: Curved swords.

18. *Revising Barrister*: A state official who drew up lists of eligible voters, the function being taken over by the town clerk in 1915.

19. *King's evidence*: Testimony in favour of the Crown by a witness who confesses his guilt, usually as an accomplice.

20. *Speisesaal*: German, 'dining hall'.

21. *jujube*: A gelatine fruit-flavoured lozenge.

22. *Charlemagne*: Holy Roman Emperor (reigned 800–814) who, to many historians, embodied the ideal requirements for a Christian king.

23. *Morris wall-papers*: The florid wallpaper designs of William Morris were exclusive and cultured during the Victorian period but have since been copied to such a grotesque and excessive degree they have become clichéd. The company Arthur Sanderson and Co., which acquired the original woodblocks, have continued to manufacture Morris-styled wallpapers.

24. *verbum sat.*: Latin, used at the end of a statement, implying that further comment is unnecessary.

25. *Rapscallions*: Rascals.

26. *by Jingo*: A seventeenth-century phrase, probably derived from 'By Jesus!'; see headnote to *HMS Pinafore*.

27. *soubrette*: Coquettish maid in a play or comic opera.
28. *merry as a grig*: This should perhaps be 'merry as a Greek', a sixteenth-century saying.
29. *tollolish*: Nonsensical word introduced to rhyme with 'polish'.
30. *cithara*: An ancient instrument of the lyre family.
31. *Lesbian wine*: Wine made with grapes from Lesbos.
32. *hyporchematic*: Like a Greek choral lyric.
33. *choreutae*: Greek, 'chorus'.
34. *criticaster*: Inferior critic.
35. *choregus*: Greek, 'choir master'.
36. *oboloi*: Greek coin worth one-sixth of a drachma.
37. *Kalends*: The first day of the month in the Roman calendar, when the head of the household conducted a ceremony involving ritual bathing, the kissing of hands and the burning of incense.
38. *Periphrastic*: Using an excessive number of words.
39. *Socratic*: During the time of Socrates, the Greek philosopher from the fifth century BC.
40. *ἄριστον*: Ariston, Greek for 'breakfast'.
41. *τρέπεσθαι πρὸς τὸν πότον*: Trepesthai pros ton poton, Greek for 'they would turn to the wine'.
42. *Corybantian*: Priests of Classical antiquity who indulged in orgies in honour of the goddess Cybele.
43. *Dionysiac*: Of Dionysus, the Thracian god of wine. 'O Cyclops, son of the sea-god, come see what kind of divine drink this is that Greece provides from its vines, the gleaming cup of Dionysus', Euripides' *Cyclops* (c. 412 BC).
44. *Bacchic*: Of Bacchus, the god of wine, the Roman version of Dionysus.
45. *Dithyrambic*: The dithyramb was a wild choral hymn, especially in honour of Dionysus.
46. *Mrs Grundy*: A character in Tom Morton's comedy *Speed the Plough* (1798) cast as the epitome of moral righteousness.
47. *Coan silk*: Silk from the Greek island of Cos.
48. *hardbake*: Sweetmeat made of boiled brown sugar with almonds and flavoured with orange or lemon juice.
49. *viragoes*: Violent or ill-tempered women.
50. *leman*: Archaic word for a lover or mistress.
51. *epithalamia*: Lyrical odes in honour of a bride and bridegroom.
52. *Marsala*: The Sicilian town which produces a dark, sweet, fortified wine.
53. *All is darksome – all is dreary*: Gilbert had evidently been reading Alexander Pope again, this time 'Eloisa to Abelard' (1717), which shares a number of words and sounds with the libretto.

54. *Pommery seventy-four*: The 1874 vintage from the celebrated champagne house of Pommery and Greno in Reims, France.

55. *Principality*: Monaco in the south of France is a principality. Monte Carlo is a city within Monaco.

56. *Mentone*: Mentone is the Italian name for Menton, a town near Monte Carlo.

57. *Allons, encore . . .*: The French in the three French verses translates as: 'Let's go again – Boys and girls – Your golden coins – Your cart wheels! Hey there! Place your bets – Come on, children – Time is getting on – The bank is closing – No more bets! Seventeen black, odds you lose! Hey there! long live the bank! . . . Come on, people! The ball's rolling – Time's running out – No more bets! Thirty-five red – odds you win! Well done, students . . . If you've lost – In the past – You'll win today! – No more bets! Tra la la la! Double zero! You've lost the lot, my noble heroes . . .'

58. *prétendant*: Suitor.

59. *Merovingian period*: The Frankish dynasty *c.* 500–750, founded by Clovis.

Further Reading

Baily, Leslie, *The Gilbert & Sullivan Book* (London: Cassell, 1952).

Baily, Leslie, *Gilbert and Sullivan and Their World* (London: Thames and Hudson, 1973).

Bradley, Ian, (ed.), *The Complete Annotated Gilbert and Sullivan* (Oxford: Oxford University Press, 1996).

Bradley, Ian, *Oh Joy! Oh Rapture! The Enduring Phenomenon of Gilbert and Sullivan* (Oxford: Oxford University Press, 2005).

Dark, Sidney, *Gilbert, His Life and Letters* (London: Methuen and Co., 1923).

Dunn, George, *A Gilbert and Sullivan Dictionary* (London: G. Allen and Unwin, 1936).

Ellis, James (ed.), *The Bab Ballads* (Cambridge, Mass.: Belknap Press, 1970).

Godwin, A. H., *Gilbert and Sullivan, A Critical Appreciation of the Savoy Operas* (London: J. M. Dent and Sons, 1926).

Goodman, Andrew, *Gilbert and Sullivan's London* (London: Faber, 2000).

MacGeorge, Ethel, *The Life and Reminiscences of Jessie Bond, the Old Savoyard, As Told By Herself* (London: Bodley Head, 1930).

Pearson, Hesketh, *Gilbert and Sullivan: A Biography* (London: Macdonald and Jane's, 1975).

Sullivan, Herbert, and Flower, Walter, *Sir Arthur Sullivan, His Life, Letters and Diaries* (London: Cassell, 1927).

Wren, Gayden, *A Most Ingenious Paradox: The Art of Gilbert and Sullivan* (Oxford: Oxford University Press, 2001).

The following websites are recommended:
http://www.doylycarte.org.uk/Operas/TheMikado.htm
http://math.boisestate.edu/gas/pirates/html/index.html
http://members.aol.com/gsvloc/glossary.htm
http://homepages.ihug.co.nz/_melbear/gondoliers.htm

PENGUIN CLASSICS

THE BEGGAR'S OPERA
JOHN GAY

> 'Whore and rogue they call husband and wife:
> All professions be-rogue one another'

The tale of Peachum, thief-taker and informer, conspiring to send the dashing and promiscuous highwayman Macheath to the gallows, became the theatrical sensation of the eighteenth century. In *The Beggar's Opera*, John Gay turned conventions of Italian opera riotously upside-down, instead using traditional popular ballads and street tunes, while also indulging in political satire at the expense of the Prime Minister, Sir Robert Walpole. Gay's highly original depiction of the thieves, informers, prostitutes and highwaymen thronging the slums and prisons of the corrupt London underworld proved brilliantly successful in exposing the dark side of a corrupt and jaded society.

Bryan Loughrey and T. O. Treadwell's introduction examines the eighteenth-century background of musical theatre and opera, the changing cityscape of London and the corruption of the legal system. This edition also includes a note on the music in *The Beggar's Opera* and suggestions for further reading.

Edited by Bryan Loughrey and T. O. Treadwell

PENGUIN CLASSICS

THE MOONSTONE
WILKIE COLLINS

'When you looked down into the stone, you looked into a yellow deep that drew
your eyes into it so that they saw nothing else'

The Moonstone, a yellow diamond looted from an Indian temple and believed to
bring bad luck to its owner, is bequeathed to Rachel Verinder on her eighteenth
birthday. That very night the priceless stone is stolen again and when Sergeant
Cuff is brought in to investigate the crime, he soon realizes that no one in Rachel's
household is above suspicion. Hailed by T. S. Eliot as 'the first, the longest, and
the best of modern English detective novels', *The Moonstone* is a marvellously taut
and intricate tale of mystery, in which facts and memory can prove treacherous and
not everyone is as they first appear.

Sandra Kemp's introduction examines *The Moonstone* as a work of Victorian
sensation fiction and an early example of the detective genre, and discusses the
technique of multiple narrators, the role of opium, and Collins's sources and
autobiographical references.

'Enthralling and believable … evokes in vivid language the spirit of a place' P. D.
James, *Sunday Times*

Edited with an introduction and notes by Sandra Kemp

PENGUIN CLASSICS

OUR MUTUAL FRIEND
CHARLES DICKENS

> 'Has a dead man any use for money? …
> What world does money belong to?
> This world. How can money be a corpse's?'

Our Mutual Friend centres on an inheritance – Old Harmon's profitable dust heaps – and its legatees, young John Harmon, presumed drowned when a body is pulled out of the River Thames, and kindly dustman Mr Boffin, to whom the fortune defaults. With brilliant satire, Dickens portrays a dark, macabre London, inhabited by such disparate characters as Gaffer Hexam, scavenging the river for corpses; enchanting, mercenary Bella Wilfer; the social climbing Veneerings; and the unscrupulous street-trader Silas Wegg. Dickens's last completed novel is richly symbolic in its vision of death and renewal in a city dominated by the fetid Thames, and of the corrupting power of money.

This edition uses the text of the first volume edition of 1865, and includes the original illustrations, a chronology, a list for further reading, and appendices on the illustrations and serial plans. Adrian Poole's introduction examines biblical allusions and the central themes of *Our Mutual Friend*.

'The great poet of the city. He was created by London' Peter Ackroyd

Edited with an introduction and notes by Adrian Poole

PENGUIN CLASSICS

JANE EYRE
CHARLOTTE BRONTË

> 'I am no bird and no net ensnares me.
> I am a free human being with an independent will'

Having endured humiliation and loneliness in the home of her heartless Aunt Reed, and the harsh regime of Lowood, a charity boarding school, the orphaned Jane Eyre survives her childhood unbroken in spirit and integrity. When she takes up a post as a governess at Thornfield Hall, she also finds love with her employer, the dark and sardonic Mr Rochester. But her discovery of Rochester's terrible secret forces Jane to follow her own moral convictions, even if it means giving up her chance of happiness. Although many were shocked by its depiction of a woman's bold and passionate search for independence and love on her own terms, *Jane Eyre* was an immediate success when it appeared in 1847 and remains one of the most popular of all English novels.

In his introduction, Michael Mason discusses the literary critical history of *Jane Eyre*. This edition includes suggestions for further reading, notes and a new chronology.

'The masterwork of a great genius' William Makepeace Thackeray

Edited with an introduction and notes by Michael Mason

Penguin Classics

MIDDLEMARCH
GEORGE ELIOT

Edited with an introduction and notes by Rosemary Ashton

George Eliot's most ambitious novel is a masterly evocation of diverse lives and changing fortunes in a provincial community. Peopling its landscape are Dorothea Brooke, a young idealist whose search for intellectual fulfillment leads her into a disastrous marriage to the pedantic scholar Casaubon; the charming but tactless Dr Lydgate, whose pioneering medical methods, combined with an imprudent marriage to the spendthrift beauty Rosamond, threaten to undermine his career; and the religious hypocrite Bulstrode, hiding scandalous crimes from his past. As their stories interweave, George Eliot creates a richly nuanced and moving drama, hailed by Virginia Woolf as 'one of the few English novels written for grown-up people'.

This edition uses the text of the second edition of 1874. In her introduction, Rosemary Ashton, biographer of *George Eliot*, discusses themes of change in *Middlemarch*, and examines the novel as an imaginative embodiment of Eliot's humanist beliefs.

'The most profound, wise and absorbing of English novels ... and, above all, truthful and forgiving about human behaviour' Hermione Lee

PENGUIN CLASSICS

THE IMPORTANCE OF BEING EARNEST AND OTHER PLAYS
OSCAR WILDE

LADY WINDERMERE'S FAN/SALOMÉ/A WOMAN OF NO IMPORTANCE/
AN IDEAL HUSBAND/A FLORENTINE TRAGEDY/THE IMPORTANCE OF
BEING EARNEST

> 'To lose one parent may be regarded as a misfortune;
> to lose both looks like carelessness'

The Importance of Being Earnest is a glorious comedy of mistaken identity, which ridicules codes of propriety and etiquette. Manners and morality are also victims of Wilde's sharp wit in *Lady Windermere's Fan*, *A Woman of No Importance* and *An Ideal Husband*, in which snobbery and hypocrisy are laid bare. In *Salomé* and *A Florentine Tragedy*, Wilde makes powerful use of historical settings to explore the complex relationship between sex and power. The range of these plays displays Wilde's delight in artifice, masks and disguises, and reveal the pretensions of the social world in which he himself played such a dazzlingly and precarious part.

Richard Allen Cave's introduction and notes discuss the themes of the plays and Wilde's innovative methods of staging. This edition includes the excised 'Gribsby' scene from *The Importance of Being Earnest*.

'Beneath the wit there is always an intense emotional reality. He criticized his audience while he entertained it' Peter Hall, *Guardian*

Edited with an introduction, commentaries and notes by Richard Allen Cave

PENGUIN CLASSICS

CRANFORD
ELIZABETH GASKELL

'It is very pleasant dining with a bachelor ... I only hope it is not improper; so many pleasant things are!'

A portrait of the residents of an English country town in the mid-nineteenth century, *Cranford* relates the adventures of Miss Matty and Miss Deborah, two middle-aged spinster sisters striving to live with dignity in reduced circumstances. Through a series of vignettes, Elizabeth Gaskell portrays a community governed by old-fashioned habits and dominated by friendships between women. Her wry account of rural life is undercut, however, by tragedy in its depiction of such troubling events as Matty's bankruptcy, the violent death of Captain Brown and the unwitting cruelty of Peter Jenkyns. Written with acute observation, *Cranford* is by turns affectionate, moving and darkly satirical.

In her introduction, Patricia Ingham discusses *Cranford* in relation to Gaskell's own past and as a work of irony in the manner of Jane Austen. She also considers the implications of the novel as to class and empire. This edition also includes further reading, notes and an appendix on the significance of 'Fashion at Cranford'.

Edited with an introduction and notes by Patricia Ingham